English
Writing and Skills

CORONADO EDITION

HOLT, RINEHART AND WINSTON
SECOND COURSE

Critical Readers and Contributors

The authors and the publisher wish to thank the following people, who helped to evaluate and to prepare materials for this series:

Charles L. Allen, Baltimore Public Schools, Baltimore, Maryland
Kiyoko B. Bernard, Huntington Beach High School, Huntington Beach, California
Sally Borengasser, Rogers, Arkansas
Deborah Bull, New York City, New York
Joan Colby, Chicago, Illinois
Phyllis Goldenberg, North Miami Beach, Florida
Beverly Graves, Worthington High School, Worthington, Ohio
Pamela Hannon, Kirk Middle School, Cleveland, Ohio
Lawana Indermill, San Diego State University, San Diego, California
Carol Kuykendall, Houston Public Schools, Houston, Texas
Wayne Larkin, Roosevelt Junior High School, Blaine, Minnesota
Nancy MacKnight, University of Maine, Orono, Maine
Catherine McCough, Huntington Beach Union School District, California
Kathleen McKee, Coronado High School, Coronado, California
Lawrence Milne, Ocean View High School, Long Beach, California
Al Muller, East Carolina University, Greenville, North Carolina
Dorothy Muller, East Carolina University, Greenville, North Carolina
Arlene Mulligan, Stanley Junior High School, San Diego, California
John Nixon, Santa Ana Junior College, Santa Ana, California
Jesse Perry, San Diego City Schools, California
Christine Rice, Huntington Beach Union School District, Huntington Beach, California
Linda C. Scott, Poway Unified High School District, Poway, California
Jo Ann Seiple, University of North Carolina at Wilmington, Wilmington, North Carolina
Joan Yesner, Brookline, Massachusetts
Seymour Yesner, Brookline Education Center, Massachusetts
Arlie Zolynas, San Diego State University, San Diego, California

Classroom Testing

The authors and the publisher also wish to thank the following teachers, who participated in the classroom testing of materials from this series:

David Foote, Evanston High School East, Evanston, Illinois
Theresa Hall, Nokomis Junior High School, Minneapolis, Minnesota
Carrie E. Hampton, Sumter High School, Sumter, South Carolina
Pamela Hannon, Proviso High School East, Maywood, Illinois
Wayne Larkin, Roosevelt Junior High School, Blaine, Minnesota
Grady Locklear, Sumter High School, Sumter, South Carolina
William Montgomery, Hillcrest High School, Jamaica, New York
Josephine H. Price, Sumter High School, Sumter, South Carolina
Barbara Stilp, North High School, Minneapolis, Minnesota
Joseph Thomas, Weymouth North High School, East Weymouth, Massachusetts
Travis Weldon, Sumter High School, Sumter, South Carolina

Teachers of the Huntington Beach Union High School Writing Program

Cassandra C. Allsop	Carol Kasser	Catherine G. McCough
Eric V. Emery	Patricia Kelly	Cathleen C. Redman
Michael Frym	Stephanie Martone	Christine Rice
Barbara Goldfein	Lawrence Milne	Michael D. Sloan
Joanne Haukland	Richard H. Morley	S. Oliver Smith
Don Hohl	John S. Nixon	Glenda Watson
Sandra Johnson		

Dorothy Augustine, District Consultant in Writing

English
Writing and Skills

CORONADO EDITION

W. Ross Winterowd
Patricia Y. Murray

HOLT, RINEHART AND WINSTON
AUSTIN NEW YORK SAN DIEGO CHICAGO TORONTO MONTREAL

The Series:

English: Writing and Skills, First Course

English: Writing and Skills, Second Course

English: Writing and Skills, Third Course

English: Writing and Skills, Fourth Course

English: Writing and Skills, Fifth Course

English: Writing and Skills, Complete Course

Also available for each title:

Teacher's Edition

Workbook

Test Book

Teacher's Resource Binder

Computer Test Generator

Computer Scoring Program

W. ROSS WINTEROWD is the Bruce R. McElderry Professor of English at the University of Southern California. Since 1975, Dr. Winterowd has traveled widely as a writing consultant for numerous schools in North America.

PATRICIA Y. MURRAY is Director of Composition at DePaul University in Chicago. Dr. Murray taught junior and senior high school English in the Los Angeles city schools. She is also a consultant in curriculum development and teacher training.

Copyright © 1988, 1985 by Holt, Rinehart and Winston, Inc.

All rights reserved. No part of this publication may be reproduced or transmitted in any form or by any means, electronic or mechanical, including photocopy, recording, or any information storage and retrieval system, without permission in writing from the publisher.

Requests for permission to make copies of any part of the work should be mailed to: Permissions, Holt, Rinehart and Winston, Inc., Orlando, Florida 32887

Printed in the United States of America

ISBN 0-03-014629-1

Contents

1 Writing

1 The Writing Process

What Is Good Writing? **2**
Defining the Writing Process **3**
Prewriting to Find Ideas **5**
Questioning for Greater Depth **10**
Changing Viewpoints **13**
Revising **16**
Proofreading **18**

Sentence Combining: Using Connectors **20**

2 Keeping a Writer's Notebook

The Writer's Notebook **28**
Using Sensory Details **32**
Using Specific Words **35**
Writing About Feelings **38**

Sentence Combining: Subordinators, Commas, and *and* **40**

3 Writing a Personal Narrative

Writing About Your Life **48**
The Narrator **48**
Writing About Places **50**
Writing About People in Your Life **54**
Writing About Events **58**

Sentence Combining: Arranging Parts and Using a Colon **65**

4 Developing Expository Paragraphs

Writing Paragraphs   70
Using a Pattern: The TRI Paragraph   72
The TI Paragraph   75
Using Examples to Develop Paragraphs   76
Using Facts to Develop Paragraphs   78
Using Reasons to Develop Paragraphs   80
Using Incidents to Develop Paragraphs   83
Choosing a Method of Development   86
Writing a Well-Developed Paragraph   87
Writing a Unified Paragraph   89
Writing a Coherent Paragraph   92

Sentence Combining: *Inserting Adjectives*   98

5 Writing Compositions

Composing for a Purpose   104
Deciding on a Topic   104
Gathering and Recording Information   107
Selecting Information to Make a Point   108
Organizing Information into an Outline   110
Parts of a Composition   114
Writing a Descriptive Composition   114
Writing a Narrative Composition   119
Writing an Expository Composition   122

Sentence Combining: *Using* Who, Which, *and* Where   127

6 Research Writing

Writing a Summary   134
Selecting a Topic for a Research Report   142

Finding Sources   143
Recording Information   145
Organizing Information   148
Reading a Research Report   151
Writing a Research Report   154
Writing a Bibliography   155

Sentence Combining: *Using* with, -ing, *and* Possessives   158

7 Persuasive Writing

Persuasive and Expository Writing   167
Becoming an Effective Persuader   170
Writing Persuasion   179

Sentence Combining: Where, When, *and* How *Details*   187

8 Imaginative Writing

Building a Short Story   192
Reading a Short Story   196
Poetry   206
Figurative Language   211
Imagery in Poetry   215
Poems to Express Feelings   217

Sentence Combining: *Inserting to Tell* Something   222

9 Writing Letters

Writing Friendly Letters   228
Writing an Interesting Letter   231
Form for Friendly Letters   233
Mailing Your Letter   236
Folding Your Letter   238

Writing Social Letters   **240**
Writing Thank-You Letters   **240**
Writing Letters of Invitation   **242**
Writing an Answer   **244**
Writing Business Letters   **247**
Addressing Business Envelopes   **251**
Writing Letters of Application   **252**
Writing Letters of Request   **254**
Writing Order Letters   **256**

Sentence Combining: *Using* to + verb   **260**

10 Filling Out Forms

Order Forms   **262**
Library Card Application   **264**
Job Application Form   **267**
Preparing for a Job Application   **272**
Preparing for a Job Interview   **273**

Sentence Combining: *Placement and Choices*   **277**

2   *Grammar*

11 Nouns

Understanding Nouns   **284**
    Defining Nouns
    Grouping Nouns by Classes
    Finding Nouns by Their Features

Using Nouns   **292**
    Noun Plurals
    Irregular Noun Plurals
    Compound Noun Plurals
    Noun Possessives
    Capitalizing Proper Nouns

Writing Focus: *Using Specific Nouns in Writing*   **308**

12 Pronouns

Understanding Pronouns   **310**

    Defining Pronouns
    Grouping Pronouns by Classes
    Finding Pronouns by Their
        Features

Using Pronouns   **324**

    Pronouns and Antecedents
    Indefinite Antecedents
    Avoiding Common Problems
    Using Subject Pronouns
    Using Object Pronouns
    Using *Who* and *Whom*

Writing Focus: *Using Pronouns in Writing*   **338**

13 Verbs

Understanding Verbs   **340**

    Defining Verbs
    Grouping Verbs by Classes
    Finding Verbs by Their Features

Using Verbs   **349**

    Simple Verb Tenses
    Perfect Verb Tenses
    Using Irregular Verbs
    The Progressive Forms of Verbs
    Verb and Subject Agreement
    Avoiding Problems in Agreement
    Agreement with Compound
        Subjects and Collective Nouns
    Agreement with Pronouns
    Verbs Often Confused

Writing Focus: *Using Vivid Verbs in Writing*   **374**

14 Adjectives

Understanding Adjectives   **376**

    Defining Adjectives
    Grouping Adjectives by Classes
    Finding an Adjective by Its
        Features

Using Adjectives   **388**

    Comparative and Superlative
        Forms of Adjectives
    Irregular Comparisons

Writing Focus: *Using Fresh Adjectives*   **394**

15 Adverbs

Understanding Adverbs 396

    Defining Adverbs
    Grouping Adverbs by Classes
    Finding an Adverb by Its Features

Using Adverbs 406

    Comparative and Superlative
    Irregular Comparisons
    Choosing: Adjective or Adverb
    Avoiding Double Negatives

Writing Focus: *Using Exact Adverbs In Writing* 417

16 Prepositions

Understanding Prepositions 420

    Defining Prepositions
    Prepositions Used as Other Parts of Speech
    Prepositions with Compound Objects
    Prepositional Phrases as Modifiers

Using Prepositions 428

    Pronouns as Objects of Prepositions
    Using Troublesome Prepositions In Edited Standard English
    Prepositional Phrases as Adjectives
    Prepositional Phrases as Adverbs

Writing Focus: *Using Prepositional Phrases in Writing* 438

17 Conjunctions

Understanding Conjunctions 440

    Defining Conjunctions
    Grouping Conjunctions by Classes

Using Conjunctions 448

    Coordinating and Correlative Conjunctions
    Subordinating Conjunctions

Writing Focus: *Using Conjunctions in Writing* 454

18 Interjections

Understanding Interjections 456

Using Interjections 457

Writing Focus: *Using Interjections in Writing* 459

19 Verbals

Understanding Verbals 462

    Participles
    Gerunds

Writing Focus: *Using Verbals in Writing* 468

20 Sentence Structure

Understanding Sentences 470

    Defining Sentences
    Purposes of Sentences
    The Parts of a Sentence
    Understood Subjects
    Compound Subjects
    Subjects in Inverted Order
    The Predicate
    Compound Verbs
    Sentence Patterns
    Classifying Sentence Structures

Using Sentences 494

    Avoiding Sentence Fragments
    Avoiding Run-On Sentences

Writing Focus: *Improving Sentence Structure in Writing* 500

21 Phrases

Understanding Phrases 502

    Defining Phrases
    Grouping Phrases by Classes

Using Phrases 509

    Punctuation with Phrases
    Placing Participial Phrases

Writing Focus: *Using Phrases in Writing* 514

22 Clauses

Understanding Clauses 516

    Defining Clauses

Using Clauses 524

    Punctuating Independent Clauses

Distinguishing Clauses
Kinds of Clauses
Types of Subordinate Clauses

Punctuating Adjective Clauses
Punctuating Adverb Clauses

Writing Focus: *Using Clauses in Writing*   531

3   *Mechanics*

23 *Punctuation*

Punctuation Marks   534
The Period   535
The Question Mark   537
The Exclamation Point   537
The Comma   538
Paired Commas   543
The Semicolon   546
The Colon   547
The Dash   550
The Hyphen   550
Quotation Marks   554
Underlining (Italics)   556
The Apostrophe   559
Parentheses   562

Writing Focus: *Improving Punctuation in Writing*   566

24 *Capitalization*

Capitalization   568

Writing Focus: *Improving Capitalization in Writing*   583

4 Language Resources

25 Vocabulary and Spelling

Vocabulary **586**
Words in Context **586**
Word Structure **589**
Using Synonyms **593**
Spelling **596**
Good Spelling Habits **596**
Helpful Spelling Rules **598**

26 Changes in Language

The Dawn of the English Language **606**
Language Changes **607**
Word Borrowing **608**
Other Word Sources **609**
Language Differences: Dialects **611**
Standard American English **612**
Choosing Your Language **613**

27 Library Skills

The Dewey Decimal System **616**
Call Numbers **618**
Biographies and Autobiographies **618**
Fiction **620**
The Card Catalogue **621**
Finding Books on the Shelves **625**
Using the *Readers' Guide* **627**
Finding Periodicals in Your Library **630**

28 Reference Works

Dictionaries   632
Finding a Word in the Dictionary   632
Main Entry Words   635
Dictionary Pronunciations   635
Accent Marks   637
Abbreviations   639
Parts of Speech and Plural Form   639
Word History   640
Definitions   641
Words in Context   644
Synonyms   645
How Dictionaries Differ   646
Other Reference Works   647
Using Encyclopedias   647
Using Special Reference Books   649

29 Speaking and Listening Skills

Preparing a Speech   650
Choosing a Topic   650
Closing in on Your Topic   651
Preparing an Informative Speech Outline   653
Dividing the Speech   654
Outlining the Body of the Speech   654
Planning the Introduction   656
Planning the Conclusion   657
Delivering a Speech   659
Listening to Speeches   662

Glossary of Terms   665
Index of Authors and Titles   669
Index   671
Skills Index   683

1
Writing

1 The Writing Process

What Is Good Writing?

The following paragraphs begin the short story "The Medicine Bag." As you read, notice which parts especially catch your interest.

Model: Writing to Interest Readers

My kid sister Cheryl and I always bragged about our Sioux grandpa, Joe Iron Shell. Our friends, who had always lived in the city and only knew about Indians from movies and TV, were impressed by our stories. Maybe we exaggerated and made Grandpa and the reservation sound glamorous, but when we'd return home to Iowa after our yearly summer visit to Grandpa we always had some exciting tale to tell.

We always had some authentic Sioux article to show our listeners. One year Cheryl had new moccasins that Grandpa had made. On another visit he gave me a small, round, flat, rawhide drum which was decorated with a painting of a warrior riding a horse. He taught me a real Sioux chant to sing while I beat the drum with a leather-covered stick that had a feather on the end. Man, that really made an impression.

We never showed our friends Grandpa's picture. Not that we were ashamed of him, but because we knew that the glamorous tales we told didn't go with the real thing. Our friends would have laughed at the picture, because Grandpa wasn't tall and stately like TV Indians. His hair wasn't in braids, but hung in stringy, gray strands on his neck and he was old. He was our great-grandfather, and he didn't live in a tepee, but all by himself in a part log, part tar-paper shack on the Rosebud Reservation in South Dakota. So when Grandpa came to visit us, I was so ashamed and embarrassed I could've died.[1]

Think and Discuss

1. What parts of these paragraphs from "The Medicine Bag" left pictures in your mind?

---

[1] From "The Medicine Bag" by Virginia Driving Hawk Sneve from *Boys' Life,* March 1975, published by the Boy Scouts of America.

2. Did the last line surprise you? Why or why not?
3. What parts of the story would you like to know more about?

If someone said, "Those paragraphs are excellent because they are neatly printed," you would think that the speaker was joking. You know that the term *good writing* refers to more than neatness. If someone said, "That's the most interesting writing I've ever read, because it has no spelling or grammatical errors," you would be sure that the speaker was joking. You know that correct grammar and mechanics are important, for readers often assume that errors in grammar and mechanics indicate sloppy thinking. But you also know that neatness and correctness alone do not make good writing.

Good writing sparks a reader's interest.

Defining the Writing Process

The *writing process* includes everything you do to make your writing not only neat and correct but also interesting. This book divides the writing process into three stages: *prewriting, writing,* and *postwriting.* In this chapter you will learn more about these stages of the writing process. Then, in the chapters that follow, you will use what you have learned in a variety of writing forms, including stories, letters, and reports.

Prewriting

Prewriting is the stage of getting ideas. Energy builds up when you try to think of a story idea or an essay topic. Students often describe finding an idea as an explosion occurring, releasing energy. Kaboom! An idea!

Creative ideas may come to you when you aren't thinking about a writing assignment at all. Or you may be using prewriting methods already, without realizing it. Do you talk about writing ideas with friends or family members? Do you visualize an idea and then write it down? Do you get inspiration from books, movies, music, or art? All of these are prewriting methods.

You can often speed up the process of finding good writing ideas by using prewriting techniques such as clustering, brainstorming, and free writing. In this chapter you will learn about and practice each of these prewriting techniques.

Writing

Writing is the stage of forming ideas into sentences and paragraphs. When you find a writing idea, you'll have the urge to write fast and furiously, and you should. As you write, new ideas will come to you. Writing is a solitary activity, and often hard work, but there are surprises in store when you finish. Many writers read their completed rough drafts in amazement

and say, "I didn't know I knew that!" Through writing, you may discover hidden thoughts and develop your thinking.

Postwriting

Postwriting involves making changes in your writing and sharing it. Classmates and teachers can help at this point by reading your writing and telling you which parts are more interesting and which are less interesting to them. You then make changes by *revising* (improving the content and organization of your writing) and by *proofreading* (correcting errors in spelling, mechanics, grammar, and usage). After your writing has been revised and proofread, it is ready to share with a wider audience.

Prewriting to Find Ideas

When you write about a subject you know well, you may not find it difficult to think of ideas. Sometimes, however, writing ideas do not come easily. When this happens, the prewriting activities that follow can help.

Brainstorming

When you *brainstorm,* you try to think of all the things you know about a subject or all the possible ways of solving a problem. Although brainstorming can be done alone or in a group, a group can usually gather more information than an individual because there are several people to contribute ideas and information. What one person cannot see, another might be able to understand, and one person's ideas often suggest ideas to others.

To brainstorm, free your mind of everything except the subject. Then allow your mind to roam freely over the subject, letting one idea touch off another. Thinking about what you have read or heard about the subject will help ideas come. Your ideas may come as single words, groups of words, or even sentences. For example, suppose you are brainstorming the subject of UFO's. As you let your mind wander over the subject, you might have thoughts like these:

   Little green people with antennae and eight arms

   Spaceship that glows

   I once saw a movie called *Close Encounters of the Third Kind* about visitors from outer space.

Writing

> Reports about seeing UFO's from all over the world
>
> Reports often aren't believed
>
> Government agency that collects reports on UFO's
>
> A man in Mississippi claims he was taken aboard a ship from outer space.

When you brainstorm by yourself, jot down ideas on a sheet of paper. For group brainstorming, listen to the other people and use their thoughts as springboards for your own. As ideas begin to come, have one member of the group record them.

Brainstorming can be useful to you in many ways. If your subject is a large one, you can narrow it by brainstorming. Another brainstorming session will help you discover what you already know about these reports. A third important use of brainstorming is to find out what you do not know, but need to research.

Writing Practice 1: *Brainstorming*

Select one of the subjects from the list below or make up one of your own. Then, by yourself or in a group, brainstorm the subject. If you brainstorm by yourself, jot down ideas on a sheet of paper as they come. In a group, assign one member to write down ideas.

1. An invention to make life easier for the teenager of today
2. The ideal school
3. Pneumonia
4. A plot for a science fiction movie
5. Endangered animals
6. The value of sports in the school curriculum
7. Hurricanes
8. Snakes
9. How television affects our lives
10. Hot-air balloons

Clustering

Connecting ideas by writing them on paper and drawing lines and circles between them will help you "see" your subject.

When you think, sometimes one idea will trigger another idea, and that one in turn will make you think of another idea. This process can be transferred to paper by writing words and phrases that come to mind as you think about your subject. As you write one word or phrase, let it suggest another idea. Then write that one near it, circle both, and draw a connecting line between them, like this:

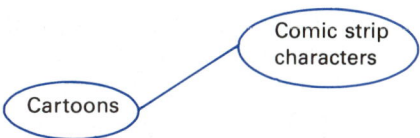

The process starts with a central idea or subject word, such as *cartoons*. If you were to continue, you would think of ideas about cartoons that you associate with the word. Each of these associations is written and connected to the central word.

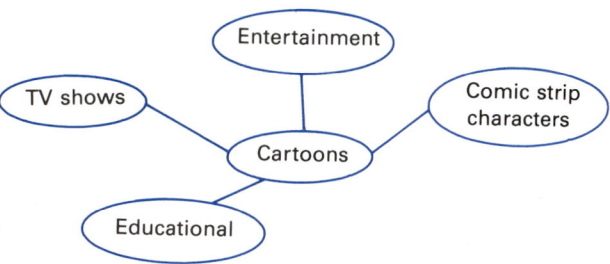

Soon each word in your cluster of words will suggest even further ideas, which are written and connected too. As you go through the process, let your mind wander over the subject freely, as you do in brainstorming.

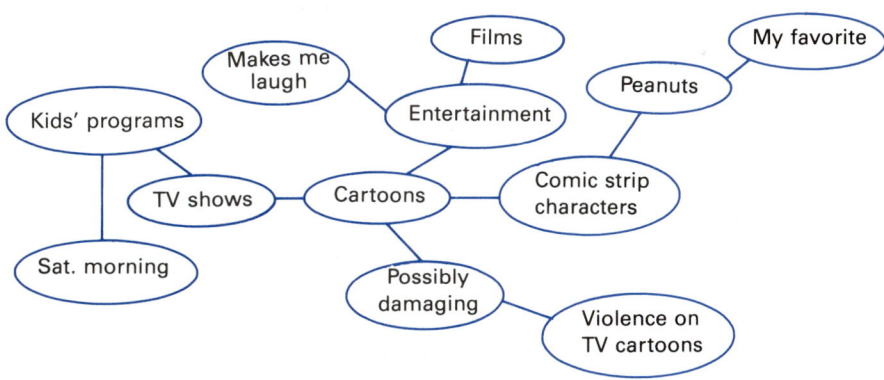

Writing

Now you have several possibilities for talking or writing about cartoons. You may not want to use everything you have written, or you may want to choose just one part of the cluster of words to discuss or write about, but you do have many ideas to work with and specific key words and phrases to use in your writing or discussion.

Writing Practice 2: *Clustering*

Either with your classmates or by yourself, select a key word or phrase with which to begin a cluster of connecting ideas. You may select one of the words below or choose one of your own. Then write that word or phrase in the middle of a sheet of paper and begin to connect more words to it. Work for two or three minutes and then stop and look at the writing possibilities you have.

1. Fun
2. Trash cans
3. Water
4. Pilgrims
5. Storms
6. Mondays
7. The future
8. Stars
9. Quiet
10. Popcorn

Then, using all or some of the words and phrases, write a short paragraph about your subject. Save your work.

Free Writing

Original ideas and new ways to express them fill your mind much more often than you realize. But concern about writing correctly can stop you from getting your words and thoughts down on paper. Free writing is a way to avoid this problem. To free write, set a time limit—five minutes is usually enough—and write continuously during that time. As you write, do not worry about correctness or even about making sense; just write whatever comes into your mind. Do not read what you have written until after the time is up. Then, as you read, underline the parts of your free writing that are good ideas or that seem especially vivid and original. Later, during the writing stage, you can form your free writing material into sentences and paragraphs.

Read the following free writing Greg did about the time he hurt his hand using the power mower.

Model: *Free Writing*

Notice that Greg does not use logical order, correct grammar, or even complete sentences. Yet he comes up with vivid memories of the event. After he finished free writing, Greg underlined the words and phrases that he wanted to use later.

> Turned mower off. Stuck hand in and felt around for grass, blades still turning, pulled out hand and thought it was a nick, but it was red and bloody. Went across the street. The kid looked at me like I was a monster. Gave me a towel and I felt guilty about bleeding on it. Sat in car and looked at finger. Could see the bone, but it didn't hurt. The nurse gave me a shot and I got sleepy, finger felt hard and cold. Couldn't sleep. Nightmares of cast. No exercising. Remembered the lawn mower. Happened real fast. Didn't seem real. Didn't feel pain. Put head down and closed eyes so blood wouldn't come so fast. Didn't want to touch hand. Washed with cold water. Calmer than I thought I would be. Here we go again. Third cast. Worried parents, too much money. Thought being called "Fingers" Cleveland would be cool.
>
> Looked at finger. Saw the bone in middle surrounded by red filet of me. Thought it was neat to see inside my finger—always wanted to see my bones.

Even though you may not use all your free writing material later, free writing can help you discover your own way of expressing yourself.

Writing

Writing Practice 3: *Free Writing*

Take five minutes and free write on a subject of your own choice (you may use the cluster you wrote in Writing Practice 2) or one of the following topics. Write everything you have to say: empty your brain onto paper! Then read your free writing and underline the parts you like best. Save your work.

1. An observation of nature
2. A new idea that has occurred to you
3. A recent event
4. A decision you've had to make

Questioning for Greater Depth

After you have used brainstorming, clustering, or free writing to find ideas for writing, you may need to gather more details. Two in-depth prewriting techniques, *questioning* and *changing viewpoints*, can help you discover details you already know about your subject.

The Six Basic Questions

The basic set of *who? what? why? when? where?* and *how?* questions can help you discover information about many subjects. For example, suppose you are given an assignment to write about safety in your home. To discover what you already know about this subject, ask yourself these basic questions:

1. *Who* is responsible for making sure my house or apartment is a safe place to live?
2. *What* can I do to make sure my house or apartment is a safe place to live?
3. *Why* should I be concerned about safety when there are police and fire departments nearby in case something happens?
4. *When* is the best time to check areas of the house or apartment for potential dangers?
5. *Where* in my house or apartment are accidents most likely to occur?

6. *How* can I tell if there is an unsafe condition in my home?

With these basic questions, you discover what you already know about your subject. Here are one writer's answers:

1. I am responsible, since I want to live safely, but each person in my family should be responsible also.

2. I can make sure I don't touch an electrical appliance while taking a shower or bath or while washing my hands in the sink. I can use knives and scissors carefully and put them away when I'm through. I can be certain that medicine bottles have tops my younger brothers and sisters can't open and that dangerous products such as drain cleaners are kept out of their reach. I can check to see if stored papers might be a fire hazard.

3. Fires and explosions happen so fast sometimes that I might not be able to escape or get to the phone to call help. Slipping and falling might make me or someone in my family unconscious and helpless.

4. Any time is a good time to be alert for dangers in my house or apartment. Maybe a routine check once a month would be a good idea.

5. Accidents can happen anywhere—in the bathroom, kitchen, stairway, basement, bedroom. Probably the worst places are the bathroom and kitchen.

6. Sometimes, I can tell there might be a danger, such as that loose rug in the hallway I keep slipping on. I probably should get some information about what to do to make my home a safer place, however.

Writing

When you use questions such as these, remember there is often more than one answer to each one. Think about each question for several minutes before moving on to the next, since the more information you can gather, the better your paper is likely to be. Also, use the questions to find out what you do not know but need to read about or research before beginning your paper.

Writing Practice 4: *The Six Basic Questions*

Select one of the subjects listed below or make up one of your own (you may use the subject you wrote about in Writing Practice 3). Then make a list of the six basic *who? what? when? where? why?* and *how?* questions to discover what you already know about the subject and write your answers to the questions. You may write the answers as notes or as complete sentences.

1. The importance of recycling
2. Saving energy
3. Planning a camping trip
4. Space travel in the year 2500
5. Bicycle safety
6. Being a success in school
7. Earning money
8. Training a pet
9. The effects of TV commercials
10. Good summers

Changing Viewpoints

Viewpoint can mean at least two different things. First, it can mean how you look at something from a physical location. For example, if you stand on top of a high hill, you can see long distances all around you. On the other hand, if you are in a small elevator with other people, your view is limited to close-ups of heads and shoulders and the four walls of the elevator. You probably cannot see all of the elevator at once.

The second kind of *viewpoint* refers to the way you think about something and understand it. You can discover many things to say about a subject by asking these three viewpoint questions:

1. What is the subject like as itself?
2. What is the subject like as part of a larger group of similar subjects?
3. How does the subject change?

Viewpoint 1—What Is It Like?

If you think about a subject *as itself,* you describe and define it. If you were examining a river, for example, you could view it as itself, different from other rivers, with features that no other river has. Perhaps it is long, deep, freshwater, winding, flowing from north to south, perhaps filled with catfish. Maybe it has a deep blue-green color or is gray and muddy. Perhaps its banks are shallow and often overflowing. If you think about the river as itself, you describe how it looks, how it acts, where it is located, how deep or long it is, and so on.

Writing Practice 5: *What Is It Like?*

Choose an ordinary household object such as a radio, a stove, or a table and describe it clearly as an individual object. You might ask questions such as these about the object:

1. What does it look like?
2. Who is its owner (if any) or user?
3. How does it operate or work?
4. When and where is it used?

5. Why is it important in this household?

Viewpoint 2—How Does It Fit In?

If you think about a subject as *part of a larger group* of similar subjects, you compare it with other subjects in the group or show how it fits into a larger system. The river, for example, can be described as part of a larger system of rivers in a region or country. It belongs to a group called "waterways" or "large, flowing bodies of water." It is like other rivers because, like them, it flows, contains billions of cubic feet of water, has a source, and empties into a larger body of water such as an ocean. Also, the river can be considered part of a transportation system, since it moves boats up and down from port to port.

Writing Practice 6: *How Does It Fit In?*

Choose an institution or organization in your community and describe how it is part of a system. You might choose a museum, a zoo, a dairy farm, a grocery store, a school, or a fire department. Ask questions such as these about it:

1. How does it fit into the community as a service?
2. Why is it important to the community?

Viewpoint 3—How Does It Change?

If you think about a subject as *a changing thing,* you show how it grows, decays, or changes through time or space. Because a river is not "frozen" in time or space, it is forever changing. In one season it may be slow and sluggish; in another, fast-moving and dangerous. Its color changes as it picks up soil or rubbish from boats. It even means different things to people: a good place to fish for those who like to fish, a "road" over which a ship's captain can move cargo, or a research laboratory for the scientist.

Writing Practice 7: *Changing Viewpoints*

With your teacher and classmates, apply the three viewpoint questions to each of the following subjects. Your teacher may want you to list the answers as you and your classmates discuss them. Study the example first.

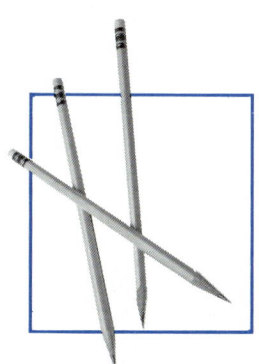

Example

Subject: **a pencil**

1. What is the subject like as itself?	2. What is the subject like as part of a larger group of similar subjects?	3. How does the subject change?
It's red and blue.	It's a tool.	It gets shorter as it is used.
Has teeth marks	Used for writing, a system of communication	The point disappears as it is used.
Eraser is missing	It has soft lead, wood cover, and eraser on top.	Becomes older, less bright

1. A tree
2. A four-year-old child
3. An automobile
4. A book
5. A record player

Revising

Writing for an impersonal audience is different from writing for a personal audience such as a close friend. One difference is that you must often explain people, places, and events that your readers might not know or understand. Another difference is that you should *revise* your writing—that is, make changes that will make your writing clearer and more interesting.

There are four kinds of changes you can make in your writing:

You can *delete* (or take out) words, sentences, or even whole paragraphs.

Original: The man who was sitting in the seat in front of me was so tall that I couldn't see the screen.

Deletion: The man ~~who was sitting~~ in the seat in front of me was so tall that I couldn't see the screen.

Revised: The man in the seat in front of me was so tall that I couldn't see the screen.

You can *add* words, sentences, and paragraphs.

Original: I was enjoying the holiday.

Revised: I was enjoying the holiday, *lying on the grass with sun warming my back while I listened to music.*

You can *rearrange* words, sentences, and paragraphs.

Original: I enjoy watching double feature horror movies on Halloween evening.

Revised: *On Halloween evening* I enjoy watching double feature horror movies.

You can *substitute* words, sentences, and paragraphs.

Original: Aunt Ellen is a *doctor*.

Revised: Aunt Ellen is an *orthopedic surgeon*.

Revision is not a last-minute job to do before you hand in your paper. Many writers, in fact, revise constantly as they go along. They may write a sentence and then decide that the sentence should be improved before writing another one. Other writers write an entire first draft and then revise that

1 The Writing Process

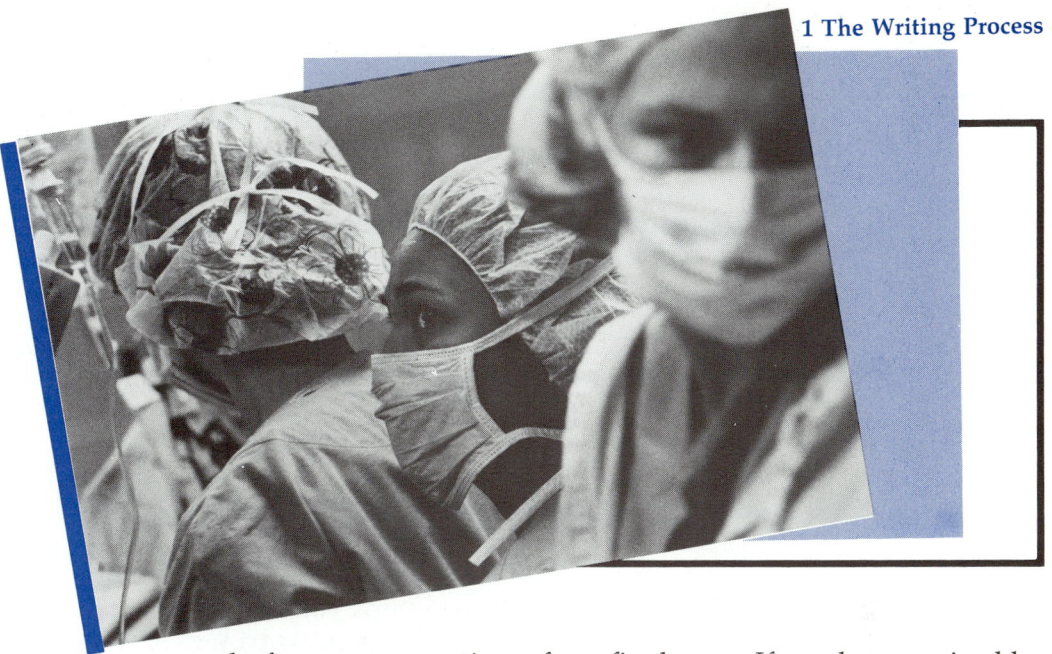

draft one or more times for a final copy. If you have revised by adding words or sentences between lines, or by crossing out words and sentences, recopy your paper so your readers will be able to read easily what you have written.

As you revise to make your writing clear and interesting, think about your purpose. Your purpose in most writing is to share an experience or an idea with readers. To accomplish this, you must use specific details, and you must explain people, places, and events that readers might not understand. When you revise, think about whether you need to add details or give readers more information. The following checklist can be a helpful guide for revision.

Checklist for Revising

1. Does my writing have a clear focus?
2. Do I need to add more details?
3. Is my writing organized in a way that makes sense?
4. Are there unnecessary parts I should leave out?
5. Is my writing style appropriate for my purpose and audience?
6. Have I chosen the most specific words possible?
7. Do my sentences vary in length and pattern?

Proofreading

In the process of publishing a book, typed pages, *manuscript,* are sent to a printer who sets it in type and makes copies, *proofs,* of the typeset material. Because it is almost impossible for a publisher and a printer to produce a work without making some errors, people known as *proofreaders* check the proofs.

In your English classroom you will usually be your own proofreader, checking errors in grammar and usage, spelling, punctuation, and capitalization. You should begin proofreading only when you have finished revision. If possible, put your paper aside for a few hours, or even days, before proofreading. Otherwise, you will not look at what you have actually written; you will look at what you think you have written. To proofread, cover your writing with a piece of paper, exposing only the bottom line. Now move the cover sheet up one line so that you are reading your paper opposite the way you wrote it. With this technique you are more likely to spot errors.

For more information on punctuation and capitalization, see pages 534–584.

Checklist for Proofreading

1. Each sentence begins with a capital letter and ends with a period, question mark, or exclamation point.
2. Each word is spelled correctly.
3. All proper nouns and adjectives are capitalized.
4. Personal pronouns used as subjects are subject forms; personal pronouns used as objects are object forms. All pronouns agree with antecedents in number and gender.
5. A singular verb is used with each singular subject, and a plural verb with each plural subject.
6. Commonly confused verbs, such as *lie/lay, sit/sat,* and *rise/raise,* are used correctly, and commonly confused adjectives and adverbs, such as *bad/badly, easy/easily,* and *good/well,* are used correctly.
7. Double negatives are avoided.
8. Sentences are correctly structured, with no run-ons or fragments.
9. The paper is neat.

> ### For Extra Help
>
> For additional help with any proofreading problems, see the following chapters.
>
> | | |
> |---|---|
> | Capitalization | Chapter 24 |
> | Punctuation | Chapter 23 |
> | Spelling | Chapter 25 |
> | Subject/Verb Agreement | Chapter 13 |
> | Pronoun Usage | Chapter 12 |
> | Sentences | Chapter 20 |

Writing Practice 8: *Revising and Proofreading*

Following the steps listed below, revise the paragraph you wrote for Writing Practice 2.

1. Cross out any words or sentences that you think are unnecessary.
2. Write between the lines to add words and sentences.
3. Rearrange words and sentences between lines.
4. Substitute words and sentences between lines.
5. When you have completed your revision, recopy your paper.

Finally, proofread your work, using the checklist on page 18.

Proofreading Marks

Mark	Meaning	Example
≡	Use a capital letter	mr. Murchison
lc/	Use a lowercase letter	lc in the Doghouse
ℒ	Take it out	I saw saw it.
∧	Add	Where is it?
¶	Indent paragraph	¶ When my friends discouraged
SpO	Spell correctly	Do you beleive Sp

Sentence Combining: Using Connectors

The Flow of Words

Sentences are linked to one another in the flow of a conversation, the development of a story, or a sketch of description.

Model: The Flow of Words

As you read the following paragraph from H. G. Wells' *The War of the Worlds,* an imaginative story about Martians arriving on earth, notice how the arrangement of sentences helps you visualize the creature.

Terrestrial means "of this earth."

Luminous means "shining like a light."

> I think everyone expected to see a man emerge—possibly something a little unlike us terrestrial men, but in all essentials a man. I know I did. But, looking, I presently saw something stirring within the shadow—greyish billowy movements, one above another, and then two luminous disklike eyes. Then something resembling a little grey snake, about the thickness of a walking-stick, coiled up out of the writhing middle, and wriggled in the air towards me—and then another.[1]

This writer wants readers to feel the suspense as the creature emerges and to imagine its unusual appearance. Suppose H. G. Wells had written the same description this way:

> I think everyone expected to see a man emerge. The man is something a little unlike us terrestrial men. The man is in all essentials a man. I know I did. I was looking. I presently saw something stirring within the shadow. I saw greyish billowy movements. They were one above another. I saw two luminous eyes. They were like disks. Something coiled up out of the writhing middle. It resembled a little grey snake. It was about the thickness of a walking stick. It wriggled in the air towards me. Then another wriggled towards me.

[1]From *The War of the Worlds* by H. G. Wells. Reprinted by permission of A. P. Watt Ltd.

Sentence Combining

The second version is full of unnecessary repetition and short, choppy sentences that slow you down as you read. In the first version, however, ideas are joined into sentences that help the writer achieve his purpose. The exercises that follow will help you learn how to write such mature sentences.

Using Connectors to Join Sentences

For more information on sentence connectors, also called conjunctions, see pages 440-455.

One way that you can improve your sentences is to combine them with *sentence connectors:* the words *and, but, or, for, so, yet, nor*. These words join two ideas of equal importance, as the following examples show. The words in parentheses after the second sentence in each set are called *signals*. The signals tell you which connector to use in making the combinations. (Note that a comma usually separates sentences joined by a sentence connector.)

Sentences: Uncle John raised the tent poles.
Aunt Lisa tied the support lines. (*and*)

Combined: Uncle John raised the tent poles, *and* Aunt Lisa tied the support lines.

Sentences: Maria loves to play the piano.
She does not enjoy practicing every day. (*but*)

For more information on using commas with sentence connectors, see page 539.

Combined: Maria loves to play the piano, *but* she does not enjoy practicing every day.

21

Writing

Nor is also a sentence connector, but it causes a change in word order. In addition, since *nor* means "not," the word *not* in the second sentence is removed:

Sentences: Four-year-old Billy had not eaten his dinner.
He had not drunk his milk. (*nor*)

Combined: Four-year-old Billy had not eaten his dinner, *nor had he* drunk his milk.

Another kind of connection between sentences of equal importance can be made with a *pair of connecting words* such as *either . . . or*. (*Either . . . or*) is the signal for this combination.

Sentences: You will take this medicine.
You will be very ill. (*Either . . . or*)

Combined: *Either* you will take this medicine, *or* you will be very ill.

Sentences: That is a perfect gift for Danielle.
I do not know my sister's taste at all. (*Either . . . or*)

Combined: *Either* that is a perfect gift for Danielle, *or* I do not know my sister's taste at all.

Sentence connectors are also called *conjunctions*.

> For more information on pairs of connecting words, also called correlative conjunctions, see pages 443-444.

Exercise 1: *Adding Sentence to Sentence*

On a sheet of paper combine the following sets of sentences. Use the signals for 1–5. For 6–10, decide which connector is best. Study the examples before you begin.

Examples

a. The cherry trees were in bloom.
The fragrance of their blossoms reached everywhere. (*and*)
The cherry trees were in bloom, and the fragrance of their blossoms reached everywhere.

b. The old typewriter barely functioned.
Dan could not part with his machine to have it repaired.
The old typewriter barely functioned, but Dan could not part with his machine to have it repaired.

Sentence Combining

1. James carved a happy face on his Halloween pumpkin.
   He did not want to frighten his little sister. (*for*)
2. The man stopped the bus at the railroad crossing.
   He could see whether or not a train was approaching. (*so*)
3. The championship game was still two weeks away.
   Our football team had never been better prepared to win. (*but*)
4. Principal Rollins scolded the entire school for not keeping the grounds clean.
   The students listened respectfully. (*yet*)
5. You will eat nutritious meals.
   You will feel tired. (*Either . . . or*)
6. Alfredo took Roberto to see the circus.
   He taught his little brother the names of many strange animals there.
7. We visited historic Fort Laramie.
   We did not see the ruts made by passing wagon trains over one hundred years ago.
8. Mr. Nguyen will teach English at the high school.
   He will work in the adult school program.
9. Sandra must do her homework every night.
   She will lose her high grade point average.
10. Richard did not follow the recipe closely.
    His pizza did not taste as good as his brother's.

Adverbs That Connect Sentences

Another group of sentence connectors are adverbs such as *however, therefore, instead, besides, furthermore, nevertheless, consequently, moreover, on the other hand, indeed,* and *in fact*.

These adverb connectors show different relationships between the sentences they connect into one statement.

For more information on adverb connectors, also called transitions, see pages 94-95.

however instead on the other hand nevertheless	Show that the second sentence is the opposite idea of the first sentence
therefore consequently	Show that the second sentence is a conclusion or result of the first sentence
besides furthermore moreover	Show that additional information will be given in the second sentence
indeed in fact	Show that the second sentence will illustrate or prove information in the first

Adverb connectors require the use of a semicolon (;) just in front of them. They are usually followed by a comma; *in fact*, this sentence is an example of how they should be used.

Study the following examples of adverbs that work as sentence connectors. The signal in parentheses tells which connector to use.

For more information on semicolons with adverb connectors, see pages 546-547.

Sentences:	The police inspector questioned the neighbors. She could find no new evidence. (*however*)
Combined:	The police inspector questioned the neighbors; *however*, she could find no new evidence.
Sentences:	The ski chairs swayed crazily in the breeze. Many skiers decided to avoid that lift for a while. (*consequently*)
Combined:	The ski chairs swayed crazily in the breeze; *consequently*, many skiers decided to avoid that lift for a while.

Exercise 2: *Adverbs That Connect Sentences*

On a sheet of paper numbered 1–5, combine the following pairs of sentences with one of the adverb connectors. For unsignaled sets, decide which adverb connector is best. Remember to use correct punctuation. Study the examples before you begin.

Example

a. Soccer was the most demanding sport Fred ever played.
Nothing else involved him so completely. (*in fact*)
Soccer was the most demanding sport Fred ever played; in fact, nothing else involved him so completely.

1. The airport noise offended nearby homeowners.
New landing patterns were created to lessen flights over residential areas. (*consequently*)

2. Math was always a difficult subject for David.
He was very surprised when he was asked to help Kiyo. (*therefore*)

3. Georgia O'Keeffe was a famous American artist.
Her paintings of western deserts are known all over the world. (*in fact*)

4. French trappers helped to settle the Rocky Mountains.
The name of the Grand Teton mountain range is evidence of their presence.

5. World energy supplies are in short reserve.
This is a problem that all must work to solve.

Writing

Using a Semicolon

For more information on semicolons, sentence connectors, see pages 546-547.

Sometimes, the two sentences that combine to make a single statement have equal importance. In such cases a semicolon (;) alone can be an effective connector.

Sentences: Paul was a junior at Jefferson High School. His sister Ellen was an eighth-grader at Washington Junior High School. (;)

Combined: Paul was a junior at Jefferson High School; his sister Ellen was an eighth-grader at Washington Junior High School.

Sentences: The deserted gas station stood like a lonely sentinel. The new highway had routed traffic away from the once-busy corner.

Combined: The deserted gas station stood like a lonely sentinel; the new highway had routed traffic away from the once-busy corner.

Exercise 3: A Special Connector

Combine the following sets of sentences using a connecting adverb or a semicolon alone. Signals are given for sets 1–5; for sets 6–10, you must decide the best way to make the combinations. On a sheet of paper numbered 1–10, write your new sentences. Be sure to study the examples before you begin working.

Examples

a. The cowhand stood lonely vigil under the starry western sky.
Only the coyote, yowling mournfully at the moon, was company. (;)
The cowhand stood lonely vigil under the starry western sky; only the coyote, yowling mournfully at the moon, was company.

b. Canyon de Chelly contains many prehistoric Indian sites.
Most of them cannot be seen from the rim of the canyon.

Sentence Combining

Canyon de Chelly contains many prehistoric Indian sites; however, most of them cannot be seen from the rim of the canyon.

1. Julio loves to read scientific studies about the moon.
   He enjoys a good detective story every now and then. *(on the other hand)*
2. Danny dislikes taking out the garbage.
   He does his chores without complaining. *(however)*
3. Backpacking in Glacier National Park is Robert's dream.
   He plans to make his wish a reality after graduation. *(furthermore)*
4. Tania ran for secretary of the class.
   She really wanted to be president. *(however)*
5. My favorite film is *The Empire Strikes Back*.
   Jerry likes *The Black Stallion*. *(;)*
6. Many people thought Mount St. Helens would not erupt.
   Scientists who studied volcanoes knew its time was near.
7. Melissa is tidy about her personal appearance.
   Her room looks like a disaster zone.
8. Use the dictionary regularly.
   It is a helpful tool for improving your use of language.
9. John Steinbeck's *Of Mice and Men* facinated Raoul.
   He admired the devotion one human being showed to another.
10. Dr. Carstens was willing to teach Fred how to paint.
    She set aside an hour each evening to help him get started.

Writing Practice: *Using Connectors to Join Sentences*

For more information on punctuation, see pages 534-567.

Reread the free writing that you did for Writing Practice 3 in Chapter 1. Write two paragraphs based on your free writing. As you write, use conjunctions, adverbs, and semicolons to join sentences. Be sure to use correct punctuation. Vary the lengths and patterns of your sentences.

2 Keeping a Writer's Notebook

The Writer's Notebook

A Writer's Notebook is a record of the writer's thoughts, feelings, and observations.

There are many reasons to keep a Writer's Notebook. It can be a place to record your thoughts, feelings, and observations to share with others. As a record of experiences, your notebook can be a helpful source of ideas for other kinds of writing. In this chapter you will practice writing a notebook to share with your teacher and classmates. (If you want to write about private thoughts and experiences, consider keeping a private notebook at home—one that only you will read.)

Each time you write in your notebook, you write an *entry*. Entries may be only a few lines long, or they may be entire stories, writing exercises, or anything else you wish to write.

Model: *A Writer's Notebook Entry*

The following entries are from the book *A Snake-Lover's Diary*, by Barbara Brenner. (A *diary* is similar to a Writer's Notebook.) The first entry tells why the writer began keeping a diary and the second tells about her capturing a water snake.

April 17

I may as well begin by telling the reason for this diary. I've started it because of something special that happened today. It was when I was taking Shalom for his afternoon walk down in that old farm field. The two of us were walking along, enjoying all the signs of spring, when Shalom's good old retriever nose caught a whiff of something. He high-tailed it over to a log and began sniffing and digging around it. I didn't see anything, but knowing Shalom's nose, I figured something had to be there. So I picked up one end of the log and looked under it. There, coiled tightly in a little ring, was a Garter Snake.

I reached down and picked it up. It hardly moved. Just stayed in my hand, still groggy from its long winter sleep. I

turned it over and over, looking at the even white stripes that ran along its tan body, and the two small, perfect yellow dots on its head.

Now, I've seen snakes before. Even caught some. But somehow, this one was different. Maybe it was suddenly coming on something alive after the deadness of winter. Anyway, it was as if I'd never *really* seen a snake before. I decided then and there to take it home.

With Shalom bounding at my heels, I headed for the house. On the way, the plan began to take shape. I decided that I'd start a scientific study of snakes, and keep a diary of my findings. The Garter Snake would be my first specimen. I promptly named him Specimen A.

May 22

My quiet, peaceful spot wasn't so quiet today. I went down there after school. As soon as I got to the river, I spotted a Water Snake on a log in the sun.

Water Snakes found around here aren't poisonous, so I felt free to take off my sneakers and wade into the water after this new specimen. Shalom came right with me; he went around one side of the log and I went around the other.

Writing

Naturally, that snake wasn't going to sit there and wait for us to surround him. He slid into the water and just as he went under, I grabbed him. He was heavier than I thought, and before I knew it I'd slipped and sat right down on that gooey bottom. Clouds of mud came up all around me. I couldn't even see the snake but I still had hold of him. I slowly pulled myself out of the ooze, hanging on to the wriggling brown and black mass. When I finally staggered to my feet I was clutching four feet of slippery Water Snake. And was he mad! Before I could get to my snake bag, and stow him safely away, he bit me. I was more surprised than anything when I looked down and saw him hanging onto my arm with his teeth.

Almost without thinking, I reached down and pried his teeth loose. Then, as I held him, I got another shock. He let me have it with secret snake weapon number two, a smelly, oily secretion from the gland at the base of his tail. All over my pants, my shirt, my hands. Ugh![1]

Think and Discuss

1. What details does the writer use to convey what she saw, felt, heard, and smelled? For example, she describes touching "four feet of slippery Water Snake." What other details of feeling does she use? What visual details? What details of smell?

For more information on verbs, see pages 340-375.

2. These two entries are packed with specific words. For instance, Barbara Brenner writes in the first paragraph that the dog, Shalom, ". . . *high-tailed* it over to a log," instead of using the more general verb *went*. What are some of the other specific verbs Barbara Brenner uses? What effect do they have? What other specific words does she use?

3. What ideas does the writer convey in these entries?

Writing Practice 1: *Writing a Notebook Entry*

Think about an experience that was important because of its effect on you. Perhaps it excited you; made you feel especially angry, sad, or happy; or taught you a lesson. Write about this experience in a notebook entry to share with your teacher and classmates.

If the experience you write about happened long ago, you may not remember it exactly, but you can ask yourself a series

---

[1]Barbara Brenner, *A Snake-Lover's Diary*, © 1970, Addison-Wesley, Reading Massachusetts. pgs. 9, 10, 26, 27, 28 and 29 (text only.) Reprinted with permission.

of questions to help you recall it. As you answer them, make notes on a sheet of paper and use the notes as ideas for your entry.

1. What exactly was the experience?

2. Where did the experience happen? Did the place have any effect on the experience? (For example, if you were saying good-bye to a good friend who is moving to a distant place, would saying good-bye in your friend's empty house make the experience seem sadder?) What are important details about the place?

3. Who were the people involved in the experience, and what part did they play in it?

4. When did the experience happen? Did the time have anything to do with the experience or with its effect? (For example, if you were once left alone late at night and became very frightened, did the fact that it was dark make you more afraid?)

5. Why did the experience happen? What caused it to happen?

6. How did the experience make you feel? Did it change you in some way?

These questions will help you discover what you already know about the event, but your entry should be more than a list of answers. Use Barbara Brenner's entry on pages 28–30 as a model for your own.

Writing

Using Sensory Details

Becoming a good observer and learning how to record your observations are important for notebook writing. As you experience the physical world, your body takes in information through the senses, and you respond to sights, sounds, tastes, textures, and smells. Later, as you write in your notebook, use specific words, as Barbara Brenner did, to re-create what you experienced through your senses.

Sensory details re-create sights, sounds, tastes, smells, and textures for the reader.

Model: Using Sensory Details

Susan Magoffin, the first woman to cross the American plains, kept a record of her journey, which was later published. As you read the following entry from it, think about the sights and sounds she describes and notice how she expresses her thoughts and feelings.

Noon. No. 20. Little Arkansas River. June 30th
 Now, about dark, we came into the musquito regions, and I found to my great *horror* that I have been complaining all this time for nothing, yes absolutely for *nothing*; for some two or hundred or even thousands are nothing compared with what we now encountered. The carriage mules became so restless that they passed all the wagons and swishing their tails from side to side, as fast as they could, and slaping their ears, required some strength of our Mexican driver to hold them in.
 About 10 o'clock the mules became perfectly frantic, and nothing could make them stand. They were turned out to shift for themselves, and Magoffin seeing no other alternative than to remain there all night, tied his head and neck up with pocket handkerchiefs and set about having the tent stretched.
 I drew my feet up under me, wraped my shawl over my head, till I almost smothered with heat, and listened to the din without. And such a noise as it was, I shall pray ever to be preserved. Millions upon millions were swarming around me, and their knocking against the carriage *reminded me of a hard rain*. It was equal to any of the plagues of Egypt.
 I lay almost in a perfect stupor, the heat and stings made me perfectly sick, till Magoffin came to the carriage and told me *to run if I could*, with my shawl, bonnet and shoes on (and

Stupor means "a daze."

32

without opening my mouth Jane said, for they would *choke* me) straight to bed.

When I got there they pushed me straight in under the musquito bar, which had been tied up in some kind of a fashion, and oh, dear, what a relief it was to breathe again. There I sat in my cage, like an imprisoned creature frightened half to death.

Magoffin now rolled himself up some how with all his clothes on, and lay down at my side, he dare not raise the bar to get in. I tried to sleep and towards daylight succeeded. On awakening this morning I found my forehead, arms and feet covered with knots as large as a pea.[1]

Think and Discuss

1. Though her spelling is peculiar, Susan Magoffin records the sights and sounds around her so accurately that modern readers experience an event that happened one hundred years ago. Readers see the mules swishing their tails and hear the insects knocking against the wagons. What other sense experiences does the writer share?

2. Which of the senses does Susan Magoffin emphasize most in this passage?

Writing Assignment I: *Using Sensory Details*

A. Prewriting

For this assignment, which will help you sharpen your powers of observation, you need paper and pen and twenty to thirty minutes. Follow these directions:

Step 1. Select a place where you are likely to find a number of people and much activity, such as a nearby shopping center, a playground, a gym, or your school lunchroom.

Step 2. Spend five or ten minutes observing the people and activity around you, concentrating not only on what you see, but also on what you *hear, taste, feel,* and *smell.* Be aware of how you think and feel about what is happening.

Step 3. Aften ten minutes or so, make a list of the *sights, sounds, tastes, textures,* and *smells* you experience as shown in the example on the next page.

---

[1] Reprinted by permission of Yale University Press from *Down the Sante Fe Trail and into Mexico: Diary of Susan Shelby Magoffin 1846-1847,* edited by Stella M. Drumm.

Writing

Reptile House at City Zoo

Sights

Large boa constrictor draped over limb of tree

Corn snake that seems to watch the people watching it

Sounds

Keeper chatting away to snake whose cage she's cleaning

Soft "plop" as one snake slides into pool

Textures

Feel of garter snake the keeper holds out for people to touch

Smells

Roasted peanuts on sale outside

Damp smell of reptile house

Tastes

Roasted peanuts

B. Writing

Using your prewriting notes and observations, write a description of the place you observed. Include in your description some details about each of the senses: sights, sounds, tastes, textures, and smells.

C. Postwriting

Share your description with a small group of classmates. After they have read your composition, ask your classmates to point out examples of sensory details that helped them to visualize or imagine the place you described.

Using Specific Words

Imagine that the year is 2000, and scientists have made it possible for people to read minds. You have just returned from a trip to the moon, and your memory is filled with your strange experiences. You remember that, because of the moon's low gravity, you and your friends bounced into the air with each step. When you talked with your friends over your helmet intercom, your voices sounded as though they came from underwater. The pizza pill you had for lunch tasted of meat and cheese and tomato sauce. Now, back on Earth, you want to share your experience with your parents and friends, so you simply tune your thoughts into their minds.

Because people cannot yet read each other's minds, your job as a writer is to re-create your experiences for readers with words. For this reason the words that you use to describe must be carefully chosen. For example, suppose you write this sentence about your trip to the moon:

It was an *interesting* experience.

The word *interesting* is a general word; it describes many different experiences but does not help your reader to imagine this particular one. You could, however, write these sentences about your moon trip:

> Every time we took a step, we floated upward about a foot because of the moon's low gravity. For almost an hour we bounced around like four small children jumping on a mattress.

Now you have used *specific* words—words that tell about particular parts of an experience and give readers concrete information.

Writing

Model: Using Specific Words

As a teenager in the early 1800s, Nathaniel Hawthorne recorded in his notebook a ghost story that he had heard from a peddler in his uncle's store. Here is the entry he wrote about the ghost story:

> A peddler named Dominicus Jordan was today in uncle Richard's store, telling a ghost story. I listened intently but tried not to seem interested. The story was of a house, the owner of which was suddenly killed. Since his death the west garret window cannot be kept closed, though the shutters be hasped and nailed at night; they are invariably found open the next morning and no one can tell how or when the nails are drawn.
>
> There is also on the farm an apple-tree, of the fruit of which the owner was particularly fond, but since his death no person has been able to get one of the apples. The tree hangs full nearly every year; but whenever any individual tries to get one, stones come in all directions, as if thrown from some secret infernal battery or hidden catapult, and more than once those making the attempt have been struck. What is more strange, the tree stands in an open field, there being no shelter near from which tricks can be played without exposure.
>
> Jordan says that it seems odd to strangers to see that tree loaded with apples when the snow is four feet deep; and what is a mystery, there are no apples in the spring; no one ever sees the wind blow one off, none are ever seen on the snow, nor even the vestige of one on the grass under the tree; and that children may play under and around it while it is in blossom, and until the fruit is large enough to tempt them, with perfect safety. But the moment one of the apples is sought for, the air is full of flying stones.

Hasped means "fastened with a metal bolt or lock."

A **catapult** is a machine for throwing objects long distances.

Terra firma **means "firm land."**

He further says that late one starlight night he was passing the house and, looking up, saw the phantom walk out of the garret window with cane in hand, making all the motions as if walking on terra firma, although what appeared to be his feet were at least six yards from the ground; and so he went walking away on nothing, and when nearly out of sight, there was a great flash and an explosion as of twenty field-pieces—then—nothing!

This story was told with seeming earnestness, and listened to as though it was believed. How strange it is that almost all persons, old or young, are fond of hearing about the supernatural, though it produces nervousness and often fear. I should not be willing to sleep in that garret, though I do not believe a word of the story.

Think and Discuss

1. In this passage Hawthorne makes use of specific adverbs to clarify his writing. For instance, he writes that he listened *intently*. What are some other examples of specific adverbs used? What specific verbs, adjectives, and nouns are used?

2. Although Hawthorne's style differs from ours today, it is clear and concise. For example, he writes, "The tree hangs full almost every year." What are some other examples of specific but slightly unusual phrases in the passage?

Writing Practice 2: *Using Specific Words*

Think of a hobby, a sport, or another way of spending time that you enjoy. In a notebook entry, describe a specific experience with your subject, using specific and vivid details to communicate your enjoyment to your readers. If you like, imagine that your notebook is one of those listed below:

1. Notebook of a Football Player (or a participant in any other sport)
2. Observations of a Star Gazer
3. Notes of a Nature Lover
4. Experiences of a Pet Owner
5. Science Fiction Fantasies
6. Memoirs of a Student
7. Responses of a Reader
8. A Moviegoer's Reviews

Writing

Writing About Feelings

If you keep a private notebook, you may write about feelings that you do not want to share. When you keep a Writer's Notebook to share with others, you can still write about less private feelings.

A good writer helps readers share feelings.

Model: Writing About Feelings

Nina Kosterina, a Russian girl, kept a notebook in which she wrote about her experiences as a teenager and young adult in Russia during the 1930s and 1940s. From her notebook, readers learn what it was like to grow up in Communist Russia, and they get a valuable insight into the inner life of a young girl. In the entry, written when she was fifteen, the writer describes a feeling she experienced during a summer at camp. As you read, look for specific details used to set the scene. (*Kutlya* and *Krutitsa* are two Russian place names mentioned in the entry.)

September 3, 1941

It is hard to say what is more beautiful: the tall, slender pines in the pensively severe woods or the gay birches, festive as a ring of peasant girls. I am closer in spirit to the sullen pine woods. One place in my woods, my domain, is especially deeply etched in my memory.

It is on the way to Kutlya, beyond the ravine near Krutitsa. There the pine forest spreads a little, letting a narrow road run through the gap. When I discovered the spot, it struck me with its beauty.

I came out upon the road and stopped, with a sudden ache in my heart. I was so moved that I burst into tears, and those tears were both bitter and sweet. It was a difficult time for me, but I cried myself out in the woods, in the shadow of the stern, listening pines, and felt the better for it. I was calmed by the majestic beauty of the woods. They seemed to whisper to me wise words about how good life is. Ah, how good it is to live! "Even in your pain and sorrows there is the joy of living! Don't cry, little human!" I looked up with gratitude. The crowns of the pines swayed lightly, and the road ran on and on, and no one was around. . . .[1]

[1] Reprinted from *The Diary of Nina Kosterina* translated by Mirra Ginsburg. © 1968 by Mirra Ginsburg.

Think and Discuss

1. Nina Kosterina helps readers see and hear the surroundings where she experienced her feelings by using details. She writes, for example, about "stern, listening pines." What other specific details does she use in this entry?

2. What feelings does the writer convey? How does she reach you with her feelings?

Writing Practice 3: *Writing About Feelings*

Think of a time you felt an emotion you can share with others, perhaps happiness, fear, sadness, or embarrassment. Maybe in the middle of a party you have felt lonely. Maybe you have had to move, and your first day at your new school was a disaster. Or maybe you have worked up the courage to try something new and had a spectacular success. Describe your feelings and your surroundings at the time with specific, vivid details.

One way to discover ideas is to simply let your thoughts roam over your subject. You can do this most effectively by sitting in a quiet place with paper and pencil ready. Try to empty your mind of everything except your subject. As thoughts come, jot down notes about them and use these notes to write your entry.

For example, perhaps you can recall the first day in a new school or the first day in your present grade. As you think about the feeling you had on that day and the experiences that caused it, thoughts such as these might come to mind:

Being lost

Don't know anyone here yet

I got on the wrong bus this morning and almost didn't reach school on time.

So many students here! This isn't at all like my old school.

Feeling that I will like it here, once I get acquainted

Wonder if this school has a marching band?

Smell of wet clothing on people taking shelter in the hallways from the rain

Bright orange and yellow posters telling students where to register for classes

Notes such as these help you gather specific details about your feelings and about your surroundings during that time.

Sentence Combining: Using Subordinators, Commas, and *and*

Connecting Sentences with Subordinators

For more information on subordinators, also called subordinating conjunctions, see pages 450-453.

In this lesson you will learn how to join two ideas that are *not* of equal importance. The less important idea is introduced by words called *subordinators*, such as *as, because, although, since, after, before, if, as if, just when, as soon as, even though,* or *until*. A subordinator does two things:

1. It makes one sentence less important than the other.
2. It makes one sentence dependent upon the other for complete sense.

Sentences: I like to eat an apple for a midafternoon snack. I come home from school. (*when*)

Combined: I like to eat an apple for a midafternoon snack *when* I come home from school.

For more information on subordinate clauses, see pages 518-522.

When is the subordinator in the above example. It shows a time relationship between the two sentences, and it makes the second sentence dependent upon the first. (See also the sections on adverb clauses in Chapter 22.) The sentence that begins with the subordinator *when* would not make sense by itself. Other subordinators will show different relationships, but they will always make one sentence depend upon the other for its meaning. Study the following examples.

Sentences: Anthony bought earphones to use with the family stereo.
He likes to listen to loud music. (*because*)

Combined: Anthony bought earphones to use with the family stereo *because* he likes to listen to loud music.

Sentences: The hurricane's winds did not diminish.
They moved inland sixty miles. (*until*)

Combined: The hurricane's winds did not diminish *until* they moved inland sixty miles.

Sentence Combining

For more information on punctuating subordinators, see pages 538-540.

In the two preceding examples no punctuation was necessary to join the second sentence to the end of the first one with a subordinator. However, when you *begin* a sentence with the subordinator, use a comma between the two sentences, as this example shows:

Sentences: You want to have extra spending money. (*since*) You will have to get a part-time job.

Combined: *Since* you want to have extra spending money, you will have to get a part-time job.

Exercise 1: Connecting Sentences of Unequal Importance

On a sheet of paper numbered 1–5, combine the following pairs of sentences with the subordinator that appears as a signal in parentheses. If the signal follows the first sentence of the pair, put the subordinator in front of that first sentence. If the signal follows the second sentence, put the subordinator between the two sentences when you join them. Study the examples before you begin.

Examples

a. Luis Mendez listened carefully to the teacher's instructions. (*although*)
He could not solve the math problem.
Although Luis Mendez listened carefully to the teacher's instructions, he could not solve the math problem.

b. Dalton River was greatly swollen.
The mountain snows had begun to melt. (*because*)
Dalton River was greatly swollen because the mountain snows had begun to melt.

1. You go camping. (*when*)
Be sure to carry first-aid equipment with you.

2. Desert turtles live longer in their natural habitat. (*although*)
Some people insist on taking them home for pets.

3. Harvey asked his older brother to pick him up after the show.
He did not want to have to walk home alone. (*because*)

4. Melissa studied her lines carefully.
She would make no mistakes on opening night. (*so that*)

41

5. You do what the doctor asks you to do. (*unless*)
   You may never regain the full use of your fractured leg.

Combine the following sets of sentences with a subordinator. No signals are given, so you must decide which one to use and where to put it in the combined sentence.

6. I will make my special pizza.
   You will join us for dinner.

7. You remember to do your chores without being reminded. (*until*)
   You will not get your allowance.

8. I plan to go to the library this afternoon.
   I will not mind returning your books.

9. Father and I were excited to discover an old plantation house hidden in the woods.
   We could not convince Grandmother to hike there to see it.

10. An owl hooted in the distance.
    The clouds parted and the moon shone through on the lonely farmhouse.

Adding Sentences with Commas and *and*

In this lesson you will learn how to join more than two sentences into a single statement. In order to do these exercises, you need to know a new signal (X) and a new term, *base sentence*. The first sentence in each set of three or more sentences is the *base sentence*. The base sentence does not change, but parts of the other sentences are added to it.

The signal (X) through a word means to remove it from the combined sentence. Study the following examples to see how the combinations work.

Base Sentence: The kitten lapped up the milk in its dish.

Add: T̶h̶e̶ k̶i̶t̶t̶e̶n̶ purred contentedly.

Add: T̶h̶e̶ k̶i̶t̶t̶e̶n̶ rubbed against Sarah's ankles.

Combined: The kitten lapped up the milk in its dish, purred contentedly, and rubbed against Sarah's ankles.

For more information on commas and coordinating conjunctions, see pages 440-443.

Notice that in the combined sentence the words *the kitten* have been removed from the two sentences that were added to the base sentence. Commas and the word *and* were placed between the base and the added sentences to keep them from running together. In this section the signals (,) and (, *and*) tell you to add a comma, or a comma and the word *and*, to the combined sentence. Study the following examples.

Base Sentence: Barbara Ashton was born in Kentucky.

Add: B̶a̶r̶b̶a̶r̶a̶ A̶s̶h̶t̶o̶n̶ moved to Georgia when she was three years old. (,)

Add: B̶a̶r̶b̶a̶r̶a̶ A̶s̶h̶t̶o̶n̶ went to high school in Ohio. (, *and*)

Combined: Barbara Ashton was born in Kentucky, moved to Georgia when she was three years old, *and* went to high school in Ohio.

Base Sentence: Brightly colored leaves fluttered down from the branches.

Add: T̶h̶e̶y̶ swirled across the yard. (,)

Add: T̶h̶e̶y̶ transformed the lawn into a beautiful red and gold carpet. (, *and*)

43

Writing

Combined: Brightly colored leaves fluttered down from the branches, swirled across the yard, *and* transformed the lawn into a beautiful red and gold carpet.

If you are not used to writing sentences as long as the ones in these examples, read the combined sentences aloud to yourself to hear how they sound. In that way you will gain a sense of the smooth, flowing quality of these new sentences.

Exercise 2: Adding Sentences in a Series

Combine the following sets of sentences, using the signals given in each. When you have finished each one, read the sentence to yourself to hear how the new pattern fits ideas together. Remember that the first sentence in each set is the base sentence. Write each new sentence on a sheet of paper numbered 1–5. Study the example before you begin.

Example

a. Tammy watched a horror film on Friday evening.
She became too terrified to sleep. (,)
She spent the whole night tossing and turning. (, *and*)
Tammy watched a horror film on Friday evening, became too terrified to sleep, and spent the whole night tossing and turning.

Sentence Combining

1. Richard watched the diving instructor very carefully.
   Richard pulled the mask into place over his eyes and nose. (,)
   Richard slipped noiselessly into the clear deep waters. (, *and*)

2. Grandmother heard the car turn into her driveway.
   She hurriedly put the finishing touches on the meal. (,)
   She rushed outside to greet the holiday guests. (, *and*)

3. The new car rolled slowly down Maple Street.
   It turned right on Via Linda. (,)
   It stopped in front of Rosa's house. (, *and*)

4. Rain poured off the eaves and down the front of the house.
   It was painting the old building with watery strokes. (,)
   It was drumming a careless rhythm on the tin roof. (,)

5. Three bicyclists pulled ahead of the other racers.
   They were straining every muscle. (,)
   They were each determined to cross the finish line ahead of all of the others. (,)

Combine the sets of sentences on the next page, leaving out repeated words and inserting punctuation when necessary. Remember that the first sentence in each set is the base sentence, and the other sentences are added to it. Write each new sentence on a sheet of paper numbered 6–10. Study the example before you begin.

45

Writing

Example

a. Palms swayed wildly in the fierce wind.
   They bent nearly to the ground.
   They lost large fronds as the gale increased.
   Palms swayed wildly in the fierce wind, bent nearly to the ground, and lost large fronds as the gale increased.

6. As John lifted the rock above it, the snake raised its head.
   It rattled its tail in warning.
   It suddenly scurried to safety between two boulders.

7. The policewoman was talking to the school children.
   She was gesturing with her hands.
   She was teaching them the signals to use when they ride their bikes.

8. Mr. Wong offered to take the boys backpacking over spring vacation.
   He helped them to find ways to earn money for the trip.
   He charted a course for the hikers to follow.

9. Boxes of books were stacked by the door.
   They were tied with strong cord.
   They were waiting for the movers to load them on the van.

10. The bargain hunters rushed into the department store.
    They jostled one another.
    They argued over prices with the unhappy clerks.

Writing Practice: *Using Sentence Combining*

Choose one of the following topics or make up one of your own, and write a short explanation of how to do or make something. Use the sentence-combining skills you have learned.

1. Making a special type of kite
2. Installing a special accessory on a bicycle
3. Taking care of records
4. Preparing a simple meal
5. Bathing a cat
6. Performing a magic trick
7. Teaching a three-year-old how to tie a shoelace
8. Organizing a clothes closet
9. Doing a simple science experiment
10. Reporting an emergency to the police or fire department

3 Writing a Personal Narrative

Writing About Your Life

Writers often record the important parts of their lives by telling about the people, places, and events that have affected them most. By writing about their experiences, they can learn more about themselves and share their knowledge about life with others. In this chapter you will learn how writing about your experiences can be helpful to you.

The Narrator

When you write about your own experiences, you are the narrator. The *narrator* is the person who tells, or *narrates*, a story.

Even though you write about other people, places, and events, you are telling the story and may use the word *I* many times. Realizing that you are the narrator is important because you are telling the story from your *point of view*.

Point of view is a way of looking at someone or something and may be both physical and mental.

Physical point of view means the location from which you observe something or someone. Watching a basketball game from high in the stands gives you a very different point of view from watching it from the bottom row of the bleachers. When you are positioned at a distance from a place, you have a different viewpoint from the one you have when you move closer to it.

Mental point of view is the way you think and feel about something or someone. Many small children, for example, are afraid of the dark and often imagine strange creatures lurking in the shadows. Usually they lose this fear as they grow older and realize the monsters exist only in their minds. Age changes their point of view.

Experience may also affect a person's mental point of view. For example, perhaps you remember your first impression of school. At that time school may have seemed a strange, frightening place, but as you had experiences there, it began to seem more comfortable. Knowledge of a person, place, or event often causes a change in viewpoint. Spectators at a soccer game who do not know the rules may see nothing more than people running around on a field kicking a ball, but people who know the rules probably see something much different.

As you mature, your point of view changes continually. Even during this past year you have probably changed some thoughts and feelings. You may have learned to like someone you did not care about earlier, or you may have decided you like a food you thought you hated.

Writing Practice 1: *Describing an Object*

Make a list of objects that were important to you when you were younger. Choose one object and write a description of it as it appeared at that time. Include your thoughts and feelings about it and tell why it was special to you.

Then write a second paragraph explaining how your point of view has changed about the object now that you are older. If the object itself has changed over time, describe it as it looks now. Explain how your thoughts and feelings toward it have also changed. Is it still as important to you as it was when you were younger?

Writing About Places

Because they help make you the person you are today and the person you will become, places are important in your life. Your school, for example, may affect the way you feel about education for the rest of your life. Even places you have visited only once, such as the hospital room where you stayed to have your tonsils removed, may be important if they had an effect on you.

By describing places of importance to you, you help readers share your experiences.

One way to share the experiences of a place is to use specific, vivid details. Think what sights, sounds, smells, textures, and tastes you remember about the place. When you remember a hospital room, for example, you may think how bare the room looked without rugs on the floor or posters on the wall, and you may recall the squeaking of the nurses' shoes on the tile floor and the faint smell of disinfectant. Record these details in your place descriptions.

Recall the people who were part of the place.

People are important in your memories of places. When you think back to your first-grade classroom, you may remember such things as the colorful alphabet posters that lined the walls and the fat pencils you used, but your memories would not be complete without recalling the people also. You may remember the teacher who smiled when you were frightened or the bully who pushed you into a mud puddle on the first day and ruined your new clothes. Describing people like these helps readers share your experiences.

Tell your thoughts and feelings about the place and the people there.

How did you feel alone in a room full of strangers? When you lost the new notebook you had taken care of since August? When you saw a classmate drop crayons into the goldfish tank?

Model: A Description of a Place

In Jesse Stuart's short story "Dark Winter," a young boy is sent out in the middle of a winter night to fetch a doctor for his seriously ill father. While reading this part of the story, look for specific, vivid details that describe the place the boy is passing.

    I am in the saddle. I do not need the lantern. When the moon turns dark I may not be able to follow the path without it. I tie it to the saddle. It is too cold to hold it in my hand. I blow out the tiny flame. I have matches in my pocket to relight it with if the moon goes down before I get back. I rub Fred's neck and say to him: "Now, boy, let's go. A straight piece of road. Slow here, Fred boy. Slow. Slow. Slow. It's a bad place. Take it easy." The stars are in the sky above me. The bull bat screams. I can hear the hoot owl laughin' under such cold moon and such cold sky filled with stars. I have to pass a graveyard and I am afraid of a graveyard at night. There are the white tombstones among the briars and brush that loom wiry and black above the snow. There are the broken-top trees at the edge of the graveyard and the old iron fence bare of snow. And I think, "What if Pop has to come here and sleep in this quiet place with only the wind to blow over him and the bull bats to try to wake him with their screams and the hoot owls to sit up there in bare chestnut tree tops and laugh all night over nothing."

    Fred gets his breath hard. He is wet around the saddle. I have to hold a tight rein. He is wiry and wants to tear up the mountain path. The snow crunches beneath his feet.[1]

---

[1] From "Dark Winter" from *A Jesse Stuart Harvest* by Jesse Stuart. Copyright © 1936 by Jesse Stuart. Reprinted by permission of the Jesse Stuart Foundation.

Writing

Think and Discuss

1. Because Jesse Stuart uses specific, vivid details, readers can share in the boy's experience as he passes the graveyard. They can hear the scream of the bat and see the white tombstones. With your teacher and classmates, find other specific details that the writer uses to make the graveyard seem an actual place.

2. Find specific details that tell the boy's thoughts and feelings about the place.

Writing Assignment I: *Describing a Place*

A. Prewriting

Selecting a Topic: Select a place that is important in your life, perhaps your home, school, or neighborhood. To help you get started, here is a list of places you might consider:

A place where you play baseball, stickball, tennis, soccer, or some other sport

A place where you spend enjoyable hours, such as your yard or a park

A place where you once made a new friend or lost a long-time friend

A place where you feel excitement, such as a concert or an amusement park

A place where you feel relaxed or secure

A place where you feel insecure or frightened

A place where you feel important

A place where you like to be alone

Listing Specific Details: Asking yourself *who? what? when? where? why?* and *how?* questions can help you remember a place and the people there. As you answer your own questions, make notes for yourself. Later you can make these notes into sentences and organize your writing for your readers. Here are questions and notes that might describe one writer's backyard when he or she was eight:

What sights, sounds, smells, textures, and tastes do I remember?

> Seeing the stars fade in the early light after my friends and I had talked all night
>
> Buzz of mosquito we could never catch
>
> Mildewy smell of pup tent I had left out in the rain
>
> Taste of dry crackers we sneaked from the house
>
> Itch of mosquito bites

Who else was there? *What* did they do?

> My friend Carlos, trying to frighten us with stories of great brown bears that destroyed pup tents with one slash of giant claws
>
> My parents, whose warning voices became more severe each time they asked us to quiet down

How does the place differ from other places like it? *Why* does it stand out in my mind?

> Large tree over the pup tent at night seemed like a huge forest.
>
> Our usually friendly-looking house stood white and ghostly in the moonlight.

How has the place changed, or is it unchanged?

> Pup tent no longer there
>
> Tree seems very ordinary now

What are my thoughts and feelings about the place? *How* are these changing?

> The backyard was a magic place for me. I was the range herder who slept under the stars while my cattle stirred nearby. Now my friends and I prefer our air-conditioned rooms to that small, hot, mosquito-filled backyard.

Writing

B. Writing

Using specific, vivid details, write a description of the place. Include your thoughts and feelings about the place and the people. Write your description so that your classmates will feel as though they have been there.

C. Postwriting

Read your description of a place to a small group of classmates. Ask them to respond to the following questions:

What specific details helped you visualize the place?

What details need to be omitted or added?

After hearing the responses of your classmates, revise your paper to make sure that:

1. The description uses vivid, specific details.

2. The description includes your thoughts and feelings about the place.

3. The description is directed to a specific audience (your classmates).

Use the checklist at the back of the book to proofread your writing.

Writing About People in Your Life

You are surrounded by people who have helped shape your life—your parents, grandparents, brothers and sisters, friends, classmates, teachers, and even people you have met only briefly. Without being aware of the details you observed about these people, you have probably drawn many conclusions about them. You may, for example, have made decisions such as these:

My grandmother is nice.

My friend Joan is a lot of fun.

That woman I just passed on the street seems strange.

Anna is pretty.

John is a good sport.

To make people seem real to your readers, you must do more than give readers the conclusions you have reached about them. A sentence such as *My grandmother is nice* does not make your grandmother seem real to your readers because it does not help them see and hear her. You must give details that will explain why you reached the conclusions that you did.

One way to give details about people is to describe them directly.

By using specific, vivid details to describe how people look and the way they act and talk, you can help your readers see and hear them.

Model: Specific Details in Description

As you read the following excerpt from Mary McCarthy's *Memories of a Catholic Girlhood*, look for specific details that describe the grandmother, her sister, and their houses.

> The strange lady was supposed to be my grandmother, but I did not think of her that way when I was little. She did not have white hair, for one thing, like my other grandmother—the real one, I considered her. Nor did she do embroidery or tapestry work or stare at us over her glasses. She did not have glasses, only a peculiar ornament on a chain that she put up to her eyes when she wanted to look at something. With her queer electric car that ran soundlessly and was upholstered inside in the softest grey like a jewel case, her dotted veil, her gloves, which had bumps in them (made by her rings, I

Writing

discovered later), her bell, and her descending terraces, she was a fairy-tale person who lived in an enchanted house, which was full of bulges, too—two overhanging balconies, on the lake side, and four bays and a little tower. (She had a fairy-tale sister, different from herself, tall, with white hair piled on top of her head in a long, conical shape, a towering mountain peak or a vanilla ice-cream cone; we were taken to see her one day and her house was magic also. She had a whole polar bear for a rug, and her floor shone like glass and made you slip when you walked on it; her house was like a winter palace or like the North Pole, where Santa Claus came from.) I did not love the strange lady in the electric but I loved the things she had.[1]

Think and Discuss

1. The writer begins the description of her grandmother by telling about the things the grandmother does not have or do. Then she paints an image of the woman by describing her within the setting of her house. What specific details help you, as the reader, imagine this woman, her house, and the writer's feelings about them both?

2. The description extends beyond the grandmother to include her sister and her sister's house. What details help you visualize the sister and her home?

For information on quotation marks, see pages 554-555.

Another way to describe people is to relate incidents involving them.

By showing how a person behaves you can make him or her seem real to your readers. Recording *dialogue*—conversation between two or more people—can help show what people are like, creating an especially vivid description.

Model: Using Dialogue to Describe Characters

In her book *Please Don't Eat the Daisies*, Jean Kerr describes her eight-year-old son by relating an incident involving him and by recording the dialogue.

> You take Christopher—and you *may*; he's a slightly used eight-year-old. The source of our difficulty with him lies in the fact that he is interested in the precise value of words whereas we are only interested in having him pick his clothes up off the floor. I say, "Christopher, you take a bath and put all your

---

[1] ©1957 by Mary McCarthy. Reprinted from her volume *Memories of a Catholic Girlhood* by permission of Harcourt Brace Jovanovich, Inc., and William Heinemann, Ltd. First published in *The New Yorker*.

things in the wash," and he says, "Okay, but it will break the Bendix." Now at this point the shrewd rejoinder would be, "That's all right, let it break the Bendix." But years of experience have washed over me in vain and I, perennial patsy, inquire, "*Why* will it break the Bendix?" So he explains, "Well, if I put *all* my things in the wash, I'll have to put my shoes in and they will certainly break the machinery."

"Very well," I say, all sweetness and control, "put everything but the shoes in the wash." He picks up my agreeable tone at once, announcing cheerily, "Then you *do* want me to put my belt in the wash."[1]

Think and Discuss

1. What details in this incident help you see and hear Christopher?
2. How would you describe him?

Writing Assignment II: *A Character Description*

A. Prewriting

First, select a person who has been important in your life, perhaps a relative, friend, or neighbor. Make a word cluster that includes specific details describing the person's physical appearance, habits, and personality traits. As you write your word cluster, think about the following questions.

1. What is it that you especially notice about the person's physical appearance?
2. What personality traits are reflected in the person's physical appearance, words, or actions?

Next, think of an incident involving the person. Choose an incident that reveals something about the person's character. Free write the story of the incident, including specific details that show through his or her words and actions, what the person is like.

B. Writing

Using the details from your word cluster and your free writing, write two paragraphs describing the person. Use dialogue, as Jean Kerr did in describing Christopher, to bring your character to life.

---

[1]Excerpt from *Please Don't Eat the Daisies* by Jean Kerr. Copyright 1954 by Jean Kerr. Reprinted by permission of Doubleday & Company, Inc. and Brandt & Brandt Literary Agents, Inc.

Writing

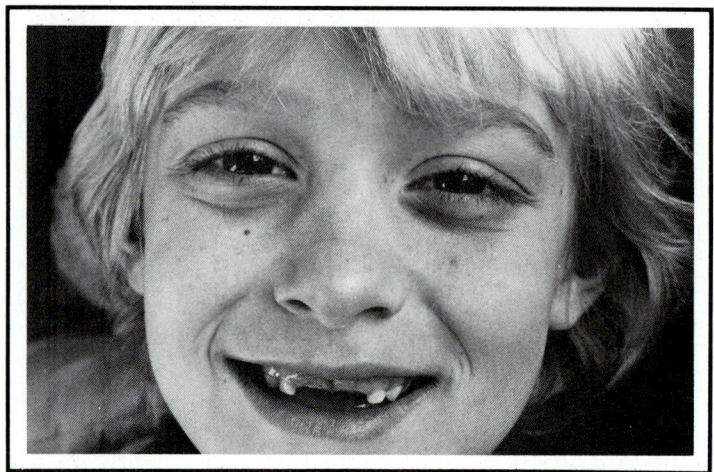

C. Postwriting

Read your description and think about changes that will make your writing clearer and more interesting to readers. Be sure that:

1. Conclusions about people are supported with specific, vivid details.
2. Descriptive details show what the person is like through his or her words, thoughts, or actions.
3. Dialogue sounds like the speech of real people.

Writing About Events

Your experiences involve more than people and places; they are also a series of events. When you write about these events as well as about people and places, you are telling an important part of your story.

Using specific details to write about events helps readers share the experience.

Here are some notes for a description of an event—the writer's first job. The notes tell about the event, about the people who were involved, and about the place where the event happened, but they do not give many details.

Got first job when in eighth grade

Helped grocery store owner take inventory

Worked on Sunday when store was closed

Counted all items on shelf

Fun at first, but later boring

Became tired, bored, and careless—made many errors

Grocery store owner talked to parents—had to do job again next Sunday

After using prewriting techniques to think of ideas, the writer begins to supply details about the event and about the people and place. As you read the following details, notice how you begin to share the writer's experience.

1. Mr. Pappas was the owner of the corner grocery store. He was a small, muscular man, completely bald, who always wore a blue bib-apron. [Details about how a person looks]

2. The store was small and grubby. The meat counter was so small that there was barely room for a tray of hamburger, a large stack of wieners, and a dozen or so pork chops. [Details about a place]

3. When Mr. Pappas told Dad that we had miscounted, Dad was very calm. The only thing he said was, "Next Sunday the counting will be done right!" [Details about how a person acts and talks]

4. The store always smelled strongly of cheese. [Detail about how a place smells]

5. Within two hours, counting shelf after shelf of cans began to bore me. I thought the day would never end. [Details about the writer's feelings]

6. On the first day of counting, Mr. Pappas let me choose what I wanted for lunch. I made myself three bologna sandwiches, drank four cartons of milk, and finished up with two bananas. [Details about what happened]

7 While I was counting, I began to think about how monotonous some jobs can be and decided to try harder in school so that I could spend my life doing interesting work. [Details about the writer's thoughts]

8. All day I could hear Mr. Pappas muttering as he counted items. [Details of sound]

Writing

Although this series of notes has more details about the event and about people and the place, it still does not have enough. For example, the writer does not give details about how the errors were made or about Mr. Pappas' reaction to them. Before writing this part of the composition for readers, the writer needs to supply these details.

The writer also needs to organize the details so that readers can easily follow the story. In the list above, for example, the writer tells about the father's reaction to the errors before telling about the day spent counting. One way writers often organize events is to tell how they happen in time, a method called *chronological* organization. In this way the writer would tell first about getting the job, then about the store and its owner, and then about the day's work, and so on.

Writing Practice 2: *Organizing Details About Events*

Using the list of details on page 59, write a complete account of this writer's first job. Arrange the details in time order and add missing details to make the story complete.

Model: Writing About an Event

In the following excerpt from Harry Mark Petrakis' autobiography, *Stelmark*, the Greek-American author tells about an event that happened when he was young. As you read, look for specific details he uses to help readers share his experience.

There was one storekeeper I remember above all others in my youth. It was shortly before I became ill, spending a

good portion of my time with a motley group of varied ethnic ancestry. We contended with one another to deride the customs of the old country. On our Saturday forays into neighborhoods beyond our own, to prove we were really Americans, we ate hot dogs and drank Cokes. If a boy didn't have ten cents for this repast he went hungry, for he dared not bring a sandwich from home made of the spiced meats our families ate.

One of our untamed games was to seek out the owner of a pushcart or a store, unmistakably an immigrant, and bedevil him with a chorus of insults and jeers. To prove allegiance to the gang it was necessary to reserve our fiercest malevolence for a storekeeper or peddler belonging to our own ethnic background.

Malevolence means "ill will."

For that reason I led a raid on the small, shabby grocery of old Barba Nikos, a short, sinewy Greek who walked with a slight limp and sported a flaring, handlebar mustache.

We stood outside his store and dared him to come out. When he emerged to do battle, we plucked a few plums and peaches from the baskets on the sidewalk and retreated across the street to eat them while he watched. He waved a fist and hurled epithets at us in ornamental Greek.

An *epithet* is an unpleasant descriptive name.

Aware that my mettle was being tested, I raised my arm and threw my half-eaten plum at the old man. My aim was accurate and the plum struck him on the cheek. He shuddered and put his hand to the stain. He stared at me across the street, and although I could not see his eyes, I felt them sear my flesh. He turned and walked silently back into the store. The boys slapped my shoulders in admiration, but it was a hollow victory that rested like a stone in the pit of my stomach.

At twilight, when we disbanded, I passed the grocery alone on my way home. There was a small light burning in the store and the shadow of the old man's body outlined against the glass. Goaded by remorse, I walked to the door and entered.

The old man moved from behind the narrow wooden counter and stared at me. I wanted to turn and flee, but by then it was too late. As he motioned for me to come closer, I braced myself for a curse or a blow.

"You were the one," he said, finally, in a harsh voice.
I nodded mutely.
"Why did you come back?"
I stood there unable to answer.
"What's your name?"
"Haralambos," I said, speaking to him in Greek.
He looked at me in shock. "You are Greek!" he cried. "A Greek boy attacking a Greek grocer!" He stood appalled at the immensity of my crime. "All right," he said coldly. "You are here because you wish to make amends." His great mustache bristled in concentration. "Four plums, two peaches," he said.

Writing

"That makes a total of seventy-eight cents. Call it seventy-five. Do you have seventy-five cents, boy?"

I shook my head.

"Then you will work it off," he said. "Fifteen cents an hour into seventy-five cents makes"—he paused—"five hours of work. Can you come here Saturday morning?"

"Yes," I said.

"Yes, Barba Nikos," he said sternly. "Show respect."

"Yes, Barba Nikos," I said.[1]

Think and Discuss

1. The problem Harry Mark Petrakis faced was not a physical problem—it was the inner conflict he experienced in learning to accept his Greek ancestry. Describe how this conflict affected the writer and what he did as a result of it.

2. To help readers see and hear the grocer and the boys, Petrakis uses specific details. For example, he writes that Barba Nikos was "a short, sinewy Greek who walked with a slight limp and sported a flaring, handlebar mustache." What other specific details help you imagine this event?

3. Petrakis uses chronological order in this story. What words and phrases that he uses refer to time?

For Your Writer's Notebook

> Harry Mark Petrakis eventually learned to cherish his Greek ancestry, and he never forgot the man who helped him do this. Imagine that you are young Petrakis and have been involved in this event or one similar to it that you make up. Then write an entry describing your role in the episode, including your thoughts and feelings about the event.

Writing Assignment III: *Writing About an Event*

Using material from your Writer's Notebook, write about an important event in your life. Use specific details to describe the event, the people involved, and the place where it happened.

---

[1]From *Reflections: A Writer's Life—A Writer's Work.* Published by Lake View Press, Chicago, IL, 1983. Copyright by Harry Mark Petrakis.

A. Prewriting

Read through the entries in your Writer's Notebook for ideas about important events in your life. You can also talk with people who remember events and your role in them, and you can use a questioning system like the six basic questions.

Questions like these will help you think of ideas for writing about events and about the people and places involved in them:

1. What happened? Briefly list the steps in the event, one after the other.

2. Who was involved? Write down what you can see, hear, touch, and smell about these people. What do you remember about facial features, hands, hair, movements, voices, clothing?

   What did these people do? What were their actions? What did they say? What place or places do you associate with these people?

   What are some details about these places?

3. Where did the event take place? Write down what you can see, hear, taste, touch, and smell about the place.

   How does the place differ from other places like it? What makes it stand out in your mind? What part did the place play in your life? Why was it important to you?

4. Why did the event happen? What was the reason for it, or the cause?

5. What were your thoughts and feelings during and just after the event? How have these thoughts and feelings changed over the years?

You probably will not use all of the details you gather with these questions, and you may remember and add more details as you write. With practice you will learn which details will best enhance or clarify your narrative.

B. Writing

Write about the details of the event in chronological order, the order they occurred in time. Include your thoughts and feelings about the event. Use your prewriting notes to guide your writing.

Writing

C. Postwriting

Reread what you have written to make sure that:

1. Specific details are used about the events to make them seem real to readers.
2. Specific details are used to describe people and places that are part of the events.
3. Details are organized so that readers can easily follow what happens.
4. Details include those of sound, touch, taste, and smell, as well as sight.
5. Your thoughts and feelings about the event are included.
6. Readers are given the information they need to understand people, places, and events.

Use the checklist at the back of this book to proofread your writing assignment.

Sentence Combining:
Arranging Parts And Using A Colon

Arranging Sentence Parts

Sentence parts do not always have to be added to the *end* of the base sentence, as the following examples show.

For more information on verbal phrases, see pages 504-507.

Base Sentence: The tuba players marched behind everyone.
Add: The tuba players were raising their horns above the rest of the band.
Combined: *Raising their horns above the rest of the band,* the tuba players marched behind everyone.
or
Combined: The tuba players marched behind everyone else, *raising their horns above the rest of the band.*

Base Sentence: The lone scout glided upriver.
Add: He was paddling his canoe silently.
Add: He was unsuspected by the enemy.
Combined: *Paddling his canoe silently,* the lone scout glided upriver, *unsuspected by the enemy.*
or
Combined: *Unsuspected by the enemy,* the lone scout glided upriver, *paddling his canoe silently.*

For more information on using commas with introductory phrases, see pages 539-540.

Exercise 1: *Arranging Sentence Parts*

On a sheet of paper, combine the following sets of sentences by adding to the beginning or end of the base sentence. Let the sense of the final combined sentence be your guide. For unsignaled sets, decide which words to leave out of the combined sentences. Study the example before you begin.

Example

a. The pilot eased the plane down gently.
~~She was~~ hoping to pass the licensing exam.
~~She was~~ unaware that the landing strip was under repair.

65

Hoping to pass the licensing exam, the pilot eased the plane down gently, unaware that the landing strip was under repair.
or
Unaware that the landing strip was under repair, the pilot eased the plane down gently, hoping to pass the licensing exam.

1. Thomas' pet spaniel greeted him at the door.
   ~~It was~~ wagging its tail excitedly.
   ~~It was~~ eager for its dinner.

2. The students watched the clock anxiously.
   ~~They were~~ hoping the teacher would forget to give their history test.

3. The rancher drove the cattle to market.
   ~~He was~~ unaware that prices had fallen drastically.

4. Mother went to her science class.
   She was pleased that she understood the lesson.

5. The trapeze artist walked the high wire twice a day.
   He was performing without a net.
   He was thrilling the crowds below.

A Special Connector: The Colon

For more information on using colons to join sentences, see pages 547-550.

A colon may also join sentences, but it has a specific use, as the following examples show. The signal (:) in parentheses after the second sentence tells you to join the sentences with a colon.

Sentences: Marty's pet hamster loves to eat certain fresh vegetables.
Those vegetables are lettuce, carrots, cabbage, and spinach. (:)

Combined: Marty's pet hamster loves to eat certain fresh vegetables: lettuce, carrots, cabbage, and spinach.

Sentences: Coach Osaka demanded that the team practice three skills during every practice.
Those skills were dribbling the ball, passing while moving, and shooting free shots. (:)

Combined: Coach Osaka demanded that the team practice three skills during every practice: dribbling the ball, passing while moving, and shooting free shots.

The colon signals that a list of things will follow in the rest of the sentence. This list names or gives an example of the idea in the first part of the sentence. Notice that the sentence that comes before the colon is a complete sentence, but the words that follow the colon need not form a complete sentence by themselves.

Exercise 2: Using Colons to Join Sentences

On a sheet of paper, combine the following sentence sets. Only sets 1–3 give the signal (:), but the colon can be used to join sentences in each set. Remember that the first sentence in each set is the base sentence. Put the colon between the base sentence and the part of the second sentence that follows. Leave out any unnecessary words when you make the combination. Study the example before you begin.

Example

a. Mrs. Hawkins misplaced several items of jewelry. These items were her gold watch, an antique brooch, and a charm bracelet. (:)
   Mrs. Hawkins misplaced several items of jewelry: her gold watch, an antique brooch, and a charm bracelet.

1. The bus driver asked the children not to do three things. These things were put their hands out the window, stand while the bus is moving, and talk loudly. (:)

2. Margaret enjoyed all of her classes at Johnson Junior High School.
   Her classes were English, geography, mathematics, French, home economics, and physical education. (:)

3. Five members of our committee were unable to attend the November meeting.
   The members were Ms. Kolesa, Mr. Waroski, Dr. Gyven, Ms. Perkins, and Ms. Merriweather. (:)

4. Joe and Uncle Jonathan managed to bring home enough fish for the whole family to enjoy.
   The fish were three bass, five bluegills, and one pike.

5. George dreams of achieving great feats of strength and endurance.
These feats are swimming the English Channel, climbing Mount Everest, and diving for lost Spanish galleons off the coast of Haiti.

Exercise 3: *Using a Variety of Signals*

Combine these sets of sentences. For unsignaled sets, decide which of the sentence combining methods you have learned works best. When you have finished, you will have a seven-sentence paragraph. Study the examples below and read them in paragraph form before you begin.

Examples

a. It was her first day at the middle school. (*because*)
Sarah was uneasy.
Because it was her first day at the Middle School, Sarah was uneasy.

b. She did not know any of the other students.
She did not know how to find her classes. (,)
She did not know even where to eat lunch! (,*or*)
She did not know any of the other students, how to find her classes, or even where to eat lunch!

c. So she spent her lunch hour touring the school grounds.
She was eating as she walked. (,)
So she spent her lunch hour touring the school grounds, eating as she walked.

d. Sarah knew things would get better.
She wanted this uncomfortable time to pass quickly. (*but*)
Sarah knew things would get better, but she wanted this uncomfortable time to pass quickly.

Paragraph Form

    Because it was her first day at Jefferson Middle School, Sarah was uneasy. She did not know any of the other students, how to find her classes, or even where to eat lunch! So she spent her lunch hour touring the school grounds, eating as she walked. Sarah knew things would get better, but she wanted this uncomfortable time to pass quickly.

1. The St. Lawrence River in Canada may seem like an unlikely place for sunken ships.
   There may be as many as 10,000 vessels on the river's bottom. (*but*)

2. These ships are many kinds.
   These ships are flat-bottomed barges, stately old clippers, and more modern fishing boats. (:)

3. In recent years divers have explored these sunken ships.
   They are finding chests of gold and silver. (,)
   They are uncovering trunks of merchandise intended for trade with people in North America. (*,and*)

4. A British ship hit rocks and sank.
   It was sailing upriver in 1759. (,)

5. Even earlier, in 1565, a Basque galleon sailed into the mouth of the St. Lawrence.
   It sank from unknown causes.

6. The presence of a Basque ship makes some people think that the Basques may have sailed to the North American continent even before Columbus.
   No one has yet proved that to be true.

7. Whatever their reasons for sailing up the St. Lawrence, thousands of ships have met their fate.
   They are resting at last on the river's deep bottom.

Writing Practice: *Using Sentence Combining in Description*

Write a paragraph describing what it might be like to explore a sunken ship, an underwater cave, a coral reef, or some other unusual and interesting place. Tell about what you might find and what dangers there might be in exploring the place. Include details about what you see, hear, smell or taste, and feel.

As you write, use some of the sentence-combining skills you have practiced in this section.

4 Developing Expository Paragraphs

Writing Paragraphs

A paragraph is a group of sentences dealing with one topic. You learned many years ago to recognize a paragraph because the first line is indented a few spaces from the left margin. Indentation is the visual signal that a new idea is about to be discussed. A well-written paragraph also has three internal characteristics: unity, coherence, and development. *Unity* means that only one idea is discussed in the paragraph. *Coherence* means that the sentences are arranged logically and are connected by the use of transitions, pronouns, and the repetition of important words. *Development* means that enough specific information is given so that the idea is completely understandable.

There are different kinds of paragraphs, but most that you will write in school are called expository paragraphs. The root word from which the adjective *expository* is formed is *expose*, so expository writing *exposes*, or makes clear and explains. You, then, will be asked to write an idea about a topic (a *topic sentence*) and then to explain your idea. The other sentences in the paragraph (*illustration sentences*) will give details to help readers understand the main idea. Because writers must use enough details to develop an idea, expository paragraphs are usually several sentences long. In this chapter you will learn how to write expository paragraphs.

Model: The Expository Paragraph

Charles Kuralt is a television correspondent who travels across the United States and reports his observations on American life. The following essay from his book *Dateline America* is about Tule Lake, California. As you read, look for the main idea in each paragraph and for Kuralt's explanation of the idea.

TULE LAKE, CALIFORNIA. This is a sight to stop your heart. In this one place at this one time, two million water

The *Klamath Basin* is an enclosed water area made by the Klamath River.

***Babel* means "a confusion of sounds."**

birds are flying in from the north in formations that stretch as far as the eye can see. They bank out of the sun, glide toward this lake, spread their wings, and splash gently down. The Klamath Basin on the Oregon-California border is the greatest waterfowl area in the world. Right now I am looking at more than 100,000 snow geese. I have to turn in my tracks to see all of them.

This place is the neck of an hourglass. Geese from the west turn inland and cross the Cascades to get here. Birds from the Northwest Territories change course at the Snake River in Idaho to join the convention. Other birds come from still farther east, across the prairie provinces, across the Great Salt Lake, to add their gabble to the Babel of the Klamath Basin in November.

What are they doing here? They might ask what *we* are doing here. The geese got here first. Long before there were any Russians in Siberia, the geese came south from Siberia. Long before there were any Canadians in the Northwest Territories or Alaskans in Alaska, the geese came south from there. And long, long before there were any of us in California or Oregon, the snow geese from Siberia and Alaska and Canada, winging south across what are now international

Writing

boundaries, stopped here at this lake to feed and rest. The Russians think of the Siberian geese as theirs, and the Canadians consider the geese of the Yukon theirs, and we say, "Look! Our geese are coming in from Alaska!" But the geese carry no passports. The geese speak the same language.

Probably the snow geese think of the northern nesting ground as *theirs* and of the flyways and this lake as belonging to them, even though lately they have met strange obstacles during their autumnal flight. Jet planes hurtle past, and sometimes through *their* flights at *their* altitude. Tall buildings with bright lights rise into their flyway to confuse them. Ribbons of concrete slice through the virgin forests along their route. And here, at their resting place of centuries, men intent on mundane earthly pursuits such as growing barley have pumped their lakes and marshes nearly dry.

Nearly, but not quite. To the north there's a town. To the east there's a highway. To the south there's a mountain range. To the west there's a line of hunters. At this one place there's a sign. It says, "National Wildlife Refuge." The sign says this tiny spot still belongs to the geese.

So that's what so many geese are doing here all at once. There's no other place left for them to go.[1]

Think and Discuss

1. Charles Kuralt divides his essay on Tule Lake, California, into six paragraphs. The topic of the first is the awesome sight of the snow geese. What are the topics of the next three paragraphs?

2. The last two paragraphs in the above essay are much shorter than the others. Why do you think the writer separates these two paragraphs from the rest of his essay?

Using a Pattern: The TRI Paragraph

A *pattern* is a model or plan you use to build or put something together. If you sew, for example, you may use a sewing pattern, cutting your material according to outlines and sewing the material together according to instructions. Although there are many ways to develop an idea, one way is to follow a pattern in a paragraph called *Topic-Restriction-Illustration,* or *TRI.*

---

[1]From *Dateline America* by Charles Kuralt. © CBS Inc. 1979. Reprinted by permission of CBS News, a Division of CBS Inc.

4 Developing Expository Paragraphs

The *topic* of TRI is a sentence that states the topic, or the main idea, of the paragraph. *Restrictions* are sentences that limit the topic by making the subject narrower or more focused than it was in the topic sentence. *Illustrations* are sentences that explain the topic and show something specific about it by giving examples, including details, presenting facts, or using figures.

Model: *The TRI Paragraph*

As you read, look for the topic (sentence 1), the restriction (sentence 2), and the illustrations (sentences 3–6).

Topic

Restriction

Illustrations

Prehistoric monuments have fascinated travelers in Europe for hundreds of years. The most often visited prehistoric monument in England is Stonehenge, dating from the Stone Age, about 2000 B.C. Stonehenge is visited by more than a quarter of a million people every year. What visitors see now is a circular arrangement of huge, standing stones, some weighing as much as forty tons. For a long time scientists believed that the structure was built by a group of people called the druids and that it had some religious significance. Today, however, scientists know that the monument was built long before the druids arrived in England and that it probably served as a giant stone calendar.

The preceding paragraph begins with a general statement of the topic: prehistoric monuments in Europe. The restriction sentence narrows the topic from *all* monuments in all of Europe to just *one* monument in *one* country. The four illustration sentences tell how and why Stonehenge is visited each year, enabling readers to learn something about it.

Writing Practice 1: *Developing a TRI Paragraph*

Each of the sets of sentences below has a topic and a restriction sentence. Select one of these or make up a set of your own, and then write three or four illustration sentences to complete the paragraph. Be prepared to explain how your illustration sentences give specific information about the paragraph topic.

1. *Topic*: By the year 2500 life will be much different from the way it is now.
   Restriction: Perhaps scientists will have thought of new products to make life easier for teenagers.

2. *Topic*: Any sport can be dangerous if people don't follow some common-sense rules of safety.
   Restriction: Bicycle riders, for example, sometimes do foolish things that result in serious injury.

Each of the following sentences is a topic sentence. Select one of these. Then write the topic sentence, a restriction sentence, and three or four illustration sentences.

3. Some television commercials are so ridiculous they make me angry.

4. In my many years of riding the bus to school, I've had some interesting experiences.

5. Playing football (or some other sport) is important to me in many ways.

The TI Paragraph

Not all paragraphs are built according to the topic-restriction-illustration plan. One way to change the pattern is to begin with a topic sentence and then follow immediately with illustration sentences.

Model: *The TI Paragraph*

Here is an example of the *topic-illustration* plan for building a paragraph:

Restricted topic — One of the most remarkable things about Stonehenge is the way its builders were able to carry out difficult transportation and engineering feats with primitive tools.

Illustrations — Ditches, pits, and the holes for the stones were all dug with pickaxes made from the antlers of deer. The chalk that filled low spots was scraped up with the shoulder blades of cattle, carried in baskets, and dumped where needed. The huge stones were moved by boat and raft as far as possible, then hauled overland. Once on site the stones were tipped into holes and hauled upright by people pulling on ropes. When the stone had settled in the ground, the top was made level by pounding the rock away.

The topic-illustration pattern should be used only when the topic sentence is already limited. In the model TRI paragraph the topic sentence is about all prehistoric monuments in Europe and needs limiting. In the paragraph you have just read, however, the topic sentence is already limited because it is about the difficult job of building one particular monument called *Stonehenge.* Each illustration sentence gives specific information about how the temple was built.

Both *Topic-Restriction-Illustration* and *Topic-Illustration* are patterns for building paragraphs. Many writers change these patterns, and some do not use them at all. For example, you will read, and sometimes write, paragraphs where the topic sentence comes at the end of the paragraph or even where there is no topic sentence at all. Most expository paragraphs that you write, however, should begin with a topic sentence.

Writing Practice 2: *Using the TI Pattern*

Select one of the topic sentences on the following page, or make up one of your own. Then write four or five illustration

Writing

sentences that give specific information about the topic. You may include the topic sentence at the beginning or the end of the paragraph.

1. I'm not the same person I was five years ago.
2. Popcorn can be lots of fun.
3. I've already given a lot of thought to what I want to do when I finish school.
4. Saturday is my favorite day of the week.

Using Examples to Develop Paragraphs

Illustration sentences, as you have learned, are used to explain the topic. One kind of illustration is the *example*. An example is one item taken from a larger group or concept. The blue chair in your living room is an example of the furniture in your house. Smog is an example of pollution. The smile on Jim's face when he receives a bicycle for his birthday is an example of happiness.

Model: Paragraph Developed by Examples

In the following paragraph from a book about solar energy, the writer uses two examples with specific details to develop the topic sentence.

Restricted topic
Illustrations

Some ways of harnessing solar energy were discovered long ago. It has been said that centuries ago the Greek mathematician Archimedes used sunlight concentrated by many large reflectors to set fire to invading Roman ships. Early scientists knew that very intense heat could be generated by using sunlight. In 1772 the French scientist Antoine Lavoisier built a solar furnace hot enough to melt a number of metals. His concentrator was a huge lens that focused sunlight into a small area. With it he was able to conduct many chemical experiments needing high temperatures which only sunlight could then provide.[1]

In the topic sentence, the writer states that some ways of using solar energy were known long ago. The specific examples are the Greek mathematician Archimedes and the French

[1] From *Solar Energy* by John Hoke. Copyright 1968, 1978 by Franklin Watts, Inc. Reprinted by permission of the publishers.

scientist Lavoisier. Notice that the examples themselves are not enough to make the paragraph clear; *relevant* (specifically meaningful) details about the examples are necessary. For example, while readers need to know how Archimedes used solar energy to burn enemy ships, we do not need to know that the ships were painted with bright colors. While we need to know how Lavoisier built a solar furnace, we do not need to know that he was twenty-nine years old at the time. Even though these details may be interesting, they are not relevant to the main idea of the paragraph.

Writing Practice 3: *Developing a Paragraph with Examples*

Select one of the topic sentences below or make up one of your own. Then write a paragraph developing the topic sentence with one or more examples. Use relevant details with each example you include.

1. Noise is a problem in my school's hallways.

2. A good book can let you explore faraway worlds.

3. Television can be educational as well as entertaining.

4. A *fad* is a style that comes and goes in a short time. (Continued on page 78.)

Writing

Reread the paragraph to make sure that:

1. Each sentence in the paragraph gives specific information about the topic sentence.
2. The paragraph is well developed with enough specific information about the topic.
3. The examples make the general statement in the topic sentence more exact.
4. Details about the example make it clear and interesting.
5. Details about the examples are relevant and appropriate to the topic sentence.

Use the checklist at the back of this book to proofread your paragraph.

Using Facts to Develop Paragraphs

Ideas may be explained in different ways, but readers are more likely to understand your idea if you use facts in your development or illustration sentences. A *fact* is something that can be proven true. Facts can be checked and verified. It is a *fact* that John F. Kennedy was the President of the United States from 1961 to 1963. You can verify this fact in many ways. For example, you can talk to people who knew John Kennedy, you can see and hear him on videotape, and you can read about him in books and magazines.

Model: *Paragraph Developed with Facts*

The following paragraph uses facts to explain the accomplishments of Mary McLeod Bethune. As you read, think about which statements could be proven and which could not.

Topic

Restriction

Illustrations

Many black women down through the centuries have stood out as pathbreakers, but one black woman has always been especially revered. Mary McLeod Bethune, who on July 11, 1974, became the first black (or white) woman to have her statue placed in Lincoln Park in Washington, D.C., was born in 1875 in Mayesville, South Carolina, one of seventeen children. Education became her crusade. Through hard work and faith she founded the Bethune-Cookman Institute at Daytona Beach in 1904. She was adviser to four presidents on a wide range of issues. She was a member of the Planning Commission for a National Conference on the Education of Negroes in 1933, administrator of the Office of Minority Affairs of the National Youth Administration, special consultant at the United Nations Charter Convention in San Francisco, and founder of the National Council of Negro Women. In making the presentation of the Bethune Statue in 1974, Miss Dorothy Height, herself an outstanding black woman leader and President of the National Council of Negro Women, pointed out that Mrs. Bethune's statue was a recognition of both blacks and women.[1]

Think and Discuss

1. This paragraph about Mary McLeod Bethune states the fact that she was the first woman, black or white, to have her statue placed in Lincoln Park. What other facts about her are stated in the paragraph?

2. How could these facts about Ms. Bethune be verified?

Recognizing Facts and Opinions

Suppose the writer of the paragraph on Mary McLeod Bethune had written the following sentence: *Mary McLeod Bethune was the greatest woman who ever lived.* While the writer may believe this statement to be true, she cannot prove it. Therefore, the statement is an *opinion,* not a fact.

Writing Practice 4: *Developing a Paragraph with Facts*

Select one of the following topic sentences or make up one of your own. Then write a paragraph using facts to develop the topic sentence you selected. Use such sources as encyclopedias or almanacs to find the facts you need.

1. The 1965 Los Angeles Dodgers baseball team included several award-winning individuals.

2. People do some silly things to establish a world record.

3. Because of their outstanding service to the nation, America's greatest military leaders were promoted to the rank of General during World War II.

(Continued on page 80.)

[1] Reprinted from "The Black Revolution" from *A Pictorial History of Women in America* by Ruth Warren. Text copyright © 1975 by Ruth Warren. By permission of Crown Publishers, Inc.

Writing

Reread your paragraph to make sure that:

1. Each sentence in the paragraph gives specific information about the topic sentence.
2. The paragraph contains enough information to make the topic clear to readers.
3. Facts, rather than opinions, are used to develop the paragraph.
4. All facts have been checked for accuracy.

Using Reasons to Develop Paragraphs

Giving reasons is another way to illustrate or develop paragraphs. Many topic sentences give the writer's personal opinion. Suppose, for example, that you write a paragraph with the topic sentence *Today's movies are better than ever*. The topic sentence states an opinion that may or may not be shared by others. If you wish others to accept your opinion, you will have to explain why you think as you do.

Reasons answer the question *why*? Why do you believe movies are better than ever? Here are some possibilities; you may have other reasons of your own:

Reason: The new 70-mm film makes images on the screen appear larger than life.

Reason: A new sound system filters out background noise and makes the audience feel they are actually in the scene, listening to what's going on.

Reason: With improved technology, movie producers can create spectacular special effects.

Your opinion is more valuable to others if it is based on evidence. Reasons supported by evidence may contain facts, the statement of an authority (a person who knows a great deal about the subject), or your own observation or experience. Reasons, then, are not just stated; they are supported by details. Some details may be facts, some opinions. It is a fact that movies are now made with 70-mm film, but an opinion that the sound system makes the audience feel included. Details help to make the reasons clear and the paragraph more interesting.

Model: Paragraph Developed with Reasons

In the following paragraph about television violence from the book *The Incredible Television Machine*, the topic sentence is *Television is too violent*. As you read, look for reasons that support this opinion.

Restricted topic
Illustrations

Television is too violent. This includes Bugs Bunny's putting his finger in Elmer Fudd's shotgun, which blows up in Elmer's face, as well as whatever happens on any of the police dramas—the killings and the beatings, especially. All this violence, critics say, has an influence on you, making you think that human beings aren't very important and that life is not especially valuable, to say the least. They also say that the loud, fast, violent action will make you more aggressive. Some researchers have reported that children seem to get meaner toward each other after watching shoot-'em-ups. If a program has a great deal of action—people shooting each other, many fist fights and karate chops—you may notice that afterwards you feel even more irritated than usual when your parents say it is time to wind up your television viewing. Or, if your brother has played one of your records without your permission, you may get angrier than you did when the same thing happened a while back.[1]

---

[1] From "Television is Too Violent" from *The Incredible Television Machine* by Lee Polk and Eda Le Shan. Copyright © 1977, Lee Polk and Eda Le Shan. Reprinted with permission of Macmillan Publishing Co., Inc. and Ann Elmo Agency.

Writing

Think and Discuss

1. These writers develop the topic sentence *Television is too violent* with two main reasons. The first is that television violence makes viewers feel that human life does not have much value. What is the second reason?

2. Notice the use of details. In the second sentence, for example, the writers give specific details of violence on television. Later in the paragraph the writers give specific details about *how* they believe television makes you more aggressive. What are those details?

Writing Practice 5: *Developing a Paragraph with Reasons*

Select one of the topic sentences below, use a topic sentence from a previous Writing Practice, or make up one. Write a paragraph developing the topic sentence with reasons, using details to make the reasons clear and interesting.

1. We need (or don't need) a dress code in our school for faculty as well as students.
2. Because of energy problems, the legal age for beginning drivers should (or should not) be raised to eighteen.
3. The city (or county) government should (or should not) sponsor free rock concerts for teenagers.
4. Watching television for many hours a week is (or is not) harmful to teenagers.
5. All students should (or should not) be required to participate in at least one sport.

Reread your paragraph to make sure that:

1. Each sentence in the paragraph gives specific information about the topic sentence.
2. The paragraph is well developed with enough specific information about the topic.
3. Details make the reasons clear and interesting.
4. Reasons are supported with evidence, either facts, authority, or observations.

Use the checklist at the back of the book to proofread your paragraph.

Using Incidents to Develop Paragraphs

People love stories. One way to illustrate your topic sentence and to capture your reader's attention is to develop your paragraph by telling a brief story, or an *incident*. An incident may be something that happened to you, or it may be something you have read or heard about. Incidents may be serious or humorous, factual or fictional. You may use one incident to explain your topic, or you may use several.

Model: *Paragraph Developed with Incidents*

The paragraph that follows is from an article on strong animals and has the topic sentence *Another animal that has frightening strength is the crocodile.* As you read, look for the incidents the writer gives to develop the topic sentence.

Restricted topic
Illustrations

Another animal that has frightening strength is the crocodile. This reptile often needs great strength to subdue its prey. An Australian farmer once had a fine, big draft horse sent

Writing

from England. It weighed a ton all by itself. One day, this splendid beast wandered close to the river. It may have stepped into the shallow water for a drink. A crocodile snapped its jaws shut on one of the horse's legs. No matter how hard the huge horse pulled, the croc, it is said, pulled harder and finally dragged the horse right into the water and drowned it. In East Africa, a hunter once witnessed a similar tug of war between a crocodile and a black rhinoceros. Nobody had a chance to weigh or measure the rhino, but this animal can be more than eight feet long and weigh up to three tons. According to the British army captain who saw the battle, the rhino lost, and it, too, was dragged under the water by the crocodile.[1]

Think and Discuss

1. One incident the writer gives to develop the topic sentence involves the horse that was pulled into the water by a crocodile and drowned. What other incident does the writer give?

2. By giving details about the incidents, the writer makes them clear and interesting to readers. For example, the writer gives specific details about the horse, telling what it looked like and what it was doing when the crocodile pulled it into the water. In the second incident, what specific details does the writer give?

3. The way you organize your illustration sentences can be very important. The events in an incident are usually organized in *chronological order*—the order in which they happened. For example, the incident about the horse and crocodile above is organized chronologically. What happened first in the incident? What happened next?

4. One way to help readers follow a chronological order is to use words about time: such words as *first, second, third, then, when, last, as soon as, until, soon, the next day, tomorrow,* and so on. These words are called *transition* words because they help readers make a *transition,* or movement, from one event to the next. What transition words are used in the paragraph about crocodiles?

[1]From "Strongest Animals of All" by George Laycock from *Boys' Life,* August 1979. Reprinted by permission of George Laycock.

Writing Practice 6: *Writing a Paragraph with Incidents*

Select one of the topic sentences below or make up one of your own. Not all of the sentences need to be restricted, but if the one you choose does, write a restriction sentence to follow it. Then write a paragraph developing your topic sentence with one or more incidents told in chronological order. Use specific details to make the incident clear and interesting. Use time words to help your readers follow the movement of events.

1. Growing up involves making hard decisions.
2. My pet is special.
3. Something funny happened to me on my way to school this morning.
4. Even the best trained athletes sometimes have bad days.
5. People can sometimes learn a lot from making a mistake.
6. Clothing styles change from year to year.
7. The Nobel Peace Prize has been awarded to people from all over the world.
8. Movies are better today than they were twenty-five years ago.

Reread your paragraph to make sure that:

1. If necessary, the topic sentence is restricted by another, more specific sentence.
2. Each sentence in the paragraph gives specific information about the topic sentence.
3. The paragraph contains enough information to make the topic sentence clear to readers.
4. The incident or incidents develop the topic sentence of the paragraph.
5. Specific, relevant details about the incident make it clear and interesting to readers.
6. Details in the incident are arranged in chronological order, and time words help readers follow the organization of details.

Use the checklist at the back of the book to proofread your paragraph.

Choosing a Method of Development

You have learned four specific ways to develop expository paragraphs and have practiced each method. Topic sentences have been provided for you. When you write other assignments, you will write your own topic sentences and choose your own methods of development. The method you choose to develop a paragraph depends upon your purpose in writing.

Using Facts

Facts may be included in any paragraph, but a paragraph developed mainly by facts answers the questions *who? what? when? where?* and *how?* Consider, for example, the following sentence about George Washington: George Washington (*who?*) was named head of the Continental Army (*what?*) in 1775 (*when?*) in Philadelphia (*where?*) by an act of the Second Continental Congress (*how?*).

Using Examples

When you generalize about a group or an idea, develop your paragraph with examples. Paragraphs developed mainly with examples answer *who specifically? what specifically? where specifically? when specifically?* or *how specifically?* A topic sentence about fathers (generalization) could be illustrated with sentences about Jane's father (specific), Arnold's father (specific), and Tim's father (specific). If you were writing about equality (generalization), you might give examples of political equality (more specific) or social equality (more specific).

Using Reasons

Paragraphs developed with reasons answer the question *why?* Suppose your topic sentence was *Teenagers too young to drive automobiles should have a moped.* Why? *Mopeds are economical, give teenagers practice in observing laws,* and *relieve parents of the need to drive their teenagers to so many places.* The sentence of illustration gives reasons for the assertion made in the topic sentence.

Using Incidents

When you want to tell what happened, relate an incident. Suppose your history teacher asks on a test, *What happened at Gettysburg in 1863?* Your paragraph might begin: *In Gettysburg, Pennsylvania, on July 1 to 3, 1863, one of the most decisive battles of the War Between the States was fought.* Then you could illustrate your paragraph with sentences that tell in chronological order what happened each day of the battle.

Writing Practice 7: *Choosing a Method and Developing a Paragraph*

1. You have been asked to explain in a paragraph why you were late for school today. Do so, using a suitable method of development.
   or
2. Your health teacher has asked you to write about the effects of such illegal drugs as marijuana, heroin, or LSD on the human body. Choose a suitable method of development and write a paragraph on this topic.

Writing a Well-Developed Paragraph

You have written paragraphs using facts, examples, reasons, and incidents. This chapter has emphasized the use of specific details in each method so that your ideas will be clear and interesting to readers. Chapter 1 taught you how to discover detailed information for writing. By using these methods, you can write well-developed paragraphs.

Read the beginning sentences on the next page from a paragraph about how lizards use their tails for protection:

Writing

> A lizard's tail is often useful for protection. Many lizards have brittle tails that are easily broken off. The lizard isn't hampered by the loss of its tail very long, because it can grow a new one in a few weeks.

The topic sentence is *A lizard's tail is often useful for protection.* The next two sentences are sentences of illustration but do not give much specific information. The paragraph is not well-developed because it has not told you why or how lizards use their tails for protection.

Model: *A Well-Developed Paragraph*

Below is the paragraph by George F. Mason. Notice how much more specific information is contained in the illustrations.

Restricted topic
Illustrations

> A lizard's tail is often useful for protection. Many lizards have brittle tails that are easily broken off. The lizard isn't hampered by the loss of its tail very long, because it can grow a new one in a few weeks. Even though it can grow another, you may wonder what useful reason there can be for having a brittle tail that comes off so easily. Isn't it better for the lizard to suffer the temporary loss of a tail than to lose its life? Most of these brittle-tailed lizards are preyed upon by birds or other animals, and very often one of them is seized by its long tail as it scampers away. The attacking animal usually succeeds in capturing only a section of the lizard's tail. There are some lizard tails that actually flip and wriggle around after they are broken off, thus holding the attention of the captor while the lizard escapes unharmed, except for the temporary loss of its tail.[1]

Now you have specific information about *why* and *how* lizards use their tails for protection. The *reason* they do so is that they often are prey for birds and other animals. The *way* they use their tails is that when the predator—the animal chasing the lizard—captures the tail, the rest of the lizard scampers away, and the predator is left holding only the tail.

Writing Practice 8: *Writing a Well-Developed Paragraph*

Choose a paragraph from one of the previous writing practices and revise it by adding more information. Add a sentence or two and use more specific words in the existing sentences.

---

[1]Excerpt from *Animal Tails* by George F. Mason. Copyright © 1958 by George F. Mason. By permission of William Morrow & Company.

4 Developing Expository Paragraphs

Writing a Unified Paragraph

As mentioned earlier, a *unified paragraph* has only one main idea, and every explanatory sentence in the paragraph helps to illustrate that idea. If there are sentences in a paragraph that do not develop the main idea, the reader may be confused.

Writing a unified paragraph requires discipline because, in writing as in conversation, we often change the subject. Remember when Uncle Joe started to tell about his fishing trip to Alabama, but the story you heard was more about the hinges falling off the back gate? Or perhaps you wrote a paragraph intending to describe Disney World's Fantasyland, but instead you wrote about the cute person serving hamburgers in Adventureland. Your paragraph was not unified, and your reader was probably left confused.

The paragraph on the next page, from the book *Beyond Tomorrow* by D. S. Halacy, Jr., is about replacing human eyes lost because of disease or injury. The topic sentence, which is enclosed in brackets, is not part of the original paragraph.

89

Writing

Model: A Unified Paragraph

Restricted topic

Illustrations

[For hundreds of years doctors have attempted to replace human eyes lost because of injury or disease.] Early doctors learned to replace the missing orbs with glass "marbles" or artificial eyes that were more ornamental than useful. It was a brave surgeon who in 1853 actually tried to implant a piece of clear glass in a diseased cornea to restore vision for his patient. Although it failed, the effort is historically of great importance. For the first time, an artificial substitute had been tried for a living complex organ. Later attempts were made using not glass but living cornea—from a pig! Amazingly, the patient was claimed to have seen through a pig's eye for upwards of a year. Slowly the success of corneal transplants improved, substituting human eye tissue for the animal cornea. Temporarily, then, the direction of progress moved away from the artificial replacement and toward another technique called "transplanting."[1]

In unified paragraphs each sentence develops the main idea. Here is the way each sentence in the above paragraph develops the topic of replacing eyes:

Sentence	**How Sentence Develops Topic**
1. Early doctors learned to replace the missing orbs with glass "marbles" or artificial eyes that were more ornamental than useful.	This sentence tells about early attempts to replace eyes.
2. It was a brave surgeon who in 1853 actually tried to implant a piece of clear glass in a diseased cornea to restore vision.	This sentence tells about a specific attempt to replace part of an eye with a piece of glass.
3. Although it failed, the effort is historically of great importance.	This sentence tells that the attempt in the last sentence failed, but was still important.

[1] From *Beyond Tomorrow* by Dan S. Halacy. Copyright © 1965 by Dan S. Halacy. Reprinted by permission of the author.

4. For the first time, an artificial substitute had been tried for a living complex organ.	This sentence tells why the attempt in Sentence 2 was important.
5. Later attempts were made using not glass but living cornea—from a pig!	This sentence tells about later attempts to replace eyes.
6. Amazingly, the patient was claimed to have seen through a pig's eye for upwards of a year.	This sentence gives specific information about the attempt in Sentence 5.
7. Slowly the success of corneal transplants improved, substituting human eye tissue for the animal cornea.	This sentence tells about more successful attempts to replace eyes.
8. Temporarily, then, the direction of progress moved away from the artificial replacement and toward another technique called "transplanting."	This sentence tells about the new direction in attempts to replace human eyes.

Writing Practice 9: *Writing a Unified Paragraph*

Select one of the following topic sentences or make up one of your own. Decide on a method (examples, reasons, incidents, or facts) to develop the topic sentence and then write a paragraph using that method. When you have finished, copy each sentence of your paragraph on a separate line of a sheet of paper. After each sentence write a brief statement explaining how the sentence develops the topic of the paragraph.

1. Teenagers should (or should not) be allowed to drive at the age of fourteen.
2. I have changed in many ways during this past year.
3. Spring (summer, fall, winter) is my favorite time of year.
4. School in the year 2500 will be much different from the way it is now.
5. The characters in my favorite book are like real people.

As you revise, think about these guidelines for writing paragraphs:

1. Topic sentences that need restricting are followed by a restriction sentence.
2. The method of development suits the topic sentence.
3. Specific details are used to make examples, reasons, and incidents clear and interesting.
4. Facts and figures used to develop the paragraph are accurate.
5. The paragraph is well-developed.
6. The paragraph is unified.

Use the checklist at the back of the book to proofread your paragraph.

Writing a Coherent Paragraph

Paragraphs need not only to be well-developed and unified, but also to be *coherent*. In a coherent paragraph, all the sentences show their relationship to one another.

One way to achieve coherence is to arrange the sentences

in a logical order. *Logical order* means arranging sentences for a reason. For example, if you write about events as they happen, it is logical to use chronological, or time, order. If you describe an object or a place, it is logical to arrange details spatially, by the way they appear in space. If you write using facts, examples, or reasons, it is logical to arrange them according to order of importance.

Paragraphs without coherence are difficult to read. The following sentences from the book *DNA: The Ladder of Life,* by Edward Frankel, tell about a researcher named Fred Griffith, who found a clue to the mystery of heredity when he was performing an experiment with bacteria that cause pneumonia. At the time of this experiment, people believed that only coated germs could cause pneumonia. As you read the sentences, try to understand the experiment. (It cannot be done unless you rearrange the sentence order.)

1. Back in 1928, Fred Griffith, an English bacteriologist, was experimenting with pneumonia organisms.
2. What was that something?
3. Not one of these animals became sick.
4. Moreover, while the bodies of these dead mice swarmed with coated pneumonia germs, the harmless, uncoated ones could not be found.
5. From what was then known about these microbes, the mice should have remained alive and healthy.
6. Apparently the dead germs were really dead.
7. Instead, the animals developed pneumonia and died.

Writing

8. Using heat, he killed some of the coated germs and then injected mice with a mixture of these killed coated ones and live, harmless, uncoated microbes.

9. He therefore injected other mice with only some dead germs from the original batch.

10. Griffith thought perhaps the killed coated germs which he injected were not really dead.

11. Evidently the dead germs passed something on to the living microbes that changed them and their offspring.

12. In some mysterious way, the uncoated microbes acquired a coat and became deadly.

Although each of these sentences comes from the same paragraph, they are not arranged in any logical order, so it is difficult to understand the experiment. For example, Sentence 2 asks a question that Sentence 1 does not prepare for. Neither Sentence 1 nor Sentence 2 says anything about animals, but Sentence 3 mentions "these animals."

Model: A Coherent Paragraph

Here is the paragraph as it actually appears in *DNA: The Ladder of Life*. As you read it, notice how the sentences follow the steps in the experiment.

> Back in 1928, Fred Griffith, an English bacteriologist, was experimenting with . . . pneumonia organisms. Using heat, he killed some of the coated germs and then injected mice with a mixture of these killed coated ones and live, harmless,

uncoated microbes. From what was then known about these microbes, the mice should have remained alive and healthy. Instead, the animals developed pneumonia and died. Moreover, while the bodies of these dead mice swarmed with coated pneumonia germs, the harmless, uncoated ones could not be found. Griffith thought perhaps the killed coated germs which he injected were not really dead. He therefore injected other mice with only some dead germs from the original batch. Not one of these animals became sick. Apparently the dead germs were really dead. In some mysterious way, the uncoated microbes acquired a coat and became deadly. Evidently the dead germs passed something on to the living microbes that changed them and their offspring. What was that something?[1]

The paragraph as Frankel wrote it contains certain devices to help the reader understand the topic sentence. Transition words such as *instead, moreover,* and *therefore* help you understand how the sentences are related to each other. Also, the writer uses pronouns and repeats important words and important phrases to help readers understand how sentences are related. For example, the first sentence in the paragraph is about Fred Griffith. When the writer uses the pronoun *he* in the second sentence, you know that the *he* is Fred Griffith. In the second sentence Edward Frankel mentions microbes and in the third sentence uses the words *these microbes*.

Think and Discuss

1. What are the important words in the model paragraph?
2. What examples can you find of Frankel's use of transition words, pronouns, and repetition of important words and phrases?
3. What would the paragraph sound like if only nouns, and no pronouns, were used?
4. What would be the effect if no transition words were used?

Writing Assignment I: *Writing an Expository Paragraph*

A. Prewriting

Select one of the subjects listed on the next page, or one of your own on which to write a paragraph.

---

[1]From *DNA: Ladder of Life* by Edward Frankel. Copyright © 1964 by Edward Frankel. With the permission of McGraw-Hill Book Company.

Writing

Holidays	Money	Earthquakes	Floods
Music	Hospitals	Girls	Hobbies
Movies	Pets	Boys	Grandparents
Libraries	Doctors	Food	War

Using one or more of the methods for discovering ideas for writing, generate as much material as you can on the subject you have chosen. After you have details for your paragraph write a sentence that states the main idea you want to explain.

B. Writing

Choosing one of the four methods of development you have learned, begin with your topic sentence and write a well-developed, unified, and coherent paragraph.

C. Postwriting

If your teacher directs you to do so, meet with one or two of your classmates and share your paragraph with them. Then ask them the following questions:

1. What is the topic of my paragraph?
2. How is my topic limited?
3. What is my method of development?
4. What are my examples, reasons, incidents, or facts?
5. What kinds of details do I need to add to make my paragraph clearer and more interesting?

4 Developing Expository Paragraphs

Next revise your paragraph, paying attention to your classmates' suggestions. Think about these characteristics of good paragraphs as you revise your paragraph:

Checklist for Revising a Paragraph

1. The topic sentence is restricted if it needs to be.
2. The method of development suits the topic sentence.
3. Specific details make examples, reasons, or incidents clear and interesting.
4. Facts have been checked for accuracy.
5. Each sentence in the paragraph explains the main idea.
6. The paragraph is arranged in a logical order.
7. The paragraph is coherent because of the use of transition words, pronouns, or repeated words or phrases.

For information on punctuation, see pages 534-567.

Finally proofread your paragraph, using the checklist at the back of this book.

97

Sentence Combining:
Inserting Adjectives

Combining Sentences by Inserting Adjectives

In this section you will practice inserting one or more sentences or parts of sentences into a *base sentence*. *To insert* means "to place one thing inside another." For example, you insert a letter into an envelope before you mail it, and your doctor inserts a needle into your arm to give you a shot. Inserting sentences into each other involves taking *part* of one sentence and placing that part into a *base sentence*. The inserted part may be changed in some way in order to form the combined new sentence.

For more information on using hyphens, see pages 550-553.

Base Sentence: The beautiful doll was an heirloom.
Insert: The doll was hand painted.
Combined: The beautiful *hand-painted* doll was an heirloom.

For more information on adjectives, see pages 376-395.

Base Sentence: Trying to find shelter from the rain, the campers ran toward the cave.
Insert: The rain was cold and pounding.
Insert: The campers were weary.
Insert: The cave was distant.
Combined: Trying to find shelter from the *cold and pounding* rain, the *weary* campers ran toward the *distant* cave.

Notice that only the adjectives—the words from the insert sentences that describe a word in the base sentence—are used in the combined sentence.

Remember that the first sentence is always the base sentence. In exercises where no signals are given, you must decide which parts of the other sentences in the set to use in making the combination. The following is an example of how unsignaled sentence sets will look.

Sentence Combining

A package was left on our front doorstep.

The package was suspicious looking.

The doorstep was the front one.

In writing the new combined sentence, you will use the words *suspicious looking* because they describe the package, and the word *front* because that describes the doorstep. Your result will be this sentence:

A *suspicious-looking* package was left on our *front* doorstep.

Exercise 1: *Inserting Adjectives*

Combine each set of sentences. For sets 1–5, the words to be inserted are underlined; for sets 6–10, decide which parts to insert into the base sentence (the first sentence).

Example

a. The night ended with an incident.
   The night was terror filled.
   The incident was tragic.
   The terror-filled night ended with a tragic incident.

1. Tanta Delia polished her oak table.
   The oak table was antique.

2. San Antonio is a city of many landmarks.
   The landmarks are cultural and historical.

Writing

3. Hens scratched in the barnyard.
   The hens were <u>speckled</u>.
   The hens were <u>black and white</u>.

4. The garden contained plants.
   The garden was a <u>vegetable</u> garden.
   The plants were <u>tomato and green pepper</u> plants.

5. Bushes bloomed along the path.
   The path was <u>nearby</u>.
   The path was a <u>boathouse</u> path.

6. The aquarium sat on the desk in front of a window.
   It was a freshwater aquarium.
   The window was sunny.

7. What Dad likes is food.
   The food is spicy.
   The food is Chinese.

8. History is Yoshiro Tanaka's subject.
   The history is ancient.
   Yoshiro Tanaka is young.
   The subject is the favorite one.

9. The industry in Arizona is undergoing a development.
   The industry is construction.
   The development is rapid.

10. The cat moved her kittens to the barn.
    The cat was a mother.
    The kittens were newborn.

Inserting Several Adjectives

For more information on using commas with the word and, *see pages 538-539.*

When you insert several adjectives into a base sentence, it is often necessary to put commas or the word *and* in the combined sentence. If the sentence set has signals, watch for the signals (,) or (*and*) or (,*and*) at the end of the insert sentence. Place a comma, the word *and*, or a comma and the word *and* before that sentence part in the newly combined sentence.

Grandfather is proud of his African violets.
The African violets are huge.
The African violets are healthy. (,)

Grandfather is proud of his *huge, healthy* African violets.

Sentence Combining

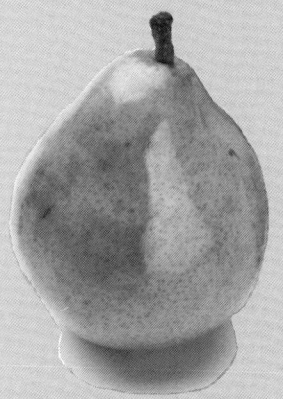

The branches of the tree offer a harvest every October.
The branches are fruit laden.
The tree is ancient.
The tree is a pear.
The harvest is rich.
The harvest is abundant. (*and*)
The *fruit-laden* branches of the *ancient pear* tree offer a *rich and abundant* harvest every October.

If the sentence set does not have signals, use your own judgment in deciding where to place commas and the word *and* in the newly combined sentence.

Exercise 2: *Inserting Several Adjectives*

After studying the example, combine each of the following sentence sets. Write the new sentences on a sheet of paper numbered 1–10. For the first five sets follow the signals in deciding where to place commas and the word *and*. Use your own judgment for the last five unsignaled sets.

Example

a. The swamp was a haven for the outlaws.
The haven was dangerous.
The haven was frightening. (*and*)
The outlaws were weary.
The outlaws were desperate. (,)
The swamp was a dangerous and frightening haven for the weary, desperate outlaws.

101

Writing

1. Three sharpened pencils lay beside the paper.
   The paper was clean.
   The paper was unlined. (,)

2. Little Miss Muffett eyed the spider warily.
   The spider was shiny.
   The spider was brown. (,)
   The spider was fiddle shaped. (,)

3. The brook meandered through the meadow.
   The brook was ice-cold.
   The brook was spring fed. (,)
   The meadow was warm.
   The meadow was sunny. (and)

4. The mechanic changed the tires on our car.
   The tires were threadbare.
   The tires were mismatched. (,)

5. Mrs. Morgan sold apple butter at the fair.
   The apple butter was delicious.
   The apple butter was homemade. (,)

6. Paintings cover the museum walls.
   The paintings are oil ones.
   The paintings are watercolor ones.
   The walls are high.
   The walls are wide.

7. The attendant filled the truck's tank with fuel.
   The attendant was young.
   The attendant was attractive.
   The attendant was female.
   The fuel was clean burning.
   The fuel was diesel.

8. Elephants paced back and forth across the zoo's yard.
   There were four elephants.
   The elephants were gigantic.
   The elephants were slow moving.
   The yard was dusty.
   The yard was well trodden.
   The yard was the pachyderm one.

9. The doctor X-rayed the bones.
   The doctor was young.
   The doctor was brilliant.
   The bones were broken.
   The bones were shin bones.
   The bones were ankle bones.

10. The cartoonist Al Capp created Li'l Abner and other characters.
    The cartoonist was popular.
    The cartoonist was clever.
    The cartoonist was widely read.
    The other characters are lovable.
    The other characters are uneducated.

Writing Practice: *Inserting Adjectives*

Write a paragraph explaining a process—how to do, make, or operate something. Choose a topic you know enough about to explain clearly and one that interests you, perhaps making a papier-mâché figure or a special kind of kite. Or you might tell how to repair a hole in a knit sweater or how to plant a garden. When you write your paragraph, use some of the sentence-combining skills you have practiced in this section.

5 Writing Compositions

Composing for a Purpose and an Audience

The word *composition* comes from a Latin word meaning "a putting together." Today the word means "putting together a whole by combining parts." The musician who *composed* your favorite song did so by putting together sounds. Writers *compose* by joining words, sentences, and paragraphs.

In school the word *composition* usually means a short paper of several paragraphs.

According to your purpose in writing, compositions may be classified as *narrative, descriptive,* or *expository*. The purpose of a *narrative* composition is to tell a story; of a *descriptive* composition, to describe people, places, objects, or events; and of an *expository* composition, to explain something.

Musicians, artists, and writers have something in common: they decide how to put the parts together so that the whole composition achieves its purpose. In this chapter you will learn how to bring words, sentences, and paragraphs together to form a composition that achieves your purpose.

When you write a composition, you write for a specific audience. The audience is the person or people who will read what you write. Depending on your audience, you might use the same general topic for different purposes. For example, if you are writing a composition about baby-sitting for potential employers, you might try to *persuade* them that you are fond of children and know what to do in an emergency. If, on the other hand, you are writing about baby-sitting to *entertain* your friends, you might choose to write about the weird food you have encountered in other peoples' refrigerators.

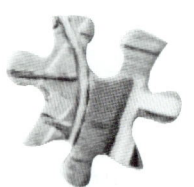

Deciding on a Topic

Almost any subject can become the basis for a composition. You may think of such subjects as clothes, sports, music,

or movies, but thousands of books have been written on each of these subjects. Each subject is too large for a school composition, so you must decide how to narrow the subject to a topic. A *topic* is a limited subject that can be discussed with specific details.

Some of your ideas for writing may already be topics for a short paper. Although *clothes* is too large a subject for your purposes, your feelings about your school's dress code would not be. You could explain why you feel your school should (or should not) have a dress code. *Sports* is also too large, but one exciting event in sports is not. You might narrate the story of the frightening moments when the quarterback of the football team lay injured on the field. Likewise, the subject of *music* could be limited to a description of a jazz concert that you recently attended.

Before deciding on a topic for writing, ask yourself what might interest readers. A good way to begin is to think about your experience or knowledge on a subject. Some experiences that everyone shares make enjoyable reading. For example, most people would like to be rich, attractive, and happy, and they enjoy reading about how to achieve these goals. Some of the best-selling books today have titles such as *A Sure-Fire Way to Lose Weight*, *How to Be a Millionaire Before Thirty*, and *How to Bring Happiness into Your Life*.

Most unusual experiences are of interest to readers. If you have studied about magic and know how some of the great magicians' tricks were done, you might write a composition titled *How Houdini Survived Being Buried Alive*. Even everyday experiences can be interesting if you write about them in an unusual or humorous way. Brushing your teeth is an ordinary experience, but if you have a dog that constantly hides your toothbrush, forcing you to search the house each morning and evening, you have the basis for a humorous paper on the subject.

Writing Practice 1: *Deciding on a Topic*

Each of the following subjects is too large for a short paper. From this list select three subjects with which you have had some experience. For each subject think of one topic for a descriptive composition, one for a narrative composition, and one for an expository composition.

Space travel
Hobbies
School
Earning money
Weekends

Robots
Games
Appearance
People
The newest fad

Gathering and Recording Information

Once you have decided on a topic, your next step is to discover what you know about it. In the chapter "The Writing Process," you learned how to do this. Use one or more of these methods to help you think of specific information about your topic. As ideas come to you, write them down in the form of notes on a sheet of paper or on note cards. If you use note cards, write each piece of information on a separate card. These cards will be helpful to you later when you begin to organize your information.

For example, suppose you do not like the way teenagers appear on television, because they do not seem like real teenagers, so you decide to write a composition about this topic. You might begin by brainstorming the topic *Television teenagers and the real thing.* As you do, you might have thoughts like these:

Always smart and popular

I like color television better than black and white.

TV families don't have many problems.

Lead exciting lives

I remember one show where the teenage character went on a fishing trip halfway around the world.

Parents think I watch too much TV

Television teenagers almost never do anything dumb.

Usually close to brothers and sisters

Teenagers in real life aren't really this way.

They are not always smart and popular, and their families may have problems.

Using the basic set of six questions, you might ask yourself questions like these:

1. *Who* are the teenagers on TV?
2. *What* is wrong with the way they are portrayed?
3. *When* are these teenagers on television?
4. *Where* do these teenagers live? What are their homes like?
5. *How* do they solve their problems?

6. *Why* don't television producers make these teenagers more like real people?

When you write down the answers on a sheet of paper, you find that the questions help you find specific information about your topic. Your answers to Question 1 give the names of specific characters and the shows in which they appear. When you answer Question 2, you realize that many teenagers compare themselves to those on television and feel that something is wrong with their own lives. The answers to Questions 4 and 5 tell you more about the lives these make-believe teenagers live. Question 6 introduces reasons why television teenagers are portrayed so unrealistically.

From your television viewing you have absorbed more information than you realize. These methods of gathering information help you discover what you already know and help you realize also that you need more information. For example, you may decide that you would like more specific information about teenagers on one particular show. By watching this show and taking notes on what you see, you gather the information you need.

Writing Practice 2: *Gathering and Recording Information on a Topic*

Select one of the topics you wrote for Writing Practice 1. Then, to discover what you already know about the topic, use at least two different prewriting methods. Write the information you gather on a sheet of paper or on note cards.

Selecting Information to Make a Point

Nearly all writing you do in school will be to make or illustrate a point. Description may be written to convey sense impressions only. And narration may be written to tell a story only. However, you will often use description and narration, as well as expository writing, to make or illustrate a point.

Once you have discovered and collected information on your topic, you can decide what point you want to make. Your point, or main idea, is called a *thesis*. A *thesis sentence* controls all information you include in your composition in the same way that a topic sentence controls all information you include

5 Writing Compositions

in a paragraph. For example, you observed that teenagers on television are unlike real teenagers. Therefore, you might write as your thesis sentence, "Teenagers on television are portrayed unrealistically." Your composition would develop that thesis sentence.

Look back at the information you have on the topic *Television teenagers and the real thing*. Included in the list are *I like color television better than black and white* and *Parents think I watch too much TV*. Although both these items have to do with the general subject *television*, neither relates to the specific topic *Television teenagers and the real thing*, nor to the thesis that television portrays teenagers unrealistically. Because neither piece of information develops the topic, both should be removed from the list. The topic of your paper is a specific part of a general subject, and the thesis is the point you want to make about the topic. When you select information for your paper, be certain it relates to the specific topic and that it supports your thesis.

Writing Practice 3: *Selecting Information to Make a Point*

First, using the information you collected in Writing Practice 2, decide what point you want to make about your topic. Then

109

Writing

write a thesis sentence that states the point you want to make. Last, cross out any information that does not support your thesis.

Organizing Information into an Outline

After gathering information, writing a thesis, and selecting appropriate details, the next step in planning a composition is to arrange the information. One way to do so is by writing an informal outline. An *informal outline* shows the arrangement of major ideas and supporting details.

Suppose your grandmother has told you many stories about her childhood on an Illinois farm, and you decide to write a composition on that topic. Through brainstorming and talking with your grandmother, you develop a list of information from which you write the thesis, "During her childhood on a farm, my grandmother's life was busy and productive." You then select the following details:

Went to square dances in church hall once a month

Had eight brothers and sisters

Helped to milk the cows and lead them to pasture in the morning

During the summer she had to hoe thistles, and she hated that.

Listened to radio programs

Went on hayrides in the fall

She taught some lessons to the first-grade students and listened to their reading.

Liked to go on sleigh rides in the winter

The chickens were her responsibility.

Fed chickens

Gathered eggs

Helped mother bake twelve loaves of bread every Saturday morning

In summer she drove the tractor that pulled the hayrack.

No cafeteria at school

Brought lunch from home

School had only books—no films or records

Loved to read and traded books with her friends

The first step in organizing an outline is to identify the major ideas. As you examine the details about your grandmother's farm life, you notice that some details are about summer, while others are about fall or winter. You think you might organize your information under three major ideas: farm life during the summer, the fall, and the winter. However, a second look at your list of information shows that some details are not related to a season of the year and that only one detail is about the farm in winter. You notice that some details are about your grandmother's farm chores, some are about her school, and some are about what she did in her free time. Finally, you decide you can best arrange your information about your grandmother's busy and productive childhood under three major ideas:

1. Grandmother's farm work
2. Grandmother's school
3. Grandmother's recreation

The next step is to add details that support the major ideas. In an *informal* outline, details are indented under the major ideas, as the following outline for the topic *Grandmother's Farm Life* shows.

Writing

Grandmother's Farm Life

Grandmother's farm work
    Caring for the chickens
    Milking the cows
    Hoeing thistles
    Driving tractor
    Baking bread

Grandmother's school
    Walking to school
    Studying
    Teaching younger students

Grandmother's recreation
    Radio
    Books
    Square dances
    Hayrides and sleigh rides

Notice that some details from the list of information (such as *Had eight brothers and sisters*) are omitted from the preceding topic outline. Since the writer's goal is not only to present interesting information but also to organize information clearly for readers, details are sometimes not included because they are unrelated to the major ideas.

This sample outline is called a *topic outline* because it has short topics rather than complete sentences. (All the items in a

topic outline have the same form. The items may be stated in phrases or as single words, but they should not be complete sentences.) The writer might have chosen to write a *sentence outline* in which all the items are complete sentences. An informal sentence outline for the topic *Grandmother's Farm Life* would look like this:

Grandmother's Farm Life

My grandmother helped with work on the farm.
    She cared for the chickens and gathered the eggs.
    She milked three cows and led them to pasture.
    She hoed thistles in the cornfield under a hot summer sun.
    She drove the horses as they pulled the hayrack.
    She helped her mother bake twelve loaves of bread every Saturday.

My grandmother studied in a one-room country school.
    She rode twelve miles on a bus.
    There were only books in the school and no films or records.
    She carried her lunch in a small tin pail.
    She helped the younger students with their lessons.

My grandmother still had time for recreation.
    After dinner she listened to the radio.
    She loved to read and traded books with her friends.
    Once a month she went to the square dance held in the church hall.
    She enjoyed hayrides in the fall and sleigh rides in the winter.

The two outlines in this section are *informal* outlines. In the chapter "Research Writing," you will learn about the formal outline, another way of arranging information.

An informal outline can help you arrange information and ensure that you have not left out important details. Later, when you write your composition, you can make each major heading a topic sentence developed by the supporting ideas.

Writing Practice 4: *Organizing Information Into an Outline*

Prepare an informal outline. Use the thesis and details you selected for Writing Practice 3.

Parts of a Composition

Compositions nearly always have three main parts: introduction, body, and conclusion. The first paragraph is often an *introduction*—a paragraph that introduces the topic, says something interesting about it, and states the thesis. Following the introduction are several paragraphs called the *body*. These paragraphs give readers specific information about the topic, supporting and developing the thesis. The *conclusion*, which is often one paragraph, gives readers a final, interesting point to think about.

Although some compositions do not have separate introductory or concluding paragraphs, all good compositions are organized carefully with a beginning, middle, and end. They are well developed with examples, facts, incidents, or reasons to make the point clear. In the models that follow, notice how the authors organized and developed their descriptive, narrative, and expository compositions.

Writing a Descriptive Composition

A descriptive composition describes a person, place, object, animal, or event. When you write this kind of composition, your purpose is to make your point by using specific, vivid details presented in a logical manner.

Model: A Descriptive Composition

When Maya Angelou was small, she and her brother Bailey were sent to live with their grandmother in Stamps, Arkansas. *I Know Why the Caged Bird Sings*, the title of her autobiography, describes the writer's experiences growing up in this small town.

The following portion of Maya Angelou's autobiography is a composition describing her brother Bailey. As you read it, look for the thesis and the details that make Bailey seem like a real person.

Introduction Bailey was the greatest person in my world. And the fact that he was my brother, my only brother, and I had no sisters to share him with, was such good fortune that it made me

5 Writing Compositions

Lauded means "praised."

Body

want to live a Christian life just to show God that I was grateful. Where I was big, elbowy and grating, he was small, graceful and smooth. When I was described by our playmates as being dun color, he was lauded for his velvet-black skin. His hair fell down in black curls, and my head was covered with black steel wool. And yet he loved me.

When our elders said unkind things about my features (my family was handsome to a point of pain for me), Bailey would wink at me from across the room, and I knew that it was a matter of time before he would take revenge. He would allow the old ladies to finish wondering how on earth I came about, then he would ask, in a voice like cooling bacon grease, "Oh Mizeriz Coleman, how is your son? I saw him the other day, and he looked sick enough to die."

Aghast, the ladies would ask, "Die? From what? He ain't sick."

And in a voice oilier than the one before, he'd answer with a straight face, "From the Uglies."

I would hold my laugh, bite my tongue, grit my teeth and very seriously erase even the touch of a smile from my face. Later, behind the house by the black-walnut tree, we'd laugh and laugh and howl.

Bailey could count on very few punishments for his consistently outrageous behavior, for he was the pride of the Henderson/Johnson family.

His movements, as he was later to describe those of an acquaintance, were activated with oiled precision. He was also

115

Writing

able to find more hours in the day than I thought existed. He finished chores, homework, read more books than I and played the group games on the side of the hill with the best of them. He could even pray out loud in church, and was apt at stealing pickles from the barrel that sat under the fruit counter and Uncle Willie's nose.

Once when the Store was full of lunchtime customers, he dipped the strainer, which we also used to sift weevils from meal and flour, into the barrel and fished for two fat pickles. He caught them and hooked the strainer onto the side of the barrel where they dripped until he was ready for them. When the last school bell rang, he picked the nearly dry pickles out of the strainer, jammed them into his pockets and threw the strainer behind the oranges. We ran out of the Store. It was summer and his pants were short, so the pickle juice made clean streams down his ashy legs, and he jumped with his pockets full of loot and his eyes laughing a "How about that?" He smelled like a vinegar barrel or a sour angel.

After our early chores were done, while Uncle Willie or Momma minded the Store, we were free to play the children's games as long as we stayed within yelling distance. Playing hide-and-seek, his voice was easily identified, singing, "Last night, night before, twenty-four robbers at my door. Who all is hid? Ask me to let them in, hit 'em in the head with a rolling pin. Who all is hid?" In follow the leader, naturally he was the one who created the most daring and interesting things to do. And when he was on the tail of the pop the whip, he would twirl off the end like a top, spinning, falling, laughing, finally stopping just before my heart beat its last, and then he was back in the game, still laughing.

Conclusion

Of all the needs (there are none imaginary) a lonely child has, the one that must be satisfied, if there is going to be hope and a hope of wholeness, is the unshaking need for an unshakable God. My pretty Black brother was my Kingdom Come.[1]

Maya Angelou's description is well organized and well developed. She begins her composition with her thesis, "Bailey was the greatest person in my world." Her first paragraph introduces Bailey by describing his appearance. Because Angelou wants her readers to know about more than Bailey's appearance, she leads them into the next part of her description by saying, "he loved me."

The second through ninth paragraphs describe Bailey's character, showing how he loved Maya and some of the reasons why he was so important in his sister's life. They make

---

[1] From *I Know Why the Caged Bird Sings*, by Maya Angelou. Copyright © 1969 by Maya Angelou. Reprinted by permission of Random House, Inc.

up the body of the composition. Paragraphs two through five give an example of how Bailey would get revenge on the adults who made unkind remarks about Maya. Paragraph seven describes Bailey's movements and activities, giving specific examples of how he spent his days. Paragraph eight tells an incident, a time when Bailey stole pickles from their uncle's store. Paragraph nine gives examples of Bailey's leading the other children in games during the evening hours after chores were done.

Paragraph ten is the conclusion of the composition. Maya Angelou says that she was a lonely child and that Bailey gave her what she needed to be a happy person. Bailey was like God to Maya. This comparison reinforces the thesis that Bailey was the greatest person in her world.

Think and Discuss

1. One way the writer makes her brother seem real is by using specific details to describe him physically. In the first part of the composition she writes that Bailey had "velvet-black skin." What are other specific details the writer uses about her brother's appearance?

2. What specific details does she use to describe Bailey's character?

3. Although this is a descriptive composition, Angelou develops some of her paragraphs with narration. Why do you think she develops some paragraphs in this way? Give several examples of Angelou's use of narration.

Writing Practice 5: *Writing a Descriptive Composition*

A. Using either a new topic or one you have already selected, write a descriptive composition, including an introductory paragraph.

B. Be sure to plan your composition before you write:

1. Select a subject.

2. Narrow the subject to a topic.

3. Discover your ideas about the topic through brainstorming, clustering, or jotting notes.

4. From the information you have gathered, decide what point (thesis) you want to make.

Writing

    5. Put your thesis into one statement.

    6. Eliminate any details that do not support your thesis.

    7. Organize your material into an informal outline.

C. These guidelines for writing a descriptive composition will help you think about revising your paper:

    1. The topic is limited enough to be developed in a short paper.

    2. The topic will interest readers.

    3. The topic is developed with enough specific information to make it clear to readers.

    4. Each item of information in the paper develops the topic.

    5. The composition begins in an interesting way.

    6. Specific, vivid details help readers share in the topic described.

    7. The composition is well organized.

    8. The composition concludes in an interesting way.

When you have finished revising your paper, use the checklist at the back of the book to check your paper for errors in grammar, usage, and spelling.

Writing a Narrative Composition

A narrative composition tells a story either about you or about someone else. The purpose of a narrative composition is to make a point by telling the story in a logical way. In order to make your narrative interesting, develop it with specific, vivid details.

Model: *A Narrative Composition*

In the following composition Walt Kelly, creator of the comic strip *Pogo*, tells what happened when he and some friends decided to go into business. As you read, try to determine the point, or thesis, of the narrative.

    Cranberry Campbell, Binney Robertson, and I started an outdoor candle factory one time. We dug a hole in the backyard and built a fire in it, then laid a piece of metal screening over the flames and placed a pot on that. Into the pot we put pieces of paraffin filched from our mothers. (They used paraffin to seal the jars of homemade jellies, jams, peach preserves, and cooked string beans that ladies in those days prepared during the summer.) After the paraffin was melted, we poured it into a short piece of pipe which had a string stretched through its interior, and when the stuff cooled we had a candle, or so we considered it—sometimes with a few ants imbedded in the dirty wax and with smoky stripes giving it a kind of glum decoration.
    Getting the candle out of its mold posed a problem at first, but American know-how in the person of Binney Robertson, the inventor, showed us how to heat the outside of the pipe and pull the wax monstrosity out by its string. True, we pulled a lot of strings right out of the candles, but Robertson invented a system for rethreading the wick.
    We peddled the candles around the neighborhood at five cents each, starting out that morning with high hopes and ten candles and figuring what we would do with the fifty cents we were sure to get. Most of the mothers looked at the candles with distinct distaste and at noon we still had ten. So we declared a fire sale and slashed the price to two cents each. Asked why it was a fire sale, we truthfully replied that the goods were a little damaged by smoke. "Also by ants," said Mrs. Knott as she bought two.
    Mrs. Campbell and my mother were having coffee in our kitchen when we approached with the reduction in price.

Cranberry explained to his mother that this was her chance to snap up the remaining eight. I pointed out that they were handmade and therefore worth a great deal more than store candles, which at the time were selling at two for a nickel. We described how much more valuable the wax was now than in its original form, but my mother put an end to the pitch by trying one of the candles. It burned with a sputtering blue and dismal flame for about three seconds and finally wilted, leaned gently sideways, and went out. We left, closing the screen door as quietly and as quickly as we could.

Cranberry suggested that we should try all the candles down in the cellar and sell only those that were guaranteed to stay lighted. Not one did, and in addition, they smelled pretty bad. We decided to try chewing them. But even this attempt at salvage was no good. They tasted pretty bad, too.[1]

Like other stories, a narrative composition involves characters and action. The action of the story is interesting because it leads somewhere; it has a point. For example, in Walt Kelly's composition the main characters, Cranberry, Binney, and Walt Kelly, build an outdoor candle factory, make candles, and try to sell them. The point of the story, which is not stated directly, is the utter failure of their "enterprise."

Because a narrative tells a story, events may be arranged in chronological order. Walt Kelly and his friends first build the candle factory, then make the candles, and then try to sell them. However, writers sometimes change this sequence in order to attract the attention of readers, beginning with the middle or even the end, and then going back to relate the first part of the story.

In narrative writing, the point of view of the person who tells the story is important. Walt Kelly chooses to speak as himself in his composition. He uses a *first-person* point of view, using the pronoun "I" when he refers to himself. (However, the "I" in first person narration is not always the author himself. In books such as *David Copperfield* and *Treasure Island*, the "I" refers to a specific character.) In other narratives you may notice that the author takes a more objective point of view, writing with the pronouns *he* and *she*. This is called *third-person* point of view. *Second-person* point of view uses the pronoun "you" and is taken when an author wants to speak directly to readers.

If you, as the narrator, want to be close to readers, use first-person point of view. If you want the narrator to stand away from readers and be more objective, use third-person

[1]From "Enterprise" by Walt Kelly in *Five Boyhoods* edited by Martin Levin. Copyright © 1962 by Martin Levin. Reprinted by permission of Mrs. Walt Kelly.

point of view. When you give directions, you may use second-person point of view. Once you decide on a point of view, do not change to another. Such changes confuse readers.

Think and Discuss

1. This narrative composition has no separate introductory paragraph. The first sentence introduces the characters and states what the story is about. The remainder of the composition tells in time order what happened to the boys' business venture. Kelly concludes with, "They tasted pretty bad, too." Do you think Walt Kelly needed to have separate paragraphs for his introduction and conclusion? Why or why not?

2. Earlier in this chapter you were advised to state the point you want to make when you write compositions. Why does Walt Kelly not state his point? Would you have understood the story better if he had said explicitly that their attempt to begin a business failed? If Walt Kelly had written a sentence that said the attempt failed, where should it have been placed in the narrative? Why?

For Your Writer's Notebook

> Perhaps you once began an enterprise (publishing a neighborhood newspaper or walking dogs) that failed. Write about that experience in your Writer's Notebook. Give details about your early hopes, your hard work, and your final feelings of disappointment.

Writing Practice 6: *Writing a Narrative Composition*

A. Using either a new topic or one you have already selected, write a narrative composition.

B. Plan your narrative composition by following the steps in Writing Practice 5.

C. Follow the guidelines in Writing Practice 5 to revise your composition. Additional specific guidelines for narration follow on the next page.

Writing

1. Events in the story are arranged so that readers can easily follow them.
2. Point of view is consistent throughout the entire composition.

Use the checklist at the back of the book to proofread your composition.

Writing an Expository Composition

An expository composition explains a topic. It may explain how to do something, why something works as it does, or why the writer has a certain opinion.

Model: An Expository Composition

An expository composition conveys information to clarify something that might be unfamiliar or difficult to understand. The following composition by Jack London explains the difficulties faced by an Alaskan "grub cook" in a prospectors' cabin during the winter of 1899. As you read it, make a list of these difficulties. How many can you find?

Introduction

Housekeeping in the Klondike—that's bad! And by *men*—worse. Reverse the proposition, if you will, yet you will fail to mitigate, even by a hair's-breadth, the woe of it. It is bad, unutterably bad, for a man to keep house, and it is equally bad to keep house in the Klondike. That's the sum and substance of it. Of course men will be men, and especially is this true of the kind who wander off to the frozen rim of the world. The glitter of gold is in their eyes, they are borne along by uplifting ambition, and in their hearts is a great disdain for everything in the culinary department save "grub." "Just so long as it's grub," they say, coming in off trail, gaunt and ravenous, "grub, and piping hot." Nor do they manifest the slightest regard for the genesis of the same; they prefer to begin at "revelations."

Body

Yes, it would seem a pleasant task to cook for such men; but just let them lie around cabin to rest up for a week, and see with what celerity they grow high-stomached and make sarcastic comments on the way you fry the bacon or boil the coffee. And behold how each will spring his own strange and marvelous theory as to how sour-dough bread should be mixed and baked. Each has his own recipe (formulated, mark you, from personal experience only), and to him it is an idol of brass, like unto no other man's, and he'll fight for it—ay, down to the

5 Writing Compositions

last wee pinch of soda—and if need be, die for it. If you should happen to catch him on trail, completely exhausted, you may blacken his character, his flag, and his ancestral tree with impunity; but breathe the slightest whisper against his sour-dough bread, and he will turn upon and rend you.

From this it may be gathered what an unstable thing sour dough is. Never was coquette so fickle. You cannot depend upon it. Still, it is the simplest thing in the world. Make a batter and place it near the stove (that it may not freeze) till it ferments or sours. Then mix the dough with it, and sweeten with soda to taste—of course replenishing the batter for next time. There it is. Was there ever anything simpler? But, oh, the tribulations of the cook! It is never twice the same. If the batter could only be placed away in an equable temperature, all well and good. If one's comrades did not interfere, much vexation of spirit might be avoided. But this cannot be; for Tom fires up the stove till the cabin is become like the hot-room of a Turkish bath; Dick forgets all about the fire till the place is a refrigerator; then along comes Harry and shoves the sour-dough bucket right against the stove to make way for the drying of his mittens. Now heat is a most potent factor in accelerating the fermentation of flour and water, and hence the unfortunate cook is constantly in disgrace with Tom, Dick, and Harry. Last week his bread was yellow from a plethora of soda; this week it is sour from a prudent lack of the same; and next week—ah, who can tell save the god of the fire-box?

Some cooks aver they have so cultivated their olfactory organs that they can tell to the fraction of a degree just how sour the batter is. Nevertheless they have never been known to bake two batches of bread which were at all alike. But this fact casts not the slightest shadow upon the infallibility of their theory. One and all, they take advantage of circumstances, and meanly crawl out by laying the blame upon the soda, which was dampened "the time the canoe overturned," or upon the flour, which they got in trade from "that half-breed fellow with the dogs."

Conclusion

The pride of the Klondike cook in his bread is something which passes understanding. The highest commendatory degree which can be passed upon a man in that country, and the one which distinguishes him from the tenderfoot, is that of being a "sour-dough boy." Never was a college graduate prouder of his "sheepskin" than the old-timer of this appellation. There is a certain distinction about it, from which the newcomer is invidiously excluded. A tenderfoot with his baking-powder is an inferior creature, a freshman; but a "sour-dough boy" is a man of stability, a post-graduate in that art of arts—bread-making.[1]

An expository composition must be clear and well organized. It should contain a main idea, or thesis, in the opening paragraph, which is developed fully and logically in the following paragraphs. In this composition, notice how the opening sentences immediately grab the reader's attention while effectively introducing the author's main idea at the same time.

The body paragraphs of an expository composition explain and develop the thesis. The second paragraph of the model composition explains—through the use of specific examples—the difficulties of pleasing the men being cooked for. The next paragraphs present the problems involved in baking a good sour-dough bread. The final paragraph gives added emphasis by expounding upon the pride a good grub cook feels in overcoming all these hardships and being recognized as a "sour-dough boy."

Think and Discuss

1. Notice the *process description* in paragraph 3, an explanation of how to make sour-dough bread. Do you think you could make it successfully by following the step-by-step method given there? What additional specific information might you ask for?

---

[1] Jack London, "Housekeeping in the Klondike," from *Harper's Bazaar*, September 15, 1900, as printed in King Hendricks and Irving Shepard, eds., *Jack London Reports* (New York: Doubleday & Co., 1970), pp. 322–23.

2. From his references to men's housekeeping and lifestyle and to the "fickle coquette," what can you deduce about the author's background and point of view?

3. Expository compositions should be unified, coherent, and well developed. Using specific examples, tell how this composition meets (or falls short of) each of these criteria.

4. What are the transitional devices the author uses to make his writing coherent? Compile a list of ten examples.

5. In this composition there are a number of fairly difficult vocabulary words. List and define them. What is the effect of using "difficult" words to write about a "simple" topic, such as housekeeping and baking bread?

Writing Assignment I: *Writing an Expository Composition*

A. Prewriting

1. Select a subject from this list or choose one of your own for an expository composition.

    Disadvantages (or advantages) of being an honor roll student

    The easiest way to learn computer programming

    What you learn in school that doesn't come from books

    Ways to increase your own self-esteem

    Sports is more than just a physical activity.

    How honest should people be?

    Why I will never be unemployed for long

    How to tell who your true friends are

    The five most important things to teach your child

2. Limit the subject to a topic that can be developed in a five-paragraph paper.

3. Decide your purpose and audience in writing this exposition. Do you want to explain how to do something or why you have a certain opinion? What point will your explanation make clear?

For more information on purpose and audience, see page 104.

4. Discover what you know about the topic by using one of the prewriting methods you have learned.

5. Write your thesis sentence.

6. Eliminate any details that do not support your thesis.

7. Organize your material into an informal outline.

B. Writing

Use your informal outline to write your composition. Be sure to include specific, vivid details. Also be sure that each paragraph develops your thesis in a different way. Write a powerful concluding paragraph.

C. Postwriting

Use the checklists for revising and proofreading at the back of the book to make your final product the best it can be. Then form groups composed of students who wrote on the same topic. Share your work, and appoint a group secretary to write down as many examples as the group can find of:

1. Strong, creative thesis statements
2. Logical, clear paragraph development
3. Vivid, lively language
4. Clever use of transitional devices
5. Powerful or effective conclusions

Have the group secretaries share with the entire class a few of the examples they have recorded.

Sentence Combining: Using Words Like Who, Which, *and* Where

Combining with (Who) *and* (Which)

Just as you can insert descriptive words into a sentence base, so can you insert groups of words that tell *who* somebody is or *which* person or object the sentence is about. Look carefully at the examples below and on the next page to see how the combinations are made. The combining signals (*who*) or (*which*) follow the sentence to be inserted. The part that is inserted may appear in the middle of the combined sentence or at its end.

Base Sentence: Mr. Kubrick was absent during fifth period today.

Insert: Mr. Kubrick is almost never ill. (*who*)

Combined: Mr. Kubrick, *who is almost never ill*, was absent during fifth period today.

Base Sentence: Rolling grasslands stretched as far as the eye could see.

Insert: The grasslands were covered with vast herds of bison. (*which*)

Combined: Rolling grasslands, *which were covered with vast herds of bison*, stretched as far as the eye could see.

Base Sentence: Gabriela listened attentively to the guest speaker.

Insert: The guest speaker had traveled around the world. (*who*)

Combined: Gabriela listened attentively to the guest speaker, *who had traveled around the world*.

Base Sentence: Tourists viewed the Aztec calendar.

Insert: The Aztec calendar was carved in a large circle of rock. (*which*)

Writing

Combined: Tourists viewed the Aztec calendar, *which was carved in a large circle of rock.*

For more information on punctuating adjective clauses, see pages 526-527, and 544.

Use commas to separate the words introduced by *who* or *which* from the rest of the sentence.

Exercise 1: *Combining with* (Who) *and* (Which)

Combine the following sets of sentences on a sheet of paper. The first sentence is the base sentence; the second sentence is the insert. For the first five sets use the signals (*who*) and (*which*) at the end of the insert sentences to guide you in making the combinations. Decide for yourself whether to use *who* or *which* for the last five sets. (Remember to put commas wherever they are needed.) Study the examples before you begin.

Examples

a. The castle was protected by natural rock formations.
   The castle stood high on the hill. (*which*)
   The castle, which stood high on the hill, was protected by natural rock formations.

b. The President boarded the aircraft carrier.
   The President is the Commander-in-Chief. (*who*)
   The President, who is the Commander-in-Chief, boarded the aircraft carrier.

1. I studied my math book for three hours before taking Mr. Hardman's exam.
   Mr. Hardman's exam was a midterm. (*which*)

2. Mrs. Chu will schedule Mike's recital when he has mastered his two new assignments.
   Mrs. Chu is Mike's music teacher. (*who*)

3. Our old oil lamp is a valuable antique.
   The lamp has been stored in the attic for many years. (*which*)

4. Swimming provides exercise for almost every muscle in the body.
   Swimming is the one physical activity I love. (*which*)

5. After the play the cast gave a dozen red roses to Mrs. Shaw.
   Mrs. Shaw is the drama coach at Wilson Junior High School. (*who*)

Sentence Combining

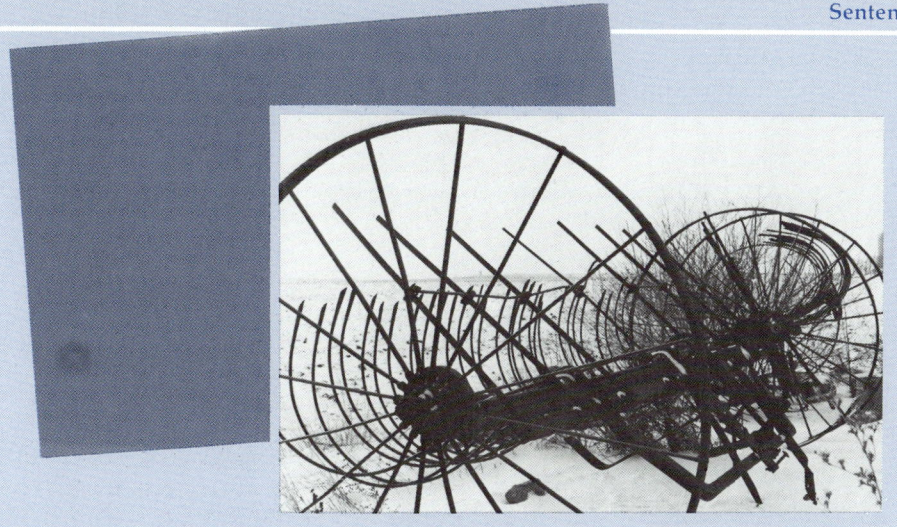

6. John and Estella played cards and ate popcorn.
   Popcorn is the one snack Mother permits.

7. At times the farmer wonders what an office job would be like.
   The farmer works from dawn to dusk seven days a week.

8. David Lonetree agreed to speak at the rally.
   David Lonetree is a native American by descent.

9. The Eskimo feed fresh meat to the dogs.
   The Eskimo depend on animals for transportation.

10. Grandmother and Grandfather could not afford to buy the new townhouse.
    The townhouse was a modern, two-story model.

Using Commas with (Who) and (Which/That)

In (*who*) and (*which*) combinations, commas show that the inserted information could be taken out of the base sentence without affecting its main idea.

Sometimes, however, the inserted information is absolutely necessary to the meaning of the base sentence. In these cases, particularly in (*that*) combinations, no commas are placed around the inserted information.

The horse *that Uncle Tobias took to the Kentucky Derby* has been retired to pasture now.

Writing

The *italicized* words in the sentence are essential because they tell exactly which horse is now spending its days in pasture. Because no commas are placed around the *italicized* words, the reader knows that they express an essential thought.

The Jeffersons' barn, *which has a silo attached to it*, was built in 1929.

In the above sentence the *italicized* words from the insert are not necessary to the main idea of the base sentence. The commas around this insert show that the information is not essential. In formal usage *that* is used when the information is essential and *which* when it is not.

In your own writing you must decide when the inserted information is essential. Notice how the meaning of the following sentence changes as commas are added:

Teachers who always expect students to do their homework cause me many hours of hard work.

Teachers, who always expect students to do their homework, cause me many hours of hard work.

In the first version the insert identifies a specific type of teacher—only teachers who expect students to do their homework—and is essential to the meaning of the sentence. The second sentence, however, is about all teachers. The insert set off by commas simply adds additional information and is not essential.

For more information on essential clauses, see pages 526-527, and 544.

Exercise 2: *Using Commas with* (Who)

In the following sets of sentences, decide whether to add commas as you insert the second statement into the base sentence. All of the insert statements begin with *who,* but only the first three sets give the *who* signal. Write the new sentences on a sheet of paper. Study the examples first.

Examples

a. I gave the book to my friend.
   My friend loves to read. (*who*)
   I gave the book to my friend, who loves to read.

b. Give the kitten to someone.
   Someone will care for it.
   Give the kitten to someone who will care for it.

1. The man lived over 500 years ago.
   The man has been haunting the castle. (*who*)

2. The person is my uncle.
   The person has had a great influence on my life. (*who*)

3. The cook in our cafeteria has put three children through college and another one through law school.
   The cook is a remarkable woman. (*who*)

4. Sarah Jo asked her sister to participate in our school's graduation ceremonies.
   Her sister is a well-known actress.

5. When he returned, Grandfather asked the children to explain their behavior.
   The children were sitting in the closet.

Combining with (Whose), (Where), (When), and (Why)

For more information on using commas with clauses, see pages 519-524, 526-530, and 544.

In this section you will combine sentences using the words *whose, where, when,* or *why* in place of the repeated word or words in the insert sentence. The process is the same as used with the (*who*), (*whom*), and (*which/that*) combining signals. Again, you will decide when to use commas in the combined sentence.

Base Sentence: The cosmetologist gave customers the very latest hairstyles.

Insert: The cosmetologist's own hair was always unkempt. (*whose*)

Combined: The cosmetologist, *whose own hair was always unkempt*, gave customers the very latest hairstyles.

Base Sentence: Cinderella's fine coach and horses turned back into a pumpkin and field mice at the moment.

Insert: The clock struck midnight at the moment. (*when*)

Combined: Cinderella's fine coach and horses turned back into a pumpkin and field mice at the moment *when the clock struck midnight*.

Writing

Exercise 3: *Combining with* (Whose), (Where), (When), *and* (Why)

On your own sheet of paper, combine the following sets of sentences. Follow the signals for sets 1–5. For sets 6–10 decide for yourself which of the four words to use. Write the new combined sentences on a sheet of paper numbered 1–10. Study the two examples before you begin.

Examples

a. Mrs. Berman introduced me to an explorer.
The explorer's life had been one long adventure. (*whose*)
Mrs. Berman introduced me to an explorer whose life had been one long adventure.

b. Mrs. Berman first met the explorer many years ago. He was in her class at school. (*when*)
Mrs. Berman first met the explorer many years ago when he was in her class at school.

1. Paul Bunyan was a mythical American hero.
Paul Bunyan's deeds showed superhuman strength and skill. (*whose*)

2. Tom looks forward to the time.
He will be able to drive his own car. (*when*)

3. Although it did not frighten us, there was no reason.
The door of the old, empty mansion began to swing back and forth on its hinges. (*why*)

4. Respectfully, the students shook hands with the principal.
The principal's encouragement and trust had changed their outlook on life. (*whose*)

5. The restaurant host politely explained the reason.
We could not be seated immediately. (*why*)

6. Pruning and fertilizing should be done at that time of the year.
Plants enter a dormant period of growth.

7. Galloping on her horse through the park in the late afternoon, Hester forgot the reason.
She had been angry with her mother.

Sentence Combining

8. Returning to the stables, Hester looked for the attendant.
   She had rented his horse from the stables.

9. Dismounting easily, Hester turned to see the man.
   The man's training had made her into a superb young horsewoman.

10. Hester and Old Willy dreamed of the time.
    Hester would win a championship event.

Writing Practice: *It Really Happened!*

Using vivid details to explain how, when, where, and why something happened, write two paragraphs describing one of the following situations. As you write, include several of the sentence-combining skills you have been practicing.

1. Losing a valuable item and finding it in an unusual place
2. Discovering that someone has stolen an item that belonged to you and trying to recover it
3. Trying to find out who has done a kind deed for you
4. Waking up one morning to find that the house or apartment building next to yours has disappeared

6 Research Writing

When you write about yourself, your purpose is to help readers share your experiences, thoughts, and feelings. In writing a research report, however, your main purpose is to present information, although your teacher may ask you to say what you think or feel about the subject.

Much of the information in a research report comes from sources such as books, magazines, and interviews. One important skill in writing a research report is knowing how to get and record such information. In this chapter you will learn how to summarize, how to use outside sources, and how to write a research report.

Writing a Summary

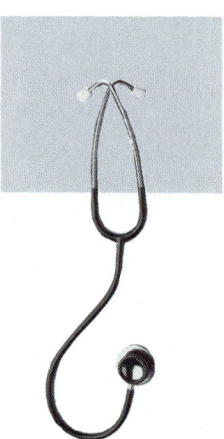

Suppose you are telling a friend of an interesting television show about a young woman who was paralyzed in a skiing accident. The bell is about to ring, and you do not have much time, so you leave out unimportant details. You tell only about the main events—how the accident happened and how the courageous young woman overcame her disability. What you give your friend is a *summary* of the story.

A *summary* is a concise retelling or rewriting of the main ideas in a book, article, story, or speech. It answers the six basic questions: who, what, when, where, why, and how. Because a summary gives only the most important ideas from the original source, it is no more than one-fourth to one-third the length of the original.

Model: Summary of a Short Piece

As you read the following paragraphs, ask yourself the *who? what? when? where? why?* and *how?* questions that apply.

Original:
Mary Edwards Walker (1832–1919), an ardent advocate

of women's rights, was the only woman ever to be awarded the bronze Medal of Honor for her distinguished service as a physician in the Union Army during the Civil War. Working tirelessly and courageously among wounded men at the battlefront, Dr. Walker was taken prisoner of war and held four months before being released in a Confederate prisoner exchange.

Dr. Walker raised eyebrows wherever she went with her blatant defiance of conventional standards for women's dress. Unheard of in her time, she wore men's trousers and a long frock coat, changing to a full men's dress suit for evening wear and lecture appearances. She bore the brunt of jeers and ridicule from men and women alike—having been arrested several times for "masquerading in men's clothes."

Following the Civil War, Dr. Walker continued her outspoken campaign for electoral reform and women's suffrage while opening her own medical practice—in a day when the only profession open to women was teaching. A brilliant and innovative thinker, she wrote two books and is credited with several inventions, including the design of the inside neckband on men's shirts and the return postcard for registered mail.

In 1917 Dr. Walker was asked to return her Medal of Honor by a review committee questioning its official authorization. Her indignant reply was, "Over my dead body!" She continued to wear her medal with pride and gentility until the day of her death in 1919. The medal was subsequently officially reinstated in 1977.

Summary:

Dr. Mary Edwards Walker was an early champion of women's rights during and after the Civil War. Although she won the Medal of Honor for her courageous service as a physician in the Union Army, she suffered criticism for defying conventional standards on women's dress and behavior.

Here are some answers you may have thought of as you read the paragraphs above:

The *who* is Mary Edwards Walker. The *what* is the activities that brought her recognition. *When* is during and following the Civil War. *Where* is the United States. *Why* is Dr. Walker's belief in women's rights. *How* is what Dr. Walker did to advocate her beliefs.

When writing a summary of a longer article or book, you can remember important information by taking notes. Use the *who? what? when? where? why?* and *how?* questions to find the most important information.

Model: Summary of a Longer Piece

The following selection about Jesse Owens is from Zander Hollander's book *Great Athletes of the 20th Century*. Read the passage carefully and then read the summary of it that follows. As you read the summary, notice which parts of the original piece were left out.

Original

At the age of six, James Cleveland Owens had been picking cotton in an Alabama field. But his family, like so many other Southern Negro families, had spent enough of their lives as sharecroppers and had moved to the north. The Owens family moved to Cleveland, Ohio. When James Cleveland attended his first day of classes in his new grammar school, his teacher asked him his name.

"J.C., ma'am," he answered, because that was what his family called him.

"Jesse?" she said, confused by his drawl.

"Yes, ma'am," he said, eager to agree with anything his new teacher said. And so he began his new life with a new name, a name that someday would be known the world over: Jesse Owens.

Jesse first showed his great running ability when he was a teenager. At a high-school track meet, he crouched down in the starting blocks, burst forward and ran a 100-yard dash in 9.4 seconds, setting a national scholastic record that would stand for thirty years. Soon he was setting records not only in 100-yard dashes, but also in 200-yard dashes and in the broad jump. And he was doing it on an empty stomach.

Food was scarce in Jesse's home all the time he was in high school. His father had been injured in an auto accident and was not able to work. The family just managed to get along.

Jesse's life was still difficult when he became a student at Ohio State University. Though he had been a prominent high-school track star, he did not receive an athletic scholarship. He operated an office building elevator from 5:00 P.M. until 12:30 A.M. for $150 a month. After work he traveled home by trolley car, ate dinner and slept until 6:30 A.M. He attended classes from eight in the morning to three in the afternoon, then practiced with the track squad until it was time to tend his elevator. He studied during the weekends and at spare moments in the elevator.

Despite the stiff schedule, he did well in his classes and in athletics. In 1933 he broke the world indoor broad-jump record, then began starring in outdoor competition. About a week before the Big Ten outdoor meet, he pulled back the covers of his bed and discovered a dead snake on the sheets. He found out who had played the joke on him, and tracked the fellow down with a bag of water. He hit the jokester over the head with it, then turned to run away. He slipped and tumbled down a flight of stairs.

Writing

Jesse wrenched his back in the tumble and was in pain all week long. The day of the Big Ten meet he drove to the University of Michigan stadium with pain shooting through his back, thighs and knees. At the stadium he dispensed with his warm up to conserve his energy for the actual competition. When broad jumpers were called to the pit, he walked there slowly. Then with pain still shooting through his body, he raced down the approach strip and leaped into the air. He leaped 26 feet, 8¼ inches, a world record.

Then he ran the 100-yard dash in 9.4 seconds, tying the world record. After that he ran the 200-yard dash in a record 20.3 seconds and the 220-yard low hurdles in a record 22.6 seconds. Despite his agony, he had won four events, set three world records and tied one.[1]

Summary:

James Owens was born in Alabama, but his family moved to Cleveland, Ohio, when he was young. In his new school James Owens' teacher did not understand him and pronounced his name *Jesse*. He did not correct her, and his name became Jesse Owens from that time on.

Jesse Owens began to set records for the 100-yard dash, 200-yard dash, and broad jump while he was still in high school. His family was poor, and Jesse's life was hard, but he went on to Ohio State University. To earn money, he worked as an elevator operator, but still managed to do well in both his classes and athletics.

Jesse Owens broke the world indoor broad-jump record in 1933, but injured his back before an important outdoor event. In great pain he competed anyway, setting a new outdoor broad-jump record. At the same time he tied a world record for the 100-yard dash and set records for the 200-yard dash and the 220-yard low hurdles.

Think and Discuss

1. In the first part of the Jesse Owens article, the writer records the dialogue between Jesse and his teacher that caused his name to be changed from James to Jesse. The writer of the summary, however, leaves it out and summarizes the incident. What are three other places in the summary where the writer does not include information from the original?
2. Why do you think this information was left out in the summary?

---

[1]From "Jesse Owens" by Steve Gelman from *Great American Athletes of the 20th Century*, by Zander Hollander. Copyright © 1966 by Random House, Inc. Reprinted by permission of Random House, Inc.

Writing Practice 1: *Writing a Summary*

The following is an article about Matthew Alexander Henson, the first man actually to reach the North Pole, from Charlemae Rollins' book *They Showed the Way*. Before you write, read the article once to get a general idea of what it is about. Then read the article a second time, this time taking notes on the important ideas. Finally, write a summary, no more than one-fourth to one-third the length of the original, using your notes as a guide.

> The first man to stand at the top of the world was Matthew Alexander Henson. As a trailbreaker for Rear Admiral Robert E. Peary, Henson reached the North Pole forty-five minutes before the leader of the expedition, on April 6, 1909. But he had spent years preparing for that moment.
> Henson was born in Charles County, Maryland, in 1866. He was orphaned quite young, and at the age of eleven he ran away from a cruel stepmother. He went to Washington, where he worked as a dishwasher. His immense longing to become a sailor led him to tramp to Baltimore. He wandered among the huge docks and warehouses, and gazed at the ocean-going vessels. He signed as cabin boy on the *Katie Hines*, bound for Hong Kong.
> The captain showed an interest in young Matthew, and taught him not only a great deal about navigation and piloting a ship, but also reading and writing. He spent five years sailing on the *Katie*, only leaving when the captain died.

Writing

Matt came ashore, and while working as a handy man in a clothing shop met Robert E. Peary, an engineer for the Navy. Peary liked the boy, and asked Matt to accompany him to Nicaragua as his personal attendant. Matt accepted, and was soon promoted to the surveying crew as field helper. He and Peary worked and traveled together for the next twenty-three years.

On their return from Central America, Peary told Henson that he planned to go to Greenland to explore the northern ice cap, but that he had no money to pay his companion because he had failed to find financial backing for the expedition. Matt offered to go without pay.

In 1888 Peary, Henson, and a number of other explorers set out for Baffin Bay. Henson soon proved himself the most useful member of the party; he handled a hammer and saw easily, drove the dog teams well, and picked up the Eskimo language quickly. Much of what he learned on this first trip was invaluable in their later Arctic explorations. When they returned to New York, Peary was determined to raise funds for an expedition to the North Pole.

Peary and Henson together made seven unsuccessful attempts to reach the Pole, and Peary made one alone. Between trips, Peary lectured throughout the country on the Arctic, while Henson worked in the Arctic section of the Museum of Natural History in New York. They had brought two huge meteorites and many other scientifically important contributions to the museum. During these years many people became interested in an American expedition to the North Pole, sufficient funds were raised, and Peary was provided with a ship, the *Windward*. Their failures only made the two men even more determined to reach their goal.

On July 8, 1908, Peary and Henson sailed again, this time in a new ship, the *Roosevelt*. They established a base on Cape Columbia, four hundred uncharted miles from the top of the world. Six months later, they were only one hundred and thirty miles from their objective. The supporting party was sent back to the base and Henson pushed ahead as trailblazer. Peary and

four Eskimos brought up the rear. By April 5 they were only thirty-five miles from their goal. Now they were more aware than ever that a sudden Arctic storm, a miscalculation of direction, or separation in the vast wastes, might end in death for them all.

On April 6, 1909, however, Peary wrote in his logbook: "Arrived here today, 27 marches from Cape Columbia, I have with me 5 men, Matthew Henson, colored, Ootah, Egingwah, Seegloo, and Ooqueah, Eskimos; 5 sledges and 28 dogs. The expedition under my command has succeeded in reaching the POLE . . . for the honor and prestige of the United States of America."

As he surveyed the frozen wilderness, Peary turned to Matt Henson, and said: "This scene my eyes will never see again. Plant the Stars and Stripes over there, Matt—at the North Pole."

And so Matthew Henson, who had been indispensable in this great discovery, planted the American flag where there is no east, no west, no north—only south.

Peary was honored by being made a rear admiral. Henson was decorated by Congress and received a gold medal from the Chicago Geographical Society; a building on the campus at Dillard University in New Orleans was named for him. On the forty-fifth anniversary of the discovery of the North Pole, the Negro explorer was honored by President Eisenhower at the White House.

Young Americans, too, can take pride in Henson's and Peary's tremendous courage, for exploration into the Arctic wastes was as hazardous then as flight into outer space is now. Henson belongs to that small company of searchers into the mysteries of our world and of our universe for whom our admiration must be unbounded.[1]

If necessary, revise your summary to make sure that:

1. The summary includes the important ideas of the original source.

2. The summary answers *who? what? when? where? why?* and *how?* about the original source.

3. The summary is written in your own words.

4. The summary is no more than one-fourth to one-third the length of the original.

Use the checklist at the back of the book to proofread your summary.

---

[1] "Matthew Alexander Henson" from *They Showed the Way: Forty American Negro Leaders*, written by Charlemae Hill Rollins. Copyright © 1964 by Charlemae Hill Rollins. By permission of Thomas Y. Crowell, Publishers.

Selecting a Topic for a Research Report

One way to find a topic for a research report for school is to think about your own interests and experiences. Although a research report uses information outside your experience, you can use personal experience as a starting point to get ideas.

For example, if you want to write about sports, you might write a research report on how football (or some other sport) began. However, you would not write about how you threw a winning pass. Or suppose you are a mystery fan. Your favorite mystery show on television would not be an appropriate topic for a research report, but a famous Scotland Yard murder case would be appropriate.

In selecting a topic, remember that you need to use outside sources for information, so before you make a decision, check to be sure you can find the sources you will need. For instance, you may be interested in writing a report on the video disk, but your library may not have that information.

Remember, too, that a *topic* is a limited subject that can be discussed with specific details in a short paper. *Continents* is a broad subject, not a topic for a short paper. However, *Atlantis, the Lost Continent* is a topic because it focuses on the story of Atlantis, a continent that some people say once existed. You could develop this topic with specific details from questions such as these:

1. Where did Atlantis exist?
2. When did Atlantis exist?
3. Why did Atlantis vanish?
4. Why do some people say this continent never existed?

Writing Practice 2: *Choosing and Limiting a Topic*

Each of the items in the list on the next page is a subject for a factual report. For each one write at least one topic that focuses on a more limited part of the subject. If you can think of more topics related to the subject, write those also. Read the example before you begin.

Example

Subject
Life in the desert

Topic
1. How camels survive in the desert
2. Snakes of the desert

1. The Revolutionary War
2. The history of comic books
3. Special effects in movies
4. How holidays began
5. Famous monsters

Finding Sources

In Chapter 1 you learned how to find information you already know about subjects. Sometimes you will know something about your subject for a research report and can use one of the methods in Chapter 1. At other times, however, you will know very little and will need to go directly to outside sources.

Reference books, including encyclopedias, dictionaries, and almanacs, are good places to begin your search for information. The information in these books is very general, but will lead you to sources such as magazines and books that can give you more specific information. You can locate magazine articles about your topic, for instance, in the *Readers' Guide to Periodical Literature.* (See Chapter 27, "Library Skills.")

At the end of each article, some encyclopedias list names of specific books relating to the subjects of that article. You can also use the subject cards in your library's card catalogue to find books. If you do not find a subject card with your exact topic, try a closely related topic. For example, suppose you want to write a report on *holography*, a way of making three-dimensional pictures. Checking the subject cards, you find that your library does not have a book on holography, but it does have a book on laser lights. Since laser lights are used to make these three-dimensional pictures, you think this book might have information on holography.

When you want to know if a book has information on your topic, check its index. The *index* is an alphabetical listing at the back of the book of all topics covered in it and the page

Writing

numbers where they can be found. Following this paragraph is a sample from the index of Herman Schneider's book *Laser Light*.[1] In the *H* section you find the topic *holography* and learn that you can read about this topic on pages 88–93 of that book.

---

112 · INDEX

absolute zero, 47
ammonia clock, 61–65
amplifiers, amplification, 63–64, 65–67
atom, 33–49
   in excited states, 39–42, 55
   exploring by resonance, 33–36
   in ground state, 38–39
   model of, 36–38
   and molecule, compared, 69
   population, 56–58
   population inversion, 58–59, 63

candle, 5–6
carrier waves, 105–106
cladding, 105
coherence, *see* light, coherent
conductors, electrical, 74

Einstein, Albert, 23, 56
electrons, 38–42
   see also excited states; ground state
energy:
   levels of, 56
   quantum theory of, 40–42
   sources of, 39
   trading of, 46–47, 51–56
ether, 13, 22–23
excited states, 39–42
experiments:
   bullets and chairs, for particle theory, 18–19
   film projectors, for particle theory, 12
   Michelson-Morley, for ether theory, 13–16, 22–23
   pendulum, for resonance, 33–35

Polaroid lenses, for wave theory, 21–22
string and chairs, for wave theory, 18–20

fiber optics, 85–86, 103–106
firefly, 10
florescence, *see* tube, florescent
frequency, 28–29
   changing of, 31–32
   and color of light, 44–45
   of maser, 66

Gabor, Dennis, 91
Gould, Dr. G., 61
glowworm, 10
ground state, 38–39

holography, 88–93
   beam splitter in, 91–92
   cancellation in, 92
   reference beam in, 91
   subject beam in, 92
Huygens, Christian, 12–13

incandescence, *see* light, thermal sources of
interference fringes, 98
interference patterns, 17
interferometer, 2, 99–102

Lampyridae (firefly), 10
laser:
   carbon dioxide, 69–71
   destructive potential of, 110
   helium-neon, 67–69
   light, qualities of, 77–80
   name explained, 54–56
   ruby, 71–73
   semi-conductor, 73–77

Writing Practice 3: *Finding Sources*

For this assignment use a topic you wrote for Writing Practice 2, or choose another limited topic about which you would like to write a report. Save your work for a later assignment.

---

[1]From *Laser Light* by Herman Schneider. Copyright © 1978 by Herman Schneider. With the permission of McGraw-Hill Book Company.

In your school library or resource center, first read an encyclopedia article; then use the *Readers' Guide to Periodical Literature*, the subject cards of the card catalogue, and book indexes to find three sources of more specific information about your topic. Write each of the sources below on a piece of paper, giving the following information:

For a Magazine Article

1. The author and title of the article
2. The name and date of the magazine
3. The page numbers for the article

For a Book

1. The author and title
2. The city where the book was published, the name of the publishing company, and the year of publication
3. The page numbers for the information about your subject

Recording Information

Taking notes for a research report is much like taking notes for a composition. With the research report, however, it is important to keep a good record of where you get your information. The easiest way to do so is to write

each piece of information, in your own words, on a separate note card. Then, on the bottom of the card, write the information about your source. Later, when you begin to write, you will know the exact source for each piece of information. (One way to be certain you are using your own words is to complete the reading and then look away from your source while writing the notes.)

Model: Note Cards for a Research Report

> Holography was invented by an engineer named Dr. Dennis Gabor.
>
> <u>World Book Encyclopedia</u>
> Volume 9, p. 263

> To make holographic pictures, a laser light is split into two beams.
>
> <u>Laser Light</u>
> by Herman Schneider
> New York: McGraw-Hill, 1978
> p. 91

> NASA officials can make holograms of objects found on other planets. These holograms can be transmitted back to earth for study.
>
> <u>Future Life</u> magazine
> July, 1979
> "Holography", by James C. Odell
> p. 23

Taking notes is easier if you have some idea of what you want to find. Once you have some general information about your topic from a source such as an encyclopedia, begin asking yourself questions to help you find information as you read other sources. For example, suppose you decide to write a research report on Matthew Alexander Henson, who accompanied Admiral Robert Peary to the North Pole and was actually the first person to reach the top. Using the *who? what? when? where? why?* and *how?* questions, you discover some of what you need to find out about your topic:

1. *Who* was Matthew Alexander Henson?
2. *What* was his role in the expedition?
3. *What* had he done before the expedition?
4. *When* was he born?
5. *When* did he and Admiral Peary begin the expedition?
6. *When* did he reach the North Pole?
7. *Where* was Matthew Alexander Henson from?
8. *Where* did he first meet Admiral Peary?
9. *Why* did Matthew Alexander Henson accompany Admiral Peary on the expedition?
10. *Why* was he the first person to reach the North Pole?
11. *Why* isn't more known about Matthew Alexander Henson,

since he was the first person to reach the top?

12. *How* did Matthew Alexander Henson feel about this accomplishment?

Writing Practice 4: *Recording Information*

Using the topic you selected for Writing Practice 3, follow each of the steps listed below.

1. Find some general information about your topic in an encyclopedia or almanac. Using your own words, make notes about this information on note cards.

2. Using the general information you now have about your topic, write a list of questions about it.

3. Using your library's card catalogue and *Readers' Guide to Periodical Literature*, find two other sources of information about your topic—books, magazines, or pamphlets.

4. If your source is a book, check the index to see where in the book your topic is covered. Write these page numbers on a piece of paper.

5. Using the questions you prepared for Step 2, read over your sources to find the information you need, taking notes as you answer the questions. If you find useful information that was not covered in your questions, make notes on this information also.

6. Save your work.

Organizing Information

Once you have collected your information, you are ready to begin organizing it. When you look back over your notes, you will find that the notes fall into general headings. For example, look back at the three sample note cards on the topic of holography. The first note card is about the invention of holography, the second how holography works, and the third the practical uses of holography. The rest of the notes the writer takes on this subject fall into these three categories. The notes you make for your research report may fall into more than three categories, but there should not be fewer than three. Having fewer than three headings now may mean that your report will not be adequately developed.

The Thesis Statement

After you have found the main categories that your report will cover, you are ready to write a *thesis statement.* This is a sentence that states the topic of your report and indicates the main points you will make about the topic. For example, a thesis statement for the report on holography outlined on pages 150-151 might be: "To those who do not understand holography, the process seems like magic, but holography is very real and has many practical uses."

This sentence lets the reader know the topic of the report—*holography*—and indicates that the report will explain how holography works and what its practical uses are. A thesis statement has two functions. First, it helps the writer to decide which details belong in the report and which are irrelevant. Second, it tells the reader what to expect from the report.

Kinds of Outlines

One way to organize your notes is to make an *informal* outline, which is a grouping of information under general headings. The information may or may not be written in sentence form. On the next page, for example, is an informal topic outline for the topic of holography:

General Information

    Dr. Dennis Gabor and other scientists invented

    Three-dimensional photographs called *holograms*

    Process that makes them called *holography*

How Holography Works

    Regular light used with ordinary camera for two-dimensional pictures

    Laser light split and beamed against film for three-dimensional pictures

Practical Uses of Holography

    Three-dimensional X-rays

    Holograms of objects on other planets

Future Uses of Holography

    Holographic television

    Holographic movies

    Holographic students

Another kind of outline you may use with a factual report is a *formal* outline, which also divides topics into major headings and items of information that develop the major heading. With a formal outline, however, you use Roman numerals (*I, II, III*) and capital letters (*A, B, C*) to show major headings and subheadings. The following is a formal outline for the topic of holography.

    I. General information
        A. Dr. Dennis Gabor and other scientists invented
        B. Three-dimensional photographs called *holograms*
        C. Process that makes three-dimensional photographs called *holography*
   II. How holography works
        A. Regular light used with ordinary camera for two-dimensional pictures
        B. Laser light used with holography for three-dimensional pictures
           1. Laser light first split
           2. Split light beamed against film
  III. Practical uses of holography
        A. Three-dimensional X-rays
        B. Holograms of objects on other planets

    IV. Future uses of holography
        A. Holographic television
        B. Holographic movies
        C. Holographic students

This outline is called a *topic* outline because it does not use complete sentences. Notice that the capital letter *A* for the first subheading comes directly beneath the first word of the major heading. When you divide the subheadings, use Arabic numerals (*1, 2, 3*) to show these divisions. The numeral *1* appears directly beneath the first word of the subheading:

    B. Laser light used with holography for three-dimensional pictures
        1. Laser light first split
        2. Split light beamed against film

If you want to make even more divisions, you show these with small letters:

    I. Major heading
        A. Subheading
            1. Subheading
            2. Subheading
                a. Subheading
                b. Subheading
        B. Subheading
    II. Major heading

Writing Practice 5: *Organizing Information*

Read over the note cards you wrote for Writing Practice 4 to see what main idea they suggest. Write a thesis statement for your report; then list headings and sort your cards into stacks according to the headings. Using these stacks of note cards, make an outline for the topic you have chosen for your research report. The outline should be structured so that your report will read smoothly and logically. (Ask your teacher what kind of outline you should make. Save your work.)

Reading a Research Report

When you finish reading the model research report on holography that follows, you should be able to say what you have learned about the topic.

Writing

Model: *A Research Report*

Holography: The Magic Picture Show

Introduction

In the first Star Wars movie the little robot R2-D2 contains a taped message from Princess Leia. When he plays the tape, a small, three-dimensional image of the princess is projected. The image, moving and talking like the real princess, asks for help to save her planet from destruction.

Body

R2-D2's princess is created by special effects artists in a movie studio, but today a photograph can produce the same effect. Thanks to the engineer Dr. Dennis Gabor and other scientists, photographs today can look as real as Princess Leia's image. These three-dimensional photographs are called holograms, and the process that makes them is called holography. To those who do not understand holography, the process seems like magic, but holography is very real and has many practical uses.

(This paragraph develops outline heading I, General information.)

(This paragraph develops outline heading II, How holography works.)

Holograms appear three-dimensional because a special kind of light, called a laser light, is used to make them. The regular light used with an ordinary camera makes only a two-dimensional picture on film. It appears to have height and width, but not depth. When a laser light is split and beamed against film, it can produce a three-dimensional picture.

(This paragraph develops outline heading III, Practical uses of holography.)

These three-dimensional images can be used in a variety of ways by modern scientists. Doctors, for example, can make holograms of the human body that give them much more information than X-rays. Holography can also help in space exploration. Scientists are already able to make holograms of objects on other planets and transmit the pictures back to earth for examination.

Conclusion

(This paragraph develops outline heading IV, Future uses of holography.)

People in science and industry continue to study the applications of holography. In the near future television viewers may share their living rooms with holographic characters. This will make television images seem far more realistic. The spaceship in science fiction movies that drifts out among the stars may soon drift out among the audience. It's even possible that, somewhere in the distant future, a student who does not feel like coming to school may send a hologram instead.

Bibliography

"Holography." World Book Encyclopedia. 1983 ed.

Odell, James C. "Holography." Future Life Magazine July 1979: 23-25.

Schneider, Herman. Laser Light. New York: McGraw, 1978.

Writing

Think and Discuss

1. The purpose of a research report is to give information about a subject. In your own words tell what holography is and how it works, based upon your reading of the sample report.

2. Where in this report is the thesis sentence?

Writing a Research Report

Writing a research report is like writing an expository composition. The first part of the report is usually the introduction. The next paragraphs, which state and develop the limited topic, are the body. The conclusion is usually a sentence or two that leaves the reader with something interesting to think about. When you plan a research report, keep your readers in mind by asking questions like these:

1. How can I interest my readers in my topic?
2. What information do I need to give my readers?
3. How can I make my report clear to readers?

If your topic is an interesting one and if you are giving your readers new information, you should be able to interest them in your report. To do this, pay special attention to your first few sentences. For example, in the first paragraph from the sample holography paper, the writer uses details that would make most readers want to continue reading:

> In the first Star Wars movie the little robot R2-D2 contains a taped message from Princess Leia. When he plays the tape, a small, three-dimensional image of the princess is projected. The image, moving and talking like the real princess, asks for help to save her planet from destruction.

The second paragraph of the model report states the limited topic and begins its development. The writer gives an example of holograms, tells who invented them, and defines two important terms that readers might not understand. Paragraph three adds to the development by defining a third term, laser light, and telling how laser light pictures are different from ones produced by regular light. The next paragraph lists practical uses of holograms, and the final paragraph tells about some of their possible future uses.

As well as organizing and developing the paper, the writer also helps readers understand the topic by using transition words and by repeating important words and phrases throughout the report. In the first paragraph, the writer uses the projection of Princess Leia as an example of what a hologram looks like. The second sentence of the second paragraph is *Thanks to the engineer Dr. Dennis Gabor and other scientists, photographs today can look as real as Princess Leia's image.* The *Princess Leia* in this paragraph refers to the *Princess Leia* of the first paragraph and helps readers see how the two paragraphs are related.

Writing a Bibliography

You should include a bibliography at the end of your report. A bibliography is a list, in standard form, of the sources you used to write the report.

Book Entries

A bibliography entry for a book consists of three pieces of information: the author, the title, and the publication data. These items appear in a particular order. Study the following

Writing

example to see the order and punctuation for a standard book entry. Also notice that the second line is indented.

> Peters, Oscar A. <u>Food for Thought</u>. New York: Random, 1976.

Note that the publisher's name appears in abbreviated form.

Magazine Article Entries

A magazine entry requires five pieces of information: the name of the author of the article (when given), the name of the article, the name of the magazine, the date of the magazine, and the page numbers that the article appears on. Study the following example of a magazine entry to see the proper form.

> Arthur, L. Michael. "Software Options." <u>The Color Computer Magazine</u>: Sept. 1984 60-65.

Encyclopedia Article Entries

An encyclopedia entry in a bibliography usually includes just three items: the title of the article, the title of the encyclopedia, and the date of the particular edition used. Here is an example:

> "Space." <u>The New Columbia Encyclopedia</u>. 1975 ed.

Writing Assignment I: *Writing a Research Report*

Using the notes, outline, and thesis you developed for Writing Practices 3–5, write a short factual report.

A. Prewriting

Gather and reread your materials from Writing Practices 3–5. Check that your thesis states the main points covered by your final outline; if it does not, revise it. Then brainstorm a few sentences that will be an interesting introduction for your report.

B. Writing

Write a first draft of your research report, using your outline and details from your note cards. Put your thesis sentence near the beginning of your report. As you write, use transitions and repetition of key words to show how your ideas are connected. End with sentences that give your readers something to think about.

For information on punctuating transitions, see pages 540, 547.

C. Postwriting

On a separate piece of paper, write a bibliography for your report. Be sure the entries are in alphabetical order. Use the model bibliography on page 153 as a guide.

The first writing of your research report is called a *first draft*. The next step is to revise your report and write a final draft.

As you revise your report make sure that:

1. The topic is focused so that it is thoroughly covered.

2. The topic is interesting to readers.

3. The topic is developed with specific information from sources such as books and magazines.

4. The report has an interesting beginning.

5. The information is explained by definitions and examples when necessary. Each paragraph is developed with specific details.

6. The ending does not leave readers dangling.

7. The report is coherent so that readers understand why it moves from one point to another.

Finally, proofread your report, using the checklist at the back of the book.

Sentence Combining: *Using* with, -ing, *and possessives*

Inserting (with) Phrases

One way to tell about a person, thing, or idea is to modify (describe) it with a *with* phrase. The word *with* plus the group of words that follow it are usually placed after the word they describe in the base sentence, although sometimes the *with* phrase can be placed at the beginning of the sentence. Study these examples to see how the combinations are made:

For more information on phrases, see pages 502-515.

Base Sentence: That huge bag of dry dog food is for Oscar the Saint Bernard.

Insert: The dog food has an odor of tuna fish. (*with*)

Combined: That huge bag of dry dog food *with an odor of tuna fish* is for Oscar the Saint Bernard.

Base Sentence: Michelle began to study and to do homework every night.

Insert: She had a strong hope of earning higher grades. (*with*)

Combined: Michelle, *with a strong hope of earning higher grades*, began to study and to do homework every night.
or
Combined: *With a strong hope of earning higher grades*, Michelle began to study and to do homework every night.

Exercise 1: *Inserting* (with) *Phrases*

Combine the following sets of sentences by making the insert sentence into a (*with*) phrase. Sets 1–5 have signals; sets 6–10 do not. Write your new sentences on a clean sheet of paper numbered 1–10. Study the example on the next page before you begin.

Sentence Combining

Example

a. The clown pretended to step on his own shoelaces.
The clown had hopes of making the audience laugh at his foolishness. (*with*)
With hopes of making the audience laugh at his foolishness, the clown pretended to step on his own shoelaces.

1. Manny thoroughly researched his science report.
Manny had the intention of doing very well on his assignment. (*with*)

2. Myra's meeting is scheduled for 3:30 P.M.
The meeting is the Animal Protection League. (*with*)

3. Sensible dieting is the surest way to lose weight.
Moderate exercise is also the surest way. (*with*)

4. The skiers rushed down the icy mountain slopes.
They had warm, woolen masks protecting their faces from the freezing air. (*with*)

5. Mr. Chung strode directly toward the hammock.
Mr. Chung had his newspaper in hand. (*with*)

6. My sack lunch looked like a banquet to my hungry eyes.
My sack lunch has its single bologna sandwich, an apple, and a thermos of hot soup.

159

Writing

7. Beckoning, Mount McKinley lured the climbers toward splendid heights and awesome views.
   Handsome, snow-capped peaks were beckoning.

8. Wearing thongs can be very dangerous.
   The thongs have broken straps.

9. The guard dog growled ferociously at the prowler.
   The guard dog had its ears laid back.

10. Oh, how I wish I had been born a talented ventriloquist!
    A ventriloquist has the ability to entertain and surprise audiences.

Inserting -ing Words

In this section you will change a verb in the insert sentence into a modifier by adding *-ing*. Then you will insert the modifier before the word it describes in the base sentence. These examples show how to make this change:

Verbs

the crow *flies*
one coach *shouts*
a verb *changes*

Modifiers

the *flying* crow
one *shouting* coach
a *changing* verb

The first step in making this combination is to identify the verb in the insert sentence. If it has an *-s* ending, drop the ending before adding *-ing*. The signal (*ing*) tells you to make this change.

Base Sentence: That toast is my breakfast!

Insert: The toast burns. (*ing*)

Combined: That *burning* toast is my breakfast!

Verbs used with a form of *be* may end in *-ing*. If such a verb appears in the insert sentence, simply drop the form of *be* and make the verb into a modifier by placing it before a noun or pronoun in the base sentence.

Base Sentence: Mari watched the car nervously.

Insert: The car was speeding. (*ing*)

Combined: Mari watched the *speeding* car nervously.

(Notice that the verb in the previous insert sentence has the *-ing* form and the helping verb *was*. When the word *speeding* describes *car*, however, it is a modifier.)

> For more information on *-ing* modifiers, also called participles, see pages 462–467.

Exercise 2: *Inserting* -ing *Words*

On a sheet of paper numbered 1–10, combine the following sets of sentences by using the *-ing* form of the verb as a modifier. In the example and in the first five sets of sentences, the word to be changed has been *italicized*. In the rest of the sets you must decide for yourself which word needs to become the modifier. Only the first five sets show the (*ing*) signal.

Example

a. Quickly, Sandy swept the snow from the room.
   The snow *melts*. (*ing*)
   Quickly, Sandy swept the melting snow from the room.

1. The crowd watched the flag as the high school band played "The Star-Spangled Banner."
   The flag *waves*. (*ing*)

2. The popular star rushed on stage, strummed his guitar, and began to play his latest hit.
   The star *sings*. (*ing*)

3. Three hens had nested in the back of the old pickup truck.
   The hens were *setting*. (*ing*)

Writing

   4. Everyone in Mr. Kang's English class passed our district's test.
      The test was to *spell*. *(ing)*
   5. Captain Shaughnessy's assistant handed out the orders to the soldiers.
      The orders *remained*. *(ing)*
   6. Bring your new shoes with you when you come to visit me in the country.
      You hike in the shoes.
   7. The award for the best actor went to my all-time favorite film star.
      The actor supports others.
   8. During the last scene of the movie, the hero must leap out of a building.
      The building burns.
   9. Rosie Grier showed the talk show host a more comfortable way to hold the needles.
      The needles knit.
   10. Half hidden behind the curtains of the empty stage, the comedian rehearsed the lines of his last performance.
       The comedian had aged.

Using the (Pos) Signal

The (*pos*) signal tells you to make a word possessive by adding an apostrophe or an apostrophe and the letter *s*:

boy/boy's   children/children's   Jeffersons/Jeffersons'

For more information on forming possessives, see pages 301-303 and 560.

In its possessive form the word becomes a modifier when placed before a noun or pronoun in the base sentence. The word *to*, *by*, or *of* in the insert sentence indicates the word to be made possessive.

Base Sentence: The team bus passed a new house.
Insert: The house belongs to Coach Corrigan. *(pos)*
Combined: The team bus passed *Coach Corrigan's new house*.

Base Sentence: Paintings show his interest in capturing light on canvas.

Sentence Combining

> **Insert:** The paintings are by Vincent van Gogh. (*pos*)
>
> **Combined:** *Vincent van Gogh's* paintings show his interest in capturing light on canvas.

Exercise 3: Using the (Pos) Signal

Combine the sentences in the following sets by changing the noun in the *to*, *by*, or *of* phrase to its possessive form. The signal appears in sets 1-5. Sets 6-10 do not have signals. After studying the example, write the new sentences on a sheet of paper numbered 1–10.

Example

a. The ribbons twisted in colorful streams as the children danced.
The ribbons were of the Maypole. (*pos*)
The Maypole's ribbons twisted in colorful streams as the children danced.

1. The basket was filled with things that Grandmother had requested.
The basket belonged to Little Red Riding Hood. (*pos*)

2. Puffing great clouds of foul-smelling exhaust, the city bus pulled in front of the bicycle.
The bicycle belonged to Uncle Jason. (*pos*)

3. We were thrilled to realize that the pitching had given us a no-hit game.
   The pitching belonged to Kathy. (*pos*)
4. Dr. Lopez scheduled a date to remove the inflamed tonsils.
   The tonsils belonged to Kevin. (*pos*)
5. The sister Princess Margaret visited Canada and Australia on a recent tour.
   The sister is of Queen Elizabeth. (*pos*)
6. A bad case of poison ivy can come from any contact with the roots, stem, or leaves.
   The roots, stem, and leaves are of the plant.
7. The pocketknife was very useful on our yearly camping trip.
   The pocketknife belonged to Hiroshi.
8. One glance at the upraised paw caused the dog to yelp in sheer terror.
   The paw belonged to the grizzly.
9. Pirates often marked their buried treasure with a head to frighten other thieves away.
   The head was of death.
10. The speech lasted much longer than our club president had planned.
    The speech was of the politician.

If the word made into a possessive form is *plural* (more than one thing or person) and ends in *s*, add only an apostrophe.

two *boys*	Two *boys'* bikes leaned against the tree.
several *records*	Several *records'* covers were ruined.
the *birds*	The *birds'* nests are in the rain gutter.
many *trees*	Many *trees'* trunks split during the frost.

If the plural does not end in *s*, however, add an apostrophe plus *s*.

three *children*	Three *children's* sleds were stored in the barn.
the *women*	When does the *women's* organization meet?
the *geese*	The *geese's* flight pattern turned south.
three *mice*	The wife of the farmer took three *mice's* tails.

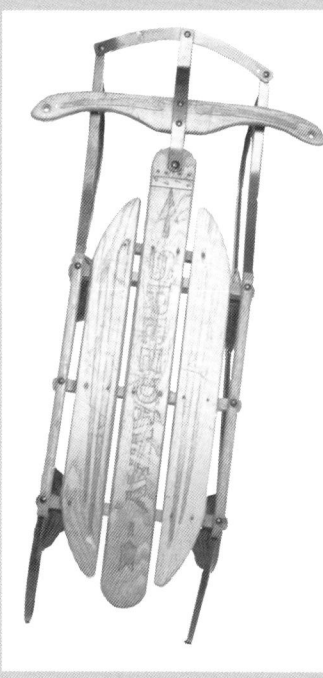

Exercise 4: *Using the* (Pos) *Signal*

On a sheet of paper, combine the following sentences by performing the *(pos)* operation on one noun, singular or plural, in the insert sentence. Only three sets are signaled. Study the example before you begin.

Example

a. The reasons for not wanting to go are good ones.
   The reasons are of the boys. *(pos)*
   The boys' reasons for not wanting to go are good ones.

1. A briefcase was left in the bus terminal yesterday afternoon.
   The briefcase belongs to a woman. *(pos)*
2. Both shops had no electrical power during the storm.
   The shops belonged to dry cleaners. *(pos)*
3. After the summer sale the records showed that he had sold over $2,000 in clothing in one weekend.
   The records belonged to the salesman. *(pos)*
4. Hunters discovered three dens in the pine forest.
   The dens were of foxes.
5. Tools were left locked in a safe place overnight.
   The tools belonged to workers.

Writing Practice: *Using Combining Skills*

Select a section from one of your textbooks and write a summary. Use the sentence-combining skills you have learned. The summary should be from one-fourth to one-third the length of the original.

7 Persuasive Writing

Here is a true-false quiz on which your score should be perfect.

		True	False
1.	The purpose of newspaper and magazine advertisements for jogging shoes is *not* to sell more of the shoes.	_____	_____
2.	Candy manufacturers advertise because they want to inform people about health food.	_____	_____
3.	Candidates for political office give speeches just to provide entertainment for the public.	_____	_____
4.	Debates in the United States Congress have no influence on what happens to you or me.	_____	_____
5.	You never try to get family or friends to agree with you about some point.	_____	_____

The answer to all of the questions above is, of course, "false." Most advertisements—for jogging shoes, candy, cameras, dishwashing or laundry detergent, diapers, hamburgers, hotels, markets, or mowers—are intended to *persuade* people to buy products or services. And candidates for political office give speeches to *persuade* voters. The debates in Congress are meant to *persuade* members to vote for this bill or to support that program; therefore, these debates often have a great influence on what happens to you and me. Finally, of course, you have tried to *persuade* family members or friends to agree with you on some point.

As the quiz shows, we live in a world of *persuasion;* others attempt to influence us, and we attempt to influence others. In this chapter you will learn techniques of persuasive writing.

Persuasive and Expository Writing

You learned in Chapter 5, Writing Compositions, that expository writing is meant to *inform*. Typical examples of expository writing are instructions (for example, how to make tamale pie), scientific reports, newspaper reports of current events, and explanations of ideas and concepts (for example, the reasons for your political beliefs). Textbooks such as this one contain primarily expository writing.

Persuasive writing also gives information, but its main purpose is to cause people to change an opinion and to take an action.

Model: *Exposition and Persuasion*

The first selection that follows is exposition; it is a report about whaling. The second selection is persuasion; it urges readers to take action to save whales from being hunted to extinction.
Exposition:

The Development of Whaling

The Basques were probably the first to hunt whales, possibly as early as the tenth century. However, a large-scale

whaling industry did not develop until the seventeenth century. But within less than 400 years, the development of the whaling industry has threatened the survival of the animals on which it depends.

In the early 1600s, the Dutch began hunting whales along the Norwegian coast. Along with the Basques, the Dutch had developed methods of *flensing* (stripping the whale of its blubber) and boiling the blubber for its oil.

For a while, the English competed with the Dutch in whaling. However, the major English whaler, the English Muscovy Company of London, collapsed in 1625. Its failure left the Dutch in control of whaling.

Within a short time, the number of whales began to decline. By about 1640, whales had become so scarce in the coastal waters that the Dutch had to sail farther and farther into the northern seas to capture the mighty creatures.

American whaling began in the coastal waters around Cape Cod and Long Island in the middle of the seventeenth century. In 1712 a Nantucket fisherman captured a sperm whale, and the superior quality of the oil from this species of whale was discovered. American whalers began sailing on long voyages to find the sperm whale. In 1791 they rounded Cape Horn, on the tip of South America, to hunt for sperm whales in the South Pacific. Whaling voyages, like the one described in Herman Melville's novel *Moby Dick*, sometimes lasted as long as three or four years.

The early whalers traveled on sailing ships. To kill a whale, they rode small, oar-driven boats out from the mother ship. The whalers stabbed the whale with sharp harpoons. But often a whale escaped, sometimes killing or injuring the hunters in the process.

More efficient methods of whaling were developed in the 1800s and 1900s. The increased efficiency further decreased the whale population. About 1856 the Norwegian Sven Foyn invented a harpoon with an explosive head. This weapon increased the odds against a whale's escaping. Modern factory ships, speedy and efficient, were built for whaling. No longer was whaling a chancy business.

By 1930 the whaling industry had reached its high point. Six shore stations, 41 floating factories, and 232 whaling ships operated in the Antarctic region. The world population of whales became seriously threatened.

After World War II most whaling nations agreed to limits on the number of whales killed. Japan and Russia, however, did not agree to restrict their whaling operations. Today, all species of whales are considered endangered.[1]

---

[1]Based on "Whaling," *The New Columbia Encyclopedia*, 1975.

7 Persuasive Writing

Persuasion:

Editor
Reno Evening Gazette
Reno, Nevada

Dear Editor:

    The great American novel *Moby Dick* tells how nineteenth-century whalers set forth in sailing ships on journeys that could last three or four years. These hardy souls were after oil for the lamps of the nation.
    Present-day whalers set forth on huge factory ships that are the ultimate in efficiency. A whale is killed by an explosive harpoon that pumps air into the carcass so that it will not sink.
    So efficient is the modern whaling industry that all species of whales are now threatened with extinction. Right whales and rorquals (including the humpback, finback, and blue whales) are endangered species, and the blue and humpback are close to extinction.
    Although whale oil still has some commercial value, the main use of these great animals is for fertilizer and pet food!
    After World War II, the United States and sixteen other nations entered an agreement called the International Whaling Convention, intended to limit the number of whales killed and to protect females with calves. However, the agreement is voluntary, and two nations in particular ignore the agreement and the possibility that some species of whales will become extinct. Those two nations are Japan and Russia.
    You can help save the whales. Write to the Russian and Japanese embassies, telling them of your concern about the effects of their whaling operations. Also write to your

Writing

representative in Congress and your senator, urging them to take action on this problem.
    Join the fight to save the whales before there are no more whales to save.

Sincerely,
Shan Stapleton

Think and Discuss

1. The first selection, "The Development of Whaling," gives you information on its topic, but it does not urge you to change your opinion or to take any action. The second selection, a letter to the editor, also gives information about whaling, but that information leads to a *persuasive* appeal, expressed in the last two paragraphs of the letter. In your own words, explain the purposes of exposition and persuasion.

2. Tell about a time when you had to use persuasion. Was your persuasion successful? Why or why not?

3. Sometimes persuaders are dishonest; they use unfair tactics and don't tell the truth. If you can think of an example of dishonest persuasion, tell about it.

Writing Practice 1: *Identifying Persuasion*

In a newspaper or magazine, find an advertisement that you think is especially persuasive. Write one paragraph explaining why you think the advertisement is effective. Bring the advertisement to class along with your paragraph.

Becoming an Effective Persuader

To be an effective persuader, you must use *sound reasoning, facts and data,* and *appropriate language.*
    Think about why the second one of each of the following pairs of passages is more persuasive than the first one.

a. Several members of the school chess club are on the honor roll. Join the chess club so that you can get on the honor roll.

b. Several members of the school chess club are on the honor roll. If you join the chess club, you will have the chance to associate with outstanding students and perhaps learn some of their study methods. I urge you to join the chess club.

a. Super Sludge, a new breakfast cereal, is a better value than Corny Creepers, another breakfast cereal. You should buy Super Sludge, not Corny Creepers.

b. Super Sludge, a new breakfast cereal, costs nine cents per ounce. It contains the daily minimum requirement of vitamins A, C, E, B-1, B-2, B-6, B-12, folic acid, niacin, and pantothenic acid. Corny Creepers costs nine and a half cents per ounce. It contains the minimum daily requirements of vitamins A, C, E, B-1, B-2, B-6, and B-12 but not folic acid, niacin, or pantothenic acid. Super Sludge is the better value.

a. Lisa Quaid, candidate for student council president, said, "Vote for me. I'll do a lot to make kids at this school happier. You know that I'm a live wire, full of good ideas."

b. Lester Quilty, candidate for student council president, said, "Vote for me. I believe that lunch periods could be staggered to eliminate the mob scene every day in the cafeteria. I will propose my plan to the principal.

"I also think that this school needs an active intramural sports program. I will support tennis, handball, volleyball, and pingpong matches and will petition the school board to provide money for playoff trophies to be awarded every year."

Writing

a. Buy the Daypacker's Economy Outfit. Now on sale. Includes daypack, canteen, first aid kit, and high-energy food.

b. Buy the Daypacker's Economy Outfit. Now on sale. Includes
   —sturdy, waterproof daypack with padded shoulder straps
   —plastic, one-quart canteen with belt loop for carrying
   —first aid kit, including assortment of bandages, mole skin, merthiolate, and elastic wrappings for sprains
   —high-energy food, including dried fruit and nut mix and date-nut bars

a. Don't vote for that wimp Lester Quilty. If you vote for that jerk, you'll just be showing your own ignorance.

b. Think carefully before you vote for Lester Quilty. He has made several promises that he probably won't be able to fulfill. If you vote for him, you may regret your decision later.

The second passage in each of the above pairs uses sound reasoning, facts and data, and/or persuasive language. In the sections that follow you will learn more about those devices.

Sound Reasoning

In sound reasoning, *conclusions* follow naturally from *premises*. Here are some examples of sound reasoning:

Premise: All members of the Drama Club at Lincoln Junior High School will attend a performance of *Man and Superman.*

Conclusion: If you are a member of the Drama Club, you will attend a performance of *Man and Superman.*

Premise: To participate in intermural athletics, students in Los Angeles schools must have a grade point average of at least *C.*

Premise: Alfonso, a Los Angeles student, has a grade point average of *B.*

Conclusion: Alfonso is eligible to participate in intermural athletics.

The science of sound reasoning is called *logic,* but a writer does not need to be a *logician* in order to use sound reasons to persuade.

When you write persuasion, use your common sense to check your reasoning. Ask yourself frequently, "Does this make sense? Does it add up?"

Writing Practice 2: *Identifying Unsound Reasoning*

Even though you have probably never studied logic, you can tell when an argument is illogical. Explain the unsound reasoning in each of the following examples.

1. Aviva drank from the fountain near the principal's office. The next day she came down with a terrible cold. She caught the cold by drinking from that fountain.

2. My neighbor, Mr. Schnurbart, comes from Germany. He likes sauerkraut. I guess all Germans like sauerkraut.

3. One glass of apple juice every day will cure dandruff. I know this is true because Mr. Gump, the crossing guard, told me so.

4. Only teenagers go to the Golden West Video Arcade. Hmung is a teenager, so he must go to the Golden West Video Arcade.

5. I can prove that New Yorkers like baseball because my friend Alvin is from New York and he's a baseball fanatic.

6. My mother told my father that if he didn't stop worrying about crabgrass in our front lawn, his hair would fall out. Well, Dad worried about that crabgrass for years, and sure enough, now he's as bald as a cue ball.

7. Pollster Elmer Stringer wanted to know how many of the 9,500 registered voters of Utopia would support Bunker for mayor. He talked to the first ten people that he met on Main Street, and all of them said that they would vote for Bunker. Since one hundred percent of the people asked said that they supported Bunker, Stringer concluded that Bunker would get at least 9,000 votes in the election.

8. All right–thinking, decent students believe that Sally Sansom should be elected class president. If you are a right–thinking, decent student, you will support Sally.

Facts and Opinions

A *fact* is a statement that can be proven to be true. For example, it is a fact that 100 divided by 5 equals 20; the laws of mathematics prove that calculation. It is a fact that English is a Germanic language; research by language scholars has proved this. It is a fact that Queen Elizabeth I ruled England from 1558 until her death in the year 1603; historical evidence supports the statement.

An *opinion* is a personal view about something. Opinions cannot be proven. For example, it is a *fact* that Bryce Canyon National Park is in southwestern Utah. A person may hold the *opinion* that Bryce is the most beautiful of the national parks. Here are some other examples of facts and opinions.

Facts	*Opinions*
Chewing gum with sugar contributes to the development of cavities.	Chewing gum in class is rude.
Both the bald eagle and the wild turkey are native American birds.	The wild turkey would be a better national symbol than the bald eagle.
Mark Twain is the author of *The Adventures of Huckleberry Finn*.	*Huckleberry Finn* is the greatest American novel.

7 Persuasive Writing

The Tutsi are cattle-raising people who live in central Africa, particularly in Burundi and Rwanda. They are an exceptionally tall group of people. Heights of seven feet or more are not uncommon.	The Tutsi are an exceptionally handsome and proud people.
Billie Jean King was the U.S. Lawn Tennis women's singles champion in 1967, 1971, 1972, and 1974.	Billie Jean King is the most dedicated athlete in the sport of tennis.

    There is hard evidence for all of the facts in the list above, and you could probably find sound reasons for some of the opinions. By showing the evidence, you can prove facts; but you must use sound reasons to convince people of opinions.
    Like almost all writing, the following selection contains both facts and opinions.
    The Great Basin is a vast area—about 125 million acres of land—covering all of Nevada, the southeastern corner of Oregon, the western part of Utah, and part of southern California. In the introduction to *Hiking the Great Basin*, John Hart tries to persuade his readers to help save the wilderness

175

Writing

areas in this region. In the following selection he describes some problems with feral horses and burros.

Model: Facts and Opinions

As you read this selection, look for important facts and opinions.

Feral Horses and Burros

Feral horses and burros are the descendants of the beasts of burden of Indians and settlers, cowboys and miners. Escaping into the wild, the horses and burros proved to be able competitors. The feral (or "gone wild") burros favor the hotter southern parts of the Great Basin; horses predominate in the central and northern parts.

The animals have just two natural enemies: starvation and people. After World War II, the herds were hunted down, with extreme brutality, for pet food. Then public opinion demanded their protection. In 1971, the Wild Free-Roaming Horse and Burro Act set rules for their future management on public land.

Since 1971, the animals have done well. Their rate of increase has been estimated at 20 percent a year. Though numbers are disputed, there are now thought to be almost 50,000 feral animals in Nevada alone.

It is hard not to root for the tough, engaging little creatures. (The horses are romantic; the burros, irresistibly *cute*.) But this latest proliferation of horses and burros is plainly bad news for the land. Where they are numerous, wide areas are savagely overgrazed. The feral animals compete with domestic stock, which ranchers don't like; they compete still more effectively with native pronghorn "antelope" and bighorn sheep. Both horses and burros tend to foul and monopolize water supplies and beat the banks of waterholes to dust. The burros' impact on bighorn sheep is particularly severe: when there is an overlap, it's the sheep that give way.

No one wants horses and burros to be driven out of existence, but it is clear that they must be controlled. The BLM [Bureau of Land Management] hopes to restrict them to herds of stable size in scattered locations; the Park Service, whose job it is to keep park landscapes in pristine condition, wants to eliminate the destructive Death Valley herd entirely.

Control is difficult, however. The law permits (but discourages) the killing of the animals; public opinion has so far permitted only live capture and deportation. The captured animals are moved to designated areas or put up for "adoption" by willing citizens; the horses, at least, do make good pets. Such measures, however, come nowhere near to

7 Persuasive Writing

solving the problem. The Park Service, reluctantly concluding that its burros must be shot, finds itself cast as a villain. Humanitarians and conservationists, frequently allied, have split on this issue.

It is a situation with no easy answer. One thing is clear: if the population explosion of feral animals can't be stopped, the desert will be a much-changed place, and a poorer one.[1]

Think and Discuss

1. Find two facts about the horses and burros. Explain why they are facts.

2. Find two opinions about the horses and burros. Why are they opinions?

3. "Since 1971, the animals have done well" is a statement of opinion. What facts does Hart use to back up his opinion?

4. The conclusion that the author reaches is this: "if the population explosion of feral animals can't be stopped, the desert will be a much-changed place, and a poorer one." Does he use sound reasoning to reach this conclusion? Explain.

5. One opinion that the author states is that "It is a situation with no easy answer." In the essay, what reasons does he give for this opinion?

---

[1] From *Hiking the Great Basin: The High Desert Country of California, Oregon, Nevada, and Utah* by John Hart. Copyright © 1981 by John Hart. Reprinted by permission of Sierra Club Books.

Writing

The Language of Persuasion

In "Feral Horses and Burros," John Hart says that the horses are "romantic" and the burros are "cute." These words help explain why people don't want to shoot or otherwise harm the animals. These are descriptive words which are important to the argument.

When you read an advertisement for orange juice, you see such words as "the sunshine drink," "refreshing," "ice cold," and "thirst quencher." An automobile advertisement might include "powerful," "quiet," and "stylish." Words that have emotional or other types of appeal are effective persuasive tools.

Which group of verbs below might be used by a conservative (a person who upholds tradition), and which might be used by a radical (a person who wants extreme changes)?

save, keep, defend, maintain, protect, support, prevent, avoid

reform, change, improve, get better, get more, reduce, stop, get rid of

Writing Practice 3: *The Language of Persuasion*

For each of the following nouns, supply two synonyms (words with similar meanings), one of which is favorable and one of which is unfavorable.

Examples

	Favorable	**Unfavorable**
a. car	limousine	rattletrap
b. restaurant	supper club	greasy spoon

1. jail
2. food
3. to work
4. rural area
5. to ask about
6. rain
7. money
8. television
9. house
10. to rest

Writing Persuasion

Writing persuasion, like most other kinds of writing, involves prewriting (finding a topic, gathering information and ideas, and planning), writing a first draft, and postwriting (revising and proofreading).

Choosing a Proposition

You would not try to persuade your classmates that basic skills in language and mathematics are valuable; everyone already agrees with that idea. However, you might try to persuade your classmates that music and art are among the basics, for not everyone agrees with that idea; some people view music and art as frills.

The point that you are trying to make—which is called the *proposition*—must not be something that is already taken for granted. It must also be specific, not general.

The following propositions could not be used in persuasive writing, either because everyone—or almost everyone—agrees with them, or because they are too general:

1. Use of seatbelts cuts down the number of fatalities in automobile crashes.

2. Students who misbehave in school should be disciplined.

3. Schools should give students the knowledge and skills needed to survive in America.

4. Watching professional football on television is one of the favorite pastimes of many Americans.

5. Computers are useful.

But the following statements might serve as propositions because they make claims that are not generally accepted and because they are specific.

1. The city should pass a seatbelt law, requiring everyone in an automobile to wear belts, and should levy a large fine against anyone caught violating the law.

2. Students who in any way destroy school property should be required to do work at the school to make up for the damage they have done.

3. Since knowledge about economics and money management is essential for survival in our society, all students in this school should be required to take two courses: economics and personal money management.

4. During the season, the television networks devote far too much time to professional football.

5. "Computer literacy" should be a statewide requirement for high school graduation.

Be ready to explain why you think each of the following propositions either *would* or *would not* serve as a good basis for a persuasive paper.

1. More and more women are assuming important roles in local, state, and national governments.

2. All students in this school should be required to develop skill in one of the arts: painting, sculpture, music, creative writing, or drama.

3. Since schools are intended to educate students, all organized sports should be abandoned in this school.

4. Teenagers should be encouraged to follow a healthy diet.

5. School officials should have the right to search students' lockers at any time.

6. Parks should be kept clean and safe.

7. All workers should be treated fairly.

8. High school students should have the right to drop out and take a job at any time.

Writing Practice 4: *Choosing a Proposition*

Suppose you have decided to write a letter to the editor of your local newspaper, of a magazine that you read, or of your school newspaper. You are not actually writing for the editor, but for the other readers of the publication. Your purpose is to persuade these readers of something.

On a sheet of paper, write three propositions that might serve as the bases for letters to the editor.

Ask yourself if all of your propositions are really arguable. Do they make claims that would not gain automatic agreement? (If not, then there is nothing to persuade your readers of, for they already agree with you.) Are they specific?

Gathering Information and Ideas

You have already learned about gathering ideas—by clustering and other prewriting methods (Chapter 1).

Wilhelmina ("Willy") van Edamer, a student at Marcus Garvey Intermediate School, wanted to write a letter to the editor of the school paper. Her proposition: *The students at Garvey should set up a car wash to raise money to help establish a neighborhood recreation and crafts center.* Her purpose was to persuade the teachers and the principal to approve the project and to persuade her fellow students to become involved.

Willy knew that she must explain exactly *what* she wanted to do and *why* she wanted to do it. She also must specify *where* the car wash could be established and *when*. Finally, she needed to state *how* the project could be carried out.

As she thought about the project and did some research, Willy used the six basic questions. She made notes that looked like those on the next page.

Writing

What

    Establish car wash to raise funds for a recreation and crafts center in the neighborhood of the school

Why

    Nearest rec center to Garvey is five miles away, too far to be used by this neighborhood's kids

    Crafts center would teach kids useful skills

    Students participating in car wash would learn about running business

    Project would be fun for participants

Where and When

    Car wash at local service stations; use a different location each Saturday

    Car wash open Saturdays from nine until five

How

    Get teachers and principal to endorse project

    Ask service station owners to approve use of facilities

    Have students work in the car wash

    Get initial funds to buy equipment—soap, sponges, polish, etc.—estimated at $30

    Advertise

Writing Practice 5: *Gathering Information for Persuasion*

Choose one of your propositions from Writing Practice 4, and gather ideas and information on it. You may want to use brainstorming, clustering, or changing viewpoints, or ask the six basic questions, as Willy did. Make notes and save them.

Organizing

Because she wanted her letter to be well organized, Willy looked over the notes she had jotted down and thought about the order in which to present her ideas in the letter. She decided that making an informal outline would help her set up the structure of her letter.

She decided to begin with her proposition, the *what:*

Proposition: Car wash to raise funds for rec and crafts center

Then she thought she should give her reasons, the *why:*

Reasons: No rec center near Garvey

Crafts center would teach kids useful skills

Students would learn about running business

Project would be fun

Next, Willy outlined the method of carrying out the project, the *where, when,* and *how:*

Method: Use facilities of local service stations each Saturday from nine until five

Get teachers and principal to endorse project

Ask service station owners to approve use of facilities

Have students work in car wash

Get start-up funds *(Where? Loan from school funds, to be paid back from profits?)*

Notice that a new idea (in *italics*) occurred to Willy as she was making her outline. She added this idea and decided not to include one idea from her original notes (*advertise*). Willy's completed outline looked like this:

Proposition: Car wash to raise funds for rec and crafts center

Reasons: No rec center near Garvey

Writing

                    Crafts center would teach kids useful skills

                    Students would learn about running business

                    Project would be fun

Method: Use facilities of local service stations each Saturday from nine until five

                    Get teachers and principal to endorse project

                    Ask service station owners to approve use of facilities

                    Have students work in car wash

                    Get start-up funds *(Where? Loan from school funds, to be paid back from profits?)*

Willy knew that she should conclude with a definite statement of what she wanted her readers to do. When you read Willy's letter, on page 185, you will find that conclusion.

Writing Practice 6: *Organizing Persuasive Material*

Organize your notes in a way that you think will be effective. Make a rough outline that shows your organization. Use these headings: *Proposition, Reasons,* and *Method.*

Writing from an Outline

When you use a rough outline to guide your writing, you need not follow the outline exactly. For example, when Willy wrote her letter to the editor, she changed her organization from the sequence in her outline. She started with two of the *reasons* and then stated her *proposition.* She also added some ideas.

7 Persuasive Writing

Model: *A Letter to the Editor*

Do you think Willy's new sequence is effective?

Sergio Gallardos, Editor
Garvey Gazette

Dear Editor:

    The area around Garvey Intermediate School badly needs a recreation and crafts center. The nearest such facility to Garvey is on Polk and 18th streets, more than five miles away. Thus, young people in this area have no place to get together for sports or dances or to learn useful crafts.
    To help raise funds for such a recreation and crafts center, I propose that Garvey students establish a car wash.
    To get under way, we will need a location or several locations. I think that owners of service stations in this area would let us use their facilities from nine to five on Saturdays. We also need an estimated $30 to buy equipment: sponges, buckets, detergent, polish, and so on. One source for this money might be a loan from school funds, which we could repay with our profits.
    Everyone involved has reasons for supporting this project. The students would gain business experience and have the fun of working together toward a worthwhile goal. The service station owners would gain the good will of the community. And, of course, the community would gain funds toward establishing the recreation and crafts center.
    I urge the teachers and the principal of this school to back this project. I also urge my fellow students to take an active part.
    Everyone interested should come to a meeting on April 13 at 3:30 P.M. in Room 201. Be sure to be there to help plan the details of the car wash fund-raising project.

                                            Wilhelmina van Edamer

For information on business letter form, see page 248.

Writing Assignment I: *A Persuasive Letter*

Using the notes and rough outline that you prepared for Writing Practices 5 and 6, write a letter to the editor of your school or local newspaper or to the editor of a magazine.

A. Prewriting

Gather and reread your notes and rough outline from Writing Practices 5 and 6. Be sure your proposition is stated clearly.

Next, evaluate the reasons that support your opinion. Do they show sound thinking? Are they based on facts? If you need more facts or stronger reasons, consult your school library for background material.

B. Writing

Here are some suggestions for writing a first draft.

1. It doesn't matter how messy your first draft is. During postwriting you will clean up the mess.
2. If you want to change plans as you write, ignore your initial outline or make a new one. Don't let the outline be a hindrance.
3. If you find it hard to get started, just begin to write; ideas and words will probably begin to come more easily. Don't try to get the beginning just right in the first draft; you can always redo the beginning when you revise.
4. Remember to conclude with a direct statement of what you want your readers to do.

C. Postwriting

Revising and Proofreading: How does a reader react to your letter? Have one of your classmates read your letter and discuss it with you, asking questions similar to the ones in the checklist below. Consider your classmate's comments as you revise.

Finally, proofread your letter, using the Checklist for Proofreading at the back of the book.

Checklist for Revising a Persuasive Letter

1. Have you used sound reasoning in your letter?
2. Does your letter need additional facts, examples, or explanations?
3. Does your letter include any information that is not necessary?
4. Would your letter be stronger if it were organized in a different way?
5. Have you chosen the best words to make your point?

Sentence Combining: Where, When, *and* How Details

Combining with (Where), (When), *and* (How)

Information telling *where, when,* or *how* something happened can be added to sentences in the following way.

>Sally Perkins visited her aunt *in Washington, D.C.* [tells where]

>Please wash the windows in your bedroom *after you come home from school this afternoon.* [tells when]

>Celia paddled through the surf, waited for the perfect wave, and mounted her board *artfully*. [tells how]

A group of words telling *where, when,* or *how* will often begin with words like those in the following lists.

Where	When	How
in	in	well
on	before	sadly
at	during	slowly
by	after	carefully
near	at	how
beyond		*most words that end in* -ly

For more information on adverb phrases and clauses, see pages 502–515 and 516–532.

Where, when, and *how* additions can sometimes appear in different places in the combined sentence without changing its meaning. (Place a comma after a long introductory *where, when,* or *how* phrase. See Chapter 23 for the section on punctuating adverb clauses.)

Base Sentence: Huck Finn told Jim to meet him.

Insert: Huck Finn would be at the boat landing. (*where*)

Combined: Huck Finn told Jim to meet him *at the boat landing*.

Writing

Base Sentence: Jim ran from town to the river's edge.
Insert: Jim ran after he had been seen doing his evening chores. *(when)*
Combined: *After he had been seen doing his evening chores,* Jim ran from town to the river's edge.
or
Combined: Jim ran from town to the river's edge *after he had been seen doing his evening chores.*

Exercise 1: *Combining with* (Where), (When), *and* (How)

On a sheet of paper, write a combined sentence for each set of sentences that follows. Insert the *where, when,* and *how* information in the base sentence wherever it makes the best sense. Only sets 1–3 are signaled. Study the example first.

Example

a. Philip Pirrip, or Pip, as he was called, had lived with his sister and her husband.
Pip had lived with them since his parents had died. *(when)*
Philip Pirrip, or Pip, as he was called, had lived with his sister and her husband since his parents had died.

1. A frightful man with leg irons grabbed him.
Pip was visiting his parents' graves in the deserted churchyard. *(when)*

2. Pip listened to the convict's demands.
Pip listened very attentively. *(how)*

3. The convict had escaped from a prison ship that was anchored.
The ship was anchored beyond the village. *(where)*

4. The escaped convict asked Pip to bring him food and a blacksmith's file.
He asked fiercely.

5. Threatening Pip with death if he failed, the convict warned Pip to return with these provisions.
Pip was to return by early the next morning.

Sentence Combining

Exercise 2: Combining with (Where), (When), and (How)

In this exercise you will insert more than one kind of information into the base sentence. Inserting the *where, when,* and *how* information where you think it makes the best sentence, follow the signals to make the combinations. For sets 6–10, which do not have signals, make the combinations the way you think best. After you have studied the example, write each new sentence on a sheet of paper numbered 1–10.

Example

    a. The escape route was cut off.
       It was at high tide. (*when*)
       It happened suddenly. (*how*)
       At high tide the escape route was suddenly cut off.

1. The palm trees swayed in the rising wind.
   The palm trees were on the beach at Key Largo. (*where*)
   They swayed gracefully. (*how*)
   They swayed gracefully at first. (*when*)

Writing

2. Heavy fronds began to break free from the bending trunks.
   They broke free suddenly. (*how*)
   They broke free as the winds reached hurricane force. (*when*)
   The trunks were bending wildly. (*how*)

3. The dangerous, thorny-stemmed fronds blew.
   They blew menacingly. (*how*)
   They blew now. (*when*)
   They blew across the sands, along the streets, and through neighborhood yards. (*where*)

4. Residents who had remained put up hurricane shutters and tied down everything that would be likely to blow away.
   They had remained on the island. (*where*)
   They had remained after storm warnings had been broadcast. (*when*)

5. The full gale whipped and pounded the small beach towns.
   The gale whipped and pounded suddenly. (*how*)
   The gale whipped and pounded forcefully. (*how*)
   The towns were on the key. (*where*)
   The towns were along the Florida coast. (*where*)

6. Mr. McCarthy opened the ancient stage trunk he had found.
   He opened it carefully.
   He had found the trunk behind his closet wall.
   He had found the trunk when he pushed the wall.
   He pushed the wall accidentally.

7. Mr. McCarthy discovered playbills and scripts from the eighteenth century.
   They were discovered as he raised the lid.
   They were discovered just inside.

8. Gazing at the relics of a past age, the actor imagined living.
   He was gazing dreamily.
   He imagined for a brief moment.
   He imagined living in those distant days.

9. Mr. Wilcox, McCarthy's director, broke the spell.
   Mr. Wilcox broke the spell suddenly.
   He broke the spell by reminding McCarthy that he had a performance to give.
   The performance would be in twenty minutes.

10. The presentation sparkled with the star's rekindled love for his profession.
    The presentation was that afternoon.
    The presentation sparkled brilliantly.

Writing Practice: *Using Sentence Combining*

Select a book of stories, a novel, or a play you have read and enjoyed recently, either during class or on your own. Then write a few paragraphs in which you describe the main idea or action of the story or play. Also tell about the characters and the setting. Your purpose is to persuade others to read the selection.

As you write, vary your sentences by inserting information that tells where, when, and how.

8 Imaginative Writing

You write for many purposes. When you fill out a form to order a poster of your favorite movie star, your purpose is practical. When you write a letter to the school newspaper asking for better school lunches, your purpose is to influence the behavior of others. If you write in a diary, your purpose may be to express your feelings. When you write compositions or research reports in school, your purpose is to explain or give information.

In this chapter you will write for still other purposes: to enjoy language for its own sake and to explore the worlds of imagination. This kind of writing, called *imaginative writing*, is found in stories, poems, and plays.

Building a Short Story

A short story is a type of narrative, but unlike the narratives you wrote in Chapter 5, "Writing Compositions," a short story does not need to make a point. Instead, the base upon which a short story is built is made up of four basic elements: characters, setting, plot, and conflict.

Characters: The people (or sometimes animals or robots) in the story

Setting: The place and time where the story happens

Plot: The events that happen in the story and the reasons they happen

Conflict: A problem that the characters experience

A series of events is not a short story. For example, the following nursery rhyme relates a series of events. It has characters and setting but no plot or conflict.

Humpty Dumpty sat on a wall;
Humpty Dumpty had a great fall.
All the King's horses and all the King's men,
Couldn't put Humpty together again.

In this narrative there are characters, but you know nothing about them. The setting is a wall, but you do not know anything about it or what part it plays in the series of events, and you do not know why Humpty Dumpty was on the wall or why he fell down. If you add these missing elements, however, you might have a story like this one:

Model: *A Story*

Humpty Dumpty's Fate

When the full moon broke free from the clouds, Humpty Dumpty stopped to catch his breath. The top of a gray stone wall stretched out in front of him, cracked and covered with moss. Humpty tried to locate any dangerous places along the edge where the rock was crumbling away, but another cloud blacked out the moon, and he was once again in darkness. A shiver ran down Humpty's eggshell, and for a moment he regretted the boast he had made back in the nest.

"You must accept your fate," Humpty's brother had said to him. "We're all going into the King's omelet in the morning. That is our purpose in life."

"Never!" said Humpty Dumpty proudly. "I'm going to escape over the wall this evening. Fate has more in store for me than being an omelet."

"Brave words," thought Humpty Dumpty as he sat alone in darkness on the decaying wall. He braced himself between two stones to wait for better light, but one gave way, and he rolled toward the edge, catching himself just in time. The jolt knocked loose a few pebbles, and their fall echoed softly through the barnyard. Sweat rolled down the back of Humpty's eggshell as he balanced precariously on the crumbling stone.

"Who goes there?" The voice of the King's guard echoed against the wall.

"It is I, Humpty Dumpty, a true egg. Never an omelet!" And so saying, he threw himself off the wall. The surprised guard sounded the alarm, and soon a whole company of the King's horsemen was standing there in the moonlight, looking down at the remains of Humpty Dumpty.

Vivid Details

Characters, setting, plot, conflict—these are the basic elements of a short story. However, a good short story is built from more. The writer of a good short story cements these four elements together with two essential materials, vivid description and suspenseful action. The result for the reader is a sense of involvement in what seems to be a real situation.

Model: Vivid Details in a Short Story

Here is the way one writer, Rudyard Kipling, uses vivid details to describe a fight between a little mongoose named Rikki-tikki-tavi and a deadly cobra named Nagaina:

> Rikki-tikki was bounding all round Nagaina, keeping just out of reach of her stroke, his little eyes like hot coals. Nagaina gathered herself together and flung out at him. Rikki-tikki jumped up and backward. Again and again and again she struck, and each time her head came with a whack on the matting of the veranda, and she gathered herself together like a watchspring. Then Rikki-tikki danced in a circle to get behind her, and Nagaina spun round to keep her head to his head, so that the rustle of her tail on the matting sounded like dry leaves blown along by the wind.[1]

The vivid details Rudyard Kipling uses help make the battle come alive. Words like *bounding*, *flung*, and *danced* help you imagine how the animals looked as they moved around. When Rudyard Kipling writes that the eyes of Rikki-tikki were *like hot coals*, you can see his little eyes glowing. When the writer tells you that Nagaina's tail sounded *like dry leaves* on the mat, you can hear this ominous sound.

---

[1] Excerpt from "Rikki-Tikki-Tavi" from *The Jungle Book* by Rudyard Kipling. Reprinted by permission of Doubleday & Company, Inc.

Suspense

Suspense is what a writer uses to keep readers involved in a story. For example, if you already know who committed the crime in your favorite television mystery, you are kept guessing about how the police will solve it. Everything that happens to make the job of the police more difficult helps to build suspense.

Every good short story, whether it is a mystery or not, is suspenseful. In almost all stories, characters face problems, and when it seems difficult for them to solve the problems, suspense builds.

Model: Suspense in a Short Story

In his story "To Build a Fire," Jack London provides a good example of a character's difficult situation and the resultant mounting suspense. This story takes place in the Yukon, an extremely cold territory in Northwest Canada. The main character, alone in an isolated place, knows he will freeze to death if he cannot build a fire. In the passage below, the main character is trying to pick up a bunch of matches he dropped in the snow. As you read, notice how the suspense builds:

> After some manipulation he managed to get the bunch between the heels of his mittened hands. In this fashion he carried it to his mouth. The ice crackled and snapped when by a violent effort he opened his mouth. He drew the lower jaw in, curled the upper lip out of the way, and scraped the bunch with his upper teeth in order to separate a match. He succeeded in getting one, which he dropped on his lap. He was no better off. He could not pick it up. Then he devised a way. He picked it up in his teeth and scratched it on his legs. Twenty times he scratched before he succeeded in lighting it. As it flamed he held it with his teeth to the birch bark. But the burning brimstone went up his nostrils and into his lungs, causing him to cough spasmodically. The match fell into the snow and went out.

The character's efforts to light a match at first meet with failure. When he finally is able to light it, the fumes make him cough and drop the match, which is extinguished in the snow. Each time this character's efforts fail the suspense grows, and readers wonder whether he will be able to survive. This kind of suspense makes readers want to continue reading the story to find out what happens.

Writing

Writing Practice 1: *Building a Short Story*

Choose one of the following series of events to build a story around. Then compose lists of details about characters, setting, plot, and conflict to go with the events. Write one or more paragraphs of a story, based on these lists, that utilizes suspense and vivid details.

1. Little Miss Muffet
   Sat on a tuffet
   Eating her curds and whey.
   Along came a spider,
   And sat down beside her,
   And frightened Miss Muffet away.

2. A spaceship circled around the Rodriguez house and then landed on the lawn. Slowly, the top of the ship opened.

3. Sherlock Holmes is trying to find the missing jewels. He interviews three people: Lord Twaddlethorpe, Lady Emmaline Twaddlethorpe, and the butler Crumley. Sherlock Holmes decides that Lady Emmaline is the only one who had a reason for stealing the jewels.

4. From a distance the figure on the horse appeared to be struggling. As the horse came closer, the townspeople saw a woman with her hands tied behind her back.

5. Sharon entered her frog in the jumping contest. It lost.

Reading a Short Story

As you read a short story, determine the nature of the suspense and note how it mounts. Also watch for details that help develop characters, setting, and plot.

Model: *A Short Story*

The following short story, "Tony Kytes, the Archdeceiver," by Thomas Hardy, is a humorous tale narrated by a native of Wessex, in southern England.

This story is largely developed with the use of dialogue. For information on quotation marks, see pages 554-555.

"I shall never forget Tony's face. 'Twas a little, round, firm, tight face, with a seam here and there left by the smallpox, but not enough to hurt his looks in a woman's eye, though he'd had it badish when he was a boy. So very serious-looking and unsmiling 'e was, that young man, that it really seemed as if he couldn't laugh at all without great pain to his conscience. He looked very hard at a small speck in your eye when talking to 'ee. And there was no more sign of a whisker or beard on Tony Kytes's face than on the palm of his hand. He used to sing 'The Tailor's Breeches' with a religious manner, as if it were a hymn. He was quite the women's favorite, and in return for their likings he loved 'em in shoals.

"But in course of time Tony got fixed down to one in particular, Milly Richards—a nice, light, small, tender little thing; and it was soon said that they were engaged to be married. One Saturday he had been to market to do business for his father, and was driving home the wagon in the afternoon. When he reached the foot of the very hill we shall be going over in ten minutes, who should he see waiting for him at the top but Unity Sallet, a handsome girl, one of the young women he'd been very tender toward before he'd got engaged to Milly.

"As soon as Tony came up to her she said, 'My dear Tony, will you give me a lift home?'

"'That I will, darling,' said Tony. 'You don't suppose I could refuse 'ee?'

"She smiled a smile, and up she hopped, and on drove Tony.

"'Tony,' she says, in a sort of tender chide, 'why did ye desert me for that other one? In what is she better than I? I should have made 'ee a finer wife, and a more loving one, too. 'Tisn't girls that are so easily won at first that are the best. Think how long we've known each other—ever since we were children almost—now haven't we, Tony?'

"'Yes, that we have,' says Tony, astruck with the truth o't.

"'And you've never seen anything in me to complain of, have ye, Tony? Now tell the truth to me.'

"'I never have, upon my life,' says Tony.

"'And—can you say I'm not pretty, Tony? Now look at me!'

"He let his eyes light upon her for a long while. 'I really can't,' says he. 'In fact, I never knowed you was so pretty before!'

Writing

"'Prettier than she?'

"What Tony would have said to that nobody knows, for before he could speak, what should he see ahead, over the hedge past the turning, but a feather he knew well—the feather in Milly's hat—she to whom he had been thinking of putting the question as to giving out the banns that very week.

"'Unity,' says he, as mild as he could, 'here's Milly coming. Now I shall catch it mightily if she sees 'ee riding here with me; and if you get down she'll be turning the corner in a moment, and, seeing 'ee in the road, she'll know we've been coming on together. Now, dearest Unity, will ye, to avoid all unpleasantness, which I know ye can't bear any more than I, will ye lie down in the back part of the wagon, and let me cover you over with the tarpaulin till Milly has passed? It will all be done in a minute. Do!—and I'll think over what we've said; and perhaps I shall put a loving question to you after all, instead of to Milly. 'Tisn't true that it is all settled between her and me.'

"Well, Unity Sallet agreed, and lay down at the back end of the wagon, and Tony covered her over, so that the wagon seemed to be empty but for the loose tarpaulin; and then he drove on to meet Milly.

"'My dear Tony!' cries Milly, looking up with a little pout at him as he came near. 'How long you've been coming home! Just as if I didn't live at Upper Longpuddle at all! And I've come to meet you as you asked me to do, and to ride back with you, and talk over our future home—since you asked me, and I promised. But I shouldn't have come else, Mr. Tony!'

"'Ay, my dear, I did ask ye—to be sure I did, now I think of it—but I had quite forgot it. To ride back with me, did you say, dear Milly?'

"'Well, of course! What can I do else? Surely you don't want me to walk, now I've come all this way?'

"'Oh, no, no! I was thinking you might be going on to town to meet your mother. I saw her there—and she looked as if she might be expecting 'ee.'

"'Oh, no; she's just home. She came across the fields, and so got back before you.'

"'Ah! I didn't know that,' says Tony. And there was no help for it but to take her up beside him.

"They talked on very pleasantly, and looked at the trees and beasts and birds and insects, and at the plowmen at work in the fields, till presently who should they see looking out of the upper window of a house that stood beside the road they were following but Hannah Jolliver, another young beauty of the place at that time, and the very first woman that Tony had fallen in love with—before Milly and before Unity, in fact—the one that he had almost arranged to marry instead of Milly. She was a much more dashing girl than Milly Richards, though he'd not thought much of her of late. The house Hannah was looking from was her aunt's.

"'My dear Milly—my coming wife, as I may call 'ee,' says Tony in his modest way, and not so loud that Unity could overhear, 'I see a young woman looking out of window who I think may accost me. The fact is, Milly, she had a notion that I was wishing to marry her, and since she's discovered I've promised another, and prettier than she, I'm rather afeared of her temper if she sees us together. Now, Milly, would you do me a favor—my coming wife, as I may say?'

"'Certainly, dearest Tony,' says she.

"'Then would ye creep under the tarpaulin just here in the front of the wagon, and hide there out of sight till we've passed the house? She hasn't seen us yet. You see, we ought to live in peace and good will since 'tis almost Christmas, and 'twill prevent angry passions rising, which we always should do.'

"'I don't mind, to oblige you, Tony,' Milly said; and though she didn't care much about doing it, she crept under, and crouched down just behind the seat, Unity being snug at the other end. So they drove on till they got near the roadside cottage. Hannah had soon seen him coming, and waited at the window, looking down upon him. She tossed her head a little disdainful and smiled offhand.

"'Well, aren't you going to be civil enough to ask me to ride home with you?' she says, seeing that he was for driving past with a nod and a smile.

"'Ah, to be sure! What was I thinking of?' said Tony, in a flutter. 'But you seem as if you was staying at your aunt's?'

"'No, I am not,' she said. 'Don't you see I have my bonnet and jacket on? I have only called to see her on my way home. How can you be so stupid, Tony?'

"'In that case—ah—of course you must come along wi' me,' says Tony, feeling a dim sort of sweat rising up inside his clothes. And he reined in the horse, and waited till she'd come downstairs, and then helped her up beside him. He drove on again, his face as long as a face that was a round one by nature well could be.

"Hannah looked round sideways into his eyes. 'This is nice, isn't it, Tony?' she says. 'I like riding with you.'

"Tony looked back into her eyes. 'And I with you,' he said, after a while. In short, having considered her, he warmed up, and the more he looked at her the more he liked her, till he couldn't for the life of him think why he had ever said a word about marriage to Milly or Unity while Hannah Jolliver was in question. So they sat a little closer and closer, their feet upon the footboard and their shoulders touching, and Tony thought over and over again how handsome Hannah was. He spoke tenderer and tenderer, and called her 'dear Hannah' in a whisper at last.

"'You've settled it with Milly by this time, I suppose,' said she.

"'N—no, not exactly.'

"'What? How low you talk, Tony.'

"'Yes—I've a kind of hoarseness. I said, not exactly.'

"'I suppose you mean to?'

"'Well, as to that—' His eyes rested on her face, and hers on his. He wondered how he could have been such a fool as not to follow up Hannah. 'My sweet Hannah!' he bursts out, taking her hand, not being able to help it, and forgetting Milly and Unity and all the world besides. 'Settled it? I don't think I have!'

"'Hark!' says Hannah.

"'What?' says Tony, letting go her hand.

"'Surely I heard a sort of little screaming squeak under that tar cloth? Why, you've been carrying corn, and there's mice in this wagon, I declare!' She began to haul up the tails of her gown.

"'Oh, no; 'tis the axle,' said Tony, in an assuring way. 'It do go like that sometimes in dry weather.'

"'Perhaps it was. . . . Well, now, to be quite honest, dear Tony, do you like her better than me? Because—because, although I've held off so independent, I'll own at last that I do like 'ee, Tony, to tell the truth; and I wouldn't say no if you asked me—you know what.'

"Tony was so won over by this pretty offering mood of a girl who had been quite the reverse (Hannah had a backward way with her at times, if you can mind) that he just glanced behind, and then whispered very soft, 'I haven't quite promised her, and I think I can get out of it, and ask you that question you speak of.'

"'Throw over Milly?—all to marry me! How delightful!'

8 Imaginative Writing

Nunny-watch is an embarrassing situation.

broke out Hannah, quite loud, clapping her hands.

"At this there was a real squeak—an angry, spiteful squeak, and afterward a long moan, as if something had broke its heart, and a movement of the wagon cloth.

"'Something's there!' said Hannah, starting up.

"'It's nothing, really,' says Tony, in a soothing voice, and praying inwardly for a way out of this. 'I wouldn't tell 'ee at first, because I wouldn't frighten 'ee. But, Hannah, I've really a couple of ferrets in a bag under there, for rabbiting, and they quarrel sometimes. I don't wish it knowed, as 'twould be called poaching. Oh, they can't get out, bless ye!—you are quite safe. And—and—what a fine day it is, isn't it, Hannah, for this time of year? Be you going to market next Saturday? How is your aunt now?' And so on, says Tony, to keep her from talking any more about love in Milly's hearing.

"But he found his work cut out for him, and wondering again how he should get out of this ticklish business, he looked about for a chance. Nearing home he saw his father in a field not far off, holding up his hands as if he wished to speak to Tony.

"'Would you mind taking the reins a moment, Hannah,' he said, much relieved, 'while I go and find out what Father wants?'

"She consented, and away he hastened into the field, only too glad to get breathing time. He found that his father was looking at him with rather a stern eye.

"'Come, come, Tony,' says old Mr. Kytes, as soon as his son was alongside him, 'this won't do, you know.'

"'What?' says Tony.

"'Why, if you mean to marry Milly Richards, do it, and there's an end o't. But don't go driving about the country with Jolliver's daughter and making a scandal. I won't have such things done.'

"'I only asked her—that is, she asked me—to ride home.'

"'She? Why now, if it had been Milly, 'twould have been quite proper; but you and Hannah Jolliver going about by yourselves—'

"'Milly's there, too, Father.'

"'Milly? Where?'

"'Under the tarpaulin! Yes; the truth is, Father, I've got rather into a nunny-watch, I'm afeard! Unity Sallet is there, too—yes, under the other end of the tarpaulin. All three are in that wagon, and what to do with 'em I know no more than the dead. The best plan is, as I'm thinking, to speak out loud and plain to one of 'em before the rest, and that will settle it; not but what 'twill cause 'em to kick up a bit of a miff, for certain. Now, which would you marry, Father, if you was in my place?'

"'Whichever of 'em did *not* ask to ride with thee.'

"'That was Milly, I'm bound to say, as she only mounted by my invitation. But Milly—'

201

"'Then stick to Milly, she's the best—But look at that!'

"His father pointed toward the wagon. 'She can't hold that horse in. You shouldn't have left the reins in her hands. Run on and take the horse's head, or there'll be some accident to them maids!'

"Tony's horse, in fact, in spite of Hannah's tugging at the reins, had started on his way at a brisk walking pace, being very anxious to get back to the stable, for he had had a long day out. Without another word, Tony rushed away from his father to overtake the horse.

"Now of all things that could have happened to wean him from Milly, there was nothing so powerful as his father's recommending her. No; it could not be Milly, after all. Hannah must be the one, since he could not marry all three. This he thought while running after the wagon. But queer things were happening inside it.

"It was, of course, Milly who had screamed under the tarpaulin, being obliged to let off her bitter rage and shame in that way at what Tony was saying, and never daring to show, for very pride and dread o' being laughed at, that she was in hiding. She became more and more restless, and in twisting herself about, what did she see but another woman's foot and white stocking close to her head. It quite frightened her, not knowing that Unity Sallet was in the wagon likewise. But after the fright was over she determined to get to the bottom of all this, and she crept and crept along the bed of the wagon, under the cloth, like a snake, when lo and behold, she came face to face with Unity.

"'Well, if this isn't disgraceful!' says Milly, in a raging whisper, to Unity.

"'Tis,' says Unity, 'to see you hiding in a young man's wagon like this, and no great character belonging to either of ye!'

"'Mind what you are saying!' replied Milly, getting louder. 'I am engaged to be married to him, and haven't I a right to be here? What right have you, I should like to know? What has he been promising you? A pretty lot of nonsense, I expect! But what Tony says to other women is all mere wind, and no concern to me!'

"'Don't you be too sure!' says Unity. 'He's going to have Hannah, and not you, nor me either; I could hear that.'

"Now, at these strange voices sounding from under the cloth Hannah was thunderstruck a'most into a swound; and it was just at this time that the horse moved on. Hannah tugged away wildly, not knowing what she was doing; and as the quarrel rose louder and louder Hannah got so horrified that she let go the reins altogether. The horse went on at his own pace, and coming to the corner where we turn round to drop down the hill to Lower Longpuddle he turned too quick, the off-wheels went up the bank, the wagon rose sideways till it was quite on edge upon the near axles, and out rolled the three maidens into the road in a heap.

"When Tony came up, frightened and breathless, he was relieved enough to see that neither of his darlings was hurt, beyond a few scratches from the brambles of the hedge. But he was rather alarmed when he heard how they were going on at one another.

"'Don't ye quarrel, my dears—don't ye!' says he, taking off his hat out of respect to 'em. And then he would have kissed them all round, as fair and square as a man could, but they were in too much of a talking to let him and screeched and sobbed till they was quite spent.

"'Now, I'll speak out honest, because I ought to,' says Tony, as soon as he could get heard. 'And this is the truth,' says he: 'I've asked Hannah to be mine, and she is willing, and we are going to put up the banns next—'

"Tony had not noticed that Hannah's father was coming up behind, nor had he noticed that Hannah's face was beginning to bleed from the scratch of a bramble. Hannah had seen her father, and had run to him, crying worse than ever.

"'My daughter is *not* willing, sir,' says Mr. Jolliver, hot and strong. 'Be you willing, Hannah? I ask ye to have spirit enough to refuse him.'

"'I have spirit, and I do refuse him!' says Hannah, partly because her father was there, and partly, too, in a tantrum because of the discovery and the scratch on her face. 'Little did I think when I was so soft with him just now that I was talking to such a false deceiver!'

"'What, you won't have me, Hannah?' says Tony, his jaw hanging down like a dead man's.

"'Never; I would sooner marry no—nobody at all!' she gasped out, though with her heart in her throat, for she would not have refused Tony if he had asked her quietly, and her father had not been there, and her face had not been scratched by the bramble. And having said that, away she walked upon her father's arm, thinking and hoping he would ask her again.

"Tony didn't know what to say next. Milly was sobbing her heart out; but as his father had strongly recommended her he couldn't feel inclined that way. So he turned to Unity.

"'Well, will you, Unity dear, be mine?' he says.

"'Take her leavings? Not I!' says Unity. 'I'd scorn it!' And away walks Unity Sallet likewise, though she looked back when she'd gone some way, to see if he was following her.

"So there at last were left Milly and Tony by themselves, she crying in watery streams, and Tony looking like a tree struck by lightning.

"'Well, Milly,' he says at last, going up to her, 'it do seem as if fate had ordained that it should be you and I, or nobody. And what must be must be, I suppose. Hey, Milly?'

Writing

"'If you like, Tony. You didn't really mean what you said to them?'

"'Not a word of it,' declares Tony, bringing down his fist upon his palm.

"And then he kissed her, and put the wagon to rights, and they mounted together; and their banns were put up the very next Sunday."

Think and Discuss

1. The *main character* in this story, Tony, seems very real. What details bring him to life as we read? Take into account all details of description, dialogue, and actions, and decide which of these work best in creating his character.

2. *Setting* is the place and time the story happens. It also includes details about how time and place affect the characters. Examine the setting of this story. Does it have a strong effect on the actions of the characters? Would the events of this story have happened on another day at another place?

3. The *plot* of a story is what happens in it and why. The events that make up the plot of a short story must be clearly tied together. There is no room for unrelated information. Summarize in your own words the action of this story.

4. *Conflict* arises when characters try to solve problems. All of the characters in this story are related by one big problem. What is it? Does each character also have minor problems springing from this major conflict? Give examples of this.

5. We usually associate suspense with horror films or ghost stories. This story is definitely not frightening, yet it still contains a high level of suspense. How does its suspense build?

Writing Assignment I: *Writing a Short Story*

Select one of the following situations or make up one of your own and develop it into a short story. Follow the steps for prewriting, writing, and postwriting.

1. Commander Alice McKrimmon was ready to give the order for blastoff from this strange planet. Before she could, however, the entire spacecraft began to rock.

2. For days Anna had thought about a good way to approach her parents. Finally, on Thursday night she worked up her courage to talk to them about what she hoped to do.

3. The old man looked around him for a long time and then slowly closed his eyes and sank onto the ground. Across the whole desolate landscape, there was not one living thing visible.

4. It had been a busy day at the service station. Cars, trucks, and even children on bicycles had been in and out in a steady stream. Carlos had been so busy that he had not stopped to count the money.

5. Making one last attempt at freedom, the young woman clawed her way through the jungle. In her desperation she failed to notice the yellow eyes following her.

A. Prewriting

Each of the above situations involves a character facing a problem or about to face a problem. Think about the situation and about how the problem might develop. Then use free writing to write as many details as you can imagine. Add other characters if you like. Underline the parts of your free writing that you will use.

B. Writing

Write a story that tells how the problem develops and how the character is or is not able to solve it. Use your free writing notes as a guide.

C. Postwriting

Read over your story to make sure that:

1. It includes details in description and dialogue, and it builds suspense.
2. The characters and action seem real so that your readers will stay interested.

Allow another person to read your story. Consider any suggestions that person may give and revise the story if you feel it is necessary.

Use the checklist at the back of this book to proofread your story.

Poetry

Poetry is another kind of imaginative writing. A poem consists of many elements, but all good poems come from writers who choose their words and arrange them carefully. Poems convey sounds that are pleasing to the ear and images that encourage the reader to perceive with all of the senses. In the sections that follow you will learn more about sound effects and images in poetry.

Sound effects add much to your enjoyment of movies. If you are watching a space adventure, you want to hear the strange voices of the aliens and the loud boom when a spaceship exceeds the speed of sound. In poetry, sound effects are also important. The sounds of words alone and the sounds of words put together in patterns create a pleasing effect when poetry is read aloud. These sound effects also help to make poetry different from forms of writing such as stories and plays.

Rhyme, alliteration, and *meter* are important sound effects in poetry.

Rhyme

Words that *rhyme* have the same ending sounds.

rh*yme* — t*ime*
mi*ddle* — f*iddle*

Model: Rhyme

As you read the poem "Pete at the Zoo" by Gwendolyn Brooks, notice which words rhyme.

Pete at the Zoo[1]

I wonder if the elephant
Is lonely in his stall
When all the boys and girls are gone
And there's no shout at all,
And there's no one to stamp before,
No one to note his might.
Does he hunch up, as I do,
Against the dark of night?

—*Gwendolyn Brooks*

---

[1]"Pete at the Zoo" from *The World of Gwendolyn Brooks* by Gwendolyn Brooks. Copyright © 1960 by Gwendolyn Brooks. Reprinted by permission of Harper & Row, Publishers, Inc.

Writing

Think and Discuss

In the poem by Gwendolyn Brooks, the last words in the second and fourth lines rhyme: *stall/all*. What are the rhyming words in the rest of the poem?

Alliteration

A second sound effect in poetry is *alliteration*, words that *begin* with the same sounds, as in these examples:

*l*ittle–*l*ady
*o*range–*o*rgan
*qu*ick–*qu*it

In lines of poetry alliteration adds to the musical quality of the words, as in this anonymous poem:

Three *g*ray *g*eese in a *g*reen field *g*razing,
*G*ray were the *g*eese and *g*reen was the *g*razing.

Model: *Alliteration*

Alliteration may also help to tie two or more lines together by repeating the beginning sound:

Then there *c*ame a *k*ing in the *c*ompany of *k*nighthood.
The might of the *C*ommune made him a ruler.
*C*ommon Wit *c*ame after and *c*reated advisers,
As a *c*ouncil for the *k*ing and for the *c*ommon safety.

— from "The Vision of Piers Plowman"[1]

Meter

When you pronounce words with more than one syllable, one syllable is spoken more loudly than the other syllables. This louder syllable, called a *stressed* syllable, is shown with a special stress mark: (').

A mer' i ca   beau' ti ful

Poets often put words together so that stressed and unstressed syllables form a regular pattern or *meter*, a third sound effect in poetry. Poems with meter often have alliteration and rhyme as well.

---

[1] From "The Vision of Piers Plowman" by William Langland in *William Langland: The Vision of Piers Plowman* translated by Henry W. Wells. Copyright 1945 by Sheed & Ward. Reprinted by permission of Andrews, McMeel & Parker. All rights reserved.

There are several different patterns of meter, and each has a different effect on the poem. One pattern, for example, is used in a humorous poem of five lines called a limerick. Read the following verse aloud until you can hear and repeat its meter.

There was a young lady named Hannah,
Who slipped on a peel of banana.
    More stars she espied
    As she lay on her side
Than are found in the Star Spangled Banner.

A limerick's regular meter gives the verse a singsong effect, which, with its rhymes, helps to make it humorous.

Model: Meter in Limericks

Some limericks are funny because of the situation; others are plays on words, letters, and numbers. As you read the following limericks, decide what makes them humorous.

There was a young man from Kent,
Whose nose was terribly bent
    One day, I suppose,
    He could follow his nose,
And no one would know where he went.

There was a young man of Typhoo
Who wanted to catch the 2:02;
    But his friend said, "Don't hurry
    Or worry or flurry,
It's a minute or two to 2:02."

To smash the simple atom
All mankind was intent.
    Now any day
    The atom may
Return the compliment.[1]

Think and Discuss

1. Identify the rhyme, alliteration and meter in the following lines from poems. (Not all poems use all three sound effects.)

---

[1] "Atomic Courtesy" from *Mice in the Ink* by Ethel Jacobson. First appeared in *Look* magazine. Reprinted by permission of Ethel Jacobson.

Writing

a. Western wind, when wilt thou blow,
   The small rain down can rain?
   　　　　—Anonymous

b. The voice of the last cricket
   across the first frost
   is one kind of good-by.
   It is so thin a splinter of singing.
   　　　　—Carl Sandburg, "Splinter"[1]

c. There lived a wife at Usher's Well,
   And a wealthy wife was she;
   She had three stout and stalwart sons,
   And sent them o'er the sea.
   　　　　—Anonymous, "The Wife of Usher's Well"

d. He clasps the crag with crooked hands;
   Close to the sun in lonely lands,
   Ringed with the azure world, he stands.
   The wrinkled sea beneath him crawls;
   He watches from his mountain walls,
   And like a thunderbolt he falls.
   　　　　—Alfred Lord Tennyson, "The Eagle"

---

[1]From *Good Morning, America,* copyright 1928, 1956 by Carl Sandburg. Reprinted by permission of Harcourt Brace Jovanovich, Inc.

2. People often use rhyme, meter, and alliteration in slogans and mottos. Advertisers use slogans with rhyme, meter, and alliteration because the slogans help people remember the products. Look through magazines or newspapers to find advertising slogans that use rhyme, meter, and/or alliteration. Bring your examples to class or copy them on a sheet of paper. Be prepared to discuss whether you think the sound effects are effective.

Rhyme, alliteration, and meter do not make a poem. Many poems, in fact, have none of these sound effects. When poets do use them, however, they add to meaning and help to create a pleasant effect for readers.

Writing Practice 2: *Using Sound Effects*

Here is a list of make-believe products. Select three of these, or make up three of your own, and write an advertising slogan for each, using rhyme and alliteration. You might even try your hand at a clever limerick that will help sell your product. If you do, read it softly to yourself to make certain it has the meter and rhyme that limericks use.

Scummo	—A cleaning product for stubborn dirt
Tingle	—A toothpaste that comes in six flavors
Seaweed	—A cologne for men that smells like the seashore
Pizazz	—An instant pizza mix
Zap	—An insect repellent
Kitty Krackers	—A snack for cats
Flip-It	—A pen that writes with blue ink on one end and black on the other
Sure Fingers	—A product that keeps your fingers and palms dry when you operate joy sticks and buttons on video games

Figurative Language

A poet once said that a poem is like a tightly coiled spring and that reading it is like letting the spring go. The poem expands,

Writing

and meanings come to you. One way a poet is able to put so much meaning into the small space of a poem is by using the sound effects of rhyme, alliteration, and meter. Another way is by using figures of speech called *similes* and *metaphors*.

Similes

A *simile* compares two different things, using the words *like* or *as*.

Although you may not realize it, you probably hear and use similes often in your everyday experience. When you say, "It's hot as an oven in this room," or "I worked like a dog on this project," you are using a simile. The first sentence compares the heat of the room with that of the oven. What two things does the second sentence compare?

Model: Simile

Poets use similes because they are a way of compressing meaning. As you read the following poem by Winifred Welles, look for the two similes in it.

Dogs and Weather[1]

I'd like a different dog
    For every kind of weather—
A narrow greyhound for a fog,
      A wolfhound strange and white,
    With a tail like a silver feather
      To run with in the night,
        When snow is still, and winter stars are bright.

In the fall I'd like to see
    In answer to my whistle,
A golden spaniel look at me.
      But best of all for rain
    A terrier, hairy as a thistle,
      To trot with fine disdain
        Beside me down the soaked, sweet-smelling lane.

—Winifred Welles

In the first stanza the speaker wants the tail of a wolfhound to be *like a silver feather;* in the second stanza the speaker

---

[1] "Dogs and Weather" from *Skipping Along Alone* by Winifred Welles, Macmillan Publishing Co., 1931. By permission of the State National Bank of Connecticut, Agent for James Welles Shearer.

wants a terrier *hairy as a thistle*. A description of the wolfhound's tail or the terrier's hair might have taken several lines without the similes. Because most readers would know what a silver feather and a thistle are like, however, the poet uses similes to convey meaning.

Metaphors

A *metaphor* conveys meaning by comparing one thing to another different thing directly, without the use of *like* or *as*.

For example, consider the metaphor *John is a clown*. Readers know that clowns amuse audiences; therefore, they picture John being amusing also.

Not all metaphors include the verbs *is* or *are* to make the comparison, as this line from Carl Sandburg shows:

This old anvil laughs at many broken hammers.[1]

An *anvil* is a block on which metal objects are hammered into shape. The key to this metaphor is the verb *laugh*. Because only human beings can really laugh, you understand that the poet is comparing an anvil to a human being. He is saying something like this: *This human being is an anvil who can take as many blows as life can give without breaking.*

---

[1] From *The People, Yes* by Carl Sandburg, copyright 1936 by Harcourt Brace Jovanovich, Inc.; copyright 1964 by Carl Sandburg. Reprinted by permission of the publisher.

Writing

Model: Metaphor

Metaphors in poetry help to condense meaning just as similes do. The next poem contains two metaphors.

Dreams[1]

Hold fast to dreams
For if dreams die
Life is a broken-winged bird
That cannot fly.

Hold fast to dreams
For when dreams go
Life is a barren field
Frozen with snow.

—Langston Hughes

Think and Discuss

In the first stanza Langston Hughes uses a metaphor when he writes that *Life is a broken-winged bird. Life is a barren field* is the metaphor in the second stanza. In your own words explain what you think the poet means by these metaphors.

---

[1]"Dreams" from *The Dream Keeper and Other Poems* by Langston Hughes. Copyright 1932 by Alfred A. Knopf, Inc. and renewed 1960 by Langston Hughes. Reprinted by permission of Alfred A. Knopf, Inc.

Writing Practice 3: *Using Similes and Metaphors*

Each of the following groups of words is about something with which you are probably familiar. For each group of words think of a simile or metaphor and then write a sentence using the group of words and your simile or metaphor.

Example

Group of Words	Simile	Sentence
Frost on a window	Like a lace curtain made of silver thread	One winter morning the frost on my window was like a lace curtain made of silver thread.

1. My room
2. The garbage cans on the street
3. My dog running for its food
4. Summer
5. Eating spaghetti
6. Growing up
7. A hippopotamus
8. Children at the circus
9. A city street at 4:00 A.M.
10. The sound of a train whistle at night

Imagery in Poetry

The poet William Wordsworth once defined poets as people who are unusually aware of the world around them. They see, hear, feel, taste, and smell more things in their world than other people. When poets describe these experiences so that readers can share them, they create *images* in their poetry.

Writing

A short poem that presents a vivid image is called a picture poem. The poem may describe a person, place, animal, object, or event, and it often has similes or metaphors that help create the image.

Model: *Imagery*

As you read the following poem by the Chinese poet Tu Fu, decide what is being described and look for the metaphor the poet uses to help develop the image. (*Egrets* are wading birds with long, white plumes.)

Brimming Water[1]

Under my feet the moon
Glides along the river.
Near midnight, a gusty lantern
Shines in the heart of night.
Along the sandbars flocks
Of white egrets roost,
Each one clenched like a fist.
In the wake of my barge
The fish leap, cut the water,
and dive and splash.

—*Tu Fu*

In the preceding poem the speaker is riding a barge on a river at night. The images in the poem help you to imagine the moonlight moving on the water and the sight of a lantern shining in the darkness. When the poet says that the egrets are *clenched like a fist*, you can picture the birds drawn up for the night. The poet also uses images to help you hear the fish leap out of the water and dive back in.

Writing Practice 4: *Writing a Poem with Imagery*

Select one of the following people, places, animals, objects, or events, or make up one of your own. Then write a picture poem describing your subject. Use specific details to help your readers imagine sights, sounds, textures, tastes, and smells.

1. Your thumbnail

---

[1]Kenneth Rexroth, *One Hundred Poems From the Chinese*. Copyright © 1971 by Kenneth Rexroth. All Rights Reserved. Reprinted by permission of New Directions.

8 Imaginative Writing

2. A mountain
3. A cat stretching in the sunshine
4. An object you kept for a souvenir
5. The hall of your school during class break
6. The area where you live during your favorite season of the year
7. A band concert
8. A person you think is especially attractive
9. An athlete you admire
10. Yourself cutting the grass or doing some other chore

Poems to Express Feelings

Think about a time you enjoyed listening to a special record because the words and music expressed how you felt. You may have felt especially happy or perhaps lonely or sad, and the music reflected these feelings for you. It may even have seemed that the person writing the song must have had you in mind. Poets, like songwriters, often write to express feelings as well as to create images.

Model: A Poem to Express Feelings

As you read the following poem by Judson Jerome, look for the feelings the poet expresses and the images he uses to express them.

Deer Hunt[1]

    Because the warden is a cousin, my
mountain friends hunt in summer when the deer
cherish each rattler-ridden spring, and I
have waited hours by a pool in fear
that manhood would require I shoot or that
the steady drip of the hill would dull my ear
to a snake whispering near the log I sat
upon, and listened to the yelping cheer
of dogs and men resounding ridge to ridge.
I flinched at every lonely rifle crack,
my knuckles whitening where I gripped the edge
of age and clung, like retching, sinking back,
then gripping once again the monstrous gun—
since I, to be a man, had taken one.

—Judson Jerome

Think and Discuss

Perhaps you have had the experience of being afraid to do something, but feeling that you must in order to appear grown

---

[1]"Deer Hunt" by Judson Jerome from *Poetry* magazine, May 1955. Copyright © 1955 by Judson Jerome. Reprinted by permission of the Editor of *Poetry* and Judson Jerome.

up. If you have, you can certainly identify with the feeling the young speaker expresses in this poem. To make the emotion real, the poet includes images such as *my knuckles whitening* and *the monstrous gun*. What other images in the poem help to express the speaker's feelings of fear and dread?

Free Verse Poems

Poems may take many forms. Free verse poems, for instance, do not have regular meter and rhyme.

Model: Free Verse

What feelings does the speaker express in this free verse poem?

Knoxville, Tennessee[1]

I always like summer
best
you can eat fresh corn
from daddy's garden
and okra
and greens
and cabbage
and lots of
barbecue
and buttermilk
and homemade ice-cream
at the church picnic
and listen to
gospel music
outside
at the church
homecoming
and go to the mountains with
your grandmother
and go barefooted
and be warm
all the time
not only when you go to bed
and sleep

—Nikki Giovanni

[1] "Knoxville, Tennessee" from *Black Judgement* by Nikki Giovanni, copyright 1968. Reprinted with permission from Broadside/Crummell Press, Detroit, Michigan.

Writing

In this poem the speaker expresses happiness and contentment with life. The poet appeals to all the senses in creating images of fulfillment and ease. Instead of rhyme or meter, the poet uses the rhythm of a young person talking.

Writing Practice 5: *Writing a Poem to Express Feelings*

Select a situation and feeling from the following list, or make up your own. Then write a poem in which you use images to express the feeling. To help get started, look again at the model poems in this section, but do not feel that your poem must copy any of them. You may use rhyme and meter or free verse.

1. Being left alone in a house at night and feeling fear
2. Being at a rock concert and feeling excitement
3. Wearing an old pair of jeans and feeling comfortable
4. Taking a test and feeling nervous
5. Having a bad day and feeling depressed
6. Having a pet die and feeling sad
7. Riding a bike or taking a walk and feeling very happy
8. Giving up something from your childhood and feeling a sense of loss
9. Being with a person you care about and feeling a sense of closeness
10. Having to eat food you hate and feeling disgust

For Your Writer's Notebook

> Perhaps you remember a time you sat by an open window on a warm day to do schoolwork. The sun was shining, and insects buzzed in the air. Instead of schoolwork, you thought about riding your bicycle or being at the beach. Think about a time when you daydreamed and imagined feeling free, playful, or sad. Then write a notebook entry describing the emotion and the time and place where you experienced it.

8 Imaginative Writing

Writing Assignment II: *Writing a Poem*

Write a poem in which you develop an image of a person, place, or experience that is important to you. Your purpose is to convey to readers how what is being described makes you feel. Describe both the emotion you experience and the causes of the emotion.

A. Prewriting

Select the subject for your poem and identify how you feel about it. Brainstorm or cluster ideas and details as they come to you.

B. Writing

Write your poem, using one or more of the sound effects of rhyme, alliteration, and meter. Next, read what you have written, looking for ways to use metaphors and similes to condense meaning and enhance sensory perception.

C. Postwriting

Reread your poem to make sure that the poem presents the image and expresses the feeling you had in mind. Finally, use the checklist at the back of this book to proofread your poem.

Sentence Combining: Inserting to Tell Something

Combining with (Who), (Where), (What), (Why), (When), (How), and a New Signal

In this section the words *who, where, what, why, when,* and *how* will be signals, but they will work together with a new signal, *something*. This example shows how the signals work together:

Base Sentence: Thomas needs to know *something*.

Insert: The lawn mower works. (*how*)

Combined: Thomas needs to know *how the lawn mower works*.

For more information on punctuating phrases and clauses, see pages 538-546.

The new signal *something* tells you to put information from the insert sentence in its place. The (*how*) signals tells you to insert information that tells *how* something is done. Consequently, the words *how the lawn mower works* replace the signal *something* in the base sentence to produce the new combined sentence. The *something* signal works in the same way with the (*who*), (*where*), (*what*), (*why*), and (*when*) signals. The signal word in the insert will always be used in the combined sentence to introduce the information.

Base Sentence: Maria heard *something*.

Insert: Mrs. Gomez said a thing about her son Richard. (*what*)

Combined: Maria heard *what Mrs. Gomez said about her son Richard*.

(Notice that the words *a thing* are omitted in the combined sentence.)

Base Sentence: Did Father see *something*?

Insert: Someone left this note on our door. (*who*)

Combined: Did Father see *who left this note on our door*?

(Notice that the word *someone* is omitted in the combined sentence.)

Sentence Combining

Base Sentence: Michael asked Evelyn *something*.
Insert: She had not done her homework. (*why*)
Combined: Michael asked Evelyn *why she had not done her homework*.

Exercise 1: Combining with a New Signal

On a sheet of paper, combine the following sets of sentences. For sets 1–5, follow the signals (*who*), (*where*), (*what*), (*why*), (*when*), and (*how*) to insert information into the base where the signal *something* appears. For sets 6–10, only the signal *something* is given; you must decide which of the six words to use. You may need to leave out repeated or unnecessary words in the insert sentence. Study the examples first.

Examples

a. Commander Robert E. Peary wondered *something*.
   His discovery of the North Pole had been challenged. (*why*)

   Commander Robert E. Peary wondered why his discovery of the North Pole had been challenged.

b. Wrongfully, Dr. Frederick A. Cook claimed he had done *something*.
   Peary had actually accomplished a thing.

   Wrongfully, Dr. Frederick A. Cook claimed he had done what Peary had actually accomplished.

223

Writing

1. On his ninth birthday Donnie had asked *something*.
   Someone would be willing to show him how to band wild ducks. (*who*)

2. Identifying birds with Uncle Charles, the naturalist, was *something*.
   Donnie wanted to do a thing most of all. (*what*)

3. Uncle Charles wanted to teach Donnie *something*.
   To sit patiently in the duck blind until the birds arrive is what he wanted to teach. (*how*)

4. From above and from the water, the ducks could not see *something*.
   The birdwatchers were hidden somewhere. (*where*)

5. Uncle Charles and Donnie could decide *something*.
   To net and band the birds was what they could decide. (*when*)

6. Our principal Ms. Bernowitz announced *something*.
   The canned-food drive would begin sometime.

7. As we had done in previous years, our entire student body voted on *something*.
   A thing would be done with the cans once they were collected.

8. The student body decided *something*.
   We would send the school's contribution somewhere.

9. Then each homeroom chose *something*.
   Someone would be its campaign director.

10. The canned-food drive helped us to remember *something*.
    Organization means something.

Combining with (The Fact That), (That), and (Join)

The signals (*the fact that*), (*that*), and (*join*) work in the same way that (*who*), (*what*), (*why*), (*where*), (*when*), and (*how*) work. Again, the signal *something*, which appears in the base sentence, indicates where to insert the information. The signal (*join*) works a little differently; the entire insert sentence is joined to the base where the word *something* appears. These sentence sets show how to use the signals:

Base Sentence:	*Something* revealed how much Andrea had enjoyed "The Tell-Tale Heart."
Insert:	She had read it three times. (*the fact that*)
Combined:	*The fact that she had read it three times* revealed how much Andrea had enjoyed "The Tell-Tale Heart."
Base Sentence:	Cleverly, Andrea guessed *something*.
Insert:	The narrator of Poe's story was insane. (*that*)
Combined:	Cleverly, Andrea guessed *that the narrator of Poe's story was insane.*
Base Sentence:	The narrator believed *something*.
Insert:	The inspectors could hear the old man's heart beating beneath the floor. (*join*)
Combined:	The narrator believed *the inspectors could hear the old man's heart beating beneath the floor.*

Exercise 2: Using New Signals

Combine the following sets of sentences in the order they are given. For the last five sets, decide whether or not to use *that* or *the fact that* to join sentences.

Example

a. *Something* made the narrator believe *something*.
   He was guilty. (*the fact that*)
   The police could see through his story. (*join*)
   The fact that he was guilty made the narrator believe the police could see through his story.

1. The passengers on the *Titanic* felt *something*.
   The great liner was unsinkable. (*that*)

2. *Something* proved this belief was ill-founded.
   The ship struck an iceberg and sank in the icy waters of the North Atlantic. (*the fact that*)

3. After the tragedy some people said *something*.
   Humans should not have challenged God by calling the liner unsinkable. (*join*)

4. *Something* made Gabriel uneasy.
   The swamp was filled with snakes and alligators. (*the fact that*)

5. He had been taught *something*.
   It is usually best to avoid disturbing the large reptiles. (*that*)

6. Still, Gabe believed *something*.
   He knew where to find the old burial ground.

7. In the book titled *The Yearling* Penny Baxter said *something*.
   His son Jody could raise a young fawn as his pet.

8. *Something* helped him to decide *something*.
   Penny had had to kill the fawn's mother.
   Jody should raise the young animal.

9. As the fawn Flag grew into a yearling, Jody suspected *something*.
   His father could not forgive it for eating the spring corn crop.

10. *Something* made Jody realize *something*.
    Flag had to be destroyed.
    It was time to set aside his childhood and assume adult responsibilities.

Exercise 3: Combining Sentences

The following sentence sets are based upon Edgar Allan Poe's short story "The Tell-Tale Heart." When you have combined each set, the new sentences will resemble those written by Poe. Using the first sentence in each set as the base sentence, make the combinations by following the signals. Write each new sentence on a sheet of paper numbered 1–5. (There are many ways to make each combination.) Study the example before you begin.

Example

a. I heard a groan.
   I heard it presently. (*when*)
   It was slight.
   I knew it was the groan. (*,and*)
   It was of mortal terror.
   Presently, I heard a slight groan, and I knew it was the groan of mortal terror.

Sentence Combining

1. It was not a groan.
   The groan was of pain.
   The groan was of grief. (*or*)
   It was the sound. (*;*)
   The sound was low.
   The sound was stifled. (*,*)
   The sound arises from the bottom of the soul. (*that*)
   The soul is overcharged with awe. (*when*)

2. It has welled up from my own bosom.
   It welled up many a night. (*when*)
   It welled up just at midnight. (*,*)
   All the world slept. (*when*)
   It deepens with its echo, the terrors. (*,ing*)
   Its echo is dreadful.
   The terrors distracted me. (*that*)

3. I say *something*.
   I knew it well. (*join*)

4. I knew *something*.
   The old man felt a thing. (*what*)
   I pitied him. (*,and*)
   I chuckled at heart. (*,although*)

5. I knew *something*.
   He had been awake. (*that*)
   It was ever since the noise. (*when*)
   The noise was first.
   The noise was slight.
   He had turned in his bed. (*,when*)

Writing Practice: *Home Sweet Home*

Imagine that you could live anywhere in the world. Write a paragraph telling your readers where that place is, what it looks like, how your life there might be, and who would share the place with you. Use words and phrases that help your readers see, hear, smell, taste, and feel the place.

As you write, use several of the sentence-combining skills you have been practicing in this chapter.

9 Writing Letters

You write letters for several reasons. Friendly letters are written to greet a friend or relative and to share something of yourself with him or her. Social letters are written to say thank you for a gift or special favor and to extend, accept, or decline an invitation. Business letters are written to apply for a job, request information, and place or correct an order, among other things.

All types of letters follow standard forms. A close friend probably cares more about what you say than how you say it, but correct letter form makes it easier for him or her to read your message. Because social and business letters may be written to people whom you wish to impress favorably, their appearance is particularly important. In this chapter you will learn the correct forms for writing friendly, social, and business letters.

Writing Friendly Letters

You write friendly letters to those people who care about you and who are interested in reading about your experiences and your thoughts and feelings. Your notebook can be an especially good source of ideas for this kind of writing.

When you write about your experiences, thoughts, and feelings, select those that will be meaningful to your reader. Experiences that the two of you have shared make good subjects. For example, if you and your friend enjoyed visiting the city zoo, he or she might like to hear about the coral snake that got loose somewhere in the reptile house or about a rare species of antelope the zoo has recently acquired. Another way to show that you have your reader in mind is to inquire about his or her activities and well-being. Such questions not only show that you care, but also give your friend a way to begin a return letter. Correspondence of this nature may greatly enrich a friendship.

Model: A Friendly Letter

Death Be Not Proud, by John Gunther, is the true story of John Gunther, Jr., who died of cancer at seventeen. It tells the story of the young man's courage on first learning about the disease and during the many months of his illness. At the end of the story, the author, John's father, included many of the letters his son had written to friends and relatives during his ordeal. The following letter from *Death Be Not Proud* is one that John Gunther, Jr., wrote to a classmate. As you read, notice how the writer, even during his illness, thinks of his reader.

Writing

May 14, 1946

Dear Steve,

 Thanks for that letter. I should like very much to clear up any misapprehensions you and the Corridor may have about my state of affairs. Frankly I think I have discovered Utopia here at the Presbyterian Hospital. No school work. No athletics. No worries. All I do is eat, sleep, and have a wonderful time generally. My parents visit me every day. (I am dictating this to my mother.) My reading is still somewhat restricted, but soon I shall be able to have any book I want.

 I had quite a serious operation. They had to drill three holes right through my skull. I'll bet you'd never guess what the trouble was—excess pressure within the brain. The most painful part of the operation occurred beforehand—they had to shave off all my hair! That hurt so much that I resolved to grow a Brahmsian beard and never shave in my life. My hair is growing back—slowly.

 Give my best to Mr. McGlyn and all the boys. Show them this letter—unless you think they'll get too jealous.[1]

A *Utopia* is an ideal situation.

***Brahmsian* describes the beard of Johannes Brahms, a German composer.**

In the preceding letter, Johnny Gunther shows that he is thinking of his reader by thanking Steve for his letter and by asking him to share it with their teacher and classmates.

Writing Practice 1: *Writing a Friendly Letter*

Think of a friend or relative to whom you would like to write. Read through your notebook to find an experience that you would like to share with him or her and then write about it in a friendly letter.

For Your Writer's Notebook

> Millions of people around the world have read the story of Johnny Gunther. He knew for several months before his death that he would die, but he never lost his enthusiasm for life or his courage. In your notebook write your reaction to his letter. How did reading it make you feel? What would you say to Johnny Gunther if he were alive today?

[1]From pp. 222–223 in *Death Be Not Proud* by John Gunther. Copyright 1949 by John Gunther. Reprinted by permission of Harper & Row, Publishers, Inc.

Writing an Interesting Letter

One of the best ways to show that you care about your reader is to take time to write an interesting letter. Such letters have specific details about people, places, events, thoughts, and feelings that help the reader share in the writer's experiences. Some preparation is needed to write a letter of this type. For instance, you can get ideas for an interesting letter by looking back at your notebook to see what you have recorded there. If you have written about an experience while it was fresh in your mind, you will have a good source of specific, vivid details. As you write, try to imagine your friend or relative sitting across from you. What specific questions might he or she have about the experience you describe? In your letter use details that answer these questions.

Model: An Interesting Letter

Here, for example, is part of a letter written in 1915 by Laura Ingalls Wilder, the author of *Little House on the Prairie*, to her husband. As she wrote the letter, Laura Wilder was on a train crossing Nevada. As you read, notice her use of specific details.

> I saw the sun rise on the desert as I lay in my berth and it was lovely. The bare, perfectly bare, rocky mountains in all kinds of heaps and piles as though the winds had drifted them into heaps and they had turned to rock, were purple in the hollows and rose and gold and pink on the higher places. There were yellows and browns and grays and the whole softly blended together. At the feet of the mountains lay the flat gray plain covered with sage brush, with patches of sand and alkali showing. Such a desolate dreary country even though beautiful in its way. All morning we have been going through the desert and now we are where there are piles of loose sand. All the way wherever there is a little spot of green someone is living, or perhaps I should say wherever someone is living there is a spot of green, but not always. I saw two houses and a windmill and one green bush between them. There was a river bottom for a little ways and corrals and cattle and a cowboy in red chaps driving a bunch of horses. We thought we were seeing water off at one side and I asked the porter what water it was. He laughed and said it looked like alkali beds. Then we saw them later close by, miles of perfectly white ground. In places it looked like water and then it looked like snow. There

Writing

was a little house and corral right out in the middle of one big bed. Not a living creature or a green thing in sight. There was a road out and it looked like a road made in about three inches of snow with dry dirt underneath. Oh, this awful, awful country we have come to now.[1]

Think and Discuss

Laura Ingalls Wilder describes her experience in a way that interests readers. To her the Rocky Mountains looked "as though the winds had drifted them into heaps and they had turned to rock." What other details do you find interesting? Are these the same details that would have helped her husband share her experience?

Writing Practice 2: *Writing an Interesting Letter*

Think of a friend or relative to whom you would like to write. Then complete each of the following steps. You may use the letter you wrote for Writing Practice 1 if you desire.

---

[1] Text excerpt from *West From Home: Letters of Laura Ingalls Wilder to Almanzo Wilder, San Francisco 1915*, edited by Roger Lea MacBride. Copyright © 1974 by Roger Lea MacBride. By permission of Harper & Row, Publishers, Inc.

1. Think of an experience both of you have shared or one that you know would interest your reader. If you are writing about an experience you can repeat, do so, and take a notebook with you to record details. For example, suppose you and your friend enjoyed riding your bicycles in the city park. Go back to the park and find a place where you can observe.

2. Divide a sheet of paper into five columns and label them *Sights*, *Sounds*, *Smells*, *Tastes*, and *Textures*.

3. In the appropriate column, list specific sensory details about your experience. You might feel a new coolness in the air, overhear the conversation of two children pretending to be robots, smell hamburgers as they cook over a grill, and so on.

4. Using the specific details from Step 3, write a friendly letter describing the experience. You might begin your description with a sentence such as "When I rode my bike in the park last Saturday, I thought of you."

Interesting details are often provided by adjectives. For more information on adjectives, see pages 376-395.

Form for Friendly Letters

While the content of your friendly letter is more important, correct form is important also. A letter carelessly written with smudge marks and crossed-out words gives a reader the impression that you do not care enough to write a neat letter.

Friendly and social letters follow the same standard form, which consists of five separate parts: heading, salutation, body, closing, and signature.

Writing

Model: Form for Friendly and Social Letters

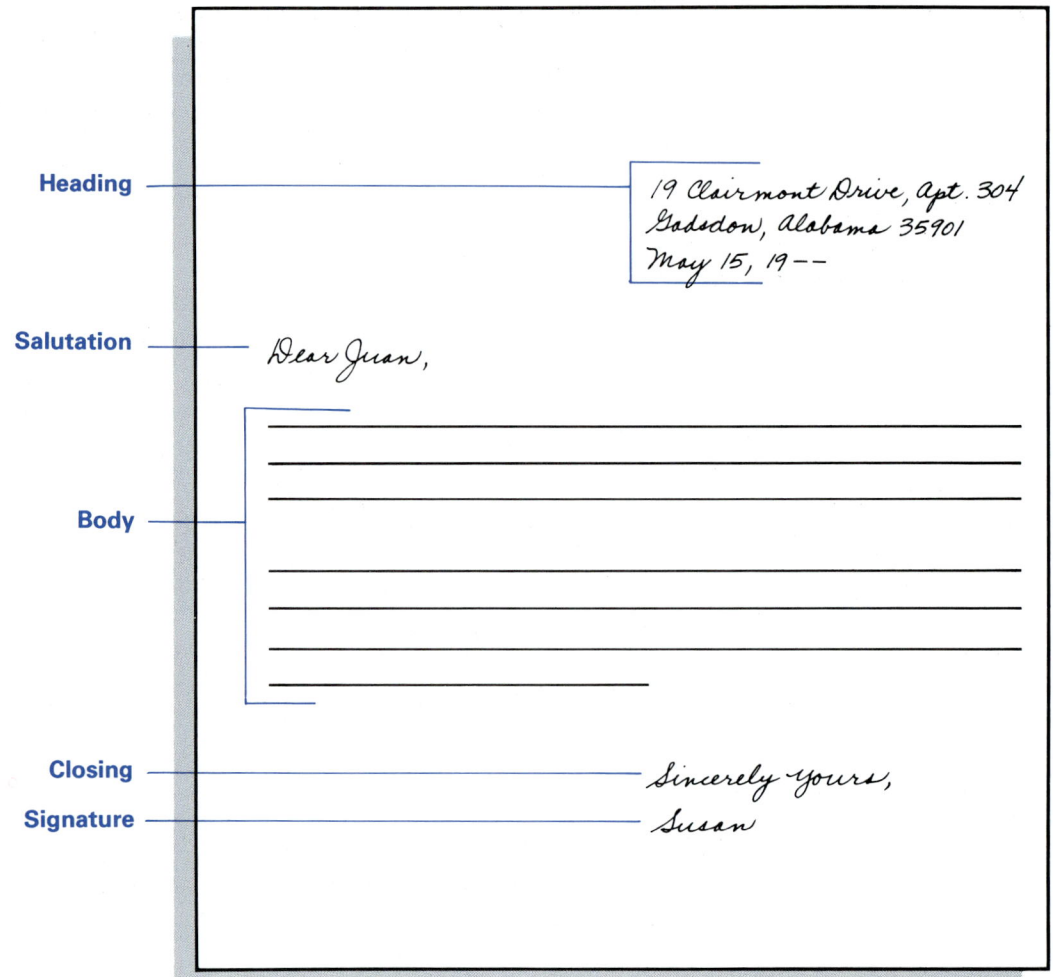

Heading

The heading consists of the address of the letter writer and the date on which the letter is written. It goes in the upper-right hand part of the page and is three lines long. The street or rural route and apartment number, if there is one, go on the first line; and the city, state, and ZIP code number go on the second line. The date belongs on the third line. Punctuation in the heading includes a comma between the street and apartment number, a comma between the city and state, and a comma between the day of the month and the year. There is no comma between the state and ZIP code.

Salutation

The salutation greets the addressee. An acceptable salutation for both social and friendly letters is *Dear,* followed by the person's name: *Dear Carlos, Dear Bobby.* In a friendly letter to a person you know well, you may use your own favorite form of address: *Dear long-lost Friend.* The first word and all nouns in the salutation are capitalized, and a comma follows the salutation. The salutation is even with the left-hand margin of the letter and begins several spaces below the heading.

Body

The body of the letter is your message. When you write a letter by hand, you usually move, or *indent,* the first line of each new paragraph a few spaces to the right. Leave a space between the salutation and the body of the letter.

Closing

The closing is almost even with the left-hand margin of the heading. There are many acceptable closings for social letters, such as *Sincerely* or *Sincerely yours.* In a friendly letter to a person you know well, you may wish to use your own special closing. Only the first word of the closing is capitalized, and a comma always follows the closing. Leave a space between the body of the letter and the closing.

Signature

If you know your reader well, you may sign only your first name. Otherwise sign your first and last names below the closing. Even if you type your letter, you should always sign your name.

Writing Assignment I: *Writing a Friendly Letter*

A. Prewriting

1. Imagine that you are in one of the photographs on page 236, taking part in what is happening.

2. Think about what you are doing, who is in the scene with you, how things look, sound, feel, or smell, and how you react to your surroundings.

3. As you create the experience in the photograph, write several notes to be used in your letter.

Writing

B. Writing

Write a friendly letter to someone you know would enjoy hearing about your experience, telling him or her about it. Since your friend cannot actually see your experience, describe it in a vivid, interesting way, using details from your notes.

C. Postwriting

Read over your letter to make sure that:

1. The heading, salutation, body, closing, and signature are included and spaced correctly.

2. Your description is vivid enough to make your friend feel involved in your experience.

Use the checklist at the back of this book to proofread your letter. Make corrections neatly. Rewrite your letter if it is smudged or messy in any way.

Mailing Your Letter

On the same day that you mail your letter, the United States Post Office will also handle millions of other pieces of mail. To make processing this huge amount of mail easier, the Post

Office asks you to follow these guidelines in preparing and addressing envelopes for mailing:

1. Do not mail letters or cards that are less than 88.9 × 127 millimeters.
2. Put the street address, Post Office box number, or rural route number on the second line from the bottom. Write the city, state, and ZIP code on the bottom line.
3. If the address is an apartment building, put the number of the apartment directly after the street address on the second line.
4. Two-letter abbreviations for states have been approved by the U.S. Post Office. If you use these abbreviations, always use a ZIP code with them. Here is a list of the approved abbreviations:

Alabama **AL**	Montana **MT**	Wyoming **WY**
Alaska **AK**	Nebraska **NE**	Canal Zone **CZ**
Arizona **AZ**	Nevada **NV**	District of
Arkansas **AR**	New Hampshire	Columbia **DC**
California **CA**	**NH**	Guam **GU**
Colorado **CO**	New Jersey **NJ**	Puerto Rico **PR**
Connecticut **CT**	New Mexico **NM**	Virgin Islands **VI**
Delaware **DE**	New York **NY**	Alberta **AB**
Florida **FL**	North Carolina **NC**	British Columbia
Georgia **GA**	North Dakota **ND**	**BC**
Hawaii **HI**	Ohio **OH**	Manitoba **MB**
Idaho **ID**	Oklahoma **OK**	New Brunswick
Illinois **IL**	Oregon **OR**	**NB**
Indiana **IN**	Pennsylvania **PA**	Newfoundland **NF**
Iowa **IA**	Rhode Island **RI**	Northwest
Kansas **KS**	South Carolina **SC**	Territories **NT**
Kentucky **KY**	South Dakota **SD**	Nova Scotia **NS**
Louisiana **LA**	Tennessee **TN**	Ontario **ON**
Maine **ME**	Texas **TX**	Prince Edward
Maryland **MD**	Utah **UT**	Island **PE**
Massachusetts **MA**	Vermont **VT**	Quebec **PQ**
Michigan **MI**	Virginia **VA**	Saskatchewan **SK**
Minnesota **MN**	Washington **WA**	Yukon Territory
Mississippi **MS**	West Virginia **WV**	**YT**
Missouri **MO**	Wisconsin **WI**	Labrador **LB**

Writing

Model: Form for Addressing Envelopes

The sample envelope below follows U.S. Post Office guidelines and is the standard form for personal letters:

```
Susan McIntosh
19 Clairmont Drive
Gadsdon, AL 35901


                    Mr. Juan Garcia
                    35 Harlan Court, Apt. 304
                    Arvada, CO 80002
```

The *return address* is the name and address of the letter writer. Write your name on the top line, but do not use *Mr.* or *Ms.* before your name. Leave some space at the top and side of the envelope. The name and address of the receiver is just to the left and below the center of the envelope. Use a title such as *Mr., Ms., Dr.,* or *Professor* with this person's name.

Addresses on the envelope are punctuated and capitalized just as they are in the letter. These abbreviations are often used on envelopes:

R.R.	Rural Route	Blvd.	Boulevard
P.O.	Post Office	Hwy.	Highway
St.	Street	Apt.	Apartment
Dr.	Drive		

Folding Your Letter

If you are using 8½ × 11 inch paper and are putting the letter into a long envelope, fold your letter in this manner:

9 Writing Letters

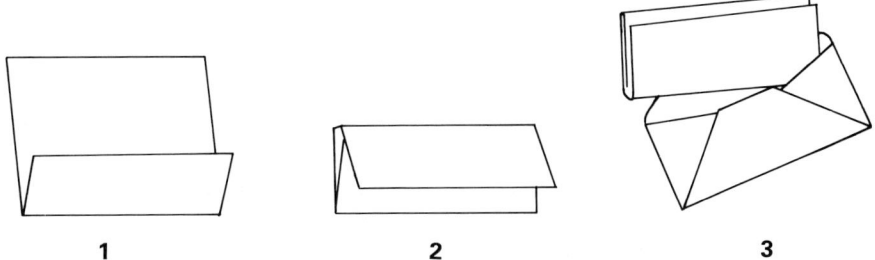

1. Fold the bottom of the paper one third of the way to the top. Make a crease.

2. Fold the top third of the page to within ¼ inch of the folded bottom. Make another crease.

3. Put the letter into the envelope with the open end up.

For a smaller envelope, fold your letter this way:

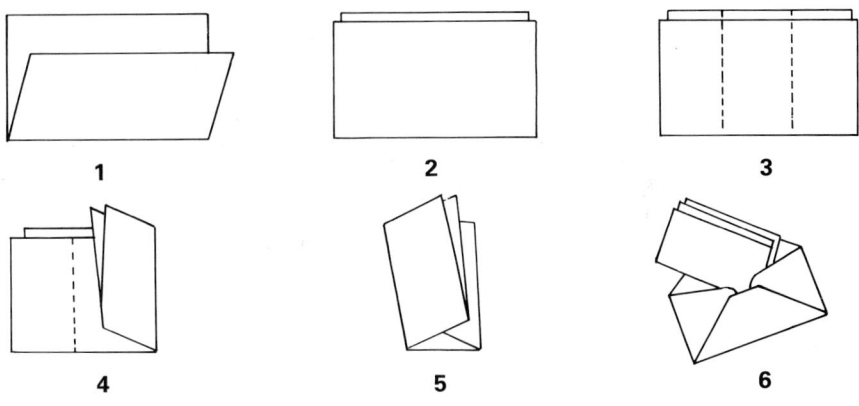

1 and 2. Bring the bottom half of the page to within ¼ inch of the top. Make a crease.

3 and 4. Fold the right third of the page toward the left side. Make a crease.

5. Fold the left third of the paper toward the right side. Make a crease.

6. Put the letter into the envelope with the open side up.

Writing

Writing Practice 3: *Addressing an Envelope*

For this writing practice use the name and address of a classmate as the receiver and your own name and address as the letter writer. On a sheet of paper, draw an outline of an envelope and then address the outline as you would an envelope to send to your classmate. Or, use a real envelope and address it to the person you wrote to in Writing Practice 2.

Writing Social Letters

Social letters and notes, which follow the same form as friendly letters, should be written on good quality, unlined paper in blue or black ink. A letter should be centered on the page, leaving an almost equal margin at the top, bottom, and sides. A short letter may be written on a note card. You should write in your very best handwriting, avoiding smudges, inkblots, and crossed-out words.

Writing Thank-You Letters

One kind of social letter is a *thank-you letter,* expressing your appreciation for a gift or special favor. A letter written to thank a host for an overnight or a longer visit is often called a *bread-and-butter letter.*

9 Writing Letters

Thank-you letters should be written as soon as possible after you have received a gift or returned from a visit. To make your letter seem more personal, mention specific reasons why you like the gift or enjoyed the visit. Write a bread-and-butter letter to the adults who were most responsible for your visit. For example, if the parents of your friend cooked your meals and drove you to the movies, write the letter to your friend's parents.

Model: A Thank-You Letter

> Route 1, Box 546
> Dallas, Texas 75247
> October 3, 19--
>
> Dear Mr. and Mrs. Fornelli,
>
> Thank you for an enjoyable weekend. I have missed Ralph and my friends very much since I moved away, and it was very kind of you to have me back to visit.
>
> Mr. Fornelli, thank you for taking Ralph and me to the model railroad exhibit. It's the biggest one I've seen, and I came back with some good ideas for my own layout. Thank you both for all that delicious food, especially the good Texas barbeque.
>
> I arrived home in plenty of time to see the television special you told me about, Mrs. Fornelli. I hope you enjoyed it as much as I did.
>
> Please tell Ralph that my parents and I look forward to seeing him here soon.
>
> Sincerely yours,
> Doug Mosel

Writing Practice 4: *Writing a Thank-You Letter*

Select one of the following situations or a situation of your own choice and write a thank-you letter. Make up any missing details.

1. You stayed at the home of an aunt or other relative while your parents were away for the weekend.
2. The parents of a classmate let you have an end-of-the-year party at their house. They also furnished paper plates, cups, and ice.
3. A relative or a friend of your parents sent you a gift of money for your birthday.

Writing Letters of Invitation

Another kind of social letter is a letter of invitation. Although printed invitation forms are widely used today, there may be times when you want to write a letter instead. If you invite a guest of honor, an older person, or a person who will have to make a great effort to attend, a letter shows special thoughtfulness.

A letter of invitation should have information about the occasion, the date, time, and place, and it should make the person being invited feel that you really want him or her to attend. In addition, you may need to include special information about directions to your house or apartment, activities that require special dress, and the guest of honor, if there is one.

9 Writing Letters

Model: A Letter of Invitation

> 2324 Wolski Drive
> Englewood, New Jersey 07631
> December 11, 19--
>
> Dear Shirley,
>
> Ever since Joyce moved, I've been trying to get her back to Englewood for a visit. I finally did it, and she will be at my house on Saturday, December 28.
>
> I am planning on having a group of last year's classmates over about 3:00 P.M. on that Saturday, and we wouldn't feel the group was complete without you. Would it be possible for you to come?
>
> If it snows enough before then, we can plan on a snowball fight, so be sure to wear old clothes.
>
> I look forward to seeing you on Saturday.
>
> Sincerely,
> Jenny Nickels

Writing Practice 5: *Writing a Letter of Invitation*

Select one of the following situations or make up one of your own and write a letter of invitation. Supply any missing details that you need to write the letter.

1. Your cat has just had eight kittens, and you are planning a party to try to give them away.

2. You have been given the job of cleaning the underbrush from a large field behind your parents' house. You plan a work party followed by a wiener roast.

3. Your parents are celebrating their twentieth wedding anniversary. You plan a small party to honor them.

4. You just learned how to make pizza in your home economics class. Your parents will furnish the ingredients, and you plan to have a party where your guests make the pizzas.

Writing an Answer

After you receive an invitation, a letter or note of response should be sent as soon as possible. If you accept, repeat the information about the time, date, and place to be certain it is correct. You should also express thanks for the invitation.

If you decline an invitation, do so courteously. Express your regret and, if possible, give specific reasons why you cannot attend. Look at the examples on page 245.

Writing Assignment II: *Writing in Response to an Invitation*

A. Prewriting

Exchange letters of invitation from Writing Practice 5 with a classmate. Decide whether or not you will accept or decline the invitation. As a class, brainstorm ways to courteously decline an invitation. Discuss also those points that are necessary to include when writing a letter to accept an invitation.

B. Writing

Write your letter of response. If you are accepting the invitation, express your thanks along with the information about the time, date, and place. If you are declining the invitation, express your regret courteously. Your teacher may want you to write two letters (one accepting, and one declining the invitation) to give you additional practice.

Model: Accepting or Declining an Invitation

C. Postwriting

As is true for any piece of writing that you are sharing with others, a social letter should represent your best effort. Revise your letter according to the appropriate points in the list below.

1. A thank-you letter mentions specific reasons for liking a gift or for appreciating a favor.

2. A thank-you letter sounds as though the writer is sincerely grateful for the gift or favor.

3. A bread-and-butter letter mentions specific reasons for having enjoyed a visit.

4. A letter of invitation includes the occasion, date, time, place, and any other special information guests might need, such as directions or the time of entertainment.

5. A letter of acceptance repeats the information about the occasion, date, time, and place.

6. A letter declining an invitation does so in a courteous way, giving, when possible, specific reasons for not being able to attend.

When you are satisfied with the content of your letter, proofread it for correctness, using the following Checklist for Proofreading Friendly and Social Letters.

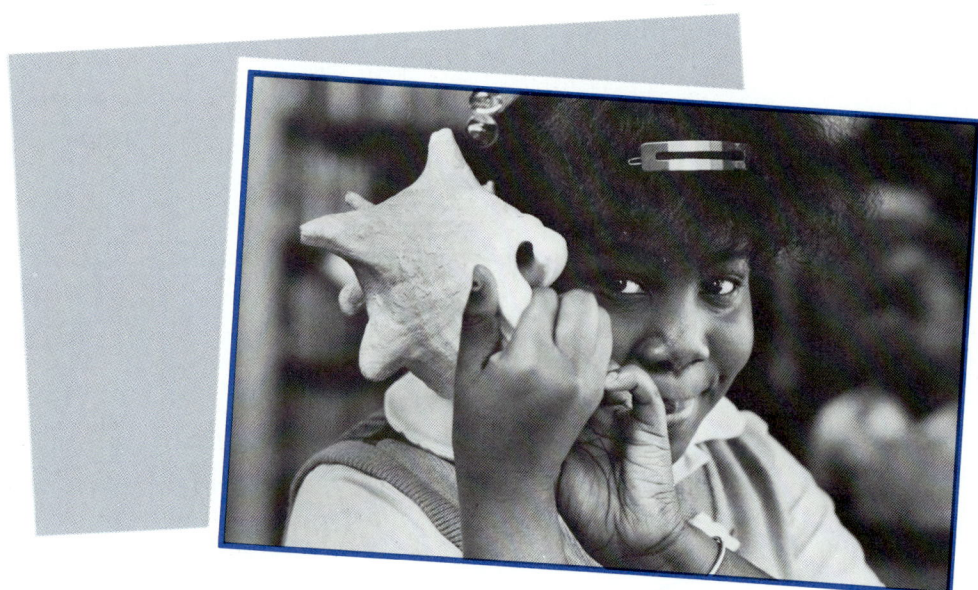

> ### *Checklist for Friendly and Social Letters*
>
> **Appearance and Form**
>
> 1. The letter is neatly written on unlined paper in blue or black ink.
> 2. The letter is centered on the page.
> 3. All parts of the letter have correct spacing.
> 4. The left-hand margin of the heading is even with the left-hand margin of the closing.
> 5. The left-hand margin of the salutation is even with the left-hand margin of the body of the letter.
>
> **Punctuation**
>
> 1. A comma comes between the city and state in the heading.
> 2. A comma comes between the day of the month and the year in the heading.
> 3. A comma follows the salutation.
> 4. A comma follows the closing.
>
> **Capitalization**
>
> 1. Names of streets, cities, and states in the heading are capitalized.
> 2. The month in the heading is capitalized.
> 3. The first word and all nouns in the salutation are capitalized.
> 4. The first word of the closing is capitalized.

Writing Business Letters

Business letters should be written on good quality, white, unlined paper of a standard size. If you type well, you may type business letters; otherwise, write them in your best handwriting. Center your letter on the page, leaving even spaces for margins around the letter. If the letter is too long for one page continue it on a second page.

Writing

Model: Form for Business Letters

Standard business letter form differs from that of friendly and social letters, as the model shows.

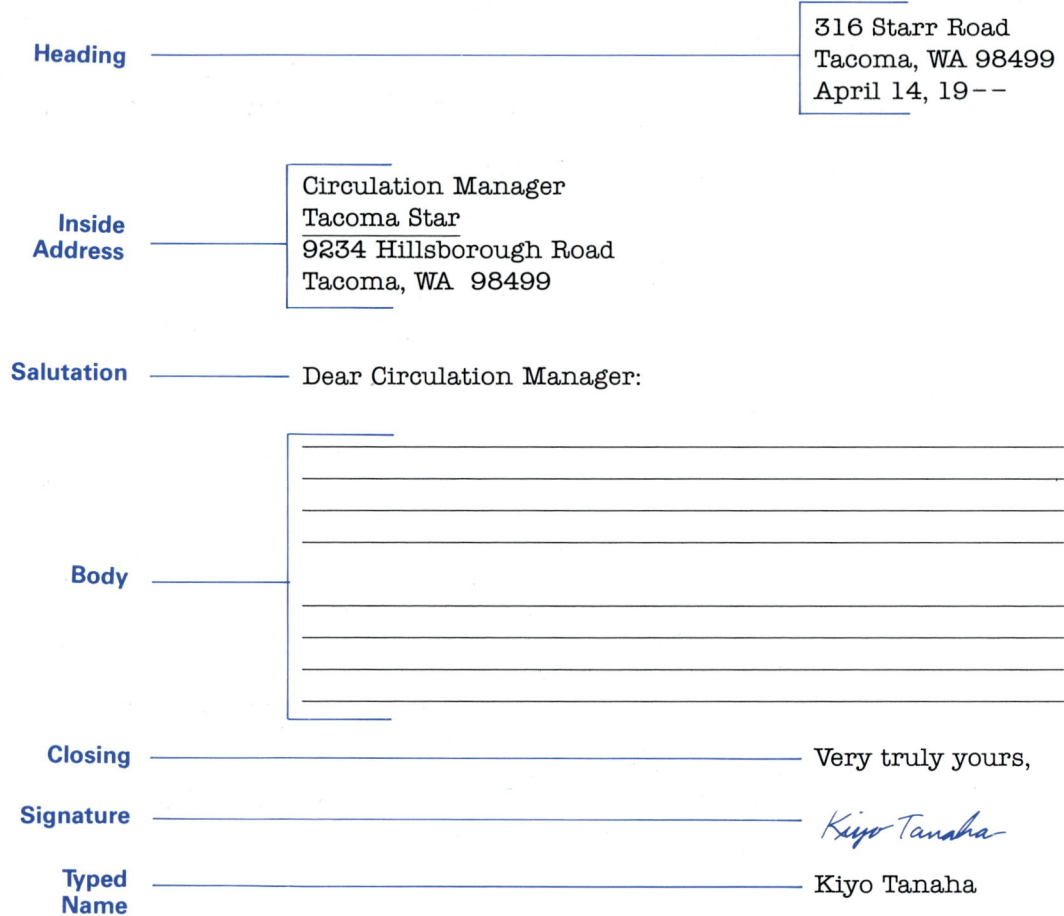

The differences between the parts of a business letter and those of a social or friendly letter are as follows.

Heading

The heading of a business letter is written in the same way as that of friendly and social letters.

Inside Address

The name and address of the person or company you are writing to make up the *inside address*. The person's name and title go on the top line. If you do not know the person's name, you may use a title or even a department: *Circulation Manager, Boys' Club Director, Advertising Department.* If the person's name and title are fairly short, you can put them both on one line: *Ms. Jane Freeman, Principal.* When the name and title would extend too far across the page, put the title on the second line:

> Mr. Luis Jiminez
> Television Advertising Director

The name and address of the company are on the next two or three lines.

Place a comma between a person's name and title, if these are on the same line, and between the city and state.

Salutation

Skip a space between the inside address and the salutation. The lefthand margins of the inside address and the salutation are even. When you know the name of the person you are writing to, the salutation is usually *Dear,* followed by the person's title and last name: *Dear Dr. Saito, Dear Ms. Fiddle.* If you do not know the person's name, the salutation presents a special problem because you do not know whether you are writing to a man or woman. In this case the traditional salutation is *Dear Sir or Madam,* but it is also acceptable to write *Dear,* followed by the person's title or by the name of the department or company: *Dear Bicycle Safety Director, Dear Advertising Department, Dear Star Motor Company.* The salutation of a business letter is always followed by a colon.

Body

The *body* of a business letter is your message. It should be brief, courteous, and to the point, and include all necessary information. Skip a space between the salutation and the body. The first line of each paragraph may be indented a few spaces to the right, depending on the style used.

Closing

Skip a space between the body and the closing of the letter. The left-hand margin of the closing is even with the left-hand margin of the heading. Acceptable closings are *Very truly yours,*

Writing

Yours truly, and *Sincerely yours.* Only the first word of the closing is capitalized, and a comma always follows the closing.

Signature

Even when you type a business letter, your name should be signed. If you type your letter, type your name four spaces below the closing and then sign your name in the space between.

Model: Block Style for a Business Letter

A particular style of business letter, called the *block style,* is most often used when letters are typed but is also acceptable for handwritten letters. The left-hand margin of all parts of this letter are even. Skip the same number of spaces between parts with this style as you do with the indented style but leave an extra space between paragraphs.

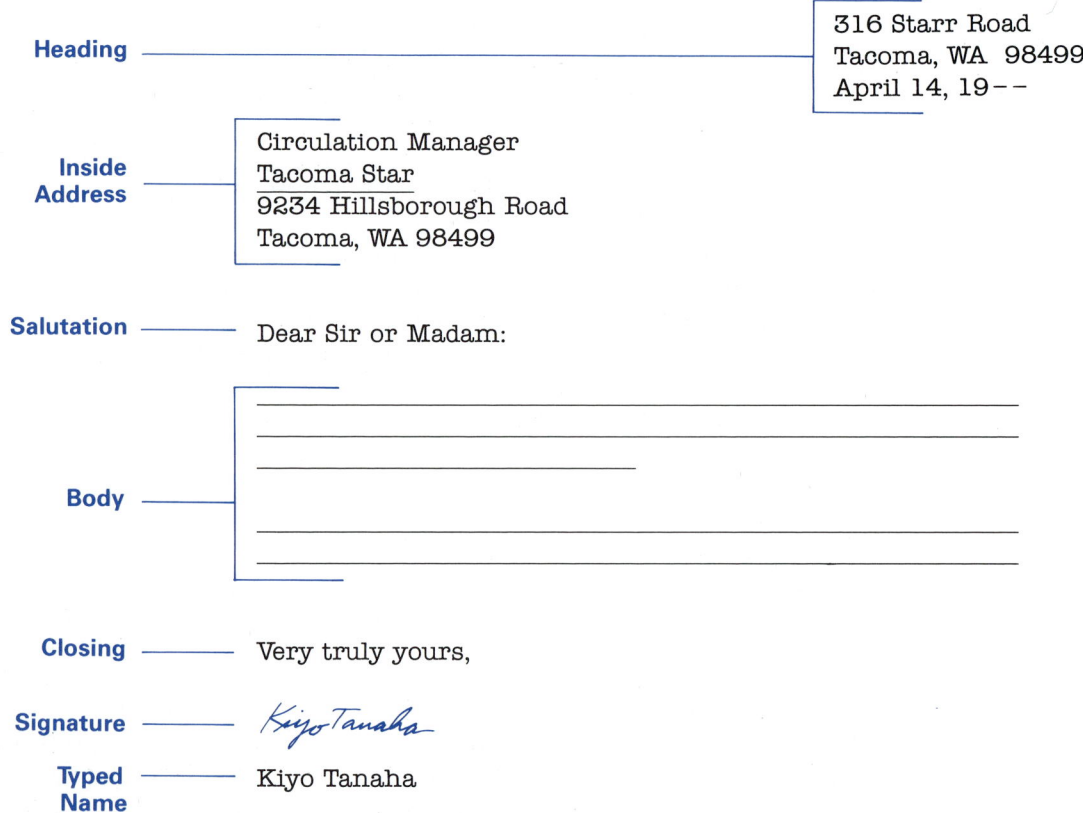

9 Writing Letters

Writing Practice 6: *Using Correct Form*

On a sheet of paper, set up the form for a business letter you might write in response to an ad in your local newspaper for delivery boys and girls. Address the letter to the circulation manager of your local newspaper. Include the heading, inside address, salutation, closing, and signature. Draw lines to represent the body of the letter. Use block or indented style.

Addressing Business Envelopes

Envelopes for business letters are addressed like those for friendly and social letters. Write your name and address in the upper left-hand corner of the envelope. Write the address on the envelope just as it appears inside the letter, beginning slightly below and to the left of the envelope center. Use a business size envelope for business letters and fold the letter according to the directions on page 239.

Writing Practice 7: *Addressing a Business Envelope*

On a piece of paper, draw an outline of a business envelope and address it as you would an envelope for the letter form you prepared for Writing Practice 6. Include your return address and name, as well as the name and address of the person or company you have written to. If necessary, use the sample envelope on page 238 as a guide.

Writing Letters of Application

When you decide that you want a job, one of your first steps may be to write a *letter of application*. The person to whom you write has probably never seen you before and will form an opinion about you from your letter. For this reason the appearance and content of your letter are very important.

The appearance of your letter includes such things as letter form, neatness, and correctness in spelling, punctuation, and grammar. The body of your application letter should include the following information.

1. Where or how you heard about the job
2. Personal data such as your age, grade in school, and grade average
3. Your qualifications for the job
4. Where and when you can be reached for an interview
5. The names and addresses of two or three people not related to you who know about your qualifications

Your qualifications for the job are reasons you think you would be a good employee and could include personal qualities such as willingness to work hard and previous experience in this and similar jobs. People who can tell about your qualifications are called *references* and may be your adult neighbors, teachers, school principal, minister, rabbi, and so on. As a courtesy, you should ask permission of your references before listing them.

9 Writing Letters

Model: *A Letter of Application*

In the following letter of application, notice how Frank includes details about his qualifications, his relationship to his references, and his availability for an interview.

16552 Polk Avenue
Memphis, TN 38116
March 14, 19--

Mr. Ronald Skyles, Director
Sav-a-Pet Shelter
1903 Lincoln Avenue
Memphis, TN 38116

Dear Mr. Skyles:

I saw your advertisement for someone to work with the animals after school on our community bulletin board. I would like to apply for the job.

I am fourteen years old and an eighth-grade student at Worth Junior High School. For the past two years my grade average has been B+. I have two dogs and a cat of my own and enjoy being around animals. Last summer I started my own pet-sitting service. I took care of my neighbors' dogs, cats, birds, and other pets for as long as two weeks at a time. This care included feeding, walking, and bathing them.

One of the neighbors I sat for is Mrs. Martha Gower, 12618 Polk Avenue, telephone 555-9058. Mrs. Gower says she will be happy to tell you about the good care I gave her dog. My school principal, Miss Marjorie Johnson, will tell you about my schoolwork. She can be reached at the school by calling 555-3093.

If you would like to talk with me, I am usually at home after four o'clock on weekday afternoons. My home telephone number is 555-1929.

Sincerely yours,
Frank Denowski

Writing

Writing Practice 8: *Writing a Letter of Application*

Look through the want ads of your local newspaper until you find an advertisement for a job you would like to have now or some time in the future. Then write a letter of application in response to that ad. If the job is one you want when you finish school, make up the qualifications you would like to have by then. Cut out the ad and attach it to your letter.

Writing Letters of Request

Another kind of business letter is the *letter of request*, which you write to ask for information, catalogues, or a special favor. For example, many government agencies and businesses often give away pamphlets and booklets with advice on saving energy, deciding on a career, or becoming a good baby-sitter. You may write a letter to an agency or business requesting a copy. You may also write to request information about a place your class plans to visit or to invite a speaker to your class.

When you write a letter of request, remember that you are asking for a favor, so be especially courteous. Remember to thank the person who will fill the request and include all information the agency or business will need to fill it. Be especially careful about writing letters of request to individuals. Many professional writers, for example, receive letters from students asking for help with reports. Respect an individual's right to privacy.

9 Writing Letters

Model: *A Letter of Request*

>1906 Ashland Avenue
>Chicago, IL 60648
>April 2, 19--

World Pen Pals
1694 Como Avenue
St. Paul, MS 55108

Dear World Pen Pals:

   I am interested in getting the name and address of a pen pal in a foreign country. I am fourteen years old and an eighth-grade student. My interests are reading, skiing, and going to baseball games.

   I am sending a stamped, self-addressed envelope for your reply. I am also sending a money order for one dollar, which is the fee for an individual listing.

   Thank you for your help. I look forward to hearing from you.

>Sincerely yours,
>*Michael Friedman*

   Michael's letter is a good example of giving all the necessary information. He has answered all the questions he anticipated the recipient might ask.

Writing Practice 9: *Writing a Letter of Request*

Think of a person that you would really like to have as a class speaker. Write a letter of request to that person, asking him or her to speak to your class. Be sure to explain why what he or she has to say is relevant to your studies, and suggest a good time for the visit.

255

Writing

Writing Order Letters

An *order letter* is a letter you write to order merchandise through the mail. The purpose in writing an order letter is to give the company the necessary information to fill your order correctly, such as where and when you saw the merchandise advertised, the size, color, price, number, and any special features.

In your letter include information about how you are paying for the merchandise. If you are sending money, write the amount and tell whether you are sending a check or money order.

Model: An Order Letter

```
                                        Route 1, Box 46
                                        Newport News, VA  23601
                                        May 5, 19--

Crunchy Cereal Company
302 2nd Avenue
New York, NY 10029

Dear Crunchy Cereal Company:

   On the back of your Fruit Chewies cereal box you
advertise a T-shirt with a picture on it for $3.95 plus
two box tops.

   I would like to order one T-shirt, blue, medium size,
with the picture I am enclosing on it. I am enclosing
a money order for $3.95 and two Fruit Chewies box
tops. As instructed in the advertisement, I will allow
up to six weeks for delivery.

                              Very truly yours,

                              Julie Curtis
```

9 Writing Letters

Writing Practice 10: *Writing an Order Letter*

Look through catalogues, magazines, and newspapers until you find an item you would like to have. Then write a letter to order it.

Writing Assignment III: *Writing a Business Letter*

A. Prewriting

1. Choose one of the situations below and write an appropriate business letter.

   a. In the local newspaper today is an ad from Jefferson's Department Store for a Countess II stereo tape cassette recorder and radio. The price has been reduced to $49.95 from the original price of $85.00. Sales tax must be added to the price. The store will accept a personal check or money order in payment. Write a letter to order the radio/recorder.

   b. You have heard that the position of Junior Counselor is available at Camp Winnewaka for six weeks during the summer. You have gone to the camp every summer since you were six years old, and your family camps out regularly. Write a letter of application, telling why you are interested in the job and how you are qualified for the position.

Writing

    c. Your family is planning a four-week tour of the west coast of the United States, and you want tour guide books from California, Oregon, and Washington. Write to your local automobile club requesting these books. If your parents are members of the automobile club, the books are free, but you must give their membership number when you write. If your parents are not members of the club, the price is $5.00 for each book plus a $2.00 mailing charge.

2. Make up any details you need to complete your letter.

B. Writing

Select a business letter style, and write the appropriate business letter.

C. Postwriting

1. Revise the letter, if necessary, to make sure that:

    a. The message is brief and to the point, but courteous.

    b. Letters of application include information about when and how the writer heard about the job and about his or her personal qualifications and references.

    c. Letters of request include information necessary to fill the request.

    d. Order letters include information about the item, such as quantity, color, price, and method of payment.

2. Use the following rules to check appearance and form:
   a. The letter is written neatly on unlined paper in blue or black ink with no smudges or crossed-out words.
   b. The letter is centered on the page.
   c. The parts of the letter have correct spacing between them.
   d. The left-hand margin of the heading is even with the left-hand margin of the closing.
   e. The left-hand margin of the inside address is even with the left-hand margin of the body of the letter.
   f. The left-hand margin of the salutation is even with the left-hand margin of the body of the letter.
   g. If block form is used, all left-hand margins are even.
3. Check for correct punctuation.
   a. A comma comes between the city and state in the heading and in the inside address.
   b. A comma comes between the day of the month and the year in the heading.
   c. A comma comes between the name of the person to whom you are writing and the person's title and department, if these are on the same line.
   d. A colon follows the salutation.
   e. A comma follows the closing.
4. Make sure you capitalize correctly.
   a. Capitalize names of streets, cities, and states in the heading.
   b. Capitalize the month in the heading.
   c. Capitalize the receiver's name and title.
   d. Capitalize the names of the department and company in the inside address.
   e. Capitalize street, city, and state names in the inside address.
   f. Capitalize the first word and all nouns found in the salutation.
   g. Capitalize the first word of the closing.

Sentence Combining:
Using to + verb

Combining with (To + Verb)

For more information on verbs, see pages 340-375.

The (*to* + *verb*) combination joins *to* plus a verb to the sentence base. The (*to* + *verb*) combination may be added to the beginning, the middle, or the end of the base sentence. Here are several examples of this connecting pattern:

Base Sentence: *Something* is every player's goal.
Insert: The players improve for each game. (*to* + *verb*)
Combined: *To improve for each game* is every player's goal.

Base Sentence: You are welcome (to do) *something*.
Insert: You clean my room for me. (*to* + *verb*)
Combined: You are welcome *to clean my room for me.*

Base Sentence: Kiyo likes *something.*
Insert: Kiyo sings solos in her church choir. (*to* + *verb*)
Combined: Kiyo likes *to sing solos in her church choir.*

When you use the (*to* + *verb*) pattern, it is sometimes necessary to change the form of the verb. For example, you would not say *to sings solos*, even though *sings* is the verb in the previous example. Instead, simply change *sings* to *sing* in order to make it work with *to: to sing.*

Exercise 1: *Using (to + verb) Signal*

On a clean sheet of paper numbered from 1–10, combine the following sentence sets by following the (*to* + *verb*) signal. Study the examples on the following page before you begin. The first five sets have the (*to* + *verb*) signal; the last five do not.

Sentence Combining

Examples

a. Nick needs (to do) *something*.
   He practices long hours every day. (*to + verb*)
   Nick needs to practice long hours every day.

b. Julia wants (to do) *something*.
   She bakes a birthday cake. (*to + verb*).
   Julia wants to bake a birthday cake.

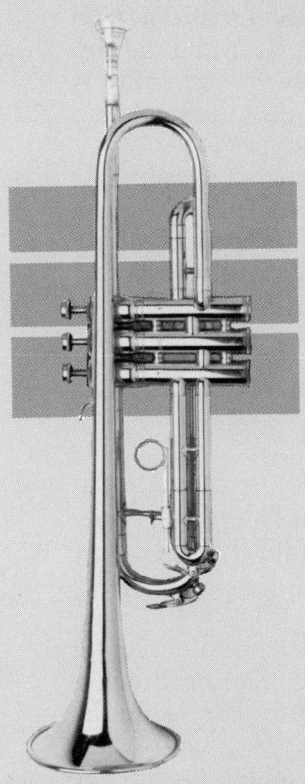

1. *Something* is his hope.
   He builds up his stamina. (*to + verb*)

2. Nick tries *something* on Sundays.
   He relaxes. (*to + verb*)

3. Nick always intends (to do) *something*.
   He does his homework on Sundays. (*to + verb*)

4. However, he usually manages (to do) *something*.
   He watches a game on television. (*to + verb*)

5. *Something* requires discipline, not television.
   He does homework. (*to + verb*)

6. Soon Nick has (to do) *something*.
   He makes a choice.

7. Do you believe for an instant that he would choose (to do) *something*?
   He turns off the television.

8. *Something* would be impossible for Nick!
   He leaves a game before it ends.

9. Nick's grandmother has learned (to do) *something*.
   She insists that he finish all of his schoolwork by Saturday evening.

10. That way, she doesn't have (to do) *something*.
    His grandmother nags at Nick.

Writing Practice: *Using Sentence Combining*

Teenagers often think and dream about what they would like to do or become when they are adults. Write a paragraph about your own dream or plan for your future. Give your ideas about how you can achieve your dream or plan and what you think the rewards will be when you reach your goal.

Use the sentence-combining skills you have learned.

10 Filling Out Forms

Forms are a simple and convenient way to gather information and to store facts and figures. For this reason they are often used by schools and businesses for ordering merchandise and for collecting information about job applicants, students, and other groups of people. The forms themselves vary greatly. A form can be a few lines asking for your name, address, and telephone number, or it can be several pages.

In school and out, you have probably had experience completing many forms. You may have used a form to register for a class, order a book, join a club, receive a refund, or apply for a summer job. In this chapter you will learn about reading and filling out forms that you are likely to encounter in your daily life.

Order Forms

Most order forms in newspapers and magazines are simple to read and complete. Usually they ask only for your name and address and require you to check or circle the item you wish to order.

Although these forms look simple, you should always read them thoroughly before completing and mailing them, a good habit that can save you problems later. For example, many clubs offering books at a discount require you to buy a certain number of books every year. A careful reading of the form will give you this information.

Model: Order Form

Most order forms label the separate spaces for your name, address, city, state, and ZIP code, as you can see in the following sample form. You should always type or print this information, since it is easier to read printing than handwriting. If the form asks for your signature, however, sign your name as you usually do.

Some order forms are postcards that you can detach and mail. Before mailing, check in the upper right-hand corner to see if it is prepaid or if you need to put a stamp on it. If the order form is to be cut out and put into an envelope, address the envelope as you would a business letter, using the mailing address given on the order form.

Order Forms

Whenever you find an asterisk (*) by a word or number in a form, look for a matching asterisk at the bottom or in the margin. In the order form on the following page, for example, an asterisk appears at the end of the second line. The asterisk after the $8.97 amount refers you to information at the bottom of the page marked with a second asterisk. There you learn that the price of the magazine subscription is higher if you live outside the United States. Always read the information marked with an asterisk, because often it tells you about restrictions or hidden costs.

Writing

Model: *Order Form with Asterisk*

```
Subscribe to NOW

15 Issues For Only $8.97*

 ✓   I'll subscribe to NOW for 30 Weeks
     (15 issues) at $8.97.

 ___ I'll subscribe to NOW for one year
     (26 issues) for $15.50.

 ✓   This is a new subscription.

 ___ This is a renewal.

 ✓   Payment enclosed (check or money order).

 ___ Bill me.

 GREGÓRIO DIAZ
 Name
      737 BELDEN
 Street
 EVANSTON        IL        60201
 City            State      ZIP

* Outside USA, send $13 for 15 issues,
  $22.50 for 26 issues
```

Writing Practice 1: *Filling Out an Order Form*

Find an order form in a newspaper or magazine. Cut out the form or copy it onto a sheet of paper and bring it to class. Then complete the form as though you were actually ordering the item.

Library Card Application

A *library card application* is a form designed to give the library information about each cardholder. The library staff keeps this information on file so that it can notify people of overdue books and let them know when books they have requested become available.

Model: Library Card Application

The following form, a sample library card application, is organized in three sections. The first section shows that the application is for a student card. The second section gives you information about filling out the card and states your responsibilities as a cardholder. The third section asks for information about who you are, where you live, and where you go to school.

Library Card Application   Wilton Public Library

STUDENT CARD

No._____ Expires_____

Complete this application in INK only. Do not write above this line. It is for library use.

I hereby agree to obey all the rules and regulations of the Wilton Public Library, to pay promptly all fines charged against me for late return, loss, or damage of library materials, and to give immediate notice of any change of name or address.

Mr. or (Ms)   *Powers*   *Jennifer*   *A.*
Circle One   Last Name   First Name   Middle Initial

1616 Artesian Bend   *555-8485*
Home Address   Home Phone

La Fayette School
School

Jennifer A. Powers
Signature

You should read an application all the way through before filling out any part of it. In many cases, as on the above application, the instructions are given at the beginning of the form. The instructions on the sample form tell you to fill out the form using ink, not pencil, and not to write above the top line. The spaces there, labeled *No.* and *Expires,* will be filled in by the librarian. Even when the instructions do not tell you to print, you should print anyway, except, of course, when you sign your name.

The second section of the sample application is a statement of your responsibilities as a library cardholder. Read this section carefully, noting that it instructs you to inform the library of any change of name or address.

Writing

The third section is divided into four lines. To fill out this application, first circle the appropriate form of address, *Mr.* or *Ms.* Then print your name, last name first, first name, and middle initial.

The second line asks for your home address. Fill in your complete address including your ZIP code. Next fill in your home telephone number.

On the third line print the name of your school. Because you are filling out a student card application, the library needs to know what school you attend.

On the *Signature* line write out your name as you usually sign it. Your signature indicates that you have read the form and agreed to everything printed on it and that the information you have filled in is correct.

Writing Practice 2: *Filling Out a Library Card Application*

Copy the library application form on page 265 onto a separate sheet of paper but do not copy the information about Jennifer Powers. Instead, fill in information about yourself or information that you make up.

Job Application Form

Most employers require you to fill out a job application form when you apply for work, giving written information about yourself that the employer uses in deciding whether or not to hire you. If no job is available when you apply, the employer may keep your application on file in order to call or write you when there is an opening.

Most companies make up their own application forms, so you may see a different form each time you apply for a job, but all of these forms request the same basic information. Usually, you will be asked to give information about six areas: (1) *Personal information* (who you are and where you live); (2) *Employment desired* (what position you want); (3) *Education* (what education you've had); (4) *Former employers* (what work experience you have had); (5) *References* (personal references you can supply); and (6) *Personal statement* (a statement of why you are a good candidate for the job).

On pages 268 and 270 are the front and back of a sample application form. As with all applications, you should read it thoroughly and be certain you understand how it is organized and how you should complete it. This application, like most other ones, has headings and labels written in shortened sentences. The following sections will give you step-by-step instructions for filling out this sample application and others like it.

Personal Information

Here, as on all applications, unless you are directed otherwise, print your answers in ink. Be careful to write the information on the lines indicated.

Social Security number. Either memorize your Social Security number or bring your Social Security card with you when you fill out a job application.

Name. Fill in your name in the order specified.

Address. Fill in your complete address, including ZIP code.

For information on punctuating addresses, see pages 541-542.

Name of parents or guardians. Guardians means the adults responsible for you, if you do not live with your parents.

Phone number. Fill in your home telephone number, including the area code.

Date of birth. Fill in your date of birth, either using numbers or writing out the month: *9/23/70 (September 23, 1970).*

Citizen of the U.S. Indicate with a *yes* or *no* whether or not you are a citizen of the United States.

Writing

Model: Job Application Form (Front)

```
APPLICATION FOR EMPLOYMENT                    THE HERALD NEWS, INC.

PERSONAL INFORMATION
                                              341-67-8379
                                              Social Security Number

Name    CAMPION        MELISSA          JANE
        Last           First            Middle

Address 649 ASBURY     AUSTIN      TX   78767
        Street         City        State ZIP Code

        MR. AND MRS. JOSEPH CAMPION    555-1992
        Name of parents or guardians   Phone number

        OCTOBER 3, 1971                YES
        Date of birth                  Citizen of U.S. (yes or no)


        If related to anyone in our employ,    Referred by
        state name and department.

EMPLOYMENT DESIRED

        NEWSPAPER DELIVERY             JUNE 15, 19--
        Position                       Date you can start

        YES                            YES
        Are you employed now?          If so, may we inquire of your present employer?

        NO
        Ever applied to this company before?   Where and when


  EDUCATION    | Name and Location of School        | Years Attended
  Elementary   | SAM HOUSTON GRAMMAR SCHOOL         | 1976-1984
  School       | 121 CENTRAL ST., AUSTIN, TX 78765  |
  High School  |                                    |
```

If related to anyone in our employ, state name and department. If you have a relative working for the company to which you are applying, give the relative's name and the department where he or she works. If you are not related to anyone at the company, leave this space blank. Some job application forms request that you leave no blank spaces. In that case, put *N/A* (not applicable) in the space provided. Then the reader of the form knows that you did not accidentally leave a blank space.

Referred by. Provide the name of the person who referred you to the job.

Employment Desired

Write your answers on the lines as indicated.

Position. Fill in the position, or job, for which you are applying.

Date you can start. Fill in the first day you can begin work.

Are you employed now? Print *yes* or *no.* Do not write in the name or address of your present employer.

If so, may we inquire of your present employer? Print *yes* if you have told your present employer that you are looking for another job and do not mind if the company calls him or her. Print *no* if for any reason you do not want the company to call your present employer.

Ever applied to this company before? Print *yes* or *no.*

Where and when. If the answer to the previous question is *yes,* tell where you applied (some companies have more than one office) and give the date.

Education

Pay special attention to the place where you write your answers in this section. The labels *Elementary School* and *High School* indicate where the information belongs. Write the information on the blanks to the right of the labels.

Name and location of school. The first line is for the name of your elementary school, and the second line is for the address. If you have attended more than one elementary school, list in chronological order all the schools you have attended. (If there is not enough room on the application you may put this information on a separate sheet of paper and write "see attached sheet" in the space on the form.) If you attend a junior high or middle school, list it last.

Former Employers

The instructions in this section say to list three employers, beginning with the most recent one. If you have not worked for

Writing

Model: Job Application Form (Back)

FORMER EMPLOYERS				
(List below your last three employers, starting with last one first)				
Date Month and Year	Name and Address of Employer	Salary	Position	Reason for Leaving
From SEPT. 1984 To PRESENT	ELMER'S FOODS 1920 WEST ROAD AUSTIN, TX 78763	$4.00 per hr.	STOCK PERSON	WANT REGULAR HOURS
From JUNE 1984 To SEPT. 1984	WILCOX FACTORY OLD RIDGE RD. AUSTIN, TX 78765	$3.75 per hr.	WINDOW WASHER	RETURNED TO SCHOOL
From JUNE 1983 To SEPT. 1983	SELF-EMPLOYED	$3.00 per hr.	BABY-SITTER	RETURNED TO SCHOOL

REFERENCES

(Give below the names of three persons not related to you, whom you have known at least one year)

NAME	ADDRESS	OCCUPATION	YEARS ACQUAINTED
1. MR. JAMES WONG,	121 Central St. Austin, TX 78765	PRINCIPAL Sam Houston Grammar School	3 YRS.
2. DR. MARIA NORIEGA,	Plaza Center, Suite 1010 Austin, TX 78760	DOCTOR,	5 YRS.
3. FATHER DANIEL COOPER,	4120 ALAMEDA, AUSTIN, TX 78763	PRIEST	4 YRS.

PERSONAL STATEMENT

(In the space below, please state why you are a good candidate for this job.)

I am a responsible, self-reliant worker. This summer I want a job with regular hours that will let me be outside. Newspaper delivery is perfect for this, and I am very enthusiastic about the job.

Melissa Jane Campion   6-15-88
Signature   Date

DO NOT WRITE BELOW THIS LINE

Interview by   Date
REMARKS: ―――――――――――――――――――

Neatness   Experience
Personality   Ability

---

three separate employers, list the one or two for whom you have worked. If you have worked at a job where you had many employers (a lawn cutter or baby-sitter, for example), write *self-employed*.

Date. In the space labeled *From*, enter the month and year you began working for this employer. In the space labeled *To*,

write the month and year you left that job. If you are still employed, write *Present* in this space, meaning "Employed at the present time."

Name and address. Write the name and address of your employer in the column opposite the date, being certain to keep your entries about each employer in the correct left-to-right columns.

Salary. Enter the salary you earned from each employer. You may give an hourly salary (*per hour*) or a weekly or monthly salary (*per week* or *per month*), but indicate which one it is on the form.

Position. In the space opposite the salary column, write in your duties for that employer.

Reason for leaving. Your reason for leaving a job can be stated briefly. If it was a summer job, the answer will most likely be, "Returned to school." Another possible reason for leaving is shown on the sample application: "Want regular hours." This means that the applicant wants to leave his or her present job because the hours are not regular.

References

References are people the employer can ask for information about you: your habits, your character, and your ability. The instructions say to give the names of three persons not related to you whom you have known at least one year. Give the names of adults—teachers, ministers, doctors, neighbors whom you have known at least one year.

Decide in advance whom you would like to list as references and ask those people for permission to list them. Never include someone as a reference without obtaining permission first. In the spaces indicated enter the name, address, and occupation of your reference and the number of years you have known him or her.

Personal Statement

The instructions tell you to state why you would be good at the job for which you are applying. Your personal statement should be clear and to the point, telling about yourself and your work habits and saying why this particular job interests you. Print rather than write, do not cross out any words, and be neat. Writing your answer first on a piece of scratch paper before writing on the application form is a good idea.

Signature. Always write out your name in a signature; never print it. By signing your name to the application, you are affirming that everything you have written on the application is true.

Date. Enter today's date opposite your signature.

On the line below your signature, you will see the instruction DO NOT WRITE BELOW THIS LINE. That space is for use by the employer and the person who will interview you. Leave it blank.

Preparing for a Job Application

Much of the information you enter on a job application is simple: your name, address, telephone number, name of school, and date of birth. However, you are often asked for information that you probably have not memorized. For this reason you should make up a sheet of information to take with you when you apply for a job. You may put this information in any order you wish, but you should include the following items.

1. Your Social Security number
2. The addresses of the schools you have attended
3. The years you attended each school
4. The names and addresses of any former employers
5. The dates of each job
6. The salary you received at each job
7. The names, addresses, and occupations of three references whom you have permission to include

10 Filling Out Forms

Writing Practice 3: *Preparing for a Job Application*

On a separate sheet of paper, make a list of all the information you will need to take with you for a job application. Title your sheet *Job Application Information* and include information about each of the seven items listed above. If you do not want to write about yourself, make up information about a fictitious person.

Preparing for a Job Interview

Most employers *interview,* or talk in person with job applicants. During such interviews you will be asked questions about your interests, work experience, and skills. Your answers will help others decide if you can handle the job. The following hints will help you during the job interview.

1. Pay attention to how you look. Dress simply and neatly. Be sure your hair is clean and carefully combed.

2. Be polite. Address the person to whom you are talking as *Mr., Miss, Ms.,* or *Mrs.* Speak clearly and distinctly. An interviewer may not want to hire someone who mumbles or seems very shy.

3. Assume a responsible and mature attitude. Avoid slang. Sit or stand with good posture, and be alert and interested in the job.

4. Answer questions completely, avoiding "yes" or "no," but do not talk too much.

5. Be honest and fair about your answers; make direct eye contact with the interviewer.

6. Do not criticize a former employer.

7. Be ready to leave when the interviewer cues you that the interview is at an end.

8. As the interview concludes, ask when you will be notified about the job, thank the interviewer for the time and consideration given to you, and shake hands with the interviewer.

You can also prepare for an interview by anticipating the questions an employer might ask. Following are some questions you should be prepared to answer.

1. Why are you interested in this particular job?

2. What kind of grades do you get in school? Will this job interfere with your studies?

3. How will you travel to and from work? Will you be dependent on someone else for transportation?
4. Have you discussed this job with your parents? How do they feel about your working?
5. Do you have any illness or allergies that would keep you from performing the job reliably? Have you been seriously ill in the past year?
6. What are your plans for the future? Do you hope to attend college or vocational school?
7. What is your previous work experience? What tasks did you perform on these jobs? Would they hire you again?
8. Would you be able to work extra hours?
9. What are your favorite (or least favorite) courses in school?
10. Can you handle instructions and criticism of your work well?
11. What school activities are you involved in? Will these interfere with your work?

The interviewer will probably ask if you have any questions, so think about what you would like to know about the job. For example, you should want to know what your hours would be, how much you would earn, and when you would be paid. If you must wear a uniform, would you be asked to buy it, or would the company supply it? Asking questions shows that you have a real interest in the job.

Writing Practice 4: *Preparing for a Job Interview*

The following are questions that interviewers often ask. First think of a job you would like and imagine that you are interviewing for that job. Then, on a sheet of paper write the answers you might give to the questions. If your teacher prefers, answer the questions aloud in class as you would in an actual interview.

1. Why are you interested in this particular job?
2. Why do you think you are qualified for this job?
3. What are your plans for the future? Have you given any thought to what you want to do as an adult and how this job might relate to that?

Writing Assignment I: *Applying for a Social Security Number*

You must have a Social Security number before you can be employed by a company. If you do not have a Social Security number, go to the Social Security office in your area and apply for one.

A. Prewriting

1. Get a copy of your birth certificate and some other proof of identification, such as a library card or student identification card, to take with you to the Social Security office.
2. Pick up the application form at the Social Security office and read it carefully all the way through.

B. Writing

Apply for a Social Security number by filling out the application form and showing your proofs of identification when the clerk asks for them.

C. Postwriting

Check over the form to make sure all information on it is correct and legible. Your Social Security card with your number on it will arrive in the mail in about four to six weeks.

Sentence Combining:
Placement and Choices

One of the advantages of sentence combining is that it helps you find many ways to say something. You also learn to choose the best possible way to say it. So far you have developed the following sentence-combining skills.

1. Adding new ideas to sentences
2. Moving parts of sentences so that you express what you want to say effectively
3. Taking out unnecessary words to make sentences clear

The remaining exercises in this chapter will help you practice writing for variety. Because the signals will become fewer, you can develop the skill of choosing the best ways to combine ideas.

Placing Sentence Parts for Variety

For more information on using commas, see pages 538-546.

Parts of sentences can be placed at the beginning, the middle, or the end of a sentence base. (Use commas to set off the inserted parts of the combined sentence.) Where you place words or groups of words may affect the meaning of the complete sentence, or the emphasis of the sentence may be changed. Notice the italicized parts of the following sentences:

The race car driver, *startled and alarmed,* pulled to the side of the track.

The race car driver pulled to the side of the track, *startled and alarmed.*

Startled and alarmed, the race car driver pulled to the side of the track.

Each of these sentences is acceptable and makes sense, but the last sentence emphasizes the *feeling* the driver experienced, by placing the words *startled and alarmed* at the beginning. The second sentence emphasizes *what* the driver did and then describes the feeling. What is the effect of the first sentence, where the driver's feeling is described in the middle?

Exercise 1: *Placing Sentence Parts for Variety*

For sets 1–5, place the *italicized* part of the insert sentence at the beginning, middle, or end of the sentence base. For sets 6–10, decide which parts to use, and where they go. Use commas where needed. Study the example before you begin.

Example

a. The woman jumped from the burning building.
She was *knowing she had no other choice*.

Knowing she had no other choice, the woman jumped from the burning building.

1. Tom, the Terrific Talent, sat for a moment with his head in his hands.
He was *recognizing that he had nearly crashed into the wall*.

2. He vowed to leave the dangerous sport of racing forever.
His heart was *beating fast and hard inside his chest*.

3. His wife Happy was delighted with her husband's final decision.
His wife was *relieved that Tom had not been hurt*.

4. Tom and Happy walked off the track together.
They were *surprising both the crowd of admirers and the reporters who were present*.

5. They didn't even look back at the disabled race car.
They were holding hands and planning a new future together.

6. The twins spotted abalone on a shelf twenty feet below.
   They were jumping off the back of the boat.
   The abalone was slightly camouflaged by rocks and weeds.

7. The shellfish taunted the snorkelers above them.
   The shellfish were clustered in great numbers.
   The shellfish were just waiting to be gathered up.

8. The twins tried again and again to dive the twenty-five feet between the surface and the shelf.
   They were wishing they had brought scuba gear.
   They dived without success.

9. The children finally gave up the quest.
   They were splashing and struggling to no avail.
   They were resting on the water's surface to catch their breath.

10. There was no way that they could overcome the buoyancy of the water.
    They were without a weight belt.
    It was a fact they would remember the next time.

Making Choices for Combining

To make a good choice in combining a set of sentences, you need to decide the most important thing the sentence has to say. That statement will be your sentence base. Then it is a simple matter of adding other ideas to that sentence base. Look at the variety that is possible in combining the following three statements:

An old ceramic container sat by the barn door now.

The container now served as a catchall for kites, children's sand shovels, and a broken umbrella.

It had always held delicious, fresh milk when Gramps had been a small boy.

Combination 1: An old ceramic container, which had always held delicious, fresh milk when Gramps had been a small boy, sat by the barn door now, serving as a catchall for kites, children's sand shovels, and a broken umbrella.

Combination 2: Serving now as a catchall for kites, children's sand shovels, and a broken umbrella, an old ceramic container sat by the barn door now; it had always held delicious, fresh milk when Gramps had been a small boy.

Combination 3: An old ceramic container sat by the barn door now and served as a catchall for kites, children's sand shovels, and a broken umbrella; but when Gramps had been a small boy, it had always held delicious, fresh milk.

Which of the three combinations do you prefer? Why? In what other ways can you combine these sentences?

Exercise 2: Making Choices for Combining

For more information on using commas, see pages 538-546.

Combine each set of sentences in this exercise in at least two ways by adding to the front, middle, or end of the base sentence, using commas wherever they are needed. Since no signals are given, use any of the sentence-combining skills you have learned. Write the new combined sentences on a sheet of paper. Study the example before you begin.

Example

a. Lenny strode into the garage.
   He was looking as if nothing were wrong.
   The group was waiting to begin the rehearsal.
   They were waiting somewhat impatiently.

   Looking as if nothing were wrong, Lenny strode into the garage where the group was waiting somewhat impatiently to begin the rehearsal.

   or

   The group was waiting somewhat impatiently to begin the rehearsal as Lenny strode into the garage, looking as if nothing were wrong.

1. Inside, Rosemary had taken her place.
   She was at the rear.
   She was holding her big bass ready.
   She was tilting her head a little.
   She tuned the instrument.

2. Carlo checked his drums.
   He was making minor adjustments.
   He was beating a nervous tattoo with the sticks.
   He showed his impatience.

3. Ken flipped pages of music.
   Ken was at the piano.
   He was to find the first piece.
   It was a popular one.
   It was sure to please the partygoers that evening.

4. Lenny was taking his guitar out of its case.
   He was slipping his head through the strap.
   He was adjusting it over his shoulder.
   Lenny signaled with his head.
   He was ready to start.
   He set the beat with his foot.
   The rehearsal began.

5. The players lost themselves.
   It was in the sounds of their music.
   Lenny's tardiness was forgotten.

Writing Practice: *Using Sentence Combining Skills*

Select one of the topics on the next page or make up one of your own and write a short composition. As you write, use the sentence-combining skills you have learned in this textbook:

Writing

Combining with connectors such as *since, on the other hand, however, furthermore, but, yet,* and *and*

Combining with (*which/that*), (*who*), (*whose*)

Combining with (*pos*) and (*ing*)

Combining with (*that*) and (*join*)

Combining with (*with*)

Combining with (*to* + *verb*)

Liken or Contrast

1. Two games you enjoy
2. Two friends you know well
3. Two stores you have shopped in
4. Two stories you have read
5. Two schools you have attended
6. Two of your favorite foods
7. Two kinds of pets
8. Two part-time jobs you have had
9. Yourself and another person
10. School today and school in the year 2500

2
Grammar and Usage

11 Nouns

Understanding Nouns

In the place where you are sitting, you should be able to name more than a dozen things. If you are in a classroom, you can probably also name most of the students. Words that name are called *nouns*.

You can learn to identify nouns in three ways: by definition, by class, and by features that distinguish them from other parts of speech.

Defining Nouns

A noun is usually defined as the name of a person, place, thing, or idea.

Marie Curie discovered radium.	[name of a person]
She was born in *Poland*.	[name of a place]
In 1903 she and her husband won the *Nobel Prize* in physics.	[name of a thing]
They had discovered the *truth* about an unknown element.	[name of an idea]

Exercise 1: Identifying Nouns

Write the sentences on the following page and underline all the nouns. Above each noun write whether it names a person, a place, a thing, or an idea.

Examples

a. Andrés Segovia played his guitar at the White House.

                person   thing   place
Andrés Segovia played his guitar at the White House.

  b. More people speak Chinese than any other language.
       person   thing   thing
  More people speak Chinese than any other language.

1. The long-eared bat sleeps in a cave.
2. Nora was elected president of her class.
3. The article discussed the dangers of skateboarding.
4. Have you seen the underground caves in Kentucky?
5. Julio wrote an editorial about equality of the sexes.
6. Scientists are studying the use of earthworms for food.
7. Patty and Mildred Hill, two sisters, wrote the famous song "Happy Birthday to You."
8. Huck Finn sailed a raft down the Mississippi River.
9. A magic kiss woke Sleeping Beauty from her long nap.
10. Chief Joseph spoke eloquently of his hope for peace.

Grouping Nouns by Classes

Nouns may be divided into four classes: *concrete*, *abstract*, *common*, and *proper*.

Concrete nouns name what you can see or touch.

People, places, and things are usually concrete nouns.

    The new *city hall* was built in 1978.

    My *aunt* planted a *tree* in the *yard*.

Abstract nouns name ideas and feelings that cannot be seen or touched.

    The *design* of the house was modern.

    The puppy brought *happiness* to my sister.

Exercise 2: Identifying Concrete and Abstract Nouns

Write the following sentences and underline the nouns. Write *C* above each concrete noun and *A* above each abstract noun.

Examples

a. The broken window was caused by childishness.

                C   A

The broken <u>window</u> was caused by <u>childishness</u>.

b. Her face was red with anger.

     C   A

Her <u>face</u> was red with <u>anger</u>.

1. This lawn is the pride of the neighborhood.
2. The safety of the passengers is the concern of the pilot.
3. The library has several books about justice that you can read.
4. My cousins and my brother help me rake the yard.
5. Freedom and equality are important values in the country we live in.
6. Our cat is not very good at obeying rules.
7. Most flowers add a sweet aroma to a room.
8. The success of our team lies in the strategy we use.
9. A dark room usually fills me with fear.
10. I always check my homework with my calculator.

Proper nouns name specific persons, places, things, or ideas. All other nouns are called *common nouns.*

The *catcher* hit a home run.

Catcher is a common noun because it does not name a specific person.

Johnny Bench hit a home run.

Johnny Bench is a proper noun because it names a specific person. Proper nouns are always capitalized; common nouns are not.

The *golfer* hit a birdie on the seventh hole.	[common noun]
Nancy Lopez won the Women's Open.	[proper noun]
She is looking for a *book* about the Civil War.	[common noun]
Jeff is reading *The Red Badge of Courage*.	[proper noun]
We plan to visit several *states*.	[common noun]
Everglades National Park is in southern *Florida*.	[proper noun]

Many proper nouns and some common nouns are *compound nouns* because they are made up of more than one word.

Compound proper nouns may be closed (spelled as one word), open (spelled as two separate words), or hyphenated.

The Red Badge of Courage	[one book]
Kansas City, Missouri	[one place]
George Washington Carver	[one person]

Compound common nouns may be closed (spelled as one word), open (spelled as two separate words), or hyphenated.

Closed: airport, earthquake, newspaper

Open: home run, post office, sea otter

Hyphenated: boy-king, cave-in, self-control

Exercise 3: Identifying Proper Nouns

Write the sentences on the following page, capitalizing each proper noun. Underline the nouns you capitalize.

Example

a. Dr. janice yin is a surgeon at walter reed hospital.
Dr. <u>Janice Yin</u> is a surgeon at <u>Walter Reed Hospital</u>.

Grammar and Usage

1. My favorite record is the one I just bought, chuck mangione's "the children of sanchez."
2. This summer willie bunch is working as a reporter for a weekly newspaper in ada, oklahoma.
3. When it is 7 o'clock in carson city, nevada, it is 10 o'clock in new hampshire.
4. The first atomic reactor was built under stagg field at the university of chicago.
5. When you ride up the major deegan expressway in the bronx, you get a good view of yankee stadium.
6. In the *odyssey* by homer, the hero odysseus blinds a one-eyed monster named polyphemus in order to escape from the monster's cave.
7. The nineteenth amendment, which gave women the right to vote, was ratified in 1920 and added to the united states constitution.
8. From the top of the eiffel tower in paris, one can see notre dame cathedral, the louvre, and the winding seine river.
9. Drama students at eleanor roosevelt junior high school are presenting *the wiz*, an adaptation of *the wizard of oz*.
10. For more than eleven years joe louis successfully defended his title as world heavyweight champion.

Finding Nouns by Their Features

The following four features can help you identify nouns. Most nouns have at least one of these features, and some nouns will have all four.

Nouns often follow *determiners*.

The most common determiners are *a*, *an*, and *the*, which are also called *articles*. Other common determiners include these:

my	his	their	this	some
our	her	these	that	many
its	your	those	each	one, two, three, *etc.*

Determiners can show ownership (*my* bicycle), tell how many (*three* bicycles), or point to a particular noun in a sentence (*this* bicycle).

Modifiers often come between the determiner and the noun.

"The Raven" is my *favorite* poem.

Our *old* house has been sold.

Nouns may be either *singular* or *plural*.

Many nouns have both a singular and plural form. The plural form is used for nouns that name more than one person, place, thing, or idea.

Singular	Plural
one ring	two rings
one toe	several toes
one bus	six buses
one crutch	two crutches

Nouns may show ownership or relationship.

Both singular and plural nouns have possessive forms that show ownership or relationship. The possessive form is shown with an apostrophe (') and -s or with an apostrophe (') only.

The camera belonging to Harry is old. *Harry's* camera is old.	[ownership]
The horn of the car was broken again. The *car's* horn was broken again.	[relationship]

Nouns may be formed with a noun suffix such as *-ation*, *-ism*, *-ment*, *-ness*, and *-ance*.

A *noun suffix* is a special ending that makes a word a noun. For example, *tender* becomes the noun *tenderness* when the

Grammar and Usage

noun suffix *-ness* is added. The endings of many words may give helpful clues that they are nouns.

organize + -ation = organization

national + -ism = nationalism

resent + -ment = resentment

Exercise 4: Identifying Nouns by Their Features

Use what you have learned about noun features to identify at least ten of the twenty-five nouns in the following paragraph. Write the paragraph and underline each noun you identify. The first one is done for you. (Your teacher may ask you which features you used to identify the nouns.)

The <u>Tomikos</u> and their neighbors planted a garden together. Mr. Tomiko cleared the land, and the remaining members of the two families planted the vegetables. After many hours of hard work, Mr. Tomiko's son-in-law strung a fence around the garden's boundaries to protect it from the rabbits. (They can really be a nuisance with their appetite for vegetables.) With this threat eliminated, the natural nourishment of the sun and rain took over and helped to provide the families with groceries.

Review: Understanding Nouns

Write sentences 1-20 and underline each noun. Your teacher may ask you how you identified each noun. Did you decide that it named a person, a place, a thing, or an idea? That it fit into one of the noun classes? That it had one or more noun features?

Example

a. On Sheridan Street the potholes look like craters on the moon.
   On <u>Sheridan Street</u> the <u>potholes</u> look like <u>craters</u> on the <u>moon</u>.

1. Richard Wagner wrote many operas based on German mythology.

2. A newborn hippopotamus weighs sixty to one hundred pounds, and older hippos weigh two or three tons.

3. Carefully Sheila climbed to the last step on the ladder to pick three grapefruits at the top of the tree.

4. Gwendolyn Brooks, a poet from Chicago, won the Pulitzer Prize for *Annie Allen*, her second book of poetry.

5. Even a self-propelled lawn mower is hard to use when the grass is this tall.

6. Toshiko Akiyoshi, a composer, wrote a song called "Tuning Up," which bands often play as their first number.

7. Last July my parents and my two uncles visited the Texas Cowboy Reunion and Rodeo in Stamford, Texas.

8. Though the ancient Greeks believed that thunder was caused by angry gods, scientists tell us that the great noise is caused when air heated by lightning expands violently.

9. In his delicatessen Nikos Kalymira sells figs, bread, olives, and the best sandwiches on Ninth Avenue.

10. Whenever the telephone rings, Ken races to answer it as if he were chasing the last out in the World Series.

11. Nicole complains that she never gets any mail, but her stack of unanswered letters keeps getting higher.

12. In some places birds tied to long ropes dive into water to catch fish for their owners.

13. Tom Sawyer, an amateur psychologist, tricked his friends into doing a job he hated.

14. Maria Teresa is saving her money to visit South American relatives, who have promised her a trip to Machu Picchu, the ancient city of the Incas high in the Andes Mountains.

15. Both Mario and Anna have earned their Senior Lifesaving Certificates from the American Red Cross.

16. The first toboggans were built by native Americans, who used runnerless sleds to carry game and other heavy objects over the snow.

17. Sojourner Truth, a former slave, traveled throughout New England and the Midwest, speaking against slavery.

18. The first compasses, invented by the Chinese about 900 years ago, were magnetic pieces of iron that floated on straw or cork in a bowl of water.

19. More coal is mined in Kentucky, West Virginia, and Pennsylvania than in the other states.

20. Owen has applied to the United States Air Force Academy, which is about five kilometers north of Colorado Springs.

Applying What You Know

In the following selection a writer describes her experiences in a one-room schoolhouse. On a sheet of paper, list the fifty-one nouns in the passage. (The first one is underlined for you.) Use what you know about their definition, features, and classes to identify the nouns.

Tucked between flat <u>cornfields</u> in northern Illinois, Willow Hill School contained one classroom and a narrow, gloomy cloakroom where we stored our dripping boots and hung our coats on black iron hooks. Inside, the desks were arranged to create four separate grades. The tiny first-graders sat up front near the reading tables, while the more mature fourth-graders ruled from the back near the washrooms. The dark, slanted tops of our wooden desks bore stains and deep marks, and our seats screeched whenever we swiveled in and out of them. Tall windows fitted with green shades faced the schoolyard, where the empty swings clanked against each other in the wind. Two low bookcases held all twenty-five volumes of our library and three large geraniums in red clay pots. The letters of the alphabet, printed on white paper, trailed around the walls above the blackboards. The only other decoration was a large picture of Benjamin Franklin and other men we couldn't identify signing the Declaration of Independence. When the bitter winters of the Midwest trapped us inside, we sang or hunted the hidden thimble in endless games of Huckle Buckle Beanstalk. At lunchtime Mrs. Schuster warmed us with the grilled sandwiches she made on a hot plate, and on the gloomiest afternoons we ate freshly popped popcorn while she read aloud.

Using Nouns

Most of the problems in using nouns involve irregular plurals and the spelling of the possessive form. In the following sections you will learn how to avoid these problems, how to form the plurals of compound nouns, and how to decide which nouns are proper and must be capitalized.

Forming Noun Plurals

The plural of most nouns is formed by adding the suffix *-s* or *-es* to the singular form. Plurals formed in this way are called *regular plurals*.

Form the regular plural of most nouns by adding the suffix *-s*.

Singular	Plural
one day	three days
one book	several books
one mistake	two mistakes

Form the regular plural of nouns ending in *s*, *sh*, *ch*, *x*, or *z* by adding the suffix *-es*.

Singular	Plural
one address	two addresses
one bush	several bushes
one porch	many porches
one box	four boxes
one buzz	several buzzes

Form the plural of nouns ending in *o* preceded by a vowel by adding the suffix *-s*; form the plural of nouns ending in *o* preceded by a consonant by adding the suffix *-es*.

Singular	Plural
a radio	two radios

Grammar and Usage

Singular	Plural
the stereo	many stereos
one potato	five potatoes
the hero	several heroes

Exception: The plural of nouns that end in *o* and have to do with music take only the suffix -*s* (altos, pianos, solos).

Exercise 5: Forming Regular Plurals

The nouns in the following sentences have been *italicized*. Write the sentences and change each italicized singular noun to its plural form by adding -*s* or -*es*. Underline the nouns you make plural.

Example

a. He sewed the *patch* on the *hole* in the *sweater*.
He sewed the patches on the holes in the sweaters.

1. The *lizard* scampered over the *bush* and *tree*.
2. Wickedly, the evil *queen* granted the *wish* of the *princess*.
3. My *cousin* rented the *studio* once occupied by the now famous *artist*.
4. Add the *tomato*, *onion*, *carrot*, and *potato* before you put the *casserole* into the oven.
5. The *kangaroo* and the *fox* escaped from the *zoo* and chased the *bus* down the *street*.
6. The *movie* made by the film *class* will be shown during the *afternoon*.
7. Near the damp *wall* of the *dungeon*, the *torch* showed the ancient *skeleton* and *pile* of *bone*.
8. When the *Jeep* broke down high on the mountain *trail*, the *mosquito* swarmed around Sylvia as she wept and scratched her *bite*.
9. The amplified *sound* of the *drum* and *guitar* greatly annoyed the *neighbor* next door.
10. The wild *throw* knocked the *batter* out of the *box* .

Forming Irregular Noun Plurals

Many nouns have an irregular plural formed by a spelling change plus the suffixes -s or -es.

Form the plural of most nouns that end in *y* preceded by a consonant by changing the *y* to *i* and adding the suffix -es.

Singular	Plural
one baby	several babies
one country	many countries
one candy	three candies

Form the plural of nouns that end in *y* preceded by a vowel by simply adding the suffix -s.

Singular	Plural
a key	several keys
one Saturday	many Saturdays
a monkey	six monkeys

Form the plural of some nouns ending in *fe* or *f* by changing the *f* to *v* and adding the suffix -es.

calf	calves	self	selves
half	halves	shelf	shelves
knife	knives	thief	thieves
life	lives	wife	wives
loaf	loaves	wolf	wolves

Grammar and Usage

Exception: Some nouns ending in *f* or *fe* form their plural by the addition of the suffix *-s*.

chef	chefs	safe	safes
chief	chiefs	reef	reefs
cliff	cliffs	roof	roofs
belief	beliefs		

If you are not sure how to spell the plural of any noun, check your dictionary.

Exercise 6: Forming Irregular Plurals

Write the following sentences and change each *italicized* noun to its plural form. Underline the nouns you make plural.

Example

   a. The *calf* wandered through the garden, trampling the *strawberry* and *daisy*.
   The <u>calves</u> wandered through the garden, trampling the <u>strawberries</u> and <u>daisies</u>.

1. The *chief* described the *life* of the Seminoles before their *treaty* with the government.
2. In the *story* about Bluebeard, his *wife* had good reason to feel nervous after their wedding *day*.
3. Throughout the long *journey* the *donkey* brayed and the *baby* cried.
4. The *family* of *osprey* perched on the *buoy* in the *bay*.
5. The *lady* from the northern *country* spoke of the *grief* caused by the long war.
6. We watched the *monkey* climb onto the *roof* and peer down the *chimney*.
7. No one replied to her *inquiry* about the *salary* of people who work in the *library*.
8. The *thief* went directly to the *shelf* in the *study*, removed the books, and opened the *safe*.

9. Juanita says that fishing from the *wharf* or *jetty* is often as good as fishing from the *dinghy* offshore.
10. The *sentry* paced along the *cliff*, guarding the *army* from any attack by their *enemy*.

Form some irregular plurals by changing a vowel sound.

Singular	Plural
woman	women
mouse	mice
foot	feet
goose	geese
tooth	teeth

Some words have the same form for both singular and plural.

A *deer* drank from the river.

A dozen *deer* drank from the river.

The following words also have the same singular and plural form.

bass	elk	salmon
carp	Japanese	sheep
Chinese	moose	trout
cod	pike	tuna

Use your dictionary to check plural forms that may be unfamiliar.

There is no pattern or rule to cover other irregular plurals. Some of these nouns form their plurals according to rules of Latin or Greek, from which the words originally came. Others add a whole new syllable to form the plural.

Grammar and Usage

Singular	Plural	Singular	Plural
alumna	alumnae	datum	data
alumnus	alumni	hypothesis	hypotheses
child	children	larva	larvae
crisis	crises	ox	oxen
criterion	criteria	phenomenon	phenomena

Exercise 7: Forming Irregular Plurals

Write the following sentences and put each *italicized* noun into its proper plural form. Underline the nouns you make plural.

Examples

a. On her first day of fishing, Danielle caught three *trout*.
On her first day of fishing, Danielle caught three trout.

b. A sleek tomcat controlled the colony of *mouse* in the barn.
A sleek tomcat controlled the colony of mice in the barn.

1. Oberlin College in Ohio was the first in the United States to admit *woman*.
2. The first transcontinental railroad was built mostly by the *Chinese*.
3. Have you collected enough *datum* to support all of your *hypothesis*?
4. At the county fair the Velasquez family entered a team of *ox* and several *goose*.
5. The *child* of *alumnus* have a slightly better chance of being accepted into some colleges.
6. Few people believe in ESP, clairvoyance, and other psychic *phenomenon*.
7. Instead of coffee breaks, the *Japanese* often take exercise breaks for group calisthenics.
8. The President spoke about energy, inflation, and other serious *crisis* affecting our nation.

9. Each spring the *man* sheared the *sheep*.
10. During the full moon off Whistle Buoy, the *fisherman* caught six Cuban snappers, which have sharp, spikelike *tooth*.

Forming Compound Noun Plurals

If a compound noun is written as one word, apply the rules for pluralizing to the last part of the compound.

Singular	Plural
one cupful	two cupfuls
one lighthouse	three lighthouses
one grapefruit	a dozen grapefruits
one housewife	several housewives
one fingerprint	many fingerprints

Exception: one passerby, two passersby.

When compound nouns are written as two or three words or are hyphenated, the plural is formed by making plural the most important word.

Singular	Plural
folk song	folk songs
sister-in-law	sisters-in-law
postmaster general	postmasters general
lieutenant governor	lieutenant governors
vice president	vice presidents
man-of-war	men-of-war
runner-up	runners-up

Grammar and Usage

Sometimes it is difficult to tell which is the most important word in a compound noun. For such nouns an *-s* or *-es* is usually added to the end of the last word to form the plural. The plural of *fourteen-year-old,* for example, is *fourteen-year-olds.* Check your dictionary if you are unsure about the plural of a compound noun.

Exercise 8: *Forming Compound Noun Plurals*

Each of the following sentences contains one or more singular compound nouns. Rewrite the sentences and change each compound noun to its plural form. Underline the compound nouns you make plural.

Examples

a. The six-year-old begged for another ride on the merry-go-round.
   The <u>six-year-olds</u> begged for another ride on the <u>merry-go-rounds</u>.

b. My parents and I drove to Peoria to see my brother and sister-in-law.
   My parents and I drove to Peoria to see my <u>brothers</u> and <u>sisters-in-law.</u>

1. The lieutenant governor met to discuss some of the problems facing Virginia, West Virginia, Kentucky and Tennessee.
2. Eighth-grader and ninth-grader can try out for cheerleader.
3. The police officer found the revolver and shotgun aboard the abandoned houseboat.
4. We kept the algae, starfish, and sea urchin in the bucketful of water.
5. Their mother-in-law will celebrate their eightieth and ninetieth birthday on the same day.
6. The Tanaka brothers and their neighbors built the tree house in the backyard with the two-by-four and other scrap lumber.
7. Unseasoned tenderizer can relieve the painful stings caused by the Portuguese man-of-war.

8. The baseball, football, and other athletic equipment are stored in the field house behind the tennis court.
9. For a great snack, mix the cupful of raisins and dried apples with the small bowlful of nuts.
10. Maria is looking for some teenager to work as baby-sitter for the three-year-old.

Forming Noun Possessives

The possessive form of a noun shows either ownership or the relationship of one noun to another. The following three rules apply to forming noun possessives.

All singular nouns form their possessive with an apostrophe (') and the letter *s*.

Singular Noun	Possessive Form
the ultraviolet rays of the *sun*	the *sun's* ultraviolet rays
the family of *Mr. Chew*	*Mr. Chew's* family
a novel by *Jane Austen*	*Jane Austen's* novel

Even when a singular noun ends with the letter *s*, the possessive is usually formed with an apostrophe and an *s*.

Singular Noun	Possessive Form
the door of the *bus*	the *bus's* door
the girlfriend of *Charles*	*Charles's* girlfriend
a poem by *Keats*	*Keats's* poem

(*Charles' girlfriend* and *Keats' poem* are also correct.)

Plural nouns that end in *s* form the possessive with only an apostrophe.

Grammar and Usage

Plural Noun	Possessive Form
the mistakes of the *players*	the *players'* mistakes
the locker room of the *girls*	the *girls'* locker room
the goal of the union *members*	the union *members'* goal

Plural nouns that do not end in *s* form the possessive with an apostrophe and an *s*.

Plural Noun	Possessive Form
the games of the *children*	the *children's* games
the owner of the *oxen*	the *oxen's* owner
the surface of your *teeth*	your *teeth's* surface

Exercise 9: Forming Noun Possessives

Rewrite the following sentences, using the possessive form of the noun in *italics*. The meaning of the new sentence should be the same as that of the original. Underline the new possessive noun.

Examples

a. The twins took apart the gold watch that belongs to their *grandfather*.
The twins took apart their grandfather's gold watch.

b. The "real" name of *Superman* is Kal-El.
Superman's "real" name is Kal-El.

c. I've read all of the stories by Arna Bontemps.
I've read all of Arna Bontemps's stories.

1. The friends of *Luis* surprised him with a party for his fourteenth birthday.
2. The tools and the supplies of the *carpenters* weighed more than forty pounds.

3. Have you read any of the books and articles of *William Armstrong?*

4. She answered only a few of the probing, intense questions of the *reporters.*

5. Next year the vacation of *Jessica* will be a visit to her family in Ireland.

6. The stories by *Isaac Bashevis Singer* are a satisfying mixture of reality, fantasy, and wisdom.

7. The arguments of the *women* for equal pay for equal work are difficult to dispute.

8. The magazines in the offices of the *doctors* are almost never recent.

9. In the museum we saw capes made from golden and blue feathers of the *birds.*

10. Every year the prices for the new *cars* drop just before the models of the next *year* appear.

Capitalizing Proper Nouns

Proper nouns name specific persons, places, and things and are always capitalized.

Common Noun	Proper Noun
my aunt	Ms. Carlita Gomez
the mayor of Logan	Mayor Jack McDaniels
my neighbor's store	Morgenthau Cleaners
the state capital	Lansing, Michigan

Capitalize all the important words in the name of a specific building, landmark, or institution.

Note: Unimportant words such as the articles (*a, an, the*), prepositions, and conjunctions with fewer than five letters are usually not capitalized.

Common Noun	Proper Noun
this building	the Museum of Science and Industry
that monument	the Statue of Liberty
her college	Massachusetts Institute of Technology

Capitalize the first and last words and all important words in the title of a book, magazine, newspaper, poem, story, song, movie, or television series.

Note: Capitalize *a*, *and*, and *the* only when these words are actually part of a title.

Common Noun	Proper Noun
book	*That Was Then, This Is Now*
magazine	*Skateboarder*
newspaper	*The Philadelphia Inquirer* but the *St. Louis Post-Dispatch*
poem	"The Song of Hiawatha"
song	"Joy to the World"
short story	"The Lady, or the Tiger?"
movie	*The Day the Earth Stood Still*
television series	*All in the Family*

Capitalize names of national origin and religions.

Common Noun	Proper Noun
a religion	Judaism
our allies	the Canadians
a people	the Iroquois

Capitalize words showing family relationship when they are used as part of a person's name or in place of a name.

> Janice visited Grandfather Martin.
> Her grandfather celebrated his eighty-fifth birthday.
>
> Can you drive us to the game, Dad?
> My dad grows his own vegetables.

Capitalize geographical sections of the country but not directions.

> Mount St. Helens is a volcano in the Northwest.
>
> Our house is northwest of the post office.

Capitalize the name of a team, an organization, or a government body.

Common Noun	Proper Noun
the team	the Boston Celtics
the organization	the National Honor Society
the government body	the Internal Revenue Service

Capitalize nouns that name school courses when they are followed by a numeral or are the title of a specific course. The names of all language courses are always capitalized.

> We used a computer in my Math II class.
>
> Mrs. Adams teaches a course called Practical Electronics.
>
> My Spanish class is really interesting.

Exercise 10: *Capitalizing Proper Nouns*

Write the sentences on the next page and capitalize each proper noun. Underline *italicized* words and the nouns that you

305

Grammar and Usage

capitalize. (Be sure to underline all of the words in a compound proper noun.)

Example

a. Sarah, did you know that uncle frank was once a judge?
Sarah, did you know that <u>Uncle</u> <u>Frank</u> was once a judge?

1. You'll find an exit for the brookfield zoo on the eisenhower expressway.
2. I enjoy american history more than I enjoy math or drafting II.
3. When the national basketball association has its play-offs, I always support the atlanta hawks.
4. Just a minute, mom, and I'll go with you to townsend's drugstore; I need a copy of *newsweek* for my history report.
5. On tuesday mayor hawkins personally congratulated the tournament champions from east central high school.
6. My brother likes the deserts of the southwest, but I prefer the beaches of the southeast.
7. If your uncle can drive us to riverfront stadium, I'm sure aunt sophie can pick us up.
8. On wednesday broward junior college offers a course on politics taught by congressman martinez.
9. My mother and father and I still watch *star trek* reruns; "in a wink of an eye" is our favorite episode.
10. Sonja's cousins marsha and yolanda are counselors at camp winnebuck in crescent lake, minnesota.

Review: Using Nouns

Write the following sentences and change each *italicized* noun to its proper plural or possessive form. Capitalize any proper nouns which are not capitalized in the sentences. Underline the nouns you change.

1. Yesterday *Wes* bicycle was stolen.
2. We found a *raccoon* footprint near the tent.

3. The organization known as the national council of teachers of english will meet next thanksgiving in phoenix, arizona.
4. Julia is reading a book about the *life* of great women writers.
5. The *men* shoe department is on the main floor across from the shirts.
6. Have you ever eaten in the *employees* lunchroom or do you always go out?
7. My brother jack has been reading roald dahl's "the landlady," a strange story about a woman who murders people.
8. Armed guards will patrol the three *countries* borders until the truce is signed.
9. The student gathered *datum* on the life systems of blue-green algae.
10. When the car overheated, we added two *pailful* of water to the radiator.
11. Two eighth-graders, margie onsager and kim suzuke, have written words and music for a song they call "it's always you."
12. The *room* only exit was not clearly marked, so we tried several doors before we got out.
13. Of all the *mouse* in the laboratory, Herman is the boldest and the most temperamental.
14. When she was only nineteen years old, edna st. vincent millay wrote her famous poem "renascence."
15. Important *belief* in this country are the freedom and dignity of the individual.
16. The *runner-up* prize in this race is a silver trophy.
17. The *passerby* stopped to watch the construction workers excavate for the building.
18. Before she moved to palestine, golda meir taught school in milwaukee.
19. In the light wind the *sheaf* of wheat rippled gently.
20. The *babies* dress on Halloween was orange blankets and green hats.

Grammar and Usage

Writing Focus: *Using Specific Nouns in Writing*

Good writers use specific nouns to paint a clear and exact picture for readers. For example, the noun *tiara* is more specific than the noun *jewelry*. As much as possible, use specific nouns in your writing.

Assignment: *Choose Mine!*

Notice the photograph on page 309. Imagine that you snapped it and wish to enter it in a photography contest. Along with the photo, you need to send a report that tells about the picture. The judges are interested in the whole context of the photograph—how you came to take it and what was happening before, during, and after you snapped it.

In one or more well-developed paragraphs, write a report about the photograph. Write for the judges of the photography contest to help them decide that your photo is the best. You must be persuasive as well as descriptive as you write. Your work will be evaluated for effective use of nouns.

Use the following steps to complete this assignment.

A. Prewriting

Study the photograph carefully. Write down several words and phrases that describe in detail what you see. Remember that nouns name ideas and emotions as well as people, places, and things. Imagine yourself being at the scene and actually taking the picture. Be sure to mention how you happened to be in that place at that particular time. Free write. (Review Chapter 1 on free writing if necessary.) If you have ever taken pictures, recall some of the things you had to consider before you actually snapped the picture. Using your imagination, write down words, phrases, or sentences about your experience. Include details that explain how you happened to be at the scene, what you saw happening, what you caught on film, and what happened after you snapped the picture. See the whole experience in your mind's eye. After ten or fifteen minutes, stop, and reread your free writing. Underline the ideas you like that describe the photograph and explain how you came to take it.

11 Nouns

B. Writing

Use your free writing to write one or more paragraphs about the photograph and how you came to take it. Choose the details that best describe and explain it. Remember to make your report clear, interesting, and even entertaining so that the judges will choose your photo as the winner of the contest. As you write, use specific nouns to make your writing precise.

C. Postwriting

Use the following checklist to revise your work.

1. Have I actually described my photograph and explained how I came to take it?

2. Do I use specific nouns to make my writing precise?

Edit your work using the Checklist for Proofreading at the back of the book. If appropriate, share your writing with your classmates by sitting in a circle to read each other's work. Compare descriptions of the photograph and discuss how you "saw" the scene.

12 Pronouns

Understanding Pronouns

Pronouns are words that take the place of nouns. Pronouns can be identified in three ways: by their definition, by the classes into which they can be grouped, and by the features that distinguish them from other parts of speech. In the following sections you will study and practice each of these methods to identify pronouns.

Defining Pronouns

A *pronoun* is usually defined as a word that takes the place of a noun or another pronoun.

A pronoun usually refers to a specific noun or to a pronoun called an *antecedent*. Antecedents usually come before the pronoun.

Tammy tried the exit *door,* but *it* was locked.

The two *neighbors* decided *they* would plant a hedge.

Sometimes an antecedent follows the pronoun.

Although *she* had missed a week of class, *Lisa* made an A.

When *he* plays *his* trumpet, *Pedro* is always applauded.

The antecedent may also appear in a preceding sentence.

Charlene waited anxiously for the *letter. She* had expected *it* to arrive last week.

A single pronoun can replace several nouns in a sentence.

The *passenger pigeon*, the *great auk*, and the *dodo* no longer exist on earth.

These are only a few of the species that have become extinct.

Sometimes a pronoun replaces a word group that functions as a noun.

The rings of Saturn, which can be observed with a telescope, can be seen tonight if the sky is clear.

A single pronoun can be used in place of an entire sentence.

Ted is kind and understanding and has a great sense of humor. *That* is why I like him.

Exercise 1: Identifying Pronouns and Their Antecedents

Write the following sentences and circle each pronoun. Then underline the antecedent to which each pronoun refers.

Examples

a. The Ugly Duckling was depressed because the other ducks made fun of him.
The Ugly Duckling was depressed because the other ducks made fun of (him.)

b. Billie Jean King beat Bobby Riggs in three straight sets. That was an important victory.
Billie Jean King beat Bobby Riggs in three straight sets. (That) was an important victory.

1. Abby, have you forgotten your lunch?
2. Flying at night with the altimeter gone, the pilot had no way of knowing his altitude over the ocean.
3. When the little girl learned to whistle, she whistled all day long.

4. Martha opened the pineapple with her Swiss army knife.
5. The twelve princesses wore out their shoes by dancing.
6. "To be, or not to be." That was Hamlet's question.
7. The photograph on the piano, which belonged to Grandmother, is more than a hundred years old.
8. When she opened her laundry bag, Lee found a dead mouse.
9. Hank thought he had a foul ball in the upper deck behind home plate.
10. Danielle says she never lies, but her brother does not think that can be true.

Grouping Pronouns by Classes

Pronouns are usually grouped into six main classes: *personal, possessive, indefinite, interrogative, demonstrative,* and *relative.*

Personal pronouns **allow speakers or writers to refer to themselves, to the people they speak or write to, and to subjects they speak or write about.**

	Singular	Plural
First Person:	I, me	we, us
Second Person:	you	you
Third Person:	he, she, it him, her, it	they, them

The pronouns *I, me, we,* and *us* are called *first-person pronouns* and are used when speakers or writers refer to themselves.

Singular	Plural
I feel wonderful.	*We* feel wonderful.
The call was for *me.*	The call was for *us.*

The second-person pronoun, *you,* refers to the person or people who are addressed.

Singular	Plural
You are late.	*You* are both late.
The call was for *you*.	The call was for both of *you*.

Third-person pronouns, *he, him, she, her, it, they,* and *them,* are used to describe other people or things.

Singular	Plural
He / *She* / *It* is late.	*They* are late.
The call was for *him.* / *her.* / *it.*	The call was for *them.*

Some personal pronouns can combine with *-self* or *-selves:*

>I can do that by *myself.*

>We should not quarrel among *ourselves.*

>Cindy planned to put *herself* through dental school.

>The parrot has taught *itself* to speak French.

Exercise 2: Identifying Personal Pronouns

Write the following sentences and underline the personal pronouns. Be prepared to explain whether each pronoun is in the first-, second-, or third-person singular or plural.

Examples

    a. Consuela will marry him in September.
    Consuela will marry <u>him</u> in September.

    b. We treated ourselves to a sightseeing tour of Boston.
    <u>We</u> treated <u>ourselves</u> to a sightseeing tour of Boston.

1. Betty and Jessica have just come back from the Yucatán Peninsula, where they visited the Mayan pyramids.

2. Twice a week I work as a volunteer in the library.

Grammar and Usage

3. To complete this application you must fill in a Social Security number.
4. She helped herself to more yogurt.
5. We never could have finished the job on time without Sid's help, but he doesn't have much confidence in himself.
6. She asked him for a date.
7. Mrs. Yang works as a night nurse, so that she is home when the children come from school.
8. Most of us had never seen a hang-gliding competition before; it was as exciting as we had expected it to be.
9. "Give me another chance," she begged them, as she picked herself up from where she had fallen.
10. When the bicyclist went through the stop sign, he crashed into the side of an oncoming car.

Possessive pronouns are the forms of personal pronouns used to show ownership or relationship.

Singular	Plural
my, mine	our, ours
your, yours	your, yours
his her, hers its	their, theirs

Some possessive pronouns can be used in front of the noun they possess.

I plan to use *her* design.

Please put *your* project on the table.

We gave *our* attention to the speaker.

Some possessive pronouns can be used alone.

I plan to use *hers* instead of *mine*.

Please put *yours* next to *his*.

We let the neighbors borrow *ours*.

Exercise 3: Identifying Possessive Pronouns

Write the following sentences and underline each possessive pronoun you find.

Examples

a. His painting is next to mine.
   <u>His</u> painting is next to <u>mine</u>.

b. The students have a right to see their records.
   The students have a right to see <u>their</u> records.

1. Anna, the last piece of chicken is yours.
2. Jumping rope is her favorite exercise.
3. Mrs. Choy said, "My oldest son is with the Peace Corps in Tanzania."
4. "These are my binoculars," Sheila said.
5. Max has forgotten the combination to his hall locker.
6. While Mr. and Mrs. Henry were on their way to work, their car ran out of gas.
7. Bud's uncle owns an art gallery, and his aunt works for the utility company.
8. Jamie picked up the lizard by its tail.
9. Fernando, is your sister coming to the dance?
10. Julie and Christopher said, "Those purple beach chairs are ours."

Indefinite pronouns do not refer to a specific person or thing. They may take the place of a noun, but they often do not have antecedents.

Below is a list of the most commonly used indefinite pronouns.

all	either	nobody
any	everybody	none
anybody	everyone	no one
anyone	few	one
anything	many	some
both	most	somebody
each	neither	someone

Grammar and Usage

Many words in this list can also be used as modifiers. Words like *each, some, many,* and *few* are indefinite pronouns only when they function as a noun.

Each of the jockeys wears the owner's silks.	[indefinite pronoun]
Each jockey wears the owner's silks.	[modifier]
Some of the books are missing.	[indefinite pronoun]
Some books are missing.	[modifier]
For *many*, Social Security benefits do not keep pace with inflation.	[indefinite pronoun]
For *many* elderly people, Social Security benefits do not keep pace with inflation.	[modifier]

Exercise 4: Identifying Indefinite Pronouns

Write the following paragraph and underline each of the fifteen indefinite pronouns. Be careful not to underline any modifiers. The first one is done for you.

    <u>Each</u> of the guests is expected to come in costume. I don't know anyone who is really happy about coming in costume, but nobody can get into the dance without one. Last year somebody came as Spider Man, only to find three more Spider Men sitting inside. All of them had bought their costumes. Many of the students make their own costumes, and some are really creative. But has anybody ever dressed as anything except an animal or a person? Someday I'd like to see someone arrive as a telephone pole or a flowerpot. Everyone would be more interested then. One of my friends is trying to convince me to come as an earthworm, with both of us sharing the same costume. I refuse. I can't imagine that either of us would enjoy the dance in an earthworm costume.

Interrogative pronouns **are used in asking questions. An interrogative pronoun stands for an unnamed person, place, or thing.**

Interrogative Pronouns

who	whose	what
whom	which	

Who is coming to the party?

Whom are you bringing?

Whose is the silver car?

Which is Kiyo's sister?

What did you say?

If an interrogative pronoun is used before a noun, it is used as a modifier, not as a pronoun.

What time is it?	[modifier]
What is it?	[interrogative pronoun]
Which is more exciting?	[interrogative pronoun]
Which ride is more exciting?	[modifier]

Exercise 5: Identifying Interrogative Pronouns

Write each of the following sentences and underline all of the interrogative pronouns. Check to be sure that these words do not modify nouns in the sentence. Some sentences may not have interrogative pronouns.

Example

a. With what will you make the salad dressing?

With <u>what</u> will you make the salad dressing?

1. Who are the two senators from your state?
2. For whom did you buy this new soccer ball?
3. Which museum has the *Mona Lisa* by Leonardo da Vinci?
4. What is the distance from the earth to the sun?
5. Which movie did you like better?
6. To whom did you speak when you applied for the job?
7. What is the real name of Marilyn Monroe?

Grammar and Usage

8. Whose is the racing bike in front of the house?
9. Whose bright idea was it to go skiing in a snowstorm?
10. Which is your favorite rock group?

A *demonstrative pronoun* is used to point out a specific person, place, thing, or idea.

This is your last chance.

That was a delicious meal.

If you want to help, carry *these*.

Are *those* the students' paintings?

Demonstrative pronouns have a singular and a plural form.

Singular	**Plural**
this	these
that	those

When the words listed above come before a noun, they are being used as modifiers, not as demonstrative pronouns.

These are Tony's cousins.   [demonstrative pronoun]

These people are Tony's cousins.   [modifier]

Exercise 6: Identifying Demonstrative Pronouns

Write each of the following sentences and underline all of the demonstrative pronouns. (Be sure that these pronouns do not modify nouns in the sentence.) Some sentences may not have demonstrative pronouns.

Examples

a. This is a very dangerous situation.
   <u>This</u> is a very dangerous situation.

b. That is the famous Brooklyn Bridge.
   <u>That</u> is the famous Brooklyn Bridge.

1. "This is ridiculous!" she cried.
2. Those are land crabs.
3. That suggestion will not help solve the problem.
4. These coins are Canadian.
5. Beth's job is much more challenging than that of her brother.
6. "This is an extremely unusual case," said the district attorney.
7. That is exactly the tone of voice I cannot stand.
8. These are the earliest drawings known.
9. Most of her mysteries are better than those you lent me.
10. Why are these so different from the other leaves on the mangrove?

> **A *relative pronoun* introduces a group of words that modifies a noun or pronoun.**

The following words are called *relative pronouns* when they are used to introduce a group of words that modifies a noun or pronoun in the sentence.

| which | who | whose |
| that | whom | what |

Keith, *who was voted the team's most valuable player*, has pitched three straight shutouts.

Janet Reno, *whom you met last night*, is the county's district attorney.

This umbrella, *which I bought at a sale*, already has three holes in it.

The painting *that hangs over my desk* is one of Norman Rockwell's.

Do not confuse relative pronouns with interrogative pronouns (which ask a question), demonstrative pronouns, or single-word modifiers.

319

Grammar and Usage

The essay *that* she wrote is about a family of Polish-Americans.	[relative pronoun]
That is the tallest lighthouse in the state.	[demonstrative pronoun]
That door has four different locks.	[modifier]
Whose is this?	[interrogative pronoun]
Whose boat is docked over there?	[modifier]
Kim, *whose* grandparents run a diving shop, is an experienced scuba diver.	[relative pronoun]
Which piece of chicken do you want?	[modifier]
Which is her apartment?	[interrogative pronoun]
The package *that* I received came from Bangkok, Thailand.	[relative pronoun]

Exercise 7: Identifying Relative Pronouns and Their Antecedents

Write the following sentences and underline each relative pronoun. Then draw an arrow from the relative pronoun to its antecedent.

Example

a. The leek, which is the national emblem of the Welsh, looks like a large green onion.

The leek, <u>which</u> is the national emblem of the Welsh, looks like a large green onion.

1. Sarah Bernhardt, whose leg was amputated when she was seventy-one, continued her stage career.
2. He suffers from xenophobia, which is a fear of strangers.
3. According to Mark Twain, cauliflower is a cabbage that has a college education.
4. Scientists who have studied bees have found indications of a language of signs and sounds.
5. In Transcaucasia, which has the world's largest population of people over one hundred years old, the word for *elderly* is *many centuried*.
6. Using flatworms, psychologist James McConnell did experiments that tried to explain the nature of memory.
7. Anna Freud, who was one of Sigmund Freud's six children, became a famous child psychoanalyst.
8. Vitamin K, which is found in green, leafy vegetables and alfalfa sprouts, is necessary for blood clotting.
9. Edgar Cayce, who died in 1945, diagnosed the diseases of people without ever seeing or meeting them.
10. Sauk Centre, Minnesota, which is 105 miles northwest of Minneapolis, is Sinclair Lewis' hometown.

Finding Pronouns by Their Features

The following three features distinguish pronouns from other parts of speech. Personal pronouns have all three of these features, and most other pronouns have at least one.

A pronoun may be singular or plural.

	Singular	*Plural*
Personal:	I, you, he, she, it, me, him, her	we, you, they, us, them
Possessive:	my, mine, your, yours, his, her, hers, its	our, ours, your, yours, their, theirs
Demonstrative:	this, that	these, those

Grammar and Usage

    Indefinite: anybody, every-one, nobody, each, one, someone   both, few, many, others, several

Pronouns may change form to show what they do in a sentence.

Only personal pronouns have both subject and object forms.

Subject Form	Object Form
I, we	me, us
you	you
he, she, it, they	him, her, it, them

She entered the contest.	[subject]
After dinner *we* met Laura's uncle.	[subject]
Raoul made a beaded ring for *me*.	[object]
Joe's sister helped *us* paint the house.	[object]

Pronouns may show gender.

Personal and possessive pronouns may be masculine, feminine, or neuter.

Masculine: he, him, his

Feminine: she, her, hers

Neuter: it, its

Some pronouns can be either masculine or feminine, depending on the speaker or writer.

    I, me, you, mine, yours

Some pronouns refer to groups of men, groups of women, or to mixed groups, depending on the meaning of the sentence.

we, our, ours, us   you, yours   they, them, their, theirs

Exercise 8: Identifying Pronouns by Their Features

Use what you have learned about the features of pronouns to identify the pronouns in the following sentences. Write the sentences and underline each pronoun. (Your teacher may ask which feature you used to identify the pronoun.)

Examples

a. We seated everyone by the number on his or her ticket.
   <u>We</u> seated <u>everyone</u> by the number on <u>his</u> or <u>her</u> ticket.

b. José found my wallet on his front porch.
   José found <u>my</u> wallet on <u>his</u> front porch.

1. Mike and I looked for the pencils, but we couldn't find them.
2. When everyone arrives, you can give each person a program.
3. Your notebook is the same as mine.
4. I hope these are the right answers.
5. Charlotte makes her own clothes; she is very clever at designing them.
6. Violin, cello, and banjo—these are all instruments my sister plays.
7. Few of the records belong to me; many of them are really hers.
8. Our house has more windows in it than yours.
9. Do you think he is as tall as I am?
10. The party was supposed to be a surprise for him, but it wasn't.

Review: Understanding Pronouns

In the fable on the next page, "Belling the Cat," there are twenty-seven pronouns. The first three are underlined for you. Write the numbers 1–20 on a sheet of paper and list at least twenty of the remaining twenty-four pronouns. (Hints: Count *one another* as one pronoun; do not count *all* as a pronoun.)

Grammar and Usage

Long ago, the mice had a general council to consider what measures <u>they</u> could take to outwit <u>their</u> common enemy, the Cat. <u>Some</u> said this, and some <u>said</u> that; but at last a Young Mouse <u>got up</u> and said he had a proposal to make which he thought would meet the case. "You will all agree," said he, "that our chief danger consists in the sly and treacherous manner in which the enemy approaches us. Now, if we could receive some signal of her approach, we could easily escape from her. I venture, therefore, to propose that a small bell be procured and attached by a ribbon round the neck of the Cat. By this means we should always know when she was about and could easily retire while she was in the neighborhood."

This proposal met with general applause, until an Old Mouse got up and said, "That is all very well, but who is to bell the Cat?" The mice looked at one another and nobody spoke. Then the Old Mouse said:

"It is easy to propose impossible remedies."[1]

Applying What You Know

From a magazine, newspaper, or book you have read, select several paragraphs and identify the pronouns. List them on a sheet of paper.

Using Pronouns

The two most common problems in using pronouns are selecting subject and object forms and making pronouns agree with their antecedents. In the sections that follow, you will learn how to avoid these problems.

Agreement of Pronouns and Antecedents

Pronouns agree with antecedents in both number and gender.

A pronoun must agree with its antecedent in number.

---

[1]"Belling the Cat" from *Aesop's Fables* retold by Joseph Jacobs. Copyright © 1950, 1978 by Macmillan Publishing Co., Inc. Reprinted with permission of Macmillan Publishing Co.

When an antecedent is singular, the pronoun used to refer to it must be singular.

Anna wrote to *her* cousin in Mexico City.
[*Anna* is the antecedent; *Anna* is singular.]

Each of the lockers has *its* own combination.
[*Each* is the antecedent; *each* is singular.]

When the antecedent is plural, a plural pronoun is used to refer to it.

The union members voted on *their* new contract.
[*Members* is the antecedent; *members* is plural.]

These are chairs my great-grandfather made.
[*Chairs* is the antecedent; *chairs* is plural.]

A pronoun must agree with its antecedent in gender.

The gender of pronouns is clear when the pronoun is singular.

Marvin's mother packed *him* a lunch.

JoAnn told Carol that *she* could join us.

Did Gene ask *his* mother to pick *him* up?

When a singular antecedent is feminine, the pronouns *she*, *her*, and *hers* are used.

Rosita said that *she* would be late for *her* lesson.

Sharon hoped the winning number was *hers*.

When a singular antecedent is neuter, the pronouns *it* and *its* are used.

This tree keeps *its* leaves in the winter.

The dog returned home when *it* got hungry and lonely, but always left again.

Grammar and Usage

A pronoun that has a *compound antecedent* (two or more nouns joined by the word *and* or *or*) follows these rules:

When two or more antecedents are joined by *and*, a plural pronoun is used to refer to them.

José, Marion, and Dave were late because *their* bus never came.

Dancers and tennis players must keep *their* legs in good condition.

When two or more singular antecedents are joined by *or* or *nor*, a singular pronoun is used to refer to them.

Justin or Dan has forgotten *his* umbrella.

He held up a copperhead or a rattlesnake and asked us to identify *it*.

When two or more plural antecedents are joined by *or* or *nor*, a plural pronoun is used to refer to them.

Lentils or dried peas are nutritious because *they* are high in protein.

Neither the Jets nor the Reds have played *their* final game.

Exercise 9: Making Pronouns and Antecedents Agree

Write each of the following sentences and supply a pronoun that agrees with the *italicized* antecedent. Underline the pronoun that you choose.

Examples

a. *Sheila Edmonson* wrote about _____ harrowing experiences in the desert.
   Sheila Edmonson wrote about <u>her</u> harrowing experiences in the desert.

b. *Amy Akibo and her sister* have built _____ own teaching machine.
   Amy Akibo and her sister have built their own teaching machine.

1. *Scheherazade*, a beautiful young woman, saved _____ own life by telling tales for a thousand and one nights.
2. *Mark* is starting _____ first year of college.
3. Either *Sara* or *Sharon* will drive _____ car to the airport.
4. The *coaches* and the *players* have done _____ best to prepare for the first game.
5. A *grackle* or a *crow* has built _____ nest in that tree.
6. *Craig* and *Lou* waited for _____ turn at the telescope.
7. *Mr.* and *Mrs. Avila* depend entirely on _____ garden for fresh vegetables.
8. Either *students* or *parents* can send _____ comments in.
9. As cooks, both *Mike* and his *brother* use _____ imaginations more often than recipes.
10. Most *dog owners* are angry about the law that requires _____ to clean up after _____ dogs.

Agreement with Indefinite Antecedents

When the antecedent is an indefinite pronoun, you must decide whether it is singular or plural in order to make other pronouns agree.

Singular			Plural	Singular or Plural
each	everyone	someone	several	all
one	everybody	somebody	few	none
either	anyone	no one	both	any
neither	anybody	nobody	many	most
much			others	some

When the antecedent is a singular indefinite pronoun, a singular pronoun is used to refer to it.

Each of the boys is in *his* room.

Neither of the girls has finished *her* report yet.

A singular indefinite pronoun sometimes refers to a mixed group of men and women. In such sentences you may use the words *his* or *her* or reword the sentence so that the antecedent is plural.

Everyone should cast *his* or *her* vote in Tuesday's election.

All of the voters should cast *their* votes in Tuesday's election.

Voters should cast *their* votes in Tuesday's election.

When the antecedent is a plural indefinite pronoun, a plural pronoun is used to refer to it.

Few of the actors had memorized *their* parts.

Several had forgotten *their* lines.

When the antecedent is an indefinite pronoun that can be either singular or plural, you must look closely at the meaning of the sentence to see how it is used.

Some of the gold was missing, and *it* was never found. [singular]

Some of the students forgot *their* report cards. [plural]

Exercise 10: Making Pronouns Agree with Indefinite Antecedents

Write each of the following sentences and choose the pronoun in parentheses that agrees with its antecedent. Underline the pronoun that you choose and be prepared to explain your choice.

Example

a. All of the boys want to know (their, his) grades on the final.
All of the boys want to know <u>their</u> grades on the final.

1. Each of the girls nominated (herself, themselves) for president of the eighth-grade class.
2. All of us want (my, our) team to win.
3. They strongly believe that (their, its) territory should be made into a state.
4. All of the women on the Olympic team have worked hard to get (themselves, herself) in shape.
5. One of the elephants raised (its, their) trunk and sprayed the crowd with water.
6. Somebody has left (his, their) sneakers in the men's locker room.
7. Everyone on the girls' volleyball team is doing (her, their) best to win the state championship.
8. Few of the boys have completed (their, his) requirements.
9. Several of the relief workers shared (his or her, their) own food and clothing with the flood victims.
10. Everyone must complete (his or her, their) assignment by Monday.

Avoiding Common Pronoun Problems

Avoid using unnecessary pronouns.

My brother goes to the University of Kansas.
[rather than *My brother he*]

Melissa makes delicious tacos.
[rather than *Melissa she*]

Grammar and Usage

Name yourself last in a series when you are speaking or writing about yourself and other people.

The first-person pronouns (*I, me, we,* and *us*) are always named after other nouns or pronouns.

Howie and *I* are interested in model railroads.
[rather than *I and Howie*]

This party is for the twins and *me*.
[rather than *for me and the twins*]

Make sure that using a pronoun makes the meaning of a sentence clear.

Unclear: Frank and Carlos will go to *his* house after school. [Whose house?]
Clear: Frank and Carlos will go to Frank's house after school.

Unclear: Edna and Dina are waxing *her* car. [Whose car?]
Clear: Edna and Dina are waxing Dina's car.

When writing in Edited Standard English, choose pronouns that are features of this dialect.

The pronouns *hisself* and *theirselves* are not features of Edited Standard English. Use the forms *himself* and *themselves* instead.

He didn't hurt *himself* when he fell.

They congratulated *themselves* on the large turnout at the dance.

Exercise 11: Correcting Problems in Pronoun Usage

Each of the following sentences has a problem in pronoun usage. Write each sentence and correct the problem.

Examples

a. Jess's Aunt Kay she swims thirty-two laps a day.
   Jess's Aunt Kay swims thirty-two laps a day.

b. I and Mari are going skating in the park.
Mari and I are going skating in the park.

1. The Democrats they will debate the issues with the Republicans.
2. When he was only twelve, my grandfather came to America by hisself.
3. I and my sister get up at 5 o'clock to deliver the morning newspaper.
4. Lori and her mother are visiting her sister in Phoenix.
5. Mrs. Orlinsky and her daughter built their patio all by theirselves.
6. Jed's stepfather he works as a mechanic for an airline.
7. Next Saturday I and my friends are going to a record swap meet.
8. When Oscar and Pete collided, his glasses broke.
9. Italian is not a difficult language for me and my friends.
10. Janice and Mary Ellen took photographs at her sister's wedding.

Using Subject Pronouns

The subject form of the personal pronoun includes these pronouns:

Subject Form	
Singular	*Plural*
I, you, he, she, it	we, you, they

Use the subject form when the pronoun is the subject of a sentence.

We picked two bushels of apples.

Kuni and *I* ran to catch the bus.

Kamau and *he* play together well.

331

Grammar and Usage

Use the subject form when the pronoun follows a form of the verb *be* and renames or identifies the subject of the sentence.

The winners were Melissa and *she*.

"This is *he*," Mr. Garcia replied.

It was *they* who gave us directions.

Sometimes, a pronoun is joined with a noun or other pronoun in a sentence. Use the form of the pronoun you would use if the pronoun were alone in the sentence.

Darren, Phyllis, and *he* were the ushers at the concert. (*He* was the usher at the concert.)

Did *you* and *she* join the swimming team? (Did *she* join the swimming team?)

When a sentence ends in an incomplete construction, use the subject form. (An incomplete construction is a sentence with part left for the reader to complete.)

My brother is taller than *I*.	[than I am]
I am older than *he*.	[than he is]

Exercise 12: Using Subject Pronouns

Write the following sentences and choose the pronoun that correctly completes each sentence. Underline the pronoun you select.

Examples

a. (Her, She) has been a court reporter for three years.
   She has been a court reporter for three years.

b. The best bowlers on our team are you and (me, I).
   The best bowlers on our team are you and I.

1. If the weather is good, Kelly and (he, him) want to play one-on-one basketball this weekend.
2. The tallest students in the class are Ted and (her, she).
3. Carlita and Paul dance better than (us, we), but (them, they) and (us, we) are still good friends.
4. (They, Them) and (we, us) are entering the Planet Ocean Contest as creatures of the deep.
5. Marcia has a better collection of stamps from Latin American countries than (them, they).
6. The soloists now are Katy, Martin, and (me, I), but (us, we) choir members will vote on the new ones soon.
7. The person in our family who is most interested in fishing is (she, her).
8. My brother and (I, me) are planning a backpacking weekend along the Appalachian Trail.
9. Are Jerry and (her, she) the two people organizing the neighborhood cleanup campaign?
10. Marilyn, Lois, and (me, I) all have the same middle name; (we, us) girls were all named Kathleen.

Using Object Pronouns

Personal pronouns have a singular and plural object form.

Object Forms	
Singular	**Plural**
me, you, him, her, it	us, you, them

Use the object form when the pronoun is the object of the verb. The object answers the question *whom?* after the verb.

Sheila invited *me* to spend the weekend.

Maria and Rosa drove *us* to the airport.

The clown squirted *them* with water.

Grammar and Usage

Use the object form when the pronoun answers the question *to whom?* after the verb.

> Dad gave *her* and *me* tickets to the concert.
>
> Julio sent *him* a postcard from Quebec.
>
> Mr. Ling gave *us* a science test on Friday.

Use the object form when the pronoun follows a preposition, such as *by*, *for*, *to*, *from*, and *with*.

> The ball came straight at *them*.
>
> A package arrived this morning for *me*.
>
> Will you sit with *us* at the game?

Exercise 13: Using Object Pronouns

Write the following sentences and choose the pronoun that correctly completes each sentence. Underline the pronoun you select.

Examples

   a. Ask Lois and (him, he) for directions.
      Ask Lois and him for directions.

   b. This package is addressed to Kiyo and (I, me).
      This package is addressed to Kiyo and me.

1. When the truck passed, it splashed mud and water on Tony and (I, me).
2. The doctor sent Mrs. Noburu and (me, I) a notice of her change of address.
3. To Anthony and (I, me) the field trips are the best part of the class.
4. Did anyone call (her, she) or (me, I)?
5. Susan's parents talk to (she, her) and (I, me) as if they like and respect us.
6. Please tell Bill and (we, us) the results of the student government presidential poll.

7. Without you and (her, she) we never would have finished the work.
8. The principal complimented the eighth-graders and (we, us) for our help in tutoring elementary school students.
9. Jan's mom always asks Jan's brother and (she, her) for their opinions.
10. Just between you and (me, I) Sally is nervous about singing on stage.

Using Who and Whom

The distinction between *who* and *whom* is disappearing in informal speaking and writing. For formal situations, however, you should know which form to use.

Who is the subject form and is used as the subject of the sentence.

Who closed the window?

Who will make the final decision?

Do you know *who* scored the tying run?

Whom is the object form and is used as a direct object, an indirect object, or an object of a preposition.

Whom did you ask for directions?

To *whom* is the book dedicated?

With *whom* did she arrive?

If the pronoun comes at the beginning of the sentence, you can often determine the correct form by mentally changing the word order, or by substituting a statement for the question.

[Who/Whom] do you want to help?

[You do want to help *whom?*]

[Who/Whom] are you going with?

[You are going with *whom?*]

Grammar and Usage

Exercise 14: Using Who and Whom

Write out the following sentences and supply the correct form of *who* or *whom*. Underline the pronoun you select.

Examples

a. _____ did you see at the meeting?
   <u>Whom</u> did you see at the meeting?

b. _____ ran the country during Woodrow Wilson's illness?
   <u>Who</u> ran the country during Woodrow Wilson's illness?

1. _____ did the committee recommend to chair the industrial project?
2. _____ fought the Battle of the Alamo?
3. By _____ was "The Star-Spangled Banner" written?
4. _____ were some of the leaders of the women's suffrage movement?
5. _____ did Chief Tecumseh attempt to unite?
6. _____ was Malcolm X?
7. On the back of a ten-dollar bill, _____ is shown?
8. _____ do you think will win the election for president of the student council?
9. For _____ is the element lawrencium named?
10. _____ did she say was calling?

Review: Using Pronouns

Write each of the following sentences and choose the correct form of each pronoun in parentheses. Underline the pronoun you have chosen.

Examples

a. The telegram was for Mr. Ignazio and (her, she).
   The telegram was for Mr. Ignazio and <u>her</u>.

b. Kiyo and (him, he) are coeditors of the newspaper.
   Kiyo and <u>he</u> are coeditors of the newspaper.

1. Mrs. Fong asked the Hendersons and (us, we) to her graduation.
2. To (whom, who) are the legislators responsible, the voters or themselves?
3. Susan and (her, she) head the special committee on environmental problems.
4. (Whom, Who) wrote the well-known, long narrative poem, "Casey at the Bat"?
5. The contractor hired (them, they) and (us, we) at three dollars a basket.
6. (Him, He) and (me, I) are taking a course in computer programming.
7. Please give the new botany catalogues to Dr. Lowe and (her, she).
8. Sherry and (them, they) are planning a barbecue to celebrate their graduation.
9. (Whom, Who) did Marcus hit?
10. Jackie's cousin Juanita and (her, she) are respiratory therapists.
11. (Whom, Who) do you have to meet after the game on Saturday?
12. Have Marcia and (her, she) taken down the tent?
13. (Whom, Who) painted the ceiling of the Sistine Chapel in Rome, Italy?
14. Without Aunt Cele and (her, she), family get-togethers wouldn't be much fun.
15. This song is dedicated to you and (him, he).
16. (Them, They) and (us, we) have been rivals for more than twenty years.
17. (Whom, Who) did you say is calling?
18. (Whom, Who) was the first Vice President of the United States?
19. Langston Hughes and (him, he) are among the best American poets of the twentieth century.
20. To (whom, who) do the eighty acres across the river from you belong?

Grammar and Usage

Writing Focus: *Using Pronouns in Writing*

You can strengthen your writing by using pronouns to avoid unnecessary repetition and to vary the structure of your sentences. Be sure that the pronouns you use are in the correct form and agree with their antecedents in number and gender.

Assignment: *My Hero*

Most of us have a special person we admire. Perhaps this person is a senator or president, an entertainer, a grandparent, a friend, a teacher, a family member, or even a literary or historical figure. This person, we feel, exhibits qualities we may wish we had. We respect, admire, and even love the person. He or she becomes for us a hero or heroine.

Write one or more well-developed paragraphs about your hero or heroine. Be specific about the qualities that make the person a hero or heroine in your eyes. Write for your classmates. Your writing will be evaluated for correct use of pronouns.

Use the following steps to complete this assignment.

A. Prewriting

Spend five to ten minutes making a list of people you admire. Choose one to write about. Use the six-basic-questions method described in Chapter 1 to generate ideas. Jot down questions like the following: *Who* is my hero or heroine? *What* qualities does this person have which make him or her a hero? *Where* did I first encounter or hear about this person? *When* did this person become my hero or heroine? *Why* did this person become my hero or heroine? *How* did this person become my hero or heroine? Keep writing down questions that help you think about all aspects of your hero or heroine. Answer your questions specifically in words, phrases, or sentences. Review your answers and group them into an organizational pattern that will help your readers follow your discussion. Part of your writing might relate in chronological order the event or events that led to your finding your hero or heroine.

B. Writing

Using your answers, write one or more paragraphs about your hero or heroine. Tell about the special person and explain how and why he or she became heroic to you. Discuss the qualities that make the person a hero or heroine. Be sure to include specific details in your account. As you write, pay particular attention to the pronouns you use.

C. Postwriting

Revise your first draft using the following checklist.

1. Have I explained fully about my hero or heroine?
2. Does each pronoun I used agree with its antecedent in number and gender?

Edit your work using the Checklist for Proofreading at the back of the book. If appropriate, share your writing with your teacher and classmates. Create and illustrate a class magazine entitled *Heroes*.

13 Verbs

Understanding Verbs

Verbs give sentences meaning by saying something about the subject. The traditional approach to identifying verbs is through their definition. Studying the classes into which verbs may be divided and looking at the features that distinguish them from other parts of speech are also useful methods. In the following sections you will study and practice each of these methods.

Defining Verbs

A *verb* is usually defined as a word that shows action or state of being.

Joanna *reached* for the pickles.	[action]
Señor Blanco *judged* the essays.	[action]
Ken *is* inside his room.	[state of being]
I *am* nervous about the audition.	[state of being]

Grouping Verbs by Classes

Verbs are usually grouped into three main classes: action verbs (transitive and intransitive), linking verbs, and helping verbs.

***Action verbs* show physical or mental action.**

Physical Action

We *hike* along the river.
They *talk* for hours.
I *wiggle* my ears.

Mental Action

Fran *dreamed* about a volcano.
Paolo *knew* the answer.
The children *believed* us.

Exercise 1: Identifying Action Verbs

Write the following sentences and underline each action verb.

Examples

a. Ellen painted the bathroom ceiling.
Ellen <u>painted</u> the bathroom ceiling.
b. Harvey thought of a solution to his problem.
Harvey <u>thought</u> of a solution to his problem.

1. Every student signed the petition.
2. Nora tells long, ridiculous jokes.
3. Michelle cleaned the work area carefully.
4. Tony often daydreams during study period.
5. Science fiction writers imagine possibilities of future life.
6. Alice tumbled down an incredibly deep hole.
7. Last Friday night they went to the Peter Frampton concert.
8. She worries too much about final exams.
9. Dick typed his science report.
10. Jim Beckwourth discovered a pass through the Sierra Nevadas.

Action verbs may or may not take objects. An object is a noun or pronoun that receives the action of the verb. Action verbs that take objects are called *transitive* verbs.

Stephanie *planted* some roses. [*Roses* is the object of *planted*.]
Tom *played* the piano all afternoon. [*Piano* is the object of *played*.]

Action verbs that do not take an object are called *intransitive* verbs.

The trees *swayed* in the breeze.
My brother *laughed*.

Grammar and Usage

Some action verbs can be either transitive or intransitive.

> Nancy shakes her piggy bank. (T)
> When frightened, animals often shake. (I)

Exercise 2: Identifying Action Transitive and Intransitive Verbs

Go back to Exercise 1. Put a T next to the sentence if the verb is transitive. Put an I if it is intransitive.

Examples

a. Ellen <u>painted</u> the bathroom ceiling. (T)
b. Harvey <u>thought</u> of a solution to his problem. (I)

Linking verbs **do not show action. Instead, they link a noun or pronoun in the first part of a sentence with a word in the second part. All linking verbs are intransitive.**

The double rainbow *was* spectacular.

The tacos *tasted* spicy.

My aunt *became* an engineer.

Practical jokes *are* my specialty.

Linking verbs include forms of the verb *be* and a few other commonly used verbs. Many linking verbs are related to the five senses.

Some Forms of **Be**		*Other Common Linking Verbs*		
am	has been	taste	look	grow
is	have been	smell	feel	appear
are	had been	sound	become	remain
was	will be	seem	stay	
were	should be			
may be	would have been			
can be	shall be			

Depending on use, some words can be either action or linking verbs.

Action: Sam *grew* corn and tomatoes last summer.

Linking: Nancy *grew* taller last year.

Action: Lisa *felt* the smoothness of the velvet.

Linking: Our morning swim *felt* refreshing.

Exercise 3: Identifying Linking Verbs

Write the following sentences, underlining each linking, or transitive, verb. Then write the words the linking verb connects.

Examples

a. The story about the vampire was scary.
   The story about the vampire was scary.
   Was connects story and scary.

b. This caterpillar becomes the beautiful butterfly.
   This caterpillar becomes the beautiful butterfly.
   Becomes connects caterpillar and butterfly.

1. During the debate Joan appeared confident.
2. Grace Yin's mother became a citizen on January 1.
3. Mrs. Garcia stayed calm during the fire.
4. Even with the door shut, your stereo sounds too loud.
5. Keith is patient with his little sister.
6. She still felt hungry after lunch.
7. Helen's favorite movie stars are Paul Newman and Robert Redford.
8. During the summer the school looks small and deserted.
9. David sounds bored with his job.
10. Paula's aunt has been a taxidermist.

Helping verbs help the main verb express action or state of being.

Karim *has* designed a mural for the cafeteria.

The officers *will* be elected on Wednesday.

Grammar and Usage

Lucia *did* speak to him about the program.

We *should have* given him the directions.

Helping verbs include the forms of *be* and many other commonly used words.

Forms of **Be**		*Other Helping Verbs*		
be	was	has	did	could
been	were	have	may	shall
am		had	might	should
is		do	must	will
are		does	can	would

Helping verbs work together with the main verb to form a *verb phrase*.

A verb phrase consists of two or more verbs that work together as a single verb.

She *should have been elected* president of the club.

Lucia *will win* the spelling contest.

I *have registered* for a ceramics course.

Exercise 4: Identifying Verb Phrases and Helping Verbs

Write the following sentences and underline each verb phrase. Then draw a second line under each helping verb.

Examples

a. Male lions can sleep as much as twenty hours a day.
   Male lions <u>can sleep</u> as much as twenty hours a day.

b. The huge St. Bernard has been trained as a rescue dog.
   The huge St. Bernard <u>has been trained</u> as a rescue dog.

1. The jaguarundi, a species of cat, can be found in South and Central America.
2. Donkeys will eat practically anything.
3. Pasht was worshiped in ancient Egypt as the cat goddess.

4. The sinister laugh of the hyena can be heard at night.
5. Because of its intelligence and keen sense of smell, the poodle was used as a hunting dog.
6. Ricardo's uncle could have photographed a large, white rhinoceros.
7. Every year defenseless seals are killed by hunters.
8. Many black bears have begged people for handouts in Yellowstone National Park.
9. The South American capybara, a giant rodent, can weigh as much as 130 pounds.
10. Groups of killer whales have been seen in all of the world's oceans.

Finding Verbs by Their Features

The following four features can help you identify verbs. A verb must have at least one of these features, and some verbs have all four.

Verbs have tense.

Tense is the time expressed by a verb. There are two kinds of tenses: *simple* and *perfect*.

Simple Tenses	Perfect Tenses
present	present perfect
past	past perfect
future	future perfect

The tense of the verb is formed from one of its three principal parts: *present*, *past*, and *past participle*.

The present form is the form of the verb used with *to*: (*to*) *do*, (*to*) *begin*, (*to*) *help*.

The *past* form is the form used to show action that occurred in the past: *did, began, helped*.

The *past participle* form of the verb is the form used with the helping verb *has, have,* or *had*: (*has*) *done,* (*have*) *begun,* (*had*) *helped*.

Grammar and Usage

Present	Past	Past Participle
open	opened	opened
play	played	played
fish	fished	fished
rain	rained	rained
hit	hit	hit
see	saw	seen
break	broke	broken
fall	fell	fallen

The following list shows how verb tenses are formed.

Simple Present:	present form of the verb	I look, he looks
Simple Past:	past form of the verb	I looked, he looked
Simple Future:	present form plus *shall* or *will*	I shall look, he will look
Present Perfect:	past participle plus *have* or *has*	I have looked, he has looked
Past Perfect:	past participle plus *had*	I had looked, he had looked
Future Perfect:	past participle plus *shall have* or *will have*	I shall have looked, he will have looked

Verbs have an *-ing* form.

The *-ing* form of a verb is its *progressive* form. The progressive form of the verb has a form of *be* plus an *-ing* verb.

Simple Present:	We *are painting* the house.
Simple Past:	We *were painting* the house.
Simple Future:	We *will be painting* the house.
Present Perfect:	We *have been painting* the house.
Past Perfect:	We *had been painting* the house.
Future Perfect:	We *will have been painting* the house.

Verbs have a singular and a plural form.

The singular or plural form of a verb is used to agree with the subject in the sentence. When the subject is singular, the ending *-s* or *-es* is added to the present tense form of the verb for third-person singular. When the subject is plural, the present tense form is used by itself. Helping verbs also have a singular and plural form.

Joseph <u>plays</u> the guitar well.	[singular]
All four students <u>play</u> the guitar well.	[plural]
A panther <u>searches</u> for food in the jungle.	[singular]
Birds <u>search</u> for berries on trees.	[plural]
Louise <u>has requested</u> a transfer.	[singular]
The employees <u>have requested</u> a transfer.	[plural]

Verbs often include suffixes such as *-fy, -ize, -ate, -ish,* or *-en.*

Horror movies may *terrify* younger children.

In our English class we *memorize* a poem each week.

Exercise 5: *Identifying Verbs by Their Features*

Write each of the following sentences and underline the verb or verb phrase. Use the features you have learned to identify the verbs.

Examples

a. Sam and Eric are washing the car.
Sam and Eric <u>are washing</u> the car.
(This verb has an <u>-ing</u> form and a form of <u>be</u>.)

b. Rhonda practices the flute every day.
Rhonda <u>practices</u> the flute every day.
(This verb has an <u>-s</u> ending for its singular form.)

1. Our cat likes fish better than liver.
2. Before the game the players will report to the gym.

Grammar and Usage

3. Julio will finish his test before anyone else in the class.
4. Finally the rain has stopped.
5. Michael Lin rides his bike two miles to school.
6. I am planting tomatoes in the garden this spring.
7. You must vacate the building immediately for a fire drill.
8. The snow has covered the front steps already.
9. Please darken the room before film time.
10. Our class was collecting aluminum cans for the recycling center.

Review: Understanding Verbs

In the following story about words, there are twenty-five verbs or verb phrases. Using what you have learned about identifying verbs in this section, find at least twenty of the verbs and verb phrases. List them on a sheet of paper. The first one is underlined for you.

    Two gangs of words <u>were hanging</u> around on opposite street corners. One group of words acted tough. The other group of words pretended they didn't care. The tough words had been flexing their muscles and telling loud jokes when their leader drove up. The leader should have been there earlier, so his gang of words ignored him. "What does this mean?" yelled the leader.
    "You could be on time once in a while," said a reasonable word.
    "Or is that too hard for you?" sneered a sarcastic word.
    "You might have phoned!" shouted an angry word.
    Then, in front of their eyes, the leader blew up like a balloon. As he got bigger, he screamed threats at his gang. "I frighten! I terrorize!"
    The other group of words quickly sneaked off down the alley. The leader's gang shrank to one small voice, "We apologize."

Applying What You Know

Select a few paragraphs from a magazine, newspaper, or book you have read. Identify the verbs and list them on a sheet of paper. Your teacher may ask you what method you used to identify them. Do they fit the definition of a verb? Do they belong to one of the verb classes? Do they have one or more features of verbs?

Using Verbs

The following sections will give you practice in forming and using the tenses of verbs and their progressive forms. You will also practice making verbs agree with their subjects and using the correct forms of verbs that are often confused.

Using the Simple Verb Tenses

Form the *present tense* with the present form of the verb.

In the present tense *-s* or *-es* is added to the third-person singular verb.

Present Tense

I show	we show
you show	you show
he she it } shows	they show

Form the *past tense* of regular verbs by adding *-d* or *-ed* to the present form.

Past Tense

I played	we played
you played	you played
he she it } played	they played

Form the *future tense* by adding *shall* or *will* to the present form.

Grammar and Usage

Future Tense	
I shall/will practice	we shall/will practice
you will practice	you will practice
he ⎫ she ⎬ will practice it ⎭	they will practice

Note: In formal English *shall* is used with first-person verbs.

Exercise 6: Using Simple Verb Tenses

Rewrite each of the following sentences and change the tense of each verb to the tense given in parentheses. Underline the verbs you form. (The verbs are regular.)

Examples

a. Halley's comet returns predictably. (future)
   Halley's comet will return predictably.

b. The eclipse is an awesome sight. (past)
   The eclipse was an awesome sight.

1. Some of the students stared in amazement. (present)
2. Elephants dance to a strange song in her dream. (past)
3. Gina lived across the street from an express subway stop. (present)
4. Fifty thousand people jam the stadium. (future)
5. In a single bound Superman jumps over tall buildings. (past)
6. Suddenly the earth moves. (future)
7. Mrs. Drzewiecki's terrier chased everything. (present)
8. On a thirty-mile bike hike Earl's legs sometimes cramp. (future)
9. Dr. Frankenstein creates a monster. (past)
10. Woody plays his drums for his friends only in the basement. (past)

Using the Perfect Tenses

The *present perfect tense* is formed with the helping verb *has* or *have* and the past participle form of the verb.

Has is used with the third-person singular form of the verb. Form the past participle of regular verbs by adding *-d* or *-ed* to the present form.

Present Perfect Tense

I have learned	we have learned
you have learned	you have learned
he / she / it has learned	they have learned

The *past perfect tense* is formed with the helping verb *had* and the past participle form of the verb.

Past Perfect Tense

I had opened	we had opened
you have opened	you had opened
he / she / it had opened	they had opened

The *future perfect tense* is formed with the helping verbs *shall have* or *will have* and the past participle form of the verb.

Grammar and Usage

Future Perfect Tense	
I shall/will have listened	we shall/will have listened
you will have listened	you will have listened
he } she } will have listened it }	they will have listened

Exercise 7: Using Perfect Tenses

Write each of the following sentences and supply the perfect tense of the verb shown in parentheses. Underline the verb phrase. (The verbs in this exercise are regular verbs.)

Example

a. Night looks darkest before the dawn. (past perfect)
Night <u>had looked</u> darkest before the dawn.

1. Lady Macbeth washes her hands. (present perfect)
2. A huge oil slick approaches the coast of California. (past perfect)
3. The ash cloud from the eruption of Mount St. Helens drifts toward Chicago. (future perfect)
4. Sam Spade solved the mystery. (present perfect)
5. Carl plays the bagpipes in every parade in his hometown. (future perfect)
6. Juanita will record four of her best songs for the album. (past perfect)
7. Peter Piper picked a peck of pickled peppers. (present perfect)
8. John Smith's friendship with Pocahontas saved the settlers just in time. (past perfect)
9. By the end of next week, we finish our reports on conservation and on writing as a means of communication. (future perfect)
10. Before he was elected President, Franklin Delano Roosevelt served two terms as governor of New York. (past perfect)

Using Irregular Verbs

Irregular verbs do not follow the regular pattern for forming their principal parts.

Some irregular verbs form their past and past participle forms with a spelling change; others remain the same in both the past and past participle forms. The following list gives the three principal parts for commonly used irregular verbs. Read over the list several times to become familiar with the words.

Present Tense	**Past Tense**	**Past Participle** [*has, have,* or *had*]
become	became	become
begin	began	begun
break	broke	broken
bring	brought	brought
build	built	built
burst	burst	burst
buy	bought	bought
catch	caught	caught
choose	chose	chosen
come	came	come
dive	dove *or* dived	dived
do	did	done
draw	drew	drawn
drink	drank	drunk
drive	drove	driven
eat	ate	eaten
fall	fell	fallen
fly	flew	flown

Grammar and Usage

Present Tense	Past Tense	Past Participle [*has, have,* or *had*]
forget	forgot	forgotten
freeze	froze	frozen
give	gave	given
go	went	gone
grow	grew	grown
keep	kept	kept
know	knew	known
lay	laid	laid
lie	lay	lain
ride	rode	ridden
ring	rang	rung
rise	rose	risen
run	ran	run
see	saw	seen
shake	shook	shaken
shrink	shrank	shrunk
sing	sang	sung
sink	sank	sunk
speak	spoke	spoken
spend	spent	spent
spring	sprang	sprung
steal	stole	stolen
strive	strove	striven
swear	swore	sworn
swim	swam	swum
take	took	taken
teach	taught	taught
think	thought	thought

Present Tense	Past Tense	Past Participle [*has, have,* or *had*]
throw	threw	thrown
wear	wore	worn
write	wrote	written

If you are not sure about the principal parts of any verb, check your dictionary. Dictionaries always list the entry words for verbs in the present tense form. If the verb is regular, its principal parts will not be listed unless there is a spelling change. For example, the past form of *hop* is listed because the *p* is doubled in *hopped*. Dictionaries do list the past and past participle forms of all irregular verbs, as the following entry for the verb *fall* shows.

fall (fôl) vi. **fell, fallen, falling**

Each verb's principal parts are given in this order: present, past, past participle. The entry word (*fall*) is in the present form. After the pronunciation, the past form is listed (*fell*). The next form is the past participle form (*fallen*). The *-ing* form may also be listed (*falling*).

The tenses of irregular verbs are formed with the three principal parts and with helping verbs.

Principal Parts

Present	Past	Past Participle
ride	rode	ridden

Simple Present (Add *-s* or *-es* in third-person singular.)

I ride	we ride
you ride	you ride
he, she, it rides	they ride

Grammar and Usage

Simple Past (past form)

I rode	we rode
you rode	you rode
he, she, it rode	they rode

Simple Future (shall or will + present form)

I shall/will ride	we shall/will ride
you will ride	you will ride
he, she, it will ride	they will ride

Present Perfect (have or has + past participle)

I have ridden	we have ridden
you have ridden	you have ridden
he, she, it has ridden	they have ridden

Past Perfect (had + past participle)

I had ridden	we had ridden
you had ridden	you had ridden
he, she, it had ridden	they had ridden

Future Perfect (shall have or will have + past participle)

I shall/will have ridden	we shall/will have ridden
you will have ridden	you will have ridden
he, she, it will have ridden	they will have ridden

Exercise 8: Using Irregular Verbs

Each of the following sentences contains an irregular verb. Write the sentences and choose the proper verb form from the choices given in parentheses. If you are unsure about which form is correct, consult the list of irregular verbs. Underline the verb form you select.

Examples

a. Paula has never (rode, ridden) with a Western saddle.
   Paula has never ridden with a Western saddle.

b. Larry (kept, keeped) six hamsters in the garage.
   Larry kept six hamsters in the garage.

1. This hand has (shook, shaken) the hand of the President of the United States.
2. She (teached, taught) us how to play backgammon in one afternoon.
3. When the temperature dropped below zero, the pipes in the basement (burst, bursted).
4. She (sprang, sprung) to her feet when the doorbell rang.
5. I (saw, seen) Mari and Hiroshi at the school dance last weekend.
6. Kiyo has (broke, broken) her grandmother's antique clock.
7. Ramon and Cleo have (gone, went) to the Knicks game.
8. Have you (did, done) anything to conserve energy?
9. Joyce will have (saw, seen) *The Empire Strikes Back* four times.
10. Mr. Ostrowsky called the police to report that someone had (stole, stolen) his 1948 car.

Using the Progressive Forms of Verbs

The progressive form can be used in all six tenses. Form each tense with the correct tense of *be* and the *-ing* form of the verb. (Add *-ing* to the present verb form. Use the spelling rules in Chapter 27 to guide you.)

Tenses of Be

Present Tense

Singular	Plural
I am	we are
you are	you are
he/she/it is	they are

Past Tense

Singular	Plural
I was	we were
you were	you were
he/she/it was	they were

Future Tense

Singular	Plural
I shall/will be	we shall/will be
you will be	you will be
he/she/it will be	they will be

Present Perfect Tense

Singular	Plural
I have been	we have been
you have been	you have been
he/she/it has been	they have been

Past Perfect Tense

Singular	Plural
I had been	we had been
you had been	you had been
he/she/it had been	they had been

Future Perfect Tense

Singular	Plural
I shall/will have been	we shall/will have been
you will have been	you will have been
he/she/it will have been	they will have been

Progressive Form

Simple Tenses

Perry *is waxing* the car.	[progressive form of present tense]
Rosa *was dancing* with Steve.	[progressive form of past tense]
We *will be waiting* in the lobby.	[progressive form of future tense]

Perfect Tenses

Kiyo *has been studying* astronomy.	[progressive form of present perfect tense]
Lucy *had been crying*.	[progressive form of past perfect tense]
By June we *will have been living* here a year.	[progressive form of future perfect tense]

Exercise 9: Using Progressive Forms of Verbs

Write each of the sentences on the following page and change the verb to its progressive form without changing its tense. Underline the new verb form.

Example

a. The Boston Red Sox led the Eastern Division.
   The Boston Red Sox <u>were leading</u> the Eastern Division.

Grammar and Usage

1. Diaz changes the oil in his car.
2. He will look for a flat that rents for less than 200 dollars.
3. She flew alone across the Atlantic.
4. Neil Armstrong had taught at the University of Cincinnati.
5. Stan fixes the leaks in the roof.
6. Mrs. Aquinatta will have taken the civil service exam.
7. Two of the employees took lie detector tests.
8. Jenny and her dad built bookcases for her room.
9. Sally Rainwater had written a letter to the editor.
10. Mari talks to her guidance counselor.

Making Verbs Agree with Subjects

A verb must agree with its subject.

Verbs and their subjects can be either singular or plural. When a subject is singular, its verb must also be singular. In the third-person singular of the present tense, the verb requires an *-s* or *-es* ending.

I *work* in the library on Saturdays.	[singular subject, singular verb]
You *work* at the drugstore.	[singular subject, singular verb]
Betty *works* every night at the bookstore.	[singular subject, singular verb]

When a subject is plural, its verb must also be plural. Most verbs drop the *-s* or *-es* ending to form the plural verb.

Mel and Janice *leave* an hour from now.	[plural subject, plural verb]
The apples *taste* crisp and juicy.	[plural subject, plural verb]

| The chimes *ring* on the hour. | [plural subject, plural verb] |

Exercise 10: Making Verbs Agree with Subjects

Rewrite each of the following sentences by changing the subject to that given in parentheses. Keep the tense of the verb the same as that in the original sentence but be certain the form of the verb in the new sentence agrees with its subject. Then underline the verb or verb phrase in the new sentence.

Example

a. The horses jump across the gully. (The horse)
The horse <u>jumps</u> across the gully.

1. Victor Chong has moved to Seattle. (Victor Chong and his family)
2. The soldier waits for letters from home. (The soldiers)
3. The waiters make twenty dollars in tips. (The waiter)
4. The next plane leaves at 8:15 P.M. (The next planes)
5. Bonnie goes to City College. (Bonnie and her sister)
6. Ernest picks vegetables and fruit in southern California. (Ernest and his wife)
7. Ms. Ling speaks Spanish, English, and Vietnamese. (Ms. Ling and Kim Ling)
8. Emiliano Zapata led a Mexican land reform movement in the early 1900s. (Emiliano Zapata and his followers)
9. Sherlock Holmes searches carefully for clues at the scene of the crime. (Sherlock Holmes and Dr. Watson)
10. The masons have finished the floor. (The mason)

Avoiding Problems in Agreement

Agreement with the subject is not changed by a phrase following the subject.

Grammar and Usage

Subjects are often followed by prepositional phrases used to further describe them. The verb does not agree with the noun in the phrase. Instead, it must agree in number with the subject.

The box of records sits in the closet. [singular subject, singular verb]

The pencils on the table need sharpening. [plural subject, plural verb]

Exercise 11: Solving Agreement Problems

Write the following sentences and choose the form of the verb given in parentheses that agrees with the subject in each sentence. Underline both the subject and the verb form that you choose.

Example

a. The flowers on the desk (smell, smells) good.
The flowers on the desk smell good.

1. The director of the city libraries (take, takes) requests for new books.
2. The construction on our streets (is, are) disturbing our peace and quiet.
3. The windows on the west side of the house (needs, need) washing.
4. Seldom do the members of our team (arrive, arrives) late.
5. That can of peanuts (are, is) stale.
6. The semester exams in our school (begin, begins) next week.
7. The fire hydrants in the center of town (was, were) painted red, white, and blue.
8. In the afternoon the trees in the backyard (cover, covers) the lawn with shade.
9. The morning air in large cities (show, shows) a large amount of visible pollution.
10. The announcer on the evening news (speaks, speak) clearly.

When *there* or *here* is used to begin a sentence, the subject often appears after the verb in the sentence. The subject and verb must still agree in number.

Here is my Spanish notebook.	[singular subject and verb]
Here are the pictures of my dog.	[plural subject and verb]
There was a storm last night.	[singular subject and verb]
There were two questions on the test.	[plural subject and verb]

When a sentence is written as a question, the subject usually follows the verb. The subject and verb must still agree in number.

Where is the set of wrenches?	[singular subject and verb]
Where are the wrenches?	[plural subject and verb]
Does Jim know the correct answer?	[singular subject and verb]
Do the Wongs have a new cat?	[plural subject and verb]

Exercise 12: Solving Agreement Problems

Write the sentences on the following page and choose the form of the verb given in parentheses that agrees with the true subject of each sentence. Underline both the subject and the verb form that agrees with it.

Example

a. Where (is, are) the keys to the apartment?
Where are the keys to the apartment?

Grammar and Usage

1. (Has, Have) one of the records been broken?
2. Where (do, does) the members of the Camera Club have their film developed?
3. There (go, goes) my hopes for passing this test.
4. Here (is, are) a painting of apples, lemons, and oranges to hang over the kitchen table.
5. (Do, Does) many students in your class complain about Mr. Grippo's daily quizzes?
6. Where (was, were) the bowl for the fruit?
7. (Is, Are) the chemicals in this bag of fertilizer safe for the plants?
8. Here (come, comes) the twins.
9. There (was, were) a swarm of bees attacking the characters in the film.
10. (Has, Have) this bag of potatoes been weighed yet?

Agreement with Compound Subjects and Collective Nouns

Subjects joined by *and* take a plural verb.

Janice and Sid *collect* movie stars' autographs.

Mother Frances Cabrini and Judge John J. Sirica *are* famous Italian-Americans.

Singular subjects joined by *or* or *nor* take a singular verb.

Jan, Donna, or Greta *has won* first prize.

A poodle or a collie *makes* a good pet for children.

Neither Carlos nor Juan *is* home.

When a singular and plural subject are joined by *or* or *nor*, the verb agrees with the nearer subject.

Neither the *employees* nor the *employer wants* a strike.	[singular]
Neither *Lou* nor his *sisters want* to move.	[plural]

Collective nouns can be either singular or plural. If they refer to a group as a unit, they are singular. If they refer to the individual members of the group, they are plural.

The jury *gives* its verdict at the end of the trial.	[singular]
The jury *are* from several different cities.	[plural]

The following list gives some of the most common collective nouns.

group	family	army	audience
flock	club	fleet	crowd
herd	class	troop	assembly
swarm	team	public	squadron

Exercise 13: Agreement with Compound Subjects and Collective Nouns

Each of the following sentences contains a compound subject or a collective noun used as a subject. Write each sentence and choose the verb form given in parentheses that agrees with the subject. Underline the verb or verb phrase.

Example

a. Either Kevin or Becky (want, wants) your old bicycle.

Either Kevin or Becky <u>wants</u> your old bicycle.

1. A canoe or a kayak (is, are) dangerous in rough water.
2. Neither wind nor snow (stop, stops) the letter carriers.
3. The coaches and the referee (discuss, discusses) the rules before the game.
4. The Vasquez family (has, have) decided to paint their house.

Grammar and Usage

5. Neither Sylvia nor her parents (has, have) met the new neighbors.
6. Flying lessons or an encyclopedia (is, are) the grand prize.
7. Heavy shoes and a knapsack (is, are) needed for the hike.
8. Meadowlark Lemon and Wilt "the Stilt" Chamberlain (was, were) Harlem Globetrotters.
9. The audience always (clap, claps) when R2-D2 is on the screen.
10. The class (go, goes) their separate ways after graduation.

Agreement with Indefinite Pronouns

When indefinite pronouns are used as subjects of sentences, their verbs must agree with them.

Some indefinite pronouns are always singular and take singular verbs.

each	either	everyone
one	neither	everybody
nobody	anyone	someone
no one	anybody	somebody

| No one in our school *speaks* Hindu. | [not one single person] |
| Everybody *needs* respect. | [every single person] |

Some indefinite pronouns are always plural and take plural verbs.

both   many   few   several

Both of my cousins *are* nearsighted.

Several of the old pennies *were* valuable.

Some indefinite pronouns can be singular or plural, depending on the "sense" of the sentence.

all	any	most	part
none	some	half	

If the pronoun refers to one person or thing, it is singular and takes a singular verb. If it refers to more than one person or thing, it is plural and takes a plural verb.

All of the garden *needs* watering.	[singular subject and verb]
All of the prices *have* gone up.	[plural subject and verb]

Exercise 14: Making Verbs Agree with Indefinite Pronouns

Write each of the following sentences, substituting the word given in parentheses for the *italicized* subject. Keep the tense of the verb the same as that in the original sentence but be sure that the form of the verb agrees with its new subject. Underline the verb in each sentence.

Example

a. Have *you* finished? (Everyone)
   Has everyone finished?

1. *The tenants* in the apartments are angry about the number of robberies and muggings. (Everyone)
2. Do *you* know the formula for the area of a circle? (Anyone)
3. *Aunt Julie and Uncle Mort* make delicious lentil soup with mushrooms and vegetables. (Somebody)
4. *Both* of the brothers want to have the job. (Neither)
5. Have *all* of the students completed the index? (Each)

Write each of the sentences on the following page and choose the correct form of the verb in parentheses. Underline the verb or verb phrase in each new sentence.

Example

a. Half of the jigsaw puzzle pieces (is, are) missing.
   Half of the jigsaw puzzle pieces are missing.

Grammar and Usage

6. Most of the treasure from King Tut's tomb (remain, remains) in Egypt.

7. Seven people were rushed to the hospital, but all (is, are) well.

8. (Do, Does) any of the guides read Hebrew?

9. Several of the pictures from the priceless collection (is, are) on display in the museum.

10. Many of the workers doing research on ground water (has, have) Ph.D. degrees.

Using Active and Passive Voices

A verb is in the *active voice* when it expresses an action performed *by* its subject. It is in the *passive voice* when it expresses an action performed *upon* its subject.

Active: The farmer harvested his crops.
[The subject, *farmer,* performs the action, *harvested.*]

Passive: The crops were harvested by the farmer.
[The subject, *crops,* receives the action, *harvested.*]

Only transitive verbs (those that take an object) can be used in the passive voice. The object of an active-voice sentence becomes the subject of the passive-voice sentence.

Active: The pitcher threw the ball.
          S   O

Passive: The ball was thrown by the pitcher.
          S

A passive voice sentence tells what is, was, or will be done to the subject. Passive voice verbs are always verb phrases; they include a form of the helper *be* and the past participle form of the main verb.

When a verb is written in the active voice, the subject performing the action is emphasized. When a verb is written in the passive voice, the emphasis is on the person or thing receiving the action.

Active: Carolyn washed the dog.
[The emphasis is on Carolyn.]

Passive: The dog was washed by Carolyn.
[The emphasis is on the dog.]

Exercise 15: Using Active and Passive Voices

Write each of the following sentences, changing the active verbs to passive, and the passive verbs to active. (It will be necessary to rearrange each sentence.) Underline the verbs you form.

Examples

a. Frank saw the ship in the harbor.
   The ship in the harbor was seen by Frank.

b. The trash was taken out by me.
   I took out the trash.

1. We were encouraged by the good news.
2. The teacher asked me to speak louder.
3. She laid the lavender flowers next to the daisies.
4. The curtains were raised by the theater manager.
5. In the rush, we forgot our gloves.

Verbs Often Confused

Lie/Lay

The verb *lie* means "to recline" or "to remain lying down." This verb can be used to describe a person who is relaxing or an object that has been placed at rest. The verb *lie* is always intransitive. The verb *lay* means "to put or place something down." When using this verb, state the object that is being put down or placed. The verb *lay* is always transitive.

Principal Parts

Present	Past	Past Participle
lie	lay	(have, had) lain
lay	laid	(have, had) laid

369

Lie

The cat *lies* on the chair by the window.	[present tense]
Yesterday the cat *lay* on the chair by the window.	[past tense]
Since dinner the cat *has lain* on the chair by the window.	[present perfect]

Lay

Yoki *lays* her tennis racket on the bed.	[present tense]
Yesterday Yoki *laid* her tennis racket on the bed.	[past tense]
Yoki *has laid* her tennis racket on the bed before.	[present perfect]

Sit/Set

The verb *sit* means "to occupy a seat," "to rest," or "to remain undisturbed." *Sit* is usually intransitive. The verb *set* means "to put or place something." When using this verb, state the object that is being put or placed. *Set* is usually transitive.

Principal Parts

Present	Past	Past Participle
sit	sat	(have, had) sat
set	set	(have, had) set

Sit

Gene *sits* nervously in the doctor's office.	[present]
The old vase *sat* on the shelf for years.	[past]
Michelle *has sat* in the same seat every day.	[present perfect]

Set

Jennifer *sets* the nails on the ledge.	[present]
Someone *set* the thermostat lower yesterday.	[past]
Earlier classes *have set* records for us to break.	[present perfect]

Rise/Raise

The verb *rise* means "to get up" or "to go up." *Rise* is always intransitive. The verb *raise* means "to lift up," "to force up," or "to bring up." When using the verb *raise*, state the object that is being lifted, forced or brought up. *Raise* is always transitive.

Principal Parts		
Present	**Past**	**Past Participle**
rise	rose	(have, had) risen
raise	raised	(have, had) raised

Rise

The price of movie tickets *rises* quickly.	[present]
The price of movie tickets *rose* again yesterday.	[past]
The price of movie tickets *has risen* three times over the past year.	[present perfect]

Raise

Nicole *raises* her hand.	[present]
Nicole *raised* her hand to answer the question.	[past]
Nicole *has raised* her hand four times.	[present perfect]

Grammar and Usage

Exercise 15: Using Verbs That Are Often Confused

Write each of the following sentences and choose the correct verb in parentheses. Underline the verb or verb phrase.

Examples

a. Katherine (laid, lay) on the raft in the lake.
Katherine lay on the raft in the lake.

b. After the rain the lake (rose, raised) six inches.
After the rain the lake rose six inches.

1. "(Lay, Lie) down," she commanded, but the cat stalked away.
2. As usual, Roger has forgotten where he (lay, laid) his glasses.
3. "Won't you (set, sit) down for a while?" she asked the joggers.
4. We (sat, set) very quietly in the shelter until the lightning stopped.
5. The audience (raised, rose) from their seats.
6. Will you (leave, let) us go to the museum?
7. (Can, May) we go to the movies tonight?
8. Please (raise, rise) and state your name and address.
9. Patty has (set, sat) on a freshly painted park bench.
10. Torri has (let, left) his club membership lapse.

Review: Using Verbs

Write each of the following sentences and choose the proper verb form from the choices given in parentheses. Underline the verb you select.

Example

a. Do you (know, knew) this material?
Do you know this material?

1. Have you (forgot, forgotten) the formula for water so soon after class?
2. When the phone (rung, rang), I (knew, knowed) it was my father.
3. How many laps have you (swam, swum) so far?
4. Have you (took, taken) the math final yet?
5. Margaret (dived, doved) gracefully from the high board into the placid pool below.
6. We (drank, drunk) all of the limeade we had (brung, brought).
7. Lefty (threw, throwed) a high curve ball to the nervous rookie.
8. The extra pencils and pen (is, are) on top of the bookcase in the hallway.
9. Either Wendy or Elena (has, have) your social studies notebook.
10. A whole shipment of flashlights and batteries (was, were) sold in an hour.
11. (Do, Does) Danielle or her brother know anything about computers?
12. The class (does, do) not agree among themselves about who should be the speaker.
13. Neither the director nor the singers (uses, use) music.
14. One of Amelia Earhart's engines (was, were) on fire during her solo flight across the Atlantic.
15. None of the committee members (agree, agrees) on the issue.
16. Each of the judges (watch, watches) the floor exercises in gymnastics.
17. In the 1700s few students (was, were) girls.
18. Some (believe, believes) that Sir Francis Bacon really wrote Shakespeare's plays.
19. Most of her work (require, requires) both patience and creativity.
20. Several of the rocks (is, are) too heavy to move without some assistance from the others.

Grammar and Usage

Writing Focus: *Using Vivid Verbs in Writing*

You can greatly improve your writing by including vivid verbs to *show* action precisely and clearly. Let the subject of your sentence *stare*, *glance*, *glimpse*, *peer*, or *peruse* rather than *look*. Avoid overusing such dull verbs as *make*, *has*, *have*, *does*, *do*, *are*, *is*, and *was*.

Assignment: *WOW!*

Notice the photograph on page 375 which has stopped the action of the parachute jump. Imagine that you can enter the photo and be part of the continuing action. You're now the parachutist, falling fast and free before your chute opens. The feeling is almost indescribable. What an experience!

Write one or more well-developed paragraphs telling about your parachute jump as though you are on it—now! Use words to paint a picture of your experience for your audience of classmates. Your writing will be evaluated for correct and effective use of verbs.

Use the following steps to complete this assignment.

A. Prewriting

Study the photograph carefully. Use your imagination to enter the picture. Pretend you're the parachutist, jumping out of the plane. Free write, described in Chapter 1, about what you are experiencing: what you see, hear, feel, think, and do. Concentrate on the details of the action and don't worry about putting them down correctly. Just let your imagination help you create the experience. Reread your free writing and underline the words, phrases, and sentences that best describe the action and convey your experience. Number them in the order that shows the action.

B. Writing

Using your free writing to help you, write one or more paragraphs telling about your parachute jump. Start your account by setting the scene. Then create a moving picture of

what happens before, during, and after the photo was snapped. Consider using the present tense of verbs to help you relate the experience as if it were happening *now*. Be certain to use vivid, specific verbs so that your readers can share the action.

C. Postwriting

Revise your first draft using the following checklist.

1. Does my account include enough specific details so that readers can experience my parachute jump with me?
2. Do I use vivid verbs to convey a clear picture of the action?
3. Is each verb in the proper tense, and does it agree in number with the subject?

Edit your work, using the Checklist for Proofreading at the back of the book. If appropriate, share your writing with your classmates to enjoy each other's "jumps."

14 Adjectives

Understanding Adjectives

Adjectives add details to your speaking and writing by describing other words. In the following sections you will learn to identify adjectives by studying their traditional definition. You will also learn two other ways to identify adjectives: by the classes into which they are grouped and by the features that distinguish them from other parts of speech.

Defining Adjectives

Adjectives are usually defined as words that modify nouns and pronouns.

Two tall, young women won *the three-legged* race.

A small, furry kitten slept on *our front* steps.

The students were *nervous* about taking *the* exam.

The calm, gentle, and *patient* mother soothed

the furious child.

Adjectives answer the questions *what kind? which one?* or *how many?* about the words they modify.

tiny ants	[What kind of ants?]
this shell	[Which shell?]
three pieces	[How many pieces?]

Exercise 1: Identifying Adjectives

Write the following sentences and underline each adjective. Draw an arrow from the adjective to the word it modifies. Your teacher may ask you which question the adjective answers.

Examples

a. The large, sunny room is our favorite place.

   The <u>large</u>, <u>sunny</u> room is <u>our</u> <u>favorite</u> place.

b. Large elm trees shade the back porch.

   <u>Large</u> <u>elm</u> trees shade <u>the</u> <u>back</u> porch.

1. The best player on the team is John.
2. A noisy and impolite mockingbird began to sing in the early daylight.
3. Jane is a tall girl with blond hair.
4. I have had these jeans for two years.
5. We bought two tickets and reserved the last available seats for the jazz concert.
6. The hungry and thirsty scouts stopped to rest after the long hike.
7. Sometimes, garden roses do not have thorny stems, but more often they do.
8. A thick, yellow mist is polluting the air.
9. In early evening a cool breeze blows through the tall pines.
10. The first thing Sojourner Truth did as a free woman was to sue a planter who had illegally bought her young son.

Grouping Adjectives by Classes

Adjectives can be divided into five classes: (1) articles, (2) proper adjectives, (3) nouns used as adjectives, (4) pronouns, and (5) predicate adjectives. Some adjectives, however, do not fit into any of these categories.

377

Grammar and Usage

The articles *a*, *an*, and *the* are the largest group of adjectives.

A and *an* are used before singular nouns; *the* modifies either singular or plural nouns. *An* is used when the following word begins with a vowel sound.

The short, elderly woman put on *a* new lure and caught *an* eight-pound fish in *the* last moments of *the* contest.

Any word that is used to modify a noun or pronoun is called an adjective. Sometimes other parts of speech are used as adjectives in a sentence. Proper nouns, common nouns, and some pronouns act as adjectives in a sentence when they are used to modify or describe a noun or pronoun.

Proper nouns used as adjectives are called *proper adjectives*.

Some proper nouns change form to become adjectives. All proper nouns and proper adjectives are capitalized.

Proper Noun	Proper Adjective
Italy	an Italian movie
France	French bread
China	a Chinese wok
Picasso	a Picasso painting

Exercise 2: Identifying Proper Adjectives and Articles

Write the sentences on the next page and circle each proper adjective. Underline each article.

Examples

a. The wooden cutting board had an assortment of Swiss and American cheeses.

14 Adjectives

The wooden cutting board had an assortment of (Swiss) and (American) cheeses.

b. Twenty-five people went on the summer European tour.

Twenty-five people went on the summer (European) tour.

1. Ruins of the Aztec civilization can be seen south of the Mexican border.
2. An Oriental vase is sometimes valuable.
3. The race was won by an Italian sports car.
4. The peaceful Bavarian village has many friendly people.
5. Diogenes, an ancient Greek philosopher, searched for an honest person.
6. In English class we read a humorous Shakespearean play called *A Midsummer Night's Dream*.
7. The New England countryside is a scenic place to drive in late autumn.
8. The equestrian competition featured an exciting performance by Arabian horses.
9. Her Persian wool coat kept her warm in the cold Chicago winters.
10. The Calgary rodeo was the highlight of our Canadian vacation.

Common nouns act as adjectives when they modify another noun or pronoun.

We plan to remodel the *recreation* room next summer.

Juliet has a valuable *stamp* collection.

Please open the *garage* door.

Note: The possessive form of a noun is not classified as an adjective but as a noun. The possessive noun is thought to possess, not modify, the noun that it precedes.

Grammar and Usage

> *Charlie's* uncle is a movie producer.
> I bought a birthday present for *Sheila's* brother.

Exercise 3: Identifying Nouns Used as Adjectives

Write each of the following sentences and underline all nouns that are used as adjectives. Draw an arrow to the noun that each modifies. (In some sentences more than one noun acts as an adjective.)

Examples

a. Although she has never seen a baseball game, Anna is a devoted Yankee fan.

Although she has never seen a <u>baseball</u> game, Anna is a devoted <u>Yankee</u> fan.

b. Karim is on a canoe trip up the Oleta River.

Karim is on a <u>canoe</u> trip up the Oleta River.

1. To play on clay courts you must wear tennis shoes.
2. Paolo's brother has been an airplane pilot for ten years.
3. Dave buys his concert tickets the day they go on sale.
4. Julio will enter the heifer he raised in the state fair.
5. Without a television set we spent more time talking and doing things as a family group.
6. The Florida primary is held in the spring of an election year.
7. Jennifer has decided to go to night school to get her college diploma.
8. On hot summer nights Robert and his brother sleep on the fire escape.
9. Potatoes, corn, tomatoes, peanuts, and peppers are some of the food plants first cultivated by native Americans.
10. She is writing her research report on local consumer agencies.

Some pronouns act as adjectives when they modify nouns or pronouns.

Demonstrative pronouns (*this*, *that*, *these* and *those*) are used as adjectives when they modify a noun or pronoun.

This is very difficult.	[pronoun]
This puzzle is very difficult.	[adjective]
These are the best stories I've read.	[pronoun]
These stories are the best ones I've read.	[adjective]

Interrogative pronouns (*which*, *what*, and *whose*) act as adjectives when they modify a noun or pronoun.

Which is your favorite subject?	[pronoun]
Which subject is your favorite?	[adjective]
What did you answer?	[pronoun]
What answer did you give?	[adjective]

Indefinite pronouns can sometimes act as adjectives if they modify a noun or pronoun.

Several of the students are late.	[pronoun]
Several students are late.	[adjective]
Both were good movies.	[pronoun]
Both movies were good.	[adjective]

Possessive pronouns (*my*, *your*, *his*, *her*, *its*, *our*, and *their*) sometimes act as adjectives to modify nouns.

Lucy found *her* hat in the closet.

The Franklins changed *their* number.

The door had a crack in *its* frame.

Grammar and Usage

Exercise 4: Identifying Pronouns Used as Adjectives

Write each of the following sentences. Underline all of the pronouns used as adjectives and draw an arrow from each pronoun to the word it modifies.

Examples

a. Most of the work was done by a few students.

Most of the work was done by a <u>few</u> students.

b. What kind of paint are you using on your project?

<u>What</u> kind of paint are you using on <u>your</u> project?

1. Several palms have died from a plant disease.
2. She said, "Your friends are as interesting as my friends."
3. Each person is responsible for completing a specific job.
4. I have seen this movie twice; the best part is its ending.
5. That is one of her many practical jokes.
6. Some of the groceries are more expensive each week, but this is cheaper today.
7. No one in my group knew about that detour.
8. Whose money is that? We must keep our cash together.
9. Which is the better of these brands of tape?
10. All students and their parents are invited to the Open House this evening at school.

Predicate adjectives **follow a linking verb and describe or modify the subject of the sentence. There may be more than one predicate adjective in a sentence.**

Your suggestion seems *workable*.

Mrs. Okano looks *worried* about something.

The boat was *long* and *sleek*.

Exercise 5: Identifying Predicate Adjectives

All of the following sentences have linking verbs. Write each sentence and underline each predicate adjective. Draw an arrow from the adjectives to the nouns or pronouns they modify.

Examples

a. We feel hot and sticky from the humidity.

We feel <u>hot</u> and <u>sticky</u> from the humidity.

b. The yogurt was thick and creamy.

The yogurt was <u>thick</u> and <u>creamy</u>.

1. Carl's voice became hoarse after his speech.
2. In the early morning the grass feels cool and wet on our feet.
3. The audience grew quiet as the voice became louder.
4. Swimming in the ocean at night is dangerous.
5. The tomatoes on that vine look ripe and delicious.
6. This apple is tasty but not very crisp.
7. My voice sounds unfamiliar on a tape recorder.
8. The dog was jittery and nervous during the storm.
9. The children look ready and eager to begin the game.
10. When she is angry or nervous, her hands become shaky.

Finding an Adjective by Its Features

Two features—degrees of comparison and suffixes—can help you identify many adjectives.

Adjectives may change form to show degrees of comparison.

Grammar and Usage

Adjectives have three degrees of comparison: *positive, comparative,* and *superlative.*

Positive [describes one thing]	Comparative [compares two things]	Superlative [compares three or more things]
long	longer	longest
wet	wetter	wettest
healthy	healthier	healthiest

She picked a *ripe* tomato.	[positive]
She looked for a *riper* tomato than this one.	[comparative]
She picked the *ripest* tomato in the garden.	[superlative]

The regular way to form the comparative and superlative forms is to add *-er* and *-est* to the end of the adjective. Sometimes there will be a slight spelling change: healthy, healthier, healthiest.

Some adjectives have irregular comparative forms.

Positive	Comparative	Superlative
good	better	best
bad, ill	worse	worst
much, many	more	most
little	less	least

Betsy writes *good* stories.	[positive]
Tamiko writes *better* stories than Betsy.	[comparative]
Neil writes the *best* stories in the class.	[superlative]

Many two-syllable adjectives and all adjectives that have three or more syllables form their comparative form with *more* and their superlative form with *most.*

14 Adjectives

Positive	Comparative	Superlative
careful	more careful	most careful
ridiculous	more ridiculous	most ridiculous
worrisome	more worrisome	most worrisome

Carlos is *intelligent*.	[positive]
Carlos is *more intelligent* than Mike.	[comparative]
Carlos is the *most intelligent* person I know.	[superlative]

Exercise 6: Identifying Degrees of Comparison

Write the following sentences. Underline only those adjectives that show one of the three forms of comparison. Label each adjective *P* for positive, *C* for comparative, or *S* for superlative.

Examples

a. The younger girl played a better game of tennis than the older girl did.

          C   C
The <u>younger</u> girl played a <u>better</u> game of tennis than
    C
the <u>older</u> girl did.

b. If you want to read a good book, read this one.

                            P
If you want to read a <u>good</u> book, read this one.

c. This is the best book I've ever read.

              S
This is the <u>best</u> book I've ever read.

1. Debbie painted her room the brightest shade of yellow she could find.
2. Our chess club has more industrious members now than it did before.

Grammar and Usage

3. The small boy hoped that some day he would be as tall as his older brother.
4. Bringing a raincoat was a smart idea, Jeff, but bringing an umbrella would have been a smarter idea.
5. Janice is the youngest of nine children.
6. The day was hot and humid until the cold front brought in cooler, drier air.
7. I think both Rosie and Jan look better with short hair than with long hair.
8. This is the darkest room in the house because it has fewer windows than the rest of the rooms.
9. Our spring storms are usually bad, but this is the earliest and severest we've had all year.
10. "You could be our best swimmer with just a little more energetic practice," encouraged the coach.

Adjectives may be formed with suffixes.

The following list gives the most often used adjective suffixes. Notice that some words have a spelling change when the suffix is added.

Noun or Verb	+	Suffix	=	Adjective
navy	+	-al	=	naval
like	+	-able	=	likable
color	+	-ful	=	colorful
fool	+	-ish	=	foolish
care	+	-less	=	careless
ghost	+	-like	=	ghostlike
wonder	+	-ous	=	wondrous
sun	+	-y	=	sunny

Exercise 7: Identifying Adjectives Formed with Suffixes

Write the following sentences and underline all of the adjectives that are formed with suffixes.

Examples

a. Pedro's dependable work is helpful to his family.
   Pedro's <u>dependable</u> work is <u>helpful</u> to his family.

b. A careful look at the trail showed us it was dangerous.
   A <u>careful</u> look at the trail showed us it was <u>dangerous</u>.

1. The soccer game was scoreless at the half, but the final score proved our ambitious effort to win.
2. The comfortable cushions on these seats make them more suitable for watching a long performance.
3. The ghostlike shadows in the forest that night caused many of us to have nightmarish dreams.
4. Jeff is a likable person because of his humorous jokes.
5. We were thankful for the balmy weather we had while staying at the coastal resort.
6. It would be foolish to leave that poisonous substance unmarked on the shelf.
7. As I approached the house, the curious shape on the windowsill became identifiable; it was a small, defenseless kitten waking from its nap.
8. The lifelike statue that the sculptor had created represented ageless beauty.
9. Mrs. Chung felt that the beautiful bouquet of flowers we gave her was a thoughtful gift.
10. The school nurse is responsible for alerting all parents when one of the students has a contagious disease.

Review: Understanding Adjectives

In the following selection from Maya Angelou's autobiography, *I Know Why the Caged Bird Sings*, the children are laughing at the author, who has forgotten a poem she was to recite. The author goes back in time and tells about the making of her new dress. Write the numbers 1–20 on a sheet of paper and list each underlined word. Beside each word write *yes* if the word is an adjective or *no* if the word is not an adjective.

The <u>children's</u> section of the Colored Methodist Episcopal Church of <u>Stamps</u>, Arkansas, was wiggling and giggling over my <u>well-known</u> forgetfulness.

The dress I wore was lavender taffeta, and each time I breathed it rustled, and now that I was sucking in air to breathe out shame it sounded like crepe paper on the back of hearses.
As I'd watched Momma put ruffles on the hem and cute little tucks around the waist, I knew that once I put it on I'd look like a movie star. (It was silk and that made up for the awful color.) I was going to look like one of the sweet little white girls who were everybody's dream of what was right with the world. Hanging softly over the black Singer sewing machine, it looked like magic, and when people saw me wearing it they were going to run up to me and say, "Marguerite [sometimes it was 'dear Marguerite'], forgive us, please, we didn't know who you were," and I would answer generously, "No, you couldn't have known. Of course I forgive you."[1]

Applying What You Know

Select several paragraphs from a book, short story, magazine, or newspaper article. Read the selection, using the definition, classes, and features of adjectives to identify each adjective. Then list the adjectives on a sheet of paper and beside each one write how you identified it.

Using Adjectives

Using adjectives correctly can help make your speaking and writing more interesting. The following sections will give you practice in using the comparative and superlative forms of adjectives. You will also learn how to form adjectives from other parts of speech.

Using Comparative and Superlative Forms of Adjectives

There are three ways in which adjectives change to show the comparative and superlative degrees:

---

[1]From *I Know Why the Caged Bird Sings* by Maya Angelou. Copyright © 1969 by Maya Angelou. Reprinted by permission of Random House, Inc.

1. With the addition of *-er* and *-est* to the positive form
2. With the words *more* and *most* placed before the positive form
3. With irregular forms that are completely different from the positive form

Most one-syllable adjectives form their comparative and superlative degrees with the addition of *-er* and *-est* to the positive form.

Positive	Comparative	Superlative
close	closer	closest
dark	darker	darkest
small	smaller	smallest

When the positive form ends in *y*, change the *y* to *i* before adding *-er* or *-est*.

Positive	Comparative	Superlative
sloppy	sloppier	sloppiest
sunny	sunnier	sunniest
wealthy	wealthier	wealthiest

If the positive degree ends in the letter *e*, drop the *e* before adding *-er* or *-est*.

Positive	Comparative	Superlative
late	later	latest
nice	nicer	nicest
white	whiter	whitest

Grammar and Usage

> If the positive degree ends in a single consonant preceded by a single vowel, double the consonant before adding *-er* or *-est*

Positive	Comparative	Superlative
flat	flatter	flattest
slim	slimmer	slimmest
thin	thinner	thinnest

> Many two-syllable adjectives and all adjectives that have three or more syllables form their comparative and superlative degrees with *more* and *most*.

Positive	Comparative	Superlative
thoughtful	more thoughtful	most thoughtful
dangerous	more dangerous	most dangerous
fortunate	more fortunate	most fortunate

> To compare lesser amounts, use the words *less* and *least*.

Positive	Comparative	Superlative
probable	less probable	least probable
significant	less significant	least significant
trustworthy	less trustworthy	least trustworthy

Exercise 8: Using Comparative and Superlative Forms of Adjectives

Write the sentences on the facing page and supply the correct form of the adjective in parentheses. Underline the adjective form you choose.

Examples

a. Gwen is the _____ person I know. (honest)

   Gwen is the <u>most honest</u> person I know.

b. Today is _____ than yesterday. (cool)

   Today is <u>cooler</u> then yesterday.

1. Tanzania is _____ to the equator than is Kenya. (close)
2. Jupiter is the _____ planet in our solar system. (large)
3. Vermont in 1777 was the _____ state to abolish slavery. (early)
4. Malcolm X, one of the _____ black leaders, was assassinated on February 21, 1965. (influential)
5. Cottage cheese is _____ than potato chips. (nutritious)
6. San Francisco's _____ earthquake destroyed the city in 1906. (intense)
7. The scorpion fish is _____ than any other fish. (deadly)
8. At more than 29,000 feet, Mount Everest is _____ than any other mountain on earth. (tall)
9. One of the _____ inventions was the toothpaste tube, invented in 1892 by a New York dentist. (useful)
10. Homemade yogurt is often _____ than commercial yogurt. (smooth)

Using Irregular Comparisons

A few adjectives change form completely to show comparative and superlative degrees.

Positive	Comparative	Superlative
bad, ill	worse	worst
far	farther	farthest

Grammar and Usage

good	better	best
little	less or lesser	least
much	more	most
many	more	most
well	better	best

Exercise 9: Using Irregular Comparisons

Write the following sentences and supply the correct form of the adjective given in parentheses. Underline the adjective form you choose.

Examples

a. She is feeling _____ than she did yesterday. (well)
   She is feeling <u>better</u> than she did yesterday.

b. Jack tries to eat _____ bread than he used to. (little)
   Jack tries to eat <u>less</u> bread than he used to.

1. Jennifer lives in the _____ house from school. (far)
2. Which do you like _____: chocolate, vanilla, or strawberry? (good)
3. Elaine is a _____ backgammon player than I am. (bad)
4. Allan has much _____ patience than his sister. (little)
5. The _____ flan I ever tasted was made by Manuela's father. (good)
6. What is the _____ movie you have ever seen? (bad)
7. Each week I have swum one lap in _____ time than the week before. (little)
8. The _____ money I have ever earned was twenty-five dollars a day. (much)
9. Because it was the championship game, _____ fans than usual were present. (much)
10. Are there _____ students studying Spanish now than there were last year? (many)

Review: Using Adjectives

Write the following sentences and choose the correct form of the adjective given in parentheses. Underline the adjective you select.

Example

a. St. Augustine is the _____ city in the United States. (old)
St. Augustine is the oldest city in the United States.

1. The country of Iceland has _____ people than the city of Baltimore. (few)
2. I think dandelions are _____ weeds. (beautiful)
3. The _____ subway in New York was powered by a large fan. (early)
4. Michelangelo was _____ as a sculptor than as a painter. (famous)
5. The _____ species of worm can be 180 feet in length. (long)
6. One kilogram is a little _____ than two pounds. (heavy)
7. Garbage has the _____ smell that I know. (unpleasant)
8. Taking lava rocks from Hawaii is supposed to bring _____ luck. (bad)
9. In 1908 a hundred thousand people died in Sicily in the _____ earthquake of modern times. (disastrous)
10. Annie Oakley was the _____ sharpshooter ever. (good)
11. Of the three states Idaho is the _____ north. (far)
12. Which do you find _____, rubber cement or glue? (effective)
13. Who is _____ in an emergency, your mother or your father? (calm)
14. Bobby Short's renditions of Cole Porter songs are much _____ than this record. (good)
15. We need a _____ and effective method of dealing with the problems of the aged. (humane)
16. What do you think was the _____ event leading up to the Civil War? (important)

17. Ripe coffee berries were used as a stimulant by ancient African warriors, but Arabs produced the _____ drink made from coffee. (early)

18. Caligula was the _____ of the ancient Roman emperors. (bad)

19. My average in math is _____ than my average in any other course. (low)

20. Paco is the _____ of the three young men. (popular)

Writing Focus: *Using Fresh Adjectives*

Fresh adjectives can give your writing life by adding specific details of sight, smell, sound, taste, and touch. However, using too many adjectives, or using stale ones such as *lovely*, *nice*, or *neat*, can deaden your writing. Use adjectives precisely.

Assignment: *Perspective*

Notice the photograph on page 395. Imagine that you are the person walking toward the structure in the water. What did the structure look like as you stood on the shore? As you came closer? Are there any similarities or differences in the two views?

Think about the preceding questions, and write one or more paragraphs comparing your views of the structure in the photo. Write for your classmates using your imagination to supply the details. Your writing will be evaluated for correct and effective use of adjectives.

Use the following steps to complete this assignment.

A. Prewriting

Divide a piece of paper into two columns: Far View and Near View. In the Far View column, list details about the structure in the photograph. You might start with one of its corners and

move around it in an orderly fashion. To the side of each point you've listed, put down in the Near View column what you see in your imagination about that point as you get closer to the structure. Go back over your list, and underline the key points or ideas that best compare the two views. Decide on an effective order for your information. You might discuss points about the structure from the far view first, then discuss the same points about it from the near view. Or you might discuss the structure from both views together under main ideas like *material*, *shape*, or *use*.

B. Writing

Write one or more paragraphs comparing the two views of the structure in the photograph. Use your columned prewriting to help you. Remember that if you discuss a point about the structure from the far view, you must discuss the same point about it from the near view. Use fresh adjectives to provide details.

C. Postwriting

Revise your first draft using the following checklist.

1. Do I use details to point out similarities and differences?
2. Do I use fresh, specific adjectives?

Edit your work using the Checklist for Proofreading at the back of the book. If appropriate, share your writing with your classmates and discuss the process of observing from two views.

15 Adverbs

Understanding Adverbs

Adverbs are words that modify by answering specific questions about other words. Adverbs can be identified by their definition, by the classes into which they are grouped, and by the features that distinguish them from other parts of speech. In the following sections you will study and practice each of these methods for identifying adverbs.

Defining Adverbs

Adverbs are usually defined as words that modify verbs or verb phrases, adjectives, or other adverbs.

Modifying a verb or verb phrase:

Peter left *early*.

Have you *always* lived in Nevada?

Modifying an adjective:

Donna is an *extremely* ambitious person.

The *clearly* visible falcon swooped toward us.

Modifying another adverb:

He does his work *somewhat* carelessly.

She opened the door *rather* cautiously.

Adverbs modify verbs, adjectives, and other adverbs by answering the questions *how? how often? when? where?* and *to what extent?*

Cinderella's stepsisters treated her *cruelly*.   [how?]

She *usually* slept in the cinders.   [how often?]

Yesterday she danced at the prince's ball.   [when?]

She left her slipper *there*.   [where?]

She had *extremely* tiny feet.   [to what extent?]

Exercise 1: Identifying Adverbs

Write the following sentences. Underline each adverb and draw an arrow to the word or words it modifies. Some sentences have more than one adverb. Your teacher may ask you which question the adverb answers and what kind of word it modifies.

Example

a. I'm more optimistic about the future than my brother is.

I'm <u>more</u> optimistic about the future than my brother is.

1. We drifted quietly until the raft hit the shore.
2. All of the contestants were noticeably tense.
3. In October people in some places turn the clock backward one hour when daylight-saving time begins.
4. She sat with her head bent forward over the ant farm.
5. Slowly and quietly the murderer opened the lantern until a single ray of light fell on the old man's eye.
6. Luis works much harder for his grades than his older brother does.
7. Juan usually finishes his homework quickly.
8. Which is the least expensive ring in the case?
9. At low tide Nicole walked steadily around the bay toward the very large lighthouse.
10. Turn the knob clockwise until you hear a click.

Grouping Adverbs by Classes

Adverbs can be divided into three classes: *interrogative adverbs, negative adverbs,* and *intensifiers.* Many adverbs, however, do not fit into any class.

Interrogative Adverbs

Interrogative adverbs often appear at the beginning of a sentence that asks a question. Each interrogative adverb is used to modify a verb, an adjective, or another adverb in the sentence.

How lucky can you be?	[modifies the adjective *lucky*]
When are you moving?	[modifies the verb phrase *are moving*]
Where were you last night?	[modifies the verb *were*]
Why is the door unlocked?	[modifies the verb *is*]

Negative Adverbs

Not **and** ***never*** **are** **negative adverbs. When used to modify a verb or verb phrase, they give a sentence a negative meaning.**

(*Not* often appears in a sentence as a contraction: *cannot* = *can't*.)

> I do *not* plan to finish this book tonight.
>
> The doctor *couldn't* find her pulse.
>
> Consuela has *never* been here before.

In a sentence that contains a one-word verb, a form of the helping verb *do* must be added to make the sentence negative.

> They live in Rochester.
> They *do not* live in Rochester.

Jennifer raises hamsters and gerbils.
Jennifer *doesn't* raise hamsters and gerbils.

The following contractions are formed by adding *n't* to the end of a helping verb.

isn't	don't	shouldn't	hadn't
aren't	doesn't	wouldn't	mightn't
wasn't	didn't	haven't	mustn't
weren't	couldn't	hasn't	

Note: will + n't = won't
can + n't = can't

Not and *never* can also be used to modify an adjective or an adverb.

Michael speaks French but *not* very well.

Never quiet except when asleep, he talks endlessly.

She usually wins but *never* easily.

Not far from here is where the fire occurred.

Intensifiers

Adverbs that modify adjectives and other adverbs are sometimes called *intensifiers*.

Intensifiers answer the question *to what extent?* and always come right before the word they modify.

The following are some commonly used intensifiers.

too	unbelievably	almost
so	quite	more
very	somewhat	most
extremely	rather	less
incredibly	fairly	least

He was *incredibly* thirsty.

Maria plays the guitar *quite* well.

The room was *so* dark that we were *rather* frightened after the lights were dimmed.

Grammar and Usage

Exercise 2: Classifying Adverbs

Write the following sentences and underline each interrogative and negative adverb and each intensifier. Some sentences may contain more than one of these adverbs.

Examples

a. Haven't you received your report card?
   Have<u>n't</u> you received your report card?

b. Why are you so irritable?
   <u>Why</u> are you <u>so</u> irritable?

1. Where did you find the missing key?
2. The food at the Greek Festival was unbelievably good.
3. An extremely small octopus, the size of a cat, washed on board the boat during the night.
4. It is exasperating to argue with people who are quite certain they are right.
5. Why didn't you ask someone for help?
6. Rosa Parks wouldn't give her bus seat to a white man on December 1, 1955.
7. Balsa logs are extremely buoyant and can float a loaded jeep.
8. Old Faithful, the largest geyser on earth, erupts regularly for about five minutes every hour.
9. An extraordinarily colorful assortment of anemones and corals makes the reef like a rock garden.
10. How carefully did you take notes at the lecture?

Finding an Adverb by Its Features

Two features—degrees of comparison and suffixes—can help you to identify many adverbs.

Some adverbs change form to show degrees of comparison.

Adverbs have three degrees of comparison: *positive*, *comparative*, and *superlative*.

Most adverbs form their comparative and superlative degrees with the words *more* and *most*.

Positive	Comparative	Superlative
loudly	more loudly	most loudly
easily	more easily	most easily
logically	more logically	most logically

The monkey chattered *loudly*.	[positive]
The dog barked *more loudly* than the monkey chattered.	[comparative]
The lion roared *most loudly* of all.	[superlative]

Some adverbs add *-er* and *-est* to form their comparative and superlative degrees.

Positive	Comparative	Superlative
far	farther	farthest
early	earlier	earliest
slow	slower	slowest

Willie hit the ball *far* into the outfield.	[positive]
Jane hit the ball *farther* than Willie.	[comparative]
Mary Lou hit the ball *farthest* of the three.	[superlative]

Exercise 3: Identifying Degrees of Comparison

Write the sentences on the following page and underline the adverbs. Label each adverb *P* for positive, *C* for comparative, or *S* for superlative degree. Read each sentence carefully; it may have more than one adverb.

Grammar and Usage

Example

a. Melissa lives close to the school.
         P
Melissa lives close to the school.

1. You can park closer to the stadium now than you can at night.
2. Kevin tries hard to win at running, but Sheila tries hardest of any of us.
3. The Wongs arrived later than the Hillarys.
4. You walk fastest because your legs are longer than mine or Harry's.
5. The North Star shines more brightly than other stars visible from the earth.
6. Far from the crowd a small child wandered alone.
7. I usually wake up earlier than anyone else in my family.
8. This plant needs watering more frequently than that one.
9. The view of the city is most clearly visible from here.
10. If you spoke louder, we could hear you better.

Adverbs may be formed with suffixes.

Many adverbs (especially those that answer the question *how?*) end in the suffix *-ly*. These adverbs are usually formed by adding the suffix to adjectives.

Adjective	**+**	**-ly**	**=**	**Adverb**
delightful	+	-ly	=	delightfully
sudden	+	-ly	=	suddenly

Adding the *-ly* suffix sometimes involves a spelling change.

witty	+	-ly	=	wittily
busy	+	-ly	=	busily
simple	+	-ly	=	simply

Not all words that end in *-ly* are adverbs. Only those words that end in *-ly and* modify a verb, an adjective, or another adverb are adverbs.

Janice is a *friendly* person.	[adjective modifying a noun]
Maria acts *friendly* to everyone.	[adverb modifying a verb]

Other adverb-forming suffixes are *-ward*, *-wise*, and *-ways*.

> Move the pawn one square *forward*.
>
> She turned the screw *counterclockwise*.
>
> We danced two steps *sideways* and one step *backward*.

Exercise 4: Identifying Adverbs Formed with Suffixes

Write the following sentences and underline each adverb that is formed with a suffix you have studied in this lesson. Draw an arrow from the adverb to the word it modifies.

Examples

a. Courageously the knight fought the last dragon.

<u>Courageously</u> the knight fought the last dragon.

b. Pam carefully placed all of the pictures in the family album.

Pam <u>carefully</u> placed all of the pictures in the family album.

1. The newscaster accurately reported the daily news.
2. We walked southward from Chicago until we were too weary to go on.
3. Fortunately we found our seats quickly before the performance began.
4. He gave me a friendly wave when I looked at him strangely.
5. Cautiously we stepped sideways along the narrow ledge.
6. We walk to the bus stop daily, but we usually get a ride home.

Grammar and Usage

7. Our paper carrier throws our paper upward and hopes it will land at the right apartment door.

8. Raking the lawn weekly means we can cut the grass more easily.

9. The teacher asked half our gym class to run clockwise.

10. The police patrol the neighborhood nightly to keep the monthly crime rate low.

Review: Understanding Adverbs

Write the following sentences. Then underline each adverb.

Examples

a. "That it will never come again
    Is what makes life so sweet."   —Emily Dickinson
   "That it will <u>never</u> come <u>again</u>
    Is what makes life <u>so</u> sweet."

b. "Speak softly and carry a big stick; you will go far."
                                                    —Teddy Roosevelt
   "Speak <u>softly</u> and carry a big stick; you will go <u>far</u>."

1. "Nice guys finish last."   —Leo Durocher

2. "All that I have I would have given gladly not to be standing here today."   —Lyndon Baines Johnson

3. "You gain strength, courage, and confidence by every experience in which you really stop to look fear in the face."   —Eleanor Roosevelt

4. "When they told me yesterday what happened, I felt like the moon, the stars and all the planets had fallen on me."   —Harry Truman

5. "I never forget a face, but in your case I'll make an exception."   —Groucho Marx

6. "Wisdom is knowing when you can't be wise."
                                                    —Paul Engle

7. "Injustice anywhere is a threat to justice everywhere."
                                                    —Martin Luther King, Jr.

8. "There is nothing so powerful as truth—and often nothing so strange."   —Daniel Webster

9. "Don't look back. Something may be gaining on you."
   —*Leroy "Satchel" Paige*

10. "There wasn't room to swing a cat there."
    —*Charles Dickens*

Applying What You Know

In the following selection from Shirley Dolph's essay "The Eye of a Deer," a young girl tells why she is happy her brother Stan did not kill a deer on that day's hunting trip. List each underlined word on a sheet of paper numbered 1–20. Remembering what you have learned about the definition, classes, and features of adverbs, decide if each underlined word is an adverb. If the word is an adverb, write *yes* beside it; if the word is not an adverb, write *no*.

I exulted silently. "He couldn't do it—I knew he wouldn't!" Stan, at twelve, was two years older than I, and, when he wasn't teasing me to the point of tears, he was my best friend. When our father died, Stan and I had become especially close. He shared my reverence for all living things, especially animals. Together we had raised, loved, and played with a variety of pets, mostly cats, dogs, and rabbits. We delighted in hanging over the rails to watch the squealing baby pigs. We'd climb trees in the woods and watch squirrels and chipmunks and imitate birds. Stan was marvelous at splinting broken wings and coaxing abandoned baby animals to eat from an eye dropper. If one of his tiny patients succumbed, we would hold a sad funeral, always with a stone-ringed grave, a small stick cross, and tenderly planted wild flowers.

Stan and I both hated the sight of blood and never watched the slaughtering of the pigs or cows on the farm. We avoided the chicken coop when we knew one of those unfortunate fowl was about to lose its head to an ax. It would run wildly about, headless, for several seconds like an unearthly creature, screaming noiselessly.

The men were eating ravenously now and talking about their plans for the next day's hunting. Stan was quiet and still avoiding my eyes. I picked at my dinner, and my thoughts went back to three months earlier. Stan and I were in a tree at the far edge of the cow pasture when Stan grabbed my arm and motioned for me to be quiet. There, cautiously edging towards a salt lick block, was the most magnificent animal I had ever seen. It was a male white-tailed deer. It stood regally, its fuzzy brown antlers resembling a velvet crown. I looked at Stan. His eyes were wide with awe and admiration, and he was holding his breath. The buck raised his head, and we could see his

Grammar and Usage

huge dark eyes. He sensed our presence then, and in two graceful leaps he was back in the woods. Stan let out his breath in a low whistle, "Whooeeee, wasn't he something!" I nodded eagerly, and Stan took my hand to help me down the tree.

My mother's concerned voice brought me back to the dinner table. I assured her that I was feeling fine and started to help clear the dishes.[1]

Using Adverbs

In the following sections you will learn how to use the comparative and superlative forms of adverbs and how to avoid double negatives. You also will learn how to distinguish between adjectives and adverbs and when to choose an adjective and when to choose an adverb in your writing.

Using Comparative and Superlative Forms

Most adverbs form their comparative and superlative degrees with the words *more* and *most*.

Positive	Comparative	Superlative
slightly	more slightly	most slightly
quickly	more quickly	most quickly
slowly	more slowly	most slowly

Adverbs can also show lesser amounts with the word *less* in the comparative and *least* in the superlative degree.

---

[1]From "The Eye of a Deer" by Shirley Dolph. Reprinted by permission of Shirley Dolph.

Positive	Comparative	Superlative
gently	less gently	least gently
firmly	less firmly	least firmly
confidently	less confidently	least confidently

Ann drives *more cautiously* than David.

Who drives *most cautiously*—Juan, Maria, or Kiyo?

She worked *less eagerly* than she did before.

Michelle works *least carefully* of all the workers.

A few adverbs form their comparative and superlative degrees by adding *-er* and *-est* to their positive forms.

Positive	Comparative	Superlative
close	closer	closest
dark	darker	darkest
deep	deeper	deepest
early	earlier	earliest
fast	faster	fastest
hard	harder	hardest
high	higher	highest
late	later	latest (or last)
light	lighter	lightest
long	longer	longest
low	lower	lowest
near	nearer	nearest

Exercise 5: Using Degrees of Comparison

Write each of the sentences on the next page and supply the proper form of the adverb given in parentheses. Underline the adverb form you have used. Remember to use the comparative

Grammar and Usage

degree to compare two things. Use the superlative degree to compare more than two.

Examples

a. Jason climbed _____ than his brother. (high)
   Jason climbed higher than his brother.

b. Can you sing _____ than an alto? (low)
   Can you sing lower than an alto?

c. This old bike chain works _____ than the new one. (efficient)
   This old bike chain works less efficiently than the new one.

1. Of all the members of his family, James stays up _____. (late)
2. Of all the candidates, Mary came _____ to winning a majority of the votes. (close)
3. She always gets more done because she works _____ of her classmates. (ambitiously)
4. Will you be able to leave _____ than the others? (early)
5. To find the buried treasure, you must dig _____ than two feet. (deep)
6. Juan has flown _____ than any of the other hang gliders. (heroically)
7. Because he wasn't wearing a seat belt, he was injured _____ in the crash than the driver. (seriously)
8. I used a _____ blue paint for the sky than I used for the water. (dark)
9. Who studies _____, you or I? (diligently)
10. Her performance was not as good as the rehearsal because she acted _____. (convincingly)

Using Irregular Comparisons

Only a few adverbs form their comparative and superlative degrees by using words that are entirely different from the

408

positive degree. Since these adverbs are often used, you must memorize their forms.

Positive	Comparative	Superlative
badly	worse	worst
far	farther	farthest
little	less	least
much	more	most
well	better	best

Nicole bowls *badly*.	[positive degree]
Dolores bowls *worse* than Nicole.	[comparative degree]
Of the three girls, Danielle bowls *worst*.	[superlative degree]

Exercise 6: Using Irregular Comparisons

Write the following sentences and supply the proper form of the adverb given in parentheses. Underline the form you choose.

Examples

a. Do you think you can see _____ from this seat than from that one? (well)
   Do you think you can see better from this seat than from that one?

b. Jennifer feels _____ nervous about the interview than Maria. (much)
   Jennifer feels more nervous about the interview than Maria.

1. Eduardo can run _____ than Frank. (far)
2. She worries _____ than she used to. (little)
3. Of all the members on the team, Fiona debates _____. (well)

Grammar and Usage

4. Mom was pleased with the award, but Dad was even _____ pleased. (much)
5. The _____ useful of all the gifts are the compass and hiking boots. (much)
6. He tried to bunt the ball, but it went much _____ than he had intended. (far)
7. Yelling is probably the _____ effective way to settle a family argument. (little)
8. Elizabeth rolls her *r*'s in Spanish even _____ than I do. (badly)
9. Perhaps my pen will write _____ than yours. (well)
10. Who do you think is _____ suitable for the job of class secretary—Pam, Beth, or Gail? (much)

Choosing Between Adjectives and Adverbs

The guide you should use in choosing between adjectives and adverbs is to remember what kinds of words each part of speech can modify.

Adjectives modify nouns and pronouns.

Adverbs modify verbs, adjectives, and other adverbs.

Bad/Badly

The adjective *bad* modifies nouns and pronouns; it may follow a linking verb.

I felt *bad* about losing your book.

This cheese tastes *bad* because it isn't fresh.

The *bad* weather spoiled our camping trip.

The adverb *badly* modifies action verbs by answering the question *how?* or *to what extent?*

410

Our team played *badly*. [how?]

The baby wren was wounded *badly* in the fall. [to what extent?]

The adverb *badly* is also used to modify adjectives.

Kiyo's knee was *badly* bruised.

The *badly* injured person received help.

Easy/Easily

The adjective *easy* can modify nouns and pronouns and may follow a linking verb.

That was the first *easy* test Mr. Chu has given us.

It was *easy* only if you had studied for it.

The adverb *easily* almost always modifies a verb or verb phrase.

I can draw the map *easily* for you.

Martha can speak *easily* about fishing.

Do not use the adjective *easy* to modify a verb.

Real/Really

The adjective *real* means "actual" or "true." It modifies nouns or pronouns.

The *real* purpose is stated at the end of the article.

Is this material *real* or synthetic?

The adverb *really* means "actually" or "truly." It modifies verbs, adjectives, or other adverbs and has the same meaning the word *very* would have.

Carlos drew a *really* fine poster for the dance.

We drove *really* far on our last gallon of gas.

Sure/Surely

The adjective *sure* modifies nouns and pronouns and has several different meanings. *Sure* means "certain," "positive," or "confident."

The weather forecaster was *sure* that it wouldn't rain.

Ricardo is a *sure* winner in the election.

***Surely* is an adverb that modifies verbs, adjectives, and other adverbs. It often has the meaning "certainly."**

That *surely* was a delicious sandwich.

Thunder and lightning *surely* frighten our dog.

Good/Well

The adjective *good* modifies nouns and pronouns and often follows linking verbs.

Holly is a *good* runner and champion diver.

Apples and cheese taste *good* together.

She is *good* at fixing things.

However, when the meaning is "in good health," use *well*.

Are you feeling *well?*

Todd's father isn't *well.*

The adverb *well* modifies verbs.

Did you sleep *well* during the thunderstorm?

The White Sox played *well* last week.

Exercise 7: Choosing Between Adjectives and Adverbs

Write each of the following sentences and choose the adjective or adverb from the pair in parentheses needed to complete the sentence. Underline your choice.

Examples

a. Ellen Jean took notes _____. (careful, carefully)
   Ellen Jean took notes carefully.

b. Fresh broccoli tastes _____ raw. (good, well)
   Fresh broccoli tastes good raw.

1. Jim is a _____ good goalie on the hockey team. (real, really)
2. After two straight sets Mike began to play _____. (bad, badly)
3. Donna Obermeyer's songs sound _____ to me. (good, well)
4. Ray can wash three cars _____ in an hour. (easy, easily)
5. The performer danced _____ across the stage. (slow, slowly)
6. Do you think the sour cream still tastes _____? (good, well)
7. The old snail inches _____ up the basement wall. (slow, slowly)
8. This new dish you prepared last night tastes _____. (bad, badly)

Grammar and Usage

9. Did you feel _____ after your typhoid shot? (good, well)

10. I am feeling _____ excited about your visit next week. (real, really)

Avoiding Double Negatives

The negative adverb *not* gives a negative meaning to verbs. (*Not* often appears in contractions: *is not* may be written as *isn't*.)

Harry is *not* going to college.

Harry *isn't* going to college.

When two negative words are used where only one is necessary, the result is a *double negative*. Not a feature of Edited Standard English, the double negative often happens when writers forget that there are several other negative words besides *not*.

The words *no, never, none, no one,* and *nothing* all have a negative meaning and can be easily remembered because they all begin with the letter *n*.

Double negatives can be changed in two ways: by removing or by changing one of the negative words.

An asterisk (*) denotes a sentence with a feature that is not a part of ESE.

*I didn't have no trouble.	[double negative]
I have no trouble.	[take out negative word]
I didn't have any trouble.	[change negative word]

A few negative words do not begin with the letter *n*. The words *hardly, scarcely,* and *barely* have negative meanings.

I have *hardly* said a word.	[*hardly* has a negative meaning]
*I have*n't hardly* said a word.	[double negative]

15 Adverbs

When the words *only* and *but* mean "no more than," they also have a negative meaning.

He had *only* one chance.	[meaning "no more than" one chance]
*He had *no* more than *only* one chance.	[double negative]
We had *but* two hours left to wait.	[meaning "no more than"]
*We had*n't but* two hours left to wait.	[double negative]

Exercise 8: *Eliminating Double Negatives*

Each of the following sentences contains a double negative. Write the sentences and make whatever changes are necessary to eliminate the double negatives. Underline the negative word that is left in each rewritten sentence.

Example

a. Frances never drinks no soda.
   Frances never drinks soda.

1. Isn't nobody home?
2. Kiyo never wants to go nowhere.
3. Because of the unusually warm weather, none of the northern cities has had no snow yet.
4. Jim can't hardly remember to cut the grass.
5. Hasn't anybody got no library card?
6. There were several pencils on the desk, but now I can't find none.
7. She didn't never give me her phone number.
8. We couldn't scarcely taste the garlic in the sausages.
9. I haven't never been to Rhode Island.
10. Nobody on the food committee brought no salad dressing to the awards banquet.

415

Grammar and Usage

Review: Using Adverbs

Each of the following sentences contains a usage error. It may be the wrong form of a comparison, an adjective or adverb used incorrectly, or a double negative. Rewrite the sentences, making the necessary corrections. Underline the changes you make.

Examples

a. Mr. Lee can wiggle his ears easily than his son can.
   Mr. Lee can wiggle his ears more easily than his son can.

b. The runner needed a drink of water bad.
   The runner needed a drink of water badly.

c. I have tried baking sourdough bread, but it didn't never come out right.
   I have tried baking sourdough bread, but it never came out right.

1. Of the three players, Manuel played well.
2. Last night's dress rehearsal was real good.
3. On December 7, 1941, nobody expected no attack on Pearl Harbor.
4. Paula earned a better grade than Lisa because Paula prepared her paper carefully.
5. Nicole thinks that she played bad in the semifinals.
6. Does the sukiyaki taste well?
7. Nobody has never captured a unicorn.
8. Anthony was good for the team's morale because, of all the team members, he spoke more enthusiastically about winning.
9. Orpheus failed to bring Eurydice back from the Underworld because he couldn't wait no longer and turned around to look at her.
10. John won the marathon because he ran fast.
11. Nicole threw the javelin as far as she could, but Michelle threw it farthest.
12. We were sure happy to find an open gas station.

13. Come quick.
14. Marty finished the job easy.
15. My glasses don't help at all; in fact, I can see most clearly without them.
16. Phrenologists once convinced a lot of people that character could be analyzed from the shape of the skull and its bumps, but nobody hardly believes that any more.
17. Bobby Short plays Cole Porter songs extremely good.
18. The twins get along very bad.
19. Who do you think writes well, Ernest Hemingway or John Steinbeck?
20. No one hardly uses the hourglass and the sundial to tell time any more.

Writing Focus: *Using Exact Adverbs in Writing*

Writers use adverbs to make their descriptions more exact and vivid, to show time and space relationships, to clarify the relationships between ideas, and, often, to help explain *how* something happens. See how much more effective your writing can be as you practice using effective adverbs.

Assignment: *A Job Worth Doing*

You've dreaded this job all week, but now it's time for you to clean the garage (or attic or your room). The task seems hopeless. Things have accumulated for ages, dust is everywhere, and you can't imagine where to begin. You really, really, really don't want to clean. The thought of doing it makes you want to go back to bed and pull the covers over your head forever. What can you do to get yourself to clean up the place? Perhaps a master plan might help.

Grammar and Usage

Write one or more paragraphs explaining how you're going to clean a large, messy, specific place. Your primary audience will be yourself, but write for your classmates as well. Be precise in telling about the steps you'll need to follow to actually clean the place so that the job will be easy, fast, and fun rather than hopeless, hard, and horrible. Your work will be evaluated for correct and effective use of adverbs.

Use the following steps to complete this assignment.

A. Prewriting

Think about all the places you've cleaned, especially the very messy ones. Imagine a garage, attic, or your room that must be cleaned—by you. Draw a picture of it. Imagine the many tasks you'll have to perform to get it spic and span and orderly. Make a list of all the equipment and steps necessary to do that. Some necessary items might include a broom, mop, and several rags. For now, don't worry about the order of the steps. Just jot down everything you can think of that will help you clean easily and quickly. Keep listing until nothing else occurs to you. Read over your list. Group and number the steps in the order you'll need to do them for maximum efficiency.

15 Adverbs

B. Writing

Using your list, write, in paragraph form, directions explaining how you are going to clean up the messy place. Begin by discussing any equipment you'll need to gather. Then take yourself through the steps you'll need to follow in the proper order. Use words like *first*, *next*, *then*, *while*, and *last of all* to help you. As you write, pay particular attention to your use of adverbs.

C. Postwriting

Use the following checklist to revise your first draft.

1. Have I included enough information so that I can complete the cleaning easily, quickly, and thoroughly?

2. Have I used exact adverbs?

Use the Checklist for Proofreading at the back of the book to edit your work. If appropriate, share your writing with several of your classmates.

16 Prepositions
Understanding Prepositions

Prepositions are words that show relationships between other words. You can learn to identify this part of speech by learning the definition and by looking at the way prepositions function in a sentence. In the following sections you will study and practice each of these ways to identify prepositions.

Defining Prepositions

A *preposition* is usually defined as a word that shows the relationship between a noun or pronoun and some other word in the sentence.

The ball sailed *over* the goalposts.
The ball sailed *under* the goalposts.
[The prepositions *over* and *under* show the relationship between the noun *goalposts* and the verb *sailed*.]

The horse *inside* the barn is Alonzo's.
The horse *behind* the barn is Alonzo's.
[The prepositions *inside* and *behind* show the relationship between the noun *barn* and the noun *horse*.]

We met *before* the show.
We met *after* the show.
[The prepositions *before* and *after* show the relationship between the noun *show* and the verb *met*.]

The following words are commonly used as prepositions.

aboard	along	below	but
about	among	beneath	by
above	around	beside	down
across	at	besides	during
after	before	between	except
against	behind	beyond	for

from	off	since	underneath
in	on	through	until
inside	onto	throughout	up
into	out	till	upon
like	outside	to	with
near	over	toward	within
of	past	under	without

The noun or pronoun used with the preposition is called the *object of the preposition*. The object of the preposition (*OP*) usually appears after the preposition (*P*).

                 P   OP

Joyce stood *under the old elm tree*.

            P OP

He waited *for them* all afternoon.

The preposition, the object of the preposition, and the object's modifiers are called a *prepositional phrase*. The prepositional phrases in the following sentences are *italicized*.

She called the number *for almost twenty minutes*.

Bill promised to meet her *during his lunch hour*.

In our backyard is a Japanese garden.

Exercise 1: Identifying Prepositional Phrases

Each of the sentences on the next page contains at least one prepositional phrase, although some have more than one. Write the sentences and underline the prepositional phrases. Write *P* above each preposition and *OP* above each object of the preposition.

Examples

a. Ricardo opened a savings account in the new bank.

                                                   P   OP

Ricardo opened a savings account <u>in the new bank</u>.

b. She leaned the shovel against the wall of the house.

                                 P   OP P   OP

She leaned the shovel <u>against the wall</u> <u>of the house</u>.

Grammar and Usage

1. The wind howled throughout the night.
2. Please hand me the scissors near the lamp.
3. Beyond our galaxy are many other galaxies.
4. My brother Dan delivers the morning paper every day at 6 o'clock.
5. Is the package in the hallway for me?
6. Kiyo swam across the lake in two hours.
7. Someone broke into the factory storeroom over the weekend.
8. What would I do without you?
9. We watched the city lights far below us.
10. When she opened the door, an ugly lizard scampered across the floor into the room.

Prepositions Used as Other Parts of Speech

Some prepositions can also be used as other parts of speech—as adverbs, as nouns, or as adjectives.

Put *down* that chair.	[adverb]
Our team made a first *down*.	[noun]
Carl is wearing a *down* vest.	[adjective]
The climber slid *down* the mountainside.	[preposition]

The word *inside* can also be used in several ways:

Please come *inside*.	[adverb]
We cleaned the *inside* of the car.	[noun]
Want to hear the *inside* scoop about the elections?	[adjective]
Good grief! Someone has locked a dog *inside* that car.	[preposition]

The word *to* is sometimes a preposition and sometimes a part of an infinitive (such as *to live* or *to swim*). When *to* is followed by a verb, it is part of an infinitive, but *to* followed by a noun or pronoun is a preposition.

Do you want *to go* with us?	[part of infinitive]
We are going *to* the baseball game.	[preposition]
To be an engineer is my goal.	[part of infinitive]
The project was assigned *to* the engineer.	[preposition]

The best way to decide whether a word is used as a preposition is to look for an object, since a preposition *always* has one.

Exercise 2: Identifying the Function of Prepositions

Write each of the following sentences and indicate whether the *italicized* word or words function as prepositions, adverbs, or parts of infinitives.

Examples

a. "I am glad the tests are *over*," she said.
over—adverb

b. The recluse hid her money *under* the mattress.
under—preposition

c. Janey wants *to* buy her own skis.
to—part of infinitive

1. Please take the garbage *out* before you leave.
2. When the baby tried to climb *from* the crib, it fell.
3. "Move *along*, folks," said the police officer.
4. Nikki Marie hopes to travel *to* Crete to see her maternal grandparents.
5. Will you please turn your stereo *down*?
6. Before we go *to* the store, bring the laundry *inside*.

Grammar and Usage

7. "I've asked you *before*," he complained, "but you never answer."
8. We glimpsed a shadowy figure *outside* the window.
9. The beach house was built on land six inches *above* sea level.
10. Look *around* carefully before you buy a car.

Prepositions with Compound Objects

Prepositions with more than one object have a compound object.

```
                          P         OP            OP
       We stacked the hay during the morning and afternoon.
                              P      OP         OP
       Do you know the girl in the jeans and red shirt?
                           P     OP        OP        OP
       He borrowed books on psychology, football, and astronomy.
```

Exercise 3: Identifying Prepositions with Compound Objects

Each of the following sentences contains one or more prepositions with compound objects. Write the sentences and underline each prepositional phrase. Above each preposition write *P* and above each object of the preposition write *OP*.

Examples

a. Yesterday I saw Henry with Burt and Earl.
                      P   OP   OP
   Yesterday I saw Henry <u>with Burt and Earl</u>.

b. On Mondays and Fridays I baby-sit for Mrs. Sanchez.
  P   OP   OP
<u>On Mondays and Fridays</u> I baby-sit for Mrs. Sanchez.

1. The children rode on the bumper cars and the merry-go-round all afternoon and evening.

2. The historical house was surrounded by hedges and a fence.
3. I like to eat crackers with cheese and peanut butter.
4. From the front and the back your costume looks absolutely ridiculous.
5. I want to take a trip to the mountains or the beach, but I want to go without my little sister and brother.
6. My grandparents traveled by boat, plane, and camel.
7. Would you rather ride in our car or theirs?
8. The obstacle course takes you through tunnels and tubes and then across water hazards and sand traps.
9. The sale on those records and tapes takes place on Thursday, Friday, and Saturday.
10. I've looked under the couch, the chairs, and the pillows, but I still can't find my glasses.

Prepositional Phrases as Modifiers

Prepositional phrases are used as modifiers in the same way adjectives and adverbs are. Prepositional phrases are adjectives when they modify nouns or pronouns and answer the questions *what kind? which one?* and *how many?*

Myra is using the book *on the table*.	[which one?]
The book *of stamps* is completed now.	[what kind?]

Prepositional phrases are adverbs when they modify verbs, adjectives, or other adverbs and answer the questions *where? how? when?* and *to what extent?*

Phillip has a job *after school*.	[when?]
Nicole works *at the grocery store*.	[where?]

Sometimes one prepositional phrase follows another prepositional phrase. In such a case the second prepositional phrase

Grammar and Usage

often acts as an adjective to modify the noun or pronoun object of the first phrase.

I mailed the letter *in the mailbox on the corner*.

The brass doorknob *on the front door of the house* is an antique.

Exercise 4: Identifying Prepositional Phrases as Modifiers

Write the following sentences and underline each prepositional phrase. Draw an arrow from the phrase to the word or words it modifies. Write *adj.* above the phrase if it acts as an adjective and *adv.* if it acts as an adverb.

Examples

a. Bright wallpaper covered the walls of the bedroom.

　　　　　　　　　　　　　　　　　　　adj.
Bright wallpaper covered the walls <u>of the bedroom</u>.

b. The horses in the corral are groomed in the morning.

　　　　　adj.　　　　　　　　　　adv.
The horses <u>in the corral</u> are groomed <u>in the morning</u>.

1. Send your reply to the sponsor of the program.
2. The car in the right lane slid through the intersection.
3. The story about the fire was printed in last night's newspaper.
4. The flowers on the table were delivered this morning.
5. During the storm the dog remained under the sofa and whimpered.
6. Will you write something funny on the last page of my autograph book?
7. The front of the house is being remodeled with great care.
8. The portrait over the fireplace was painted by my uncle.
9. In the library is a map of the city.
10. The scrambled eggs with tomatoes, onions, and cheese were served on a hot platter.

Review: Understanding Prepositions

In the following selection from *Medicine Man's Daughter*, a story about the Navaho people by Ann Nolan Clark, there are thirty prepositions. The first five are underlined for you. Number a sheet of paper and list at least twenty of the other twenty-five prepositions. (Hint: Do not confuse the preposition *to* with *to* used as part of an infinitive.)

> Air that had been, but a few days ago, hot <u>in</u> the canyons of the Tseghi, mild <u>on</u> the flat plateau, cool <u>in</u> the foothills, now <u>became</u> freezing <u>cold</u>. First snow lay white and glistening <u>on</u> the mountain peaks which were piled peak upon peak as far and as wide as one could see. The trail zigzagged up and up into the soft gray snowclouds that filled the sky and rested lightly on the pointed peaks. The horses kept on their prodding climb, but as each high point was reached, higher ones blocked the way.
> Under the tall pines, bright red berries hid in the waxy leaves of the kinnikinnick. Wild turkeys ate the berries and gobbled with curiosity at what they saw coming up the trail. Deer crashed through the ground oak, leaving heart-shaped hoof prints in the moist earth.
> In the mountain peaks the tired horses rested, cropping the sweet, wild grass, splashing through the ice-cold mountain streams, snorting with pleasure.
> Tall-Girl was always to remember this trip, her first one into the wild country of the purple peaks. She was always to treasure the gifts of the Yei that she brought back with her. She was always to believe, at least a little, in the magic that they held for her to use. But try as she would, in the years that were to come, she could not sort out what had happened into any kind of pattern or order. She could never say, in remembering, this happened first and then this and this followed.[1]

Applying What You Know

Select several paragraphs from a book, short story, magazine, or newspaper article. Use what you have learned about prepositions and prepositional phrases in the previous sections to identify the prepositions in the passage you have selected. List them on a sheet of paper and beside each one write the method you used to identify it.

---

[1] Reprinted by permission of Farrar, Straus and Giroux, Inc. Excerpt from *Medicine Man's Daughter* by Ann Nolan Clark. Copyright © 1963 by Ann Nolan Clark.

Grammar and Usage

Using Prepositions

Using Pronouns as Objects of Prepositions

Only object forms of pronouns can be used as objects of prepositions.

Object Forms

Singular	Plural
me	us
you	you
him	
her	them
it	
whom	whom

Donations for the food drive were collected by *us*.

A picture was taken of *her* and *him* during the race.

The person for *whom* I am voting is Fred.

Julius went with *me* to the recycling center.

Exercise 5: Using Pronouns as Objects of Prepositions

Write each of the following sentences, choosing the correct form of the pronouns given in parentheses to be the object of the preposition. Underline the pronouns you choose.

Example

a. A letter arrived for (she, her) and (me, I).
   A letter arrived for her and me.

1. The winning skit was performed by Anna and (he, him).
2. That free lesson was helpful for (we, us) beginners.
3. While the neighbors were on vacation, Julie collected their mail for (them, they).

4. The dog jumped over (she, her) and (we, us) as it romped through the house.
5. By (who, whom) was this picture taken?
6. José ran into (me, I) when we both tried to answer the telephone at the same time.
7. I began the letter to the company, "To (who, whom) it may concern."
8. Angelo tried to sneak behind (us, we), but we caught him.
9. Between you and (I, me) who do you think is taller?
10. Please pass the vegetables to (he, him) and (she, her).

Using Troublesome Prepositions Correctly

Among/Between

Use *between* when referring to exactly two persons or things. Use *among* to refer to more than two persons or things.

This will be a secret just *between* you and me.

Divide the assignments equally *among* the three reporters.

Beside/Besides

***Beside* refers to a position next to something. *Besides* means "in addition to" or "other than."**

The kitten lay down *beside* her.

Besides her broken leg Mari has other problems.

In/Into

***In* refers to a movement that happened "inside or within" a place, but *into* implies a movement "from outside to inside."**

Grammar and Usage

They talked for a minute *in* the cafeteria.

Joan walked quickly *into* the cafeteria.

On/Onto

On refers to a position on the top of something. Onto should be used only to refer to a movement toward the top of something.

Your notebook is *on* the kitchen table.

She climbed *onto* the ladder to change the light bulb.

Exercise 6: Using Troublesome Prepositions Correctly

Write the following sentences, choosing the correct preposition from the pair in parentheses. Underline the preposition you choose.

Examples

a. Please step (in, into) the sunlight, Count Dracula.
Please step into the sunlight, Count Dracula.

b. We will divide the money (between, among) the whole class.
We will divide the money among the whole class.

1. Who else is going to the lecture (beside, besides) Helena and me?
2. The senator stood (among, between) the two warring local politicians.
3. Cincinnati was built (beside, besides) the Ohio River.
4. When the earth shook, many people ran (in, into) the street.
5. Wonder Woman stood (on, onto) Hoover Dam.
6. There is a good deal of jealousy (among, between) the four sisters.
7. A short, bearded stranger walked (in, into) the office and demanded to see the doctor.

8. What do you like to eat (beside, besides) steak and roast beef?
9. (In, Into) the darkened theater we could see only a few people.
10. In the movie King Kong climbed (on, onto) the Empire State Building.

Using Prepositions in Edited Standard English

In this section you will study the guidelines for using prepositions in Edited Standard English.

About

Do not use *about* and *at* together in expressions of time. Use only the word that expresses the relationship you want to show.

(An asterisk [*] indicates a sentence with a feature that is not part of Edited Standard English.)

*We will arive at about 5:15.
We will arrive *at* 5:15.
We will arrive *about* 5:15.

At

Do not use *at* with *where*.

*Where does Michael work at?
Where does Michael work?

*Where did she park the car at?
Where did she park the car?

By

Do not use *by* to mean "with."

*That book is all right by me.
That book is all right *with* me.

From

Use *from*, not *than*, after the adjective *different*.

*My drawings are different than Michael's.
My drawings are different *from* Michael's.

Use *from*, not *off*, after the verb *borrow*.

*May I borrow a pen off you?
May I borrow a pen *from* you?

Of

Do not use *of* to replace the helping verb *have*.

*I couldn't of done it without your help.
I couldn't *have* done it without your help.

Off

Use just the preposition *off* instead of *off of*.

*The vase fell off of the shelf.
The vase fell *off* the shelf.

On

Use the verb *blame* by itself instead of *blame it on*.

*He always blames it on me.
He always *blames* me.

To

Do not use *to* with *where*.

*Where did you go to?
Where did you go?

*Where were you going to last night?
Where were you going last night?

Exercise 7: Using Prepositions in ESE

Each of the following sentences contains a preposition usage that is not a feature of Edited Standard English. Write each sentence, changing the preposition to conform to ESE. Underline your changes.

Examples

a. Mrs. Kraidman is very different than my grandmother.
   Mrs. Kraidman is very different from my grandmother.

b. Miriam should of come with us.
   Miriam should have come with us.

1. Betty wanted to borrow a dollar off her little sister.
2. Our bus arrives at about 10:30.
3. Michael's policy about studying is completely different than mine.
4. Would you like to come by me to the store?
5. Where have you been to since I saw you last?
6. Someone has ripped the label off of the package.
7. We should of called to see if they were home.
8. Where should we put these papers at when we finish?
9. May I borrow a piece of paper off of you to finish this test?
10. Don't blame it on Kara if her speech is too long.

Using Prepositional Phrases as Adjectives

Prepositional phrases can appear in many different positions in a sentence. In each position the prepositional phrase may have a different meaning.

We walked by a carnival *in a park*.	[tells *which* carnival]
We walked *in a park* by a carnival.	[tells *where* we walked]

Grammar and Usage

> **When a prepositional phrase is used as an adjective, it usually should be placed immediately after the noun or pronoun it modifies.**

Alice gave a speech *on vegetarian meals* to our science class.

Any other position may make the meaning of the sentence unclear.

Alice gave a speech to our science class *on vegetarian meals*. [Is the science class about vegetarian meals?]

On vegetarian meals Alice gave a speech to our science class. [Does Alice eat only vegetarian meals?]

Exercise 8: Using Prepositional Phrases as Adjectives

Each of the following sentences contains a prepositional phrase that acts as an adjective. Each sentence is unclear because the prepositional phrase does not directly follow the word it modifies. Rewrite each sentence and move the prepositional phrase to make its meaning clear. Underline the phrase you move.

Example

a. Hank sang a song for the group with a refrain.
   Hank sang a song with a refrain for the group.

1. Sarah bought a plastic pail for her baby brother with two scoops.
2. Ricardo gave a parakeet to his little brother with blue feathers.
3. How you can save energy is the topic of Mr. Yoshimo's speech in the home.
4. The windows should be cleaned today in the front of the house.
5. I used a large atlas to look up the continent of Australia in my father's office.
6. The students had several plants that needed watering on the shelf.

7. The soccer team won the championship on the bus.

8. The coat was a gift from my parents in the closet.

9. His leather boots were designed for riding horses from Spain.

10. That dog is a fine animal for hunting on my left.

Using Prepositional Phrases as Adverbs

Prepositional phrases that modify verbs can appear in a variety of positions without confusing the reader.

The meeting will be held *in the afternoon.*

In the afternoon the meeting will be held.

If the sentence contains two verbs, however, be careful to place the prepositional phrase as close as possible to the verb you want it to modify, since the phrase's location may change the meaning of the sentence.

We found the wallet that was lost *in the morning.*
[The wallet was lost in the morning.]

In the morning we found the wallet that was lost.
[The wallet was found in the morning.]

Exercise 9: Using Prepositional Phrases as Adverbs

Each of the sentences on the following page contains a prepositional phrase that acts as an adverb. The sentence is unclear because of the placement of the phrase. Rewrite the sentence and make the meaning clear by moving the phrase. Underline the phrase you move.

Examples

a. Jeremy stood and watched the ambulance go by on the front porch.
Jeremy stood <u>on the front porch</u> and watched the ambulance go by.

Grammar and Usage

  b. The student on the counter spilled the jar of glue.
   The student spilled the jar of glue on the counter.

1. We cooked dinner and sang songs over the fire.
2. Manuel cut the grass and washed the car with the new lawn mower.
3. Shelly kicked the ball and fell into the air.
4. They fried some eggs and poured some cereal on the grill.
5. Josh took the history exam and read his book with his new ball-point pen.
6. Linda took a refreshing shower and dried her hair in cold water.
7. Melissa painted a picture and rinsed the brushes with her new water colors.
8. He quickly shaved his face and brushed his teeth with an electric razor before going to work.
9. The family started a fire and sat down in the fireplace.
10. Jim ate some peanuts and drank some milk from his hand for a snack.

Review: Using Prepositions

Some of the following sentences are unclear because of the position of prepositional phrases. Others have incorrectly used prepositions. Rewrite the sentences, moving any unclear prepositional phrases or replacing any incorrect preposition with the proper one. If the sentence is correct, write *correct* on your paper. Underline the changes you make.

Examples

  a. Please distribute these papers between the committee members.
   Please distribute these papers among the committee members.

1. Charlene straightened her hair and washed her face with a comb.
2. Ty borrowed a dollar off Alexa.

3. The grasshoppers jumped from the grass on the picnic-table.
4. Who else besides Ernestine and Kamau can speak Spanish and French?
5. Susan bought the blue and white dress for the dance on the bed.
6. They went to the Lincoln Park Zoo for their holiday on the school bus.
7. We cleaned the rug with a shampooer rented from the drugstore on the floor.
8. Jessica stepped among John and Charlie, who glowered at each other, ready to fight because Charlie scratched John's bicycle.
9. The wood sculpture on the bookcase was carved by my sister in the den.
10. Between us three, there are no secrets.
11. Bob must have borrowed a whole package of notebook paper off me.
12. While in Minnesota visiting my cousin I bought a pair of moccasins.
13. The girl sat silently and watched the waves roll toward shore on the cliff.
14. Bring the records and come over to my house from your collection.
15. Raoul's views on doing daily chores are different from his father's.
16. We've been lost for an hour. Do you know where Dr. Chang's office is at?
17. The woven basket stood in the corner near the door with umbrellas in it.
18. Claire and Joe should of won first place in the dance contest.
19. It's okay by me if you wait until tomorrow to wash the windows, but the trash and the dishes have to be taken care of today.
20. At lunch we saved the bread crumbs and ate the steak for the birds.

Grammar and Usage

Writing Focus: *Using Prepositional Phrases in Writing*

As a writer, you can use prepositional phrases to make important distinctions and to add information to and show relationships between words in sentences. Use prepositional phrases to make your writing clear and precise.

Assignment: *Summer Treat*

Imagine that your grandfather has offered you a special summer treat—your choice of either a new bicycle or a two week stay at a summer camp you've always wanted to attend. What a dilemma! You must decide which treat you want and be prepared to explain your choice to your grandfather.

Use the following steps to complete this assignment.

A. Prewriting

Imagine two voices inside your head debating the dilemma. One voice could speak for the bike, and one for the stay at camp. Record the debate you hear. Write it quickly, easily, and without judging the quality of the ideas. For example, the bicycle might say, "I can give you years of pedaling pleasure and exercise," while the summer camp could respond, "But I can give you a unique and unforgettable experience." Let the two treats continue to discuss and argue their merits until you feel you have a decision. Write your decision on a separate piece of paper. Go back over your dialogue and underline three points that offer the most compelling reasons for your choice. Write them under your decision, leaving space between them. In the space, jot down details and more specific information to further explain your reasons. Number the reasons in this order: the second most important, the least important, and the most important.

B. Writing

Using your notes, write one or more paragraphs explaining your decision to accept either the bicycle or the two weeks at

camp. Be specific. As you write, use prepositional phrases to add specific details and to show relationships.

C. Postwriting

Use the following checklist to revise your first draft.

1. Does my writing clearly state my decision?
2. Have I provided adequate reasons for my choice?
3. Have I used prepositional phrases to provide details and to show relationships?

Edit your work using the Checklist for Proofreading at the back of the book. If appropriate, share your writing with your classmates. Discuss with them or your friends in general the process you use in making a decision.

17 Conjunctions
Understanding Conjunctions

Conjunctions are words that join. In the following sections you will practice identifying conjunctions by learning their definition and by looking at the way they can be grouped into classes.

Defining Conjunctions

A *conjunction* is usually defined as a word that joins words or groups of words.

The most common conjunctions—*and, but, or, nor, for,* and *yet*—are used to join individual words, word groups, or sentences. When a conjunction is used to join individual words, the words must be of the same type.

Joining Nouns:

Teachers and *students* met to discuss the new schedule.

Joining Pronouns:

She will probably choose *you* or *me* for the job.

Joining Verbs:

Melissa *draws* and *paints* well.

Joining Adjectives:

The couple from India are *friendly* but *shy.*

Joining Adverbs:

She pulled off the bandage *quickly* but *painfully.*

Nouns and pronouns may also be joined.

My *friends* and *I* enjoy listening to records.

Sometimes, the words that are joined by a conjunction have other words modifying them.

You can use the aluminum *racket* or the fiberglass *one* in the garage.

Conjunctions can also join groups of words. The groups of words can be phrases, clauses, or sentences. Groups of words joined by a conjunction must be parallel. Parallel groups of words have the same form or structure. Analyze the structure of the groups of words to make certain they are parallel.

Jessica Anthony likes to swim in the lake (and) play in the sand.

The cat is probably hiding behind the couch (or) under your bed.

Exercise 1: Identifying Conjunctions

Each of the following sentences contains conjunctions that join single words or groups of words. Write the sentences and circle each conjunction. Underline the words or groups of words that are joined.

Example

a. Their hearing will be held on Monday or Tuesday.

Their hearing will be held on Monday (or) Tuesday.

1. The chicken and dressing were done, but the potatoes weren't cooked.
2. She waited silently and sullenly for his answer which he was very slow to give.
3. The child asked a question, yet no one paid any attention.
4. Larry jogs or swims three days a week.
5. Kay is trying to get tickets to a play or a concert.
6. Without Lee and Pat life would be dreary.
7. Some time after Thanksgiving and before spring, we're planning a weekend camping trip.
8. Slowly and triumphantly she placed the last piece in the jigsaw puzzle.
9. The man in the yellow shirt and plaid jacket was extremely upset about the plane's delay.
10. Write out the sentences and circle each conjunction.

Grouping Conjunctions by Classes

Conjunctions can be classified into three groups: *coordinating, correlative,* and *subordinating.*

***Coordinating conjunctions,* the most common type of conjunctions, are used to join similar words or groups of words.**

The following list shows coordinating conjunctions.

and	nor
but	for
yet	so
or	

Elizabeth looks *angry* (and) *upset.*

Will (and) *Jim* are plowing the north ten acres.

Look for the roller skates *in the front closet* (or) *on the laundry room shelf.*

The man told us to get out of the lake, (for) *a storm was headed our way.*

We couldn't find an open gas station, (so) *we decided to go home and rest.*

When coordinating conjunctions join more than two words or groups of words, the conjunction comes between the last two items in the series and a comma is used immediately before the conjunction.

Angelo's lasagna recipe calls for *basil, bay leaves,* (and) *oregano.*

She wore *a faded pair of jeans, a red pullover sweater,* (and) *a navy blue coat.*

Exercise 2: Identifying Coordinating Conjunctions

Write the following sentences and circle each coordinating conjunction. Underline the words or groups of words that are joined.

Examples

a. Do you know Nick Grassie, or shall I introduce you?

Do you know Nick Grassie, (or) shall I introduce you?

b. Sherry has twenty-two hamsters, a gerbil, and three goldfish.

Sherry has twenty-two hamsters, a gerbil, (and) three goldfish.

1. Marsha has never missed a committee meeting, for she is dependable.
2. We raked leaves for an hour, but we still didn't finish.
3. None of the coaches nor any of the team members were passengers on the bus that collided with the truck.
4. We climbed to the top of the diving platform and jumped.
5. The crowd cheered loudly and enthusiastically after Armando's speech.
6. My calculator should be on my desk or in the top drawer.
7. Enthusiasm, confidence, and skill are what we need.
8. That mystery was long but exciting to read.
9. Susan, will you please carry the charcoal, the picnic basket, or the cooler to the car?
10. I felt a cramp in my side, so I dropped out of the race.

Correlative conjunctions always occur in pairs; they are never used alone.

In the following list of correlative conjunctions, the dots indicate that other words come between the conjunctions.

both . . . and   either . . . or
not only . . . but also neither . . . nor
whether . . . or

Like coordinating conjunctions, correlative conjunctions connect items of the same kind.

(Either) *Elissa* (or) her *brother* can baby-sit tonight for the Wongs.

Grammar and Usage

The water in the stream was (both) icy *cold* (and) *clear*.

Dave Cappaccio plays tennis (not only) *on the school team* (but also) *in a city league.*

(Either) you *have a little more patience,* (or) *I won't continue helping you.*

Sandy hasn't decided (whether) *to go to college* (or) *to look for a job.*

Exercise 3: Identifying Correlative Conjunctions

Write the following sentences and circle each pair of correlative conjunctions. Underline the words or group of words that are joined.

Example

a. Neither Celia nor Brenda has called all week.

(Neither) Celia (nor) Brenda has called all week.

1. The quilt that my grandmother made is both comfortable and decorative.
2. The Wilsons haven't decided whether to go to the beach or to visit the mountains for their vacation.
3. Mrs. Valdez coaches gymnastics not only for girls but also for boys.
4. Either the radio or the stereo is playing too loudly.
5. That popcorn is both salty and buttery.
6. On Saturdays I want neither to work nor to study, just to relax and watch television.
7. Manuel is training for the track meet by jogging not only in the morning but also in the evening.
8. Either we trim these bushes, or no one will see the stop sign on the corner.
9. I don't know whether to call Hal or to see Linda about the assignment I missed.
10. The key I found in the drawer fits neither the front door nor the back door.

Subordinating conjunctions are used only at the beginning of a subordinate clause.

The following words are commonly used as subordinating conjunctions.

after	as long as	if
although	as soon as	in order that
as	as though	provided that
as far as	because	since
as if	before	so long as
so that	unless	where
than	until	wherever
that	when	whether
though	whenever	while

Subordinating conjunctions are used to join groups of words that would otherwise be separate sentences. A subordinating conjunction may occur at the beginning or in the middle of the new sentence. See Chapter 22 for a further discussion of subordinate clauses.

We waited in line. The box office opened.
We waited in line *until* the box office opened.

Lin has made three close friends. He moved to Newark.
Lin has made three close friends *since* he moved to Newark.

The grapefruit is yellow. It still tastes sour.
Although the grapefruit is yellow, it still tastes sour.

Exercise 4: Identifying Subordinating Conjunctions

Write the following sentences and underline the subordinating conjunctions. (Some subordinating conjunctions consist of more than one word.)

Example

a. Randy has been skating since he was very young.
  Randy has been skating <u>since</u> he was very young.

1. Unless Jason sells some of his paintings, he won't enter any more art shows for a while.

2. Kevin has been successful because he is both talented and perservering.
3. When our class collects enough money, we will begin to plan our field trip.
4. Elaine is usually sick whenever there is a holiday.
5. Although the rain has stopped, the ground is still too wet to play softball.
6. As long as we have a compass, we won't get lost while we're hiking.
7. The passengers sat in the station until the train arrived.
8. The campaign will be interesting provided that the candidates stick to the issues.
9. Kathryn accepted the invitation as soon as it arrived.
10. Before it entered deep space, *Voyager* sent pictures of Jupiter back to earth.

Review: Understanding Conjunctions

Write each of the following sentences and underline the coordinating, correlative, and subordinating conjunctions. (Some sentences have more than one conjunction.)

Example

a. Pam is having a party because it's her birthday.
Pam is having a party <u>because</u> it's her birthday.

1. Neither rain nor sleet stops a mail carrier.
2. When you called with the news, Alonzo and Tom had just rung the doorbell to tell me the same thing.
3. Randy and his brother are making a kite.
4. I can go to the game as soon as I finish my chores.
5. Has anyone seen Gabriela since she graduated in June?
6. It is definitely not safe to eat all the berries and all the fruit that birds eat.
7. Do you know whether you will be able to take Spanish or French next year?

17 Conjunctions

8. Unless we leave right away, we'll miss the last bus.
9. Check for termites wherever you see piles of sawdust.
10. When Nicole's grandparents came to California, they not only spoke no English but also knew no one.
11. Either the Wongs or the Lees have a lawn mower that we can borrow at any time.
12. She felt she deserved a raise, so she didn't hesitate to ask.
13. Joe's brother joined the volunteer fire fighters' association when a forest fire threatened his home.
14. You can stay as long as you like.
15. Mrs. Levin cooked the grits on one burner while her husband finished the eggs on the other.
16. Both Vince and Mari are rehearsing for the play.
17. Try to look as if you feel relaxed and comfortable.
18. Whenever the alarm clock rings, Leslie promptly turns it off and goes right back to sleep.
19. If you feel strongly about a national issue, write to your representative or senator.
20. A wild turkey has a blue head and brown body.

Applying What You Know

Harriet Tubman: Conductor on the Underground Railroad, by Ann Petry, is the biography of Harriet Tubman, a courageous former slave who helped other slaves escape to freedom. In the following excerpt the narrator describes the slaveowners' reaction to Harriet Tubman, whom they called "Moses." Using what you have learned in the previous sections, identify the coordinating, correlative, and subordinating conjunctions in the passage. The first two are underlined for you. Find ten more conjunctions.

Along the Eastern Shore of Maryland, in Dorchester County, in Caroline County, the masters kept hearing whispers about the man named Moses, who was running off slaves. At first they did not believe in his existence. The stories about him were fantastic, unbelievable. Yet they watched for him. They offered rewards for his capture.

They never saw him. Now and then they heard whispered rumors to the effect that he was in the neighborhood. The

Grammar and Usage

woods were searched. The roads were watched. There was never anything to indicate his whereabouts. But a few days afterward, a goodly number of slaves would be gone from the plantation. Neither the master nor the overseer had heard or seen anything unusual in the quarter. Sometimes one or the other would vaguely remember having heard a whippoorwill call somewhere in the woods, close by, late at night. Though it was the wrong season for whippoorwills.

Sometimes the masters thought they had heard the cry of a hoot owl, repeated, and would remember having thought that the intervals between the low moaning cry were wrong, that it had been repeated four times in succession instead of three. There was never anything more than that to suggest that all was not well in the quarter. Yet when morning came, they invariably discovered that a group of the finest slaves had taken to their heels.

Unfortunately, the discovery was almost always made on a Sunday. Thus a whole day was lost before the machinery of pursuit could be set in motion. The posters offering rewards for the fugitives could not be printed until Monday. The men who made a living hunting for runaway slaves were out of reach, off in the woods with their dogs and their guns, in pursuit of four-footed game, or they were in camp meetings saying their prayers with their wives and families beside them.[1]

Using Conjunctions

Conjunctions are important because they connect words and ideas. They also show how one idea relates to another. In the following sections, you will practice using conjunctions.

Using Coordinating and Correlative Conjunctions

Coordinating conjunctions can join two items or a whole series of items. In a series the coordinating conjunction may be replaced by a comma.

[1] From *Harriet Tubman: Conductor on the Underground Railroad* by Ann Petry. Reprinted by permission of Russell & Volkening, Inc., as agents for the author. Copyright © 1955 by Ann Petry.

Rudy can play the drums *and* trumpet *and* guitar.

Rudy can play the drums, trumpet, *and* guitar.

Whenever a conjunction joins items in a series, the last two items are separated by a comma and a conjunction.

Do you want cantaloupe, honeydew, *or* watermelon?

I have called the office several times, written twice, *and* even visited in person.

Both coordinating and correlative conjunctions join words or groups of words of similar structure. When the structures of the words are not similar, or *parallel*, the resulting sentence sounds awkward.

Jack is witty and a sincere person.	[awkward]
Jack is witty and sincere.	[revised]
Ed doesn't like to ride a bicycle or ball.	[awkward]
Ed doesn't like to ride a bicycle or play ball.	[revised]

Exercise 5: Using Coordinating and Correlative Conjunctions

In each of the following sentences, replace conjunctions with commas wherever necessary. Then correct any awkward sentences by changing the structure of the word groups so they are parallel. Underline the coordinating or correlative conjunctions in your new sentences.

Examples

a. Beth showed us her collection of dried plants and herbs and leaves and flowers.
   Beth showed us her collection of dried plants, herbs, leaves, and flowers.

b. Mario woke up, got dressed, and big breakfast.
   Mario woke up, got dressed, and ate breakfast.

Grammar and Usage

1. Zana squinted into the dry wind that blew the tumbleweeds against the fence and thinks about her home.
2. Do you have a pencil or a ball point or a felt tip marker?
3. Sometimes I like to just sit quietly and listen to the rain or talking to a friend.
4. You must either start your research sooner or to choose a less difficult topic.
5. Michelle is not only generous but also thoughtful.
6. We found old pictures and postcards and letters.
7. Mallory loves to read, ski, and swimming.
8. During the downpour Marlene had neither boots nor was she carrying an umbrella.
9. Snow pea pods and mushrooms and Chinese cabbage are essential ingredients for moo goo gai pan.
10. Jenny is good at writing and acting and making ceramics.

Using Subordinating Conjunctions

The subordinating conjunction tells how two ideas are related.

I never forget Bryan's birthday. It is the same as my father's.
I never forget Bryan's birthday *because* it is the same as my father's.

You have already finished your work. Let's go to a movie.
Since you have already finished your work, let's go to a movie.

I'm planning a party. Phyllis comes to town in January.
I'm planning a party *when* Phyllis comes to town in January.

A subordinating conjunction is always followed by a subordinate clause. When a subordinate clause begins a sentence, the clause is followed by a comma.

A *clause* is a group of words with a subject and verb.

After we met, we dated for a year.

Unless he gets his way, Craig is impossibly moody.

Wherever we looked, we saw mushrooms growing.

When the subordinate clause appears at the end of a sentence, however, a comma is usually not necessary.

We dated for a year *after we met.*

Craig is impossibly moody *unless he gets his way.*

We saw mushrooms growing *wherever we looked.*

Exercise 6: Combining Sentences Using Subordinating Conjunctions

Pairs of sentences are given below. Join the two sentences by using the subordinating conjunction given in parentheses and write each new sentence.

Examples

a. The pictures didn't come out. The film was overexposed. (because)
The pictures didn't come out because the film was overexposed.

b. I called Carla. She sounded so happy with her new school. (when)
When I called Carla, she sounded so happy with her new school.

1. Many people left the movie starring the new actor. It was over. (before)
2. Please call Marlene or William. You can't come to the party. (if)
3. We searched all around the spot. We had camped in the woods. (where)
4. We try to talk. We end up fighting. (whenever)
5. You should stay in bed. Your temperature is normal. (until)

6. Mrs. Kim says there will be no homework over the vacation. All of the students turn in their research papers. (provided that)

7. Michael found homes for all the kittens. Maria decided she wanted one. (after)

8. This is not the right house. I am lost. (if)

9. She finished singing her solo. Her throat was terribly sore. (although)

10. Emperor Nero played his violin. Rome burned. (while)

Review: Using Conjunctions

Rewrite each of the following sentences. Whenever necessary, replace conjunctions with commas and correct awkward structures. If a subordinating conjunction is given in parentheses, use the conjunction to combine pairs of sentences.

Examples

a. Lee's parents argue. It upsets her. (whenever)
Whenever Lee's parents argue, it upsets her.

b. Mrs. Wong appointed Jerry and Pete and Mark to organize the field trip.
Mrs. Wong appointed Jerry, Pete, and Mark to organize the field trip.

c. Pablo's hobbies are taking photographs and to draw landscapes.
Pablo's hobbies are taking photographs and drawing landscapes.

1. The elephant driver pressed his feet behind the elephant's ears. The elephant would lift the log. (so that)

2. Cecilia has applied to a department store and a nursery school and a bookstore for a summer job.

3. The luxury liner *Titanic,* with hundreds on board, sank. It hit an iceberg. (after)

4. The names of many states and cities and rivers come from native American languages.

5. The first capital of Texas was Washington-on-the-Brazos. Texas declared its independence from Mexico. (after)

6. The duckbill platypus is a mammal. It nurses its young. (because)
7. Tornadoes occur most frequently in Kansas and Oklahoma and Texas and Missouri and less frequently on the East and West Coasts.
8. The Delaware nation lived on the present site of Philadelphia and Delaware. The Europeans arrived in the early 1600s. (before)
9. The offspring of a tiger and lion is called a *tiglon* or *tigon* or *liger*.
10. Microscopic animals and plants called *plankton* are an important food source for marine animals. Bodies of water exist. (wherever)
11. The Spanish explorers introduced potatoes to Europe in the 1500s. They found them being cultivated by the Incas in South America. (after)
12. Humans began to cultivate land. Plant seeds were scattered by wind or animals or water. (before)
13. They are birds. Penguins and turkeys and ostriches cannot fly. (although)
14. Oleander and foxglove and mountain laurel are poisonous to people.
15. The Battle of Lookout Mountain is also called the "Battle Above the Clouds." Lookout Mountain is more than 2,000 feet above the city of Chattanooga which is in the state of Tennessee. (since)
16. Most of the world's tin is mined in Malaysia and Bolivia and Indonesia and Thailand. Some tin is mined in Africa. (although)
17. A pregnant woman gains too much weight or smokes or drinks or takes drugs. Her baby's life and health are endangered. (when)
18. Police officers in training study psychology and sociology and law and use of weapons.
19. You will need a compass, and some graph paper, and a protractor. You can complete your math assignment correctly. (so that)
20. Petrified wood is formed. Water seeps through mud or sand that covers buried tree trunks. (when)

Grammar and Usage

Writing Focus: *Using Conjunctions in Writing*

Good writers use conjunctions to connect thoughts and to make their writing flow smoothly. Conjunctions tell readers how one idea or event relates to another, and they allow writers to express themselves in mature and complex ways.

Assignment: *Magic*

A popular character in many stories is the magician who changes people into other forms or shapes. Imagine for a moment that you have your own personal "Merlin the Magician." Who or what would you like to be? What might life as your new self be like?

Write one or more well-developed paragraphs describing an hour's existence as your new transformed magical self. Write for your classmates. Give concrete details of your new appearance as well as your movements and experiences during the hour. Bring your readers into your enchanted world. Your writing will be evaluated for effective use of conjunctions.

Use the following steps to complete this assignment.

A. Prewriting

Use brainstorming, described in Chapter 1, to generate details about your new appearance and experiences. Concentrate on including details that appeal to the senses. Look back over the items on your brainstorming list, and jot down any experiences you might have in your new form. Does the fact that you can fit inside a match box lead you into an adventure in someone's pocket, for example? Underline the details and associations that best describe the magical you and your experiences. Number them in the order that captures movement through the hour's time.

B. Writing

Using your brainstorming list to help you, write one or more paragraphs describing an hour's experiences as a transformed self. Begin your description with the magician changing your

appearance. Then move to the experiences you had during an hour. Include details that paint a moving picture. As you write, use conjunctions to combine ideas and to make relationships between ideas clear.

C. Postwriting

Use the following checklist to revise your first draft.

1. Have I included enough details so that my readers can actually imagine my hour as a transformed person?
2. Have I combined short sentences by using conjunctions?
3. Have I used the appropriate conjunction to show the relationship between my ideas? Are my ideas properly coordinated or subordinated?

Edit your paragraphs, using the Checklist for Proofreading at the back of the book. If appropriate, share your work with your classmates by reading it aloud.

18 Interjections
Understanding Interjections

Interjections are usually defined as words that show a strong or sudden feeling (such as joy, sorrow, anger, or pain) and that have no relationship to other words in the sentence.

> Hey! Watch where you're going.
>
> Wow! Look at that T-shirt!

Some interjections are very mild.

> Oh, did you want to talk to me?
>
> Well, what did you expect?

The following words are also used as interjections.

alas	help	no way
dear me	hooray	ugh
good grief	my	whew
goodness	never	yippee
great	nonsense	

Some interjections may be used as other parts of speech.

"*Never!*" she cried.	[interjection]
We will *never* be friends.	[adverb]

Exercise 1: Identifying Interjections

Write the following sentences and underline each of the interjections.

Example

a. "Hey!" Glenna called. "Wait for me."
"<u>Hey!</u>" Glenna called. "Wait for me."

b. Good grief! Jogging two miles is more difficult than I expected.
<u>Good grief!</u> Jogging two miles is more difficult than I expected.

1. No way! I'll never work there again.
2. When Chico scored the touchdown, the coach slapped him on the back and yelled, "Hooray! You're terrific!"
3. Wow! Will you look at that costume.
4. Every time I see him, Uncle Joe says, "My, you certainly have grown."
5. Well, I guess we'd better say good night.
6. Ugh! This cough medicine tastes terrible.
7. Diane wrote, "Great! I'd love to come to your party if it's on a Friday."
8. When she fell overboard, the child cried, "Help! I can't swim!"
9. Whew! Am I glad that my final examinations will be over this week!
10. Hamlet looked at the skull and said, "Alas, poor Yorick, I knew him well."

Using Interjections

When you talk, your voice shows whether you are expressing strong or mild feelings, but in writing, punctuation marks must convey the level of emotion. An interjection followed by an exclamation point indicates strong feeling, and one followed by a comma indicates mild emotion.

Well! If that's the way you feel, I'll leave right now! [strong feeling]

Well, it must be about time to leave. [mild feeling]

Notice that the word following the exclamation point is capitalized because it begins a new sentence. When a comma is used with an interjection, however, the word that follows is not capitalized.

Grammar and Usage

Interjections that are part of a direct quotation should never have both a comma and an exclamation point together. Either one or the other mark of punctuation is used—not both.

In a direct quotation the word that follows the interjection is not capitalized unless it begins a new sentence.

"Golly!" *she* cried.

"Golly! *Where* did you get that hat?" she cried.

Exercise 2: Punctuating Interjections

Each of the following sentences contains an interjection. Write the sentences and place an exclamation point after the interjections that show a strong or sudden feeling. Use a comma after those that express a milder emotion. (Remember to capitalize the first word following an exclamation point if that word begins a new sentence.)

Example

a. "Never" she cried. "I will never marry you!"
   "Never!" she cried. "I will never marry you!"

b. Yippie we won the relay.
   Yippee! We won the relay.

1. My it's a lovely day.
2. Aha so you're the thief!
3. "Hooray" she yelled.
4. "Well shall we dance?" he asked his sister without enthusiasm.
5. Help the building is on fire!
6. Dear me I did not realize it was so late and I have so much left to do.
7. Oh were you talking to me?
8. Hey watch where you point that gun!
9. "Good grief the last train has left and everybody's gone!" Maria moaned.
10. Ugh get that Limburger cheese away from me before the smell makes me sick.

Writing Focus: *Using Interjections in Writing*

Interjections are used to express strong emotions or sudden feelings, usually in dialogue. When you write dialogue, use interjections that are appropriate for the speaker. Your friends, for example, probably don't use the same interjections that your parents do.

Assignment: *A Strange Sight*

Notice the photograph below. Imagine that you and some friends have just come upon the scene represented in the picture. "Yikes! What's that?" one of you asks. "Hey, what's going on?" questions another.

Grammar and Usage

    Write the conversation/dialogue that you and your friends might have as you view the scene. In it show your personality and the personalities of your friends through topics of conversation and the use of interjections. Let your audience of classmates and teacher have a glimpse of your lives and your responses to the sight. Your work will be evaluated for effective and correct use of interjections.

    Use the following steps to complete this assignment.

A. Prewriting

Study the photograph carefully. Imagine coming on the scene with your friends. Make a list of topics of conversation you might discuss. (What the sight is might be one fascinating topic!) Now make word clusters, described in Chapter 1, about the conversation. Put your name and the names of your four friends in separate word cluster circles. Add bits of conversation about the sight and any other topics you'd like to write about around each name that would be appropriate to that person. Let your imagination help you create this dialogue about the strange scene.

18 Interjections

B. Writing

Write a short dialogue that might occur among you and your friends as you come upon the scene represented in the photograph. Begin with a few sentences that explain where you were and what you were doing just before you saw the sight. Then write the dialogue, using the ideas and bits of conversation from your word clusters. Let the dialogue develop naturally as you and your friends discuss the scene. Include appropriate interjections.

C. Postwriting

Revise your first draft using the following checklist.

1. Does my dialogue sound realistic for the situation?
2. Have I used interjections accurately to express emotion?
3. Have I punctuated and capitalized the interjections and other elements of the dialogue correctly?

Edit your draft using the Checklist for Proofreading at the back of the book. If appropriate, share your dialogue with your classmates, and discuss the different ideas that students had about the scene.

19 Verbals

Understanding Verbals

Although not a part of speech, *verbals* are an important word group. A *verbal* is a word that is formed from a verb but acts as another part of speech in a sentence. In the following sections you will study two kinds of verbals: *participles* and *gerunds*.

Participles

Participles **are verb forms that act as adjectives in a sentence. Participles may be either** *present* **or** *past*.

Present Participles

Present participles are verb forms ending in *-ing* that act as adjectives by modifying nouns or pronouns. They may appear either before or after the word they modify.

The *dancing* witches cast their spells into the black pot.

The witches, *dancing* in a circle, cast their spells into the black pot.

To avoid confusing present participles with verbs, look for the noun or pronoun that the participle modifies. Also, remember that a verb phrase with a helping verb is not a participle.

The *dying* embers were still dangerous.	[participle]
The embers *were dying* slowly.	[verb phrase]
Carl can run a *printing* press.	[participle]
The child *is printing* her name.	[verb phrase]

Exercise 1: Identifying Present Participles

Write each of the following sentences and underline the present participles used as adjectives. Draw an arrow from each participle to the noun or pronoun it modifies.

Examples

a. The blizzard, howling wildly, kept us inside the house for several days.

The blizzard, <u>howling</u> wildly, kept us inside the house for several days.

b. George watched the glowing sunset.

George watched the <u>glowing</u> sunset.

1. The fire fighters saved the burning house, but couldn't save the furniture.
2. Miss Perez showed us a flying squirrel that was in her backyard.
3. The deer, bounding away, cleared the fence.
4. Melissa chased the buzzing fly out of the house.
5. The piglets, squealing loudly, demanded their supper.
6. I got a blistering sunburn at the beach.
7. John, opening his gym locker, noticed something strange inside.
8. We stared in terror at the roaring funnel cloud.
9. Outside the door stood my sister, laughing at my friends and me.
10. The rising sun awoke the birds sleeping in their nest on my windowsill.

Past Participles

The *past participle* is one of the three principal parts of a verb. The past participle of regular verbs is formed with *-d* or *-ed* added to the present tense form of the verb: *talk, talked; train, trained*. The past participle of irregular verbs must be learned separately. (A list of irregular past participles is in Chapter 13.)

Grammar and Usage

A past participle can be used as either a verb or an adjective. If a helping verb is used with a past participle, the participle is being used as a verb.

The spaniel *has broken* its toy.	[verb]
The colt *was startled* by the noise.	[verb]

If a past participle is used by itself to modify a noun or pronoun, the participle is being used as an adjective.

The spaniel had a *broken toy*.	[adjective]
The *startled* colt galloped away.	[adjective]

Exercise 2: Identifying Past Participles

Each of the following sentences contains at least one past participle used as an adjective. Write the sentences and underline the past participles. Then draw an arrow from each past participle to the noun or pronoun it modifies. Leave enough space on your paper for the arrows.

Examples

a. Someone sat down on our completed project and ruined it permanently.

Someone sat down on our <u>completed</u> project and ruined it permanently.

b. Mary patched the punctured tire and put it back on the car immediately.

Mary patched the <u>punctured</u> tire and put it back on the car immediately.

1. A lost cat came to our house and wouldn't leave after we fed it.

2. The car jolted down the rutted road until we reached the paved section.

3. The sparrows ate the scattered crumbs we threw onto the ground.
4. We could have baked chicken for supper, or would you prefer broiled fish?
5. The satisfied cows grazed in the lush meadow with their calves.
6. Garrett Morris is a trained singer as well as a funny comedian.
7. The hijacked bus didn't stop for us but rushed past at a high speed.
8. The startled fisherman caught a large bass and a speckled trout.
9. A good breakfast would be fried eggs, bacon, and juice.
10. Police officers recovered the stolen property from the convicted felons.

Gerunds

A *gerund* is a verb form ending in *-ing* that is used as a noun. A gerund can be used in a sentence in any way that a noun can. (Remember that nouns do not modify other words.) Verb forms ending in *-ing* that modify nouns or pronouns are "participles used as adjectives," not gerunds.

Swimming is Rosa's favorite sport.	[noun: gerund]
The *swimming* snake was not poisonous.	[adjective: participle]
Sandy went *hiking* in the mountains.	[noun: gerund]
You'll need *hiking* boots for this trip.	[adjective: participle]

Exercise 3: Identifying Gerunds

Write each of the sentences on the following page and underline the gerund. Be certain that the word you underline is being used as a noun.

Examples

a. Skydiving seems dangerous to me.
   <u>Skydiving</u> seems dangerous to me.

b. Riko likes reading.
   Riko likes <u>reading</u>.

1. Biking is good exercise.
2. These shoes are good for running, tennis, and basketball.
3. Mark's best rodeo sport is roping.
4. Tina likes canoeing on unspoiled rivers in the wilderness of Colorado.
5. Unfortunately, Michael considers his singing quite good.
6. A great experience is camping in the wilderness.
7. Our dog enjoys barking just to get our attention.
8. Jesse Owens won many awards for running and the broad jump.
9. Fishing relaxes the body and the mind, and sometimes even provides a meal.
10. Paula's best subject was spelling.

Review: Understanding Verbals

Write each of the following sentences and underline the verbals. Write *P* over the verbal if it is a participle. Write *G* if it is a gerund.

Examples

a. The first practical typing machine was invented in 1867.

                          P
The first practical <u>typing</u> machine was invented in 1867.

b. In my opinion multiplying is much less difficult than dividing.   G
In my opinion <u>multiplying</u> is much less difficult than
     G
<u>dividing</u>.

1. The fighting trout was hard to land but we were successful after several minutes.
2. We caught a quick glimpse of a shooting star.
3. The losing team had two injured players.
4. I am buying some frozen beans and a dozen ears of corn for supper.
5. The trained seal balanced a ball on its nose.
6. Screaming is a natural response to a frightening movie, though it makes listening difficult.
7. Those burning coals are dangerous.
8. The broken handle makes getting inside the car even more difficult than I had expected.
9. The boiling liquid bubbled like lava.
10. The runners crossed the finish line panting and with drooping bodies.
11. Going to the movies can be a relaxing experience.
12. Writing is a good way of expressing yourself.
13. Only a torn curtain covered the shattered window.
14. The experienced bowlers are using the lanes today so we must wait until tomorrow.
15. My weekend job is baby-sitting the Norton children.
16. My mother did the driving while the rest of us slept.
17. Eric's goal in life is winning at everything he does, and he is usually successful.
18. Those fried eggs are just too cold.
19. Diving is the next scheduled event in the meet.
20. Arranging the fresh flowers was a pleasing task that I must do more often.

Applying What You Know

Select several paragraphs from a book, short story, magazine, or newspaper article. Using what you have learned about verbals, identify the participles and gerunds in the selection. List them on a sheet of paper, and beside each one write the method you used to identify it.

Grammar and Usage

Writing Focus: *Using Verbals in Writing*

Verbals function almost like a part of speech. They have the vitality of verbs but can do more than verbs alone. By using participles and gerunds in sentences, you can make your writing more lively, varied, and concise.

Assignment: *Batten Down the Hatches*

Imagine that you're a tour guide responsible for presenting facts of history and geography, anecdotes, and statistics as well as pointing out sights of interest to a group of excited tourists. Your group is taking an hour's tour under the ocean aboard a brand new double decker submarine. This is your first tour, but you're well prepared. You know the ocean floor like the back of your hand.

Write one or more well-developed paragraphs explaining what the passengers are seeing as they move through the deep ocean aboard the submarine. Direct their attention to particular sights. Use your imagination, and be specific in your running commentary as you both inform and entertain your group. Your writing will be evaluated for correct and effective use of verbals.

Use the following steps to complete this assignment.

A. Prewriting

Recall any tours you've taken. Remember sitting or walking and listening to the tour guide explain what you were seeing. Now imagine yourself as a tour guide for the ocean floor. Use your imagination to draw a map of it; include plants, rock formations, sunken ships or cities, and any new strange life forms. Use the six basic questions method described in Chapter 1 to generate information about the ocean depths. Jot down questions like the following: *Who* lives in the ocean? *What* does the ocean contain? *Where* did that particular fish come from? *When* was that rock cave formed? *Why* did giant eels evolve in this area? *How* do the inhabitants of the deep get food? Answer your questions specifically in words, phrases, and sentences.

Review your answers and group them into chronological and spatial order.

B. Writing

Using your answers, write one or more paragraphs explaining to your passengers what they are seeing on their tour of the ocean floor. Include specific details so that people not on the tour can also "see." You might begin sentences with phrases like "Coming up on your right . . . ." to help your passengers orient themselves in space and time. As you write, use verbals to make your writing clear and varied.

C. Postwriting

Use the following checklist to revise your work.

1. Does my writing contain the kind of information that explains the sights of the ocean floor and entertains the passengers?
2. Have I used verbals correctly and effectively?

Edit your work using the Checklist for Proofreading at the back of the book. If appropriate, share your writing with classmates by sitting in a circle to read each other's work. Create and illustrate a student pamphlet entitled *Strange Water Worlds*.

20 Sentence Structure

Understanding Sentences

An important skill in learning to write is recognizing and using complete sentences. In this chapter you will learn to do this by studying the definition of a sentence, by looking at the kinds of sentences, and by examining the structure of sentences to see how they are put together.

Defining Sentences

A *sentence* is usually defined as a group of words that expresses a complete thought.

Incomplete Thought:	Mows lawns on weekends [Who mows lawns on weekends?]
Sentence:	Jill mows lawns on weekends.
Incomplete Thought:	Both Harold and Ed [What did both Harold and Ed do?]
Sentence:	Both Harold and Ed went fishing in Fence Lake.

A group of words that does not express a complete thought is called a *sentence fragment*.

Exercise 1: Identifying Sentences

Some of the following groups of words are sentences; some are not. On a sheet of paper list the numbers 1–10. If the group of words is not a sentence, write *NS* next to its number. If the group of words is a sentence, write the sentence. Capitalize the first word of the sentence and supply the appropriate end punctuation.

Example

    a. the movie begins at 7:30
       The movie begins at 7:30.

1. when we reached the detour sign
2. the door creaked noisily
3. usually on cold, snowy nights
4. my cousins are arriving for a visit today
5. neither the cats nor the dogs in our neighborhood
6. after Pablo played his drum solo
7. did you finish last night's math homework
8. the tomatoes, cucumbers, and squash in the garden
9. because our hike was delayed
10. the leaves turn to a brilliant autumn gold

Purposes of Sentences

A sentence may serve any one of four purposes. According to its purpose, a sentence is classified as *declarative*, *imperative*, *interrogative*, or *exclamatory*.

A *declarative sentence* makes a statement.

A declarative sentence ends with a period.

    Peanut butter was invented in St. Louis.

    My sister eats peanut butter sandwiches for lunch every school day.

An *imperative sentence* gives a mild command or makes a request.

An imperative sentence ends with a period.

    Tell me where peanut butter was invented.

    Try this peanut butter soup, Lisa.

Grammar and Usage

An *interrogative sentence* asks a question.

An interrogative sentence ends with a question mark.

>Where was peanut butter invented?
>Who invented peanut butter?

An *exclamatory sentence* expresses a strong or sudden feeling.

An exclamatory sentence ends with an exclamation point.

>Oh, no, he dropped the peanut butter!
>What a mess this peanut butter is!

Exercise 2: Identifying the Purpose of Sentences

Write the following sentences and place the correct punctuation at the end of each. Label the sentence according to its purpose.

Examples

a. Turn down the music, please
   Turn down the music, please.
   imperative

b. There's a shark behind you
   There's a shark behind you!
   exclamatory

1. Will you come to my party
2. Our teacher can speak three languages
3. Always put the ZIP code on the envelope
4. Great Scott, a flying saucer has landed
5. My cousin visited Israel
6. Would you like another orange
7. Don't open this before your birthday
8. My sister has a pet parakeet

9. Please put all litter in the trash cans
10. You've won first prize

The Parts of a Sentence

> **A sentence has two basic parts: a *subject* (S) and a *predicate* (P).**

     S   P
The bird on the windowsill / nests in the oak tree.
     S   P
The grammar of a language / gives rules for putting words together.

The *subject* of a sentence identifies the person, place, thing, or idea that is being spoken about in the rest of the sentence. In all of the following sentences the subjects are underlined.

<u>Clare</u> plays drums in the marching band.
<u>The shabby old boxcar</u> needed painting.
Where is <u>Akron, Ohio</u>, on this map?

The *simple subject* is the main word (or combination of words) naming the subject of the sentence. In the following sentences the subjects are underlined, and the simple subjects are *italicized*.

<u>The reference *book*</u> was heavy.
<u>*No one* in the room</u> raised a hand.

The *complete subject* is the main word plus its modifiers. In the following sentences the complete subjects are underlined.

<u>The short man with the gray mustache</u> is my grandfather.
<u>The last bus to the beach</u> leaves in ten minutes.

Exercise 3: Identifying Complete and Simple Subjects

Write each of the sentences on the following page and underline the complete subject. Draw a circle around the simple subject.

Grammar and Usage

Examples

a. The next game will decide the championship.

The next (game) will decide the championship.

b. The restaurant on the corner serves great hot dogs.

The (restaurant) on the corner serves great hot dogs.

1. A large, yellow cat peered out of the window.
2. One of my aunts is a policewoman for the city of New Orleans.
3. The tall girl in the tan coat is Maria.
4. The best student in class will receive a college scholarship.
5. The voice of the coyote echoed through the night air.
6. The best medicine for a cold is plenty of rest.
7. The members of the basketball team had their pictures taken.
8. My friend's older sister attends Howard University.
9. The people in the audience cheered and clapped.
10. A huge castle of stone stood on the hill.

Understood Subjects

The subject of a sentence can be *you* understood.

Understood subjects do not actually appear in the sentence. Instead, the reader understands that the subject is the person being addressed: *You*. Imperative sentences usually have understood subjects.

Get down from there right now.
(*You*) get down from there right now.

Fasten your seat belt.
(*You*) fasten your seat belt.

> **Even when the sentence names the person or group being addressed, the subject is still *you* understood.**
>
> Tell us your plans again, Sarah.
> (*You*) tell us your plans again, Sarah.
>
> Class, exchange papers.
> Class, (*you*) exchange papers.

Exercise 4: Identifying Complete, Simple, and Understood Subjects

Write the following sentences. Underline the complete subject and circle the simple subject. If the simple subject is *you* understood, write (*You*) after the sentence.

Examples

a. Joggers on city streets should watch for cars.

(Joggers) on city streets should watch for cars.

b. Always wear shoes while using lawn mowers.
   Always wear shoes while using lawn mowers. (You)

1. Don't go near water during a thunderstorm.
2. Telephones are also dangerous during electrical storms.
3. Lightning usually strikes the highest object in an area.
4. People in open areas should crouch close to the ground for protection.
5. Do not lie flat, however.
6. You often hear stories of people being struck while standing under trees.
7. Students, never stand under a tree when lightning is present.
8. In an automobile roll up the windows and remain inside with the doors closed.
9. Very few people have been able to survive a direct hit by lightning.
10. Follow the safety procedures and save your life.

Grammar and Usage

Compound Subjects

> A *compound subject* consists of two or more connected subjects that have the same verb.

Compound subjects are usually connected by coordinating conjunctions.

Cheese, butter, and *milk* are dairy foods.
[The complete subject is *Cheese, butter, and milk*. The compound subject is *Cheese/butter/milk*.]

A *herd* of sheep and one black *goat* grazed on the hill.
[The complete subject is *A herd of sheep and one black goat*. The compound subject is *herd/goat*.]

All the doors and *most* of the windows are locked.
[The complete subject is *All the doors and most of the windows*. The compound subject is *all/most*.]

In two of the above sentences, part of the compound subject is followed by a prepositional phrase that modifies it (A herd *of sheep;* Most *of the windows.*) Do not confuse the simple subject (*S*) with the object of the preposition (*OP*).

    S   OP   S   OP
Several *of the students* and many *of the teachers* were present.

    S   OP   S   OP
Two girls *from our school* and one boy *from another school* were selected.

Exercise 5: Identifying Compound Subjects

Each of the following sentences has a compound subject. Write the sentences, underlining each complete subject. Then circle each of the nouns that make up the compound subject.

Examples

a. Ice-skating and hockey are my favorite sports in the winter Olympic games.

(Ice-skating) and (hockey) are my favorite sports in the winter Olympic games.

b. The man in the green shirt and the one in the tan jacket are my uncles.

The (man) in the green shirt and the (one) in the tan jacket are my uncles.

1. Our neighbors and their friends have a block party each year.
2. Alaska and Hawaii were the last two states admitted to the Union.
3. The Abominable Snowman and the Loch Ness monster are often spoken about but seldom seen, which makes photographs of them rare.
4. R2-D2 of *Star Wars* and HAL of *2001: A Space Odyssey* are famous "machine" actors.
5. Courage and self-discipline are closely related.
6. All of the boys and most of the fathers survived the hike up Mount Rainier.
7. Sharon, Greg, or Kathy will be the outstanding math student.
8. The director of the school choir and a few of the singers had colds.
9. Bicyclists, joggers, and roller skaters may endanger pedestrians on crowded streets.
10. Newspapers, magazines, television, and radio give people easy access to news.

Subjects in Inverted Order

When the predicate comes before the subject, the sentence is said to be in *inverted order*. Questions are often in inverted order.

Which flavor do you want?
[*You* do want which flavor?]

Where should I put this letter?
[*I* should put this letter where?]

Grammar and Usage

> **A sentence that begins with a prepositional phrase is often in an inverted order.**

Into the silent valley rode the horseman.
[The *horseman* rode into the silent valley.]

Above the courthouse flew the flag.
[The *flag* flew above the courthouse.]

Restating the sentence will help you to locate the subject in an inverted sentence.

Exercise 6: *Identifying Subjects in Inverted Sentences*

Write the following sentences and underline each complete subject. Then circle the simple subject.

Example

a. Where is my frog?

Where is my (frog)?

1. From the window peered a sinister face that frightened my little sister.
2. Did you find your ticket?
3. In back of the old barn sits a beat-up jalopy.
4. Where should we put the receipts from the ticket sales?
5. In the middle of the pen crouched the smallest puppy of the whole litter.
6. From somewhere in the middle of the crowd erupted a furious demonstration.
7. Why was our team penalized?
8. How can we put this puzzle together, with four pieces missing?
9. The mountain peak we had come to climb loomed far above us.
10. Near the stream in the middle of the woods sat the last survivor on earth.

The Predicate

> **The *predicate* of a sentence is the part that says something about the subject.**

In the following sentences the predicates are underlined twice.

    The black horse <u>pranced across the ring</u>.

    Hundreds of firecrackers <u>exploded against the dark sky</u>.

The *simple predicate* is the verb or verb phrase in the complete predicate. The predicates in the following sentences are underlined twice, and the simple predicates are *italicized*.

    David <u>*has calculated* the answer</u>.

    Sally <u>*was* late for her piano lesson</u>.

Adverbs such as *not, never,* and *ever* sometimes separate the parts of the simple predicate. These adverbs are not part of the simple predicate.

    John <u>*did* not *call* me last night</u>.

    We <u>*should*n't *have* any problem</u>.

Exercise 7: Identifying Complete and Simple Predicates

Write each of the following sentences, underlining the complete predicate twice. Circle the simple predicate.

Examples

    a. The school band practices every day.

        The school band <u>(practices) every day</u>.

    b. That calf will win a blue ribbon.

        That calf <u>(will win) a blue ribbon</u>.

1. Gary wrote a letter to the mayor.
2. Rita climbed a mountain last summer.
3. Ray Charles recorded this album.

Grammar and Usage

4. Carol and Ron work on the school newspaper.
5. Crazy Horse was a great leader of the Oglala Sioux.
6. The students did not make their costumes for the play.
7. Our family could not camp by the lake.
8. Jeff can't draw cartoons very well.
9. The leaves were turning red, gold, and brown.
10. The class is studying the planet Mars.

Compound Verbs

A *compound verb* consists of two or more connected verbs or verb phrases that have the same subject.

Compound verbs are joined by a conjunction and sometimes by commas as well.

We went to the museum (and) saw the African masks.

Myra cleaned, polished, (and) displayed her collection of coins.

The scouts walked two miles (or) ran four.

A sentence with a compound verb may also have a compound subject.

Paul and Mark washed but never waxed the car.

Exercise 8: Identifying Compound Verbs

Each of the following sentences has a compound verb. Write the sentences, underlining each simple subject once and each verb twice.

Examples

a. The plane leaves at 8:15 and arrives at noon.
   The plane leaves at 8:15 and arrives at noon.

b. Al jogged and worked with weights.
   <u>Al</u> <u>jogged</u> and <u>worked</u> with weights.

1. The dancers wore bright costumes and carried spears.
2. John plays his guitar or reads after school.
3. Lisa speaks and reads Chinese.
4. Pete and Tina like movies and see many.
5. Jim cleaned the trout and fried it in butter.
6. Miss Sosa, Mr. Brown, and Mrs. Kim came to our school and spoke in the assembly.
7. Pat breeds, raises, and sells tropical fish.
8. My grandmother jogs or bicycles four miles a day.
9. Melissa and Sue went to Washington and visited Mount St. Helens.
10. John and Sheila grow vegetables and keep chickens.

Sentence Patterns

By identifying their parts, you can see that sentences follow five basic patterns:

1. **S–V**
   Subject–Verb

2. **S–V–DO**
   Subject–Verb–Direct Object

3. **S–V–IO–DO**
   Subject–Verb–Indirect Object–Direct Object

4. **S–LV–PN**
   Subject–Linking Verb–Predicate Noun

5. **S–LV–PA**
   Subject–Linking Verb–Predicate Adjective

The groups of words that follow the subject and verb in a sentence are called *complements*.

A *complement* is a part of the predicate that completes the thought begun by the subject and verb.

S–V Sentence Pattern

Some groups of words can express a complete thought with just a subject and verb. Each part of the sentence may have modifiers, but the pattern remains the same.

   S V
  John ran.
       S   V
  The black cat has disappeared again.
        S   V
  A large brown toad with warts hopped into our picnic basket.

S–V–DO Sentence Pattern

A *direct object* is usually defined as a noun or pronoun that follows an action verb and answers the question *what?* or *whom?* about the subject and verb.

  S   V   DO
Mr. Wolfe raises Dalmatians. [Mr. Wolfe raises *what?*]

  S V DO
He asked us to the game.   [He asked *whom* to the game?]

A sentence may have more than one direct object.

    S   V   DO   V   DO
  Melissa found her keys and opened the door.
      S   V   DO DO   DO
  The chief of police discussed safety, crime, and justice at the assembly.

Direct objects receive the action of the verb or show the result of that action. They cannot follow forms of the verb *be* or linking verbs.

Exercise 9: *Identifying S–V–DO Sentence Patterns*

Write the following sentences, labeling the sentence patterns used in each sentence. Underline the words you label.

Examples

a. The workers repaired the street.

        S   V   DO
The <u>workers</u> <u>repaired</u> the <u>street</u>.

b. Every night Pat makes popcorn.

                S   V   DO
Every night <u>Pat</u> <u>makes</u> <u>popcorn</u>.

1. All day long I called her at work.
2. To save energy we rode our bikes to the beach.
3. Ginger dropped them in the bottom of her purse.
4. After the party we cleaned the house and washed the dishes.
5. Mr. Osaka rescued my cat from the roof of the house.
6. At the zoo Karen met us by the snake house.
7. Herb was studying his math last night.
8. For snacks we always eat fruit or cheese.
9. While on vacation Grandfather bought a parrot for my brother and me.
10. Before the next class Mr. Lopez will correct our tests and projects.

S–V–IO–DO *Sentence Pattern*

An *indirect object (IO)* is a noun or pronoun that answers the question *to what? for what? to whom?* or *for whom?* about the subject, verb, and direct object.

The indirect object always appears between the verb and the direct object.

S V   IO   DO
He <u>gave</u> the <u>hospital</u> some <u>money</u>.   [gave *to what?*]

S   V   IO   DO
She <u>showed</u> <u>us</u> her new <u>colt</u>.   [showed *to whom?*]

Grammar and Usage

```
       S    V    IO         DO
      Dad grilled Joe some hamburgers.        [grilled for whom?]
```

Indirect objects are never part of a prepositional phrase. If the prepositions *to* or *for* occur in a sentence, the noun or pronoun that follows is the object of the preposition, not the indirect object of the verb.

Exercise 10: Identifying S–V–IO–DO Sentence Patterns

Write the following sentences, labeling the sentence patterns. Underline the words you label.

Example

a. They sold us a cactus.

```
   S    V   IO    DO
  They sold us a cactus.
```

1. You gave me your cold.
2. Al wrote the newspaper a letter.
3. Mr. Seng made us popcorn.
4. The wolf brought its pups meat.
5. Pete told Mike the new joke.
6. Katy made her father a wallet.
7. Ms. Chavez told us stories about the Incas.
8. The fans gave Hank Aaron a tremendous cheer.
9. The clown threw the crowd peanuts.
10. In the last seconds Lucas passed Brewer the ball.

S–LV–PN Sentence Pattern

A *predicate noun* or *predicate pronoun (PN)* is the noun or pronoun that follows a linking verb and explains or identifies the subject of the sentence.

Because they complete the meaning of the subject in the sentence, predicate nouns and pronouns are *complements*.

        S   LV   PN
The woman was an astronaut.

      S   LV   PN   PN
The writers of the skit were Lisa and I.

 S LV   PN
Emile is my cousin from Minnesota.

Personal pronouns used as predicate nouns should always be in their subject form.

      S   LV PN   PN   PN
The winners are Les, Maria, and he.

       S   LV   PN   PN
The dancers in the play were she and I.

Exercise 11: Identifying S–LV–PN Sentence Patterns

Write the following sentences and label the sentence patterns. Underline the words you label.

Examples

a. The youngest people there were José and I.

                 S   LV   PN   PN
The youngest people there were José and I.

b. Fritz has been a good leader on this camp-out.

 S   LV   PN
Fritz has been a good leader on this camp-out.

c. A most peculiar fisherman was he.

                     S   LV PN
A most peculiar fisherman was he.

1. The best swimmers are Michael, Terry, and she.
2. Ted remained champion of the high jump.
3. Jedediah Smith was a hunter, a trapper, and an explorer.
4. Rosa will be the youngest actress in the play.
5. George Washington Carver was a scientist and writer.

Grammar and Usage

6. The outstanding science student will be either Kortney, Teresa, or he.
7. Chris Evert Lloyd was the winner at the Wimbledon tennis tournament.
8. Our visitors were the Johnsons and they.
9. An important native American writer was Charles Eastman.
10. Old Blue was a fine pet and good watchdog.

S–LV–PA *Sentence Pattern*

A *predicate adjective (PA)* is an adjective that follows a linking verb and modifies the subject of the sentence.

```
           S     LV    PA
The lizard looks sleepy.
          S    LV     PA
The cave remains cool during the summer.
              S    LV   PA    PA      PA
In a crisis Pedro stays calm, cool, and collected.
            S    LV    PA
The highway looked watery in the hot sunlight.
```

Exercise 12: *Identifying S–LV–PA Sentence Patterns*

Write the following sentences and label the sentence patterns. Underline the words you label.

Example

a. Grandmother stays active and alert.

```
    S         LV    PA        PA
Grandmother stays active and alert.
```

1. That color looks very good on you.
2. From the grandstand the players on the court looked rather small.
3. That movie was too scary for me.

4. Nobody seemed very interested in the clowns.
5. Your luck is quite amazing.
6. Sometimes, Ralph became disgusted with his friends.
7. The paper dragon in the parade was large and colorful.
8. Robert Heinlein's books are always popular with science fiction fans.
9. The king grew more selfish and greedy for power as the kingdom prospered.
10. Mayor Chin will be firm and forceful on that point.

Classifying Sentence Structures

Depending on the type of clauses they contain, sentences can be classified in one of four ways: *simple, compound, complex,* or *compound-complex.*

Simple Sentences

A *simple sentence* contains only *one* independent clause and *no* subordinate clause.

> S V
> The wind blew.

The subject and the verb in a simple sentence may be modified and may have complements.

> S V DO
> The wind blew the leaves all over the yard.

The simple sentence may have a compound subject, a compound verb, or both, but it still remains a simple sentence. The compound elements are part of one independent clause and belong to no other clause.

Lucy, Mike, and June write stories and compose poems.
[The compound subject is *Lucy/Mike/June*. The compound verb is *write/compose*.]

Compound Sentences

A sentence that has more than one independent clause and no subordinate clauses is called a *compound sentence.*

> Ostriches are birds, but they cannot fly.
> [This sentence contains two independent clauses: *Ostriches are birds* and *they cannot fly.* The coordinating conjunction *but* joins the clauses.]

The independent clauses may have compound subjects and verbs, but they must be two separate independent clauses.

> Ostriches and emus are birds, but they cannot fly or even glide.
>
> [The compound subject of the first independent clause is *Ostriches/emus. Can fly* and *glide* are the compound verbs in the second independent clause.]

Exercise 13: Identifying Simple and Compound Sentences

Write the following sentences, underlining the simple subjects once and the verbs twice. Below each sentence, label the structure as *simple* or *compound*.

Examples

a. Marty and Sherry looked quite surprised.
   Marty and Sherry looked quite surprised.
   simple

b. After dinner we watched television, but I fell asleep.
   After dinner we watched television, but I fell asleep.
   compound

1. The coach and the team members will practice tonight and rest tomorrow before the game.

2. Maggie made the invitations herself and mailed them yesterday.
3. The hurricane ruined our screened-in porch, but our insurance paid for the damage.
4. Michael, Susan, and Rosita are our class officers.
5. The plants turned brown and dry inside the house.
6. My brother and sister hid behind the door and surprised Anna and me.
7. Our history test was canceled for tomorrow, but Ms. Chu rescheduled it for Monday.
8. Will the band march in the parade, or will it play from the bleachers?
9. Mike called the operator and asked for assistance.
10. Tonight we could study at my house, or we could go to the library.

Complex Sentences

A *complex sentence* contains only one independent clause and at least one subordinate clause.

(For an explanation of subordinate clauses, see Chapter 22.)

> After Rachel waxed the car, she cleaned the windshield. [The independent clause is *she cleaned the windshield*; the subordinate clause is *After Rachel waxed the car*.]

A complex sentence may have several subordinate clauses but only one independent clause.

> After Doris saw the movie, she waited impatiently until she could go again.
> [The subordinate clauses are *After Doris saw the movie* and *until she could go again*.]

Exercise 14: Identifying Clauses in Complex Sentences

Write each complex sentence on the next page. Underline the independent clause once and the subordinate clause twice.

Grammar and Usage

Example

a. Cory recited a speech that had been given by Chief Joseph.

<u>Cory recited a speech</u> that had been given by Chief Joseph.

1. The picture that Kim painted was of a Korean sun bear.
2. When her sister left for college, Martha gained a room of her own.
3. Toussaint L'Ouverture, who was born a slave, led the fight for Haiti's independence.
4. My father has not seen his old friend since they were children.
5. Pat made a wish that summer vacation would never end.
6. The woman who won the door prize was delighted.
7. As soon as Betty filled one hole under the fence, the dogs dug another one.
8. While people make out their income tax forms, they sometimes grumble and groan.
9. Unless we develop new energy resources, our lives will change drastically.
10. Because they increase litter, throwaway bottles are outlawed in this state.

Compound-Complex Sentences

A *compound-complex sentence* contains more than one independent clause and at least one subordinate clause.

In the following sentences the independent clauses are *italicized*; the dependent clauses are underlined.

<u>Before they go to school each morning</u>, *Jesse washes the breakfast dishes*, and *Marla makes the beds*.

Carlos called the police, and *Anna called an ambulance* <u>when the accident occurred</u>.

Exercise 15: Identifying Clauses in Compound-Complex Sentences

Write the following compound-complex sentences. Underline each independent clause once and each subordinate clause twice.

Examples

a. Because we have not conserved wildlife, the passenger pigeon is extinct, and the eagle is an endangered species.
<u>Because we have not conserved wildlife</u>, <u>the passenger pigeon is extinct</u>, and <u>the eagle is an endangered species</u>.

b. We wanted a small dog that would be comfortable in the studio apartment, but we ended up with a large Siamese cat.
<u>We wanted a small dog</u> <u>that would be comfortable in the studio apartment</u>, but <u>we ended up with a large Siamese cat</u>.

1. If you leave food outside your tent, raccoons will bother you at night, and ants will have a picnic for a week.
2. The flowers that you planted are lovely, but they need more water when the weather is this warm.
3. After they finish work, Mom plays racquetball, and Dad goes jogging.
4. Although Chris and Everett are both honor students, Chris finds time for swimming, and Everett is on the basketball team.
5. When the power went out during the storm, the food in the refrigerator spoiled, and we were unable to cook.
6. Michael hoped that it would snow, but Rosa hoped that it would not.
7. After we pitched our tents, Terry dug a firebreak and I took a nap.
8. As soon as the alarm sounded in the middle of the night, my brother yelled, and I jumped out of bed.

9. I read two of the books that you lent me last month, but I have not had time to read the third.//
10. Because the day was wet and rainy, plans for the picnic were altered, yet everyone seemed to have a wonderful time.

Review: Understanding Sentences

Write each of the following sentences, underlining the complete subject once and the complete predicate twice. Circle each simple or compound subject and each verb or verb phrase. If the subject is *you* understood, write (*You*) next to the sentence.

Examples

a. Danielle and Bob are visiting their grandparents.

(Danielle) and (Bob) (are visiting) their grandparents.

b. The playful kittens found the ball of yarn and unraveled it.

The playful (kittens) (found) the ball of yarn and (unraveled) it.

1. The umbrellas and raincoats are in the hall closet where they belong.
2. Close the door on your way out.
3. Which book are you reading?
4. The loud ambulance raced down the street to the nearest hospital.
5. The answers to the problems can be found at the back of your book.

Write the following sentences and label the sentence patterns. Underline the words you label.

Examples

a. Mel slipped on a banana peel.

   S   V

Mel slipped on a banana peel.

b. The boy told the teacher the truth.
      S   V   IO   DO
   The boy told the teacher the truth.

6. Yeni showed us her puppets.
7. The singers at the concert were Charlie Pride and Freddie Fender.
8. Grandfather Storm made my two brothers and me a new clubhouse.
9. All evening long the thunder rumbled.
10. Pete packed his backpack carefully.
11. Rosaria read her little brother a story.
12. Marty loves her old jeans.

Write the following sentences. Below each sentence, write whether the sentence is declarative, interrogative, imperative, or exclamatory. Then write the word that is the simple subject of the sentence.

13. Clark got new glasses.
14. Where is Timbuktu?
15. A goblin is out there!
16. Never skip breakfast.

Write the following sentences. Underline each independent clause once and each subordinate clause twice. Below each sentence, tell how it should be classified according to structure.

Example

a. The plant that you bought Saturday is an African violet.
   The plant that you bought Saturday is an African violet.
   complex

17. The moon rose, and the crickets began to chirp.
18. Queen Victoria of England was also the Empress of India.
19. Do you want to ride the bus home, or do you want to walk?
20. Do you want an apple or an orange?

Grammar and Usage

Using Sentences

Two common problems in using sentences are the *sentence fragment* and the *run-on sentence*. The following sections will give you practice in correcting both of these problems.

Avoiding Sentence Fragments

A *sentence fragment* is a separated part of a sentence that does not express a complete thought.

A sentence fragment results when end punctuation is used before a thought is completed. To be complete a sentence must have a subject, a verb, and sometimes a complement.

*Before the end of the first inning	[fragment]
We arrived before the end of the first inning.	[sentence]
*A store my nephew likes	[fragment]
A store my nephew likes is called Circus World.	[sentence]
*Singing a popular song	[fragment]
Joseph entered the room, singing a popular song.	[sentence]

Even with a subject and verb, a group of words may not express a complete thought.

*In the morning the ocean looks [*what* or *how?*]	[fragment]
In the morning the ocean looks calm.	[sentence]
*Since the bus is late [*what?*]	[fragment]
Since the bus is late, I'll have to walk.	[sentence]

Many sentence fragments are caused by punctuating participial phrases or subordinate clauses as sentences.

An asterisk (*) denotes a sentence with a feature that is not part of Edited Standard English.

Participial Phrases

*Mary, *singing in the rain.*	[fragment]
Mary, singing in the rain, caught cold.	[sentence]
**Driving carelessly*, the people.	[fragment]
Driving carelessly, the people skidded and spun out.	[sentence]

Subordinate Clauses

**As soon as we have the chance.*	[fragment]
We'll leave as soon as we have the chance.	[sentence]
**If nothing happens.*	[fragment]
If nothing happens, Dwight has an alternate plan.	[sentence]

Exercise 16: *Correcting Sentence Fragments*

Some of the following groups of words are sentences; some are fragments. Number a sheet of paper 1–10. If the group of words is a sentence, write *sentence* next to its number on your paper. If the group of words is a fragment, add the words necessary to make it a complete thought. Write the new sentence on your paper and underline the words you add.

Example

a. Sewing the emblem on my jacket.
   Sewing the emblem on my jacket, I stuck my finger with the needle.

1. Amused by the monkey swinging in the cage.
2. Suddenly out of the middle of the lake!
3. Having won the tennis match, the player jumped over the net to shake hands.
4. Hiking up the face of the rugged mountain.
5. Looking up those addresses took a long time.
6. Often when I see my friends at the lake.

Grammar and Usage

7. Washing windows is not a favorite chore of mine.
8. On the side of the building was a poster advertising the circus.
9. Lost in the crowd, the young child began to cry.
10. High on the top step of the winding staircase.

Avoiding Run-On Sentences

A *run-on sentence* consists of two or more sentences incorrectly separated by a comma or by no mark of punctuation.

*Scientists have discovered and named over 1,200 different species of bats, they are found all over the world except in polar regions.	[run-on]
Scientists have discovered and named over 1,200 different species of bats. They are found all over the world except in the polar regions.	[correction]
*Since they are creatures of the night, bats are seen only rarely, during the day they sleep in caves, in trees, or even in houses.	[run-on]
Since they are creatures of the night, bats are seen only rarely. During the day they sleep in caves, in trees, or even in houses.	[correction]

Run-on sentences can be corrected by separating the sentences with end punctuation, by joining them with a comma and a conjunction, or by joining them with a semicolon. They may also be corrected by making one of the sentences into a subordinate clause or participial phrase.

*Last week Lorraine said I could have a ride with her to swimming practice, I just knew she would forget, I should have reminded her.	[run-on]

Last week Lorraine said I could have a ride with her to swimming practice. I just knew she would forget; I should have reminded her.	[correction]
*Angelo and I want to join the baseball team, practice is after school when we deliver newspapers.	[run-on]
Angelo and I want to join the baseball team, *but* practice is after school when we deliver newspapers.	[correction]
*I walked down the hall, I talked to my friend, and then I turned the corner to use my locker, and then I bumped into Roberto, and then we both dropped our books!	[run-on]
I walked down the hall, *talking to my friend. When I turned the corner to use my locker*, I bumped into Roberto; we both dropped our books!	[correction]

Exercise 17: *Correcting Run-On Sentences*

Read each of the following groups of words carefully. Correct run-on sentences by adding end punctuation after complete thoughts or by joining related ideas with commas and conjunctions or with semicolons. Write the corrected sentences on your paper.

Examples

a. After the storm a rainbow appeared, it was the first double rainbow I had ever seen.
   After the storm a rainbow appeared. It was the first double rainbow I had ever seen.

b. I played my radio softly, I didn't want to disturb Harold's studying.
   I played my radio softly, for I didn't want to disturb Harold's studying.

1. Rosa never walks under a ladder, she's either superstitious or just careful.

Grammar and Usage

2. That must be a popular movie, the ticket line is a block long.
3. Coach Larson says people should swim more often, it will improve their muscle tone.
4. This intersection is dangerous, three accidents occurred here last month.
5. My sister enjoys being a camp counselor, the job keeps her outside most of the summer.
6. On our class field trip we visited the city newspaper, we toured the pressroom, talked to some of the reporters, and watched the evening edition being run on the presses.
7. My sister and I like to watch comedies on television, my parents prefer news programs.
8. Why was a crowd gathering on the corner, she rushed out the door to see what was happening.
9. My uncle owns a pet store in the shopping center, he specializes in tropical fish.
10. Always try to be on time, it's only polite.

Review: Using Sentences

Read each of the following groups of words carefully. Some groups are fragments, some are run-ons, and some are complete sentences. Number your paper 1–20. If a sentence is correct, write *correct* next to its number. If the group of words is a fragment or a run-on, rewrite the words as a correct sentence or sentences.

Examples

a. Sliding into third base.
   Sliding into third base, Matthew was safe.

b. Everyone in our neighborhood filled out the census questionnaire.
   correct

c. Karl brought the mustard, ketchup, hamburgers, and buns, he forgot the charcoal for the grill.
   Karl brought the mustard, ketchup, hamburgers, and buns, but he forgot the charcoal for the grill.

1. Under the creaking wooden steps in the basement.
2. Dressed in Batman and Robin costumes for the party.
3. When I woke, the ground was covered with a fresh blanket of snow.
4. Karen wished her legs were longer, she really wanted to run the hurdles.
5. Amazed that she did so well on the science test.
6. Joan did have the leading role in our spring play, she broke her arm in a gymnastics competition a week before the performance.
7. Convinced that the witness was telling the truth.
8. After my last checkup, the dentist suggested that I snack on fruit and raw vegetables.
9. Don't try to carry in all of those packages at once, I'll help you in a minute.
10. The only difference between Mary Ann's gold wedding ring and mine.
11. Armando is a talented artist, he drew a portrait of his mother for her birthday.
12. That coin completes my collection for the neumismatists' convention next week.
13. When the stray dog followed Doug home.
14. I really woke up late this morning, I forgot to set my alarm clock and missed the train.
15. The directions on the package were so very confusing that the recipe was unintelligible.
16. The parakeets that we gave my grandparents for their anniversary.
17. You did the whole assignment wrong, next time read the directions carefully.
18. Terry put her charcoal sketch where no one in the house would smudge it.
19. Because she was an outstanding math student.
20. Last summer we planted an orange tree in the backyard, this summer we're drinking fresh orange juice as often as we choose.

Grammar and Usage

Writing Focus: *Improving Sentence Structure in Writing*

You can strengthen your writing style by using a variety of simple, compound, complex, and compound-complex sentences. Make sure your sentences are complete sentences and not fragments or run-ons.

Assignment: *Surprise!*

You and your friends have decided to give a surprise birthday party for your favorite teacher. The timing and festive activities must be planned carefully so that the teacher will be surprised. Each of you has ideas about what to do to make the celebration a good one.

Write one or more well-developed paragraphs explaining your plans for the party. Explain to your friends the steps you think are necessary to ensure a wonderful surprise party for the teacher. Be as precise as you can. Your paragraphs will be evaluated for correct and varied sentences.

Use the following steps to complete this assignment.

A. Prewriting

Think about surprise parties you've heard about or have actually attended. Make a list of all the items you can imagine needing for a successful party. Then list the steps you'll need to follow in order to have the party in the classroom on the teacher's birthday. Don't worry about the order of the steps. For now, just jot down everything you can think of that will help get food, a present, entertainment, students, and the teacher together without the teacher's knowing about the party. Use specific details. Finally, group and number the steps in the order they will need to be performed.

B. Writing

Using your list, write one or more paragraphs explaining how the party should be planned. Begin by discussing any items that will need to be assembled or made. Then go through the

steps of what must be done in the proper order. Use words like *first*, *next*, *then*, *while*, and *last of all* to help organize your plans. As you write, pay particular attention to using a variety of complete sentences.

C. Postwriting

Revise your first draft, using the following checklist.

1. Have I included enough information so that my friends and I could give a successful surprise party for our teacher?

2. Do my steps have a logical organization? Does each step follow the one before?

3. Have I varied the structure of my sentences?

Edit your draft using the Checklist for Proofreading at the back of the book. If appropriate, share your writing with your classmates to compare party planning strategies.

21 Phrases

Understanding Phrases

Defining Phrases

A *phrase* is usually defined as a group of words that act as a single part of speech and that do not have a verb or a subject.

     Verb Phrase Adverb Phrase
Karem *might have gone to the library*.
      Adjective Phrase
This book *about science* is interesting.

Grouping Phrases by Classes

Phrases can be grouped into four main classes: *verb phrases, prepositional phrases, verbal phrases,* and *appositive phrases.* Each kind of phrase functions as a single part of speech in a sentence.

A *verb phrase* includes the main verb and its helping verb and functions as a single verb in a sentence.

  The drama club *has been practicing* all afternoon for the opening of the play.

  The stage *might collapse* with all that weight.

  You *could have called* us from the station.

A *prepositional phrase* includes a preposition, its object, and any modifiers. A prepositional phrase can function either as an adjective or as an adverb in a sentence.

If a prepositional phrase modifies a noun or pronoun, it functions as an adjective in the sentence.

This book *about World War II* is very informative.

Anna is my cousin *from Boston*.

She is the one *about whom* we have heard.

If a prepositional phrase modifies a verb, an adjective, or an adverb, it functions as an adverb in the sentence.

Ty will practice *after school*.	[modifying verb]
He is careful *with his money*.	[modifying adjective]
We study later *in the evening*.	[modifying adverb]

Exercise 1: Identifying Classes of Phrases

Write the following sentences. Beneath each sentence write the verb, adjective, or adverb phrases within it and identify the class to which each phrase belongs.

Examples

a. Jo Ann was reading a story about pioneers.
Jo Ann was reading a story about pioneers.
was reading—verb phrase
about pioneers—adjective phrase

b. Bart will call before Saturday.
Bart will call before Saturday.
will call—verb phrase
before Saturday—adverb phrase

1. We were watching a movie about dolphins.
2. My brother will play the tuba in the band.
3. The owl in the pine tree had been hooting.
4. Tony had run up that big hill.

5. Our bus may be delayed by the accident.
6. Joan has seen whooping cranes near the lake.
7. His pursuer had been a hound with a ghostly howl.
8. Rosa will work her way through college.
9. Les could have gone to Camp Cucamonga for a month.
10. Gasoline for our trip will be costly.

> **A *verbal phrase* includes a verbal with its modifiers or complements working as a single part of speech.**

The two kinds of verbal phrases that you will be studying in the following sections are *participial phrases* and *gerund phrases*.

A *participial phrase* includes a present or past participle with its modifiers. A participial phrase is used as an adjective to modify a noun or pronoun. A *present participial phrase* includes the *-ing* form of the verb with its modifiers. The modifiers are usually prepositional phrases or adverbs.

Waving frantically, the man flagged down the train.
[*Waving* is the present participle; *frantically* is an adverb modifying *waving*. *Waving frantically* modifies the noun *man*.]

The owl, *sleeping in the tree*, nodded suddenly.
[*Sleeping* is the present participle; *in the tree* is a prepositional phrase modifying *sleeping*. *Sleeping in the tree* modifies the noun *owl*.]

A *past participial phrase* includes the third principal part of the verb with its modifiers. The modifiers are usually prepositional phrases.

Caught in the net, the eel wriggled desperately.
[*Caught* is the past participle; *in the net* is a prepositional phrase modifying *caught*. *Caught in the net* modifies the noun *eel*.]

The dog *trained by my uncle* won the trophy.
[*Trained* is the past participle; *by my uncle* is a prepositional phrase modifying *trained*. *Trained by my uncle* modifies the noun *dog*.]

Exercise 2: Identifying Participial Phrases

Write the following sentences and underline the participial phrases. Draw an arrow from each participial phrase to the noun or pronoun it modifies.

Examples

a. The horse led by the jockey belongs to my cousin.

The horse <u>led by the jockey</u> belongs to my cousin.

b. The bees swarming around the tree frightened the picnickers away.

The bees <u>swarming around the tree</u> frightened the picnickers away.

1. These hard hats are for visitors touring the factory.
2. Akira replaced the windows shattered by the hail.
3. Burning with anger, the coach strode over to the umpire.
4. The monster sneered at the tanks blocking its path.
5. This book is for the pupils studying African history.
6. The mayor, quite concerned about the serious problem, sent for her advisers.
7. Mother likes almost any movie starring George C. Scott or James Earl Jones.
8. The regional tournament won by Central High School will be televised tomorrow night.
9. The students taking biology must dissect a frog.
10. Elena, knowing Spanish, translated the note.

A gerund phrase includes the present participial (-ing) form of the verb with its modifiers.

A gerund phrase looks like a present participial phrase but is used as a noun. (Remember that participial phrases are always used as adjectives.)

Because a gerund is part verb, it can have a direct object in its phrase and can be modified by an adverb.

Grammar and Usage

Climbing these hills can be hard work.
[*These hills* is the object of the gerund *climbing*.]

Swimming fast is Elisa's talent.
[*Fast* is an adverb modifying the gerund *swimming*.]

Because a gerund is part noun, it can be modified by a single-word adjective or by a prepositional phrase used as an adjective.

The chattering of the birds woke us.
[*Of the birds* is an adjective phrase modifying the gerund noun *chattering*.]

I enjoy *the singing of folk songs*.
[*Of folk songs* is an adjective phrase modifying the gerund noun *singing*.]

Gerund phrases can be used in any way that a noun can be used in a sentence.

Playing the piano came naturally to Otis.
[*Playing the piano* is a gerund phrase used as a subject.]

Terry's biggest surprise was *winning the sweepstakes*.
[*Winning the sweepstakes* is a gerund phrase used as a predicate noun.]

We were puzzled by *the eerie glowing of the footprints*.
[*The eerie glowing of the footprints* is a gerund phrase used as an object of a preposition.]

We watched *the raising of the flag*.
[*The raising of the flag* is a gerund phrase used as a direct object.]

Exercise 3: Identifying Gerund Phrases

Each of the following sentences contains a gerund phrase. Write each sentence and underline the gerund phrase it contains.

Examples

a. The cloning of human beings isn't possible yet.
   The cloning of human beings isn't possible yet.

b. They accused us of putting a skunk in their tent.
   They accused us of putting a skunk in their tent.

1. Repainting the car was a long task.
2. Willy admired the playing of Rod Carew.
3. The best part of being in a band is marching in parades.
4. President Lincoln enjoyed telling funny stories.
5. Nobody likes hearing bad news.
6. We listened to the weird wailing from the haunted house.
7. Watching old movies sparked Phil's interest in films.
8. Mary loves tinkering with machines.
9. Max earned money by mowing lawns.
10. My family's favorite sport is hiking through the woods.

An *appositive phrase* includes an appositive and its modifiers. All the words in an appositive phrase work together as a unit to describe or identify a noun or pronoun.

An *appositive* is a noun or noun substitute set beside another noun or pronoun to describe or identify it.

Our destination, *Timbuktu*, is still very distant.

I drew a picture of our state bird, *the cardinal*.

Gooseberries, *pale green berries with a sour taste*, make a tangy treat.

My cousin, *a gymnast in the 1972 Olympics*, won a bronze medal.

Occasionally an appositive phrase will come before the word it modifies.

A great and gallant horse, Ruffian had too short a career.

Exercise 4: Identifying Appositive Phrases

Write the sentences on the following page and underline the appositive phrases. Then draw an arrow from each phrase to the noun or pronoun it modifies.

Grammar and Usage

Examples

a. I talked to Ms. Nelson, the scout leader.

I talked to Ms. Nelson, the scout leader.

b. Corrine, the girl next door, has a pet ferret.

Corrine, the girl next door, has a pet ferret.

1. Jim Beckwourth, the famous frontiersman, led an exciting life.
2. The magician, Gaspar the Great, sawed his assistant in half.
3. Dave and Imat made us *sati*, a delicious Indonesian dish.
4. We read about the *Titanic*, a truly tragic ship.
5. Dan was born in El Campo, a small city in Texas.
6. Rosa has a black belt, the highest rank in karate.
7. Mo, the brown and white dog, is my favorite.
8. I read an excellent book, *Black Elk Speaks*.
9. Most of us know too little about Canada, our northern neighbor.
10. Alexandre Dumas, the French author, wrote *The Three Musketeers*.

Review: Understanding Phrases

Twenty phrases are underlined in the following selection. Write each phrase on a sheet of paper numbered 1–20. Beside each phrase write verb, adjective, adverb, participial, gerund, or appositive to indicate its type.

Canoeing, an ancient form of navigation, is my grandfather's greatest pleasure, but Indians on the river years ago would not have recognized his canoe. Two bicycle wheels, castoff parts of an old ten-speed, whirl in the air behind him. In the front the handlebars and fender of a moped are visible. This strange combination of moped, wheels, and canoe has a practical purpose. My grandfather, an early riser, loves canoeing at dawn. However, finding transportation to the river became a problem. Solving this was an easy task for Grandfather, an inventive individual. The first step involved attaching the old wheels to the top of the canoe. Flipped upside down, the canoe balanced smoothly on the wheels. Next Grandfather hitched this contraption to his moped. The moped with its attached canoe-on-wheels is an amusing sight, but it gives Grandfather freedom. At the river he slides the canoe into the water and arranges the moped in its prow. With the situation reversed and the canoe transporting the moped, he paddles toward his destination, a quiet spot near the old mill. There, he again reverses the situation and before the rest of the awakening world has stirred, he is headed home pulling his silvery canoe-on-wheels behind him.

Applying What You Know

Select several paragraphs from a book, short story, magazine, or newspaper article. Identify each phrase in the selection. List each phrase on a sheet of paper and tell what kind it is.

Using Phrases

Where a phrase appears and how it is punctuated can make an important difference to the meaning of a sentence. In the following sections you will practice placing and punctuating phrases correctly.

Using Punctuation with Phrases

The punctuation you use with participial and with appositive phrases is important to the meaning of your sentences.

A participial phrase used at the beginning of a sentence should always be followed by a comma.

Swatting its tail from side to side, the tiger stalked away.

Lashed by the storm, the old tree tossed and swayed.

A participial phrase that is not necessary to the main idea of the sentence is called a *nonessential phrase*. A nonessential

Grammar and Usage

phrase adds detail but not important meaning and is set off by commas.

> The volcano, *rumbling in the distance*, was now visible over the treetops.
> [The volcano was now visible over the treetops.]
>
> The horse entered the rodeo ring, bucking furiously.

A participial phrase that does add important information to the meaning of the sentence is called an *essential phrase*. If an essential phrase is removed from a sentence, the meaning of the sentence is no longer clear. Essential phrases are *not* set off by commas.

> Everyone *working with that mule* gets kicked regularly.
> [*Everyone gets kicked regularly* would not have the same meaning.]
>
> The man *wearing the red bow tie* is the mayor.
> [*The man is the mayor* would not identify the mayor clearly.]

Exercise 5: Punctuating Participial Phrases

Write the following sentences and underline the participial phrase in each sentence. If the phrase occurs at the beginning of the sentence or is nonessential, add the appropriate comma or commas.

Examples

a. The goose honking and hissing chased the cat away.
   The goose, honking and hissing, chased the cat away.

b. My uncle is the man wearing the chef's hat.
   My uncle is the man wearing the chef's hat.
   (*essential phrase—no punctuation needed*)

1. Standing on the curb Rita watched the fire fighters.
2. The woman taking the tickets will help you.
3. Mario tired of waiting got up and went home.
4. All people having coupons will get a free piggy bank.
5. Leaning over the bridge railing Scott watched the boats.
6. Packages damaged in the mail should be brought to the postal inspector.

7. The fans cheering wildly carried the champion on their shoulders.
8. The woman stamping the books is the head librarian.
9. We gave our passes to the man sitting at the desk.
10. My shoes soaking from the rain began to squeak.

Appositive phrases are generally set off from the rest of the sentence by commas.

Appositives of more than one word and appositives that refer to a proper noun are also generally set off by commas.

I mowed the yard, *a jungle of tangled weeds*.

We climbed the area's highest mountain, *Old Baldy*.

Mr. Quill, *the secretary*, wrote the report.

Sometimes, commas are not used for one-word appositives or for appositives that are closely related to the words they refer to.

Our cat *Felix* eats olives.

The composer *Beethoven* became deaf at an early age.

Exercise 6: Punctuating Appositive Phrases

Write the following sentences and underline the appositives and appositive phrases. Add a comma or commas where needed.

Example

a. A skull and crossbones a symbol for poison was on the label.

A skull and crossbones, a symbol for poison, was on the label.

1. The Amazon a river in South America has many treacherous waterfalls.
2. Miguel the fastest runner in our class was selected for the all-star team.
3. Second prize at the science fair was won by my best friend David.

Grammar and Usage

4. Only three people the driver and two passengers were saved in the accident.
5. Invite your brother Tom to come with us.
6. Ms. Jenkins won a trip to Hawaii the island of her dreams.
7. Have you ever been to Missouri the "show-me" state?
8. Our family had a birthday party for our dog Red.
9. A good source of iron liver is important to your diet.
10. Alfred Hitchcock a director made many famous mystery films.

Placing Participial Phrases

Participial phrases that are used as adjectives should be placed close to the words they modify.

An introductory participial phrase should always modify the noun or pronoun that immediately follows it.

Mooing with fear, the cow fled from the farmer.

Fried crispy, the chicken was served by Grandmother.

When the correct noun or pronoun does not immediately follow the participial phrase or when there is no noun or pronoun for the phrase to modify, the result is a *dangling modifier*.

Covered with mosquito bites, the tent looked good to the scout. [dangling modifier]

Covered with mosquito bites, the scout thought the tent looked good. [correct]

Stuck deeply in the mud, a helicopter came to the rescue of the jeep. [dangling modifier]

Stuck deeply in the mud, the jeep was rescued by a helicopter. [correct]

Review: Using Phrases

Each of the following sentences needs proper punctuation for phrases, rewriting to correct dangling modifiers, or both. Rewrite each sentence, making the necessary corrections.

Examples

a. Speaking half a dozen languages, Lisa watched the UN interpreters.
Lisa watched the UN interpreters speaking half a dozen languages.

b. Plodding up the hill, my house looked strange in the evening light.
Plodding up the hill, I thought my house looked strange in the evening light.

1. The bloodhound sniffing furiously located the trail.
2. Pete reading a new novel didn't want to be disturbed.
3. Neglected for years the house now needed many repairs.
4. Sitting on the phone wires John spotted the pair of birds.
5. Puzzled by the child's crying the baby-sitter called the parents.
6. The next event the relay race is the one we have been waiting for.
7. Swimming in the lake a rock cut Sean's foot.
8. My sister jogging after dinner witnessed a robbery.
9. Cawing loudly the crow drove off the intruding squirrel.
10. The car sputtering and coughing could not last much longer.
11. Our biggest mistake one we lived to regret was not preparing for rain.
12. We saw a herd of buffalo driving to Wyoming.
13. Digging in his spurs, the horse carried Kyle over the line.
14. James Earl Jones an actor played the role of Othello.
15. Laura hurrying to school forgot her lunch money.
16. I accidentally put in too much pepper frying the chicken.
17. Luis watching carefully made his way through the brush.

Grammar and Usage

18. Morris found a spider putting on his shoes.
19. Crashing onto the beach the waves broke and foamed.
20. The cat a valuable Siamese was probably "catnaped."

Writing Focus: *Using Phrases in Writing*

Many different types of phrases are available to you as a writer—verb, adjective, adverb, appositive, gerund, participial, and infinitive. To strengthen your writing style, choose appropriate phrases to add details, to combine sentences, and to vary sentences.

Assignment: *Camping Out*

Your club has decided to celebrate the last meeting of the year by camping out in a forest. After you've put up your tent, eaten hot dogs around the fire, and sung some old favorite songs, you settle down for the night.

Write one or more well-developed paragraphs describing your experience as you lie in your tent in the forest on the verge of sleep. Include details that appeal to the senses as well as accounts of any happenings that occur so that your audience of classmates can share your experience. Your writing will be evaluated for correct and effective use of phrases.

Use the following steps to complete this assignment.

A. Prewriting

Picture a cool, dark night in the forest, a dozen tents ringing a dying fire. Imagine being in one of the tents and drifting into sleep. Make a separate word cluster, described in Chapter 1, for each of your senses. Add words or phrases around each that describe what you experience. What do you see, hear, smell, feel, or taste as you lie in the dark getting drowsy? Does an owl hoot? Does the lingering smell of popcorn make your stomach

growl? Does the sound of a footstep start your heart pounding? How do you feel emotionally as you lie in the tent in the forest? Choose the details from each cluster that most accurately and vividly capture your experience. Consider their order of presentation. You might use a chronological approach or one that provides a dominant impression.

B. Writing

Using your clusters, write one or more paragraphs describing your experience in your tent in the forest. As you write, use various kinds of phrases to add details, combine sentences, and vary sentences.

C. Postwriting

Revise your first draft, using the following checklist.

1. Have I included sufficient details so that my readers can "experience" what I did?

2. Have I used and punctuated phrases correctly?

Use the Checklist for Proofreading at the back of the book to edit your work. If appropriate, share your writing with your classmates and compare descriptions.

22 Clauses

Understanding Clauses

In this chapter you will learn to identify clauses by their definition and by the way they are classified into types.

Defining Clauses

A *clause* is usually defined as a group of words that contains a subject (*S*) and a verb (*V*) and is used as a part of a sentence.

    S V   S V
We liked the movie / because it was funny.
  S   V   S   V
I vacuumed the rug / while Harold washed the windows.

Distinguishing Clauses from Phrases

A *clause* is a group of words that has its own subject and verb. A *phrase* is a group of words acting as a single part of speech that does not have its own subject and verb.

After supper Linda read her history assignment.	[phrase]
S V *After she finished supper*, Linda read her history assignment.	[clause]
I fixed the bike *with the broken chain*.	[phrase]
S V *When the chain broke*, I had to fix the bike.	[clause]

Exercise 1: Distinguishing Clauses from Phrases

Write the following sentences, identifying the *italicized* words as either a clause or a phrase. If the group of words is a clause, write S over the subject and V over the verb. Underline the group of words you identify.

Example

a. *When Maria saw the rattlesnake,* her blood froze.

        S   V
<u>When Maria saw the rattlesnake,</u> her blood froze. (clause)

1. Jane was alone in the old house *when she heard a strange sound.*
2. *Since gasoline is expensive,* Rosa rides a bicycle to work.
3. The squirrel, *sitting on the high limb,* teased the dogs barking at it.
4. Raoul groaned *as he remembered his unfinished chores.*
5. Lydia wondered about the note *in her locker.*
6. Alonzo gave up his paper route *because he got a better job.*
7. The person *who put the dead fish in the teacher's lounge* will be severely punished.
8. The tire *that I patched* had another leak before the week ended.
9. *After Alice in Wonderland,* Lewis Carroll wrote a book about mathematics.
10. *When Hank Aaron hit his 500th home run,* the fans went wild.

Kinds of Clauses

Clauses may be either *independent* or *subordinate*.

> An *independent clause* is a group of words that has a subject and verb and expresses a complete thought.

Grammar and Usage

Also called the *main clause* of the sentence, the independent clause can stand alone because it expresses a complete thought.

We liked the movie because it was funny.

Independent Clause:	S V We liked the movie	[complete thought]
Subordinate Clause:	S V because it was funny.	[not a complete thought]

A sentence can have more than one independent clause joined by a coordinating or correlative conjunction.

　　　　　S　　　V　　　　　　　　　　S　　V
The restaurant was beautiful, *but* the food was bad.

　　　　　　　S　　　V　　　　　　　　S　　V
Either these apples must be picked, *or* they will rot.

A *subordinate clause* is a group of words that has a subject and verb but does *not* express a complete thought.

A subordinate clause cannot stand by itself because it does not express a complete thought. To make its meaning clear it must be used with an independent clause.

　　S　V　　　　　　　　　S　　V
We left the beach *after the rain began.*

Independent Clause:	We left the beach	[complete thought]
Subordinate Clause:	*after the rain began.*	[incomplete thought]

　　S　　　V　　　　　　　　S　　V
Pat received the letter *that Meg sent.*

Independent Clause:	Pat received the letter	[complete thought]
Subordinate Clause:	*that Meg sent.*	[incomplete thought]

Exercise 2: Identifying Independent and Subordinate Clauses

Each of the following sentences contains two clauses. Write the sentences. Beneath each sentence, list each independent clause and each subordinate clause. (Remember that a subordinate clause cannot stand alone as a sentence.)

Examples

a. Joe mended the stairs so no one would trip.
   Joe mended the stairs so no one would trip.
   Joe mended the stairs—independent clause
   so no one would trip. —subordinate clause

b. When the sun rose, we went fishing.
   When the sun rose, we went fishing.
   When the sun rose, —subordinate clause
   we went fishing. —independent clause

1. Raoul built a fire while Michael unpacked the food.
2. I was late because our car had a flat tire.
3. You should usually look before you leap.
4. If aliens landed here, they might be friendly.
5. Uncle Bob found a fishing spot where the bass are huge.
6. Although an ostrich has wings, it cannot fly.
7. Fred couldn't go to the party until he cleaned his room.
8. Since my cousin saw the movie, he has been afraid of vampires.
9. After you finish your spinach, you may have another vegetable.
10. As Jan looked at the painting, she noticed something odd.

Types of Subordinate Clauses

In the following sections you will study two types of subordinate clauses: *adjective* and *adverb*.

Grammar and Usage

> **A subordinate clause used to modify a noun or pronoun is called an *adjective clause*.**

All of the words in an adjective clause work together to modify a noun or pronoun in the independent clause. Most adjective clauses begin with a *relative pronoun—who, whom, which, that,* and *whose—*that relates the adjective clause to the word it modifies.

The rat, *which is a very hardy rodent*, has survived for centuries.

We visited the studio *where Star Wars was filmed*.

Luis is the boy *who won four blue ribbons*.

We saw the meteor *that fell at the edge of town*.

Exercise 3: Identifying Adjective Clauses

Write the following sentences. Underline each adjective clause and draw an arrow from the relative pronoun to the noun or pronoun that the clause modifies.

Examples

a. We saw the woman who was the president of the company.

   We saw the woman <u>who was the president of the company</u>.

b. The husky, which is a very sociable dog, is unhappy alone.

   The husky, <u>which is a very sociable dog</u>, is unhappy alone.

1. The whooping crane, which is an extremely beautiful bird, is almost extinct.
2. We met our new neighbors, who are Vietnamese.
3. My aunt hopes to marry a man who likes to cook.

4. John read the book that Ms. Washington recommended.
5. The students who have a *B* average will not have to take the final exam.
6. We like to go to the movie theater that is decorated with Egyptian designs.
7. The man whom Ralph bumped into was very polite about the incident.
8. The model of the Hopi village that Rosa made was put on display in the office.
9. An advertisement for frogs who wished to be rich and famous appeared in the paper.
10. Mr. Cagney, who used to play professional football, won the poetry contest.

A subordinate clause that acts as a unit to modify a verb, an adjective, or an adverb is called an *adverb clause*.

Adverb clauses answer the questions *how? when? where? why?* and *under what conditions?* about the words they modify.

The sky looked *as if it were night*.
[*How* did the sky look?]

After the assembly was over, Pat hurried to her locker.
[*When* did Pat hurry?]

The crew of the spaceship boldly went *where no person had gone before*.
[*Where* did the crew go?]

Mark couldn't do his homework *because he had broken his glasses*.
[*Why* couldn't Mark do his homework?]

We'll go swimming Saturday *unless it rains*.
[*Under what conditions* will we go swimming?]

Adverb clauses can also modify adjectives or adverbs in the independent clause to which they are joined.

Grammar and Usage

> Sasha was smarter *than most dogs are*.
>
> You wear that shirt more often *than you do any other one*.

Adverb clauses are linked to the rest of the sentence with a *subordinating conjunction*. Subordinating conjunctions perform two functions: they link the adverb clause to the independent clause, and they show the relationship between the clauses.

The words in the list below are commonly used as subordinating conjunctions. Notice that some subordinating conjunctions consist of more than one word. These compound conjunctions function as a unit and work just like a one-word subordinating conjunction.

after	if	though
although	in order that	until
as far as	provided that	when
as if	since	whenever
as long as	so long as	where
as though	so that	wherever
because	than	whether
before	that	while

Exercise 4: *Identifying Adverb Clauses*

Write the following sentences and underline each adverb clause. Then draw an arrow from the subordinating conjunction to the word or words the clause modifies.

Example

a. Since the snow paralyzed all traffic, school is closed.

<u>Since the snow paralyzed all traffic</u>, school is closed.

1. Jackson will sing the solo because he has the best voice.
2. Carla got to school earlier than her teacher did.
3. My brother treats his records as though they were the world's most precious treasure.
4. The noise in our engine became louder than it was before.
5. The fire started where some oily rags had been piled.

6. Juan wears his helmet whenever he rides his motorbike.
7. Glenda is even better at karate than Joe is.
8. We can go to the jazz concert if the tickets haven't been sold.
9. After we saw the movie, we were certain that space aliens were around us everywhere.
10. Shana drank the buttermilk, although she didn't like its taste.

Review: Understanding Clauses

Write the following sentences and underline each subordinate clause. Identify each type of subordinate clause by writing *adjective* or *adverb* after the sentence.

Examples

a. The girl who sits next to me in math comes from Oklahoma.
   The girl <u>who sits next to me in math</u> comes from Oklahoma. —adjective

b. My brother's tooth became looser than it was before.
   My brother's tooth became looser <u>than it was before</u>. —adverb

1. As we walked into the cave, we saw a strange and eerie light far ahead of us.
2. Myron uses his seat belt whenever he rides in a car.
3. As soon as I finish the assignment, I want to read *Lord of the Rings*.
4. We used the map that Uncle John gave us.
5. After the rain stopped, the game was resumed.
6. Gene talks to his goldfish as though it were a person.
7. Students who have a failing average will have to attend summer school.
8. *The Outsiders*, which many students have read, was written by S. E. Hinton at age sixteen.
9. Jeff will design the poster because he is good in art.

Grammar and Usage

10. Although we missed the bus, we still arrived at school on time.
11. I accepted the package for my neighbors, who are away on vacation.
12. President John F. Kennedy once said, "All free men, wherever they may live, are citizens of Berlin."
13. We found the clue that we needed to solve the mystery.
14. Whenever she reads in bed, Chris falls asleep with the light on.
15. The science project that I made was displayed in the lobby.
16. The story is about a young girl who was abandoned on an island.
17. The house in Amsterdam where Anne Frank hid for two years now houses an institute devoted to the cause of world peace.
18. The Declaration of Independence was written so that Americans would have equal rights.
19. If the weather improves, we can hold the concert outside.
20. I hope to find a job that pays well.

Using Clauses

Punctuating Independent Clauses

Two independent clauses can be joined with a coordinating conjunction. (The coordinating conjunction is not considered part of either clause.)

When a coordinating conjunction is used to join two independent clauses, a comma (,) usually follows the first independent clause.

Queen Elizabeth I was highly respected, *for* she was a strong ruler.

Pam wanted to go on the trip, *yet* Ted made her refuse.

Another method of joining two independent clauses is to replace both the comma and conjunction with a semicolon (;).

Charles Forte was a rebel; he challenged many scientific statements.

A tall woman entered first; a distinguished gentleman followed.

Only independent clauses with a close relationship should be joined with a semicolon. If you wish to express a special relationship, such as a result or cause-effect, use the appropriate coordinating conjunction.

Exercise 5: *Punctuating Independent Clauses*

Rewrite each of the following pairs of sentences, making them into one sentence with two independent clauses. First decide what relationship the joined clauses should have and then select either a comma with the appropriate conjunction, or a semicolon.

Examples

a. My dog is a nuisance. Yours isn't much better.
My dog is a nuisance; yours isn't much better.
(close relationship between ideas)

b. Marge wanted to go to the concert. Unfortunately the tickets were sold out.
Marge wanted to go to the concert, but unfortunately the tickets were sold out.
(*But* shows a contrast.)

1. Rosa likes fried liver. Her brother detests it.
2. Mother wanted to go back to work. She got a job at the hospital.
3. Pedro was going to buy a bicycle. He bought a stereo instead.
4. A blind student graduated from medical school. The newspaper ran an article about him.

5. The Nuyen sisters don't seem like twins. They look nothing alike.
6. The stagehands worked hard. The set was not finished on time.
7. Wright Morris is a writer. He is an excellent photographer as well.
8. The Appaloosa is a beautiful breed of horse. Its strength and stamina, first recognized by the American Indian, are also impressive.
9. Our family dog Lancelot is frightened of the lawn mower. He always hides under the porch when anyone uses the machine.
10. To reach another galaxy we would have to travel at the speed of light. This would be impossible.

Punctuating Adjective Clauses

An adjective clause that does *not* add information important to the meaning of the sentence is called a *nonessential clause*.

Commas are used to separate a nonessential adjective clause from the rest of the sentence.

Loretta Lynn, *who is a coal miner's daughter*, has won many awards for her music.

The man on the stage, *whom we met yesterday*, is the coach at the high school.

When an adjective clause adds information that is important to the meaning of the independent clause, it is called an *essential clause*. An essential adjective clause is *not* set off by commas.

Everyone *who drinks this potion* will become invisible.
[*Everyone will become invisible* does not have the same meaning.]

Our town has a police chief *who used to be a stunt man in the movies*.
[*Our town has a police chief* does not convey the important idea of the sentence.]

Exercise 6: Punctuating Adjective Clauses

Each of the following sentences contains either an essential or a nonessential adjective clause. Write each sentence and underline the clause. If you think the clause is nonessential, insert a comma or commas to set it off from the rest of the sentence. Circle the commas you supply.

Example

a. Ms. Gomez who teaches art lent Malcolm some books.

Ms. Gomez, <u>who teaches art</u>, lent Malcolm some books.

1. I envy people who can sing well.
2. Julie's brother who is an Eagle Scout helped her learn to tie knots.
3. The painting that won first prize was a picture of an old trapper.
4. Tony who is good at math kept track of the ticket sales.
5. Even Michelle who likes all food couldn't eat the chocolate-covered sardines.
6. We visited Joslyn Art Museum which has a fine collection of native American art.
7. Marcia got the best dog that she ever owned at the dog pound.
8. The man whose watermelons were being stolen set a trap for the thieves.
9. Jupiter which is the largest planet has several strange moons.
10. The person who wrote *Frankenstein* was Mary Shelley.

Punctuating Adverb Clauses

When an adverb clause appears at the beginning of a sentence, it is followed by a comma.

Grammar and Usage

When Juanita dusts, her little brother helps her.

After the Alfred Hitchcock thriller was over, Dale was afraid to go to bed.

When an adverb clause appears at the end of a sentence, a comma is usually *not* used.

David hurt his leg *when he slid into third base*.

Jenny visited with us *after she attended her convention*.

Certain subordinating conjunctions *are* preceded by commas when they introduce an adverb clause at the end of the sentence. A comma is used before adverb clauses that begin with *though* and *although* and before *as* and *since* when they mean "because."

Pete can't eat taffy, as it sticks to his braces.

Lena sometimes wears earrings, although she usually doesn't like to.

We didn't mind leaving our old house, since it had been too small.

Chris likes shrimp, though Terry hates them.

Exercise 7: Punctuating Adverb Clauses

Write the following sentences and add commas according to the rules you learned in the previous section. Underline the subordinate adverb clauses and circle the commas you insert.

Examples

a. Whenever my cousin goes near ragweed he sneezes.

<u>Whenever my cousin goes near ragweed</u>(,) he sneezes.

b. We decided not to go fishing as it was getting dark.

We decided not to go fishing(,) <u>as it was getting dark</u>.

1. Although Karen's mother comes from Hungary Karen can't speak Hungarian.

2. The coach gave our team much praise although we certainly didn't deserve it.

3. After Jane read *Have Space Suit, Will Travel* she wanted to be an astronaut.
4. Alice Scutter attended a college night course when she was ninety years old.
5. When Abraham Lincoln emancipated the slaves he asked Frederick Douglass to be his adviser.
6. Dr. Charles Drew helped save many lives because he established the blood bank.
7. The hikers reached the mountaintop later than they had expected.
8. Lisa never swims where there is not a certified lifeguard on duty.
9. Rita can keep her job although she must maintain her grades.
10. Whenever she has spare time Riko reads her books on astronomy.

Review: Using Clauses

Write the following sentences. Underline each adjective clause and draw an arrow from the relative pronoun to the noun or pronoun the clause modifies. Then add a comma or commas where necessary to set off a nonessential clause from the rest of its sentence. Circle the commas.

Examples

a. John Ford who made many fine Westerns was a great Hollywood director.

John Ford(,) who made many fine Westerns(,) was a great Hollywood director.

b. Paul McCartney who is a musician was a Beatle.

Paul McCartney (,) who is a musician (,) was a Beatle.

1. The students who illustrated the class magazine were Leslie, Terry, and June.
2. The basketball coach would like to meet some students who are seven feet tall.

Grammar and Usage

3. The bold geese that our neighbor keeps are as good as watchdogs as far as we are concerned.
4. Carolyn who was high scorer in the game got the Most Valuable Player Award.
5. The Aztecs who were excellent astronomers invented a very accurate calendar.
6. Fred who has trouble waking up got a much bigger and louder alarm clock.
7. The cowboy star Will Rogers was famous for the rope tricks that he did.
8. Janice has an antique music box that plays a Viennese waltz.
9. We ended up in Galena which was more than fifty miles out of our way.
10. Edgar Allan Poe was an early writer who helped develop the detective story.

Write the following sentences, adding all necessary punctuation. Underline each adverb clause and circle the commas you insert.

11. When Sojourner Truth died she was given the biggest funeral ever held in her city.
12. After women graduate from the Lady Carpenter Institute they can operate power saws, drills, and sanders.
13. Nobody likes houseflies since they spread disease.
14. Fred's new alarm clock rings much more loudly than his old one did.
15. Many coyotes are uselessly slaughtered as ranchers mistakenly believe they kill sheep.
16. Marcia is happiest when she is outdoors.
17. Whenever a bluegrass music festival is held Carrie goes and takes her guitar.
18. Since you and Elizabeth got all the answers right you both get an *A +*.
19. Josefina can use her parents' car if she buys her own gasoline.
20. After the knight saw the fire-breathing dragon he decided the princess should get another suitor.

Writing Focus: *Using Clauses in Writing*

You can improve your writing by using clauses to add details, to combine sentences, to show relationships, and to vary sentence structure. Pay attention to the punctuation of clauses. To decide whether a clause should be set off by punctuation, determine its position and function in the sentence.

Assignment: *Have You Seen Our Teacher?*

Watching movies like *Star Trek* and *Star Wars* can spark our imaginations about living centuries in the future. What would life be like? More specifically, what might a particular aspect of life, one we take for granted, be like? How would you imagine a day at school to be in the future? What would you study? How would you do your homework? Who would be your teacher?

Write about a day at school in the future. Your paragraphs will be evaluated for correct and effective use of clauses. Use the following steps to complete this assignment.

A. Prewriting

Think about living centuries in the future. Imagine yourself at school. Use the six basic questions technique, described in Chapter 1, to help you generate ideas. Use the questions *who? what? where? when? why?* and *how?* to explore the school day from different angles. For example, questions like the following which begin with *what* may start you thinking: What does the classroom look like? What do teachers do to teach? What do students do to learn? What facilities are available? What supplies are used? List and answer as many questions as you can for each of the six words. Go back over the list and notice the many different ways of thinking about and describing the school day. Underline the details you wish to write about, and number them in an order that will help describe the day.

B. Writing

Using your questions and answers, write one or more paragraphs. Provide details about everything. Make sure your

readers (your classmates) have a clear picture of the activities that occur during the day. As you write, vary your sentences by using clauses in different ways.

C. Postwriting

Using the following checklist, revise your first draft.

1. Do the paragraphs include specific details?
2. Have I used clauses effectively to vary the structure of my sentences?
3. Are there sentence fragments or short sentences that can be combined by using clauses?
4. Have I punctuated each clause correctly?

Edit your revision, using the Checklist for Proofreading at the back of the book. If appropriate, share your writing with classmates and discuss your opinions about education.

3
Mechanics

23 Punctuation

Punctuation Marks

Communicating effectively in speech is easy for most people. Speakers can pause, lower or raise their voices, gesture with their hands—even stop to ask if the audience understands. Written communication, however, is often a much more challenging task, since writers cannot use such aids. For this reason writers depend on symbols called *punctuation marks* to convey meaning.

Writers of Edited Standard English use punctuation marks in the same way—that is, they follow certain rules in their use of punctuation. In this chapter you will study these rules.

Punctuation marks separate.

Some marks of punctuation separate words, phrases, or entire sentences, telling the reader that certain elements should not be run together. One use of the period, for example, is to separate a sentence from a sentence following it.

Charles Lindbergh made the first solo flight across the Atlantic. He flew from Long Island to Paris.

Punctuation marks link.

Several marks of punctuation can be used to link words, phrases, or entire sentences. The semicolon, for example, often joins two independent clauses that are closely related.

Amelia Earhart was the first woman to fly the Atlantic; her trip took about fifteen hours.

Punctuation marks enclose.

Punctuation marks can enclose words or groups of words that act as a unit. Quotation marks, for example, are used to enclose words in certain titles.

We learned a lot about sea life from the story "The Sea Devil."

Punctuation marks show omission.

A few marks of punctuation are used to indicate that letters have been left out. The apostrophe, for example, identifies the place in a contraciton where letters have been omitted.

Hasn't that paint dried yet, Wayne?

The Period

The *period* is used most often to separate one sentence from another, but it is also used to show that letters have been omitted in an abbreviation.

Use a period after a sentence that makes a simple statement (declarative sentence) or mild command (imperative sentence).

Enrique washed all the porch windows Saturday.

Please wash the windows, Enrique.

Use the period in some abbreviations to show that letters have been omitted.

Abbreviation	*Meaning*
Mr.	a title before a man's name
Mrs.	a title before a married woman's name
Ms.	a title used before a woman's name
Rev.	reverend
Sr.	senior
Jr.	junior
etc.	*et cetera* (and so forth)
dept.	department
A.D.	*anno domini* (in the year of the Lord)

535

Mechanics

Abbreviation	Meaning
B.C.	before Christ
lb.	pound

Note: The dictionary lists most abbreviations and their meanings. A period is not used with abbreviations for many government agencies, two-letter abbreviations for states in addresses, or metric units:

NASA	National Aeronautics and Space Administration
FBI	Federal Bureau of Investigation
ICC	Interstate Commerce Commission

NY	New York	TX	Texas
VA	Virginia	PA	Pennsylvania
IL	Illinois	CA	California

10 cc	cubic centimeters
5 kg	kilograms
3 km	kilometers

Some common abbreviations are now written without periods. Television networks and large companies, for example, often prefer to write their abbreviated names without periods. The abbreviations that follow are all written correctly without periods.

PBS	Public Broadcasting System
mpg	miles per gallon
rpm	revolutions per minute
fm	frequency modulation
IBM	International Business Machines

The Question Mark

Use a question mark to end a sentence that asks a question.

Does your sister Helen enjoy her work as a landscape architect? The job sounds very challenging.

When a declarative sentence contains a quotation that is also a question, place the question mark inside the closing quotation marks.

Lisa turned to me and asked, "Would you like more salad?"

"Do you enjoy working with animals at the clinic?" the interviewer asked the veterinarian.

When an interrogative sentence contains a quotation, place the question mark outside the quotation marks.

Weren't you shocked when George said, "You can begin work today"?

Wasn't it exciting when the race announcer said, "Start your engines"?

The Exclamation Point

Use an exclamation point to end a sentence or an expression that shows strong feeling.

You almost hit your head on that beam!

Stop it! You've been whistling that song over and over for the last thirty minutes!

Note: When a declarative sentence contains a quotation that is also an exclamation, place the exclamation point inside the closing quotation marks.

The first thing my brother Tom said when he got home was, "We won!"

Mechanics

Exercise 1: Using the Period, Question Mark, and Exclamation Point

Read the examples below then write the following sentences. Place the appropriate mark of punctuation at the end of each sentence. Be sure to capitalize the first word in each sentence. Circle the marks you insert.

Examples

a. The earliest train to Atlanta leaves at 9 A M and doesn't arrive until late in the afternoon

The earliest train to Atlanta leaves at 9 A⊙M⊙ and doesn't arrive until late in the afternoon ⊙

b. Goodness, that hurts

Goodness, that hurts !

1. Watch your step these stairs are rather steep
2. Our family vacationed in Washington, D C, last month
3. Surely this recipe isn't right it calls for six lbs of flour
4. A close friend of my mother's, Dr Cecilia Gomez, took us to Mount Vernon for the day
5. About 100 B C a Roman architect first developed the concept of the elevator
6. Could you hold my books for a second I have to tie my shoe
7. Hurray That basket means we've won the game
8. Ouch Why didn't you tell me the pan was hot
9. Sam turned to Rover and asked, "Why can't you learn to roll over"
10. Did that sign really read, "Canaries for sale—cheep"

The Comma

The *comma* is used most often to separate words, phrases, or clauses from other elements in a sentence.

Use a comma to separate words or word groups that are a series of three or more items.

Vincente wore a flannel shirt, long underwear, and a heavy jacket to the football game.

Numerous plays, short stories, and novels have been written about the lovely Pocahontas.

To refinish old furniture correctly one must strip off the old finish, sand the bare wood, and apply a new finish.

Use a comma to separate two or more adjectives when they precede a noun.

The frolicking, tanned children built castles in the sand.

My cousins were fascinated by the noisy, bustling atmosphere of downtown New York.

If the conjunction *and* makes sense between the adjectives, use a comma.

The frolicking *and* tanned children built castles in the sand.

My cousins were fascinated by the noisy *and* bustling atmosphere of downtown New York.

Use a comma to separate independent clauses that are joined by the coordinating conjunctions *and*, *but*, *or*, *for*, *nor*, *so*, and *yet*.

Carlos works at the library after school, *and* on Sunday he plays the organ at church.

We can't afford a new chair, *so* my grandmother is sewing slipcovers for the old one.

I have gone out of my way to be courteous and helpful to customers, *yet* my boss doesn't seem to notice.

Use a comma to separate introductory adverb clauses, participial phrases, and long prepositional phrases from the rest of the sentence.

While she waxed the kitchen floor, Linda reviewed the vocabulary words for her Spanish exam.
[introductory adverb clause]

Mechanics

Playing calmly and skillfully, Carlotta pivoted and made a quick basket.
[introductory participial phrase]

After the long wait to pick up our luggage, we headed toward the parking lot.
[long introductory prepositional phrase]

Use a comma to separate short introductory elements from the rest of the sentence.

Follow mild interjections and words such as *yes*, *no*, *why*, *well*, *still*, and *now* with a comma when they introduce a sentence.

Well, I'm not really worried about the weather.

Now, I can't promise you anything, but I'll talk to my parents about the trip.

Follow an introductory noun of address with a comma.

Girls, let's go in there and win this game!

Senator, do you support all of the President's economic policies?

Follow introductory transitional expressions such as *however*, *thus*, *consequently*, *accordingly*, *yet*, *hence*, *therefore*, and *besides* with a comma.

Consequently, the town council will meet Saturday afternoon rather than Wednesday night.

Therefore, the decision on the recycling center will be postponed until next month's meeting.

Use a comma to separate a direct quotation from the rest of the sentence.

Mr. Thurman asked, "What candidate will you vote for next Tuesday?"

"I'm thinking of casting my vote for Anna Juarez in the mayoral contest," Ms. Thurman responded.

Note: Do not use a comma when a person's words are used in an indirect quote.

Mrs. Thurman says she will vote for Anna Juarez.

Exercise 2: Using Commas

Write each of the following sentences. Place commas wherever they are needed. Circle the commas you insert.

Examples

a. The tough strong-willed Mary Harris was one of America's early labor reformers.

The tough, strong-willed Mary Harris was one of America's early labor reformers.

b. Mary Harris organized labor unions helped the poor and educated workers.

Mary Harris organized labor unions, helped the poor, and educated workers.

1. The gray overcast day ruined the children's plans for a picnic in the yard.
2. Fresh fruit is a quick tasty dessert our whole family enjoys.
3. Shelling fresh peas from the garden takes time but fresh peas certainly taste better than canned ones.
4. Mother wants us to paint the front porch but not the front door.
5. My youngest sister is teaching us to knit to crochet and to embroider.
6. No I have no idea if Tom will be home for dinner.
7. Susan this award proves you're one of the best writers in school.
8. Therefore oil prices will continue to rise unless the American consumer learns to conserve.
9. "Dad you've already served us tuna casserole three times this month" Otis complained.
10. Working skillfully and carefully Rosa installed several new shelves in her closet.

Use a comma to separate parts of geographical names and items in an address.

Mechanics

> We moved to Cleveland, Ohio, in 1979.
>
> My cousin Sara's new address is 45 Whitehorse Boulevard, Missoula, Montana 59801.

Note: When used in a sentence, the entire address is followed by a comma.

> We have lived at 221 Oaklawn Drive, Chicago, for two years.

A comma is not used between a building number and street name, nor between a state and a ZIP code.

> Send your request to the museum director at
> 108 Main Street
> West Chicago, IL 60185

Use a comma to separate a person's name from a degree, a title, or an affiliation that follows it.

> Jerry Musich, Ph.D.
>
> Martin Luther King, Jr.
>
> Cyrus Vance, Secretary of State

Note: When used in a sentence, the degree, title, or affiliation is also followed by a comma.

> At the state fair Dr. Clara Stevenson, D.V.M., told our scout troop about her experiences as a veterinarian.

Use a comma to separate items in dates.

> Jill was born on March 8, 1977, at Sandwich hospital.
>
> The income tax return must be mailed by Wednesday, April 15, to comply with federal law.

Note: Do not use commas when words appear between the items.

> I believe that April 15 falls on a Wednesday in 1981.

Exercise 3: Using Commas

Read the examples on the next page and then write the following sentences. Place commas wherever they are necessary. Circle the commas you insert.

Examples

a. The first public museum in America opened on January 12 1773 in Charleston South Carolina.
The first public museum in America opened on January 12 ⌢ 1773 ⌢ in Charleston ⌢ South Carolina.

b. Francisco's new college address is 120 Healey Avenue Champaign Illinois 61820.
Francisco's new college address is 120 Healey Avenue ⌢ Champaign ⌢ Illinois 61820.

1. On Labor Day 1981 we moved into the house we built ourselves.
2. This book on child care was written by Carmen Rivera R.N., an authority on children.
3. Sandra Tong M.D. has done extensive research on the link between poor nutrition and birth defects.
4. Did you know that Reno Nevada is farther west than Los Angeles California?
5. Mary Goddard was appointed the first postmaster of Baltimore Maryland in 1775.
6. The new fuel conservation law will become effective on Friday October 1.
7. Andrea Stephenson said to write to her at the Easter Seal Society at 2023 W. Ogden Ave. Chicago Illinois 60612.
8. The colonies were first termed the *United States* on July 2 1776.
9. According to this label these are home movies of Thanksgiving Day 1949.
10. Our Saint Bernard puppy was born on Wednesday August 8 1979.

Paired Commas

Clauses, phrases, and other expressions that appear in the middle of a sentence need more than one comma to separate them from the rest of the sentence. *Paired commas* (one comma at the beginning and one at the end) are used to separate these items from other words.

Use paired commas to separate nonessential clauses and phrases from the rest of the sentence.

Nonessential clauses and *phrases* are those not absolutely necessary to the meaning of the sentence.

Mrs. Smith, *who is an expert on sewing*, gave our drama director some good advice on altering patterns.

The sweater, *made of wool*, is six sizes too large.

Because they are necessary to a sentence's meaning, *essential clauses* and *phrases* are not set off by commas.

The clerk *who is an expert on sewing* gave our drama director better advice on altering patterns than did any of the other clerks.

The sweater *that she knit herself* is much larger than the one her aunt sent.

Rules for commas with phrases are in Chapter 21. Rules for commas with clauses are in Chapter 22.

Use paired commas to separate nonessential appositives and appositive phrases from the rest of the sentence.

If an appositive merely adds information and could be eliminated without changing the meaning of the sentence, it is nonessential and should be set off with paired commas.

Sacajawea, *a Shoshone woman*, was a skillful guide for Lewis and Clark on their explorations in the Louisiana Territory.

Meriwether Lewis and William Clark, *the famous explorers*, began their expedition into the Louisiana Territory in 1804.

When an appositive distinguishes the noun it refers to from similar items or others in the same group, the appositive is essential and is not set off by paired commas.

The Shoshone woman *Sacajawea* guided Lewis and Clark during their exploration of the Louisiana Territory.

The famous explorers *Meriwether Lewis and William Clark* began their expedition into the Louisiana Territory in 1804.

For more information about appositives, see Chapter 21.

Use paired commas to separate parenthetical expressions from the rest of the sentence.

Parenthetical expressions interrupt the flow of the sentence but add nothing to its essential meaning.

Common parenthetical expressions include *I think* (*believe, know, hope*), *I am sure, on the other hand, by the way, incidentally, after all, on the contrary, to be sure, in fact, for example,* and *to tell the truth.*

We could, *on the contrary*, run into bad weather during this hiking trip.

My aunt, *by the way*, is a reporter for the newspaper you just mentioned.

My blind friend is a better chess player, *in fact*, than almost anyone I know.

Use paired commas to separate nouns of address from the rest of the sentence.

I'm not sure, *Juanita*, if we can go to the concert.

Are you wondering, *Coach*, if we'll win this game?

Use paired commas to separate transitional expressions from the rest of the sentence when these expressions merely interrupt the flow of the sentence.

The worst part of the project, *then*, was knocking down the old plaster walls.

It is not your responsibility, *however*, to saw the wood for the fireplace.

Exercise 4: Using Commas

Write each of the sentences on the following page. Place single or paired commas wherever they are necessary. Circle the commas you insert.

545

Mechanics

Examples

a. Money it is said can't buy happiness.

Money⌢ it is said⌢ can't buy happiness.

b. Charles Dickens who wrote numerous books about poor but ambitious boys created the hero called Oliver Twist.

Charles Dickens⌢ who wrote numerous books about poor but ambitious boys⌢ created the hero called Oliver Twist.

1. Senator John Kennedy who later became President of the United States won the Pulitzer Prize for his book *Profiles in Courage*.
2. We'll be late I'm afraid if we stop for dinner.
3. Crispus Attucks one of the men killed in the Boston Massacre was probably one of America's earliest heroes.
4. The umbrella developed to ward off sunburn was quickly adapted for other purposes.
5. The cheetah I believe can run sixty miles per hour.
6. Storing paint for example anywhere near your furnace can be extremely dangerous.
7. Phillis Wheatley a slave published a volume of excellent poetry in 1773.
8. It is ironic that two Presidents Thomas Jefferson and John Adams both died on the Fourth of July in 1826.
9. These two Presidents died in fact on the fiftieth anniversary of the signing of the Declaration of Independence of the United States of America.
10. You believe then that solar energy is an important energy alternative?

The Semicolon

The *semicolon* signals a more distinct break in thought than the comma and creates a longer pause when read aloud.

Use a semicolon to link independent clauses when they are not joined by a coordinating conjunction.

> The first Western cattle drive was in 1866; cowhands drove hundreds of thousands of cattle from Texas to Kansas.
>
> In 1867 Secretary Seward purchased Alaska from the Russians; the United States paid two cents per acre for this territory.

Use a semicolon to link independent clauses when the second independent clause begins with a transitional adverb.

> This suit costs far too much; *besides*, the fabric is not washable.
>
> Poverty and physical handicaps blocked her path; *however*, Wilma Rudolph overcame these obstacles to become an Olympic track star.

Note: A semicolon is also used to link independent clauses when the second clause begins with *in fact*, *on the other hand*, *on the contrary*, or similar transitional phrases.

Use a semicolon to separate items in a series when one or more of the items contain commas.

> The junior high band will march this summer at parades in Gary, Indiana; Kenosha, Wisconsin; and Bloomington, Illinois.
>
> To qualify for service abroad with our bank, an applicant must speak French, German, and one other language; possess excellent math skills; and have a college degree in finance.

The Colon

The *colon* is used to separate elements within a sentence. Like an arrow pointing forward, the colon directs the reader's attention to the word, phrase, or list that follows it.

Use a colon to separate a list of items from an introductory statement containing a specific number or the words *these*, *the following*, *as follows*, and *all of the following*.

Four students won blue ribbons in the state music contest: Antonio Alvarez, Rachel Burnstein, Andy Smith, and Alice Willett.

The spices I have in the cupboard are as follows: oregano, dill, marjoram, cinnamon, and dry mustard.

Among the items donated to the white elephant sale were the following: a plaid hammock, a paisley piano scarf, and an old tuba.

Use a colon to separate an introductory statement from an explanation, an appositive, or a quotation.

She learned one thing from her coaching experiences: how to be more patient.	[explanation]
In 1868 an exciting new product appeared on the American market: compressed yeast.	[appositive]
The humorist Josh Billings once commented about solitude: "It's a good place to visit but a poor place to stay."	[quotation]

Use a colon to separate the salutation from the body in a business letter.

Dear Homeowner:

Dear Senator Lopez:

Use a colon to separate the hour from the minute in expressions of time.

the 8:15 bus

at 7:20 P.M.

23 Punctuation

Exercise 5: Using Semicolons and Colons

Write the following sentences. Place semicolons or colons wherever they are necessary. Circle the marks you insert.

Examples

a. In 1844 the first bathtub was installed in an American hotel however, bathtubs were still prohibited in Boston at that time.

In 1844 the first bathtub was installed in an American hotel(;) however, bathtubs were still prohibited in Boston at that time.

b. The formal essay should include all of the following an introduction, a thesis statement, several paragraphs of development, and a conclusion.

The formal essay should include all of the following(:) an introduction, a thesis statement, several paragraphs of development, and a conclusion.

1. The first three women to run for Vice President were Mary Stowe, in 1892 Marie Brehm, in 1924 and Grace Carlson, in 1948.

2. Harriet Quimby was America's first female aviator she was also an outstanding magazine writer.

3. We couldn't afford to put up aluminum siding therefore, the whole family devoted their time to stripping and repainting the house.

4. Vernon Smith, my uncle Anita Smith, my aunt and Hiram Otis, my grandfather, are all pharmacists.

5. I have always admired Paula she is an outstanding counselor who is dedicated to her work with teenagers.

6. All of the following are native American words that have become part of our vocabulary *tomahawk, moccasin, toboggan,* and *tepee*.

7. I can think of only one way to describe my bedroom wall-to-wall chaos.

8. We will leave Chicago tomorrow on the 11 30 train and reach Minneapolis by 8 30 P.M.

Mechanics

9. The four languages with the largest number of native speakers are the following Mandarin, English, Russian, and Spanish.

10. Henry David Thoreau once wrote these words "Dreams are the touchstones of our characters."

The Dash

The *dash* is used to separate elements within a sentence. Like an arrow pointing backward, it directs the reader's attention to the word, phrase, or list that precedes it.

Use a dash to separate an introductory series or thought from the part of the sentence that further develops it.

A few quiet days at the beach—that's what I really need.

Strong leadership, courage, and intelligence—those are the qualities we need in a President.

To watch the Packers in the Super Bowl—that's his one dream.

Use a dash to separate an abrupt or unexpected change in thought from the rest of the sentence.

Be careful—that chair doesn't look very sturdy.

Myron is here—we can begin now.

The Hyphen

The *hyphen* is used to link the parts of some words. When you are uncertain about how a hyphen should be used in a word, consult a dictionary.

Use a hyphen to link the parts of some compound nouns.

Use a hyphen to link the parts of compound nouns that begin with the prefixes *ex-*, *self-*, and *all-*.

ex-soldier

self-control

all-star

Use a hyphen to link the parts of compound nouns that end with the suffix *-elect*.

President-elect

mayor-elect

Use a hyphen to link the parts of a compound noun that include a prepositional phrase.

jack-*in-the-*box

man-*of-war*

Use a hyphen with the prefix *great-* when it is part of a compound noun expressing family relationship.

great-grandfather

great-uncle

Note: Remember that some compound nouns are not hyphenated at all (*tennis shoe, real estate, school day*), while some other compound nouns are written as a single word (*typewriter, homemaker*). Dictionaries indicate how a compound noun is written.

Use a hyphen to link the parts of some compound adjectives.

Use a hyphen to link the parts of compound adjectives that are an adjective and a noun.

all-purpose

low-income

Use a hyphen to link the parts of compound adjectives when the last word is capitalized.

all-American

pre-Revolutionary

post-Darwinian

Mechanics

Use a hyphen to link the parts of a compound adjective when one part is a number and the other part is a noun or an adjective, and to link the parts of a compound adjective that is a fraction.

    four-page letter

    five-dollar bill

    one-third inch

    three-eighths foot

Note: The hyphen may be omitted when the fraction is used as a noun.

    Three fourths of our class is going on the field trip.

Use a hyphen to link the parts of a compound adjective when the second part of the adjective is a participle.

    good-natured neighbor

    quick-drying paint

Note: A hyphen is not used between the parts of a compound adjective when the first part is an adverb ending in *-ly*.

    slowly moving storm

Use a hyphen to link the parts of the compound numbers between twenty-one and ninety-nine.

    thirty-nine cents

    twenty-two children

Use a hyphen to link the syllables of a word begun on one line of writing and continued on the next line. Use the hyphen only between syllables.

My parents have always taught that preserving the *envi-ronment* is a personal responsibility.

Because the elbow was still stiff when the cast was *re-moved*, her doctor suggested some physical therapy.

Since a hyphen is used only between syllables, words of one syllable are not hyphenated, and a hyphen is not used if one letter would be left standing alone on either line. (An asterisk [*] denotes a sentence with a feature that is not part of Edited Standard English.)

*My sister said that right now she is ranked a-
bove 90 percent of the students in her class.
[*Above* should not be hyphenated.]

My sister said that right now she is ranked *above* 90 percent of the students in her class.

Words already containing a hyphen should be divided only at the hyphen.

*Cleaning up the oil slick off the coast will be a *heart-rend-
ing* task.
[*Heart-rending* should be divided only at the hyphen.]

Cleaning up the oil slick off the coast will be a *heart-
rending* task.

Exercise 6: *Using Dashes and Hyphens*

Write each of the following sentences. Place dashes and hyphens wherever they are necessary. Circle the marks you insert.

Examples

a. There are only two things you can't eat for breakfast lunch and dinner.

There are only two things you can't eat for breakfast— lunch and dinner.

b. In 1925 Henry Ford introduced the first eight hour workday.

In 1925 Henry Ford introduced the first eight-hour workday.

1. The trip to the Aleutian Islands was great but let's get my luggage.
2. Two tickets to a pro football game now that's a real treat.
3. Skydiving that's what I call a jumping good time.
4. Our ill fated trip to Florida ended with Dad's appendicitis attack.

Mechanics

5. Do you think the development of atomic weapons will eventually bring about our self destruction?
6. The pre Revolutionary War era is often called the Colonial Period.
7. To finish this crossword I need a six letter word for *happy*.
8. I will need a four foot piece of rope to tie up this wood.
9. We used several two by fours to frame in the doorway of our family room.
10. This bookcase looks a little top heavy; perhaps we should move some of these books to the bottom shelf.

Quotation Marks

Quotation marks have two major uses in writing: they enclose direct quotations and some titles.

Use quotation marks to enclose a direct quotation—that is, the exact words of a writer or speaker.

According to Ralph Waldo Emerson, "Who so would be a man, must be a non-conformist."

"With a fresh coat of paint," Mother said, "these chairs will look fine."

"Well, I'm afraid you're wrong about the weather," she responded.

Note: Quotation marks are only used when the *exact* words of a writer or speaker are recorded.

In one of his essays Ralph Waldo Emerson stated that anyone who would call himself a man must be a non-conformist.	[indirect quotation]

Use quotation marks to enclose the titles of short stories, short poems, songs, essays, lectures, and speeches.

Reading Edgar Allan Poe's "The Black Cat" really gave me the shivers.	[title of short story]
When we read "Blue-Butterfly Day," I displayed my butterfly collection and gave a short talk.	[title of poem]
All the fans joined in when the organ played "Take Me Out to the Ball Game."	[title of song]
Henry David Thoreau's essay "Civil Disobedience" is said to have influenced both Mahatma Gandhi and Martin Luther King, Jr.	[title of essay]
The museum director delivered her lecture, entitled "Using Your Museum Resources," at the convention of the Wisconsin Historical Society.	[title of lecture]
My history teacher read us a portion of Lincoln's "Cooper Union Speech" in class today.	[title of speech]

Use quotation marks to enclose the titles of magazine and newspaper articles, chapter titles in a book, and episodes of radio and television programs.

I found a newspaper article called "Preserving Our Wilderness Areas" that might help you with your social studies report.	[article in a newspaper]
The chapter "American Folk Heroes" discusses Davy Crockett, Paul Bunyan, and John Henry.	[chapter in a book]
The most touching episode of *The Waltons* last season was "Olivia's Homecoming."	[television episode]
The best remembered episode of Orson Wells' Mecury Theater on the Air is "The War of the Worlds."	[radio episode]

Mechanics

Underlining (Italics)

A writer uses underlining most frequently to set off the titles of some works of art. A printer uses a special type (*italics*) to indicate underlining. *The words you are now reading are in italics.*

Underline the titles of books, plays of any length, very long poems, newspapers, magazines, and pamphlets.

Mr. Ciardullo will help direct the sixth-grade play, <u>Cheaper by the Dozen</u>.	[title of play]
I'm going to read <u>Charlotte's Web</u> to my little brother as soon as he gets it from the library.	[title of book]
My mom is reading a long poem called <u>Canterbury Tales</u>; she says it's about a group of people who take a journey together.	[title of long poem]
I found out about these hanging plastic shelves from an ad in <u>Home Decorator</u> magazine.	[title of magazine]
Every Tuesday Mr. Thomas, who is in his eighties, sets the type for the weekly issue of the <u>Macon County Recorder</u>.	[title of newspaper]
When we canned these tomatoes, we just followed the directions in the government pamphlet <u>Safe and Easy Home-Preserving</u>.	[title of pamphlet]

Note: Underline the articles *a, an,* and *the* only if they are actually part of the title.

> The story about Humaweepi is from <u>The Man to Send Rain Clouds</u>.
> My mom has been a reporter for the <u>Cleveland Tribune</u> for about five years.

Underline the titles of films, record albums, and radio and television series.

I still think Charlie Chaplin's <u>Gold Rush</u> was the greatest comedy film ever made.	[title of film]
"Jitterbug Baby" is the best song on the album <u>Great Favorites of the Fifties</u>.	[title of record album]
Mr. Juarez, who plays the classical guitar, recently played several numbers on the <u>Tonight</u> show.	[title of television series]
You can listen to the show <u>Jazz Forum</u> every day at two o'clock.	[title of radio program]

Underline the titles of paintings, sculptures, ballets, operas, and musicals.

Every night this week Carlotta plans to work on the sets for the community theater's production of <u>West Side Story</u>.	[title of musical]
When we are in Philadelphia, we hope to see the opera <u>The Magic Flute</u>.	[title of opera]
My watercolor of the lilies was influenced by Vincent van Gogh's <u>Sunflowers</u>.	[title of painting]

Underline the names of ships, aircraft, and spacecraft.

Rose's great-grandfather worked as an engineer on the <u>Queen Mary</u> for over twenty years.	[name of ship]

Mechanics

| According to the records of Viking 1, the temperature of the planet Mars at dawn is over one hundred degrees below zero. | [name of spacecraft] |
| Aboard the Lame Duck Albert Read and a crew of five made the first transatlantic flight in 1919. | [name of aircraft] |

Exercise 7: Using Quotation Marks and Underlining

Write each of the following sentences. Use quotation marks or underlining wherever they are required.

Examples

a. Benjamin Franklin once commented: One today is worth two tomorrows.
Benjamin Franklin once commented: "One today is worth two tomorrows."

b. Because they enjoyed reading Huckleberry Finn so much, Felice and her father have decided to build a raft.
Because they enjoyed reading Huckleberry Finn so much, Felice and her father have decided to build a raft.

1. Do you like stories like The Lady, or the Tiger, which leave the reader up in the air?

2. Rosa must memorize This Land Is Your Land; This Land Is My Land for our program on folk music.

3. The first daily comic strip, called Mr. Mutt, began in 1907 in the San Francisco Chronicle.

4. Who's responsible for the old saying: It's Greek to me?

5. Hard work and integrity, the speaker commented, have always marked this nation's progress.

6. My grandfather has a copy of the Tribune issue that announced the election of Franklin D. Roosevelt.

7. I learned to make this flute from a pamphlet called Make Your Own Musical Instruments.

8. Did you know that Theresa's short story will be in the May issue of Creative Writer, the magazine we get at school?
9. Dad got the whole family tickets for the musical You're a Good Man, Charlie Brown.
10. One of my favorite television programs, Nova, is broadcast on PBS.

The Apostrophe

Use an apostrophe to show where letters have been omitted to form a contraction.

I'll try to return these books to the library this afternoon.	[I + will]
Could you meet me in the reference room at four o'clock?	[of + the + clock]
Sharon, weren't you nervous when you accepted the conference trophy?	[were + not]

Note: Avoid confusing some contractions with the possessive forms of personal pronouns. It will help if you remember that a contraction always contains an apostrophe; ask yourself whether the word you want to use is a contracted form of two words.

Contraction	Possessive Form
it's [it + is]	its nose
they're [they + are]	their clothes
you're [you + are]	your mother
there's [there + is]	the puppy is theirs
who's [who + is]	whose car

Use an apostrophe to show that the first two numbers of a year have been omitted.

Mechanics

> My report will deal with the stock market crash of '29.
>
> This little storm is nothing in comparison to the blizzard of '78.

When a noun is singular, use an apostrophe and an *s* to show possession.

Singular Noun	Possessive Form
Agatha	Agatha's mystery
child	child's sweater
horse	horse's mouth
Dickens	Dickens's novel

(*Dickens' novel* is also correct.)

When a plural noun does not end in *s*, use an apostrophe and an *s* to show possession.

Plural Noun	Possessive Form
people	people's wishes
oxen	oxen's tails
alumni	alumni's contributions

When a plural noun ends in an *s*, use only an apostrophe to show possession.

Plural Noun	Possessive Form
babies	babies' cries
the Hobsons	Hobsons' farm
automobiles	automobiles' hoods
planets	planets' orbits

Exercise 8: Using Apostrophes

Write the following sentences. Place apostrophes wherever they are needed in contractions and in the possessive forms of nouns. Circle the apostrophes you insert. (Some sentences may not need apostrophes.)

Examples

a. I dont want to miss the special program dealing with energy conservation that will be on tonight.

I don⊙t want to miss the special program dealing with energy conservation that will be on tonight.

b. Look at the junior class float; theirs is certainly the best in the parade.
Look at the junior class float; theirs is certainly the best in the parade.
(No changes—theirs is a possessive pronoun.)

1. We cant afford a second car, so my dad rides his bicycle to the train station.
2. Theres an excellent chance that Yolanda will make the Olympic track team this year.
3. The foreign students speech has really improved, and she is already starting to pick up slang expressions from the other students.
4. Theres nothing to do in a tornado but take cover in ones basement and hope.
5. Walt Disneys first cartoon, released in 1928, was called *Plane Crazy*.
6. In 1940 womens nylon stockings were marketed for the first time.
7. Autograph experts value Julius Caesars signature at about $2 million.
8. If you dont keep up with your Spanish, youre certainly not going to keep your *A* average.
9. All the businesses support will be necessary if the city Street Festival is to be a success.
10. The girls gymnasium will be closed next week so the floor can be repaired.

Parentheses

Use parentheses to enclose supplementary or explanatory material that is not closely related to the rest of the sentence.

> The length of the standard football field (including 10 yards of end zone at each end) is 120 yards.
>
> Louis Armstrong (1900–1971) is still considered one of the greatest jazz musicians who ever lived.
>
> To prolong one's life an English gerontologist (a doctor who is an expert on aging) recommends walking one mile a day.

Note: Both paired commas and parentheses can be used to enclose nonessential material. Paired commas are usually used to enclose material that is still somewhat related to the sentence. Parentheses usually enclose material that is only loosely connected to the sentence and could easily be placed in another sentence altogether.

Use parentheses to enclose letters or numbers that identify listed items within a sentence.

During the recent flood the city advised all residents to (a) boil all drinking water, (b) report all fallen electrical wires, and (c) call City Hall in emergencies.

The topic sentence of a paragraph can be developed with any of the following: (a) specific details, (b) examples, (c) facts and statistics, and (d) an incident.

Exercise 9: Using Parentheses

Write each of the following sentences, placing parentheses wherever they are necessary. Circle the parentheses you insert.

Examples

a. The Yangtze China, the Amazon South America, and the Nile Africa are the three longest rivers in the world.

The Yangtze (China), the Amazon (South America), and the Nile (Africa) are the three longest rivers in the world.

b. The city of Chicago the name is from a native American word suffered a disastrous fire in 1871.

The city of Chicago (the name is from a native American word) suffered a disastrous fire in 1871.

1. Add clarified butter directions for clarifying butter are on page 48 to the eggs and stir in the flour a few spoons at a time, keeping the batter smooth.

2. In his three Presidential races Grover Cleveland was elected 1884, defeated 1888, and finally elected again 1892.

3. John Quincy Adams was born in Braintree now called Quincy, Massachusetts.

4. Even for a short hike in a wilderness area, the following items are essential: 1 a compass and map of the area; 2 a small first-aid kit, knife, and matches; 3 concentrated food and a canteen of water; and 4 a poncho or a lightweight nylon jacket.

5. Mother's Day the second Sunday in May was suggested by Anne Jarvis, who wanted a day on which to honor her mother.

6. In order to pass the English midterm, you must be able to correctly define three terms: *simile* a comparison using the word *like* or *as*, *metaphor* a comparison not using the word *like* or *as*, and *meter* the rhythm of words.

7. The Feldhoffers' dog an Irish setter and Tim's a Labrador retriever have been nicknamed the Trashbusters because of their regular nighttime raids on the garbage cans in the alley behind their houses.

8. Eleanor Cameron she began by writing stories to amuse her son is the author of several award-winning novels, including *The Court of the Stone Children* and *A Room Made of Windows*.

9. In the Battle of Ayacucho 1824 the heroic General Antonio José de Sucre 1795-1830 defeated a large Spanish force and declared Peru's independence from Spain.

Mechanics

10. When he finally cleaned his room, Keith discovered the following items under his bed: a dried-up banana peel this was from the time he and his friend Gary staged a banana-eating contest, a copy of *Conan the Barbarian* this belonged to his older brother, and five mismatched socks.

Review: Using Punctuation

Write the following sentences. Place punctuation marks wherever they are needed. Circle the marks you insert.

Examples

a. As I searched through my locker I found the following a rotten apple a pair of dirty socks and my ex boyfriends picture.

As I searched through my locker(,) I found the following(:) a rotten apple(,) a pair of dirty socks(,) and my ex(-)boyfriend(')s picture.

b. Is it true that today's weather report forecasts clouds rain and possibly even sleet if the temperature drops.

Is it true that today's weather report forecasts clouds(,) rain(,) and possibly sleet if the temperature drops(?)

1. On June 15 1981 we moved from Houston Texas to a small farm.

2. The sloth a mammal from Central and South America travels from tree to tree upside down.

3. Dr I M Payne 1910–1974 was the first person to successfully transplant an appendix.

4. His parents careers in medicine and pharmacy influenced Tonys decision to become a physical therapist.

5. The rangers family spent the whole winter in a log cabin in the national forest near here.

6. The department store in town is having a special sale on ladies coats and childrens snowsuits.

7. The quarterbacks inability to throw a long pass shouldnt affect Sundays game between El Pasos rival schools, Palo Verde High School and Buena Vista High School.

8. Our family dog Snippy a six month old golden retriever usually drags her dish around in a circle when its empty and shes hungry.

9. For several years the PTA Parent-Teacher Association has opposed violence on television because of its harmful effect on viewers young viewers in particular.

10. Katharine Hepburn won Academy Awards for her performances in Morning Glory 1933 Guess Whos Coming to Dinner? 1967 and The Lion in Winter 1968.

11. I guess this just wasnt my lucky day the unhappy Vernon moaned.

12. These are common mistakes students make in their writing a run-on sentences, b fused sentences, and c sentence fragments.

13. Your research paper should include the following 1 a sentence outline, 2 a bibliography, 3 correct footnotes, and 4 a title page.

14. Denim the fabric from which blue jeans are made was first manufactured in Nîmes France not in the United States as many believe.

15. Blanche Scott 1892–1970 was Americas earliest automobile saleswoman the first female pilot and an early star in silent films.

16. Blanche Scott commented I shaped my life and career on the single idea that a woman can do anything within reason that a man can do.

17. Slim Jim one of Jonathan Sullivans many aliases is so popular remarked Uncle Tex that every sheriff in the state wants him.

18. One of the best books about the American frontier is Giants in the Earth by Ole Rölvaag.

19. I have discovered that there are several similarities between Ole Rölvaags intriguing book and the moving film The Immigrants.

20. While we were at the hospital Dad requested Please speak softly.

Mechanics

Writing Focus: *Improving Punctuation in Writing*

Punctuation marks are road signs that writers use to guide readers. The marks can slow readers down, make them stop, and even point out items of interest. Like drivers who must learn to read and follow road signs to avoid accidents and to keep traffic flowing smoothly, writers must learn to use punctuation to avoid confusion and to make their writing easy to read.

Assignment: *A Clio for Sure*

Commercials have been an important, though sometimes aggravating, part of television ever since its early days. A baby models diapers, a woman shakes her glossy hair, a fully dressed man falls into a pool unexpectedly—different commercials for different products, some more effective than others.

Imagine that you have been chosen to make a television commercial for a new book-size student computer/word processor. Write a letter to your producer, explaining and describing how you want your commercial to be presented. Include information about the product, your choice of spokesperson(s) (if any), music, scenes, action, dialogue, and so on. Discuss your commercial in detail. Your writing will be evaluated for correct punctuation.

Use the following steps to complete this assignment.

A. Prewriting

Think about all the commercials you've seen over the years. Free write (described in Chapter 1) about ones you've liked or approaches you've thought worked well on television. Now think about selling a new book-size student computer/word processor. Consider your audience. Continue free writing for at least five or ten minutes about your commercial. Add details about the name, music, or skits. Include facts that help explain, describe, and sell your product. Reread your free writing, and underline the details you wish to use in your letter.

B. Writing

Write a letter to your producer describing or explaining how you want your commercial to be presented. Use your free writing to help you. Follow the guidelines for letter writing by including a heading, inside address, salutation, body, and closing. Make the body of your letter as detailed as possible so that the producer can actually visualize the commercial. As you write, pay particular attention to using correct punctuation.

C. Postwriting

Use the following checklist to revise your first draft.

1. Is my letter in the correct form?
2. Have I provided sufficient details to explain or describe my commercial?
3. Is my punctuation correct?

Use the checklist at the back of this book to proofread your work. Share your letter with your classmates. Create a classroom folder entitled *Award-Winning Commercials,* using student work.

24 Capitalization

Capitalization

Capital letters are used to separate and emphasize important words and word groups.

Capitalize the first word of a sentence.

Capitalize the first word of a sentence to separate it from the sentence before it.

Mrs. Lance is eighty years old and very active. She has a large vegetable garden, so she cans and freezes many types of vegetables.

She is also a charming woman with a good sense of humor. Would you like to meet her?

Capitalize the pronoun *I*.

Saturday I want to teach my cousin a new song on the guitar.

Mrs. Sanchez, do you think I could organize a neighborhood cleanup campaign?

Capitalize the names of specific people.

Langston Hughes, Gwendolyn E. Brooks, and Richard Wright have all written poetry.

John and Angie are taking a course in cardiopulmonary resuscitation.

Capitalize words showing family relationship when they replace a person's name and when they directly precede a person's name.

Frequently words such as *Dad, Mom,* and *Grandfather* are used in place of a person's name.

> Usually when we have a family problem, Mom and Dad discuss it with all of us.

> At school I call Grandmother Mrs. Chan, but at home I call her Gram.

Note: Do not capitalize a word showing family relationship when it is preceded by a possessive noun or pronoun.

> Yesterday afternoon my mom and I cooked rhubarb from the garden.

> Did you know Mike's grandfather was both a sailor and a cowhand?

Capitalize a title when it is used in place of a person's name.

> Without your help, Sergeant, this accident could have been very serious.

> There is a real need, Mayor, for a lower speed limit in the area of the hospital.

> Could you help me with this math problem, Professor?

Note: When a title is used in a general sense, it is not capitalized.

> Do you think the mayor understands the need for a lower speed limit?

> Without the police sergeant's excellent help the accident could have been very serious.

Capitalize a title when it directly precedes a person's name and abbreviations that are part of a person's name or title. *Mr., Miss, Mrs.,* and *Ms.* are considered titles.

> Ms. Wong is a good teacher, Capt. Juarez is a fine pilot, and Dr. Cousins is a dedicated psychologist.

> I believe the woman in the blue suit is Senator Alvarez.

> Since she took over the local paper, Editor Winslow has increased the coverage of sports events.

Mechanics

On Saturday afternoons Rev. Loomis often referees our neighborhood baseball games.

Capitalize the titles *president* and *vice president* when they refer to the highest officers of the national government.

In 1939 Franklin Roosevelt became the first President to appear on television.

An announcement from the White House indicated that the Vice President will return shortly from his overseas trip.

Exercise 1: Using Capital Letters

Write the following sentences. Capitalize names, words showing family relationships, and titles. Circle each word you capitalize. Some sentences may not need new capital letters.

Examples

a. Do you know, dad, when aunt joyce's bus will arrive?
Do you know, (Dad,) when (Aunt Joyce's) bus will arrive?

b. My mother is thinking of working as a volunteer for senator rice.
My mother is thinking of working as a volunteer for (Senator Rice.)

1. The game of basketball was invented by dr. james a. naismith in 1891.
2. I think tim's mom taught him how to macramé.
3. My sister janice wants rev. vernon to perform her wedding ceremony.
4. Sometime I'd like you to meet my friend, mr. oswald.
5. When she served as a state senator, grandmother worked hard to gain more support for day-care centers.
6. The first image transmitted by television was that of general j. j. carty.

7. Carlotta does an excellent job as captain of the swimming team.
8. When you call the fire department about the inspection, ask for lieutenant romero.
9. Do you think tom's mom will be elected president of the local chamber of commerce?
10. Will our state be declared a national disaster area, governor, because of the damage caused by the tornadoes?

Capitalize the names of geographical places, including special regions, and monuments.

Continents, Countries:	Asia, Guatemala
States, Counties:	New Mexico, Livingston County
Cities, Towns:	Tampa Bay, Plainfield
Bodies of Water:	Bitteroot Lake, Atlantic Ocean
Islands, Points of Land:	Washington Island, the Adirondacks
Special Regions:	the Midwest, the Orient
Streets, Roadways:	Route 47, Brighton Road
Parks:	French Creek State Park, Phillips Park
Buildings, Monuments:	the Monroe Clinic, the Biograph Theater, the Washington Monument

Capitalize the words *north, south, east, west,* and their compounds to name a specific region or when they are part of an address.

We enjoy the warm, dry climate of the Southwest.

The university bookstore is at 4455 North Milwaukee Avenue.

Note: Do not capitalize *north, south, east,* and *west* for compass directions.

The new hospital will be built on the north side of the city.

We are traveling west, aren't we?

Mechanics

Capitalize the names of nationalities and peoples.

> Juan really enjoys Chinese foods, but Anita likes to eat in German restaurants.
>
> I believe this river is named after a native American people—the Delaware.

Capitalize the names of languages and other proper adjectives derived from proper nouns.

> Many of the Canadians we met on our trip spoke French.
>
> Her mother is an instructor of Slavic languages at the college.

Exercise 2: Using Capital Letters

Write each of the following sentences. Insert capital letters wherever they are needed. Circle each word you capitalize.

Examples

   a. Aren't the andes the famous mountains in peru?

      Aren't the (Andes) the famous mountains in (Peru?)

   b. The tallest building in new york is no longer the empire state building but the world trade center.

      The tallest building in (New York) is no longer the (Empire State Building) but the (World Trade Center.)

1. The hottest spot in the world is thought to be timbuktu, which is located in mali.
2. I think I might enjoy operas more if I understood italian better.
3. White lines were first used to indicate traffic lanes in trenton, michigan, in 1911.
4. The cherokee man Sequoya spent twelve years developing the first native american syllabary.
5. The lumberyard you want is located at 1600 south archer avenue.

6. The moose is a common sight in the woods of north america.
7. When we were in alabama, we hunted shells and swam in the ocean at the gulf island national seashore.
8. Many people consider british tea the best in the world.
9. You can find the brainerd monument about six miles north of doylestown on route 611.
10. Mrs. Sanchez sang a beautiful spanish song at the summer festival celebrating our hispanic heritage.

Capitalize the names of specific institutions, businesses, organizations, and their abbreviations.

We saw several paintings by female artists in the new exhibit at the Chicago Art Institute.	[specific institution]
My mom saved several dollars by buying all the nails for the new family room at Bailey Hardware and Appliance.	[specific business]
When my little brother outgrows his clothes, we usually send them to the Salvation Army.	[specific organization]

Note: Do not use a capital letter when an institution, a business, or an organization is referred to in a general sense.

Which junior high school do you attend?

My aunt will begin her job with the museum this fall.

Mr. Arturo Gomez owns the local construction company.

Capitalize the trade names, brand names, and trademarks of specific products.

Because it's meant to be diluted in water, this Vitafresh fertilizer is very inexpensive.

I like the whole-wheat bread from Butterfarm Breads because there are no chemicals in it.

Mechanics

> **Capitalize the names of political parties (but not the word *party*) and the names of government agencies, departments, and bureaus, and their abbreviations.**

My cousin gave up farming to work for the USDA. [United States Department of Agriculture]

In 1855 Congress voted funds to establish the United States Camel Corps.

This is a strong Republican county; the Democratic party has not won a county election in over fifty years.

Exercise 3: Using Capital Letters

Write each of the following sentences. Place capital letters wherever they are needed. Circle each word that you capitalize. Some sentences may not need new capital letters.

Examples

a. Grandpa said his family once had a packard auto just like the one on display at speedee auto repair.

Grandpa said his family once had a (Packard) auto just like the one on display at (Speedee Auto Repair.)

b. Mrs. Fernandez is a sales representative for the foremost automobile association.
Mrs. Fernandez is a sales representative for the (Foremost Automobile Association.)

1. I think you can get a good booklet about the moving companies in the area from the interstate commerce commission.

2. The organization called care has helped many poor and homeless people throughout the world.

3. My family shops at bill's produce market every week because the fresh fruits and vegetables are of such good quality.

4. Miriam A. Ferguson, a democrat, was elected governor of Texas in 1924.

5. My mother is giving a talk on energy conservation at the next meeting of the american association of university women.
6. Benjamin Franklin served as the first postmaster of the united states post office.
7. I'm going to write to the bureau of consumer protection about the faulty wiring in this quick 'n' dry hair dryer that I just bought.
8. Jeanette has applied for a job as a stock clerk at johnson's hardware.
9. With the scholarship she received from the united negro college fund, Angie will be able to start nurses' training in the fall.
10. Every season the green bay packers play several games in Milwaukee.

Capitalize the names of the months, the days of the week, and specific calendar holidays.

According to this book the Panama Canal was opened on October 10, 1913.

Because the truck with the fireworks didn't arrive, our city's Fourth of July celebration had to be postponed until Saturday.

Capitalize the titles of specific historical periods and events.

The Battle of Bunker Hill, an important event in the Revolutionary War, lasted about ninety minutes.

Roberta is doing a special report on the art and literature of the Middle Ages.

Capitalize the titles of specific special events.

The first World Series occurred in 1903.

Unfortunately, Ron Riegel is remembered for carrying the ball seventy yards in the wrong direction during the 1929 Rose Bowl.

Mechanics

Exercise 4: Using Capital Letters

Write each of the following sentences. Place capital letters wherever they are needed and circle each word that you capitalize.

Examples

a. Congress signed the first income tax law on august 5, 1861.

Congress signed the first income tax law on (August) 5, 1861.

b. Was it Abraham Lincoln who signed the law making thanksgiving day the third thursday in november?
Was it Abraham Lincoln who signed the law making (Thanksgiving Day) the third (Thursday) in (November?)

1. The families on my block are having a garage sale this saturday.
2. We usually start going back to school the week after labor day.
3. At the wisconsin state fair this summer Sheila hopes to exhibit the calf she raised.
4. Felicia's family is remodeling an old farmhouse built during the civil war.
5. According to the weather bureau, a hurricane will hit the coast of Florida either wednesday night or early thursday morning.
6. Do you know if the middle ages occurred before or after the renaissance?
7. If the miami dolphins play in the super bowl, there won't be a seat left for the opposition.
8. The gold coast art fair is an event held in Chicago every summer.
9. In our city the public pools, parks, and beaches officially open on memorial day weekend and close the last week in august.
10. Many movies at the festival are based on life during the first world war.

Capitalize the names of specific religions, religious groups, deities (beings regarded as holy or exalted by a religious group), and holy books.

Members of the Islamic faith worship in buildings called *mosques.*

In Italy we saw many paintings of the Virgin Mary.

The Methodists in Bayfield have organized a day-care center at their church.

The Torah is the holy book of Judaism.

Note: When the word *god* does not refer to the name of a specific deity or when it refers to a deity no longer worshiped, it is not capitalized.

The ancient Egyptians worshiped a great number of gods.

Mercury was the Roman messenger god.

Capitalize the names of the planets, stars, and other heavenly bodies.

Isn't Jupiter the largest planet in our solar system?

The seven stars of the constellation Ursa Major are commonly known as the Big Dipper.

Note: The words *sun, moon,* and *earth* are rarely capitalized and never after *the.*

A solar eclipse occurs when the moon comes between the sun and the earth.

The sun filtered through the curtains and brightened the dingy room.

Capitalize the names of specific ships, trains, and airplanes.

In 1960 the *Triton* became the first atomic sub to circle the globe underwater.

The first balloon to successfully cross the Atlantic was the *Double Eagle II.*

The first American satellite was named *Explorer I.*

Mechanics

Exercise 5: Using Capital Letters

Write each of the following sentences, placing capital letters wherever they are needed. Circle each word you capitalize. Some sentences may not need new capital letters.

Examples

a. The religion founded by muhammad is called islam.

The religion founded by (Muhammad) is called (Islam.)

b. The brightest star in the northern hemisphere of the sky is arcturus.

The brightest star in the northern hemisphere of the sky is (Arcturus.)

1. In 1804 the schooner *reynard* brought the first shipment of bananas to the United States.
2. Many followers of buddhism live in the United States.
3. The ill-fated spacecraft named *skylab* fell into the sea on July 11, 1979.
4. Did you know that it takes eight minutes for light from the sun to reach the earth?
5. The last time halley's comet appeared was in April of 1986.
6. The unsinkable *titanic* sank on its first voyage in 1912.
7. It takes nearly twelve years for jupiter to travel around the sun.
8. Moses is an important figure in the jewish, muslim, and christian religions.
9. America was greatly influenced by the religious beliefs of the puritans.
10. When I visited my cousin in New York, I attended mass at the catholic church.

Capitalize the titles of specific school courses, especially those followed by a number. Capitalize languages used as course titles.

The new course on immigration is listed as History 102 in your course description booklet.

Will we study printmaking in Introduction to Art?

I have finished my Spanish assignment, but I forgot to bring home my health book.

Capitalize the first word, last word, and all important words in the titles of the following works of art.

Books, short stories, plays, and poems

Essays, short articles, and student themes

Speeches and lectures

Radio and television programs and films

Magazines, newspapers, and pamphlets

Paintings, drawings, and sculpture

Dances, songs, record albums, and other musical works

Do you think the library might have a copy of *Guitar Playing for Beginners?*	[title of book]
I hope we can find some spirituals and folk songs for our report on this album called *Great American Music*.	[title of record album]
I really enjoyed "They Called Her Moses"; it's the first story I ever read about Harriet Tubman.	[title of story]

Note: The first and last words in a title are always capitalized, but prepositions, articles, and conjunctions with fewer than five letters are usually not capitalized.

"Something Worth Living For"

"Stopping by Woods on a Snowy Evening"

Travels with Charley
A Farewell to Arms

Ten Years Before the Mast

Mechanics

> **Capitalize the specific titles of smaller parts included in larger works of art (such as chapters in a book, articles in a magazine, columns in a newspaper).**

Now that my sister has her own apartment, Dad cuts out the "Hints from Heloise" column and sends it to her.	[column in a newspaper]
I thought the most interesting chapter in *The People's Almanac* was "The Old Curiosity Shop."	[chapter in a book]

> **Capitalize nouns followed by a number or letter.**

I'm reading Chapter 9 in *Huckleberry Finn* during my study hall today.

The class will meet in Room 24.

> **Capitalize the first word and each noun in the salutation of a letter and the first word in the closing of a letter.**

Dear Dr. Johnson   Dear good Friends   Dear Danielle
Very truly yours   Sincerely yours   Fondly

Exercise 6: Using Capital Letters

Write each of the following sentences. Add capital letters where necessary and circle the words you capitalize.

Example

a. Maya Angelou's *I know why the caged bird sings* is a touching book about the life of a young girl.

Maya Angelou's (*I Know Why*) the (*Caged Bird Sings*) is a touching book about the life of a young girl.

580

1. My brother and sister both enjoyed the book *space argonauts in distress*.
2. David will sing a really funny song called "poor jud is daid" in the spring musical *oklahoma*.
3. When my mother was in junior high school, she studied both latin and french.
4. My cousin Rosa took all the photos in the pamphlet "early antiques of america."
5. Is it true that Margaret Mitchell spent ten years writing the novel *gone with the wind?*
6. José had trouble with algebra I, but he really enjoys his geometry class.
7. Saturday I'm going to take my little sister and her friend to see the movie *cinderella*.
8. I love to listen to Marian Anderson's recording of "my lord, what a morning" on this album.
9. We just learned that we live in fire district 405.
10. Today in history class we had a chance to look at a copy of the *iroquois county herald* that was dated July 19, 1908.

Review: Using Capital Letters

Write the following sentences. Capitalize all words as needed and circle the words you capitalize.

Example

a. my brother bill plays in the jazz band at harrison high school.

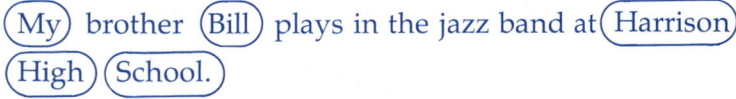

1. wayne's canary died in a chicago apartment fire on saturday, may 24.
2. the *monitor*, a ship used during the civil war, was designed by a swedish engineer.
3. the record high temperature occurring in this country was recorded in death valley, part of the mojave desert, which lies in southern california near los angeles.

Mechanics

4. in 1816 james monroe was elected president of the united states; he was formerly a lieutenant under general george washington in the american revolution.

5. on july 20, 1969, neil armstrong and edwin aldrin first stepped onto the surface of the moon.

6. the roman city of pompeii was covered over by volcanic lava from vesuvius in A.D. 79.

7. a *mosque* is a house of worship for muslims, people who believe in the religion of islam and who study the koran.

8. the highest mountain in north america is mount mckinley in the alaska range of mountains.

9. the gutenberg bible, the first book to be printed with movable type, is displayed in the library of congress.

10. the month of march is named after the roman god mars, and june is named for the goddess juno.

11. on saturday the ann arbor strawberry festival begins with mayor conlin leading the parade down prospect avenue.

12. aunt susan and uncle robert own robinson's hardware on mannerly boulevard in lubbock, texas.

13. after school i have an appointment with dr. r. s. gomez at the harris medical center.

14. Each year tourists visit the geyser called old faithful in the west's oldest national park, yellowstone national park.

15. "i'd like to thank you, sergeant, for your assistance after our accident on the chesapeake bay bridge," replied rev. fisher.

16. the navaho people, who migrated to the southwest from canada, are the largest group of native americans in the united states today.

17. the person who serves in the position of secretary of the navy is a civilian appointed by the president.

18. in december, 1964, dr. martin luther king, jr., received the nobel peace prize for his work in civil rights.

19. an award given to the author of the most distinguished contribution to american literature for children is called the newbery medal.

20. the voters of martin county elected congresswoman jordan of the democratic party in last monday's election.

Writing Focus: *Improving Capitalization in Writing*

In English, many single words and word groups are capitalized. The convention of capitalization helps both writers and readers recognize the beginning of sentences and the names of specific people, places, and things. Capitalize correctly to keep your writing clear.

Assignment: *My Kind of Town*

You have just won a trip to the city of your choice anywhere in the world. Where will you go? Why will you go there? What natural and architectural landmarks will you see? Will you travel by car, boat, plane, or bus? Will you go alone or with friends? Will you visit anyone? What will you do?

Write one or more paragraphs telling about your proposed trip. Include details about where you will go, why you chose that particular city, what you intend to do, and who and what you expect to see. Present your items in chronological order. Write for your classmates, telling them as much as you can about your upcoming trip. Your work will be evaluated for correct capitalization.

Use the following steps to complete this assignment.

A. Prewriting

Imagine you have just won a trip to the city of your choice anywhere in the world. Make a list of all the cities you have ever thought about visiting. Choose the one you most want to

Mechanics

visit. Now make a word cluster (described in Chapter 1) about your trip to the city. Include words and phrases about the city, landmarks, modes of transportation, activities, and people involved. When your cluster is complete, go back over it and number the items in the order you'll do them on your trip.

B. Writing

Use your word cluster to help you write one or more paragraphs telling about the trip to your favorite city. Don't just list the sights, people, and activities that will occupy your time; instead present your plans in a conversational way. Help your readers visualize your city and trip. As you write, pay particular attention to correct capitalization.

C. Postwriting

Revise your first draft using the following checklist.

1. Is my work an interesting account of my city and trip rather than just a list of sights, people, and activities?
2. Have I used capital letters correctly?

Proofread your work using the checklist at the back of the book. If appropriate, share your paragraphs with your classmates. Draw a map of the world and place colored pins in it to represent all the cities students chose.

4
Language Resources

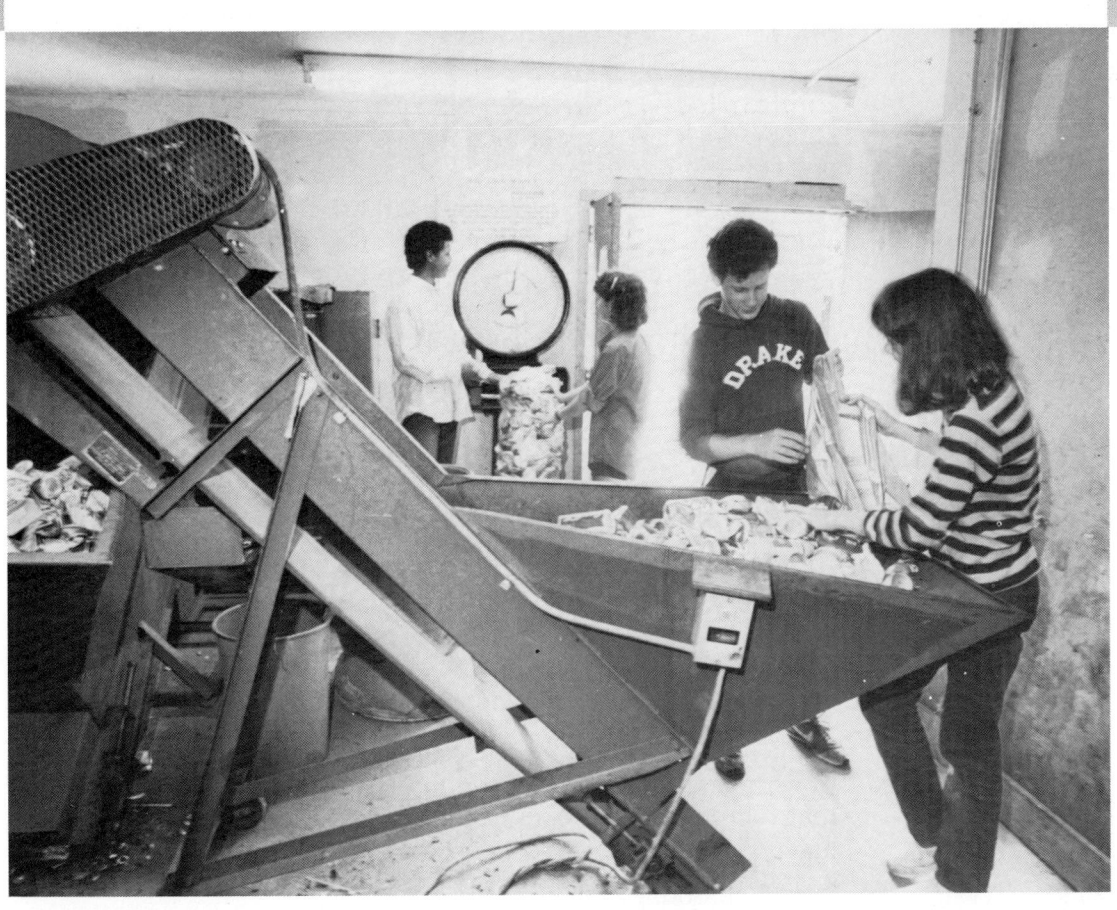

25 Vocabulary and Spelling

Vocabulary

Besides using the dictionary, there are two main ways you can learn the meanings of words: by looking at words in *context* or by examining them for their *structure*. When you look at a word in context, you study the word in its sentence and paragraph surroundings. When you look at a word's structure, you analyze the way the word is put together.

Words in Context

Context is the setting of a word—the other words that surround it.

Looking at words in their different *contexts* is important because the meanings of many words change with different settings. To understand a word you must know its context. For example, the word *dump* has different meanings in each of the following sentences.

The cleanup truck headed for the city *dump*.

Sam likes to *dump* all his clean socks in one drawer.

In the first sentence above, the word *dump* is a noun meaning "a place where refuse is left." In the second sentence *dump* is a verb with the meaning "to place carelessly." You cannot give a specific meaning for the word *dump* and for many other words unless you know their contexts.

Using Context Clues

You may not know the meanings of the *italicized* words in the following sentences, but the context of each word gives a clue to its meaning. Read each sentence and study the explanation that follows in parentheses.

The angry father *upbraided* his two children for leaving their room in such a mess.

(Even if you do not know the word *upbraided*, you do know that the father was angry at his children, so you can guess that the word has a negative meaning, such as "scold.")

It was the beginning of summer vacation, and we were *ecstatically* happy.

(You can guess from your own feelings about summer vacation that the word *ecstatically* has a positive meaning here.)

The painting was done in a *myriad* of colors, reminding me of a beautiful rainbow.

(You can guess at the meaning of *myriad* because of the comparison. If a *myriad* of colors reminds someone of a rainbow, the word must mean "many," as in "many colored.")

I will show the jury that this crime was *premeditated*, in fact, planned months before it took place.

(Here the word is almost defined in the sentence. The speaker adds that the crime was planned months ahead of time, so *premeditated* must mean "planned beforehand.")

The fabric store downtown sells only *synthetics*, like dacron, nylon, and polyester.

(There are two clues in this sentence. First, a *synthetic* must be a kind of material since the store sells fabric. Second, the sentence gives examples of synthetic materials: *dacron*, *nylon*, and *polyester*.).

Most teachers advise their students to avoid *clichés* in writing, such as "cold as ice" or "nice as can be."

(Here again are two examples of the *italicized* word. You know that "cold as ice" and "nice as can be" are often-heard phrases, and that is the definition of *cliché*.)

Mr. Osaka answered us *superficially*, with none of his usual attention to detail.

(This sentence gives a clue through contrast. Mr. Osaka usually paid attention to details, but answered in a *different* way. From this you can guess that *superficially* means "with no attention given to details.")

We expected to see only a pale light through the clouds, but the sun shone *radiantly* over the valley.

(This sentence also gives a clue through contrast. People expected to see a pale light, *but* they saw the sun shining *radiantly* instead. *Radiantly* means "brightly.")

Language Resources

The newborn kitten felt *fragile* as an eggshell.

(The clue here is a comparison with an eggshell. You know that eggshells are light and easily broken, and that is the definition of *fragile*.)

Even though Superman is supposed to be *invincible*, he can be conquered with Kryptonite.

(Because Superman can be conquered with Kryptonite, he is not *invincible*. But he is supposed to be *invincible*, so the word *invincible* must mean "unconquerable.")

Exercise 1: Using Context Clues

The following selection from an eighth-grade history book is about cowhands in the Old West. Read the selection carefully and guess the meanings of the underlined words from their context. On a sheet of paper numbered 1–10, write the meaning of each underlined word next to its corresponding number.

The Cowhand

That colorful figure, the cowhand, was the master of the long drive and the roundup. Mexican-Americans were the first cowhands. These vaqueros invented almost all of the tools of the cowhand's trade, from his broad-brimmed felt hat, his cotton bandana, and his rope lariat to his special western saddle. The word rodeo is the Spanish word for "roundup."

A cowhand's life was a hard one. The men worked long hours and received lower wages than most factory workers. Their legs became bowed from long days in the saddle. They developed permanent squints from peering into the glaring sunlight of the treeless plains. Their faces were lined and leathery, their hands calloused from constantly handling coarse ropes.

Not all cowhands were the strong, silent types portrayed in the movies by white actors. Many came from poor families or from groups outside the mainstream. About one-third of the men who worked cattle on the open range were either Mexican-Americans or Blacks.

Every item of the cowhand's clothes and equipment served a necessary function. The wide brim of his "ten gallon hat" could be turned down to shade his eyes or drain off rainfall. His bandana could be tied over his nose and mouth to keep out the dust raised by the pounding hooves of countless cattle. The bandana also served as a towel, a napkin, a bandage, and a handkerchief. Cowhands sometimes wore leather trousers, called chaps, over regular overalls. Chaps were fastened to a broad belt buckled at the back. They protected a rider's legs from injury if he fell from his horse or when he had to ride through cactus, sagebrush, or other thorny plants.

The cowhand's western saddle had a sturdy horn, or pommel, for help in roping powerful steers and horses. These western saddles were heavy, but comfortable. A cowhand could sleep in the saddle while he rode. At night his saddle became a pillow and his saddlecloth a blanket when he stretched out beside the campfire and settled down to sleep.

Cowhands drank potfuls of thick, strong coffee to stay awake on the trail. They ate mostly stews, kidney beans, biscuits, and cornbread.

It was a lonely life. This explains why cowhands were famous for letting off steam when they reached cattle towns such as Dodge City, Kansas, the "Cowboy's Capital." Many cowhands were big drinkers and heavy gamblers when they came to town. Sometimes there were brawls and gunfights. But the violence and disorder have been exaggerated. Life in the West was much calmer and more orderly than it is usually pictured in the movies. Nevertheless, many cattle towns did have "boot hills"—cemeteries for those who "died with their boots on," either from overwork or on a spree.[1]

Word Structure

Studying the *structure* of a word means examining its different parts.

Word parts are called *roots*, *prefixes*, and *suffixes*. The word *root* means "source" or "origin." Just as plants grow from their roots, words can grow from roots also. For example, the word *play* is a root. By adding the letters *re-* to this root, you make the word *replay*, or by adding the letters *-ful*, you make *playful*. What are the roots in each of the following words?

goodness	premature	unthinkable
joyous	review	unable

The roots in the preceding words are *good, joy, think, mature, view,* and *able*. New words can be made by putting groups of letters either before or after the root.

---

[1]From *American History* by John Garraty, copyright © 1982 by Harcourt Brace Jovanovich, Inc. Reprinted by permission of the publisher.

Language Resources

> **Letters added before a root are called** *prefixes*. **Letters added after the root are called** *suffixes*.

In the words below, the prefixes and suffixes are in **boldface**. How do the roots of these words differ from those in the list on page 589?

consider   dep**th**
defy   port**able**
examine   mak**er**

Removing the prefixes or suffixes from the above words leaves these roots: *-sider, -fy, -amine, dep-, port-, mak-*. Not all roots are complete words by themselves.

Prefixes

The meanings of prefixes do not change when they are added to different word roots. For example, the prefix *pre-* always has the meaning "before." *Preschool* means "before school"; *preview* means "to see before"; *preflight* means "before a flight," and so on. The prefixes in the list below are some of the often-used ones. Knowing these prefixes and their meanings can help you understand the meanings of many new words. The spelling of a root word does not change when a prefix is added to it.

Prefix	Meaning	Example
auto-	self	automatic
bi-	twice *or* two	bicycle
circum-	around *or* on all sides	circumference
de-	reversal *or* undoing	decrease
dis-	not *or* lack	distrust
ex-	removal out of *or* from	exclude
extra-	outside a boundary *or* scope	extraordinary
im-	not	impolite
mis-	error *or* wrongness; lack of	mistrust
multi-	many *or* much	multimedia

pre-	before	prevent
semi-	half *or* partly	semicircle

Exercise 2: Using Prefixes

Each of the *italicized* words in the following sentences is formed with a prefix. Using the meanings for these prefixes given above, guess the meaning of the *italicized* word. Then write your definition on a sheet of paper numbered 1–10.

Examples

a. This year our basketball team made it to the *semifinals*. Semifinals means the next to the last round of games.

b. The forecasters *misjudged* the outcome of the poll. Misjudged means guessed incorrectly.

1. A paper with George Washington's *autograph* would sell for a fortune.
2. The *bicolored* map showed each of the countries in the world.
3. We tried to *circumvent* the rules, but we were told there would be no exceptions.
4. Some people believe that *extraterrestrial* beings in UFO's have visited the earth.
5. The fire fighter was *demoted* because of his poor performance on duty.
6. The crowd looked on with *disbelief* as George Willig, the "human fly," climbed the tall building.
7. The *ex-President* of the United States maintains an office at government expense.
8. An old television show, *Mission Impossible*, is now being *rerun* on many television stations.
9. Because of a *miscalculation* the capsule carrying the astronaut back to earth landed many kilometers from the ship.
10. The woman succeeded beyond her wildest dreams, becoming a *multimillionaire* before she was thirty.

Suffixes

Prefixes and suffixes both add meanings to word roots, but suffixes can also change a word from one part of speech to another. For example, the verb *write* becomes the noun *writer* when the suffix *-er* is added. The adjective *happy* becomes the adverb *happily* with the suffix *-ly*.

The meanings of suffixes stay the same when they are added to different words, but the spellings of the root words sometimes change. When the suffix *-ly* is added to *happy*, for example, the *y* changes to an *i: happily*. When the suffix *-fy* is added to *dignity*, the *ty* is dropped: *dignify*. The following list presents some of the most frequently used suffixes and their definitions.

Suffix	Definition	Example
-ness	a quality *or* state of being	silliness
-ity, -ty	state *or* quality	humidity
-ment	product, action, *or* state	amusement
-ish	like	childish
-able, -ible	capable, worthy of, *or* inclined to	knowledgeable
-er, -or	one who	jogger
-en	to be; made of	brighten
-fy	making *or* forming into	beautify
-ize	cause to be *or* become; make into	terrorize
-ous	full of *or* having	joyous

Exercise 3: Using Suffixes

The *italicized* word in each of the following sentences is formed with a suffix. Using the above list of suffixes and definitions, decide what each *italicized* word means. On a sheet of paper numbered 1–10, write the suffix in each word and its meaning. Then write the meaning of the word with its suffix. Use your dictionary to check your answers.

Example

a. The *possibility* of the computer's taking over the spaceship worried Commander Medley.

Suffix and Its Definition **Definition of Word**

-ity: state or condition   condition of being possible

1. Just over the finish line, one of the *runners* collapsed from exhaustion.
2. When Carlos saw the half-eaten roast on the floor and the *sheepish* look on the dog's face, he knew immediately what had happened.
3. Eating a hot dog while watching a good baseball game was Martha Jean's idea of *enjoyment*.
4. The *denseness* of the fog made it impossible for Count Dracula to see his old enemy.
5. When he thought of the *immensity* of the job before him, David was ready to give up.
6. When the plane hit the water, the passengers were wearing *inflatable* life preservers.
7. While the policewoman worked to free him, the victim, his face *ashen*, begged her to hurry.
8. So she would not *jeopardize* her chance at the scholarship, Joanna studied hard every night.
9. The huge, old trunk was almost *unmanageable*, but the movers were finally able to struggle up the stairs with it.
10. The park ranger was already angry, and he felt his anger *intensify* when the tourist began to tease the bear.

Using Synonyms

Synonyms are words that have similar meanings.

No two words mean exactly the same thing, so it is important to understand how synonyms differ. For example, consider the following sentences.

Language Resources

"It is time for dinner," *shouted* Allen.

"It is time for dinner," *screamed* Allen.

Shout and *scream* are synonyms because they share the meaning "a loud cry." Yet you probably know from experience that *shout* and *scream* are not identical. *Shout* is used when people are far away and cannot hear; *scream* is used to show anger or fright.

You can usually tell which synonym to use by looking at the word's context. For example, in the three sentences below, Carlos is in a hurry to meet someone. Which of the *italicized* synonyms is best for this context?

Carlos *walked* down Central Street.

Carlos *ambled* down Central Street.

Carlos *strode* down Central Street.

Walk by itself is not a very descriptive word. *Amble* means "to walk slowly, without purpose" and does not fit the context of the sentence. *Carlos strode* gives the best picture of Carlos hurrying down the street, because *stride* means "to walk with long steps."

In the three sentences below, the scouts try to keep warm. Which of the *italicized* words best describes what they did?

The scouts *gathered* together for warmth under the tent.

The scouts *crowded* together for warmth under the tent.

The scouts *huddled* together for warmth under the tent.

The *italicized* words are synonyms, and all make sense in the context of the sentence. Only the word *huddled*, however, has the extra meaning "moving together for protection," so *huddled* is the best choice for this sentence. Whenever you are unsure about a synonym, check your dictionary for the exact meaning of each word.

In some cases, even though words are synonyms, they cannot be substituted for one another. For example, the words *fell* and *toppled* are synonyms because they share the same basic meaning of "falling," but *toppled* is a more exact word. In which of the sentences below is a synonym used incorrectly?

The rain *fell* on the roof.

The rain *toppled* on the roof.

The rain toppled on the roof does not sound right because *topple* has the specific meaning of "something falling over because it is *top*heavy." A tree may *topple*, bowling pins may *topple*, but not rain.

The words *dodge* and *flinch* share the same basic meaning of "moving away from something," but the word *flinch* is more specific because it means "moving away from something painful." You would write, "The girl did not *flinch* when it was her turn to be vaccinated," but not "The girl did not *dodge* when it was her turn to be vaccinated."

Exercise 4: Choosing Synonyms

In each of the following sentences, there are two synonyms in parentheses. On a sheet of paper numbered 1–10, copy each sentence, inserting the appropriate synonym. Underline the one you chose. Your teacher may ask you to explain your choice.

Examples

a. Many gardeners feel that the orchid is the (cutest/most beautiful) flower they grow.
Many gardeners feel that the orchid is the most beautiful flower they grow.

b. The determined pilgrims had a long and arduous (journey/trip) ahead of them.
The determined pilgrims had a long and arduous journey ahead of them.

1. My father taught me that it is wrong to (lie/falsify).
2. For almost fifty years the criminal kept (hidden/covered) the secret of the buried treasure.
3. The store manager said that she would (dispatch/send) someone over with the keys this afternoon.
4. The rabbit stayed motionless except for a quick (jerk/twitch) of its nose.
5. The doctor gave the newborn infant a quick (slap/hit) to start its breathing.
6. As president of the student council, I am happy to (give/present) your class this year's award for exemplary behavior.

7. All that day Joseph moved deeper into the woods, (looking for/stalking) the wild deer.

8. Before a big test I am usually so (excited/nervous) that I can hardly eat breakfast.

9. The prisoners were led one by one to the enormous (dungeon/prison) beneath the castle.

10. It is easy to get lost in the desert because the (moving/drifting) sands cover your footprints right away.

Spelling

Whether you write just a few sentences or several paragraphs, one of the first things a reader often notices is your spelling. Correct spelling suggests that the writer is responsible and concerned; poor spelling conveys the opposite impression. In this chapter you will learn how to improve your spelling skills.

Good Spelling Habits

Keep a list of the words that are spelling problems for you.

Write the word as you misspelled it; in a second column write the correct spelling. Then underline the letters in the word that are causing you difficulty. (You may want to keep track of the number of times you misspell the word, in a third column.) Review your personal spelling list frequently. When you proofread a piece of writing, check the list closely to be certain you avoid making the same errors you made in the past.

Pronounce words correctly.

You may be misspelling some words because you are not pronouncing them correctly. For example, if you pronounce *surprise* as *suprise*, *athlete* as *athalete*, or *grapefruit* as *greatfruit*, you may also misspell these words. Make a list of any words that you mispronounce and work on saying them clearly and correctly every day for a week. Remember that a dictionary provides information about pronunciation immediately after the entry word.

Learn to spell by analyzing the word's structure.

Spelling a long word is usually easier if you separate it into syllables. Most syllables have only three or four letters, and often only one syllable may cause the spelling problem. If the longer word is formed from a root word to which a prefix or suffix is added, keep the spelling rules for the addition of prefixes and suffixes in mind.

Consult your dictionary frequently.

Look up the word as you have spelled it. If it does not appear in the dictionary under that spelling, you are probably misspelling it. Think of other ways the word might be spelled and look up these. Remember the different letter or letter combinations that make the same sound. Once you become familiar with the dictionary, looking up a word takes only a few seconds.

Always proofread what you write.

When they write a first draft, most writers concentrate on expressing their ideas, but careful writers also reread what they have written, looking closely at the spelling of each word. When they are not sure a word is spelled correctly, they circle or underline the word lightly and check with a dictionary.

To understand the spelling rules in this chapter, you should be familiar with the following terms, which are used to describe words and word structure.

Vowel:	The letters *a, e, i, o, u,* and sometimes *y* are the *vowel* sounds in the English alphabet.
Consonant:	Letters of the English alphabet other than vowels are called *consonants*.
Syllable:	A *syllable* is a unit of language, is spoken in one breath, and contains a vowel sound (*pat·tern, sand·pa·per*).

Language Resources

Accent: *Accent* is the stress or emphasis placed on one syllable of a word to make that syllable sound louder than the other syllables (*san·i·ta'·tion, tan'·ta·lize*).

Prefix: A *prefix* is a group of letters that is added to the beginning of a word and that changes the meaning of that word: *un-* (prefix) + *like* (root word) = *unlike*; *re-* (prefix) + *charge* (root word) = *recharge*.

Suffix: A *suffix* is a letter or group of letters that is added to the end of a word and that alters the meaning or use: *truth* (root word) + *-ful* (suffix) = *truthful*; *happy* (root word) + *-ly* (suffix) = *happily*.

Helpful Spelling Rules

The following spelling rules will help you to improve as a speller. Although there are exceptions to some of them, the rules are true in many cases. Learn each rule and then concentrate on the few exceptions.

Words with ie, ei, *and the* seed *Sound*

When a word contains an *ei* or *ie* combination that sounds like the long *e* in *meet* (ē), write *ie* except after *c*.

ie sounded as long *e*:	*belief, relief, yield*
ei after *c*:	*conceive, receive, ceiling*
Exceptions:	*either, neither, leisure, seize, sheik*

When a word contains an *ei* or *ie* combination that does not sound like a long *e* (ē), write *ei*, especially if the sound is long *a* (ā).

ei not sounded as long *e*:	*foreign, their*
ei sounded as long *a*:	*weight, eight, rein*
Exceptions:	*mischief, handkerchief, friend*

Words ending with a final syllable that is pronounced like the word *seed* are spelled in one of three ways:

1	2	3
supersede	exceed	accede
	proceed	concede
	succeed	recede
		secede

Only one word in the English language—*supersede*—is spelled with a *-sede* ending. Only three words (*exceed, proceed,* and *succeed*) are spelled with a *-ceed* ending. (Concentrate on remembering that the *-ceed* ending is used only with these three common words.) All other words with an ending that sounds like the word *seed* fall into Column 3 and are spelled with a *-cede* ending.

Exercise 5: Spelling Words with ie, ei, *or the* seed *Sound*

Write each of the following sentences and supply the correct *ei* or *ie* combination or *-cede, -ceed,* or *-sede* in each underlined word. Underline the completed word.

Examples

a. Could you give me a br__f explanation of this process so I can include it in my report?

Could you give me a brief explanation of this process so I can include it in my report?

b. Michael got a ticket for ex____ing the speed limit.

Michael got a ticket for exceeding the speed limit.

1. Several of her fr__nds visited my sister during her stay in the hospital.

Language Resources

2. Manuel's uncle, who is a pr___st, has offered to conduct the marriage ceremony.

3. My family and I have always bel___ved that hard work is its own reward.

4. Yesterday my grandmother showed me how to paint the c___ling in my bedroom.

5. What exactly is the h___ght of the mountain we will be hiking up tomorrow?

6. Because my brother works out with weights, his strength super___s mine.

7. After much practice, I have finally suc___ed in beating my father at tennis.

8. The campaign speeches of the candidates pre___ our voting.

9. When the tide re___s, many beautiful shells are left on the beach.

10. After the face-off, the hockey game will pro___.

Adding Prefixes

A prefix added to a root word does not change the spelling of the root word.

Prefix +	Root	
dis-	appear	Juan's latest magic trick is making his rabbit *disappear*.
dis-	satisfied	Because she was *dissatisfied* with the electrician's previous work, my mom fixed the lamp herself.
im-	mobilize	Broken bones heal very quickly when they are *immobilized* in a cast.

When a prefix is added to a proper noun or proper adjective, a hyphen follows the prefix. The prefix is not capitalized.

25 Vocabulary and Spelling

Prefix	+	Root	
anti-		Nazi	anti-Nazi
pre-		Revolutionary	pre-Revolutionary
un-		American	un-American

When the prefix *re-* is used to mean "again," a hyphen follows the prefix if the word could be confused with another that is spelled the same way.

re-cover	=to cover again	recover	= to get back or to regain one's health
re-creation	=a second creation	recreation	=a diversion
re-lease	= to lease again	release	= to free

Exercise 6: Spelling Words with Prefixes

Write each of the sentences on the next page, supplying a word in each blank with the same meaning as the words in parentheses. (The word you supply should be a combination of one of the following prefixes and the *italicized* word.) Underline your answer. Use a dictionary for help with the meanings of prefixes.

Prefixes

anti-	im-	over-
dis-	in-	re-
il-	mis-	un-

Examples

a. It is _____ to burn leaves in most cities. (not *legal*)
   It is <u>illegal</u> to burn leaves in most cities.

b. I think our new puppy whimpers because it's still _____ with its new surroundings. (not *familiar*)
   I think our new puppy whimpers because it's still <u>unfamiliar</u> with its new surroundings.

601

Language Resources

1. The writing in this hundred-year-old diary is so faint it's almost _____. (not *legible*)
2. Because it was still spotty, Tom and I _____ the silverware before the party. (*cleaned* again)
3. I think I've _____ my math book; it's not at home and it's not in my locker. (*placed* incorrectly)
4. It is _____ that Ms. Helm will return from her business trip before Saturday's meeting. (not *likely*)
5. After I saw Emanuel's paintings, mine seemed ordinary and _____. (not *imaginative*)
6. I believe their company voluntarily installed _____ devices on all its heavy equipment. (against *pollution*)
7. This _____ electrical outlet is something we must change; it's a dangerous fire hazard. (*loaded* too greatly)
8. Most of the eighth-grade class agreed that the two students' comments during assembly were rude and _____. (not *mature*)
9. Although she is still _____ with some of the power tools, Andrea is quickly becoming a good carpenter. (not *experienced*)
10. The student council at our junior high school has decided to set up a _____ center in the downtown area. (*cycling* again)

Adding Suffixes

When a root word ends with an *e*, drop the final *e* before adding a suffix beginning with a vowel.

Root Word +	Suffix	
drive	-ing	Mother is no longer *driving* to work; she says it is more economical to take the bus.
fame	-ous	I just read an excellent biography about the *famous* Dr. Martin Luther King, Jr.

Note: When the suffix begins with a consonant, do not drop the final *e* from the root word.

care	+	-ful	Be very *careful* where you store this flammable paint remover.

Exceptions: (words that keep the *e*): *mileage, noticeable, peaceable*

(words that drop the *e*): *ninth, argument, duly, judgment, truly*

When a root word ends with a *y* preceded by a consonant, change the *y* to *i*.

Root Word	+	Suffix	
marry		-ed	My parents were *married* during a hurricane.
hurry		-ed	I *hurried* upstairs to comfort the crying baby.

Exceptions: *daily* (day + ly), *dryly* (dry + ly), *gaily* (gay + ly), *shyly* (shy + ly), *slyly* (sly + ly), *wryly* (wry + ly)
Note: When the suffix begins with an *i*, do not drop the final *y*.

Root Word	+	Suffix	
worry		-ing	I think David is *worrying* too much about Saturday's championship game.
bury		-ing	*Burying* nuts is vital to a squirrel's survival during winter.

When a root word of one syllable ends with a single consonant preceded by a single vowel, double the final consonant before adding a suffix beginning with a vowel.

Language Resources

Root Word	+	Suffix	
plan	+	-ing	Mrs. Chen, our neighbor, has been appointed to the city's *planning* commission.
slip	+	-ery	If the sidewalk is *slippery*, sprinkle some salt on the icy spots.

Exercise 7: Spelling Words with Suffixes

Read the examples below and on a sheet of paper write each of the following sentences and supply the correctly spelled form of the root word and suffix given in parentheses. Underline the word you form.

Examples

a. Petunia is one of the _____ cats I've ever seen; all she does is sit in the sun and sleep. (lazy + est)

Petunia is one of the <u>laziest</u> cats I've ever seen; all she does is sit in the sun and sleep.

b. The walls of the canyon _____ abruptly to the raging river below. (drop + ed)

The walls of the canyon <u>dropped</u> abruptly to the raging river below.

1. Almost _____ students from our local college have volunteered to help run the Special Olympics the city is sponsoring. (nine + ty)

2. My cousin Tania, who is blind, always enjoys ice-_____ with my brother and me. (skate + ing)

3. Let's move the _____ boxes first before we get too tired. (heavy + est)

4. Shortly after his _____ with Fernando, Tom decided that being upset with his friend was one of the _____ mistakes he'd ever made. (argue + ment), (silly + est)

5. No one has ever fully explained the _____ disappearance of the _____ aviator, Amelia Earhart. (mystery + ous), (fame + ous)

6. Because we _____ our trip so carefully, it was a complete success. (plan + ed)
7. Dad will be _____ either corn or broccoli for dinner. (cook + ing)
8. Carlotta caught a fly ball and _____ in three runs in Saturday's game. (bat + ed)
9. My aunt says the hardest part of working for a newspaper is _____ the deadlines. (meet + ing)
10. I am _____ an unusual book for my English class. (read + ing)

26 Changes in Language

The Dawn of the English Language

The country you know today as England was called *Britannia* 1,500 years ago. The people who had lived there the longest at that time, called the *Celts*, had been ruled for several hundred years by the Roman Empire. About 1,500 years ago, however, the Romans began to withdraw from Britannia, and tribes called the *Picts* and *Scots* began raiding the country. Needing help, the Celts turned to the *Saxons*, *Angles*, and *Jutes*, tribes from northern Europe. The Picts and Scots were defeated, but the Saxons, Angles, and Jutes did not go home when the job was completed; instead, they remained to settle in Britannia.

All of the people in this area were descendants of the Indo-Europeans. The Saxons, Angles, and Jutes spoke forms of the Indo-European language called *Germanic*. When they settled in Britannia, this Germanic language, which came to be called *Anglo-Saxon* or *Old English*, replaced the Celtic language. *Old English* is the earliest form of the English language you speak and write today.

The Old English of 1,500 years ago looks and sounds very different from Modern English, but many words in your everyday vocabulary were first used hundreds of years ago by people speaking the Old English language. The words changed in form over the years but can be traced back to their Old English source. Each time you speak or write one of these words, you strengthen the link that holds you to your language past.

Exercise 1: *Identifying Old English Words*

Each of the words in Column A is an Old English word; the words in Column B are the forms of those words you use today. Find the word in Column B that is the Modern English form of each word in Column A. Then on a sheet of paper numbered 1–10, write the Modern English word that evolved from each Old English word.

Example

a. fōt = foot

A. Old English Words
1. cild
2. æppel
3. uppe
4. swingan
5. dēad
6. twā
7. mūs
8. fether
9. fēawe
10. thurst

B. Modern English Words
swing
dead
feather
child
two
few
thirst
up
apple
mouse

Language Changes

The stages in the development of the English language are called *Old English*, *Middle English*, and *Modern English*. In each of these stages, the language was English, but it changed in many ways.

A *living language* is a language that is being spoken and written. Because the English language has been a living language for some 1,500 years, it has undergone many changes. Word meanings, spellings, and pronunciations have changed.

Speakers are often unaware of how meanings change because the change is so slow. For example, in Old English the word *mōd* meant many things: heart, mind, spirit. Its modern form is *mood*, and the modern meaning is "a mental state." Here are other examples of how words have changed their meanings from very early times to the present:

silly: In Old English the word *sælig* meant "happy" or "blessed." Later the word came to mean "blessed fool" and finally just "fool" or "foolish."

nice: In Middle English the word *nice* meant "strange," "lazy," or "foolish." Today the word has a positive meaning.

awful: In Middle English the word *awful* meant "very impressive." Today the word may mean "terrible" or "frightening to an extreme degree."

Language Resources

Exercise 2: Finding Original Word Meanings

The following words have changed meanings over the years. Use your dictionary or the unabridged dictionary in your library to find the earliest meanings of these words. Write these meanings on a sheet of paper.

1. villain
2. craft
3. corn (the plant)
4. person
5. rival
6. gray
7. cup
8. thing
9. steward
10. govern

Word Borrowing

Over the years many Old English words were lost, but many thousands more were added, some by "borrowing" from the vocabularies of other languages.

In 55 B.C. Julius Caesar, a Roman emperor, sent soldiers to establish a colony on the island of Britain. During the 400 years or so that they remained, the Romans built cities, roads, fortresses, and theaters; set up a system of government; coined money; and helped to change the English language. In the fifth century A.D. the Romans left England, but by that time the British had adopted many Latin words into their own language.

Another influence on the English language during those early years was the Scandinavian languages. The Vikings, an adventuresome people from today's countries of Norway, Sweden, and Denmark, began to invade England about the last part of the eighth century. Gradually, however, they settled in England, becoming a part of the British population. Their language mixed in with English, giving the English language some of its most-used words.

Then, in A.D. 1066, a French-speaking people from Normandy, an area in northern France, conquered the English. For nearly 300 years after that, both French and English were spoken in England, with the result that many French words became part of the English language.

About this same time Europeans were beginning to explore other parts of the world. British admirals and soldiers led expeditions to Africa, western Europe, Asia, and the North and South American continents, where they learned to speak the native languages or at least adopted some of the words into English. Crusaders went on pilgrimages to the Holy Land of Palestine, where they saw for the first time spices, cloths, and perfumes that they often had to use a Turkish or Arabic word to describe. These words also became a part of English.

Exercise 3: *Understanding Word Borrowing*

Below is a list of words the English language "borrowed" from other languages. Use your dictionary to find the language from which the word came into English and the meaning of the word in that language.

1. algebra
2. hula
3. coyote
4. cyclone
5. puppy
6. alibi
7. yam
8. tulip
9. kindergarten
10. curfew

Other Word Sources

Not all words in the English language are old; new words are created every day. These words may be acronyms, compound words, shortened words, or people's names. Brand names that become a part of everyday vocabulary are another source of the many new entries into the English language.

An *acronym* is a word made up of the first letters of a series of words. For example, *scuba*, as in *scuba diving* or *scuba gear*, is made up of the first letters of these words: *self-contained underwater breathing apparatus*. UNESCO stands for **U**nited **Na**tions **E**ducational, **S**cientific, and **C**ultural **O**rganization; radar stands for **ra**dio **d**etecting **a**nd **r**anging.

Two or more existing words are sometimes combined to make a compound word. Words that came into English this way are *broadcast, baby-sit, Boy Scout, kickoff, loudspeaker, airplane, pan-fry,* and *bowlegged*.

New words often come into the language when longer words are shortened. The word *bus*, for example, was originally *omnibus*. Since the new word is made by clipping, or shortening, the old one, these new words are called *clipped forms*. Here are more examples of clipped forms:

Clipped Form	**Original Word**
wig	periwig

Language Resources

Clipped Form	Original Word
pants	pantaloons
phone	telephone
zoo	zoological garden
car	motorcar
ad	advertisement
lab	laboratory
exam	examination
flu	influenza

Another interesting source of words is people's names. *Saxophone*, a musical instrument, has this name because a man named Sax invented it. The word *sideburns* came into English because a general named Ambrose E. Burnside, who fought for the North in the Civil War, wore his hair in front of his ears. He was much admired, and his hairstyle was copied. Later, people reversed the word and called hair worn in this way *sideburns*. If you have ever owned a *teddy* bear as a child, you owe that name to President Theodore Roosevelt, the twenty-sixth President of the United States, who once refused to shoot a small bear. The story circulated, and toy makers made the "teddy bear."

Words that were once *brand names* (product names owned by a company), sometimes become new, common words in the English language. The word *aspirin*, for example, was once a brand name for one company's pain reliever; today the word means any brand of pain reliever. Companies are usually pleased when their brand names are used this way. Here are other words that were once brand names but are now commonly used:

calico	kerosene	nylon
cellophane	linoleum	raisin bran
escalator	mimeograph	trampoline

Exercise 4: Understanding Word Sources

Following is a list of words that came into the English language as new words. Use your dictionary to find out how each word became a part of the English language. If your teacher asks you to, write two or three sentences describing the origin of each word.

1. derringer
2. hamburger
3. pasteurize
4. maverick
5. supersonic
6. AWOL
7. science fiction
8. Uncle Sam
9. pro
10. spaceport

Language Differences: Dialects

The speech of your classmates probably sounds more like your own than that of teenagers living in other parts of the country. If it does, it is because you share the same group *dialect*.

A *dialect* is a way of speaking shared by a group of people.

If you went to England today, you would find British speech very different from yours because *American English* is a separate dialect from *British English*. The first English settlers brought their British English with them when they came to the United States, but once they were isolated from their native country, this language began to change. Over the years the British English of the early settlers changed to become American English.

A *regional dialect* is a way of speaking shared by people living in a particular area.

Regional dialects are the reason New Englanders speak differently from people living in the West or the South. People from different regions often differ in their pronunciation. Pronunciation includes such things as how fast or slow a person speaks, how he or she pronounces vowel and consonant sounds, and whether or not certain sounds are dropped or added. Scholars who study dialects can usually determine a person's origins, or perhaps even the current residence, by listening to his or her speech.

Dialects also differ in vocabulary. In the northeastern states you might carry a *pail*, but Southern and Midland speakers carry a *bucket*. A New England *johnnycake* is what a person from Kansas calls *corn bread*. In the Great Lakes region and northern Mississippi Valley area, people sit on their front *stoops*, but in the South the structure is called a *verandah* and in the Midwest a *porch*.

Dialects also differ in grammar and usage. In Charleston, South Carolina, you might hear, "He lives *in* King Street" and "We stood *on* line." The Midland dialect includes, "I *clumb* up the ladder" (past tense for *climb*) and "That's *all the further* I'll go," instead of "That's *as far as* I'll go." In the Northern states you might hear, "She isn't *to* home," rather than "She isn't *at* home."

Everyone has some regional dialect, with the kinds of differences you read about in this section. When people go to school, however, or when they move from place to place, they tend to lose some of their dialects, which is why you may hear someone say about a person, "She's from the South, but she doesn't talk like a Southerner."

Standard American English

In the United States today many people believe Standard English to be the *preferred* dialect. This means that it is the dialect most accepted in schools and businesses. It is also the dialect most often used by radio and television commentators and by newspaper reporters.

Standard English has its roots in fourteenth-century London. During the fourteenth century, London, the largest city in England, was the cultural center of the country. For that reason, the London way of speaking was adopted by many educated Britishers as the "standard" dialect. When early settlers from this area brought the London speech with them, it retained its status, and although it became "Americanized," it was the early form of what is today called Standard American English. Standard British English has, of course, changed over the years.

Standard English, like other dialects, has rules for producing sentences, which you studied in Unit II, "Grammar and Usage." Although it is important to learn the features of Standard English, it would be incorrect to think of this dialect as "better" than any other. In fact, the words *good* and *bad* have nothing to do with dialects; they have more to do with how language is used. A person who uses language in harmful ways can do so in any dialect, and a person who uses language creatively can do so in any dialect.

In this book the term *Edited Standard English* (*ESE*) is used to refer to the written form of Standard American English. ESE is writing that has been carefully checked for errors and is the writing that you use in school, will use in other educational settings, hear on the radio and TV, read in publications, and will later use in your dealings with the business world. In Unit II of this book, "Grammar and Usage" you learned the features of ESE.

Choosing Your Language

Dialects are only one reason people sound different from each other. Another reason that people sound different is that they may choose between *informal* and *formal* English.

***Informal English* is the English you use most often when talking with friends and relatives or when writing personal letters and notes to friends.**

Informal English usually has short sentences and many *colloquial* and *slang words*. *Colloquial words* are widely used informal words, such as *act up* and *the creeps:* "He's always acting up." "She gives me the creeps." *Slang words* are words that are used within groups of people. Sometimes, slang words become an accepted part of English, but often they are forgotten after several years. In the 1920s, for example, young people who wanted to express approval might have said, "It's the bees' knees"; in the 1970s, however, young people probably would have said, "That's neat."

Model: *Informal English*

Informal English may also have features that are not a part of Edited Standard English. Following is an example of informal English from the book *I Wish I Could Give My Son a Wild Raccoon*, a collection of interviews by students with people from across the country. In the interview a man named Jack Pate from Albany, Texas, talks about wanting to be a cowboy.

> I've been riding more or less all my life. I was just like all kids. I was always doing something I shouldn't-a done. I used to run off from school and things like that. The first day's work I ever drew wages for in my life, oh, I was probably nine. All I did was hold cuts. I got a dollar a day. I was in the money! I

Language Resources

helped them five days and that five dollars looked like five big bicycle wheels to me.[1]

Notice that Jack Pate uses the informal word *kids* for children and the word *cuts*, a cowboy slang word for cattle that have been separated from the herd. The speaker also uses features that are not a part of Edited Standard English: "I shouldn't-a done."

Formal English **is the English you use most often in the writing you do now in school and will do later in the business world.**

Formal English has few colloquial words, no slang words, and has almost all of the features of Edited Standard English.

Model: Formal English

Here is an example of formal English from J. Frank Dobie's book *A Vaquero of the Brush Country*. This piece of writing is also about cowboys, but the English differs from that in Jack Pate's interview. What are the differences?

> Many a cowboy has spread his bandanna, perhaps none too clean itself, over dirty, muddy water and used it as a strainer to drink through; sometimes he used it as a cup towel, which he called a "drying rag." If the bandanna was dirty, it was probably not so dirty as the other apparel of the cowboy, for when he came to a hole of water, he was wont to dismount and wash out his handkerchief, letting it dry while he rode along, holding it in his hand or spread over his hat. Often he wore it under his hat in order to help keep his head cool. At other times, in the face of a fierce gale, he used it to tie down his hat. The bandanna made a good sling for a broken arm; it made a good bandage for a blood wound.[2]

Exercise 5: Using Formal and Informal English

Each of the situations in the following list calls for a decision about the kind of English to use. Select one of them and decide

---

[1] Excerpt from "I'd Rather be a Cowboy Than Anything" by Jack Pate from the book *I Wish I Could Give My Son a Wild Raccoon* by Eliot Wigginton. Copyright © 1976 by Reading Is Fundamental. Reprinted by permission of Doubleday & Company, Inc.

[2] From *A Vaquero of the Brush Country* by J. Frank Dobie. Copyright 1929; copyright © renewed 1957 by J. Frank Dobie. By permission of Little, Brown and Company.

whether you should use formal or informal English. Then do the writing called for in that situation. Make up any information that you need.

1. A personal letter to a friend about your experiences at school this week
2. A letter of application for a part-time job you want this summer
3. A note to a parent, explaining why you will be home late from school tomorrow afternoon
4. A report to your principal from your student council committee, explaining why you think the lunch period should be longer
5. A note to your teacher, explaining why your homework is late
6. A short report for your science class on the "radar" used by bats
7. A note to a neighbor, apologizing for having ridden your bicycle through a flower bed
8. A note to an ill classmate about work missed during the last two weeks of English class
9. A thank-you note to a relative who sent you a birthday gift
10. An entry in your Writer's Notebook

27 Library Skills

The many kinds of materials libraries have are arranged so that they are easy to find and use. The word *arrange* comes from a Latin word meaning "to set in a row," and that is exactly how libraries keep their books in order. In this chapter you will learn the system many libraries use to file books and other materials so that it will be easy for you to find just what you are looking for.

The Dewey Decimal System

In 1876 a librarian named Melvil Dewey improved his library's filing system by inventing what is known as the *Dewey decimal system* of classification, a system still used by most school libraries today.

The Dewey decimal system is for works of nonfiction only.

The Dewey decimal system divides all nonfiction books into ten categories, with a range of numbers for each category. The categories and numbers are usually posted in the library so that you can easily refer to them. The following list gives the major categories and their numbers:

000–099	General Works	Reference books, such as encyclopedias, magazines, and journals
100–199	Philosophy	Includes psychology
200–299	Religion	Includes Holy books, such as the Bible and the Koran, and works on religion and mythology

300–399	Social Sciences	Includes economics, education, government, law, fairy tales, folklore, and legends
400–499	Language	Includes English and other dictionaries and grammars
500–599	Science	Includes animals, anthropology, astronomy, biology, botany, chemistry, mathematics, and physics
600–699	Technology	Includes agriculture, home economics, health, aviation, business, television, and engineering
700–799	The Arts	Includes fine arts, painting and sculpture, movies, photography, recreation, and sports
800–899	Literature	Includes poetry, plays, essays, and literary criticism
900–999	History	Includes travel history, geography, and collective biography

Exercise 1: Using the Dewey Decimal System

On a sheet of paper numbered 1–10, write the correct Dewey decimal category number and name for each of the following nonfiction books.

Examples

a. *The Sculpture of Michelangelo*
   700–799   The Arts
b. *Italian Folktales*
   300-399 Social Sciences

1. *How to Stay Young and Healthy*
2. *The Greek Gods*
3. *Lives of the Great Explorers*

Language Resources

4. *Pecos Bill: An American Legend*
5. *Latin American Poetry*
6. *The Black Hole Theory of Stars*
7. *Human Psychology*
8. *Traveler's Guide to the German Language*
9. *The Encyclopedia of Cats*
10. *Boxing: The Dangerous Game*

Call Numbers

Books that are filed under the Dewey decimal system are numbered with a *call number*.

Perhaps you know that out of the billions of people in the world, no two people have identical fingerprints. Call numbers are like fingerprints: out of the many hundreds of books in your library, out of all those published every year, no two call numbers are the same. For example, *The Illustrated Book of World War II* by Peter Simkins has the following call number: 940.53
S145i

The number on the first line, *940.53*, is the *classification number*. That means the book is listed under this number in the Dewey decimal system. Below the classification number is the author's number, *S145*, which is made up of the first letter of the author's last name plus a special number for that book. After the author's number you may find a small letter, which is the first major word in the book's title. (The words *a, an,* and *the* do not count as major words because they occur so often in titles.)

Biographies and Autobiographies

Libraries do not list biographies and autobiographies in the same way that they list nonfiction books. *Biographies* are true stories about real people, and an *autobiography* is a person's own account of his or her life. Libraries group these two kinds of books together in a special way.

Biographies and autobiographies are usually labeled using one of two methods:

Biographies and autobiographies may be labeled with a *B*.

Below the *B* is the first letter of the last name of the person the book is about. For example, *Shooting Star* is a biography of John Wayne and has the call number *B*.
W

Biographies and autobiographies may be labeled with the Dewey decimal category number *921*.

Under the *921* is the first letter of the last name of the person the book is about. In some libraries John Wayne's biography *Shooting Star* has the call number *921*.
W

(For autobiographies the book's subject and author are the same.)

Collective biographies are books about the lives of several people and are arranged by the last name of the author.

Collective biographies have the classification number *920*, plus the first letter of the author's last name. For example, *Lives of the Poets* by Samuel Johnson is a collective biography and has the call number *920*.

Biographies are treated in a different way from other nonfiction books for a good reason. Suppose you wanted to find a book about Pablo Picasso, a famous artist. If biographies were classified under the regular nonfiction system, you would have to know the authors of biographies about him. However, the subject of the book, in this case, is more important than the author.

Exercise 2: Biography and Autobiography

On a sheet of paper numbered 1–10, list the biographies and autobiographies on the next page in the order they would appear on a library shelf.

Language Resources

1. *Autobiography of Mark Twain*
2. *My Lord, What a Morning: An Autobiography* (of Marian Anderson)
3. *Fifth Chinese Daughter* (autobiography of Jade Snow Wong)
4. *Wilt Chamberlain* (biography by K. Rudeen)
5. *Harriet Tubman: Conductor on the Underground Railroad* (biography by Ann Petry)
6. *Barrio Boy* (autobiography of Ernesto Galarza)
7. *The Story of My Life* (autobiography of Helen Keller)
8. *I Know Why the Caged Bird Sings* (autobiography of Maya Angelou)
9. *The Names* (autobiography of N. Scott Momaday)
10. *Jack London: The Pursuit of a Dream* (biography by Ruth Franchere)

Fiction

Fiction comes from a word that means "to form." Works of fiction are books formed mostly from the author's imagination and are not meant to be reports of events exactly as they happen. Books of poetry and all novels, for example, are fiction. Fiction books have been a source of pleasure for people in all walks of life for years. They provide lasting entertainment since they may take several hours to read and since they may be reread any number of times. Most libraries put books of fiction in an area separate from books of nonfiction.

The Dewey decimal system numbers do not apply to works of fiction. Instead, these books are arranged alphabetically by the last name of the author. When two authors have the same last name, their books are arranged alphabetically by their first names. For example, books by Anne Morrow Lindbergh are listed before books by Charles Lindbergh.

Books by the same author are arranged alphabetically by the first major word in the title. Jessamyn West, for example, has written *The Friendly Persuasion, Cress Delahanty,* and *The Massacre at Fall Creek.* These books would be arranged in this order: *Cress Delahanty, The Friendly Persuasion,* and *The Massacre at Fall Creek.*

Exercise 3: Fiction

The following is a list of books by five authors. On a separate sheet of paper, write them in the order that you would find them in the library.

Scott O'Dell:	*Tia*
	Island of the Blue Dolphins
	Sing Down the Moon
Susan Hinton:	*The Outsiders*
	That was Then, This Is Now
	Tex
Arthur C. Clarke:	*A Fall of Moondust*
	Expedition to Earth
	The City and the Stars
Toni Morrison:	*Sula*
	The Bluest Eye
	Song of Solomon
Thomas Hardy:	*Far From the Madding Crowd*
	The Mayor of Casterbridge
	Tess of the D'Urbervilles

The Card Catalogue

The *card catalogue* is the guide to finding books in the library.

The card catalogue is a large cabinet of long drawers with cards filed in alphabetical order. A tag on each drawer tells which cards are filed there. The following illustration shows how the first three drawers of a card catalogue might look.

A — AMY
AN — AZ
B — BIO

The card catalogue has three kinds of cards: *author*, *title*, and *subject*. In some libraries the different cards are mixed together in the same card catalogue; in others, there are separate cabinets for each kind of card.

Author Cards

The following sample card is the author card for the book *Early Moon*.

```
811.4                  Sandburg, Carl, 1878-1967.
Sa 56e

       Early Moon. by Carl Sandburg, illustrated by James
       Daugherty. New York, Harcourt, Brace and company
       (c1930)

       136, (1) p. incl. front., illus., plates. 23½cm

       A selection of the author's poems for young people. "First edition."


       I. Daugherty, James Henry, 1889—illus. II Title.
                                                                    30-28479
       Library of Congress          PS3537.A618E3    1930

       _____  _____  Copy 2.
                                                                    811.5
       Copyright A 29398    ( 5-5)
```

The author's name is at the top of the card, last name first, followed by the book's title. The number to the left is the *call number*. If an author has written more than one book, there will be a separate card for each book, arranged alphabetically by the first major word in each title. Author cards are helpful when you know the name of a writer but not the names of particular books.

Exercise 4: Locating Author Cards

For this exercise you will need to use your library's card catalogue. On the next page is a list of ten authors whose books are often found in school libraries. Locate a card for each author. Then on a sheet of paper numbered 1–10, write the name of each book your library has by that particular author. If your library does not have books by an author, write *not listed* in that space on your paper.

1. Pearl Buck
2. Gwendolyn Brooks
3. Langston Hughes
4. Marjorie Kinnan Rawlings
5. J. R. R. Tolkien
6. Isaac Asimov
7. Paul Zindel
8. Maureen Daly
9. Fred Gipson
10. Isaac Bashevis Singer

Title Cards

The following sample card is the title card for *The Robot Book*.

```
TJ                    The Robot Book.
211
.M34           Malone, Robert.

         The robot book / by Robert Malone; editor, William E.
      Mloney; producer, Jean-Claude Suares; design director,
      Seymour Chwast; designer, Richard Mantel; created and
      produced by Push Pin Press.—New York: Harcourt Brace
      Jovanovich, c1978.
         159 p.: 111.; 28 cm.—(A Harvest / HBJ book)

      "A Push Pin Press book."
      Bibliography: p. 158.
                                              (Cont. on next card)
                                                     77-92555
         01418                551349                        8348
```

The book title is listed at the top, and the author's name, last name first, is just below. The number to the left is the *call number* which we discussed earlier in this chapter. Title cards are filed in alphabetical order by the first major word of the title.

Exercise 5: *Locating Title Cards*

For this exercise you will need to use your library's card catalogue. On the next page is a list of ten titles often found in

Language Resources

school libraries. Locate each title in the card catalogue. On a sheet of paper numbered 1–10, write the name of the book's author. If your school does not have that title, write *not listed* in that space on your paper.

1. *To Be Young, Gifted and Black*
2. *Island of the Blue Dolphins*
3. *Johnny Tremain*
4. *The Other Side of the Mountain*
5. *Swiftwater*
6. *Only Earth and Sky Last Forever*
7. *Flowers for Algernon*
8. *By the Highway Home*
9. *From the Mixed-Up Files of Mrs. Basil E. Frankweiler*
10. *The Incredible Journey*

Subject Cards

The following sample card is the subject card for *The Navajos: The Past and Present of a Great People*.

970.3   NAVAHO INDIANS—HISTORY

Terrell, John Upton, 1900–

The Navajos; the past and present of a great people. New York, Weybright and Talley (1970)

B-13792

Subject cards are filed alphabetically by the subject. This subject is listed at the top of the card, followed by the author's name, last name first, and the book's title. The *call number* is in the upper left-hand corner of the card.

Each nonfiction book in the library should have at least one subject card or more than one if the book covers two or more subjects. A book about soccer might be listed under "Sports," "Athletics," and "Soccer." Books on training dogs might be listed under "Animals," "Pets," and "Dogs."

Exercise 6: Locating Subject Cards

Select five subjects from the following list and locate each of them in your library's card catalogue. On a sheet of paper numbered 1–10, list the book titles your library has for each of the subjects.

1. astrology
2. magic
3. football
4. science fiction
5. jazz
6. space travel
7. World War I
8. bicycling
9. cooking
10. animals

Finding Books on the Shelves

In most libraries books that are fiction are shelved in one part of the library, and biographies and autobiographies are shelved in another. All of these books are arranged alphabetically on the shelves. Books of fiction are arranged by the author's last name, and biographies and autobiographies are arranged by the last name of the person the book is about.

Language Resources

> **Nonfiction books, which are about real people and events, are usually kept in a separate area of the library and are arranged on the shelves by their Dewey decimal numbers.**

Some libraries label their bookshelves by the names of their Dewey decimal classification. In these libraries you simply walk to the shelves that read *History, Science,* or whatever subject you want. Most libraries, however, use only the Dewey decimal numbers on the shelves, so you must identify the shelf that contains the call number you are trying to find. The books are shelved in numerical order.

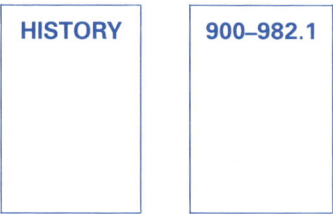

The following list is a step-by-step guide to finding nonfiction books arranged by Dewey decimal numbers. Suppose that you want to read a book about animals. Under the "Animals" subject card in the card catalogue, you find a book with the call number 542
    K64i

First step: Go to the stacks. (Stacks refers to the place the books are shelved.) Begin with the first number, *542*, and locate the correct shelf. If nonfiction shelves are labeled with names, the name on the shelf will be *Science.* Shelves labeled with numbers might read *500–550.78* or *531.79–599.* (The numbers on the shelves can change as the number of books in your library grows.)

Second step: Once you are at the right shelf, find the row of books with the top number of the call number. In this case the number is *542.* There will be many books with this same top number.

Third step: Now move on to the first letter in the call number, in this case the letter *K.* (As previously pointed out this is the first letter in the author's last name.) You will pass books with such labels as 542 and 542 before you come to the books labeled 542.   A   J
    K

Fourth step: The next part of the call number is *64*. Keep looking along the shelf until you find a *64* book. This book might be the one you are looking for, but you still have one more step to go.

Fifth step: Check the last part of the call number—the small letter to the right of the lower letter and number, in this case the letter *i*. Continue along the row of books until you come to that letter. When numbers and letters match up, you have found the book you are looking for. This method is like finding two puzzle pieces that must fit together perfectly.

Exercise 7: Using the Library

On a sheet of paper, list each of the ten Dewey decimal categories by name and numbers. Go to your library and look through the shelves to find the title of one book in each of the separate categories. Write down the title and call number for each of the ten books.

Using The Readers' Guide

Periodical **is a general name given to magazines and journals that are published at fixed time "periods."**

Some people read magazines every day for pleasure, but magazines are also excellent places to look for information on many subjects, from history to rock music, from car racing to world events. Because they are published so frequently, magazines often have more recent information than books.

The *Readers' Guide to Periodical Literature* is the guide to finding information in periodicals.

Using the *Readers' Guide to Periodical Literature* to find an article is like using the card catalogue because the *Readers' Guide* lists author and subject alphabetically. Author entries tell you the articles a particular author has written; subject entries list articles written on a subject. The following is a sample page from the *Readers' Guide to Periodical Literature*.

READERS' GUIDE TO PERIODICAL LITERATURE March 1977–February 1978

MOTHERWELL, Robert—*Continued*
Motherwell atelier. A. A. Cohen. il por Vogue 167: 230-3 + Mr '77
Paris prodigal son returns: retrospective at the Museum of Modern Art of the City of Paris. R. Hughes. il por Time 110:50-1 Jl 18 '77

MOTHS
Are you what you eat? il Chemistry 50:22 My '77
Batesian mimicry: selective advantage of color pattern. J. G. Sternburg and others. bibl il Science 195:681-3 F 18 '77
My useful friend, the cinnabar moth. V. H. Davis. Org Gard & Farm 24:89-90 My '77
  See also
  Caterpillars
  Codling moths

MOTION aftereffects. *See* After images.

MOTION in art. *See* Action in art

MOTION perception
Perception of moving targets. R. Sekuler and E. Levinson. il Sci Am 236:60-4 + Ja '77

MOTION picture acting
Reflections on the face in film. L. Shaffer. il Film Q 31:2-8 Wint '77

MOTION picture actors and actresses
Reel life heroes, excerpts from articles, 1938-1956. il Sat Eve Post 249:58-9 Jl '77
Spotlight. E. Miller. *See* issues of Seventeen
Year of the actress. C. Michener and M. Kasindorf. il por Newsweek 89:56-64 + F 14 '77
  See also
  Academy Awards (motion pictures)
  Children as actors and actresses
  Screen Actors Guild
    also names of Motion picture actors and actresses, e.g. J. Crawford

Photographs
Bridge to the past: cast of Bridge too far pictured in their youth. il Ladies Home J 94:34 Jl '77

Political activities
Politics under the palms. B. Burlingham. il pors Esquire 87:47-52 + F '77

MOTION picture adaptations
Book, movie people gear up for the upcoming Raggedy Ann & Andy animated musical feature. il Pub W 211:112 F 28 '77
Hollywood and American literature: the American novel on the screen. H. Jay. Engl J 66:82-6 Ja '77
Humiliation in Hollywood: film version of The last tycoon. S. Koch. il Harpers 254:102-4 Mr '77
Out of Pandora's box: silent film of Lulu. D. Newlin. por Opera N 41:20 + Ap 2 '77
Rights and permissions. P. S. Nathan. *See* issues of Publishers weekly
Semi-tough goes to the movies. D. Jenkins. il Sports Illus 47:78-82 + N 7 '77

MOTION picture advertising. *See* Motion picture industry—Advertising

MOTION picture authorship
Béla Balázs in German exile. J. Ralmon. bibl il por Film Q 30:12-19 Spr '77
Faulkner filmography. B. F. Kawin. bibl il Film Q 30:12-21 Summ '77
Four-letter screenwriter: Slap shot writer. N. Dowd. J. Maslin. il por Newsweek 89:68-9 Mr 7 '77
Sylvester Stallone's rocky road to Rocky: interview. ed. by P. Perry. S. Stallone. il pors Writers Digest 57:29-30 Jl '77
You ought to be in pictures. E. S. Stevens. Writers Digest 57:43-5 O '77

Motion picture awards
  See also
  Academy Awards (motion pictures)

MOTION picture cameras
Complete shopping guide to super single 8 sound cameras. D. Sutherland. il Pop Phot 81:120-1 + O '77
Equipment report:
Beaulieu 5008-S multispeed super 8 sound camera. T. Galluzzo. il Mod Phot 41:65-8 + Mr '77
Bell & Howell Filmosonic 1237 XL super 8 sound camera. il Mod Phot 41:45-6 S '77
Capon auto zoom 512XL super 8 camera. T. Galluzzo. il Mod Phot 41:42 + F '77
Canon 514XL-S. T. Galluzzo. il Mod Phot 41:42 + My '77
Elmo 350SL super 8 sound camera. il Mod Phot 41:95-6 + N '77
Eumig 880 PMA super 8. T. Galluzzo. il Mod Phot 41:44-5 O '77
Funca ZXM500 single 8 sound camera. T. Galluzzo. il Mod Phot 41:56 + D '77
Minolta XL-660 super 8 sound camera. T. Galluzzo. il Mod Phot 41:26 + Jl '77
First look: Kodak Ektasound 260. L. Drukker. il Pop Phot 81:121 S '77
Focus-free sound emerges: Elmo's 360SL. T. Galluzzo. il Mod Phot 41:26 + Jl '77
Good things in small packages: a case for the compact super 8. T. Galluzzo. il Mod Phot 41:40 + S '77
Guide to current XL cameras. Pop Phot 80: 114-15 My '77

Movie cameras and projectors. L. Drukker. il Pop Phot 80:126-7 + Je '77
Take underwater movies from above the waves. I. Berger. il Pop Mech 147:18 Ap '77

Purchasing
Movie cameras. Consumer Rep 42:257-8 D '77

Sound equipment
Home-movie sound that sounds good. D. Sagarin. il Pop Mech 149:66-7 Ja '78

Testing
Test of time: is your camera and projector on the button? T. Galluzzo. il Mod Phot 41:54 + D '77

MOTION picture cameras, Instant print
At long last. Land's instant movies. il Time 109:66 + My 9 '77
From Polaroid: instant-color movies. L. Drukker. il Pop Phot 80:244 Je '77
How Polavision really works. D. Leavitt. il Pop Phot 81:103-7 + O '77
Inside Polaroid's instant-movie system. E. H. Ortner. il Pop Sci 211:96-8 + Ag '77
Instant movies: Polavision. E. H. Ortner. il Pop Sci 211:42 Jl '77
Instant movies: shoot now, see now; Polavision. H. Fantel. il Pop Mech 148:94-5 + Ag '77
Land's new wonder: Polavision. L. Langway and others. il por Newsweek 89:75 + My 9 '77
Moving instant: Polaroid movies from camera to screen in less than two min. T. Galluzzo. il Mod Phot 41:20 + Jl '77
Schwalberg at large: Polavision movies. B. Schwalberg. il Pop Phot 81:42 + Jl '77

MOTION picture cartoons. *See* Motion pictures—Animated cartoons

MOTION picture censorship
  See also
  Motion pictures—Moral and religious aspects

MOTION picture critics and criticism
Kind word for critics: excerpt from The films in my life: tr by L. Mayhew. F. Truffaut-Harpers 255:95 + O '77

MOTION picture directors
Cost of freedom: the director's function. S. Kauffmann. New Repub 177:26-8 O 1 '77
Finders keepers: casting directors. J. Maslin and M. Kasindorf. il Newsweek 89:92 + Mr 14 '77
  See also
  Altman, R.
  Angelopoulos, T.
  Antonioni, M.
  Bergman, I.
  Bertolucci, B.
  Bresson, R.
  Buñuel, L.
  Cassenti, F.
  Coppola, F. F.
  DePalma, B.
  Fassbinder, R. W.
  Fellini, F.
  Flaherty, R.
  Godard, J. L.
  Herzog, W.
  Lucas, G.
  Mankiewicz, J. L.
  Oshima, N.
  Pechter, W. S.
  Peckinpah, S.
  Poitier, S.
  Polanski, R.
  Resnais, A.
  Rohmer, E.
  Ross, H.
  Russell, K.
  Scola, E.
  Scorsese, M.
  Smith, H.
  Spielberg, S.
  Tanner, A.
  Truffaut, F.
  Vertov, D.
  Watkins, P.
  Wenders, W.
  Wertmüller, L.
  Women motion picture directors

MOTION picture festivals
Conspirator in Berlin. P. Bogdanovich. Esquire 88:96 + D '77
Festival rites: New York Film Festival. D. Ansen. il Newsweek 90:102 + O 17 '77
Film festival: fifteenth New York Film Festival. H. Clurman. Nation 225:378-80, 412-14 O 15-22 '77
Film: second International Craft Film Festival. D. Hare. Craft Horiz 37:6 + D '77
Film: the American Film Festival. D. Hare. Craft Horiz 37:6 + O '77
Films that probe beneath the surface: New York Film Festival. J. M. Wall. Chr Cent 94:899-901 O 12 '77
In its way a great leap forward: International Ski Film Festival. A. Verschoth. il Sports Illus 47:60 O 17 '77

The words *See* and *See also* in the preceding sample page indicate *cross-referencing*. *See* means that all the information on that subject is listed somewhere else in the *Readers' Guide*. For example, if you are writing a report on movie cartoons, you would look in the *Readers' Guide* under the heading titled "Motion Picture Cartoons." There you find a note to *See* "Motion Pictures–Animated Cartoons," which means that you will find information about your cartoons under the heading "Motion Pictures–Animated Cartoons."

See also means you will find additional information about your subject under another listing or listings. For example, under the heading "Moths," three articles are listed, but there is also a *See also* that tells you to look under the headings "Caterpillars" and "Codling moths" for more articles on the subject.

The *Readers' Guide* is published in many volumes covering different months and years.

When you are looking for information, be certain to investigate all of the volumes of the *Readers' Guide* that might have the information you need. Articles on "Motion picture directors," for example, might be found in many different volumes.

Abbreviations are used frequently in the *Readers' Guide* because it contains so much information. At the front of the *Readers' Guide* are two *keys* that will help you decode the abbreviations: *Abbreviations of Periodicals Listed* and *Abbreviations*. *Abbreviations of Periodicals Listed* gives abbreviations for the names of the magazines used in the *Readers' Guide,* and *Abbreviations* lists the meanings of any other abbreviations. Some of these you may already know, such as the abbreviation *co.* for *company,* but others are more difficult to understand. For example, can you tell what *D* stands for? In the *Readers' Guide to Periodical Literature, D* means "December." Any time you are unsure of an abbreviation, check the keys at the front of the *Readers' Guide.*

Exercise 8: Understanding the Readers' Guide

For this exercise use the sample page from the *Readers' Guide* on page 628. Based on the information you find on that page, answer the questions on the following page. Use a sheet of paper numbered 1–10.

Language Resources

1. What is the title of the first article listed under the heading "Moths"?

2. Where would you look to find an article on "Motion aftereffects"?

3. Who is the author of the article titled "My Useful Friend, the Cinnabar Moth"?

4. Look under the name Robert Motherwell located at the top of the right hand column. If you were going to look up an article about him under a general subject heading, what would it be?

5. Which magazine would you look in to find the article "Year of the Actress"?

6. Name three motion picture directors listed on the sample page.

7. Under what other heading would you look to find an article about motion picture censorship?

8. Under what other heading would you look to find information about motion picture awards?

9. How many articles are listed about purchasing movie cameras?

10. Under which heading would you find articles about people who write motion pictures?

Finding Periodicals in Your Library

The *Readers' Guide* lists hundreds of magazines, but your library may not carry all of them. Most libraries post a list of the magazines they have, along with the number of years those magazines cover. If your library does not display such a list, ask the librarian for help.

Here is an example of a magazine article you might want to find:

MOTION PICTURE actors and actresses
Reel life heroes; excerpts from articles, 1938–1956.
il Sat Eve Post 249: 58-9 Jl '77

With the help of the abbreviations key at the front of the *Readers' Guide,* you can "translate" the information in the entry:

1. *Il* is the abbreviation for *illustrated;* that means the article has pictures.
2. *Sat Eve Post* is an abbreviation for the *Saturday Evening Post* magazine.
3. *249:58–9* is the volume number of the magazine (*249*) and the pages of the magazine where the article can be found (pages 58–59).
4. *Jl '77* is the month and year of the magazine: July 1977.

Now you know that you are looking for the July 1977, edition of the *Saturday Evening Post*. The next step is to find whether or not your library has this magazine and then to find where it is shelved. In general, only current issues of magazines are left out in racks. Back issues are put into large binders, labeled by name and date, and stored on the library shelves just like books. They are filed alphabetically by the name of the magazine. Sometimes, however, back issues are put on a special kind of film. In this case ask your librarian for help.

Exercise 9: *Using the* Readers' Guide

Below is a list of subjects you will find in the *Readers' Guide*. Using the *Readers' Guide*, find one article on three of the subjects. Copy the entry for each of the articles just as it appears in the *Readers' Guide*. Then use the abbreviation key in front of the *Readers' Guide* to write out the information that follows.

a. The name of the article
b. The name of the author of the article
c. The full title of the magazine or journal where you will find the article
d. The date of the magazine or journal
e. The volume number of the magazine or journal
f. The page numbers in the magazine or journal where you will find the article

1. comedy
2. whales
3. space travel
4. Muhammad Ali
5. computers
6. holography
7. hang gliding
8. cars
9. politics
10. Georgia O'Keeffe

28 Reference Works

Dictionaries, encyclopedias, and other books that are sources of general information are called *reference works*. In this chapter you will learn how to use such reference works.

Dictionaries

The man who was to write one of the most important dictionaries in the English language was born in a bookstore in 1709, the child of impoverished parents. Early in his childhood Samuel Johnson developed an illness that left him partially blind and paralyzed. But in spite of this great poverty and sickness, he lived to become one of the greatest writers in English history. Dr. Johnson, as he was known, wrote essays, plays, poetry, novels, and the *Dictionary of the English Language*.

His dictionary was two volumes long and took eight and one-half years and the help of six assistants to complete. The completed dictionary defined 40,000 words. It was the first dictionary in English to define words precisely and thoroughly. More important, Samuel Johnson made his dictionary special by printing quotations under words to illustrate how they were used at that time. In this way he showed that English is a living language, one that changes as people speak and write it.

The *Dictionary of the English Language* was a great success and still continues to influence the writing of dictionaries.

Finding a Word in the Dictionary

All dictionaries list their words in alphabetical order.

Following is a page from *Webster's New World Dictionary*.

Dictionary entries and the pronunciation key reproduced in this chapter are taken, with permission, from *Webster's New World Dictionary*, Second College Edition. Copyright © 1984 by Simon & Schuster, Inc.

Language Resources

> *Guide words* are the two words in boldface (dark print) at the top of the page.

Guide words show the first and last words on the page. On the sample page, **follower** is the first word defined, and **foolhardy** is the last word. Some words that come in between the two guide words are *following*, *fond*, *food*, and *fool*.

Dictionaries sometimes help you to find words by notching pages for each different letter or by printing the letters in color at the edge of the pages.

To find the word you want, turn to the page showing the same first letter as your word. Keep on turning the pages until you come to the right set of guide words, and then look down the page to find your word.

Exercise 1: Understanding Guide Words

In List 1 below are four sets of guide words. List 2 has words that fit between the guide words. Divide a sheet of paper into four parts. At the top of each part, write one pair of guide words. Under each part write the words from List 2 that you would find on the page with those guide words. List the words in alphabetical order.

Example

captive   carbon
    capture
    car
    carat
    carbine

List 1

1. **decant**   decibel
2. **decide**   declarer
3. **decoy**   deep
4. **defense** defoliate

List 2

decent
declare
deed

December
decision
dedication

deflate
defer
decrease
decimal
decathlon

define
deceit
decimeter
dedicate
defiant

Main Entry Words

Words arranged in alphabetical order in the dictionary are called *main entry words*.

The main entry word is usually printed in boldface and gives the word's correct spelling.

The main entry word with all the information about that word is called the *main entry*, as the following example shows.

sloth (slôth, slōth, släth) *n.* [ME. *slouthe* < *slou*, slow, used for older *slewthe, sleuthe* < OE. *slæwth*, sloth < *slaw*, slow: see SLOW & -TH[1]] **1.** disinclination to work or exert oneself; indolence; laziness **2.** [Now Rare] slowness; delay **3.** any of several slow-moving, tree-dwelling mammals (family Bradypodidae) of tropical Central and South America that hang, back down, from branches and feed on fruits and vegetation: the **three-toed sloth** (genus *Bradypus*) has three toes on each front foot, and the **two-toed sloth** (genus *Choloepus*) has two

SLOTH
(22–27 in. long, including tail)

Dictionary Pronunciations

Dictionaries show pronunciation with a code in parentheses after the main entry word. In the following example the pronunciation code is (sēz).

seize (sēz)

The pronunciation code includes *simplified spelling* and *pronunciation marks*. A simplified spelling leaves out (omits) letters that are not pronounced. For example, in the word *seize*, the *i* and final *e* are silent, so the simplified spelling is *sēz*. The pronunciation marks or symbols look like this: ā, ə, ü, o͞o, î, each one with a different meaning. Most dictionaries print two keys to help you use the pronunciation marks. A full-length key at the front of the dictionary gives the most complete information, as the following example from *Webster's New World Dictionary* shows.

```
B. Key to Pronunciation
An abbreviated form of this key appears at the bottom of
every alternate page of the vocabulary.

Symbol   Key Words              Symbol   Key Words
  a      asp, fat, parrot         b      bed, fable, dub
  ā      ape, date, play          d      dip, beadle, had
  ä      ah, car, father          f      fall, after, off
                                  g      get, haggle, dog
  e      elf, ten, berry          h      he, ahead, hotel
  ē      even, meet, money        j      joy, agile, badge
                                  k      kill, tackle, bake
  i      is, hit, mirror          l      let, yellow, ball
  ī      ice, bite, high          m      met, camel, trim
                                  n      not, flannel, ton
  ō      open, tone, go           p      put, apple, tap
  ô      all, horn, law           r      red, port, dear
  o͞o     ooze, tool, crew         s      sell, castle, pass
  o͝o     look, pull, moor         t      top, cattle, hat
  yo͞o    use, cute, few           v      vat, hovel, have
  yo͝o    united, cure, globule    w      will, always, swear
  oi     oil, point, toy          y      yet, onion, yard
  ou     out, crowd, plow         z      zebra, dazzle, haze

  u      up, cut, color          ch      chin, catcher, arch
  ʉr     urn, fur, deter         sh      she, cushion, dash
                                 th      thin, nothing, truth
  ə      a in ago                th      then, father, lathe
         e in agent              zh      azure, leisure
         i in sanity              ŋ      ring, anger, drink
         o in comply              '      [see explanatory note
         u in focus                      below and also For-
  ər     perhaps, murder                 eign sounds below]
```

In the full-length key the word *symbol* means "a sound." *Key Words* are the example words listed and are usually words that you already know how to pronounce. Vowel sounds are listed on the left-hand side, consonant sounds on the right-hand side. You read the "Key to Pronunciation" in this way:

Pronounce *a* as you pronounce the *a* in the words *asp, fat*.

Pronounce *ā* as you pronounce the *a* in the words *ape, date*.

Pronounce *ä* as you pronounce the *a* in the words *ah, car, father*.

You can usually find a shorter version of the key at the bottom of every other page in the dictionary. The key below is from the bottom of page 683 in *Webster's New World Dictionary*.

fat, āpe, cär; ten, ēven; is, bīte; gō, hôrn, to͞ol, look; oil, out; up, fʉr; get; joy; yet; chin; she; thin, then; zh, leisure; ŋ, ring; ə for *a* in *ago*, *e* in *agent*, *i* in *sanity*, *o* in *comply*, *u* in *focus*; ' as in *able* (ā'b'l); Fr. bal; ë, Fr. coeur; ö, Fr. feu; Fr. mon; δ, Fr. coq; ü, Fr. duc; r, Fr. cri; H, G. ich; kh, G. doch. See inside front cover. ✰ Americanism; ‡foreign; *hypothetical; < derived from

The preceding key reads in the same way that the longer "Key to Pronunciation" reads:

fat   *a* with no marks is pronounced like the *a* in *fat*.

āpe   *a* with a bar is pronounced like the *a* in *ape*.

cär   *a* with two dots is pronounced like the *a* in *car*.

Continue reading the shorter "Key to Pronunciation" in the same way.

Exercise 2: Understanding Dictionary Pronunciations

Number a sheet of paper 1–10. In the "Key to Pronunciation" on page 636, find one word that is an example of how to pronounce each of the following symbols. Write the word on your paper next to the corresponding number.

Example

a. ō
   open

1. e   3. ô   5. ur   7. th   9. z
2. ī   4. oo   6. r   8. zh   10. g

Accent Marks

The *accent mark* is another kind of code to help you pronounce words. The following main entry is from *Webster's New World Dictionary*.

no·tice (nōt′is) *n.* [LME. < MFr. < L. *notitia* < *notus*: see NOTE] **1.** information, announcement, or warning; esp., formal announcement or warning, as in a newspaper [a legal *notice*] **2.** a brief mention or critical review of a work of art, book, play, etc. **3.** a written or printed sign giving some public information, warning, or rule **4.** *a)* the act of observing; attention; regard; heed; cognizance *b)* courteous attention; civility **5.** a formal announcement or warning of intention to end an agreement, relation, or contract at a certain time [to give a tenant *notice*] —*vt.* **-ticed, -tic·ing 1.** *a)* to mention; refer to; comment on *b)* to review briefly **2.** *a)* to regard; observe; pay attention to *b)* to be courteous or responsive to **3.** [Rare] to serve with a formal notice —*SYN.* see DISCERN —**serve notice** to give formal warning or information, as of intentions; announce —**take notice** to become aware; pay attention; observe

The pronunciation symbol ō in (nōt′is) tells you how to pronounce the *o* sound in the word. With the pronunciation key you can tell that ō is pronounced like the *o* in *go*. The other symbol after the first syllable is called an *accent mark* (′).

Accent marks tell you which syllables to emphasize.

The part of the word spoken more strongly is called the *stressed* or *accented* syllable. In the sample word *notice*, the slanted mark after the first syllable means that the word is pronounced with a stress or accent on that syllable.

The *Webster's New World Dictionary* and some other dictionaries use the slanted accent marks that always *go after* the stressed syllable. Other dictionaries, however, use straight accent marks (′) that always go *in front of* the stressed syllable. For example, depending on the dictionary, the simplified spelling for the word *notice* could be written in either of two ways: *nōt′ is* or *′nōt is*. Look in your own dictionary to see which way is used.

Accent marks are also clues about the meaning of each word. Depending on which syllable is stressed, the word *minute* can have one of two meanings:

min′ ute or ′min ute	I will be ready in just a *minute*.
mi nute′ or mi ′nute	The scientist added a *minute* quantity of a new chemical to the test tube.

The word *record* is another example of a word with meanings that depend on its pronunciation. Explain what the differences are between the words *rec′ ord* and *re cord′*.

Some long words, such as the word *dictionary*, have two accent marks. The syllable spoken most strongly is called the *primary* stress or accent. The other emphasized syllable is called the *secondary* stress or accent. Most dictionaries show secondary accent marks in one of the two following ways.

1. A slant mark in lighter ink than the primary accent (dik′ shə ner′ ē).

2. A lowered straight mark, when the primary accent is shown by a raised straight mark (′dik shə ‚ner ē).

Abbreviations

Abbreviations **are another code dictionaries use.**

Abbreviations are listed in the front of the dictionary. The following list gives some of the more common ones.

adj.	adjective	*incl.*	including
adv.	adverb	*interj.*	interjection
Am.	American	*L.*	Latin
ant.	antonym	*lit.*	literally
Brit.	British	*n.*	noun
cap.	capital	*prep.*	preposition
conj.	conjunction	*pron.*	pronoun
e.g.	for example	*pronun.*	pronunciation
Eng.	English	*pt.*	past tense
esp.	especially	*sp.*	spelled
exc.	except	*specif.*	specifically
ff.	following	*syn.*	synonym
Fr.	French	*v.,vb*	verb
i.e.	that is	*var.*	variant

Parts of Speech and Plural Form

Main entries also give information about a word's *part of speech* and its *plural form*. The following main entry for the word *dictionary* is from *Webster's New World Dictionary*.

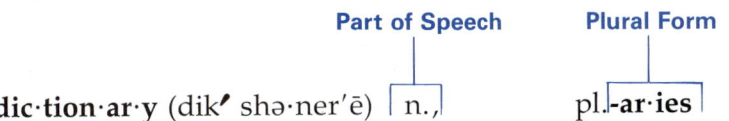

dic·tion·ar·y (dik′ shə·ner′ē) n.,   pl. **-ar·ies**

Part of Speech

The parts of speech are *noun, pronoun, verb, adjective, adverb, conjunction, preposition,* and *interjection.* The *n.* in the main entry for the word *dictionary* means that this word is a noun.

Plural Form

Pl. is the abbreviation for *plural.* All nouns have one or more plural forms, and some dictionaries show how to spell these

Language Resources

forms. For example, you can tell by reading the main entry that the plural of *dictionary* is *dictionaries*. Some plural forms are easy, but others, such as those of *octopus* or *deer*, do not follow the usual pattern. Use your dictionary to check for unfamiliar plural forms.

Exercise 3: *Using the Dictionary*

Look up each of the following words in a dictionary. Number a sheet of paper 1–10. For each word write (a) its pronunciation code, including accent marks, (b) its part of speech, (c) its plural form or forms.

Example

carnival
a. kär′ nə vəl, b. noun, c. carnivals

1. yak
2. theory
3. beach
4. traveler
5. ketchup
6. epic
7. airplane
8. handkerchief
9. luncheon
10. almanac

Word History

After the main word entry and the simplified spelling, most dictionaries give information in brackets about the word's history. The following main entry for *person* is from *Webster's New World Dictionary*.

> **per·son** (pur′s'n) *n.* [ME. *persone* < OFr. < L. *persona*, lit., actor's face mask, hence a character, person, prob. < Etruscan *phersu*, a mask] **1.** a human being, esp. as distinguished from a thing or lower animal; individual man, woman, or child **2.** [Chiefly Brit.] an individual regarded slightingly, as one of a lower status **3.** *a)* a living human body *b)* bodily form or appearance *[*to be neat about one's *person]* **4.** personality; self; being **5.** *Gram. a)* division into three sets of pronouns and, in most languages, corresponding verb forms, the use of which indicates and is determined by the identity of the subject: see FIRST PERSON, SECOND PERSON, THIRD PERSON *b)* any of these sets **6.** [Archaic] a role in a play; character **7.** *Law* any individual or incorporated group having certain legal rights and responsibilities **8.** *Theol.* any of the three modes of being (Father, Son, and Holy Ghost) in the Trinity —**in person** actually present —**per′son·hood′** *n.*

To read the abbreviations used to explain a word's history, turn to the list of abbreviations in the front of the dictionary. To learn about the history of the word *person*, for example, you need to know the meanings of these abbreviations and symbols: *ME., OFr., L., lit., prob.,* and <. In the list of abbreviations you can find the information you need:

ME.	Middle English
OFr.	Old French
L.	Latin
lit.	literally
prob.	probably
<	comes from (or) is derived from

Dictionaries list word histories with the most recent meanings first. The following example shows how to translate the abbreviations and symbols into complete sentences.

The word *person* comes from a word spelled *persone* in Middle English. The Middle English word was taken from an Old French word, which in turn was taken from the Latin word *persona*. The Latin word *persona* had the literal meaning of "the face mask worn by an actor," and so it came to be used as a word for a character or person. The Latin word probably comes from the Etruscan word *phersu*, which meant "a mask."

Exercise 4: Using the Dictionary

Choose five of the ten words listed below and look up each one in your dictionary. On a separate sheet of paper, write a short history of each word in complete sentences. Use the list of abbreviations in the front of your dictionary to assist you.

1. cargo
2. deck
3. king
4. drama
5. cartoon
6. circus
7. dinosaur
8. garage
9. moose
10. zero

Definitions

The word *define* comes from a Latin word meaning "to limit." Definitions set the limits of words, telling how they may be used. When words have more than one definition or meaning, the dictionary lists them all, as the following example shows.

catch (kach, kech) *vt.* **caught, catch′ing** [ME. *cacchen* < Anglo-Fr. *cachier* < VL. *captiare* < L. *captare*, to try to seize < pp. of *capere*, to take] **1.** to seize and hold, as after a chase; capture **2.** to seize or take by or as by a trap, snare, etc. **3.** to deceive; ensnare **4.** to discover by taking unawares; surprise in some act *[*to be *caught* stealing*]* **5.** to strike suddenly; hit *[*the blow *caught* him in the arm*]* **6.** to overtake or get to in time; be in time for *[*to *catch* a train*]* **7.** to intercept the motion or action of; lay hold of; grab or snatch *[*to *catch* a ball*]* **8.** *a)* to take or get as by chance or quickly *[*to *catch* one's attention, to *catch* a glimpse*] b)* [Colloq.] to manage to see, hear, find, etc. *[*to *catch* a radio program*]* **9.** to take or get passively; incur or contract without intention, as by exposure *[*to *catch* the mumps*]* **10.** *a)* to take in with one's mind or senses; understand; apprehend *b)* to show an understanding of by depicting *[*the statue *catches* her beauty*]* **11.** to captivate; charm **12.** to cause to be entangled or snagged *[*to *catch* one's heel in a rug*]* ☆**13.** *Baseball* to act as catcher for (a specified pitcher) —*vi.* **1.** to become held, fastened, or entangled *[*her sleeve *caught* on a nail*]* **2.** to take hold or spread, as fire **3.** to take fire; burn **4.** to take and keep hold, as a lock **5.** to act or serve as a catcher —*n.* **1.** the act of catching **2.** a thing that catches or holds **3.** the person or thing caught **4.** the amount caught **5.** a person worth catching, esp. as a husband or wife **6.** a snatch, scrap, or fragment *[catches* of old tunes*]* **7.** a break in the voice, caused by emotion ☆**8.** a simple game of throwing and catching a ball ☆**9.** [Colloq.] a hidden qualification; tricky condition *[*a *catch* in his offer*]* **10.** *Music* a round for three or more unaccompanied voices **11.** *Sports* a catching of a ball in a specified manner —*adj.* **1.** designed to trick; tricky *[*a *catch* question on an exam*]* **2.** attracting or meant to attract attention or interest —**catch as catch can** with any hold, approach, technique, etc.: originally said of a style of wrestling —**catch at 1.** to try to catch **2.** to reach for eagerly; seize desperately —**catch it** [Colloq.] to receive a scolding or other punishment —☆**catch on 1.** to grasp the meaning; understand **2.** to become fashionable, popular, etc. —**catch one's breath 1.** to return to normal breathing after exertion **2.** to rest or pause —**catch oneself** to hold oneself back abruptly from saying or doing something — **catch up 1.** to take or lift up suddenly; seize; snatch **2.** to show to be in error **3.** to come up even, as by hurrying or by extra work; overtake **5.** to fasten in loops —**catch up on** to engage in more (work, sleep, etc.) so as to compensate for earlier neglect
SYN.—**catch,** the most general term here, refers to a seizing or taking of a person or thing, whether by skill or cunning, and usually implies pursuit; **capture** implies a greater measure of resistance or elusiveness than **catch** and therefore stresses seizure by force or stratagem *[*to *capture* an outlaw*]*; **nab,** an informal word, specifically implies a sudden or quick taking into custody *[*the police *nabbed* the thief*]*; **trap** and **snare** both imply the literal or figurative use of a device for catching a person or animal and suggest a situation from which escape is difficult or impossible *[*to *trap* a bear, *snared* by her womanly wiles*]*

Each number in **boldface** listed under *catch* shows a different meaning of the word. To make your search easier the dictionary groups definitions by parts of speech. The definitions under *catch,* for example, are separated into those for *catch* as a verb, those for *catch* as a noun, and those for *catch* as an adjective. You will find the different parts of speech with their abbreviations in the list at the front of the dictionary.

In the main entry for *catch,* the abbreviation *vt.* means that the first group of definitions is for *transitive verbs.* (A transitive verb takes an object; an *intransitive* verb does not.) With some definitions the dictionary lists an example of the word used in a phrase or sentence, thus making the meaning of the word clearer. For example, definition Number 7 for *catch* under *vt.* is "to intercept the motion or action of; lay hold of; grab or snatch." After the definition is the phrase in parentheses "to *catch* a ball."

The next set of definitions is for *catch* as an *intransitive verb*, abbreviated *vi.* For each part of speech, the numbers begin again with *1.* The first definition listed in this set is "to become held, fastened, or entangled." The phrase illustrating this definition is "her sleeve *caught* on a nail."

Nouns, abbreviated *n.,* make up the next group of definitions. The first one reads "the act of catching." No example is provided because this is a commonly used form of the word.

The fourth group of definitions is for *catch* as an adjective, abbreviated *adj.* Following that are frequently heard phrases using the word *catch,* including "*catch* as *catch* can," "*catch* it," and "*catch* one's breath."

Exercise 5: Using the Dictionary

First, read through the definitions for the word *catch* on page 642. Then copy each of the following five sentences onto a separate sheet of paper. After each sentence write the part of speech and the definition number for *catch* as it is used in the sentence. Read the example before you begin.

Example

a. Ricardo felt certain he was not going to *catch* a cold that winter.
Transitive verb, Number 9.

1. If a player *catches* you attempting to steal home plate, you will be out.
2. If we get home after 11 o'clock, we are going to *catch* it from our parents.
3. The *catch* in his voice showed that Luis was overcome by emotion.
4. The crowd applauded wildly, but the player knew it was just a lucky *catch.*
5. The group pushed closer to *catch* a glimpse of the famous former actor.

Words in Context

One way to decide on the correct meaning of a word when it has many definitions is to look at it in context. Looking at the *context* means that you see all the words as they fit together in a sentence. Sometimes, the only way you can know the definition of a word is by seeing it in a setting, as this main entry for the word *cradle* demonstrates:

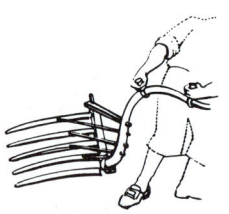

cra·dle (krā′d'l) *n.* [ME. *cradel* < OE. *cradol* < *kradula* little basket, akin to OHG. *kratto*, basket < IE. base *ger-*, to twist, turn, whence CART] **1.** a baby's small bed, usually on rockers **2.** the earliest period of one's life; infancy **3.** the place of a thing's beginning or early development [the *cradle* of civilization] **4.** [Poet.] a place of rest [rocked in the *cradle* of the deep] **5.** anything resembling a cradle or used somewhat like a cradle for holding, rocking, etc.; specif., *a)* a wooden or metal framework to support or lift a boat, ship, aircraft, etc. that is being built or repaired ☆*b) same as* CREEPER (sense 7) *c)* the support on which the handset of a telephone (**cradle telephone**) rests when not in use *d) Agric.* a frame fastened to a scythe (**cradle scythe**) so that the grain can be laid evenly as it is cut *e) Med.* a frame for keeping bedclothes raised over an injured limb, etc. ☆*f) Mining* a boxlike device on rockers, for washing the gold out of gold-bearing sand —*vt.* **-dled, -dling 1.** to place, rock, or hold in or as in a cradle **2.** to take care of in infancy; nurture **3.** to cut (grain) with a cradle scythe **4.** to support or lift (a boat, etc.) in or on a cradle ☆**5.** *Mining* to wash (gold-bearing sand) in a cradle —*vi.* [Obs.] to lie in or as in a cradle —**rob the cradle** to take as one's sweetheart or one's spouse a person much younger than oneself

CRADLE SCYTHE

Some of the meanings the dictionary gives for *cradle* are "a baby's small bed," "the place where something begins," and "a place of rest." In the following sentence which definition of *cradle* makes the most sense?

The ancient country of Mesopotamia is often thought to be a *cradle* of civilization.

The word *cradle* in the preceding context clearly means "the place where something begins." If you are trying to decide among definitions in the dictionary, always look first at how the word is used in a sentence.

Exercise 6: Using Context Clues

Look up the *italicized* words in the following sentences in your dictionary. Select the correct definition for each word by looking at it in context. Then on a sheet of paper numbered 1–10, write the correct definition of each word.

Example

a. When I asked Anna what she had been doing all day, she gave me a *blank* look.
   blank—without interest or expression

1. Mountain climbing will *try* anyone's strength.
2. It would be better to let the whole matter *rest*.
3. We are *pressed* for time because the movie is at 8 o'clock.
4. At the sight of the large players on the other team, we felt our courage *wilt*.
5. Kiyo inspected the row of pots to make certain that they were of *uniform* quality.
6. Just before sunset we saw an eagle *sweeping* across the sky.
7. I had the strange *impression* that I had been there before.
8. Christine admired the *rough* drawings.
9. The government is taking *measures* to protect the air.
10. If Lisa's exercise was not right, she always did it *over*.

Synonyms

Synonyms are words that have closely related meanings.

Dictionaries often include a section on *synonyms* after the definitions for each word. The following list of synonyms comes at the end of the main entry for *catch*.

> **SYN.—catch**, the most general term here, refers to a seizing or taking of a person or thing, whether by skill or cunning, and usually implies pursuit; **capture** implies a greater measure of resistance or elusiveness than **catch** and therefore stresses seizure by force or stratagem [to *capture* an outlaw]; **nab**, an informal word, specifically implies a sudden or quick taking into custody [the police *nabbed* the thief]; **trap** and **snare** both imply the literal or figurative use of a device for catching a person or animal and suggest a situation from which escape is difficult or impossible [to *trap* a bear, *snared* by her womanly wiles]

As you can learn from the guide to abbreviations, *Syn.* stands for *synonym.* The synonyms under *catch* include the words *capture* and *trap.* The words *catch, capture,* and *trap* are synonyms, but they do not have exactly the same meaning. For this reason you must be certain that the synonym you choose fits the meaning of your sentence. For example, "The police officer *caught* the thief" and "The police officer *captured* the thief" are very close in meaning, but even though you can *catch* a cold, you do not *capture* one.

Exercise 7: Identifying Synonyms

Look up each of the following words in the dictionary. Then on a sheet of paper numbered 1–10, write down a synonym for each word. Then write a sentence of your own using each of the synonyms. Underline each synonym.

Example

a. calm
 tranquil
 The boat drifted slowly on the smooth and <u>tranquil</u> water.

1. bright
2. answer
3. care
4. comfortable
5. error
6. frown
7. glow
8. heavy
9. intelligent
10. tell

How Dictionaries Differ

All regular dictionaries define words, but some give more information than others, so take time to look through a dictionary before deciding that it is the right one for you.

One way that dictionaries differ is that some are *abridged*, and some are *unabridged*.

Abridged simply means "shortened." In general, the unabridged dictionaries are the largest and contain the most information, a point to remember when you need to study something thoroughly. The abridged dictionaries are good for everyday use.

Dictionaries often include special kinds of information, such as a table of chemical elements and guides for better writing. In the back of the *Webster's New World Dictionary*, for example, you can learn how to make the astronomer's sign for a comet, how to make the symbols for the signs of the zodiac, and how to convert an inch into a millimeter.

Exercise 8: Locating Special Dictionary Sections

Using either your classroom dictionary or one from your library, locate the beginning of the *A* section and the end of the *Z* section. Then look through the pages before and after the main entry words to find the special information in that particular dictionary. On a sheet of paper, make a list of special sections found in your dictionary.

Other Reference Works

Using Encyclopedias

The word *encyclopedia* was first a Greek word meaning "well rounded," as in a "well rounded education." Encyclopedias can help give you a well rounded education because they contain information on almost every subject.

General information encyclopedias may come in one volume or in many volumes. The *one-volume* encyclopedia is a large volume with articles alphabetically arranged from A to Z. The following entry on Calamity Jane is from *The Concise Columbia Encyclopedia*, a one-volume encyclopedia.

Calamity Jane, c. 1852–1903, American frontier character, b. Princeton, Mo. Her real name was Martha Jane Canary, and the origin of her nickname is obscure. Little is known of her early life beyond the fact that she moved with her parents to Virginia City, Mont., in 1865 and that she grew up in mining camps and rough frontier communities. In 1876 she appeared in Deadwood, S. Dak., dressed in men's clothes and boasting of her marksmanship and her exploits as a pony-express rider and as a scout with Custer's forces. In her later years she toured the West in a burlesque show and appeared at the Pan-American Exposition in Buffalo, N.Y. She died in poverty and obscurity in Deadwood, where she is buried beside Wild Bill Hickock. See biographies by Duncan Aikman (1927) and Mrs. Glenn Clairmonte (1959); R.J. Casey, *The Black Hills and Their Incredible Characters (1949)*.[1]

One-volume encyclopedias give a large amount of information in a short space. The article on Calamity Jane, for example, is useful if all you need to know are a few facts about her life. When you want to learn more, use an encyclopedia published in many volumes.

Most encyclopedias include many volumes arranged in alphabetical order. Each volume is labeled by letters, words, or parts of words. For example, *The World Book Encyclopedia* organizes its volumes like this: *A, B, C–CH, CI–CZ, D,* and so on. *Colliers Encyclopedia* labels this way: *A to Ameland; Amen to Artillery; Art Nouveau to Beetle; Beeville to Charm;* and so on. Because these encyclopedias are much longer than one-volume encyclopedias, their articles contain more information. For example, the article on Calamity Jane in *The World Book Encyclopedia* is several paragraphs long; besides containing extra information, it also includes a picture.

Two additional volumes, the *Index* and the *Yearbook,* will help you make the best use of your library's encyclopedias. Usually, both are published as separate volumes. The *Index,* an alphabetical list of all the subjects included in the encyclopedia with page numbers telling where to find them, helps you to locate every article the encyclopedia has about any subject. The *Yearbook* is also very important because encyclopedias are so large and complex that they are not published every year. The *Yearbook* is published every year and includes the most recent information about subjects in the encyclopedia.

Exercise 9: Using an Encyclopedia

On the next page is a list of subjects you will find in almost any encyclopedia. Using an encyclopedia from your school library, select a subject and look it up. On a sheet of paper, write in your own words what the encyclopedia says about your subject.

[1]Entry for "Calamity Jane" from the *Concise Columbia Encyclopedia* edited by Harris and Levey. Reprinted by permission of Columbia University Press.

1. Crow Indians
2. Carlsbad Caverns National Park
5. macadamia
6. Rocky Marciano
7. Hasidim
3. basenji
4. Diogenes
8. pepper
9. Alice Marble
10. Penelope

Using Special Reference Books

Your library probably has many more reference books than you realize. The following encyclopedias, for example, are often found in reference areas.

The Encyclopedia of the Animal World

Baseball: Sports Encyclopedia

Encyclopedia of Rock

Encyclopedia of World Literature

Scientific Encyclopedia

World Encyclopedia of Comics

Many other special reference books covering a wide range of interests and hobbies are available in some libraries. The following list gives just a few of them.

Lincoln Library of Sports Champions

Video Games

Roget's International Thesaurus

Great Documents in Black American History

The Complete Guide to Middle Earth

Articles on Women Writers

Who's Who in Science Fiction

National Geographic Atlas of the World

Exercise 10: Locating Special Reference Books

Look in the reference section of your library to find what special reference books are kept there. List five of these books on a sheet of paper.

29 Speaking and Listening Skills
Preparing a Speech

Three purposes for speaking are *to persuade, to entertain,* and *to move to action.* The President of the United States tries to persuade Congress to support a program or pass a law. A comedian tells jokes in order to entertain. Coaches give pep talks at halftime, encouraging their teams to perform better.

Although most people speak for these purposes every day, the purpose behind most speeches is *to inform.* In this chapter you will learn how to prepare and deliver an informative speech.

Choosing a Topic

Choosing a topic is often the hardest part of preparing a speech. "What can I talk about?" is a question that must be answered first.

Choose an interesting topic.

While there is really no such thing as a boring topic, some topics are more interesting to certain groups than to others. You may be interested in sports, but if your classmates do not share your enthusiasm they will not want to listen to a speech about the World Series. However, you can still choose a topic about sports if you relate it to the interests of your audience.

You can make a topic interesting by first asking yourself what your listeners might find appealing and then approaching the topic from their viewpoint. If your audience is more interested in learning about famous athletes than in the games themselves, then design your speech to suit this interest.

Choose a newsworthy topic.

To inform means to add to the knowledge of your listeners by sharing new information with them. A speaker who tells you that two plus two equals four is giving you information that is not newsworthy. However, if you know little or nothing about the origin of Halloween customs, information about those customs would be news to you.

Choose a topic for which there is information.

Nothing is more frustrating than discovering that you cannot find information on the topic you have selected. Before making a final decision, check your library to be certain that you can find information about your topic.

Exercise 1: Choosing a Topic

Brainstorm with your classmates to think of some appealing topics. Hobbies, musical groups, television characters, favorite books—all of these and others are possibilities for an informative speech. Have one person keep a list of speech topics. Select one of the topics you think is interesting and newsworthy. Then look the topic up in the *Readers' Guide to Periodical Literature* in the library. (See Chapter 27 for information on using the *Readers' Guide.*) On a sheet of paper, write down important information about three articles on your topic. Include the author and title for each article, the name and date of the magazine, and the page numbers of the articles. Keep the list for use later.

Closing In on Your Topic

Imagine that you are to give an informative speech on the topic *Television reruns.* The topic itself is not new, but you think that there might be newsworthy ways of approaching it. You also think that you can make it interesting to your classmates, especially since so many of them watch reruns at one time or another. Finally, you have checked to see that there is material in the library on this subject. What should you do next?

Gather sources.

Find all the sources that have information about your topic, such as books, magazine articles, and newspaper stories. Other materials, such as pamphlets, filmstrips, phonograph

Language Resources

records, tapes, vertical files, and reference books, may help also. If you do not know where to find such materials, ask your teacher or librarian for help. In gathering sources, remember your conversations with others. Interviews with knowledgeable people can provide you with much background material.

After gathering your sources, record the results of your research. On a note card for each source, include the essential information about the author, book title, article title, date, and page numbers. Also keep a record of the time, place, and date of any interviews.

Collect details.

Sometimes, beginning speakers try to write a speech using only one or two pieces of information. When they give their speeches, however, they find they do not have enough information. They have to repeat their few facts, and listeners soon lose interest.

A good informative speech includes specific, detailed information. As you read or interview others about your topic, look for answers to the questions *who? what? where? when? why?* and *how?* Look for examples, quotations, explanations, statistics, descriptions, definitions, and brief stories relating to your topic. The more detailed information you have, the easier it will be to put the speech together. You may not use all of the information, but you will have a good supply from which to choose.

Record details.

A convenient way to record details is to put one fact or idea on each note card. Then you can sort and shuffle information when you write your speech outline. A label in the upper left-hand corner of the card will help you, for easy reference. On the bottom of the card, include the source of the material so that you can give proper credit, as the sample card on the next page shows.

Make connections.

To connect the pieces (details) of a topic to form a meaningful picture, lay out your note cards in front of you and read the details that you have gathered. Are there any details that fit together? Are there any that do not seem to belong?

Limit the topic.

After grouping the details, you may find that you have more details than you need. For instance, *Television reruns* is a

> Birth order—personality profile (Explanation)
>
> If you are an only child, your best traits are good verbal skills and self-confidence. However, you must watch out for feelings of loneliness and for a desire for perfection.
>
> <u>Seventeen</u>, June, 1976, p. 48

broad topic. If you have only five minutes to speak, you may find that you must choose only one part of this topic, such as explaining how the reruns are selected.

Exercise 2: Limiting the Topic

Working alone or in a group, write down as much information as you can about the topic *Pizza*, a favorite food of many Americans. Anything that seems to relate to this topic should be included on the list. Next group together closely related ideas about pizza and list the groups in separate columns on a sheet of paper or on the chalkboard.

Finally make a list of possible speech topics about pizza, based on your connecting of details. You should find many ways to "slice" this topic and therefore to limit its range.

Preparing an Informative Speech Outline

You may have listened to someone speak and felt enthusiastic about the speaker's ideas. You paid attention, enjoyed the speech, and laughed at the speaker's humorous stories. Later, however, you could not remember much about the speech. The speaker talked in such a rambling way that you really could not follow his or her ideas. Unless the speaker organizes ideas in a speech, you probably will not remember its content.

Speakers need to plan their speeches carefully so that they are both interesting and easy to remember. Listeners usually do not have the patience to piece together unrelated bits of information provided by a poorly organized speaker. Since your purpose in giving a speech is to have listeners hear, enjoy, and remember what you have to say, it is necessary to outline your speech's content.

Dividing the Speech

All speeches have three parts: a beginning (*introduction*), middle (*body*), and an end (*conclusion*).

The *introduction* starts the speech by capturing the listeners' attention and by telling them what the speech is about. The *conclusion* ends the speech by refocusing the listeners' attention on the central idea. The *body*, however, *is* the speech, because in this middle segment details about the topic are explained and described. It is the body, then, that first needs to be outlined.

Outlining the Body of the Speech

Outlining the body of the speech helps you arrange the ideas in some order.

The outline's purpose is to make connections between related thoughts in a sensible pattern. The following steps will help you in outlining the body of your speech.

Phrase your controlling statement.

When you phrase your controlling statement, you write out specifically what your speech is about. This statement tells what your topic is, limits what you will talk about, and gives the purpose of the speech. *I want to inform my listeners about phobias (fears that cause extreme panic in some people)* is an example of a controlling statement. This statement includes the purpose (*to inform*) and the topic *Phobias*.

Find the main points.

The main points explain the general topic, describe it, or give facts about it. A main point often answers one or two of the *who? what? where? when? why?* and *how?* questions. Although a speech usually has between two and five main points, the exact number depends on the speech's length. Five main points are usually enough because listeners have trouble remembering more than that.

For a speech on the topic *Phobias*, the first step is to decide the major divisions of this topic. The following topic outline will help you visualize the main points of the topic *Phobias*.

Phobias

I. Types of phobias
II. Causes of phobias
III. Symptoms of phobias
IV. Cures for phobias

Find the minor points and details that support them.

Minor points explain the main points, just as main points explain the general topic. You can also have more specific details about minor points. If you can explain, describe, or give facts about minor points, then you are using the smallest of units—*minor details*. Examine the first part of the following *Phobias* outline again, this time with minor points and minor details added:

Phobias

I. Types of phobias (Main point)
   A. Fear of an object (Minor point)
      1. People (Minor detail)
      2. Animals (Minor detail)
      3. Books (Minor detail)
      4. Daylight (Minor detail)
      5. Self (Minor detail)
   B. Fear of situation (Minor point)
      1. Going to bed (Minor detail)
      2. Being stared at (Minor detail)
      3. Being in enclosed places (Minor detail)
      4. Having to speak (Minor detail)
      5. Being married (Minor detail)

Language Resources

Exercise 3: Outlining a Speech

Select a familiar topic, such as shooting a basketball, cleaning a room, or mowing the lawn. Then develop two to five main points. Add at least two minor points for each main point. Also add two minor details about each minor point. Now write an outline showing these points and details.

Planning the Introduction

After you have outlined the body of the speech, you can direct your attention to the introduction and conclusion. The purpose of the introduction is to get your listeners' attention, give them the purpose of the speech, and cause them to feel favorably toward you and your topic. A good first impression will help you keep your listeners' attention until the very end.

There are several ways to introduce an informative speech. Study these five common ways to see which ones will be best for your speech:

1. **Refer to your audience.**

    Immediately appealing to the needs, the interests, or the situation of your audience is an excellent way of introducing a speech.

    > I'm sure that all of you have been afraid before. When you were young, you may have been afraid of the dark. Maybe now you're afraid of taking a test or having to speak in front of a group. These fears are common and are a part of your daily life. But what happens to people whose fears cause them to panic and actually prevent them from thinking straight? These people have fears that are known as *phobias*, which prevent them from having a normal life as you and I may have.

2. **Use a direct approach.**

    Going directly to the heart of your topic and defining it for your audience is a good way to begin a speech.

    > A phobia is a fear that causes a person to panic. This panic happens even though there is no real danger. To understand why a person becomes so frightened you must be aware of the types, causes, symptoms, and cures of phobias.

3. **Use an illustration.**

Using an example or a story, or a series of examples and stories, will catch your audience's attention.

>Julio turned down a job to work in a warehouse. He was sure that it was spider infested, and he could not stand the thought of spiders crawling all over him. Maggie was afraid to leave her house. She just "knew" that she would die if she left. Kuni would not visit the doctor because the doctor's office number was 1313. These are just three of many people who suffer from some unnatural fear, known as a *phobia*. The actual number of people who have phobias is unknown. But being phobic is a serious problem that we all should understand.

4. **Cite a statistic.**

A numerical fact can be used as an opening statement.

>Statistics from the National Institute of Mental Health show that seven to eight percent of all Americans suffer from phobias. As more people admit to suffering from extreme fears, this percentage grows. It is now time to understand this problem, which affects so many people.

5. **Begin with a quotation.**

Repeating someone else's words is especially good for an informative speech's opening.

>Franklin Roosevelt once said, "We have nothing to fear but fear itself." To a person with a phobia this statement is not true. A phobic will find that the list of fears ranges anywhere from fear of self to fear of worms.

Exercise 4: Preparing an Introduction

Using a topic you have developed or one you make up, write an introduction with one of the five methods you have studied in the previous section. Keep the introduction for later use.

Planning the Conclusion

Last impressions are like first impressions in a speech: both need to be planned. Leaving your listeners with a favorable impression means redirecting their attention to the speech's central idea and leaving them with a good feeling about the speech. This is why the conclusion to your speech is important.

Redirect your listeners' attention.

To start your conclusion give a summary of your material. Remind your listeners of the speech's purpose and its content. This can be done by a main point summary or a single-sentence summary.

In a main point summary you review all of those ideas identified in the outline by a Roman numeral.

> To truly understand the topic of phobias, you must be aware of their types, causes, symptoms, and cures.

In a single-sentence summary, redirect your audience's attention to the central purpose and idea of your speech.

> I've tried today to share with you some of the information about phobias.

Provide a final thought.

End your speech with a thought that ties up all loose ends, using one of the same five methods you used in your introduction.

1. *Refer to your audience.* You can once again appeal to the needs, interests, or situation of your audience to provide your speech's final note.

    > After hearing me talk about phobias, you may find that you have nothing to fear. What I've described may not apply to you, but that does not mean that you should ignore this topic. Chances are that you know someone who is phobic, and your understanding could be very helpful to that person.

2. *Use a direct approach.* Defining your topic once again is a second way to clinch a speech.

    > As I have said before, a phobia is a fear that causes a person to panic when there is really no danger present. Yet the fear itself becomes a real danger for the person who feels its hold.

3. *Use an illustration.* Tying up the loose ends with an example or a story can give your listeners a feeling of completeness.

The way a girl named Jennifer reacts to her fear of crossing a bridge is typical of most phobics. She doesn't want anybody to know about her fear. She feels that people will merely laugh at her and think that she is strange. Therefore, she doesn't receive the help she needs. But Jennifer and other phobics can be cured. The first step in that cure is realizing that their fears should be shared with others.

4. *Cite a statistic.* Give your listeners one more number to consider as you conclude.

    In Ohio alone there are an estimated 750,000 people with some type of phobia. Multiply that number by fifty and you will find quite a few Americans suffering either mildly or severely from fear.

5. *Begin with a quotation.* The final method you can use to end your speech is quotation.

    JoAnn Neuroth, a psychiatrist, summed up the phobic situation best when she wrote: "Phobics actually are afraid of two things. One is the fear of an object or situation which can panic them. The second is the fear of the panic itself."

Exercise 5: Preparing a Conclusion

Using the introduction you prepared for Exercise 4, write a conclusion for the same topic. Use one of the five methods discussed in the previous section. In front of your classmates, deliver the introduction again and then deliver the conclusion.

Delivering a Speech

Once you have chosen a topic and organized your speech, you are ready to prepare for delivery. How you give a speech is as important as what you have to say in it. Your delivery can either make your ideas come alive, or it can ruin an audience's interest in them.

A speaker's delivery is both verbal and nonverbal. Be effective verbally. Sometimes, the topic for the speech is interesting, but the speaker's voice is dull, monotonous, and flat. When the speaker's voice lacks life, so does the speech.

Language Resources

Since you do not hear yourself as others do, you may not know how effective your voice is. One solution is to record your voice on tape and then listen to how you sound. If you cannot do so, read your prepared speech aloud to a friend or classmate. In either case think about the following questions.

Will your listeners have to strain to hear you?

Speakers often forget that they must speak louder than usual, since volume suited for face-to-face conversation is not enough for an audience of ten or more listeners.

Are your words spoken clearly and distinctly?

Your listeners must be able to distinguish your words in order to understand what you say. Be especially careful to pronounce unfamiliar words slowly and carefully.

Does your voice vary?

A robot's voice never changes; its beeps and signals are flat and monotonous. In order to keep your audience's attention vary your pitch, rate of speed, and volume. Try to sound as natural as possible, not like the unchanging tone of a mechanical robot.

Do you speak too fast or too slowly?

Your listeners will lose interest if your pace is too slow, and they will not be able to follow if you race through your speech too fast. Take your time when you speak, but avoid too many pauses and too dull a pace.

Exercise 6: Expressing Emotion

Select an advertisement from a newspaper or telephone book and practice reading it aloud until you are familiar with it. Then choose one of the following emotions and read the ad so that you express that emotion. Share your reading with your classmates.

joy	boredom	anger	irritation
love	doubt	horror	eagerness
fatigue	sadness	pain	surprise

Nonverbal Communications

Your actions are the nonverbal language of a speech. You communicate through words with your listeners, but they learn from more than just those words. They see the messages your body sends. Your posture, body movement, facial expression, and eye contact all say something about you and your speech. The key to a good speech is to make the nonverbal language say what you want it to say, so check your physical appearance with the following questions.

What does your posture say to your listeners?

In order to get and hold your listeners' attention, you want them to see you as interested, energetic, and poised. Avoid rocking back and forth on your feet, leaning on the lectern or table, or standing stiffly with your hands folded behind your back. Communicate confidence and ease to your audience by standing with your weight on both feet and by being relaxed in that stance.

Does your body movement detract from your speech?

An audience's eyes follow your movement, which can call attention to itself if it is not natural and meaningful. Wringing your hands, twisting your notes, cracking your knuckles, and gesturing stiffly are all movements that distract. Gesture and move as you would in normal conversation.

Does your face reflect the meaning of your words?

Sometimes, beginning speakers have one of two facial expressions: a blank look or a pained look. Listeners read your face as they listen to your words. They believe your facial expression before they believe what you have to say; therefore, let your face reflect your intent.

Do you look at your listeners?

Looking at your listeners involves them in your speech. Talking directly to them makes them feel as if you are interested in them and lets you see how they are responding. Avoid staring out into space or at your notes. Direct eye contact is one of the best ways to let your listeners know that you want them to be interested in what you are saying.

Exercise 7: Delivering a Speech

Using what you have learned in this chapter, prepare and deliver a four- to six-minute informative speech. Use a topic you have already worked with or make up a new one.

Listening to Speeches

More time is spent listening than reading, writing, or speaking, yet most people remember only about twenty five percent of what they hear. One reason for this is that they do not really listen; another is that they may not know how to use their listening time effectively.

A speech helps you develop listening skills as well as speaking skills. You have already learned how to develop your speech skills. In this section you will learn how to develop your listening skills as well.

Prepare to listen.

To hear a speech you must focus your entire attention on the speaker. Get ready to listen before the speaker utters the first word, by resisting all distractions. If you have your mind somewhere else, you will not listen well. Preparing to listen to a speech involves getting comfortable in your seat, looking at the speaker, being curious about his or her ideas, and thinking of yourself as a participant in a conversation with the speaker.

Record the introduction.

After you prepare to focus on the speaker, you can prepare to record what you hear. Your first step in doing so is to remember that the speech will consist of an introduction, a body, and a conclusion. In the introduction the speaker will share the speech's purpose and sometimes its main points. As you listen to the introduction, mentally repeat the speech's purpose and topic as you jot them down on paper. Write down only the key words that will help you remember these points.

Record the body.

Next, jot down the main points in the body of the speech as you hear them and record the minor ideas that support those main ideas. Remember that the main points will be general ideas, while minor points will be more specific.

Use the conclusion.

Finally, listen to the conclusion to see if you have followed the speech accurately. The speech's purpose and topic will be mentioned again; main ideas may be restated as well. If your notes parallel the speaker's final thoughts, then you have recorded the information accurately. You also have improved your listening ability because you have been actively involved with the speaker's message.

Evaluate the speech.

You will remember more about a speech if you also evaluate it. As you listen and record information, ask questions about what you hear and see. Asking and answering such questions will help you to focus on the speech more effectively and to listen critically. As you discover what is effective or ineffective about the speech, you can share with the speaker what you have learned.

Some of the questions to ask yourself as you listen are the following ones:

Is the speech factual, or does the speaker give his or her opinions?

Is the speaker specific about ideas, or does he or she talk in generalities?

Are the facts accurate? Are the sources for the facts presented?

Does the speaker seem to know the topic well?

Is the speech's purpose clear?

Is the speech organized and easy to follow?

Does the topic of the speech relate well to the listeners' interests?

Are the introduction and conclusion imaginative?

Does the speaker have good posture, eye contact, facial expression, and body movement?

Is the speaker's voice lively, clear, and easy to hear?

If you can answer the preceding questions after listening to a speech, then you have done a good job of both evaluating and listening.

Exercise 8: Listening Well

Have someone read a magazine article to the entire class and ring a bell five or six times during the reading. Each time the bell rings, everyone should jot down on paper the idea being expressed at exactly that moment. Check to see how attentive and accurate everyone is.

Glossary of Terms

Abridged dictionary A dictionary that has been shortened and has fewer words than an unabridged dictionary

Acronym A word made up of the first letters of a series of words

Adjectives Words that modify nouns and pronouns

Adverbs Words that modify verbs or verb phrases, adjectives, other other adverbs

Alliteration The repetition of a sound in a group of words

Almanac A reference book that gives information with current facts and figures on a wide number of subjects

Apostrophe The punctuation mark (') used to show the omission of letters and to show possessives

Appositive A noun or noun substitute set beside another noun or pronoun to describe or identify it

Autobiography A writer's story about his or her own life

Biography A true story about the life of a real person

Body The paragraphs of a composition that follow the introduction and give specific information about the topic

Brainstorm To think of all the things one knows about a subject or all the possible ways of solving a problem

Business letter Letter written to apply for a job, request information, and place or correct an order

Call number The number used on a book filed under the Dewey decimal system

Card catalogue A large cabinet with drawers of cards in alphabetical order, each card listing the author, the subject, or the title of the books in the library

Character A person in a story

Chronological order The order in which events happen

Clause A group of words that has its own subject and verb

Coherent paragraph A paragraph in which the relationship of sentences to one another is obvious

Colloquial words Widely used informal words

Colon The punctuation mark used to separate elements within a sentence and to direct the reader's attention to what follows it

Comma The punctuation mark used to separate words, phrases, or clauses from other elements in a sentence

Complement A part of the predicate that completes the thought begun by the subject and the verb

Complex sentence A sentence with one independent clause and at least one subordinate clause

Composition A short paper of at least several paragraphs, all developing the same topic

Compound sentence A sentence that has more than one independent clause and no subordinate clauses

Compound-complex sentence A sentence with more than one independent clause and at least one subordinate clause

Conflict A struggle or problem that the characters in a story experience

Conjunction A word that joins words or groups of words

Context The setting of a word—the other words that surround it

Dash The punctuation mark used to separate elements within a sentence and to direct the reader's attention to what precedes it

Declarative sentence A type of sentence that makes a statement

Delete Take out words, sentences, or paragraphs from a piece of writing

Descriptive composition A composition that describes people, places, objects, or events

Dewey decimal system A system used in libraries for classifying nonfiction books in ten categories

Dialect A way of speaking shared by a group of people

Dialogue A conversation between two or more.

Direct object A noun or pronoun that follows an action verb and answers the question *who?* or *whom?* about the subject and verb

Edited Standard English (ESE) The written form of Standard English

Encyclopedia A reference book that gives information on almost every subject

Example An illustration that makes a general statement clearer and more exact

Exclamation mark The punctuation mark used to end a sentence or expression that shows strong feeling

Exclamatory sentence A sentence that expresses a strong or sudden feeling

Expository composition A composition that explains something

Factual report A composition that presents clear and accurate information gathered from outside sources

Fiction Writing formed mostly from the author's imagination and not meant to report events exactly as they happen

First-person point of view The point of view of the writer who chooses to speak directly to the reader and uses the pronoun *I*

Formal English The English used for writing in school and in business

Formal outline An outline that divides topics into major headings marked by Roman numerals and subheadings marked by capital letters

Friendly letter A letter written to greet a friend of relative

Gerund A verb form ending in *-ing* that acts as a noun

Gerund phrase The present participial (*-ing*) form of the verb with its modifiers, used as a noun

Guide words The two words in boldface (dark print) at the top of each page of a dictionary, showing the first and last words on that page

Hyphen The punctuation mark used to link the parts of some words

Imaginative writing The kind of writing found in stories, poems, and plays

Imagist poem A short poem that presents a vivid image

Imperative sentence A sentence that gives a mild command or makes a request

Independent clause A group of words that has a subject and verb and expresses a complete thought

Indirect object A noun or pronoun that answers the question *to what? for what? to whom?* or *for whom?* about the subject, verb, or direct object

Informal English The English used for talking with friends and relatives or for writing personal letters

Informal outline An outline that groups information under general headings

Interjection A word that shows strong or sudden feeling and has no relationship to other words in the sentence

Interrogative sentence A type of sentence that asks a question

Linking verb A verb that links a noun or pronoun in the first part of the sentence to a word in the second part

Main entry words The words arranged in alphabetical order in a dictionary

Manuscript The typed pages of a piece of writing

Mental point of view The way one thinks and feels about someone or something

Metaphor The comparison of two different items without the use of *like* or *as*

Meter A regular pattern of stressed and unstressed words

Narrative A composition that tells a story

Narrator The person who tells, or narrates, a story

Nonfiction books Books about real people or events

Noun The name of a person, place, thing, or idea

Paragraph A unit of writing made up of sentences that relate to the same topic

Paragraph pattern A model or plan, such as TRI—Topic, Restrictions, Illustrations—used to build a paragraph

Parentheses The punctuation mark used to enclose supplementary or explanatory material that is not closely related to the rest of the sentence

Participial phrase A present or past participle with its modifiers, functionig as an adjective

Participle A verb form that acts as an adjective in a sentence

Parts of speech The eight classes into which the words of the English language are divided

Period The punctuation mark used to separate one sentence from another or used with an abbreviation

665

Periodical A magazine or journal published at fixed time periods

Phrase A group of words that act as a single part of speech and do not have a verb or subject

Physical point of view The location from which one observes something or someone

Plot The events that happen in a story and the reasons they happen

Point of view A way of looking at someone or something

Predicate adjective An adjective that follows a linking verb and modifies the subject of the sentence

Predicate noun or predicate pronoun A noun or pronoun that follows a linking verb

Predicate of a sentence The part of the sentence that says something about the subject

Preposition A word that shows the relationship between a noun or pronoun and some other word in the sentence

Prepositional phrase A preposition, its object, and any modifiers, functioning as an adjective or an adverb in a sentence

Pronoun A word that takes the place of a noun or another pronoun

Proof A copy of typeset material

Proofreading Checking errors in grammar, usage, spelling, punctuation, and capitalization

Punctuation marks Symbols used in writing to separate, link, enclose, and show omission

Question mark The punctuation mark used to end a sentence that asks a question

Quotation marks Punctuation marks used to enclose direct quotations and some kinds of titles

Reference books A book that is used to find specific information

References People listed on an application form so that an employer can ask them about the applicant

Regional dialect A way of speaking shared by people living in a particular area

Revise Change writing to make it clearer and more interesting

Rhyme The repetition of sounds in words

Run-on sentence Two or more sentences incorrectly separated by a comma or not separated by any punctuation mark

Semicolon The punctuation mark used to signal a more distinct break in thought than the comma, and to create a longer pause when read aloud

Sentence A group of words that express a complete thought

Sentence fragment A separated part of a sentence that does not express a complete thought

Sentence outline An outline with the topics written as complete sentences

Setting The place and time where a story happens

Simile The comparison of two different things, using the words *like* or *as*

Simple sentence A sentence containing one independent clause and no subordinate clause

Slang words Words used informally within groups of people

Social letter Letter written to thank someone or to extend, accept, or decline an invitation

Specific details Details that tell about particular parts of an experience and give readers concrete information

Standard English The dialect most accepted in schools and businesses

Stressed syllable A syllable spoken more loudly than the other syllables in a word

Subject of a sentence The part of the sentence that identifies the person, place, thing, or idea spoken about in the rest of the sentence

Subordinate clause A group of words that has a subject and verb but does not express a complete thought

Summary A shortened retelling or rewriting of a book, story, article, speech, or the like

Synonyms Words that have related meanings

Third-person point of view The point of view of the writer who stands back from the story objectively and uses the pronoun *he* or *she*

Topic A limited subject that can be discussed with specific details

Topic outline An outline of short topics rather than of complete sentences

Topic sentence A sentence that states the main idea, or topic, of a paragraph

Underlining (italics) The punctuation mark that is used to set off titles of some works of art; in printing a special type called *italics* is used in place of underlining

Unified paragraph A paragraph in which each sentence develops the main idea

Verb A word that shows action or state of being

Verb phrase The main verb and all of its helping verbs, functioning as a single part of speech in a sentence

Verbal A word formed from a verb but acting as another part of speech in a sentence

Vivid details Details that describe sensory experiences and help readers see, hear, feel, smell, and taste what the writer describes

Writer's Notebook A record of the writer's thoughts, feelings, and observations

Index of Authors and Titles

Aesop, 324
American History, from, 589
Angelou, Maya, 116, 387–388
Animal Tails, from, 88
Atomic Courtesy, 209

Belling the Cat, 324
Beyond Tomorrow, from, 90
Black Revolution, The, from, 78–79
Brenner, Barbara, 28–30
Brimming Water, 216
Brooks, Gwendolyn, 207

Clark, Ann Nolan, 427
Concise Columbia Encyclopedia, from, 647

Dateline America, from, 70–72
Dark Winter, from, 51
Death Be Not Proud, from, 230
Deer Hunt, 218
Diary of Nine Kosterina, The, from, 38
DNA: Ladder of Life, from, 94–95
Dobie, J. Frank, 614
Dogs and Weather, 212
Dolph, Shirley, 405–406
Down the Santa Fe Trail and into Mexico, from, 32–33
Dreams, 214

Eagle, The, from, 210
Enterprise, from, 119–120
Eye of a Deer, from, 405–406

Frankel, Edward, 94–95

Garraty, John, 589
Gelman, Steve, 136–138
Giovanni, Nikki, 219
Gunther, John, 230

Halacy, Dan S., 90
Hardy, Thomas, 107–204
Harriet Tubman: Conductor on the Underground Railroad, from, 447–448
Hart, John, 176–177
Hawthorne, Nathaniel, 36–37
Hiking the Great Basin: The High Desert Country of California, Oregon, Nevada, and Utah, from, 176–177

Hoke, John, 76
Housekeeping in the Klondike, 122–124
Hughes, Langston, 214

I Know Why the Caged Bird Sings, from, 114–116, 387–388
I Wish I Could Give My Son a Wild Raccoon, from, 613–614
I'd Rather Be a Cowboy than Anything, 613–614
Incredible Television Machine, The, from, 81

Jacobs, Joseph, 324
Jacobson, Ethel, 209
Jerome, Judson, 218
Jesse Stuart Harvest, A, from, 51

Kelly, Walt, 119–120
Kerr, Jean, 56–57
Kipling, Rudyard, 194
Knoxville, Tennessee, 219
Kosterina, Nina, 38
Kuralt, Charles, 70–72

Langland, William, 208
Laser Light, from, 144
Laycock, George, 83–84
London, Jack, 122–124, 195

Magoffin, Susan Shelby, 32–33
Mason, George F., 88
Matthew Alexander Henson, 139–141
McCarthy, Mary, 55–56
Medicine Bag, The, from, 2
Medicine Man's Daughter, from, 427
Memories of a Catholic Girlhood, from, 55–56

New Columbia Encyclopedia, from, 168

Pate, Jack, 613–614
Pete at the Zoo, 207
Petrakis, Harry Mark, 60–62
Petry, Ann, 447–448
Please Don't Eat the Daisies, 56–57
Polk, Lee, and Eda LeShan, 81

Reader's Guide to Periodical Literature, from, 628
Reflections: A Writer's Life, A Writer's Work, from, 60–62
Rikki-Tikki-Tavi, from, 194

Sandburg, Carl, 210, 213
Schneider, Herman, 144
Snake-Lover's Diary, from, 28–30
Sneve, Virginia Driving Hawk, 2
Solar Energy, from, 76
Splinter, 210
Stelmark: A Family Recollection, from, 60–62
Strongest Animals of All, from, 60–62
Stuart, Jesse, 51

Tennyson, Alfred Lord, 210
The People, Yes, from, 213
To Build a Fire, from, 195
Tony Kates, the Archdeceiver, 107–204
Tu Fu, 216

Vaquero of the Brush Country, A, from, 614
Vision of Piers Plowman, The, from, 208

War of the Worlds, The, from, 20
Warren, Ruth, 78–79
Webster's New World Dictionary, from, 633, 636, 637, 639, 640
Welles, Winifred, 212
Wells, H.G., 20
West From Home: Letters of Laura Ingalls Wilder to Almanzo Wilder, San Francisco 1915, from, 231–232
Whaling, 167–168
Wife of Usher's Well, The, 210
Wilder, Laura Ingalls, 231–232

Index

Bold numbers feature basic definitions and rules.

A

A and *an*, use of, 288–289
Abbreviations
  in dictionaries, 639, 641
  on envelopes, 237–238
  explaining word history, 640–641
  government agencies and, 574
  part of name or title, 569, 574
  periods in, 535–536
  in *Readers Guide*, 629
  state, two-letter, 237
About, use of, 431
Abridged dictionaries, 646–647
Abstract nouns, defined, **285**
Accent marks, 637–**638**
Accented syllable, **598**, **638**
Acceptance, letter of, 244
Acronyms, **609**
Action
  moving to, as purpose for speech, 650
  verbs, **340**–342
Address, nouns of, paired commas with, **545**
Address of letter, 237–238, **249**, 251
  inside, **249**
  return, **238**
Addresses, commas in, **541**–542
Adjective clauses, 519–**520**
  punctuating, **526**
  relative pronoun, 520
Adjectives, **376**–395
  adverbs formed from, 402
  adverbs modifying, 396–399
  after linking verb, **382**–383
  and adverbs, choosing between, 410–413
  articles, 378
  commas separating, 100, **539**
  common nouns as, **379**–380

comparative forms, 383–385, 388–**389**, 390–392
compound, hyphen in, **551**–552
degrees of comparison, 383–385
demonstrative pronouns as, **381**
features of, 383–386
formed with suffixes, 386
grouping by classes, 377–381
irregular comparisons, 384–385, **391**–392
as modifiers, 376–382
participles used as, 462
positive forms, 384–385
possessive pronouns as, 381
predicate, **382**
prepositional phrases as, 425–426, 433–**434**
pronouns as, **381**
proper, 378
proper, capitalizing, 378, 572
superlative forms, 384–385, 388–**389**, 390–392
understanding, 376–386
using, 388–392
Adverb clauses, 519, **521**–523
  introductory, comma used to set off, **539**–540
  punctuating, **527**–528, **539**
  subordinating conjunction, 522
Adverb phrase, 502
Adverbs, **396**–419
  and adjectives, choosing between, 410–413
  adverbs modifying, 396–399
  comparative forms, 401, 406–409
  degrees of comparison, **400**–**401**, 406–409
  ending in *-ly*, 402–403
  features of, 400–403
  formed from adjectives, **402**

formed with suffixes, 402–403
grouping by classes, **398**–**399**
intensifiers, **399**
interrogative, **398**
irregular comparisons, 408–409
modifiers, **396**–399
negative, **398**–**399**, **414**–415
prepositional phrases as, 425, 435
sentence connectors, 24–25
superlative forms, 401, **406**–409
to combine sentences, 24–25
understanding, 396–403
using, 406–415
Agreement
  subject/verb, **360**–367
  of verbs and indefinite pronoun, **366**–367
Agreement of pronoun and antecedent, **324**–328
  antecedents joined by *and* or *or*, 326
  each, either, everyone, etc., **327**–328
  Edited Standard English, 330
  in number and gender, 324–325
  plural indefinite pronouns, 327
  singular indefinite pronouns, **327**
Agreement of subject and verb, **360**–367
  after *here, there*, **363**
  collective nouns, 364–**365**
  compound subjects joined by *and*, **364**
  compound subjects joined by *or* or *nor*, 364–365
  each, either, neither, etc., **366**
  indefinite pronouns as subjects, 366–367

plural subjects, **364**–365
several, few, many, both, **366**
singular subjects, **364**
some, most, any, none, all, part, **367**
All, number of, 327
All-, hyphenation of words beginning with, 551
Alliteration, 206, **208**
American English, 612–613
Among and *between,* using, 429
And, antecedents joined by, **326**
Anecdotes (incidents), developing paragraphs with, 83–85
Anglo-Saxon, **606**
Answering letter of invitation, 244
Antecedent, **310**–311
  agreement of pronouns with, **324**–328
  compound, **326**
  indefinite pronouns as, 327–328
Any, number of, 327
Anybody, number of, 327
Anyone, number of, 327
Apostrophe
  contractions, **559**
  possessive of plural noun, **164**
  possessive of singular noun, **560**
  uses of, 164–165, **559**–561
Appeals to emotion, language of persuasion, 178–179
Application
  job, form for, 267–272
  letters of, 252–253
  library card, 264–266
Appositive phrases, **507**
  commas with, **511**, **544**
  nonessential, **544**
Appositives, **507**
  colon with, **548**

nonessential, paired commas with, **544**
Argumentative writing. *See* Persuasive writing
Articles
  magazine, locating, 627–629
  summary, writing, 134–136
  titles, quotation marks enclosing, **555**
Articles (grammar), **288**
  as adjectives, 378
Asking questions
  point-of-view questions, 13–15
  who?, what?, when?, where?, why?, how? 10–12
At, 431
Atlas, 649
Audience, **104**
  See also Reader
Author cards, 622
Autobiographies, arrangement in library, 618–619
Auxiliary verbs. *See* Helping verbs

B

Bad and *badly,* using, 410
Base sentence, 43–47, 65, 98
  inserting sentences into, 98–101, 127–133, 158–165, 187–191, 222–227, 260–261
Be
  conjugation of verb, 358–359
  forms of, 342
  as linking verbs, 342
  in progressive form, 358–359
  tenses, 358–359
Beside and *besides,* using, 429
Between and *among,* using, 429
Bibliographies, 155–156
  book entries, 155–156
  encyclopedia article entries, 156

magazine article entries, 156
model, research paper, 153
Biographies, arrangement in library, 618–619
Body
  of business letter, 249
  of composition, 114
  of letter, 235, 249
  movement, 661
  of speech, 654–655
Books
  arrangement in library, 616–621
  call numbers, 616–619
  card catalogue, **621**–625
  finding on library shelves, 625–627
  index, **143**–144
  reference, 632–649
  titles, underlining, **556**
Both, number of, 327
Brainstorming, 5–6
Brand names, **573**
Business letters
  of application, 252–253
  block form, 250
  body, 249
  capitalization in, 259
  closing, 249–250
  envelopes for, 251
  folding, 238–239
  form, 248–250
  heading, 248
  inside address, 249
  models, 248, 250
  order letter, 256
  parts of, 249–250
  proofreading, 259
  punctuation, 248–249, 259
  of request, 254–255
  revising, guidelines for, 258–259
  salutation, 249
  salutation, colon in, 548
  signature, 250

671

state abbreviations, 237
But, only as negative words, 415
By, 431

C

C, ei after, **598**
Call numbers, 616–617, **618**–619
Capitalization, 568–584
   in business letters, 259
   in friendly and social letters, 235
   of brand names of products, **573**
   of businesses, **573**
   of calendar items, **575**
   of compass directions, **571**
   of first word of a sentence, **568**
   of geographical places, **571**
   of geographical regions, **571**
   of historical periods and events, **575**
   of names of people, **568**
   of nationalities, **572**
   of organizations, government agencies, **574**
   of *president* and *vice president* titles, **570**
   of pronoun *I*, **568**
   of proper nouns, 286–287, **303–305**
   of school subjects, **578**–579
   of ships, planes, and trains, **577**
   of special events, **575**
   of specific titles, **580**
   of titles of books, magazines, etc., **580**
   of titles of persons, **569**–570
   of words referring to religions, the Deity, and holy books, **577**
   of words showing family relationship, **568**–569
Card catalog
   author cards in, 622
   information given in a card catalog, 622–625
   subject cards in, 624–625
   title cards in, 623
-ceed, -cede, -sede (spelling rule), **599**

Changes in thought, dash, with, **550**
Changing viewpoints, 10, 13–14
Chapters, titles of, **555**
Character description, in personal narrative, 54–58
Characters, 192–196, 204
Checklist
   for proofreading, 18, 685
   for proofreading business letters, 259
   for proofreading friendly and social letters, 247
   for revising, 686
   for revising a paragraph, 97
   for revising a persuasive letter, 186
Chronological organization, 120
Classification number, 618
Classifying (arranging) information, 110–113
Clauses, **516**–532
   adjective, 519–**520**
   adverb, 519, **521**–522
   at beginning of sentence, **527**–528
   commas used to set off nonessential, **526**
   distinguishing from phrases, **516**
   essential, **526**
   independent, **517**–518, **524**–**525**
   introductory, **527**–528
   kinds of, 517–518
   nonessential, punctuation with, 526, 544
   subordinate, 517, **518**
Clear thinking. *See* Reasoning
Clipped forms of words, **609**–610
Closing of letter, **235**, **249–250**
   of business letter, **249–250**
   capitalizing, **580**
Clustering, 6–8
Coherence
   model of coherent paragraph, 94–95
   in writing paragraphs, 92–95
Collective nouns,
   agreement with, 364–**365**
   list of, 365
   singular or plural, **365**
Colloquial words, **613**–614
Colon

after salutation of business letter, **548**
as sentence connector, 66–67
before list of items, **548**
between hour and minute, **548**
to separate an introductory statement from an explanation, an appositive, or a quotation, **548**
uses of, **547**–548
Combining sentences
   adjective and adverb clauses, 520–522
   inserting adjectives, 98–103
   inserting adverbs, 24–25
   using colons, 66–68
   using *either/or*, 22–23
   using *-ing* words, 160–162
   using *nor*, 22
   using *(with)* phrases, 158–160
   using semi-colons, 26–27
   using sentence connectors, 21
   using subordinators, 40–42
   using *who*, and *which*, 127–130
   using *whose, where, when, why*, 131–133
   using *where, when, how*, 187–191
Comma fault. *See* Run-on sentence
Comma splice. *See* Run-on sentence
Commas
   closing of business letter, **250**
   dates, **542**
   direct quotation, **540**
   names followed by Jr., Ph.D., etc., **542**
   with adjective clauses, **526**
   with adverb clauses, **527**–528
   with appositive phrase, **511**, **544**
   connecting sentences, 21
   with geographical names in an address, **541**–542
   in independent clauses, **524**–**525**
   paired, **543**–545
   with nonessential clauses and phrases, **544**
   with nouns of address, **545**
   with parenthetical expressions, **545**

with participial phrase, **509–510**, **539**
with prepositional phrases, **539**–540
replacing conjunction, **448**–**449**
in run-on sentences, **496**
separating adjectives preceding a noun, **539**
separating introductory elements from rest of sentence, **540**
separating items in a series, **449**, **539**
single, **538–542**
with transitional expressions, **545**
uses of, **538–542, 543–545**
Common nouns, **286–287**
as adjectives, **379**
Communication, nonverbal, 660–661
Comparative degree of comparison
of adjectives, **384–385, 388–392**
of adverbs, **401, 406–409**
Comparison
degrees of, **383–385, 400–401**
irregular; **384–385, 408–409**
Comparison. *See* Degrees of comparison
Complements, **481–482, 484**
direct object, **482**
indirect object, **483**
predicate adjective, **486**
predicate noun, **484**–485
predicate pronoun, **484**–485
subject and verb, **487**
Complete predicate, **479**
Complete subject, **473**
Complex sentences, **489**
Compound-complex sentences, **490**
Compositions, **104**
body, 114
conclusion, 114
descriptive, 104, 114–117
details for, 119
expository, 104, 122–125, 167
gathering and recording information for, 107–108
introduction, 114
narrative, 104, 119–121

outline for, 110–113
parts of, **114**
selecting information for, 108–109
topic, deciding on, 104–106
writing, 104–126
Compositions. *See* name of specific type of composition
Compound adjectives, hyphen in, **551**–552
Compound antecedents, **326**
Compound-complex sentences, **490**–492
Compound nouns, **287**
hyphens in, **299**, **550**–551
rules for forming plurals, **299–300**
Compound numbers, hyphen in, **552**
Compound objects of prepositions, **424**
Compound sentences, **488**
Compound subjects, **476**
of verb, agreement with, **364–365**
Compound verbs, **480**
Compound words, 609
Conclusion
of composition, **114**
of speech, **654**, **657**–659
Conclusions, in sound reasoning, 172–173
Concrete details. *See* Specific details
Concrete nouns, **285**
Conflict, **192**–196, 204
Conjugation of verb *be*, 358–359
Conjunctions, **440**–455
coordinating, **442**, **448**–**449**, 476, 518, **524**–**525**
correlative, **443**–**444**, 449, 518
grouping of classes, 442–445
subordinating, **445**, **450**–**451**, 522, 528
understanding, 440–445
using, 448–451
Connecting ideas, 21
Connectors (connectives) to join sentences, 21–27
Connotative meaning of words, 178–179
Consonants, **597**
Context, **586**
clues, using, **586**–588

using dictionary to find, 644–645
words in, 586–588, 644
Contractions
apostrophes in, 559
with *not*, 398–399
Controlling statement of speech, 654–655
Coordinating conjunctions, **442**, **448–449**, 476, 518, **524–525**
list of, **442**
punctuation of, **442**
Correlative conjunctions, **443–444**, 449, 518
list of, **443**

D

Dangling modifier, **512**
Dash, uses of, **550**
to indicate abrupt change in thought, **550**
to separate introductory series or thought, **550**
Dates, commas in, **542**
Declarative sentence, **471**
exclamations in, **537**
period after, **471**, **535**
quotations that are questions in, **537**
Declining an invitation, 244
Definitions, 641–643
Degrees of comparison
adjectives and, 383–385
adverbs and, 400–401
irregular, 384–385, 408–409
Deities, capitalization of words referring to, 577
Demonstrative pronouns, 312, **318**
as adjectives, **381**
list of, **318**
Dependent clause. *See* Subordinate clauses
Description
in poetry, 215–216
in short story, 194
of events, 58–62
of people, 54–57
of places, 50–52
Descriptive composition, 104
revising, guidelines for, 118
writing, 114–116
writing about events, 58–62

673

writing about objects, 49–50
writing about people, 54–58
writing about places, 50–52
Details
  connecting, 652
  for informative speech, 652
  minor, in speech, 655
  organizing, 60, 110–112
  recording, 652
  specific, 35–37, 50, 55, 58–60, 76–77, 114, 119, 231
  vivid, 50, 55, 114, 119, 194
Determiners, **288**–289
Dewey decimal system, **616**–619
Dialects, 611–613
Dialogue, 56
Diary, *See* Writers Notebook
Diction, *See* Words
Dictionaries
  abbreviations in, 639, 641
  accent marks in, 637–**638**
  consulting, 597
  content and arrangement, 632–634
  definitions in, 641–643
  derivations, 640–641
  differences among, 646–647
  etymologies (word histories), 640–641
  finding words in, 632–634
  as guide to pronunciation, 635–637
  as guide to spelling, 597
  information in, 635–646
  Johnson's, 632
  parts of speech, 639–640
  special information, 647
  synonyms, 645–646
  unabridged, 646
Direct object **482**
  of gerund, **505**
  sentence patterns with, 481–484
Direct quotations
  commas with, **540**
  quotation marks with, **554**
Double negatives, avoiding, **414**–415

E

e, root word ending with, **602**–603
Each, number of, **327**

East, west, north, south, rules of capitalizing, **571**
Easy, and *easily*, using, **411**
Edited Standard English, 612–614
  pronouns used in, **330**
Education, on job application form, 269
ei and *ie* (spelling rule), **598**
-Elect, hyphen with, 551
Emotions. *See* Feelings
Employers, former, on job application form, 269–271
Employment desired, on job application form, 269
Encyclopedias, **647**–648
  additional volumes, 648
  finding information in, 647–648
  special, 649
End marks
  exclamation point, **537**–538
  period, **535**–536
  question mark, **537**
English language
  dialects, **611**–613
  history, 606–610
  informal vs. formal, **613**–**614**
English language. *See* Language
Enunciation, 660
Envelopes
  for business letters, 251
  standard form, 236–238
-er and *-est*, **384**, **407**
Essay. *See* name of specific composition
Essential clauses, punctuation of, 526
Essential phrases, 510
Etymologies (word histories)
  history of English language, 607–610
  in dictionaries, 640–641
Events
  describing, 58–62
  titles, capitalizing, **575**
Everybody, number of, **327**
Everyone, number of, **327**
-Ex; hyphenation of words beginning with, 551
Examples
  using to develop paragraphs, 76, 86

Exclamation point, 457–458, **537**
Exclamatory sentence, **472**
  punctuation in, **472**
Experience
  sense, 28, 32–33
  writing about, 28, 32–35, 48–49
  writing from, 105–106
Explanation
  colon with, **548**
  parentheses with, 562
Expository composition, 70–95, **104**, **122**–125
  brainstorming, 5–6
  choosing and limiting topics, 104–106
  classifying and arranging information, 110–113
  gathering information, 107–108
  guidelines for writing, 124
  model composition, 122–124
  outlining, 110–113
  paragraphing, 124
  purpose of, 70, **122**
  thesis, 124
  writing, 70–95, 122–126
Expository paragraphs, **70**–97
  choosing a method of development, 86–87
  development through specific information, 70
  development with examples, 76–78
  development with facts, 78–79
  development with reasons, 80–82
  development with incidents, 83–85
  guidelines for revising, 97
  writing coherent, 92–95
  writing unified, 89–91
  writing well-developed, 87–88
Expository writing. *See* Expository composition

F

Facts, **174**
  developing expository paragraphs, 78–79
  distinguishing from opinions, 174–175

using to develop paragraphs, 78–79, 86
Fallacies. *See* Reasoning
Family relationship
    words showing, **568**–569
Feelings
    expressed in poetry, 217–218
    writing about, 38–39, 50
Few, number of, **327**
Fiction, arrangement in library, 620
Figurative language
    similes, **212**–213
    metaphors, **213**–214
Films, titles of, **557**
First-person point of view, 120
First-person pronouns, **312**
    order used in, **330**
Folding a letter, 238–239
Formal English, 614
    colloquial words, 614
    Edited Standard English, 614
    slang, 614
    who and *whom*, **335**–337
Formal outline, 150–151
Former employers, on job application form, 269–271
Forms
    filling out, 262–272
    job application, 267–272
    for library card, 264–266
    order, 262–263
Fractions, compound adjectives hyphen in, **552**
Fragments. *See* Sentence fragments
Free verse, 219–220
Free writing, 8–9
French, influence on English language, 608–609
Friendly letter, **228**
    body, 235
    closing, 235
    form of, 233–235
    proofreading, checklist, 247
    salutation, 235
    signature, 235
    writing, 228–235
From, **432**
Future perfect tense
    forming, **351**–352, 356

progressive form, 346, 357–359
Future tense of verb
    forming, **349**–350
    progressive form, **346**, 357–359

G

Gender of pronouns, **322, 325,** 328
    agreement with antecedent, **325**
Geographical names, **541**–542, 571
    capitalizing, **571**
    commas with, **541**–542
Geographical regions, capitalization, **571**
Germanic languages, 606
Gerund phrases, **504, 505**–506
Gerunds, **465**
    direct object, 505
Good and *well*, using **412**–413
Great-, hyphen with, 551
Guide words, **634**
Guidelines. *See* Checklist

H

Has, had, have, **351**
Hardly, as negative word, 414
Heading, letter, 234, 248
    of business letter, 248
Helping verbs, **343**–344, **502**
    has, had, have, **351**
    shall have/will have, **351**–352
    shall and *will*, using **349**–350
His or *her*, agreements of pronoun and antecedent, **325**
Historical periods and events, capitalizing, **575**
Hyphen, uses of, **550**–553, **600**–**601**
    dividing words at end of a line, **552**–553
    in compound numbers, **552**
    with compound adjectives, **551**
    with compound nouns, **550**–551
    with prefixes *ex-, self-, all-,* 551
    with suffix *-elect*, 551

I

Ideas
    connecting, 21–26
    interesting to readers, 3
    main, in outline, 110–113
    Writer's Notebook as source of, 28
    for writing, 5–15
ie, ei, spelling rule, **598**
Illustrations, 72–76
    sentences, 72–76
    using in speech, **657**, 658
Imagery in poetry, 215–216
Imagination, writing from, 192–221
Imperative sentence, **471**
    period after, **471, 535**
    understood subject, **474**–475
in and *into*, using **429**–430
Incidents
    using to develop paragraphs, 83–84, 87
    using to describe people, 56
Indefinite pronouns, 312, **315**–316
    agreement with, **366**–367
    as antecedents, **327**–328
    list of, **315**
    number of, **327**
Independent clauses, **517**–518
    commas separating, **524–525,** **539**
    semicolon with, **525,** 547
Index
    of book, 143–144
    for encyclopedias, 648
Indirect object, **483**
    not part of prepositional phrase, 484
    sentence patterns with, **483**–484
Indo-European languages, 606
Infinitive, *to* in, 423
Informal English, **613**–614
    colloquial words, 613
    Edited Standard English, 613–614
    short sentences, 613
    slang words, 613
    who, whom, **335**–337
Informal essay. *See* Narrative composition
Informal outline, 110–113, 149–150

675

Information
  arranging in outline, 110–113
  from brainstorming and clustering, 5–9
  in dictionaries, 635–646
  in encyclopedias, 647–648
  gathering and recording, 107–108, 143–148
  inserted, essential and nonessential, 129–130
  on job application form, 267–272
  in letter of application, 252
  in letter of request, 254–255
  in letters of invitation, 242
  in order letter, 256
  in periodicals, 627–631
  organizing for research report, 148–151
  as purpose for speech, 650
  selecting, 108–109
  about speech topic, finding, 651–652
  using questions to discover, 147–148
-ing form of verbs, **346**, **465**
Inside address, letter, 249
Intensifiers, **399**
Interjections, **456**–461
  commas with, 457–458, **540**
  understanding, 456
  using, 457–458
Interrogative adverbs, **398**
Interrogative pronouns, 312, **316**–317
  who, whom, 317, **335**–337
Interrogative sentence, **472**
  punctuation of, **472**
  quotations that are questions in, 537
Interruptors, set off by commas, **543**–545
Interview, job, 273–275
Into and *in,* using, **429**–430
Intransitive verbs, **341**–343
Introduction
  of composition, 114
  of speech, **654,** 656–657
Introductory elements
  colons with, **548**
  commas with, **540**
  dash with, **550**
Invitation, letters of, 242–243
  declining, 244
  information in, 242

Irregular comparisons
  for adjectives, **384**–385, **391**–392
  for adverbs, **408**–409
Irregular plurals, **295**–298
Irregular verbs, **353**–356
  forming tenses of, **355**–356
  list of, **353**–355
Italics, **556**–558
It's and *its,* using, **559**
Its and *it's,* using, **559**

J

Jobs
  application, form for, 267–272
  application, letters of, 252–253
  application, preparing for, 272
  interview, 273–275
Journal. *See* Writer's notebook

K

Key words, 636

L

Language, 606–614
  appropriate, 613–615
  courses, names of, **578**–579
  development of English, 606–610
  dialects, 611–613
  English, history of, 606–610
  figurative, 212–214
  imagery, 215–216
  Indo-European, 606
  influence of different languages on English, 606–609
  informal vs. formal, 613–614
  Standard American English, 612–613
  varieties of English, 611–612
Latin, influence on English language, 608
Lay and *lie,* using **369**–370
Leave and *let,* using, **370**
Less and *least,* using, **406**–407
Letters
  of acceptance, 244
  address, 236–238, 251
  answering, 244
  of application, 252–253

  body, **235**, **249**
  business, 247–250
  closing, **235**, **249**–250, **580**
  declining invitation, 244
  folding, **238**–239
  friendly, 228–236, 247
  heading, **234**, 248
  inside address, **249**
  of invitation, 242–243
  mailing, 236–238
  order, 256
  of request, 254–255
  salutation, **235**, **249**, **580**
  signature, **235**, **250**
  social, 233, 240, 247
  thank-you, 240–241
  to the editor, 184–185
Levels of usage, 611–615
  See also Edited Standard English, Standard English
Library
  arrangement of books in, 616–620
  call numbers, **618**
  card catalog, **621**–625
  classification number, **618**
  Dewey Decimal System, **616**–619
  fiction, **620**–621
  finding books in, 625–627
  finding periodicals in, **627**–631
  nonfiction, 616–617
  using, 616–631
  using *Readers' Guide to Periodical Literature,* **627**–631
Library card application, 264–266
Lie and *lay,* using **369**–370
Limericks, 209
Linking expressions. *See* Transitional expressions
Linking verbs, **342**–343
  list of, **342**
  predicate adjectives following, **382**
  predicate nouns and pronouns following, **484**–485
Listening, 660, 662–663
Loaded words (persuasive language), 178–179
Logical order, arranging sentences in, 93–94
  in a paragraph, 92–93
-ly, 402–403

676

M

Magazines
　articles listed in *Readers' Guide*, 627–629
　articles, locating, 627–629
　titles of, **556**
Mailing a letter, 236–238
Main clauses. *See* Independent clauses
Main entry words, **635**
Main points of speech, 655
　summary, 658
Making connections (clustering), 6–8
Many, number of, **327**
Mental point of view, **48**–49
Metaphors, 213–214
Meter in poetry, 206, 208
Methods of paragraph development. *See* Paragraphs
Modern English, 606–607
Modifiers
　adjective clauses, **520**
　adjectives, **376**–382
　adverb clauses, **521**
　in appositive phrase, **507**
　bad and *badly*, using, **410**
　dangling, **512**
　easy and *easily*, using, **411**
　of gerund, 506
　of gerund phrase, 505–506
　good and *well*, using, **412–413**
　indefinite pronouns as, 316
　of participial phrase, 504–506
　participial phrases, **504**
　prepositional phrases, 425–426
　real and *really*, using, **411**–412
　relative pronouns, as, **319**
　single-word, 319, 506
　sure and *surely*, using, **412**
More and *most*, using, 384–385, 401, **406**
Mr., Miss, Mrs., Ms., **569**
Myself and *ourselves*, using, 313

N

Names
　capitalization, **303**–305, **568**
　commas with, **542**
　state, abbreviations, **237**
Narrative composition, 104, **119**–121
　details in, 50, 119
　order of events in, 120
　personal, 48–49
　point of view in, **48**–49, 120
　writing, 119–121
Narrative writing, purpose of, **104**
Narrative writing. *See also* Personal narrative
Narrator, **48**–49
Negative adverbs, **398**–399
Negatives, double, avoiding, **414**–415
Neither, number of, **327**
Neuter pronouns, 322
Never, **398**–399
Newspaper. *See* Periodicals
Nonessential clauses, punctuation with, **526, 544**
Nonessential phrases, **509**–510, **544**
Nonfiction
　arrangement in library, 616–619
　finding on library shelves, 625–627
Nonrestrictive clauses. *See* Nonessential clauses
Nonstandard English. *See* Informal English
Nonverbal communication, 660–661
Nor, antecedents joined by, 326
North, south, east, west, rules for capitalizing, 571
Not, **398**–399
Note cards, 146–147
Notes, taking for research report, 145–147
Noun suffix, **289**–290, **293**–296
Nouns, **284**–309
　abstract, **285**
　of address, commas with, **545**
　appositives, **507, 544**–545, **548**
　capitalizing, **286**–287, **303**–305
　collective, 364–**365**
　common, **286**–287
　compound, **287, 299**–300
　compound, hyphens in, 550–552
　concrete, **285**
　features of, 288–290
　followed by number or letter, capitalizing, **580**
　gerund used as, 505–506
　grouping by classes, **285**–287
　plurals, 289, 292–300
　possessives, **289, 301**–302, **560**
　predicate, **484**
　proper, **286**–287
　singular, 289
　suffixes, **289, 293**–296
　understanding, 284–292
　using, 292–305
Number, agreement of pronoun and antecedent, **327**–329
Numbers
　apostrophe with omitted, **559**–560
　compound, hyphen with, **552**
　first two in year, **559**–560
　part of compound adjective, **552**

O

Object
　compound, **424**
　direct, 481, **482, 483**–484
　indirect, **483**–484
　of preposition, 421, 424, **428**
Object complements. *See* Direct, indirect object
Object forms of pronouns, **322, 333**–334, **428**
Object of prepositions, 421, **428**
Of, **432**
Off, **432**
Old English, 606–608
　words, 607–608
Omissions, showing, **535**
On with blame, **432**
On and *onto*, using, **430**
One, number of, **327**
Only, but, as negative words, 415
Opinions
　distinguishing from facts, 174–175
Or, nor, antecedents joined by, **326**
Order forms, 262–263
Order letters, 256
Order of importance (organizing) in persuasive writing, 183–184
Organization
　chronological, 120

677

of information for report, 148–151
logical, 93–94
Ourselves, myself, **313**
Outline
  division of, 150–151
  formal, 150–151
  informal, 110–113, **149**–150
  sentence, 113
  for speech, informative, 653–655
  topic, 112–113, 149–151

P

Paired commas, **543–545**
Paragraphs, **70**
  checklist for revising, **97**
  coherent writing, **70**, 92–94
  developing, 70–87
  expository, 70–97
  logical order of sentences in, 92–93
  methods of development, 86–87
  importance of order in, 93
  revising, specific instructions for, **16–17**
  unified, writing, 70, **89**–90
  using examples to develop, 76, 86
  using facts to develop, 78–79, 86
  using incidents to develop, 83–84, 87
  using reasons to develop, 80–81, 87
  well developed, writing, 87–88
  writing, 70–94
Parallel structure, **441**, 449
Parentheses, uses of, **562**
  to enclose explanatory material, **562**
Parenthetical expressions, paired commas with, **545**
Participial phrases, **504**
  as sentence fragments, **494**–495
  commas with, **509**–510, **539**–540
  introductory, commas used to set off, **539**–540
  nonessential phrases, set off by comma, **544**

past participial phrase, **504**
placing, **512**
present participial phrase, **504**
punctuation with, **509**–510
used as adjectives, **504**
Participles, **462**
  distinguished from verb phrase, 462
  past, 345–346, **463**–464
  present, **462**
Parts of speech, **639**–640
Past participial phrase, **504**
Past participle, 345–346, **353**–355, **463**–464
  as principal part of verb, 345
  forming, **463**
  of irregular verbs, **353**–355
  in participial phrase, 504
Past perfect tense
  forming, **351**, 356
  progressive form, **346**, 357–359
Past tense of verbs, **345**
  forming, **349**, 356
  irregular verbs, **353–355**
  progressive form, **346**, 357–359
People
  names, capitalizing, **286**–287, 568
  titles, capitalizing, 303, **569**–570
  writing about, 54–57
Perfect tenses of verb, 345
  forming, **346**, 356
  future, **346**
  past, **346**
  present, **346**
  progressive form, **346**
Periodicals
  finding information in, 627–629
  finding in library, 630–631
Periods, **535–536**
  after abbreviations, **535–536**
  after mild command, **535**
  after simple statement, **535**
Personal information,
  on job application form, 267–269
Personal narrative, 48–64
  chronological order, 60
  describing an object, 49–50
  listing specific details, 53

model compositions, 51, 55–56, 60–62
narrator, **48**–49
using dialogue to describe characters, 56–57
writing about events, 58–64
writing about people, 54–58
writing about places, 50–52
Personal pronouns, **312**–313, **485**
  gender, **322**, **325**, 328
  list of, **312**
  object forms, **322**, **333–334**
  possessive forms, **314**
  subject forms, **322**, **331–332**
Personal statements,
  on job application form, 272
Persuasion
  checklist for revising a personal letter, **186**
  choosing a limited topic (proposition), 179–181
  facts and opinions, use of, 174–177
  language, use of, 178
  letter to the editor, 181–185
  logical thinking, 172–**173**
  outlining the argument, 183–184
  persuasive and expository writing compared, 167–170
  prewriting steps, 179–184
  propositions, choosing, 179–181
  purpose, 166–167
  reasoning, use of, 172–173
  revising a persuasive letter, checklist, **186**
  writing, 179–186
Persuasive writing. *See* Persuasion
Phrases, **502–515**
  appositive, **507**
  at beginning of sentence, followed by comma, **509**–510
  dangling modifiers in, **512**
  distinguishing from clauses, **516**
  grouping by classes, 502–507
  in sentence fragments, 494–495
  prepositional, **421**, 425–426, **502**–503
  punctuation, 509–511, 538–545
  understanding, 502–507

using, 509–512
verb, **344**, 462, 502
verbal, 462–465, **504**–505
Physical point of view, **48**
Picture poem, 216
Places
names, capitalizing, **305**
writing about, 50–52
Plot, story, 192–196, 204
Pluperfect. *See* Past perfect tense
Plural
of indefinite pronouns, 321–**322**
of nouns, **289**, 292–293, **302**
of nouns, spelling, 639–640
of pronouns, **321**, **325**, **326**, **328**
of subject and verb, **347**
suffixes, **293**–**296**
of verbs, **347**
Poetry
expressing feelings, 217–218
figurative language, 211–215
free verse, 219–220
imagery in, 215–216
limericks, 209
metaphor, 213–215
meter in, 206, **208**–**209**
quoting titles of poems, 554–555
rhyme, **206**–**208**
sensory details, vivid images, 215–217
similes and metaphors in, **212**–**213**, 214
sound and meaning in, 206
titles, 554–556
Point of view, **48**
in narrative composition, 48–49, 120–121
writing from, 13–14
Positive degree of comparison
of adjectives, **384**–**385**
of adverbs, **401**, 406–409
Possessive pronouns, 312–**314**
as adjectives, **381**
gender, **322**
Possessives
distinguishing from contractions, **559**
forming, **164**–**165**, **560**
of nouns, 164–165, 289, 301–**302**
Posture, **661**

Predicate. *See* Predicate of sentence
Predicate adjectives, **486**
Predicate noun, **484**–485
Predicate pronoun, **484**–485
Predicate of sentence, **479**
complete, **479**
simple, **479**
Prefixes, 589, **590**–**591**, 598
added to proper nouns of adjectives, **600**–**601**
added to root word, 590–591, **600**–**601**
hyphens with, **600**–**601**
meanings, **590**–**591**
spelling rule for, **600**–**601**
Premise, in persuasive writing, 172–173
Prepositional phrases, 421, 425–426, **502**–**503**
as sentence fragments, **494**–495
as adjectives, 425, 433–**434**
as adverbs, 425, **435**
functions of, 425–426
as modifiers, 425–426
Prepositions, 420–439
with compound objects, **424**
in Edited Standard English, **431**–**432**
object of, **421**, **428**
troublesome, using correctly, **429**–**430**
understanding, **420**–**426**
used as other parts of speech, **422**–**423**
using, 428–435
Present participial phrase, **504**
Present participles, **462**
as principal part of verb, 345
in participial phrase, **504**, 505
Present perfect tense
forming, **351**, **356**
progressive form, **346**, 357–359
Present tense of verb, 345
forming, **349**, 355
irregular verbs, **353**–**355**
progressive form, **346**, 357–359
Prewriting. *See* Writing process, specific type of writing
Primary accent, 638

Principal parts of verbs, **345**–**346**, **353**–**355**
Process of writing. *See* Writing process
Progressive form of verbs, **346**
tenses, **346**, **357**–**359**
Pronouns, 310–339
agreement with antecedents, **324**–**328**
antecedents, 310–311, **324**–**328**
demonstrative, 312, **318**
features of, **321**–**322**
functions, 310–311
gender, **322**, **325**, 328
grouping by classes, **312**–**320**
I, capitalizing, **568**
indefinite, 312, **315**–**316**, 327
interrogative, 312, **316**–**317**
making sentence clear, **330**
object forms, **322**, **333**–**334**, **428**
as objects of prepositions, **428**
personal, **312**–**313**, 314, 321–**322**
possessive, 312, **314**
plural, **321**, 325, 326, **328**
predicate, **484**–**485**
problems avoiding, **329**–**330**
relative, 312, **319**–320, 335, 520
singular, **321**, **325**, **326**, **327**–**328**
subject forms, **322**, **331**–**332**
understanding, 310–324
using, 324–335
who, whom, **335**–**336**
Pronunciation
accent marks, **637**–**638**
key, **636**
symbols, **636**
using dictionaries for, **635**–**638**
Proofreading, **18**–**19**
business letters, 258–259
checklist for, 18
friendly and social letters, checklist for, 247
symbols (marks), **19**
Proofreading. *See also* specific type of writing
Propaganda (appeals to emotion), 178–179
Proper adjectives, capitalizing, **378**
Proper nouns, 286–287
as adjectives, **378**
capitalizing, **303**–**305**

679

Proposition, in persuasive writing, 179–181
Punctuation, 534–535
  apostrophe, **559–560**
  in business letters, 248–249
  colon, 66–67, 547–**548**
  comma, **524–528, 538–542, 543–545**
  correcting run-on sentences, **496–497**
  dash, **550**
  exclamation point, 472, **537**
  in friendly and social letters, **234–235**, 238
  functions, **534–535**
  hyphen, **550–553, 600–601**
  with interjections, **540**
  parentheses, 562
  period, **535–536**
  with phrases, **509–511, 538–545**
  question mark, 472, **537**
  quotation marks, **554–555**
  semicolon, 24, 26, **525, 546–547**
  underlining, **556–557**, 558
Purpose, **104**

Q

Question marks, **537**
Questions
  asking to find information, 147–148
  interrogative pronouns in, **316–317**
  point-of-view questions, 13–15
  question mark with, **537**
  Six Basic, 10–11
  using to discover ideas, 10–12
Quotation marks, **554–555**
Quotations
  colon with, **548**
  direct, **554**
  direct, comma with, **540**
  questions, 537
  in speeches, 657, 659
Quoting sources, in research paper, 145–148

R

Radio programs
  episodes, quotation marks enclosing, **555**

  titles of, 557
Raise and *rise*, using, **371**
re-, hyphen following, **601**
Reader, 134
Readers' Guide to Periodical Literature, **627–629**
Real and *really*, using, **411–412**
Reasoning, 170–174
  errors in reasoning, 170–174
  sound vs. unsound, 172–174
Reasons, using to develop paragraphs, 80–81, 87
Reference books
  dictionaries, **632–647**
  encyclopedias, **647–648**
  Readers' Guide, **627–629**
  special, 649
References, on job application form, 271–272
Regional dialects, **611–612**
Regular plurals, **293–294**
Regular verbs, **340–352**
Relative pronouns, 312, **319–320**
  in adjective clauses, 520
  list of, **319**
  who, whom, **335–336**
Reports. *See* Research writing
Request, letters of, 254–255
Research for speech topic, 651–652
Research writing, 134–157
  bibliography, **155–156**
  information, recording, 145–148
  note cards, 146–147
  organizing information, 148
  outlines, 149–151
  purpose, 134
  reading, 151–154
  selecting and limiting a topic, 142–143
  sources, finding, 143–144
  summary, 134–138
  thesis sentence, **149**
  topics, selecting, 142
  writing, 154–155
Return address, 238
Revising, **16–17**
  business letters, 258–259
  checklist for, **17**
  correction symbols, **19**
  definition, **16**
  descriptive composition, guidelines for, 118

  kinds of changes, **16**
  narrative composition, guidelines for, **64**
  paragraphs, specific instructions, 16–17
  persuasive letter, checklist for, **186**
  research reports, guidelines for, 157
  rough draft (first draft), 156, 186
  social letters, guidelines for, 234–236
  summary, guidelines for, 141
Rhyme, 206, 207–208
Rise and *raise*, using, **371**
Roget's International Thesaurus, 649
Root word
  ending with *e*, suffix added to, **602–603**
  ending with *y* + consonant, 603
  prefix added to, **600–601**
Roots, word, **589–590**
Rough draft. *See* Revising
Run-on sentence, **496–497**

S

Salutation
  of business letter, 249
  capitalizing, 235, **580**
  colon with, **548**
  of friendly letter, 235
  of social letter, 235
Second-person pronouns, 312
Secondary accent, 638
Scarcely, as negative word, 414
School subjects and classes, capitalization of, **578–579**
-Sede, -ceed, -cede, spelling rules for, **598–599**
See and *See also*, 629
Self-, hyphenation of words beginning with, 551
-Self, -selves, pronoun ending in, 313
Semicolon
  with adverb connectors, 24
  combining sentences with, 26
  in independent clauses, **525, 547**
  items in a series, **547**

as sentence connector, 26
uses of, 546–**547**
Sense experiences, **32**–33
details describing, **32**
Sensory details. *See* Details
Sentence combining. *See* Combining sentence
Sentence combining methods, 20–27, 40–47, 65–69, 98–101, 127–133, 158–165, 187–191, 222–227, 260–261, 277–282
Sentence connectors, 21–26, 66–67
Sentence fragment, **470**, **494**–495
correcting fragments, 495–496
defined, **494**
phrase fragment, **494**–495
subordinate clause fragment, **494**–495
Sentence outline, 113
Sentence patterns, 481–486
Sentences, 470–501
adding in series, 43–46
base, 43–46, 98
combining, 40–47, 65–69, 127–133
complex, **489**
compound, **488**
compound-complex, **490**
declarative, **471**
direct object, 481, **482**, 484
exclamatory, 471, **472**
first word, capitalizing, **568**
fragments, **494**–495
illustrations, 70, 76
imperative, 471, **474**
indirect object, **483**–484
inserting, 98–101, 127–133, 158–165, 187–191, 222–227, 260–261
interrogative, 471, **472**
kinds of, **471**–472
parts, arranging, 65
parts, placing for variety, 277–278
patterns, **481**–486
predicate, **479**–480
punctuation, **471**–472, 534–562
run-on, **496**–497
simple, **487**
structures, **487**–490
subject, **473**–478
subjects in inverted order, **477**–478
thesis, **108**–109, 148–149

topic, 70, 76, 80–81, 89–90
understanding, 470–490
using, 494–497
Series
commas used to separate items, **539**
Set and *sit*, using, **370**–371
Setting, story, **192**–196, **204**
Shall, **349**–350
Shall have and *will have*, using, **351**–352
Short story
basic elements, **192**
building, 192–193
characters, 192–196, **204**
conflict in, 192–196, **204**
details in, 194
narrative composition as, 192
observing, 32–33
plot, **192**–196, **204**
purpose, 192
reading, 196–204
setting, **192**–196, **204**
suspense in, 195
vivid details, 194–195
Signature of letter, 235, 250
Similes, **212**–213
Simple predicate, **479**
Simple sentences, **487**
Simple subject, **473**
Simple tenses of verbs, **345**–346, 355–356
progressive form, **357**–359
Singular
nouns, **289**
pronouns, **321**, **325**, **326**, **327**–328
Sit and *set*, using, **370**–371
Six Basic Questions, 10–11
Slang words, 613–614
S-LV-PA sentence pattern, 481–486
S-LV-PN sentence pattern, 481, 484–485
Smells
observing, 32–33
Social letter, 233, 240
proofreading, **247**
Some, number of, **327**
Somebody, number of, **327**
Someone, number of, **327**
Sound
in poetry, 206–209
Sounds
observing, 32–33

South, north, east, west, rules for capitalizing, **571**
Speaking, 659–661
Speaking and listening, 650–663
Specific details, 35–37, 50, 55, 58–60, 76–77, 114, 119, 231
asking questions about, 53
in character description, 54–58
listing, 53
model using, 55–56
of people and places in personal narrative, 50
Specific information, 35
Speeches
delivering, 659–661
evaluating, 663
informative outline, 653–656
listening to, 662–663
parts of, **654**
preparing, 650–659
purposes of, 650
topic, 650–653
Spelling, 596–604
adding prefixes, **600**, **601**, 602
adding suffixes, **602**–604
-cede, -ceed, -sede, 598–**599**
consulting dictionary for, 597
good habits, developing, 596–598
helpful rules, **598**–604
ie, ei, **598**–599
irregular plurals, **295**–298
of noun plurals, **293**–294
Standard English, 612–614
formal and informal, **613**–614
State names, abbreviations, **237**
Statistics, using in speech, 657, 659
Stressed syllables, **208**, 598, **638**
Story. *See* Short story
Subject cards, 624–625
Subject forms of pronouns, **322**, **331**–332
Subject of sentence
complete, **473**
compound, **476**
in inverted order, **477**–478
simple, **473**
understood, **474**–475
Subject of verb
agreement, 360–367
compound, agreement with, **364**–365
indefinite pronoun as, **366**–367

prepositional phrase following, **361**–362
Subjects for writing
 choosing and limiting, 104–106, 142
 deciding on, 104–106
 distinguishing from topic, 105
 of interest to readers, 105
 for research report, 142
Subject-verb agreement. *See* Agreement of subject and verb
Subordinate clauses, 445, 450–451, 517, 518, 519–522
 in complex sentences, 489
 in compound-complex sentences, **490**
 nonessential, set of by commas, 544
 types of, 519–520
Subordinating conjunctions, **445**, **450**–**451**, 522, 528
 in adverb clauses, commas with, 527–**528**
 defined, **445**
 list of, **445**
 subordinate clause following, **450**–**451**
 writing with, **450**–**451**
Subordinators, 40–42
Suffixes, **590**, **598**
 added to root word, spelling rules, **592**, **602**–**604**
 adjectives formed with, **383**–**385**, **386**
 adverbs formed with, **402**–**403**
 beginning with vowel, **602**–603
 -elect, hyhen with, **551**
 -er and *-est*, **384**, **407**
 forming verbs, **347**
 -ly, forming adverbs, **402**–**403**
 meanings, **592**
 noun, **289**–**290**
Summary, **134**
 revising, guidelines for, 141
 writing, 134–141
Superlative degree of comparison of adjectives, **384**–**385**, **388**–**392**
 of adverbs, **401**, **406**–**409**
Supplementary material, parentheses with, **562**
Sure and *surely*, using, **412**

Suspense in story, **195**
S-V sentence pattern, 481, **482**
S-V-DO sentence pattern, 481, **482**
S-V-IO-DO sentence pattern, 481, **483**–**484**
Syllables, **597**
 accented, **598**–605
 hyphen linking, **552**–553
 stressed, **208**, **598**, **638**
Symbols, pronunciation, **636**
Symbols, for proofreading, **19**
Synonyms, **593**, **645**–646
 listed in dictionaries, 645–646
 using, 593–595

T

Tastes
 observing, 32–33
Tenses of verbs, 345–**346**, 349–352
Textures
 observing, 32–33
Thank-you letter, 240–241
Their, there, they're, **559**
Thesaurus, 649
Thesis, **108**–110
Thesis statement, **108**–110, 149
Third-person point of view, **120**
Third-person pronouns, **312**–**313**
Time, expressions of colon in, 548
Title cards, 623
Titles
 capitalization of words in, **304**
 following names, comma with, **542**
 quotation marks enclosing, **554**–**555**
 underlining, **556**–**557**
To
 not used with *where*, **432**
Topic, **105**
 for composition, deciding on, 104–106
 distinguishing from subject, 105
 outline, **112**–**113**
 for report, selecting, 142
 for speech, choosing, 650–651
 for speech, limiting, 651–653
Topic sentence, 70, 76, **80**–**81**, 89–90
Transitional expressions, commas with, **540**, **545**

Transitional phrases, semicolon with, **547**
Transitive verbs, 341, 343

U

Unabridged dictionaries, **646**–**647**
Underlining, **556**–**558**
 for names of ships, aircraft, spacecraft, **557**–**558**
 for titles, **556**–**557**
Understanding
 adjectives, **376**–**386**
 adverbs, **396**–**403**
 clauses, **516**–**522**
 conjunctions, **440**–**445**
 interjections, **456**
 nouns, **284**–**292**
 phrases, **502**–**507**
 prepositions, **420**–**426**
 pronouns, **310**–**324**
 sentences, **470**–**490**
 verbals, **462**–**465**
 verbs, **340**–**348**
Understood subject of sentence, **474**–**475**
Understood subjects, **474**–**475**
Using
 adjectives, **388**–**392**
 adverbs, **406**–**415**
 clauses, **524**–**528**
 conjunctions, **448**–**451**
 interjections, **457**–**458**
 nouns, 292–305
 phrases, **509**–**512**
 prepositions, **428**–**435**
 pronouns, **324**–**335**
 sentences, **494**–**497**
 verbs, 349–372

V

Verb phrases, **344**, **462**, **502**
Verb/subject agreement, **360**–**367**
Verbal phrases, **462**–**465**, **504**–**505**
 gerund phrase, **505**–**506**
 participial phrase, **509**
Verbals
 definition, **462**
 understanding, 462–465
Verbs, **340**–**375**
 action, 341
 adverbs modifying, **396**
 agreement with subject, **360**–**367**

be, conjugation of, **358**–**359**
compound, **480**
definition, **340**
features of, **345**–**347**
grouping by class, **341**–**344**
helping, 343–344, **502**
intransitive, **341**–343
irregular, **353**–**356**
lie and *lay*, using, **369**–**370**
linking, **342**–343
often confused, **369**–?
plural, **347**
principal parts, 345–**346**, **353**–**355**
progressive form, **346**, **357**–**359**
rise and *raise*, using, **371**
singular, **347**
suffixes forming, **347**
tenses, 345–**346**, **349**–**352**, **355**–**356**
transitive, **341**, 343
understanding, 340–348
using, 349–373
Viewpoints, changing, 10, 13–15
Vivid details, 50, 55, 114, 119, 194
Vocabulary
context clues, 586–587
dictionary study, 632–646
prefix, 589–**590**
root, 589
suffix, 589–**590**
word structure, 589–592
Vocabulary skills, improving, 586–595
Voice, speaking, 659–660
Vowels, **597**
suffix beginning with, **602**–**603**

W

Well, comma used to set off, **540**
West, east, north, south, rules for capitalizing, **571**
Who and *whom*, using, **335**
Who's, whose, **559**
Why, comma used to set off, **540**
Will, **349**–**350**
Will have, **351**–**352**
Words
accent marks, **637**–**638**
borrowing, 608–609
colloquial, 613–614
compound, 609
in context, 586–588, 644
definitions, **641**–**643**
English, changes in, 606–609
finding in dictionaries, 632–634
guide words, **634**
history, 640–641
hyphens in, **550**–**553**, **600**–**601**
key, **636**–**637**
loaded words, 178
main entry, **635**
origin, 640–641
parts of speech, **639**–**640**
pronunciation, using dictionaries for, **635**–**638**
rhyming, 206, 207–208
root, **589**–590
slang, **613**–614
structure, 589–590
syllables, 597, **638**
synonyms, **593**–595, **645**–646
vivid, 194–195
Writer's notebook
definition, **28**
as source of details, 28
as source of ideas, 28

using sensory details, 32–35
using specific words, 35–37
writing about feelings, 38–39
Writing
business letter, 247–250
coherent paragraphs, 70, 92–94
composition, **104**–**126**
from experience, 105–106
about feelings, 28, 38–39
friendly letter, 228–235
from imagination, 192–219
to interest readers, 2–3
with paragraphs, 70–94
about people, 54–57
about places, 50–52
research reports, 134–156
resources for, 28
revising, **16**–**17**
social letters, 233, 240–247
summary, **134**–141
unified paragraph, 70, **89**–**90**
for variety, 277–282
well-developed paragraph, 87–88
with subordinating conjunctions, **450**–**451**
Writing process, 2–18
prewriting, 3–15
writing, 3, **4**
postwriting, 3, **5**

Y

Y + consonant, root word ending with, **603**
Yearbook for encyclopedias, **648**
You, understood, **474**–**475**

683

Skills Index

Writing

Compositions
descriptive, 114–117
developing topics, 104–106
expository, 122–124
gathering information, 107–108
narrative, 119–121
outlines, 110–113
selecting information, 108–109

Expository Paragraphs
coherent paragraphs, 92–94
unified paragraphs, 89–90
using examples to develop, 76
using facts to develop, 78–79
using incidents to develop, 83–84
using reasons to develop, 80–81
writing well developed, 87–88

Forms
job applications, 267–272
library card applications, 264–265
order, 262–263

Friendly Letters
folding the letter, 238–239
form, 233–235
interesting the reader, 231–232
mailing, 236–238

Personal Narrative
describing events, 58–62
describing people, 54–57
describing places, 50–52
point of view, 48–49

Persuasive Writing
choosing a proposition, 179–181
revising, 186
using facts and opinions, 174–177
using language, 178
using sound reasoning, 172–173

Prewriting Techniques
asking questions, 10–12
brainstorming, 5–6
clustering, 6–8
free writing, 8–9
using points of view, 13–15

Proofreading
checklist for proofreading, 18
method of, 18

Research Reports and Summaries
finding information, 143–144
organizing information, 148–151
recording information, 145–147
revising, 141
selecting topics, 142
summaries, 134–138

Revising
business letters, 258
checklist for, 17
descriptive composition, 118
narrative composition, 64
research reports, 157
specific instructions for, 16–17

Social and Business Letters
application, 252–253
form of business letters, 247–250
form of social letters, 240
order letter, 256
proofreading business letters, 259
proofreading social letters, 247
request letter, 254–255

Stories
building a story, 192–195
reading a story, 196–204

Writer's Notebook
using sensory details, 32–35
using specific words, 35–37
writing about feelings, 38–39

Grammar and Usage

Adjectives
comparative forms, 383–385, 388–392
definition, classes, and features, 376–386
forming with suffixes, 386
using to be specific, 388–392

Adverbs
avoiding double negative, 414–415
choosing between adjectives and adverbs, 410–413
comparative forms, 401, 406–409
definition, classes, and features, 396–403

Clauses
definition and classes, 516–522

684

distinguishing from phrases, 516
punctuating, 524–528

Conjunctions

definition and classes, 440–445
using coordinating and correlative, 448–449
using subordinating, 450–451

Interjections

understanding, 456
using, 457–458

Nouns

capitalizing proper nouns, 303–305
definition, classes, and features, 284–290
plurals, 292–300
possessive forms, 301–302

Phrases

definition and types, 502–507
placing participial phrases, 512
using with punctuation, 509–511

Prepositions

adjective phrases, 425, 433–434
adverb phrases, 425, 435
definition, 420–421
in E.S.E., 431–432
troublesome, 429–430
with compound objects, 424

Pronouns

agreement with antecedents, 324–328
avoiding common problems, 329–330

definition, classes, and features, 310–322
object, 333–334
subject, 331–332
using *who* and *whom*, 335

Sentences

compound subjects, 476
compound verbs, 480
definition and types, 470–472
fragments, 470, 494–495
patterns, 481–486
predicate, 479–480
run-ons, 496–497
structure, 487–490
subject, 473–478

Verbals

gerunds, 465
participles, 462–464

Verbs

agreement, 360–367
definition, classes, and features, 340–347
often confused, 369–371
tenses, 345–346, 349–359

Mechanics

Capitalization

days, events, and periods, 575
first word in sentence, 568
geographical places, 571
institutions, businesses, and organizations, 573–574
names showing family relationships, 568–569
pronoun *I*, 568
school courses, 578

Punctuation

colons, 547–548
commas, 538–545
dashes, 550
exclamation marks, 537
hyphens, 550–553
paired commas, 543–545
periods, 535–536
questions marks, 537
quotation marks, 554–555
semicolons, 546–547
underlining (*italics*), 556–558

Language Resources

Library

arrangement of books, 616–620
card catalogue, 621–625
finding books, 625–627
finding periodicals, 627–631

Reference Works

using dictionaries, 632–646
using encyclopedias, 647–648
using special reference books, 649

Speaking and Listening

delivering a speech, 659–661
listening, 662–663
preparing a speech, 650–659

Spelling

developing good habits, 596–598
helpful rules, 598–604

Vocabulary

using synonyms, 593–595
word structure, 589–591
words in context, 586–588

685

Checklist for Proofreading

1. Each sentence begins with a capital letter and ends with a period, question mark, or exclamation point.
2. Each word is spelled correctly.
3. All proper nouns and adjectives are capitalized.
4. Personal pronouns used as subjects are subject forms; personal pronouns used as objects are object forms. All pronouns agree with antecedents in number and gender.
5. A singular verb is used with each singular subject, and a plural verb with each plural subject.
6. Commonly confused verbs, such as *lie/lay*, *sit/sat*, and *rise/raise*, are used correctly, and commonly confused adjectives and adverbs, such as *bad/badly*, *easy/easily*, and *good/well*, are used correctly.
7. Double negatives are avoided.
8. Sentences are correctly structured, with no run-ons or fragments.
9. The paper is neat.

Checklist for Revising

1. Does my writing have a clear focus?
2. Do I need to add more details?
3. Is my writing organized in a way that makes sense?
4. Are there unnecessary parts I should leave out?
5. Is my writing style appropriate for my purpose and audience?
6. Have I chosen the most specific words possible?
7. Do my sentences vary in length and pattern?

Symbols for Proofreading

Symbol	Meaning	Example
Cap ≡	Capitalize	Cap justice Sandra O'Connor
lc /	Lowercase letters	lc a new Justice
¶	New paragraph	¶ Justice Sandra O'Connor is the first woman to be appointed to the Supreme Court of the United States.
no ¶	No new paragraph	no ¶ In addition to having been a representative in the Arizona State Legislature, Justice O'Connor also served as a federal judge.
∧	Insert letter, word, or phrase; called a caret; also used to indicate where a change is to be made	Justice ∧Sandra O'Connor has a reputation as being a highly qualified judge.
stet	Leave as is (from the Latin phrase meaning "let it stand"); used to indicate that a marked change is not to be made.	Justice ~~Potter~~ stet Stewart resigned, leaving the vacancy that was filled by Justice O'Connor.
∽	Transpose	Justice S⁀nadra O'Connor's swearing-in ceremony was not open to the public. After the ceremony her fellow justices and Justice O'Connor posed for a ⁀photograph historic.
◠	Close up space	Justice O'Connor appeared in magazines and news◠papers once again when she announced that she would begin an exercise program in the gymnasium of the Supreme Court building. The new justice invited other women who worked in the building to join#her.
#	Insert space	
ℓ	Delete	My aunt is also a judgeℓ

Acknowledgments

CREDITS

Key: (t) top, (c) center, (b) bottom, (l) left, (r) right.

Page 1, Gregg Eisman; 2, Thomas Hooke Photography; 3(l), Steven Kiecker; 3(r), 4, Jean-Claude Lejeune; 8, 11, Vito Palmisano; 12, Jean-Claude Lejeune; 14, John Weinstein; 15, Thomas Hooke Photography; 17, 21, 23, Jean-Claude Lejeune; 24, Vito Palmisano; 28, Thomas Hooke Photography; 29(l), 29(r), Steven Kiecker; 31, Jean-Claude Lejeune; 34, Bruce Powell; 36, 39, Steven Kiecker; 41, Thomas Hooke Photography; 42, Kamila Kiecker; 44, Steven Kiecker; 45, Vito Palmisano; 46, Bruce Powell; 47, Arthur Tress; 48, Thomas Hooke Photography; 49(l), 49(r), Vito Palmisano; 51, 52, Jean-Claude Lejeune; 55, Vito Palmisano; 58, Jean-Claude Lejeune; 60, John Weinstein; 64, Jean-Claude Lejeune; 67, Thomas Hooke Photography; 70, John Weinstein; 71(l), Vito Palmisano; 71(r), Steven Kiecker; 73, Culver Pictures, Inc.; 74, Vito Palmisano; 77, Jean-Claude Lejeune; 80, Vito Palmisano; 83, Bruce Powell; 86, 89(l), Jean-Claude Lejeune; 89(r), Bruce Powell; 91, V. Lee Hunter; 93, Vito Palmisano; 94, 96, 97, Jean-Claude Lejeune; 99, Arthur Tress; 101, Thomas Hooke Photography; 102, 103, Jean-Claude Lejeune; 104, Thomas Hooke Photography; 105(l), Jean-Claude Lejeune; 105(r), Vito Palmisano; 106, Jean-Claude Lejeune; 109, Gregg Eisman; 111, 112, Steven Keicker; 115, Jean-Claude Lejeune; 116, Thomas Hooke Photography; 118, Jean-Claude Lejeune; 123(l), Thomas Hooke Photography; 123(r), Steven E. Gross; 126, Jean-Claude Lejeune; 129, Steven Kiecker; 133, Frank Siteman/The Marilyn Gartman Agency; 134, Thomas Hooke Photography; 135(l), Culver Pictures, Inc.; 135(r), Jean-Claude Lejeune; 137, UPI; 139, Culver Pictures, Inc.; 143, Thomas Hooke Photography; 145, Jean-Claude Lejeune; 149, Bruce Powell, 152, © Lucasfilm Ltd. (LFL) 1977. All rights reserved. Courtesy of Lucasfilm Ltd.; 155, Courtesy of Museum of Holography, NYC; 157, Jean-Claude Lejeune; 159, Steven Kiecker; 160, Jean-Claude Lejeune; 163, John Weinstein; 165, 166, Thomas Hooke Photography; 167(l), 167(r), Lee Youngblood; 168, 169, Culver Pictures, Inc.; 171, Jean-Claude Lejeune; 172(l), Thomas Hooke Photography; 172(r), Frank Siteman/The Marilyn Gartman Agency; 175, UPI; 177, R. Redden/Animals, Animals; 178, Bruce Powell; 180, 182, Jean-Claude Lejeune; 184, Bruce Powell; 187, Vito Palmisano; 189, Frank Siteman/The Marilyn Gartman Agency; 191, Bruce Powell; 192, Thomas Hooke Photography; 193(l), Steven Kiecker; 193(r), Thomas Hooke Photography; 196, 198, Jean-Claude Lejeune; 201, 202, 203, Steven Kiecker; 205, 207, Jean-Claude Lejeune; 210, Vito Palmisano; 213, John Weinstein; 214, Frank Siteman/The Marilyn Gartman Agency; 217, Vito Palmisano; 218, 221, Jean-Claude Lejeune; 223, Culver Pictures, Inc.; 224, Vito Palmisano; 228, Thomas Hooke Photography; 229(t), Arthur Tress; 229(c), Jean-Claude Lejeune; 232, Vito Palmisano; 233, Jean-Claude Lejeune; 236(l), Steven E. Gross; 236(r), Arthur Tress; 240, Jean-Claude Lejeune; 242, Vito Palmisano; 246, 251, 253, 254, 257, Jean-Claude Lejeune; 258, Vito Palmisano; 261, 262, Thomas Hooke Photography; 263, 266, 271, Jean-Claude Lejeune; 273, 274, Gregg Eisman; 276, Bruce Powell; 278, D. Shigley; 281(l), Thomas Hooke Photography; 281(r), Frank Loose; 282(l), 282(r), Jean-Claude Lejeune; 283, Gregg Eisman; 309, Steven E. Gross; 339, Jean-Claude Lejeune; 375, Photri, Inc.; 395, Arthur Tress; 418, 419, 439(t), Jean-Claude Lejeune; 439(cr), John Weinstein; 455, Arthur Tress; 459, 460, Jerry N. Velsmann; 469, Steve Arnam/The Marilyn Gartman Agency; 501(l), Thomas Hooke Photography; 501(r), 515, 532, Jean-Claude Lejeune; 533, Gregg Eisman; 567, Arthur Tress; 583, Vito Palmisano; 584, Bruce Powell; 585, Gregg Eisman.

2 3 4 5 6 7 8 9 0 93 92 91 90 89 88